THE RISE OF RADICALISM

THE

Rise of Radicalism

The Social Psychology of Messianic Extremism

EUGENE H. METHVIN

ARLINGTON HOUSE   *New Rochelle, N.Y.*

Library of Congress Catalog Card Number 76–189374

ISBN 0–87000–158–2

MANUFACTURED IN THE UNITED STATES OF AMERICA

FOR

Barbara Lester Methvin

WHO BLESSED ONE YOUNG UTOPIAN'S IMPOSSIBLE
DREAM WITH THE GRAND FAIRYTALE END-
ING: ". . . AND THEY WERE
MARRIED AND LIVED
HAPPILY EVER
AFTER."

TABLE OF CONTENTS

INTRODUCTION

I see now more clearly than ever before that even our greatest troubles spring from something that is as admirable and sound as it is dangerous—from our impatience to better the lot of our fellows.

—Karl Popper
The Open Society and Its Enemies
(Preface to second edition, 1950)

The French Senate once commenced an address to Napoleon with these striking words:

Sire, the desire for perfection is one of the worst maladies that can affect the human mind.

Hardly a man among the assembly had not suffered personally and poignantly from that malady during the turbulent French Revolution just behind them. They had all lived through the intoxicatingly hopeful days of 1789 and 1791; exulted with Robespierre in his dream of creating a "Republic of Virtue"; and trembled and wept as they watched that dream turn into the Reign of Terror.

How much more relevant for our own twentieth-century world is the realization that moved those sobered Frenchmen! We who have lived through the utopias-turned-to-terror proffered by Lenin and Stalin, Hitler and Mussolini, and their ideological progeny in the 1960s and 1970s, should hardly miss their meaning.

Yet in fact rare are the contemporaries who have understood. One such was the Italian historian Ferrero, who wrote sadly from his place of exile at the time of Adolf Hitler's early victories that men of our day should jettison the traditional celebration of the Fourteenth of July, Bastille Day, and make it instead a time for somber meditation on that "revolutionary apocalypse which has lasted for a century and a half and now, after having devastated Europe, threatens to spread all over the world and destroy everything."

The apocalyptic rage runs among us still. Born of a utopian expectation and lust for a new "Republic of Virtue," a tidal wave of hate and terror struck America in the 1960s. Though it seems now to

[13]

eddy, the nation shudders still. In the four summers 1964–67, America's cities were rocked by 109 major riots, insurrections and civil disorders. In the cities armed teams of snipers fought battles with police and soldiers: firebombers burned thousands of buildings. The dead totalled 130, the injured over 3,000, and estimated damages approached a billion dollars. Throughout the nightmare-holocaust, radical revolutionaries hawked their ideological wares and their handbooks of terrorism, insurrection and social demolition. "In future summers America *will* burn. . . . Götterdämmerung!" proclaimed Daniel N. Watts, editor of *Liberator*, through the *Saturday Evening Post*'s pages. Television-favorite Student Non-Violent Coordinating Committee Chairman Rap Brown told a screaming audience of 1,500 in New York that the 1967 summer riots were merely "dress rehearsals for revolution!" As he talked, radical cohorts passed anti-Semitic and Chinese communist propaganda leaflets through the crowd. In the national headquarters of Students for a Democratic Society (SDS), the secretary, Gregory Calvert, speaking beneath a beaming photograph of Che Guevara, told a *New York Times* reporter, "We are working to build a guerrilla force in an urban environment. We are actively organizing sedition. We are post-communist revolutionaries." And soon, in fact, SDS spawned a nationwide terrorist organization whose bombs blasted away from the U. S. Capitol to the University of Wisconsin to Portland's City Hall.

On the campuses the scene was no less tumultous, though less deadly. The names of the nation's most prestigious centers of learning became bywords signifying rampant revolutionary radicalism: Berkeley, Columbia, Harvard, Cornell. Thrice in two years National Guardsmen battled radical-led rioters at the University of Wisconsin; at Kent State, Ohio Guardsmen vollied into students, killing two rioters and two wholly innocent passers-by. In the aftermath hysteria drowned reason, and 700 colleges closed in the face of actual or threatened violence. Always in the vanguard were those whom the headline-writers called "the New Left," whose ideological principles as summarized by John Gardner seemed to be "rage and hate for a good cause" and "be vicious for virtue." After interviewing numbers of SDS adherents, one *Philadelphia Bulletin* reporter sadly concluded they were "super-idealists, unhappy because America fails to live up to its textbook image, upset because life is different from dreams. They are not hippies, not freaks. A generation ago they might have been communists."

What manner of process turns idealism into a raging hate that murders reason in its bed—in a university or college campus?

It is the same process that turned Moliere's *Misanthrope,* the lover of justice and worshipper of high ideals, into a hater of all men for their failure to conform to his idealism.

It is the same process that moved Trotsky, an intense young Russian intellectual, to justify revolutionary terrorism as a means for attaining and sustaining power, convinced that under his imagined post-revolutionary socialism,

> Man will become immeasurably stronger, wiser and subtler. His body will become more harmonized, his voice more musical. The average human type will rise to the heights of an Aristotle, a Goethe, a Marx.

Believe that, and it hardly seems a crime to commit murder in the name of revolution.[1]

It is the same process that led Stalin and his fellow Bolshevik revolutionaries to plot the deliberate genocidal extermination of millions of Russian kulaks. A young American diplomat who met one of Stalin's top Comintern agents, Mikhail Borodin, in Moscow in 1932 found him "the most charming murderer I ever knew." A thoroughgoing idealist, Borodin excused planned mass starvations by saying simply, "We have to sacrifice a generation in order to build the future socialist state." By such logic Hitler constructed his extermination camps, and Stalin entrained millions to the death camps of Siberia—ironically, Borodin among them.

It is the same process that enabled that survivor of the Stalinist hell, Nikita Khrushchev, even after exposing and denouncing that hell, still to declare and believe:

> We communists believe that capitalism is a hell in which laboring people are condemned to slavery. We are building socialism. We have already been successful in many respects, and we will be even more successful in the future. Our way of life is undoubtedly the most progressive in the world at the present stage of humanity's development. To use the language of the Bible, our way of life is paradise for mankind.

It is the same process that brought that stolid successor of Khrushchev and paragon of the *aparatchiki,* Brezhnev, to choke up while he was still speaking at the 24th Communist Party Congress in 1971, and to flush with tears welling in his eyes as the delegates sang "The Internationale":

> Arise, ye prisoners of starvation,
> Arise, ye wretched of the earth,
> For justice thunders condemnation,
> A better world's in birth!
> 'Tis the final conflict.
> Let each stand in his place!
> The International Party
> Shall be the human race!

It is the same process that grips New Left heroine Jane Fonda, the young movie star, and 2,000 students who cheer as she says: "If you understood what communism was, you would hope, you would pray on your knees that we could someday become communist." It moves Angela Davis, philosophical protégé of Herbert Marcuse accused (but found not guilty) of complicity in murdering a judge, to declare:

> I want to see all oppressed people throughout the world free. And the only way we can do this is by moving toward a revolutionary society where the needs and wishes of all people can be respected.

In his head man can pull apart reality and put it back together in all sorts of impossible shapes. But he may never find in reality the dream-image he forms inside his head. Man has created centaurs, unicorns, satyrs and mermaids—but he has never seen one. And he has created the post-revolutionary utopia. But he has never seen one of those, either. Yet in its name, he has committed horrendous crimes. To a ":naked ape" wont to react to frustration by blind aggression and hatred, it is terribly tempting when confronted with imperfections and deviations from the dream to lash out and kick over the whole structure. This tendency of political man was apparent at least as early as the time of Aristotle, who sadly noted: "The essence of political tragedy is to make the perfect the enemy of the good."

Revolutionary radicalism is basically thus a corruption of man's creativity and of his very nature as a thinking animal. It is idealism gone wild, just as cancer is a normal healthy growth gone wild, a malignant mutation of a healthy, necessary natural process. It is the product of a diseased, disgruntled mind whose bitter reaction to a world that will not accept his utopian vision, or fulfill it, is to conspire to seize the secular power to force humanity into his own design. Like a child who pitches a tantrum when his blocks will not defy gravity and conform to his grand architectual design, the revolutionary radical hurls himself at all creation. He sets out to destroy the secular order and remake it to his own plan. And if humanity does not conform, then so much the worse for humanity—he will crush it. He sets himself up as the sovereign, the conscience, the mind of mankind. Against his vision no one else may dare to plot his own life, seek his own dream, pursue his own vision. This breed of radical turns all men into puppets for his own pleasure and gratification. And like all burners of heretics, he will destroy any sovereign soul who dares breathe free.

The very fact that radicalism is a malignant corruption of the natural, vital process of idealism makes it doubly virulent in American society. For it is a malignant corruption of the faith that lies at the heart of our constitutional institutions. That faith was stated clearly and boldly in *Federalist* No. 1, where Hamilton insisted that men "are really capable . . . of establishing good government from reflection and choice" and that they are not "forever destined to depend for their political constitutions on accident and force." Since most Americans share with our Founding Fathers—from Hamilton to Washington to Jefferson to Tom Paine—the belief that men can and must achieve a rational ordering of society and a peaceful, prosperous and liberal civilization, we are susceptible to its malignant pathology. For this very reason, we desperately need to understand it. Else we risk losing the dream altogether.

The American susceptibility manifests itself in the very semantic confusion over the meaning of the word, "radicalism." It is a much embattled object in our history and political semantics. Many who claim the label for themselves do not fall within the tradition or definition of "radicalism" as treated in this book. They would contest our title and claim we unfairly smear "radicals" by lumping them together with those we discuss herein, who they feel should be labeled "revolutionary radicals." These homeless "nonrevolutionary radicals" have inherited a constellation of traditions and prejudices that set them against the status quo, the existing order be it monarchy, autocracy, or a constitutional regime. Their emotional ties make them frequent fellow travelers with or sympathizers to the radicals we trace in this volume. But their rational equipment also forces them to hold back, to maintain an intellectual and organizational independence, and frequently even to oppose them vigorously. Many are democratic socialists, Marxist revisionists, and liberals of varied stripes who for sentimental reasons insist upon calling themselves "radicals," while they try to cut a new definition and pin a different label on the others. One such self-styled radical contemporary is Daniel J. Boorstin, a distinguished scholar of political history if ever there was one. In the '30s, he came to consider himself a "radical," but those who do so today he insists are not "radicals" at all but "new barbarians."[2]

But such redefinitions present problems themselves. They leave the redefined term "radical" with such a broad extension it covers too much. Adam Ulam points out, "In the Second International ideological terms had their common-sense meaning: a leftist was a man who believed in revolution, a right-wing Socialist one who envisioned the achievement of his aim through evolution and nonviolent means."[3] This was the distinguishing difference: a preference for or belief in the inevitability of violent cataclysm. It is the meaning we adopt in the title of this book: *The Rise of Radicalism*. We might have called it, *The Rise of Revolutionary Radicalism*, to please the Boorstins of contemporary thought. But in the clear classic meaning, that would have been redundant. Ideological hair-splitters who try to rescue the word "radical" from today's "new barbarians" or violent messianics want to use the word like Alice: when they use it, it means precisely what they want it to mean, no more and no less. Very well. We shall use the word to apply to those who believe they can get to the root of the things and change them only through *violent* revolution, through violence applied in one form or another in the pre-revolutionary stage and afterward through the terror and coercion of a "revolutionary dictatorship," as preached by Lenin, Trotsky, Stalin, Hitler, Mussolini, Castro, Mao, and the rest. We do not object to the phrase "revolutionary radicalism," and shall indeed use it, too, but we equate it with simple "radicalism."

Boorstin adopts Karl Marx's definition:

To be radical is to grasp things by the root. But for man the root is man himself . . . the doctrine that *man is the supreme being for man.* It ends, therefore, with the *categorical imperative to overthrow all those conditions* in which man is an abased, enslaved, abandoned, contemptible being.[4]

Indeed, by Marx's own definition, the American Founding Fathers were the most radical political leaders in history. Few men have gone more to the root of human nature and government than did the Philadelphia framers. (See, e.g., Hamilton, quoted previously.) And the permanent, peaceful revolution they launched continues to be the leading radical revolution in human experience. As Jean Francois-Revel has pointed out, American society is the most fluid, fast-changing society in recorded history. America in the mid-twentieth century has produced epochal social change, amid political liberty more complete than has ever been known anywhere, enjoyed by a people with the highest level of education and consequent ability to participate that has ever existed. As Herbert Wechsler, distinguished Columbia professor of constitutional law and director of the prestigious American Law Institute, writes:

> Legal protection of the rights of conscience and expression and participation in the choice of those who exercise authority has reached its apogee in our time . . . At no time in human history have government and legal institutions been so shaped that they are more responsive to just demands.[5]

So in the broad definition represented by Marx's 1843 definition, and as Boorstin would have it, we are all radicals in contemporary America. At least anyone who falls into the school of American progressivism represented by Grover Cleveland, Teddy Roosevelt, Woodrow Wilson, Franklin D. Roosevelt or Dwight D. Eisenhower might be entitled to claim for himself the label of "radical." ("I am in every fiber of my body a radical," Teddy Roosevelt once declared.) Indeed, by such a yardstick the most radical radicals of all were those men who gathered at Philadelphia in 1787 and hammered out a practical plan for concerting action "to overthrow all those conditions in which man is a humbled, oppressed, abandoned, despised being." Their genius was that they went so far to the root of the problem of government that they recognized that any governors, even revolutionary dictators, must from time to time consult their fellow men in deciding *which* conditions are humbling and oppressive and inhumane and must be overthrown (including their own possession of power), and which should be preserved. In short, even the best shoe salesman in the world must consult his customers on where the product pinches—and so must the utopia-makers. "To be

[19]

radical means to grab the matter by its roots," said Marx. And that the Constitution-makers did indeed, very directly and boldly. And nothing Marx or his progeny ever did was more radical; in fact, as we shall see, starting from their affirmation of humanity and dignity and freedom, they arrived at the very opposite, an anti-human, anti-radical result.

Where, then, does our definitional line-drawing leave to "radicals" of Boorstin's version? They should perhaps be considered heirs to the Mirabeaus, the Girondins, and the Kerenskys of revolutionary history. Such are the dynamics of revolution and social earthquakes that in them these moderate radicals share a melancholy fate, a fate in no small measure a functional result of the same emotional biases, enchantments and ambivalences that cause them to rever and try to save for themselves the label of "radical." Their love for the word, their distaste for the existing order, their noble idealism and their paralysis before the revolutionary radicals determine their fate.

We are tracing not merely an idea. We are tracing a *delusional belief system:* that men can through a violent and apocalyptic showdown play messiahs and create the Kingdom Come; that history can be ended and men converted to angels and governments abolished with one bloody stroke; that the ideal can become real. A key to the delusion lies in the fact that there is no such thing as one ideal; men have different ideals—each his own, and even within the individual ideals change with time and experience and life's rhythmic pattern. And even if there were agreement on an ideal, statecraft and human nature are too inexactly understood to permit men to realize the ideal by deliberate, straight-line choices. Men are simply not smart enough to build utopia, even if they could agree on a design. And thus our story is a tragic epic of misspent idealism, of frustration, disappointment, and defeat.

Our tracing of this delusional belief system is not "intellectual history." It is the story of *men*—men who believed, and how they came to believe, and why. It is the story of the development of a subculture and a religious movement and a conspiracy and a political party—but always a story of men, their beliefs and behavior. It is a kaleidoscopic drama of messiahs in search of followers and followers in search of messiahs. Until 1900, the tumbling of ingredients of these messianic mass movements was more or less spontaneous, historical happenstance.

With Lenin, we find a new, systematic and empirical spirit: messiahs set down their findings and developed a body of knowledge both for building mass movements and waging social demolition. This change was a function and development of the Megamedia Age —the age of mass media audiences numbering in the millions. Megamedia audiences are a wholly twentieth-century phenomenon. They had to await developments in public health, transportation, and communications technology that permitted urban groupings of a million or more persons readily accessible to the printing press and, after 1920, broadcast media.

Indeed, revolutionary radicalism seems to be endemic in urban life from the very earliest development of cities. It seems to be a *social fact* associated with the urbanization of mankind. It is one individual and group psychological reaction to the stresses and strains of urban society, with its economic specialization, division of labor and differentiation of social roles, its speeded social interactions and collisions and impermanence. Pitirim Sorokin, in listing the causes of revolution,[6] remarked on "the difference in the revolutionary propensities of the cities as compared with the villages," which he held to be more adapted to man's nature than the modern city in which man "finds himself upon a 'bed of nails' to which his instincts are not adapted." We find here an obvious parallel to Desmond Morris's more recent study, *The Human Zoo.* Revolutionary radicalism thus may be a natural atavistic response of "the naked ape" to "the human zoo" he has created for himself in his cities. It seems to be, functionally, one way of escaping from stress and venting hostilities generated in the frustrating social collisions that randomly occur in human society— but more frequently in urban settings. It may well be an inappropriate maladaptive result of what Freud termed *Civilization and Its Discontents*, the repression that is the price man necessarily pays for being civilized. Norman Cohn and Karl Popper, as we shall see, traced revolutionary messianism and totalitarianism from Plato's Athens to the growing textile centers of the Lower Rhineland in the eleventh to the sixteenth centuries. As in the America of 1950–70, such periods of urbanization and population mobility always mean uprooting large numbers of people from age-old ties, from the stabilizing and supportive environment of the village and tribe and extended family of agrarian culture. These hurricanes of change always produced whorls and eddies of marginal people, individuals who were being squeezed out of the agricultural economy and found no comfortable place in the new urban environment. They became the tinder for some enflaming messianic preaching Apocalypse and Armageddon, the Manichean Final Clash between the Forces of Light and the Forces of Darkness.

On the historical stage we will see the messiahs attempt to stage their passion plays: Karl Marx in 1843 and 1848, Lenin in 1902 and 1905, Mussolini in 1919 and Hitler in 1920—all came on, new messiahs finding new constituencies. In 1960 Frantz Fanon stepped forth to define another new constituency: "the wretched of the earth," the urban lumpenproletariat compressed into the world's cities by the gathering technological revolution in agriculture and public health. In America first Malcolm X (assassinated February 21, 1968) and then Huey P. Newton of the Black Panther Party and the "Weathermen" of the disintegrated SDS stepped forth as the new messiahs to lead the apocalyptic army.

The psychodynamics of the messianic utopian tyrannists appear remarkably constant. Indeed, this category of psycho-pathology deserves the highest priority in man's quest for knowledge of himself and the diseases that afflict him.

Why is the embryonic phase of revolutionary radical movements so important to study?

Because that is where we first see them, and must learn to recognize and deal with them. It would have been far better to hang a few Nazis in Munich in 1923, after only 20 dead, than to wait until Nuremburg after 30 million dead. It would have been better to deal with the proto-Bolshevik band in 1905 than after the extermination of 21 million "class enemies" in planned mass murder. As Adlai Stevenson posed the problem:

> We have always known that hatred is unbearably evil. Indeed, our religions—particularly here in the West—are explicit rejections of this worst and most brutal of passions.
> Reason proscribes it and philosophy deplores it. Yet it persists. What can be done after all these thousands of years of failure to change human nature?
> Well, we do have at least one advantage which our predecessors did not have—the advantage of necessity. We will either subdue hatred or it will destroy us, and our history with us.[7]

The great task of mankind in the twentieth century has been and will continue to be peace. Ours is the century of the most horrendous wars and engines of destruction in mankind's existence. And at bottom, the problem of peace is today the problem of coping with the totalitarians: Lenin, Mussolini, Hitler, and their followers. Certainly we in the twentieth century have seen the worst results of the unlimited quest for utopia: the mass madness of the "Red Guards" and the Great Cultural Revolution of Red China; the complete megalomania and paranoia of Stalin and his genocidal purges of the Russian people; and the Götterdämmerung suicide of Hitler, a grand finale of blood and fire and Apocalypse. Mankind can choose between two results: either we will find a way to de-energize this messianic madness and consign it to the rubbish heap of history, or revolutionary radicalism will consign mankind to the rubbish heap of the universe, either as a race of slaves ruled by the New Royalists in a global concentration camp, or as ash aboard a dead cinder-planet orbiting a minor star in the teeming supergalaxies of creation.

The failure to comprehend the roots and implications of the utopian malady of the mind turned America's Camelot-hope of the gallant young President John F. Kennedy into the nightmare-holocaust of Vietnam. Because the military-diplomatic bureaucrats incorrectly assessed the psychology of the communist true believers opposing them in Hanoi and the South Vietnamese jungles, they blundered into an incredible series of international and domestic consequences for the American people: an epidemic of violence on the college campuses; open insurrections in the cities; a 20 percent debasement of the currency over four years; more dead and wounded than in any U.S. war except the two world wars; and ultimately in 1968, the fall of an American government in wartime, the first in history. The stolen top-secret documents published in the *New York Times* in June 1971 show the Johnson Administration's war planners thought that by a "rachet" action of bombing, pauses, and increased bombing they could persuade Hanoi to call off the thinly-disguised invasion of South Vietnam. Reviewing the period, former Secretary of State Dean Rusk admitted,

> I personally, I think, underestimated the resistance and the determination of the North Vietnamese. They have taken over 700,000 killed, which in relation to the population is almost the equivalent of ten million Americans, and they are continuing to come.

The error reflected a tragic level of historical ignorance and unsophistication about the nature of the revolutionary radical belief system, and no comprehension at all about the means required to dent or demolish it or render it benign. The Johnson Administration committed the same mistake as Neville Chamberlain at Munich: failing to understand the fanatical messianic mentality.

It is a mistake repeated often by decent, civilized, liberal gentlemen—by Clark Kerr at Berkeley, Grayson Kirk at Columbia, Nathan Pusey at Harvard, James A. Perkins at Cornell, Jerry Cavanagh in Detroit, John Lindsay in New York, and Ramsey Clark in Washington, among others in the 1960s, as well as the Johnson Administration leaders. The bureaucracies led by such liberal gentlemen repeat the mistake in their own way and scale wherever they confront the problem, whether it be with a college administration or a national government or a city hall.

Yet the record is plain for all who trouble to read it. We can trace the messianic mentality from Robespierre to Nechayev to Lenin to Hitler and Mao and Ho Chi Minh and Mario Savio and Mark Rudd and Rennie Davis. To avoid blood-lettings such as those blundered into by the Chamberlains and McNamaras of our time, we must read and understand.

THE RISE OF RADICALISM

Chapter 1
THE MALIGNANT DREAM

The essence of political tragedy is to make the perfect the enemy of the good.
—Aristotle (384–322 B.C.)

Everything has got to be smashed to start with. Our whole damned civilization has got to go, before we can bring any decency into the world.
—'Mourlan', in Du Gard's
Les Thibaults

It is not by comparison with the present bad state of society that the claims of communism can be estimated . . . The question is whether there would be any asylum left for individuality of character; whether public opinion would not be a tyrannical yoke; whether the absolute dependence of each on all, and the surveillance of each by all, would not grind all down into a tame uniformity of thoughts, feelings, and actions. No society in which eccentricity is a matter of reproach can be in a wholesome state.
—John Stuart Mill (1806–1873)

UTOPIA IN HISTORY   From the beginning of recorded thought men have dreamed about an ideal human society. From Plato's *Republic* to Thomas More's *Utopia* to Karl Marx's *Communist Manifesto*, philosophers have described this ideal society and pondered the means to bring it about.[1] In this dream world, man's rational and humane capacities would dominate, and his animal traits of selfishness and rage would be banished.

The very earliest literature contained utopian elements, and they were among the most beautiful and inspiring. The Greeks had their dream of the Golden Isles, but it was the Hebrew prophets who bequeathed a heritage of utopian expectation to mankind. Amos, the shepherd of Tekoa, launched the utopian tradition about the middle of the eighth century B.C. He lived in the days of Jeroboam II, king of Israel, whose long and brilliant reign had been marked by peace and prosperity. Israel had crushed her worst enemy, the kingdom of Damascus, and Jeroboam II had subjected all the neighboring kingdoms, reigning over a land extending from Hamath to the Dead Sea, the size and grandeur of which was unsurpassed since the days of David. The land flowed luxury and riches: ivory palaces, houses of hewn stone, castles and forts, horses and chariots, power and pomp, the luxurious and idle rich. In the year 760 B.C., the people at Bethel were celebrating the autumn festival in revelry and feasting of unwonted splendor.

Suddenly, Amos appeared, a lowly and plain-looking herdsman out of the stern, wild Judean hills around the Dead Sea. This brooding shepherd shattered them with his maledictions of moral decay and rottenness and his jolting prophecy of doom.

Amid the people's revels he saw false worship and social injustice, with ritualism supplanting spirituality and oppression smothering justice. He protested the feast of Bethel with its perfunctory sacrifices. It was a perversion of the Hebraic religious rites, and with true social vision he saw that the whole life of the body politic was bound up in the due performance of those rites. Through the luxury of the few he saw that the courts were corrupt and venal, justice poisoned at its source by the love of money, the poor exploited and swindled by being sold bad grain, given short weight, and charged exorbitant prices. At this despicable corruption the incensed shepherd hurled predictions of inevitable doom. With elemental power and wrath he proclaimed that a society founded upon such a social injustice could not endure.[2] And an inevitable logic brought Amos to look forward from the flawed present to a world in which service and not ceremony was the ideal, a new era of social justice. Amos proclaimed his utopianism as a frank commanding plea:

> Let justice flow like a river
> And righteousness like a perennial stream.
> —Amos 5:24

It remained for Isaiah to crown the cycle of prophets with his vision of the coming Messiah and the arrival of Heaven on Earth. The utopian Isaiah began his prophetic period in a time of trial for Israel, about 450 B.C., after the fall and in the period of exile and post-exile. Biblical scholars call him Deutero-Isaiah, for the utopian passages are found in Chapters 40 to 66 and are assigned to a separate, unknown author; hence the name Deutero-Isaiah or Second Isaiah. The prophet brought for himself and his people in this era of national humiliation and spiritual depression a message not of rebuke but of comfort, encouragement, and hope. He spoke not of doom but of coming glory, a patently escapist message. Israel was to be delivered from Babylon and her scattered and enslaved children gathered from all the corners of the earth, led back through the wildernesses to Jerusalem where the universal kingdom, the New Jerusalem, was to reign again in all its glory. It is to be an eternal city, and in it, joy everlasting, world without end. And the Jew and the Gentile, all the peoples and all nations, shall share in its glory. Violence and destruction will be no more, and peace and tranquility will reign throughout this ideal land. Rivers and fountains will break forth and the waste places will be like Eden and the deserts like gardens. Labor shall have its just reward. Happy man shall live forever.[3]

> The wolf shall lie down with the lamb, and the leopard shall dwell with the kid, and the calf and the lion and the fatling together, and the little child shall lead them. And the cow and the bear shall feed; their young ones shall lie down together; and the lion shall eat straw like the ox. And the sucking child shall play on the hole of the asp, and the weaned child shall put his hand in the cockatrice den. They shall not hurt nor destroy in all thy holy mountain, for the earth shall be full of the knowledge of the Lord, as the waters cover the sea.
> —Isaiah 11: 6–9

PLATO—THE FIRST TOTALITARIAN?   In the fifth century before Christ, after the defeat of the Persians at Marathon in 490, Athens came into its Golden Age. New-found skills in seafaring and commercialism made her the imperial city of the Mediterranean. Her population may have reached 350,000—a record high in human history to that time. Pericles led a democratic revolution against the primeval tribal and theocratic authorities. *"Although only a few may originate a policy, we are all able to judge it,"* he proclaimed about 430 B.C.

This profoundly revolutionary and democratic declaration became the foundation-stone for the philosophy of constitutionalism developed by Cicero four hundred years later, and by Adams, Madison, Washington, and Franklin 2200 years after.

Plato came onto the Athenian stage in the generation after the Periclean revolution. Born in 428 B.C., Plato in his early years was politically ambitious. Reactionary politicians, spying his talent, wooed him. Among his early writings was *The Republic*, about 370 B.C., a utopian plan for a perfect state ruled by philosopher-kings. Whether it was only a philosophical fantasy, a speculative binge, or whether it was really a political campaign platform is an issue today's scholars hotly debate. But there is no doubt that the older Plato, after he started his Academy and became a career educator with no political aspirations, was wiser and more mature, as his later work, *The*

Laws, reveals. And there is no doubt that *The Republic* was a design for a totalitarian state that would arrest all change, the very process that was continuously revolutionizing Athenian society to the distress of his displaced, disgruntled noble patrons.

The purpose of Plato's ideal state was to train the citizens to become "virtuous." Citizens would be divided into three classes according to the three dominant virtues of the soul—the governing class (whose virtue is wisdom); the military class (valor); and the industrial class (self-restraint and willing obedience). The ruler would be "the philosopher king," who seems to be in Plato's mind partly at least a copy of the tribal priest-king. For each citizen, Plato insists, true happiness is achieved only by keeping his place. The ruler must find happiness in ruling, the warrior in warring, and—we may infer—the slave in serving. Plato claims to aim not at the happiness of any individual nor of any class, but at the happiness of the whole—a concept totalitarian in character and resembling Rousseau's "General Will," which we will explore. Plato wrote:

> The greatest principle of all is that nobody, whether male or female, should be without a leader. Nor should the mind of anybody be habituated to letting him do anything at all on his own initiative; neither out of zeal, nor even playfully. But in war and in the midst of peace —to his leader he shall direct his eye and follow him faithfully. And even in the smallest matter he should stand under leadership. For example, he should get up, or move, or wash, or take his meals . . . only if he has been told to do so. In a word, he should teach his soul, by long habit, never to dream of acting independently, and to become utterly incapable of it.

Such a passage may have sounded marvelous to speculative philosophers down through the ages, but it sounds hardly so in the twentieth-century age of Stalin and Hitler that produced also Orwell and Huxley, *1984* and *Brave New World.* It was probably inevitable that the revisionists should begin to catch up with Plato.

In 1937 R. H. S. Crossman, a scholar of Greek and philosophy professor at Oxford (and later member of Parliament), published his *Plato Today,* radically reinterpreting Plato's political views. He called Plato a "failed politician" and proclaimed that "the Academy was really a school for counter-revolutionaries and *The Republic* not a timeless exposition of ultimate truths but a handbook for aspiring dictators." Plato's was "the first in a line of social philosophies revolting against civilization and giving expression to the intellectual's deep-felt dissatisfaction with a world which does not, and cannot, live up to our moral ideals and to our dreams of perfection."[4]

Plato was counter-revolutionary because he profoundly feared and disliked the Athenian democratic revolution, Crossman argues. This revolution had shaken morality and religion to their very foundations. Not only in Athens, but all over the Greek world, the destruction of aristocratic authority had brought with it a new freedom of spirit, a distrust of traditional authority not only in the political but in the religious sphere, and a reliance on human reason (and the individual) as the only proper instrument for the solution of every problem. The age differed very little from that which nourished Marx and Lenin—the Industrial Revolution that profoundly changed the old class-structure of society, Darwinism that challenged the dogmas of the churches, and political liberalism that freed men from the established authoritarian order of scientific and ethical dogma.

Karl Popper, in *The Open Society and Its Enemies* (1945), piled high the evidence against Plato and traced the social and historical roots of his reaction. He argues that *The Republic* was written as an actual political campaign document, with Plato viewing himself as a real candidate for philosopher-king. Thus did Plato launch a perennial reactionary revolt against freedom and reason in behalf of a return to tribalism, in Popper's view. The tribal form of social life emphasized the supreme importance of the tribe without which the individual is nothing at all. From it naturally grew the doctrine of the chosen people. Ultimate twentieth-century derivatives were the racialism of the Nazis, the fascism of the corporate state, and the Marxian dictatorship of the chosen class. All, from Plato to Mussolini to the American Ruddites of 1964–70, were efforts to solve or escape the problem of the changing social world and to retreat into a peaceful and stable world in which everyone "knows his place." The open society confronts individuals with personal choice—and attendant anxiety and stress. The change from tribalism for many means a serious inward struggle, and the utopian dream is an effort "to comfort themselves for the loss of a stable world."[5] "A feeling of drift seems to be a typical reaction to the dissolution of the ancient tribal forms of social life," says Popper:[6]

I believe that Plato, with deep sociological insight, found that his contemporaries were suffering under a severe strain, and that this strain was due to the social revolution which had begun with the rise of democracy and individualism. He succeeded in discovering the main causes of their deeply rooted unhappiness—social change, and social dissension—and he did his utmost to fight them . . . The medico-political treatment which he recommended, the arrest of change and the return to tribalism, was hopelessly wrong.[7]

Thus Plato sought to replace the stress of the open society with its ever-widening field of personal decisions, problems, and responsibilities, by the arrested society of philosopher-kings who resembled nothing so much as the theocratic tribal priest-kings.[8] It was a program for arresting change. His dream of unity and beauty and perfection and collectivism was a product as well as a symptom of the lost spirit of tribalism. No modern American who has left the small towns or farm communities—that until 1920 cradled half our population—for the metropolis of the mid-twentieth century can help but feel this same melancholiac longing for lost human community. Plato may well have been suffering and seeking to escape the stress of "future shock." But, says Popper:

> Excellent as Plato's sociological diagnosis was, his own development proves that the therapy he recommended is worse than the evil he tried to combat. Arresting political change is not the remedy; it cannot bring happiness. We can never return to the alleged innocence and beauty of the closed society. Our dream of heaven cannot be realized on earth. Once we begin to rely upon our reason, and to use our powers of criticism, once we feel the call of personal responsibilities, and with it, the responsibility of helping to advance knowledge, we cannot return to a state of implicit submission to tribal magic. For those who have eaten of the tree of knowledge, paradise is lost. The more we try to return to the heroic age of tribalism, the more surely do we arrive at the Inquisition, at the Secret Police, and at a romanticized gangsterism. Beginning with the suppression of reason and truth, we must end with the most brutal and violent destruction of all that is human. *There is no return to a harmonious state of nature. If we turn back, then we must go the whole way—we must return to the beasts.*

MEDIEVAL MESSIANICS PURSUE THE MILLENNIUM   Between the eleventh and sixteenth centuries Europe's poor masses repeatedly spawned swarms of hive-like messianic movements. They would separate from the rest of medieval society and follow some prophet promising the Kingdom Come, a world purged of suffering and sin. Social historian Norman Cohn traces these movements in detail in his illuminating book, *The Pursuit Of The Millennium,* subtitled: "Revolutionary messianism in medieval and Reformation Europe and its bearing on modern totalitarian movements."[10] Such movements included Tanchelm's heresy in Utrecht (1110–1115); the pseudo-Baldwin craze in Flanders (1225); Joachim of Fiore (1145–1202); the "Brethren of the Free Spirit" which recurred among the multitude of wandering preachers in the densely populated, highly urbanized areas of northern France and the Low Countries along the Rhine that were so prone to messianic excitement; the "flagellants" who massacred the Jews in the Rhineland cities during and after the Black Death (1347–1350); the Drummer of Niklashausen in 1476; Thomas Munzer in 1625; the "Ranters" in Cromwell's England, and many more. Invariably the leaders cemented their followers as an in-group by designating a visible and accessible hate target, an Antichrist onto which they could project all evils—the local clergy, the nobility or the Jews were favored.

The career of the Drummer of Niklashausen was representative. This shepherd began haranguing the peasants and artisans in the taverns and market places near Wurzburg. At first he attacked the local lords and princes, then the whole social system of his day. As his fame grew, he addressed thousands, sometimes from the top of a tub, sometimes from an upper window or a tree. He represented himself as one sent by God, and his message was always revolutionary and violently against the constituted authorities. "The Emperor is a scoundrel and the Pope is useless. Alas, poor devils that you are!" he told the people. He rallied the oppressed, impoverished and resentful in all the towns and villages along the Tauber valley, and spread such mass hysteria whenever he spoke that guards were required to keep fervid followers from crushing him to death. People snatched his clothing and treasured the pieces like relics. When the Prince-Bishop of Wurzburg sought to re-establish the Town Council's authority, bloody riots and open warfare exploded. Ultimately, the *Trommler* was tried by an ecclesiastical court, found guilty of sorcery and heresy, and burned at the stake.[11]

These messianic movements can only be described as "collective megalomania," Cohn declares, and they "throw considerable light on the sociology and psychology of totalitarian movements in their revolutionary heyday."[12] Comparing the medieval chiliastic movements and contemporary totalitarianisms, Cohn concluded: "The old symbols and the old slogans have indeed disappeared, to be replaced by new ones; but the structure of the basic fantasies seems to have changed scarcely at all."[13] The prophets and their massed messianics were early prototypes of our modern Hitlers and Lenins and their revolutionaries expecting the thousand-year Reich or the post-revolutionary utopian flowering of mankind.

Invariably these apocalyptic movements arose in similar circumstances: "when population was increasing, industrialization was getting under way, traditional social bonds were being weakened or shattered and the gap between rich and poor was becoming a chasm." Then, among the surplus population living on the margin of society, epidemics of revolutionary chiliasm would spread. The victims:

> peasants without land or with too little land even for subsistence; journeymen and unskilled workers living under the continuous threat of unemployment; beggars and vagabonds—in fact, that amorphous mass of people who were not simply poor but who could find no assured and recognized place in society at all. These people lacked the material and emotional support afforded by traditional social groups; their kinship-groups had disintegrated and they were not effectively organized in village communities or in guilds; for them there existed no regular, institutionalized methods of voicing their grievances or pressing their claims. Instead they waited for a *propheta* to bind them together in a group of their own—which would then emerge as a movement of a peculiar kind, driven on by a wild enthusiasm born of desperation.
>
> ... Then in each of these areas in turn a collective sense of impotence and anxiety and envy suddenly discharged itself in a frantic urge to smite the ungodly—and by doing so to bring into being, out of suffering inflicted and suffering endured, that final Kingdom where the Saints, clustered around the great sheltering figure of their Messiah, were to enjoy ease and riches, security and power for all eternity."[14]

The leaders who rallied these True Believers were usually themselves believers, captives of the common fantasy. The followers projected onto the Prophet the classic Good Father image, reflecting their internal needs for a herd as a home and a shepherd as a guardian. And in turn there were always men around willing for their own internal emotional reasons to accept such a projection, for they saw themselves and wished to be seen as the infallible, wonder-working savior and agent of salvation. If they did not actually regard themselves as incarnate gods, at least they felt themselves vessels of divinity and really believed their Inner Light would guide themselves and their followers to the Promised Land in which all would be made new and spared all suffering. In their common struggle as the Forces of Light against the Forces of Darkness, the Hosts of Antichrist, such crimes as robbery, rape, and massacre became not only guiltless but holy acts.[15]

These pathological messianic epidemics were regular features of medieval urbanization. In the eleventh, twelfth, and thirteenth centuries, northeast France and the Low Countries enjoyed firm governments and peace. Population grew rapidly as a result, overburdening the land and sending multitudes of displaced peasants streaming into the growing commercial and industrial centers, where textile manufacturing was beginning to prosper. Towns in Flanders grew to as many as 20,000 to 50,000 people—such urban agglomerations had not existed since the time of Rome. They teemed with beggars, street gangs, prostitutes, unemployed peasants, and, with the fluctuations of business, unemployed craftsmen and guildsmen. These were the raw tinder for flashfires of messianic crazes.

A persistent characteristic of these movements was their *antinomianism*—denial of all rules and norms. It was especially so of the continuing Free Spirit heresy that spread among small pockets of gypsy-like (or, for modern America, hippie-like) mystics. They extended from Silesia in central Europe to France and England, where they were known as the Ranters and where they generally merged into the Quakers. They appeared about the twelfth century. The adepts of the Free Spirit were the psychological antecedents of Bakunin, Nechayev, and many of our own communists, anarchists, and nihilists. They manifested their antinomianism in cheating, theft, robbery, justified violence of all sorts, ritual nakedness, promiscuity on principle, and even ritual rape and murder. Fundamentally they were a gnostic heresy, like all the other millenarians: the Free Spirit believed he had attained a perfection so absolute he was incapable of sin. He was an amoral superman, a "perfect man," and hence licensed by God, even enjoined, to do whatever was commonly regarded as forbidden. Usually that meant a sexual license; and it also usually embodied a philosophy of the abolition of private property. In practice that meant ritual seduction, vagabondage, and living by theft. And the Free Spirits usually also foresaw an early apocalyptic clash and the Millennium.*

One of the earliest messianic and utopian urban insurrections

*The medieval accounts of these wandering groups remind us of contemporary California's Charles Manson "family," whose "adepts" murdered Sharon Tate and her house guests. The resemblance is complete even to Manson's vision of an imminent "helter-skelter" race war and utopian rule by whites, with himself at their head.

was that of Cola Di Rienzi at Rome in 1347, during the exile of the popes at Avignon. Son of a tavern-keeper, Rienzi gathered supporters to the ideal of restoring a new Roman Empire and dressed in full armor he rode to proclaim a new day of glory for the imperial city. He addressed a large assembly on "the servitude and redemption of Rome." The nobles fled, and by acclamation Rienzi was proclaimed absolute ruler. He took the ancient title of Tribune of Rome. He governed sternly, in contrast to the licentiousness of the nobility, and invited all the cities and provinces of Italy to send representatives to an assembly. This fantastic ceremonial proved costly to taxpayers, and his extravagant pretensions soon excited ridicule. He lasted just under seven months before the nobles regained control, and he had to flee into hiding. Rienzi continued to plot and scheme, and from Avignon Innocence VI used him as a cat's paw until, in a new attempted coup in 1354, Rienzi was killed. Cohn summarizes his findings on the medieval messianics:

> The *propheta* himself belonged to a distinctive social type which changed little down the centuries . . . Whatever their individual histories, collectively these people formed a recognizable social stratum—a frustrated and rather low-grade intelligentsia. And it was here, in this restless world of *déclassé* intellectuals and semi-intellectuals, that eschatological lore was not only studied and conserved but also edited and elaborated until it was fit to serve as a revolutionary ideology . . .
>
> No doubt some of these people were megalomaniacs and others were imposters and many were both at once—but to all of them one thing is common: each claimed to be charged with the unique mission of bringing history to its preordained consummation. And this claim on the part of the *propheta* deeply influenced the group that formed around him. For what the *propheta* offered to his followers was not simply a chance to improve their lot and to escape from pressing anxieties—it was also, and above all, the prospect of carrying out a divinely ordained mission of stupendous, unique importance. This fantasy quickly came to enthrall them in their turn. And what followed then was the formation of a group of a peculiar kind, a true prototype of a modern totalitarian party: a restlessly dynamic and utterly ruthless group which, obsessed by the apocalyptic fantasy and filled with the conviction of its own infallibility, set itself above the rest of humanity and recognized no claims save that of its own supposed mission.[16]

Thus the Leader and the Followers were held together by a powerful psychological magnetism. In each other and in their messianic commune they found *escape* from stress, boredom, facelessness and anxiety; they satisfied their *lust for significance;* and they found *hate targets* onto which to project their subterranean frustrations and hostilities.

THE ARCHETYPAL EDEN FANTASY   The Eden fantasy is thus one of the most persistent dreams in men's imaginations through the centuries. It is the notion that in some remote past or near or distant future lies an era of perfect peace in which there would be no aggressive manifestations or stress of any kind. Many modern behavioral scientists believe it is an *archetypal fantasy*—a mental content which lies dormant in the minds of all men, and which is therefore easily activated by enthusiasts of the type who activated and joined the medieval messianic movements.[17]

Two common human frictions may ignite the individual's latent archetypal utopianism:

1. The stress of a flawed early family environment. Karl Stern, in his book *The Flight for Woman,* demonstrated that for philosophers like Descartes and Schopenhauer their very alienation from love spawned their philosophies.[18] Their need to create an ideal world was a compensation for the disappointments of reality and was rooted in maternal deprivation. Alexander Herzberg in his *The Psychology of Philosophy* traced the lives of great philosophers from the earliest times. He found their penchant for abstraction was uniformly a defensive retreat from reality, activated in some cases by a frail physical constitution, in others by super-sensitive or inhibitive personality structures.[19]

2. The continuing stress of the individual's relationship to the group. The individual human being must have a considerable aggressive drive to assert and establish his independence as he grows up. But to maintain his parents' love and support he must repress this instinctive aggression. He also must muster considerable aggression to maintain his independence from his family and tribal society, though his interdependence restrains his aggressiveness since he must live in his society and maintain himself in the group to survive. Thus he wages a never-ending war between the self and the group —a war from which inevitably at times he longs to escape.[20]

Utopianism thus seems to be an effort to escape stress—of social change, of parental criticism and threat, of the individual's combat with the group as he proceeds through the process of socialization and the cooperation necessary to survival. It is a flight from the darker side of what Freud called *Civilization and Its Discontents.* It is an intellectual reflection of the Freudian death instinct—the longing for an end to struggle and change and stress of life's hurly burly. It may also arise from a kind of weariness that Nietzsche described long ago: "weariness that wants to reach the ultimate with one leap, with one fatal leap, a poor ignorant weariness that does not want to want any more; this created all gods and other worlds." The utopian builds his dream like the little boy builds his tree house: to have a place to escape to when his mother scolds and his mundane surroundings become oppressive. The dreamer flees his own inner turmoil and escapes an agonizing introspection.

But hostility will out. And so he projects it onto those who do not fit the dream, to the evil men who prevent its realization: capitalist, Jew, Negro, any number of hate targets that may be scapegoated for the failure of the Kingdom to Come.

Accordingly, the history of the questers after Utopia and Kingdom Come is littered with horrendous crimes in the name of Man's Salvation. Writes R. A. Knox:

> Your Anabaptist or Ranter may consult the light within him, and mistake some psychological urge for a divine guidance. He will then be guilty of the most atrocious cruelties, of the most astounding profligacies, on the ground that he is not permitted merely, but ordered, to act in this way. It is very difficult to argue with him. The very outrageousness of his conduct is, in a sense, the guarantee of its supernatural inspriation. 'How could you suppose,' he will argue, 'that I would behave in such a manner so unlike myself, if a Divine command had not made it necessary?' We might, to be sure, write off these unpalatable incidents as the result of lunacy, if the 'inspiration' was felt only by a single person. But what are we to make of it, when a whole group of energumens make common cause?[21]

What indeed? Such Holy Killers manned the planned genocide of Russia's millions of kulaks after 1927 and of Germany's Jews after 1936. And they did it in the name of salvation, of building a perfect society, of their malignant dream.

The compulsive utopians, when they get serious about politics, invariably deal with reality the way Procrustes, the legendary cruel robber-giant of Attica, dealt with his victims. Procrustes would lure travelers to his home and when they would lie down on his bed, he lopped off as much of their limbs as was required to make their length equal that of his bed; or if they were too short he stretched them. Hence the word "procrustean" has come to stand for the trait of reducing events or reality to fit preconceived forms by force or mutilation, or torturing disparity into conformity or uniformity. The procrustean utopian philosopher, from Munzer to Marx to Mao, distorts the real world into his intellectual and abstract ideological molds instead of shaping thought to fit facts and events. For emotional-ideological reasons, he *procrusteanizes* his environment. If mankind will not fit the procrustean philosopher-king's vision, then individual men must be stretched on the rack or chopped on the guillotine or otherwise forced into the intellectual iron maiden in the ruler's brain.

In every case, from Plato to Munzer, from Babeuf to Marx to Lenin to Mao to Tom Hayden, Mark Rudd and Huey Newton, they were political-ideological-theological con men. They peddled a cure-all ideological snake oil, promising to arrest change and to release their true-believing followers from the ordeal of change. They offered escape from the stress of a complicated existence, from the doom of an insignificant life, from the loneliness of a rootless state. They promised to answer men's universal quest for communion and lust for significance. They offered a return to the tribal comfort of membership in the Chosen People. As with all successful con men, to greater or lesser degrees they conned themselves as well as their followers into believing that they had the True Gospel, represented the Kingdom Coming and would lead all True Believers into the Promised Land. So believing, they also believed they were themselves above the rules set for ordinary men. For leaders as well as led, with bruised egos and fragile self-esteem, self-doubt is too painful to endure.

Depressing is the regularity and similarity in these occurrences of epidemic messianic radicalism from ancient Athens to modern Berkeley and Columbia and Harvard.

I. THE FRENCH REVOLUTION

Chapter 2
ROUSSEAU: THE IGNOBLE SAVAGE

Rousseau clothed passion in the garb of philosophy, and preached the sweeping away of injustice by the perpetration of further injustice.

—T. H. Huxley: *On the Natural Inequality of Man*, 1890

Rousseau knows he is talking nonsense, and laughs at the world for staring at him.

—Samuel Johnson, 1769

You know, a guerrilla is a romantic man. He is one who live with the trees, the sunrise, the starlight, with his gun alone, bold and free, like Rousseau's magnificent savage. If you think it is all organization then you don't understand.

—A former Viet Minh guerrilla general, 1963

PARIS TO PEKING   On December 26, 1962, Peking, the capital of the world's most populous communist state, was bedecked with red flags floating over the pagodas. Under a clear blue sky thousands crowded into the city's squares to commemorate the 250th anniversary of the birth of a French writer and philosopher, Jean-Jacques Rousseau. Red China's distinguished men of government and letters toasted him as one of the world's cultural giants. The Russian-sponsored World Peace Council, too, from its headquarters in Prague, Czechoslovakia, honored Rousseau with special commemorations and programs throughout the year.

Why should modern communists pay such homage to a centuries-old philosopher?

Rousseau was the man of whom Napoleon said, "Without him the French Revolution would not have occurred."

Like comets swerving into our solar system out of the dark universe, ideas sometimes streak across the affairs of men, portending great events. These comet-like ideas engage the attention of men and obsess their souls, driving them to strain muscles, torture brains, and fight battles.

Why do these ideas appear? Occasionally the times are right, and they seem programmed to appear on the stage of history at that moment. Other times they appear by accident and are generated by change, but in turn change the whole script.

Such was Rousseau's favorite theme that man is by nature good and that his social environment is the source of all corruption. This idea was only a short step to the radical conviction that to bring to reality the imagined utopia of the future the progressive, humanitarian man must first clear the way for the New World and New Man by destroying existing society.

Rousseau hit upon this idea accidently. A dozen years later he boosted the myth that it came to him in a religious experience in 1749 as he was walking to Vincennes to visit his friend Diderot. The Grand Flash smote him prostrate along the roadside and convinced him he was Chosen to bring the Revealed Truth to all other men:

> All at once I felt myself dazzled by a thousand sparkling lights. Crowds of vivid ideas thronged into my mind . . . A violent palpitation oppressed me. I sank down beneath a tree . . . Ah, if ever I could have written a quarter of what I saw and felt under that tree, with what clarity I should have revealed all the contradictions of our social system! With what simplicity I should have demonstrated that man is by nature good, and that only our institutions make him bad![1]

But Morelley, Marmontel, and other mutual confidants of both men agree upon a different story. Rousseau was walking with Diderot—as Marmontel tells us in his memoirs[2]—and the two were discussing the prize offered by the Academy of Dijon for the best treatise on the subject: "Has the Progress of the Arts and Sciences Contributed to the Purification of Morals?" Rousseau, an unsuccessful musician, composer and poet, an unknown as a writer, told his famous friend he intended to compete.

"Which side will you take?" asked Diderot.

"The affirmative," replied Rousseau.

"That is the ass's way. All men of mediocre talents will take that route and will dispense with commonplaces. Take the other side and you will find yourself in open country, rich and fruitful, where eloquence and philosophy can be given full play."

"You are right," said Rousseau after a moment's reflection. "I will follow your advice."

"That moment," says Marmontel with profound psychological insight, "determined his character—the role he was to play and the mask he was to assume." In full accord with the psychological law of role-persistence Rousseau became henceforth the "noble savage" who glorifies the "natural man," and repudiates his own contemporary civilization.

Rousseau won the Dijon prize and created an unparalleled sensation. His essay took the artificial and crotchety French society of the day by storm. In it, he developed the famous "paradox of Rousseau," the assertion of the savage state as superior to the civilized state. He argued that civilization, arts and sciences have corrupted man's natural goodness, and glorified the "noble savage." Furthermore, only strong and virtuous countries (no examples cited) can retain primitive simplicity. His third and main point was that corruption and military defeat are the rewards of progress.

These ideas were not new. Nor were they Rousseau's alone. But he presented them concretely at one of those watershed points of history and made them a battle cry for a new age. He first expressed the modern radical's attitude toward the past. Scholars attribute his impact on the Europe of his time to the beauty of his language as much as anything else. Through this beauty, in the words of one famous scholar, Rousseau "created new modes of thought and feeling, a wholly new idiom which the artistic and social rebels of the 19th century adopted as their natural vehicle of self-expression."[3]

PLAYING THE ROLE   When Rousseau penned this essay he was thirty-eight-years old and distinguished only by his lack of success. A thoroughly alienated person, he had quarreled and floated his way through life as a compulsive vagabond and emotional cripple. Toward the end of his life he recalled:

> I became disgusted with men . . . I have never been truly accustomed to civil society, where all is worry, obligation, duty and where my natural independence renders me always incapable of the subjections necessary to whoever wishes to live among men.[4]

Rousseau as a result of his essay found himself the lion of the Paris salons. Francueil gave him a valuable post as cashier in the receiver-general's office. All Europe rang with his fame. That his newly-found success deeply influenced him is demonstrated by the way he began playing the role he had created. Because his essay glorified the "noble savage" living in a state of nature, he began living according to its maxims. To show his rejection of the rotten "Establishment" society, he discarded the fashionable gold braid, sword and white stockings, and adopted the simple garb and smaller wig of the middle class. He even gave away his watch, declaring grandly he no longer needed to know the time as time-watching was an evil manifestation of civilization. Rousseau's success convinced him that he had stumbled unwittingly upon an epoch-making truth. And what is more natural, in the Pavlovian sense of a correct response gaining a reward and thereby confirming the response?

In 1753 the Academy of Dijon offered another prize, this time for the best essay on "the origin and the causes of inequality among men." Rousseau quite naturally decided to compete again. He did not win the prize, but his "Discourse on Inequality," published in 1755, further stirred contemporary thought. He began the tract with these famous words:

> The first man who having enclosed a piece of ground presumed to say, "This is mine," and found people simple enough to believe him, was the true founder of civil society. What crimes, what wars what murders what miseries and horrors the human race would have been spared had someone but pulled up the stakes and filled in the ditch and cried to his fellow-men: "Beware, don't listen to this imposter! You are lost if you forget that the fruits of the earth belong to everyone, and that the land belongs to no one!"

With this Rousseau launched a new tirade indicting all existing civilization, the political state, and private property as perverters of man's natural innocence. He propounded anew his sentimental romantic's case for a "return to nature" as seen in savages and animals. In this natural, primitive state, Rousseau maintained, there are no inequalities of social position, rank, or inherited wealth. All development beyond this tribal period he condemned for the introduction of private property, an inequality producing a handful of the mighty rich and millions living in squalor and obscurity. Private property was based on plunder. The growth of communities only widened the gulf between the strong and rich and the helpless and poor. To bring back justice and peace these institutions and their works had to be destroyed. In mankind's original state, things were held in common, and envy and violence were absent. Return to a "state of nature" and the Golden Age will return.

This was bad anthropology, banal psychology, atrocious history, and downright absurd sociology. It was a gargantuan oversimplification and distortion of social organization. It promoted the conception of social and economic classes, of divisions of labor, as warring, conflicting, struggling elements rather than what they were in fact—cooperating specialists operating as a team for productivity. Granted, many times the input and division of the product were sadly disproportionate, and often the relationship was degrading and lacking in humane reciprocity. Nevertheless, the very organization of production requires class cooperation, not class struggle. To regard the division of labor implicit in the act of fencing off a piece of property to grow things as an act of brigandage, was a horrendous piece of sociological observation. It reflected not reality but Rousseau's own "sour grapes" reaction to an existing social structure to which he, as a compulsive vagabond, had never been able to establish an enduring attachment.

Rousseau's "Discourse on Inequality" repudiated European civilization on the basis of a myth that this civilization had changed man's natural goodness and cut him off from his heritage of equality, reason, and benevolence. It was one of the earliest and most primitive expressions of the class struggle doctrine and the Marxian theory of the capitalist state as a weapon of the wealthy exploiters in class struggle. (Marx and Engels acknowledged frankly their debt to Rousseau.) The essay was one of the earliest and clearest manifestations of a basic psychological component of modern communism and radicalism: *the absolutist, nihilistic belief that existing society is all evil, corrupt, unjust and hateful, and that to achieve the golden age, since man is naturally good, the established order must be destroyed first.*

Neither Rousseau nor anyone else in this age of the first stirrings of the Industrial Revolution understood the value of entrepreneurship—the imagination to visualize new products and the initiative to marshal the factors of production such as labor and raw materials to produce goods and satisfy wants. No one understood, either, the function of profits as the wages of good entrepreneurship and sound management. They could not foresee the tremendous benefits of such functions nor understand that economic value and wealth are created primarily by production, innovation, and entrepreneurship, not mere idle property ownership. All the Rousseauists understood was vague frustration over the sparse economic demand for their intellectual outpourings, while material rewards seemed to gravitate toward contemptible nonintellectual economic doers who were forging the new urban bourgeois society. That Rousseau—a ne'er-do-well, wandering pauper—and the generalized free-floating hatred of all society in subsequent years should express themselves in attacks on private property and property owners was natural enough. Property and their owners were the most universally available targets.

Though there was much objectively in eighteenth-century Europe to condemn, even so vicious a critic as Voltaire could not accept Rousseau's warped thinking. When Rousseau sent him a copy of his "Discourse on the Origin of Inequality," Voltaire responded:

> I have received, sir, your new book against the human species, and I thank you for it . . . No one has ever been so witty as you are in trying to turn us into brutes; to read your book makes one long to go on all fours. As, however, it is now some sixty years since I gave up the practice, I feel that it is unfortunately impossible for me to resume it.[5]

And when he saw Rousseau's passion for savagery continued in the *Social Contract,* Voltaire wrote to a friend, "Ah, Monsieur, you see now that Jean-Jacques resembles a philosopher as a monkey resembles a man."[6] He is the "dog of Diogenes gone mad."[7] If civilization were the curse of man, the logical course of Rousseau's thought was to seek its destruction. This was exactly the inference which Voltaire drew in his satire *Timon,* designed to laugh Rousseauism out of style. Unhappily for humanity, Voltaire did not succeed.

ROUSSEAU'S PSYCHOPATHOLOGY   "My birth was the first of my misfortunes," Rousseau declared in his *Confessions.*[8] "I was born a poor and sickly child, and cost my mother her life." A paternal aunt nursed him through: "My dear aunt, I pardon you for causing me to live," he wrote.

Scholars in the conventional history of philosophy and political thought spend too much effort studying *what* philosophers think and too little on *why* they think. In Rousseau's case psychology and sociology are more enlightening than merely describing his philosophy. Certainly the facts of Rousseau's life present absorbing grist for the modern psychoanalytic mill. Many biographers and historians have diagnosed him, and although differing in detail, they agree that he presents a massively pathological personality, poignant and pitiable.

Born in Geneva in 1712, Rousseau was the son of a poor man who combined the professions of watchmaker and dancing-master. His father was of unstable disposition and his attitude toward young Jean-Jacques wavered between overfondness and neglect and outright brutality—a changeability that modern psychiatrists know generates more stress, guilt and repressed rage than either extreme consistently practiced. The boy was inevitably destined to feel guilt over the fact that his birth cost his mother's life; but the father magnified it manifold: "Jean-Jacques, let's talk about your mother," he would say. And invariably, the two wound up in tears. Rousseau recorded: "He thought he saw her again in me, without being able to forget that I had taken her away from him. He never kissed me without my feeling in his sighs, in his convulsive embraces, that bitter regret was mingled in his caresses; they were all the more tender for it . . . ." Such embraces were a clear source of his latent homosexuality.

The father was capable of mindless rage and brutality, too. Once, as punishment for having torn his Latin book, he locked his son in an attic room on short rations for several days and beat him daily. No doubt such experience generated volcanic subterranean rages. They were all the more intensified by the motherless child's urgent need for love, and hence the imperative of repressing his rage and justifying his father by assuming a massive burden of compulsive guilt. The "noble savage" is born of this emotional jungle: "How could I have become wicked when I never saw anything except models of gentleness?" Rousseau writes.[9] Subjectively perhaps he never saw otherwise because he could not afford to face reality. Here is the old red thread: the need to deny and escape a hostile world and to find utopia.

The father taught the lad his letters out of Plutarch and the French seventeenth-century romances. The two remained reading in his father's shop sometimes all night until they saw the swallows flying low under the eaves. But, by and large, relatives raised the boy. Jean-Jacques received so little regular training that discipline remained anathema all his life, and probably was starved for normal parental affection and tenderness as well as a close role-model. Educated in the orthodox Calvinist fashion, he left school at the age of twelve when his father, facing trial as a result of a brawl, ran away, leaving the lad to shift for himself. Apprenticed to various trades, he hated them all. First he was a notary's helper, was fired, became an engraver's apprentice, and ran away at the age of sixteen. Then the lad wandered over the countryside in Savoy in southeast France. Will Durant describes the effect of this chaotic childhood:

> Rousseau had been a sickly youth—driven into brooding and introversion by his physical weakness and the unsympathetic attitude of his

parents and teachers; he had escaped from the stings of reality into a hothouse world of dreams, where the victories denied him in life and love could be had for the imaging. His *Confessions* reveal an unreconciled complex of the most refined sentimentality with an obtuse sense of decency and honor; and through it all an unsullied conviction of his moral superiority.[10]

Here we have another manifestation of a basic psychological component of the modern totalitarian: *compulsive belief*—born of a bruised ego needing self-esteem and a defense mechanism—*that he is endowed with moral and intellectual superiority and is fit to claim the right to rule his fellow men and make decisions for all humanity.*

Rousseau became a lackey and a clerk, then entered a Catholic seminary after a conversion he said frankly later was for wholly mercenary motives: "I could not dissemble from myself that the holy deed I was about to do was at bottom the act of a bandit." He was expelled after two months and became a lackey to a lady in Turin who died after three months. Next he took up with a Madame de Warens, a convert from Protestantism like himself, a fine lady who enjoyed a pension from Savoy's king for her services to religion. She had established in her house at Annency a refuge for Protestant youths, to which Rousseau was sent by a Savoyard priest. Rousseau called her "maman" even after she became his mistress. For the next fourteen years Rousseau led a very irregular existence, working occasionally as a footman, secretary, music teacher, and wandering about France and Savoy. Inevitably, though, he returned to the matriarchal security of Mme. de Warens' home.

In 1743 he accompanied the French ambassador to Venice as secretary, but was offended by his employer's condescending manner and returned to Paris the next year. He attempted to sue the diplomat, but soon learned that a commoner could rarely obtain redress from an aristocrat, an experience which soured him considerably.

There is general agreement that during the last ten to fifteen years of his life Rousseau was not wholly sane—and sometimes totally insane. He was a clear psychopath most of his life. At twenty-four he was seized by a neurotic nervous depression and prostration that enervated him, and made him weep over the most trivial things. He believed himself on the verge of death. After a temporary improvement, he suffered a curious attack of loud hammering at the temples and buzzing, murmuring, whistling, and knocking in the ears, accompanied by sudden deafness. The ear noises and deafness continued; a shortness of breath, insomnia, anxiety and moodiness also followed. Vertigo on bending down and shortness of breath when walking or lifting weights rendered physical activity impossible. Rousseau's hypochondria was accompanied by a passivity characteristic of masochism which he describes: "I was growing accustomed to languishing, to going without sleep, *to thinking* instead of acting."[11] (Such is the inevitable result of intense anxiety and inhibition.) Finally, Rousseau got it into his head, as hypochondriacs will, that he was suffering from a "polypus" or tumor in the heart. So he set forth to see a famous doctor at Montpellier. On the way, however, as recorded in his *Confessions,* he met a lady who showed interest in him "and then goodbye to fever, vapours and polypus—all vanished in her presence, save some few palpitations of which she would not cure me."

We have already noted Rousseau's inclination to vagabondage. He also showed masochistic and exhibitionist tendencies in his sex life and extraordinarily intense inhibitions. Of these he himself provides numerous detailed accounts. Sent to a Calvinist pastor's boarding school when he was eleven, he fell in love with his teacher, the pastor's thirty-year-old sister. When she whipped him for misconduct he felt "an admixture of sensuality which left me rather more eager than otherwise for a repetition by the same hand."[12] When he offended further he took such obvious pleasure in suffering beneath her blows that she resolved never to whip him again. This masochistic streak remained in Rousseau all his life. In later teenage he resorted to exhibitionism, slipping about in dark alleys and hidden corners and exposing his buttocks to girls and young women at a distance, and inviting whipping: "The foolish pleasure which I had in displaying this ridiculous object before their eyes cannot be described. From this there was but a step to the desired treatment; and I do not doubt that some resolute woman passing by would have given me the amusement had I had the audacity to continue." Alas, once he exposed himself to several girls, and a guardsman armed with a heavy sword leading several old women with brooms hauled him out. He lied his way free by pretending to be a deranged young nobleman.

His shyness was so intense he could not perform the simplest everyday tasks if he felt watched.

A thousand times, whilst I was an apprentice and afterwards, I have gone out with the intention of buying some sweetmeat or other. I approach the confectioner's shop; I see women at the counter; I believe that they are laughing and joking with one another at the little sugar-baby. I pass a fruit stall and cast glances at the nice pears; their fragrance attracts me. Two or three young people standing near look at me; a man who knows me is standing at the door of his shop . . . My shortsightedness causes me a thousand illusions. Every passerby seems to be an acquaintance and I am always rendered diffident, *restrained by some obstacle;* my longing grows with my hesitancy and finally I go home like a fool, consumed with desire.[13]

If he delayed a visit for a few days, fear of fulfilling his duty so late made him afraid to pay it at all. This diffidence was especially noticeable where women were involved. He had extreme difficulty making the acquaintance of women, and in their company he was often so awkward and stupid that they soon lost interest in him. When in love these traits ballooned to distraction and in situations of a certain delicacy Rousseau was frequently unable to take the lead. (When he yielded his virginity to Mme. de Warens, it was she who took the lead.) Never, even in the most impassioned love encounters, did he dare to admit his masochistic perversion to a woman. When once an Italian prostitute, whom he ardently desired and whose room he had entered, told him to sit at her feet, he threw himself down, trembling, with a cry:

But what will hardly be believed is that I dared attempt no more, not even to say a single word, to raise my eyes to her, even in my awkward position to touch her by leaning an instant against her knee. I was dumb and motionless, but certainly not calm; everything in me betrayed my agitation.[14]

Rousseau was only sixteen at the time of this scene, but he reacted exactly the same way thirty years later toward Mme. d'Houdetot, whom he loved passionately.

We had supped together and we were alone in a grove in the moonlight and after two hours of the most vivacious and tender conversation we went at midnight out of the grove and her friend's arms as untouched, as pure in body and heart as she had gone in. Reader, ponder all the circumstances! I will add nothing to them.[15]

[49]

Rousseau's massive inhibitions hindered all his relations with other people.

> Everything makes me shy and afraid; a passing fly frightens me; a word that I ought to speak, a movement that I ought to make, has first to overcome my inertia. *Fear and shame* rule me to such a degree that I should like to hide from everyone's sight. If there is something to be done, I do not know how to begin it, if there is something to be said I am at a loss to know what to say, if anyone looks at me, I am put out of countenance.[16]

Rousseau's fear and shyness made it so impossible for him to speak freely that in 1752 after he brought out a successful operetta he could not face an audience with the king that would certainly have assured a pension for him; he disobeyed the command to come to court. Such a worrier was he about his love affairs that most of them failed on that very account. His system was filled with the greatest generalized anxiety; he saw in every situation the worst possible consequences for himself, and in his youth fear of Hell caused him cruel torments.

When he was thirty-two and living in a Paris hotel, Rousseau took up with a servant girl, Therese le Vasseur. Ugly and ignorant, she could not read, write, make change, or tell time. But Rousseau lived with her for the rest of his life—not excluding other affairs—and married her 24 years after their first cohabitation. Rousseau showed in this affair that he was destitute of all the ordinary virtues. He fathered five children by Therese, all of whom he promptly delivered to a foundling home. Despite his celebrated theories on education published in 1762 in *Émile*, he was not confident enough to try them out in reality. In his *Confessions* he excused abandoning his children with the scandalously flip explanation that,

> In handing over my children to the State to educate, for want of means to bring them up myself, I thought I was behaving like a citizen and a father, and considered myself a member of Plato's Republic.

He also expressed the singular opinion that had he done otherwise "they would have been brought up to hate, perhaps to betray, their parents; it is a hundred times better that they have never known them."

In later life, Rousseau's neuroses deepened into psychosis. At age fifty he published his *Émile;* at the same time a Geneva physician published a work on education which was awarded a prize by the Haarlem Academy. Rousseau got the notion that this book was copied word for word, except for a few platitudes, from the first volume of his own work—an obviously baseless idea. He believed he had been mysteriously robbed and said that the Haarlem Academy and its prize were frauds designed to hide the theft from the public.

Émile was a romantic prescription for the education of an infant son of a nobleman, of whom Rousseau imagined himself total tutor. He built on his "noble savage" hypothesis, reflecting Rousseau's own pitiful fight from the terrible turmoil and guilt within himself which he had to deny and repress:

> Let us lay it down as an incontrovertible rule that the first impulses of nature are always right. There is no original sin in the human heart . . . Never punish your pupil, for he does not know what it means to do wrong. Never make him say, "Fogive me." Wholly unmoral in his actions, he can do nothing morally wrong, and he deserves neither punishment nor reproof. . . .

David Hume, whose sympathetic efforts to help brought him much grief, noted Rousseau's sensitivity in a remarkably perceptive letter to a friend:

> He has read very little in the course of his life, and has now totally renounced all reading; he has seen very little, and has no manner of curiosity to see . . . he has not, indeed, much knowledge. He has only felt, during the whole course of his life; and in this respect his sensibility rises to a pitch beyond what I have seen any example of, but it still gives him a more acute feeling of pain than of pleasure. He is like a man who were stript not only of his clothes but of his skin, and turned out to combat with the rude and boisterous elements, such as perpetually disturb this lower world.[17]

His nonconformist ideas on religion and religious education in *Émile* kicked up a storm among French authorities, who ordered his arrest. He fled to Switzerland, but was harried from canton to canton even there. Late in 1765 Hume offered him refuge in England. London lionized Rousseau. The English press acclaimed him, and George III granted him a pension. But Rousseau's insanity developed fully in the form of a persecution mania. He suspected Hume of being the agent of would-be assassins. In lucid moments he would realize the absurdity of his suspicions and embrace Hume, exclaiming, "No, no, Hume is no traitor." After eighteen months with Hume, his delusions grew so strong he fled suddenly, leaving behind a letter which accused Hume of conspiracy. He roamed about England and wrote to the Lord Chancellor that he wanted to leave the country but did not dare leave his house for fear of his enemies, and so requested an official guard! In a letter to General Conway he declared Hume had made him a prisoner of the state, expressed fear of being murdered, and petitioned to be permitted to leave England. He finally returned to France, and wandered about there for three years. He found lodging in the chateau of the Prince de Conti, who treated him with kindness, but Rousseau saw everyone as an enemy and part of a great conspiracy against him. A friend fell ill, and Rousseau believed himself accused of poisoning. The chateau's steward died, and Rousseau convinced himself he was regarded as a murderer and asked that an autopsy be performed. He left and found another patron early in 1769. "The floor on which I stand has eyes and the walls have ears," Rousseau wrote. "Surrounded by spies and ever-watchful attendants who wish me harm, I dash down, ill at ease and unable to concentrate, a few hurried and disconnected words on paper, but from lack of time I can hardly read them over, still less revise them."[18] This was, of course, a typical manifestation of paranoid schizophrenia.

Rousseau's delusions became more and more ridiculous. One time he believed himself involved in an attack on the life of Louis XIV; at another he accused his enemies of supplying him with colorless ink so as to make it impossible to him to write his *Confesssions*. He slaved away on that work with such a burst of paranoia that his friends—who heard him deliver it emotionally at the close of an incredible seventeen-hour reading in Paris in November 1770—concluded he was mentally deranged: "I have written the truth!" he exclaimed.

> If any person has heard of things contrary . . . he has heard calumny and falsehood . . . I publicly and fearlessly declare that anyone, even if he has not read my writings, who shall have examined with his own eyes my disposition, character, manners, inclinations, pleasures, and habits, and shall then believe me a dishonorable man, is himself one who deserves to hang.

Such absoluteness comes not from logic. It is a defense mechanism of a terrible flawed and shaky personality seeking to escape reality.

When Rousseau finally died in 1778 at sixty-six, suicide was suspected. His friend Diderot said of him:

> He was born with sensibility, and, at a distance, he loves every human being. He only hates those who approach him, because his vanity induces him to think that they are all envious of him; that they serve him only to humble him that they flatter him but to injure him; and that even those who pretend to love him share in the conspiracy. This is his disease. Interesting on account of his misfortunes, his talents, and a fund of kindness and rectitude that his heart cherishes, he would have friends, if he believed in friendship. As it is, he will never have any, or they will love him singly; for he will always distrust them. This fatal mistrust, this light and prompt facility, not only of suspecting, but of believing of his friends all that is most atrocious, most mean, and most infamous; of attributing to them baseness and perfidy, without any other proof than the dreams of an ardent and somber imagination, whose vapors cloud his distorted brain, and whose malignant influence sours and poisons his gentlest affections; in short, this delirium of melancholy and timid mind, made savage by misfortune, was most truly the disease of Rousseau, and the torment of his soul.[19]

Rousseau's political and ethical theories seem to rationalize subjective problems. His romanticism really boils down to irrationalism and primitivism. Rousseau never really tried to understand either himself or his world; rather, he exults in his irrationality, which is probably one way of coping with it.

ROUSSEAU'S POLITICAL IDEOLOGY   Rather than trying to understand the growing complexities of his rapidly changing society, Rousseau sought escape in some universal and certain rule for the just governing of men. He arrived at this in his *Social Contract*, published in 1762. The result was a totalitarian concept—a Procrustean bed into which he clearly intended to force mankind. This essay was a product of the years of increasing personality rigidity and signs of mental abberation. In 1756 he quarreled with most of his friends and retired to a cottage near the forest of Montmorency to write during the next six years. In the *Social Contract*, he unveiled his conception of the "general will." He discovers that ultimately the social order is founded on convention. We exchange primitive freedom of the jungle for civilized freedom, and we gain the equivalent of what we have lost because we create the state, an organization with a will of its own. Because each individual contributes to the general will, it is concerned with the good of all, and, therefore, with the good of the individual who contributes to it.

But Rousseau failed to foresee that in this verbal and ieological hocus-pocus, we lose something. We find him asserting that the general will *is always right and always tends to the public good.* Ergo, the state cannot err, and when the individual conflicts with the will of the state, it is the individual who must yield. Thus Rousseau arrives at the formulation that, since freedom lies in submission to the general will, he who does not submit is unfree and must therefore be *"forced to be free."* That is, the nonconformist must be forced to do what the general will, the state, requires. The general will is infallible. Thus does Rousseau raise over mankind a new tyranny far worse in practice than ever was the divine right theory of kings.

For if there is a discernible general will obviously it must be obeyed if the country pretends to government "of the people and for the people." *But it logically follows: 1. There must be some one or some group who can discern and define this general will. 2. There must be someone or group that will have the power to execute it. And these two corollaries provide the basis for modern totalitarianism. There must be a priesthood (the interpreters) and an executive of the supreme will of mankind, an anointed class that must, according to their own notions, "force men to be free."*

Present-day communism has these priests who sit in the high councils of the party. They are supreme because Rousseau's doctrine also implies that once the general will has been determined, any person who dissents from it is an "enemy of the people." Modern communists label him an ideological deviate, or in the history of religion a heretic. He must be "forced to be free." In the presence of a defined general will neither the deviationist nor the heretic has any rights. The concept of rights of the individual against the state makes no sense once the idea of an omnipotent and infallible "general will" is accepted.

Rousseau's mental rigidity kept him from accepting the ambiguity that the good of all may not always be the good of some individuals. He must have certainty and self-justification. His infallible general will is rather a wounded personality's utopian scheme than an account of how society actually governs itself. Had Rousseau concerned himself with reality, he most assuredly would have advanced concrete political suggestions. But his political writings are conspicuously deficient in *concrete proposals for concrete social situations.* Rousseau's philosophy is out of touch with the *real* world.

For example, can society afford to grant the rebel freedom *not* to conform, within certain limits? Rousseau never faced this problem. From his castle in the clouds, he could only prescribe force to crush the dissenter—to "force him to be free."

Rousseau's philosophy marched to its ultimate, practical, and bloody dénouement. For his ideological descendents—Robespierre, Marx, Lenin, Stalin, and Mao—erected out of his general will a great god, "The People," upon whose altar the high priests of the general will have in the name of the state slaughtered millions of persons.

Rousseau also twisted religion into an instrument of the state. Since some form of religion, he felt, would be necessary for governing men, the "civil religion" should be formulated by the state and imposed upon all individuals. "The dogmas of the civil religion ought to be few, simple, and precisely worded, but without explanation or commentary," he declared.

> The existence of a mighty, intelligent, and beneficent divinity, possessed of foresight and providence; the life to come, the happiness of the just, the punishment of the wicked, the sanctity of the social contract and the laws; these are its positive dogmas.[20]

Robespierre, as we shall see, attempted literally to follow this Rousseauist injunction.

Rousseau electrified Europe's intellectuals with an apocalyptical vision of imminent disaster:

> It is impossible that the great kingdom of Europe should last much longer. Each of them has had its period of splendor, after which it must inevitably decline. The crisis is approaching: we are on the edge of a revolution.[21]

The poetry of Rousseau's exaltation of freedom against externally constituted authority influenced the U.S. Constitution. But the men who wrote it were practical men grappling with concrete problems, and they rejected Rousseau's prescriptions while admiring his hymns.[22] His destructive attitude toward the past and existing society, on the other hand, deeply influenced the French and Russian revolutions, because the men who made them were out of power, and hence out of contact with the real problems of governing diverse human beings, while the problems they *were* grappling with were those of social demolition.

Rousseau was, says Bertrand Russell, "the inventor of the political philosophy of psuedo-democratic dictatorships . . . Ever since his time, those who considered themselves reformers have been divided into two groups: Those who followed Rousseau and those who followed Locke. At the present time, Hitler is an outcome of Rousseau; Roosevelt and Churchill, of Locke."[23] (Russell should have added Stalin's name to Hitler's.)

THE FIRST UTOPIA AROUND THE CORNER   Despite Rousseau's unfortunate insanity, his wholesale indictment of European society had a ring of truth and a rationale to it. To the *philosophes,* he was like a fierce Moses emerging out of the wilderness. Under Louis XV, so much was wrong, brutal, oppressive and archaic, that French society was a virtual tinderbox—and it was Rousseau who struck the match. He advanced radical attitudes akin to Voltaire's famed outbursts: *"Ecrasez l'infame!"* ("Destroy the infamous thing!") Rousseau's paradox—proclaiming the superiority of the "noble savage" over civilized man, and devaluating the established order and present time period in the name of a golden future—became the rage after his death. Revolutionaries imitated and worshipped him. His writings shaped the entire generation and fed a rising revolutionary attitude that culminated in the French Revolution.

In 1770 a book published anonymously in Amsterdam marked a milestone in mankind's intellectual drama with the idea of social perfection. It was *The Year 2440* written by an obscure and inferior dramatist named Sebastien Mercier. *This was European literature's first nonapocalyptic, seriously prophetic utopia.* Up to this time, utopian writers either projected their ideal states into a remote past or located them in a remote, vaguely-known region. "To project them into the future was a new thing," declares the distinguished historian of thought, J. C. Bury, "and when Sebastien Mercier described what human civilization would be in A.D. 2440, it was a telling sign of the power which the idea of progress was beginning to exercise."[24]

With publication of *The Year 2440,* the ideal state was imagined as not only achievable, but as an approaching event. Mercier's *2440* depicted utopia as the outcome of the "march of history." This time the writer did not regard his work as indulgent fancy, but as serious prediction. Here was a trusting forerunner of Huxley's *Brave New World* and Orwell's *1984.*

Eighteenth-century thought and urban society were jarred by two potent ideas constituting a revolutionary explosion—the idea that contemporary civilization was wholly hateful, the sole source of evil and human degradation among men who were inherently good; and the idea that perfection was attainable in history, within grasp in the foreseeable future. These two ingredients were combined and ignited by the fiery Maximilien Robespierre, a young lawyer born five years after Rousseau proclaimed in 1753 that "man is naturally good and only by institutions is he made bad." Rousseau became Robespierre's Marx, and Robespierre was Rousseauism in power, just as Lenin and Stalin, Mao and Castro are Marxism in power.

"FORCED TO BE FREE."   The same year the European and Chinese communists celebrated the 250th anniversary of Rousseau's birth, a young man named Peter Fechter, 18 years old, attempted to climb Berlin's Wall of Shame and escape from the Communist East into West Berlin. East German guards shot him, and he fell back into the Communist utopia, where he lay bleeding and crying until he died an hour later. The East Berlin City Funeral Commission sent an official state orator to explain to weeping relatives the theory of government that required such a sacrifice. The young man had made a "foolish decision," he proclaimed. Comparing life in divided Berlin to climbing a mountain, the Communist orator said, "Certain paths are blocked to ordinary people, although they might want to see the beautiful view from higher up. The authorities know these paths are dangerous. We must trust the judgment of our Government." Those who do not must be procrusteanized with bullet and bayonet— "forced to be free."

Chapter 3
ROBESPIERRE: DEMON CERTITUDE STALKS THE EARTH

Robespierre came out of the pages of Rousseau as surely as the People's Palace rose out of the debris of a novel.

—Oscar Wilde: *1889*

There is no need to endow Robespierre with fiendish foresight and calculation. The complex and the subtle explanations are entirely out of place in the case of Robespierre. His case is elementary: he was Mr. Everyman in the throes of one hundred percent certitude.

—G. J. Renier

THE TRAGEDY OF IDEALISM One summer day in the little French village of Lievre in 1770, a brooding, silent twelve-year-old lad yielded to his little sister's pleas and let her play with one of his pet pigeons. The girl carelessly left the bird out of doors that night, and a sudden thunderstorm left it drowned on the doorstep the next morning. The boy cried and cried, and for days he would not stop.

Fourteen years later, this same boy, now a judge, tormented himself so over having to condemn a man to death that he resigned his post rather then face the possibility of having to do it again. He could neither eat nor sleep for days. He kept groaning in response to his sister's consolations, "He is a criminal, no doubt, but to put a man to death!"

Yet, six years later, when he walked upon the scaffold in Paris in the Place de la Concorde and went under the guillotine, this man, Maximilien Robespierre, at thirty-six, had stamped his name in the annals of history as one of the world's bloodiest dictators. He had sent 1,200 people, including his closest friends and colleagues, to the guillotine. He blazed a revolutionary trail that would be followed later by totalitarian butchers such as Mussolini, Hitler, Lenin, Stalin, Mao, and Castro.

Robespierre was first and foremost an idealist who loved Man— though not so much his fellow men. He set out to create for all mankind an ideal state, history's first utopia realized. As student and lawyer he drank deeply of Rousseau and idolized "the people." From

Rousseau, Robespierre came to believe that all he had to do was overthrow the king and enthrone the people for virtue to reign and the millennial utopia to begin. Yet when the king was toppled, Robespierre found there were persons around who did not conform to his ideals of a virtuous state. Consequently, Robespierre reasoned, they had to be perverse, evil creatures, not just ordinary men. Hence they could not really be a part of "the people" he worshipped. And so they had to be eliminated for the ideal state to be born.

But, to Robespierre's sad dismay, these evil men kept appearing, and they came, and came, and came. And, as his guillotine chopped, and heads piled high and the streets of Paris ran with blood, fewer and fewer persons were to be found who personified his ideal of virtue. This idealist, who as a boy wept for days over the death of a pet pigeon and as a young man was so shaken by having to pass a death sentence, grew sick. He soon realized the futility of his dream and the horribleness of his crimes in pursuit of an unattainable goal. And so he condemned himself to death by suicidal inaction, delivering himself to his enemies.

Robespierre's transition from a man who trembled and was sick for days over having to condemn a man to death, to a man who sent a king and then hundreds of innocent commoners to the guillotine, shows how engaging in struggle can warp normal moral standards. In making this transition, Robespierre followed another pattern that is an integral part of the subculture of revolutionary extremism: the emotional state that causes a person, in the name of humanity, to torture human beings with abandon. The pattern persists in modern communism. In the name of building a better world in the 1960s, for example, Viet Cong guerrillas stopped school buses and chopped off the little fingers of tiny girls, as a warning to their parents to keep them away from the imperialist government's schools. And a Hanoi communist magazine in the 1950s complained indignantly, "Children of parents wrongly classed as landlords were allowed to starve," the crime being not that children were allowed to starve but that their parents were unjustly classified!

Robespierre's story is a tragedy, but with universal meaning. We are still living out the Tragedy of Robespierre. Before the curtain comes down—or the theater burns up—it may become the Tragedy of Man.

THE EMOTIONAL SCARS OF CHILDHOOD   Robespierre's entire life was a struggle with imperfect reality, and from childhood he was cursed with a supersensitivity to it.

Robespierre was born in Arras, France, in 1758. His mother died when he was but seven. Crushed by the blow, his poor father, a lawyer, gave up his practice, abandoned his four children to the care of their mother's relatives, and disappeared from their lives. Robespierre's sister, Charlotte, recorded, apropos her older brother's supersensitivity, that he could never recall his mother's memory without tears. Her death and his father's desertion turned young Robespierre, Charlotte reports, from a normally cheerful boy into an austere child. The tender young soul found refuge in books. In school, a teacher remembered that "he was a hard worker, but heavy in hand, like an ox at the plough."[1] In college Robespierre read Voltaire and other authors of the Enlightenment, whose forbidden corrupting works were smuggled in. He developed a hero worship of Rousseau. Robespierre impressed one fellow student as "silent, reserved, unbending, secretive . . . a dreamer . . . I can't remember ever seeing him smile."

As a young lawyer Robespierre displayed the tendency psychologists often note in supersensitive introverts of high intellect: escaping reality into castles in the clouds. As a lawyer defending a woman imprisoned for debt, he wandered into a crusade for women's rights. His defense of an amateur scientist persecuted by frightened neighbors for tinkering with lightning rods wandered to a crusade for science against the persecutions of Galileo, Harvey, and Descartes. He turned a deserted soldier's suit for a rich uncle's estate into a demand for a regenerated national government and an appeal to King Louis XVI to come forth as a champion of the People "to lead men through virtue to happiness . . . to forge the deathless chain which should unite us to God and our fellow-men, by destroying all causes of oppression and tyranny . . . Such, Sire, is the glorious enterprise to which you have been called!" Robespierre thought in grandiose Procrustean terms; he was unhappy unless as lawyer, legislator or ruler he could generalize and turn any proceeding into a cataclysmic clash of cosmic import. This was Demon Certitude stalking the earth.

And the French Revolution, an earth-shaking political and social cataclysm, liberated him from the ordinary social restraints in an obscure French village onto the larger stage of all humanity.

THE REVOLUTION UNFOLDS   Bad harvests in 1787 and 1788 heightened the crises confronting a decrepit monarchy struggling to reform itself. Prices skyrocketed during the winter of 1788. The king, desperate, summoned the estates-general for the first time in a century to try to raise revenue, inflating hopes of bread and reforms. Food riots erupted. The army, infected with democracy from its American service, was unreliable. When the king attempted to use troops to dissolve the runaway estates general he exposed the regime's weakness and paved the way for the destruction of the Bastille. Political uprisings continued throughout the summer. Estate owners were attacked, storehouses looted, and seignorial archives (the basis of the land tenure system) burned. The estates-general eventually became the National Constituent Assembly. With the loyal support of the king it would give France the new constitution that the nation desired. For two years reforms were carried out forming the basis of modern French life. The king, virtually a prisoner, plotted secretly to restore royal power with aristocrats who had fled to sympathetic courts beyond France's borders. In June 1791 Louis and his queen tried to sneak out, too, but were caught and hauled back to Paris. In April 1792 the king and the conservatives in the new legislative assembly declared war on Austria hoping to rally people to the throne. In August, with the Prussian army invading, Jacobin radicals in alliance with the Paris Commune engineered a mob uprising, and forced the assembly to suspend the king and call a new constitutional convention to convert France into a republic.

THE FIRST TOTALITARIAN PARTY   At Versailles in 1789 the deputies met in small like-minded caucuses to discuss Assembly strategy. Gradually those informal meetings grew into formal clubs, and the most radical of these—the one which naturally attracted Robespierre—was known officially as "The Society of the Friends of the Constitution," nicknamed the Jacobin Club because they debated nightly in a Jacobin monastery. The Jacobins admitted non-members of the Assembly, and other radical groups outside Paris affiliated. Soon the Jacobin Society covered the whole country with its "clubs." They developed a ritual, launched slogans, flaunted distinctive badges. As insurrection and invasion threatened the revolutionary regime these clubs acquired all the characteristics of the cells which today are the basic units of every totalitarian organization: fanaticism, intolerance, a readiness for violence, hero-worship, and the tremendous conformist pressures that intimidate all moderates and leave the more violent extremists to set the pace. In short, the Jacobin Society became the first modern totalitarian organization. In the nineteenth century revolutionaries studied its structure carefully and patterned their own organization after it.

ROBESPIERRE IN PARIS, 1789–1792   Campaigning for the estates-general, Robespierre issued a proclamation that begins to disclose his increasingly apocalyptic mentality:

> Our countryside offers the spectacle of unhappy people who spray with tears of despair the soil their sweat has fertilized in vain! The major part of those who inhabit towns and country are lowered by

want to that extreme degree of brutalization in which man, entirely absorbed by the worrying necessity of preserving his existence, becomes incapable of reflecting upon the cause of his miseries and of recognizing the rights he has been given by nature.

Others also idealized Man, breathed "the Enlightenment" air supercharged with worship of Reason, Progress, Science, and The People; read Newton and Voltaire; questioned the traditional social arrangements; and built mental blueprints for a "scientific" Republic of Virtue. But Robespierre added his own peculiar note: He projected these people's feelings of guilt for the evil and imperfection around them outward, onto alleged conspirators. He discovered plotters, unidentified vile creatures everywhere—those who, unlike himself, were deaf to the unuttered cry of "oppressed" masses; those, whose remedies differed from his, who were uncertain and hesitant. Robespierre possessed none of the humility that enables men to recognize that contemporary evils may be but the legacy of historical circumstance and social inertia, not the results of scheming, evil men. To him, life was simply black versus white, evil men versus the good. Cried he: "Vice, armed with unjust power, must itself learn to tremble before triumphant justice and reason!" Robespierre believed so fiercely he could stir the galleries to fever pitch with his oratory. The elder moderate statesman, Mirabeau, listened and remarked, "That man will go far: he believes every word that he says!" Soon Robespierre won the sobriquet, "The Incorruptible."

For four years his pattern was to speak, harangue, inflame. But he was not action-oriented, like Danton, the military hero who worked organizational miracles. Rather, Robespierre was content to be a legislator without responsibility or executive power. His reaction to some new crisis of practical government was not to organize, plan a policy, then execute it. No, he was more likely to retire to his study and write a long, theoretical speech on the great principles at stake. Comments one historian:

> We naturally think of those grave men who a few years before had founded the Republic in America. Jefferson served with Washington in the Virginia legislature and with Franklin in Congress, and he afterwards said that he never heard either of them speak ten minutes at a time, while John Adams declared that he never heard Jefferson utter three sentences together. Of Robespierre it is stated on good authority that for eighteen months there was not a single evening on which he

did not make to the assembled Jacobins at least one speech, and that never a short one.[2]

His eloquent words, broadcast by the revolutionary gazettes of Paris, made him the Voice of the Revolution, the Philosopher of Jacobinism, the high priest of thousands of radicals throughout France whose feelings he voiced. Robespierre became the lightning rod toward which moderates, aristocrats, and the Royal Court hurled their thunderbolts. Through such mutual assaults Robespierre and his antagonists developed a dynamic reaction of increasing extremism toward each other. Robespierre's latent persecution mania soon had him perpetually justifying himself and finding evil motives that in his view made his enemies worthy only of total obliteration.

ROBESPIERRE PROCRUSTEANIZES "THE PEOPLE"

Robespierre had been in Paris barely two months when Parisians, frightened by rumors that the king planned to abolish the National Assembly, rioted and attempted to storm the Bastille—an ancient prison fortress that symbolized the hated old regime. The king failed to send rescue forces and the commander, de Launay, opened the gates in return for a promise of safe conduct. (The "storming of the Bastille" is thus a total myth.) Vicious toughs in the mob thereupon beheaded him and killed several of his garrison. Six days later the Assembly's "middle-of-the-roaders" sought a resolution denouncing the violence and calling for vigorous law enforcement. But Robespierre could not see that a mere 900 rioters[3] could hardly represent a city of 650,000, much less a nation of 27 million.[4] He cried out bitterly against condemning mob rule:

> Revolt! But this revolt is liberty! The battle is not at its end. Tomorrow, it may be, the shameful designs against us will be renewed; and who will there be then to repulse them, if beforehand we declare the very men to be rebels who had rushed to arms for our protection and safety?[5]

Robespierre sounded this theme until his death: the revolution was threatened by evil men; the people were supreme; any action in the name of "the people" and preserving the revolution was moral, no matter how terrible. When a crowd lynched some poor baker or plundered a grocer's shop, Robespierre thought it was trying to express its faith in liberty, equality, and Rousseau's principles. After the Paris mob invaded the Tuileries on August 10, 1792, and overthrew the monarchy, Robespierre led a Paris Commune delegation to the Assembly demanding a summary trial for the survivors of the 800 Swiss guards slaughtered by the crowd:

> The people is reposing, but it is not asleep. It wills—and rightly—the punishment of those who are to blame!

A month later, on September 2, the Prussian army captured Verdun. Rumors flew that the political prisoners of Paris were waiting for volunteers to march away to meet the enemy, then break out and massacre the old, the women, and children left behind. That afternoon a crowd gathered at the Abbaye prison, and began massacring inmates. For five days the slaughter continued as mobs moved from prison to prison, held drum-head courts, and allowed ruffians to hack most of the poor wretches to pieces with sabres and pikes. Between 1,100 and 1,400 prisoners out of the 2,800 in nine prisons were slaughtered. Only a fourth, it turned out, were priests, nobles or "politicals"; the rest were common thieves, prostitutes, forgers and vagrants.[6]

The horror soon dawned on people, and they began demanding an investigation and punishment. Robespierre's response illuminates the darkest chambers of his psyche:

> It seems pretty certain that one innocent man perished. And doubtless even one is far too many. One ought to weep, and we have wept over this cruel mistake. You should weep even for the criminal victims, who fell beneath the blade of popular justice. But let your grief, like everything moral, have an end, and let us keep a few tears for tragedies that effect us more closely—the hundred thousand victims of Bourbon tyranny.[7]

Appallingly, Robespierre somehow convinced himself that only one out of 1,300 victims was undeservedly executed! This, despite the fact that 160 boys and girls at a reformatory were hacked to pieces, and at a hospital 35 women inmates were killed! Far from apologizing, Robespierre actually took pride in the massacres because he felt it was good to see "the people" taking such an active part in their own salvation!

And so it went. In all incidents between demonstrating Paris crowds and police, Robespierre *invariably took the side of the mobs.* Without exception he accused authorities and police of counter-revolutionary plots, provocation, or ill will. He continually distorted events to fit the contours of his mind, which could not tolerate ambiguity or honest disagreement and diversity. Any riot, any lynching or mob atrocity expressed the people's righteous anger; every action of the authorities was counter-revolutionary. Anyone who disagreed with "the people" was automatically venal, vicious, evil. "The People" was, by definition, "good," and Robespierre was its infallible interpreter and self-appointed spokesman. It was as if he were echoing the Islamic Muzzin and crying, "There is but one god, one will, the people, and Robespierre is its prophet!"

"General and abstract ideas are the source of the greatest errors of mankind," Rousseau had written (*Émile*, Book IV), and also: "Nothing on this earth is worth buying at the price of human blood." Yet Robespierre was about to launch a mad binge to buy his dream of a "new man" and "society of virtue" with other people's blood. Here, says J.L. Talmon, historian of the origins of totalitarianism, "we are face to face with the Messianic doctrinaire as a historic phenomenon—

> He is a compound of two things, inner fanatical certainty, and what may be called *a pencil sketch of reality*. The pencil lines represent the external facets of social existence, in fact the sinews of the institutional framework. The flesh of the intangible, shapeless living forces, traditions, imponderables, habits, human inertia and lazy conservatism are not there. They are ignored. Left out of account are also the uniqueness and the unpredictability of human nature and human conduct, which result either from the irrational segments of our being, or from man's egotism. The Revolutionary doctrinaire is convinced that his pencil sketch is the only real thing, that it sums up all that matters. He experiences reality not as an inchoate static mass, but as a denouement, a dynamic movement towards a rational solution. The amorphous fleshy mass is unreal, and can be brought into shape in accordance with the pencil pattern . . . Similarly, human idiosyncrasies and peculiarities that interfere with the rational working of the systematic, abstract pattern are not something that must be taken for granted, but an accident to be prevented, removed, or avoided . . . And so it happened that many a Revolutionary who started with and put his trust in the institutions of a pencil-sketch doctrine to solve all problems, hoping that conditions and men would fall in by themselves into the harmonious whole, ended with a desperate determination to create like Moses a new type of man and a new people . . . The doctrinaire never thinks of the pencil sketch in terms of coercion. It is not intended to interfere with freedom; on the contrary, it is designed to secure it. Only the

ill-intentioned, the selfish and perverse can complain that their freedom is violated. They are guilty of sabotage, refusing to be free, and misleading others. They cannot be given freedom to do their evil deeds, for they are at war with the pattern of freedom that continues to unfold itself till its full realization. Liberty can be restored only after this war has come to an end, only when the enemy has been eliminated and the people re-educated, that is to say, when there will be no longer any opposition. So long as there is opposition there can be no freedom.[8]

Robespierre's sister, Charlotte, who was with him often during the revolutionary years, recalls that Maximilien had distraught moods. Often he would sit in a corner of the room, during card playing or conversation, deep in thought. And sometimes he had fits of absent-mindedness. Once, Charlotte says, he helped the soup onto the table-cloth instead of his plate; and once, returning with her from a call, he walked on ahead, shut himself in his room, and when she entered it he asked where she had been.[9] In 1792 a middle-aged wife of a Jacobin colleague, who had entertained Charlotte and Robespierre at dinner, wrote:

> I was much pleased with the Robespierre family. The sister is naive and natural, like your aunts: she arrived two hours before her brother, and we chatted like two old women. I made her tell me about their domestic life: it is exactly like ours, simple and frugal. Her brother has as little to do with the 10th of August as with the 2nd of September [i.e. the prison massacres]. He is as capable of being a party leader as of catching hold of the moon. He is absent-minded, like a thinker, cold and formal, like a lawyer, but gentle as a lamb, and as somber as young. I see he has not our tender sensibility, but I believe he desires the good of the human race, though rather from justice than from love . . .[10]

KILLING THE KING CORRUPTS "THE INCORRUPTIBLE"

Mushrooming events swept Robespierre along, propelling his natural emotional predispositions toward their logical, cruel consequence—the struggle mentality. In the fall of 1792 the Jacobin leaders decided that trying the king would take the public's mind off hunger, inflation, and other social problems. Louis would make a good weapon against the moderate Girondins.

Robespierre faced a major problem of conscience. He had, after all, resigned his judgeship over having to condemn a murderer to death. Moreover, he had eloquently fought the death penalty. But his burning desire to right the world transmogrified into a necessity to rule and that meant winning the political struggle. On December 3, 1792, he told the Convention that a dethroned king permanently menaced a republican government and could become more dangerous, if time was wasted on debating his fate:

> There is no question of a trial. Louis is not a defendant. You are not judges. You are not, and cannot be, anything but statesmen, and the people's representatives. You have not to give a verdict for or against an individual, but to adopt a measure of public safety, to safeguard the future of the nation . . .
>
> If we fall back upon questions of form, it is because we have no principles. If we make a point of scruples *(delicatesse)*, it is because we lack energy: we make a show of humanity only because we are not really humane. We reverence the shadow of a king only because we have not learned to respect the people; and if we have a soft spot for our oppressors, it is only because we have no pity for the oppressed.[11]

With this "either-or" declaration, Robespierre thrusted all dissenters, who by accident of history, birth, or social circumstance opposed radical revolution, beyond the pale of the Judeo-Christian ethic of tolerance and forgiveness. Don't be squeamish, he exhorted. Let us have no "delicatesse" in this business. We can almost hear the Stalinist rationalization, "You've got to break an egg to make an omelette." A person may be individually and subjectively innocent and yet an "objective enemy of the people." Here we face a classic rationalization of totalitarianism. Robespierre concluded:

> For my own part, I detest the death penalty that your law prescribes so freely: in the Assembly I moved for its abolition, and it was not my fault if that Assembly regarded the first principles of reason as moral and political heresies. But now you propose to set aside the death penalty in the case of the one man whose death could justify it. I agree, the death penalty is, in general, a crime, and that, for the very reason that it can only be justified where it is necessary for the safety of individuals, or the body politick. But where you have dethroned a king at the heart of a revolution which is entirely held together by just laws —a king whose very name brings the scourge of civil war upon a distracted nation, neither imprisonment nor exile can prevent his presence affecting the public welfare. Such is the fatal conclusion which, however much I regret it, I cannot avoid. Because the fatherland must live, Louis must die!

The moderate Girondins, whose followers were stronger outside Paris and more sympathetic to Louis, moved to give the people a say on the king's fate by holding a referendum. This put Robespierre on the spot. He believed in "the people." But on September 20 the Republican army had defeated the invaders at Valmy, and it was probable that a nationwide referendum would refuse to condemn the king to death. So Robespierre devised the ideas of an elitist "general staff of the revolution" and a temporary "dictatorship of the proletariat." While upholding the "voice of the people" as supreme, he simultaneously fought consulting them. He demanded advance guarantees that "bad citizens, moderates, and aristocrats" would be "given no access" and would be prevented from misleading the people by playing upon their sympathies. Because the people might disagree with Robespierre, the deck must first be stacked to insure his victory or the people must not be allowed to vote! Thus, Robespierre began to develop the idea that in the name of democracy self-appointed democratic Platonic guardians may abandon its practice:

> In this so-called appeal to the people, I see nothing but an appeal from what the people has willed and done (the August 10 mob uprising) to *those secret enemies of equality whose corruption and cowardice were the very cause of that insurrection!*[12]

Robespierre was saying that the people's recorded opinions could not be taken as reflecting the true "general will," because the perfect conditions for democracy still had not yet developed. People were still ill-educated, hungry, dominated and misled by the rich and venal. So the real friend of democracy will not simply let the people speak freely and spontaneously and accept their verdict as final and absolute. Rather, his task is first to create the conditions for a "true" expression of the popular will. And that means wiping out entire classes of those who might subvert and mislead the people: evil men, capitalists—in short, all *opposition*. Only after this genocide can the people be allowed to vote! To allow popular political activity is only to give the scoundrels and counter-revolutionaries a chance to mislead the people. The vanguard must not be troubled by such hollow forms of democracy while it carries out the more urgent, cosmic task of preparing the people's paradise! *In the interim, the enlightened vanguard is the real will of the people!*

So, on January 14, 1794, Louis XVI was declared guilty; and a week later, he was beheaded. As Albert Camus, that tortured soul of modern French radical literature, wrote:

[68]

On January 21, with the murder of the King-priest, was consummated what has significantly been called the passion of Louis XVI. It is certainly a crying scandal that the public assassination of a weak but goodhearted man has been presented as a great moment in French history. That scaffold marked no climax—far from it. The revolutionaries may well refer to the Gospel, but in fact they dealt a terrible blow to Christianity, from which it has not yet recovered. It really seems as if the execution of the King, followed, as we know, by hysterical scenes of suicide and madness, took place in complete awareness of what was being done.[13]

Millions more have died and will die before the totalitarian doctrines the king's trial engendered are laid to rest. Robespierre's rationalization set a psychological pattern of incredible evil that hounds Western man even today: that it is possible to know what "the people" want and give them what's good for them without consulting them. The argument Robespierre framed has been warmed over by every dictator to follow in the post-monarchial age of democracy, from Mussolini and Hitler to Lenin, Stalin, Castro and Mao. In May 1972 Soviet Minister of Culture Yekaterina Furtseva invoked it against foreign journalists asking why Nobel literature prizewinner Alexander Solzhenitsyn's works were not published in his native Russia: "He has raised his hand against the very dignity of the Soviet people, and since we publish books not from private capital but from the people's money, why should we spend the people's money on someone who is against the people?"

The ultimate flaw in Rousseau's doctrine of the infallibility of the "general will" is that anybody can *know* it. Invariably it degenerates into a new justification for aristocratic "divine right" rule: the people must be saved from their own delusions and weaknesses by the Superman, or the Radical Elite of supermen, who alone can penetrate the schemes of real or imagined exploiters or divine what is truly good for "the people."

Chapter 4
ROBESPIERRE: FROM IDEALIST TO TYRANT

O posterity, sweet and tender hope of humanity, thou art not a stranger to us. It is for thee that we brave all the blows of tyranny. It is thy happiness which is the price of all our painful struggles. *Often discouraged by the obstacles that surround us, we feel the need of thy consolations:* it is to thee that we confide the task of completing our labors, and the destiny of all the unborn generations of men . . . Make haste, O Posterity, to bring to pass the hour of equality, of justice, of happiness!
—Robespierre, 1791

Terror is naught but prompt, severe inflexible justice; it is therefore an emanation of virtue; it is less a particular principle than a consequence of the general principle of democracy applied to the most pressing needs of the fatherland.
—Robespierre, 1794

THE GAP BETWEEN DREAM AND REALITY   In the year after Louis XVI's execution, Robespierre struggled to straddle the growing breach between his own doctrinaire concepts and an inevitably diverging reality. In bitter power struggles with moderates, he moved increasingly toward complete Leninist rationalization. As anti-Jacobin forces coalesced, Robespierre joined Marat, the ultra-radical leader of the Paris Commune who had consistently agitated for a personal dictatorship "to save liberty by violence." On April 6, 1793, the Convention created the infamous Committee of Public Safety as the Revolution's executive body. Robespierre and Marat rammed through decrees declaring whole groups "outside the law." To cries of "tyranny!" Robespierre screamed, "The people is no tyrant, and it is the people that now reign!"

"Subdue by terror the enemies of liberty!" he told the Convention. "You have the right . . . The government of the Revolution is the despotism of liberty against tyranny!"

And who are the enemies of liberty?

"He who is not for the people is against the people . . . When a man remains silent in the moment when he should speak, he is suspect . . ."

On May 26, 1793, Robespierre called for "the people" to rise. He convinced himself the time had come for the Jacobins to seize absolute power and create the Utopia. In a memorandum to himself he declared:

What we need is a single will . . . The internal dangers come from the middle classes: in order to defeat them, we must rally the people . . . This rising must continue until the measures necessary for saving the republic have been taken. The people must ally itself with the Convention and the Convention must make use of the people. The insurrection must gradually spread from place to place, on a uniform plan; the *sansculottes* (the city's small shopkeepers, laborers and vagrants) must be paid, and remain in the towns. They must be supplied with arms, aroused to anger, and enlightened. Republican enthusiasm must be inflamed by all possible means.

"Lenin himself might have penned this program," declares J. M. Thompson, a leading biographer of Robespierre. "On the political side, at least, Robespierre thus declares himself a Marxian revolutionist."[1] On June 2, 1793, the Jacobins used armed crowds to pull a lightning *coup d'état*, arresting the Girondin opposition. About this time, Robespierre wrote his terrible "Catechism," which shows his state of mind when, on July 27, he was named to the twelve-man Committee of Public Safety: "What is our aim?" Robespierre asked himself. His answer:

It is the use of the Constitution for the benefit of the people.
Who are likely to oppose us? The rich, and the corrupt.
What methods will they employ? Slander and hypocrisy.
What factors will encourage the use of such means? The ignorance of the *sansculottes*. [This word is roughly similar to the Marxist "proletariat."]
The people must therefore be instructed.
What obstacles are there to its enlightenment? The paid journalists, who mislead it every day by shameless impostures.
What conclusion follows? That we ought to proscribe these writers as the most dangerous enemies of the country, and to circulate an abundance of good literature.
The people—what other obstacle is there to its instruction?
Its destitution.
When, then, will the people be educated?
When it has enough bread to eat, and when the rich and the government cease bribing treacherous pens and tongues to deceive it; when their interests are identified with those of the people.
When will this be?
Never.
What other obstacles are there to the achievement of freedom?
The war at home and abroad.
By what means can the foreign war be ended?

[71]

By placing republican generals at the head of our armies, and by punishing those who have betrayed us.

How can we end the civil war?

By punishing traitors and conspirators, especially those deputies and administrators who are to blame; by sending patriot troops under patriot leaders to reduce the aristocrats of Lyon, Marseilles, Toulon, the Vendee, the Jura, and all other districts where the banner of royalism and rebellion has been raised; and by making a terrible example of all the criminals who have outraged liberty and spilt the blood of patriots.[2]

Robespierre proclaimed once more the messianic vision: "Our destiny, most sublime, is to found on Earth the empire of wisdom, of justice, and of virtue." And in the name of that empire the twenty-two leading Girondins were marched to the scaffold and beheaded. Robespierre had declared war on all who did not conform to the precepts of his utopian vision.

THE MURDERING IDEALIST. Next Robespierre faced factions within his own Jacobin Club. Radicals on the left, led by Jacques-René Hébert, opposed private property and religion, demanded extension of the Terror to all shopkeepers violating price controls, and favored the dechristianization of France. They wanted to execute all 28,000 who signed the royalist petitions of 1792. Against them, moderates rallied around Danton; they were a mixed crowd, including some profiteers on army contracts and grain speculators, but they were all sick of bloodshed. Robespierre reacted much as did Lenin in the 1917–18 winter when he stood between left communist radicals who wanted headlong world revolution and "reactionaries" who wanted moderate liberal democracy and slower reforms. Both dictators felt in their grasp the instruments of power —and to both, keeping hold seemed at the moment the ultimate value. Robespierre warned the factions:

> Under a constitutional regime, little is needed but to protect the individual citizen against abuse of power by the government; but under a revolutionary regime the government has to defend itself against all the factions which attack it . . . *Only good citizens deserve public protection, and the punishment of the people's enemies is death.*

By definition, he casts the cloak of virtue about his shoulders, and shakes the finger of Terror at all who do not agree completely. It was too much for Camille Desmoulins, an old friend, public admirer and champion. A moderate editor, he challenged Robespierre's theory of dictatorship for the duration of the struggle. Desmoulins asserted that even if the Committee of Public Safety were composed of the world's best statesmen, it should not expect to go uncriticized: "Let us beware of connecting politics with moral regeneration—a thing at present impracticable. Moralism is fatal to freedom."

Robespierre roared in reply:

> I assure all faithful Jacobins that *victory lies within our grasp!* There are *only a few serpents left for us to crush!* [Applause, and cries from all parts of the hall: 'They shall be crushed!'] *Let us not trouble about this or that individual, but only about the country!*

The "individual" happened to be one of Robespierre's oldest friends, a schoolmate in whose wedding Robespierre had participated. But now, Robespierre sent him to the guillotine, despite tearful letters from his wife, Lucile, and her mother, Mme. Duplessis. The mother reminded Robespierre of the warm evenings they all spent together, of the pleasure he expressed in taking little Horace, the Desmoulins' child, onto his knee and playing with him, and of the hope he had once had of becoming her son-in-law—for Robespierre considered marrying Lucile's sister, Adele. Lucile wrote: "Robespierre, how can you really carry through this fatal design, suggested (it must be) by the vile beings who surround you? Have you forgotten a friendship that Camille can never recall without tenderness? What wrong has my Camille done?" But Robespierre's mind and heart were obsessed with a cold ideal immune to warm, living human beings. Camille was executed—and Robespierre even sent his young wife Lucile to the guillotine soon after.

In March 1794 Robespierre and his cohorts formed a temporary coalition with the Dantonists, then arrested the Hébertists, guillotining nineteen. In the week following, Robespierre plotted to crush the Dantonists. Only a year before when Danton returned from his heroic military feats in Belgium to find his wife had died, Robespierre wrote condolences: "If it is any consolation in the midst of misfortunes to be certain of a warm and devoted friend that at least I can assure you. I love you more than ever, and I shall love you till I die." But now Robespierre schemed to send Danton to his death. He helped Saint-Just prepare a speech denouncing Danton; Robespierre's notes and charges are a fantastic mass of paranoid pratings.

Robespierre notes he once told Danton of a slander campaign by their enemies to which Danton replied, "What do I care? Public opinion is a prostitute." Robespierre recalls darkly Danton laughed at the word virtue. How, demands Robespierre, could such a man be a champion of freedom?

On March 30, just six days after the execution of the Hébertists, Robespierre launched his anti-Danton plan. Packed galleries and planned jeering prevented Danton and his friends from defending themselves, and the Convention voted their arrests. At the trial, Danton's dangerous eloquence in his own defense frightened the prosecutors. The court hastily adjourned. Saint-Just used reports of a plot for a prison escape to pressure the Convention into decreeing that "any person accused of conspiracy who resisted or insulted national justice" was at once *deprived of the right of defending himself.* The decree was read in court next day, and when the defendants protested, they were immediately disbarred and found guilty. Danton, roaring a protest, was dragged away. Considered by many to be the greatest hero of the Revolution, he died magnificently, theatrically, appealing to posterity and declaring:

I leave it all in a frightful welter. Not a man of them has an idea of government. Robespierre will follow me. He is dragged down by me. Ah, better be a poor fisherman than meddle with the governing of men!

Danton's execution left Robespierre the supreme dictator.

THE REIGN OF TERROR   Like a recurring Beethoven refrain is the vision of the wonderworld to be won in the struggle. The death toll rose steadily—21 in September 1793, 59 in October, 61 in November, 68 in December, 61 in January 1794, 77 in February, and 121 in March.

On February 5, 1794, Robespierre delivered his "Report on the principles of political morality which ought to guide the National Convention in the internal administration of the Republic"—one of his great convention speeches.

What is our aim? It is the peaceful enjoyment of liberty and equality, and the reign of that eternal justice whose laws are engraved, not on marble or stone, but in the hearts of every man . . . We desire an order of things in which all base and cruel feelings are suppressed, and all beneficent and generous sentiments evoked by the laws; . . . in which the country guarantees the well-being of every citizen, and every citizen is proud to share in the glory and prosperity of the country; in which every soul grows greater by the constant sharing of republican sentiments; . . . in which liberty is adorned by the arts it ennobles, and commerce is a source of public wealth, not merely of the monstrous opulence of a few households. We want to substitute, in our country, morality for egoism, honesty for love of honor, principles for conventions, duties for decorum, the empire of reason for the tyranny of fashion, the fear of vice for the dread of unimportance. We want to substitute price for insolence, magnanimity for vanity, the love of glory for the love of gold. We want to replace . . . intrigue by merit, wit by genius, brilliance by truth, and the dullness of debauch by the charm of happiness; for the pettiness of the so-called great we would substitute the full stature of humanity. In place of an easy-going, frivolous, and discontented people create one that is happy, powerful, and stouthearted; and replace the vices and follies of the monarchy by the virtues and the amazing achievements of the Republic.

Robespierre warned of the dreadful consequences he would inflict on those who failed to conform to his ideals. "Virtue is a natural quality of the people," and a wise government in normal peacetime will "trust the people and be severe upon its own agents." But when the Republic is struggling with traitors within and foes without, the rule becomes:

Manage the people by argument, and the enemies of the people by intimidation . . . If the basis of popular government in time of peace is virtue, its basis in a time of revolution is both virtue and intimidation —virtue, without which intimidation is disastrous, and intimidation, without which virtue has no power . . . Intimidation is merely justice —prompt, severe, and inflexible. It is therefore an emanation of virtue, and results from the application of democracy to the most pressing needs of the country.[3]

The inconsistency between his liberal ideal and his program of political terrorism had vanished, causing Robespierre's biographer to note: "Philosophy cannot explain this: it can only turn away from a state of mind that ought not to have existed, or hand it over to the practitioners in mental pathology."[4]

MAKING MAN GOOD A month after Danton's execution, on May 7, 1794, Robespierre unveiled a messianic scheme to establish a state religion for cultivating morality among the masses—for turning religion into a tool for the reconstruction of humanity. The statesman must realize that "everything which is useful to the world and produces good results is true." Solon, Socrates, and Rousseau all spoke of transcendent beings. Therefore, declared Robespierre, the French Republic must complete the political revolution by initiating the spiritual revolution foreseen by Rousseau the Prophet. The Convention applauded Robespierre's every phrase, and passed his decree unanimously:

ARTICLE I. The French people recognizes the existence of the Supreme Being, and the immortality of the soul.

ARTICLE II. It recognizes that the best way of worshipping the Supreme Being is to do one's duties as a man.

ARTICLE III. It considers that the most important of these duties are: to detest bad faith and despotism, to punish tyrants and traitors, to assist the unfortunate, to respect the weak, to defend the oppressed, to do all the good one can to one's neighbor, and to behave with justice towards all men.

ARTICLE IV. Festivals shall be instituted to remind men of the Deity, and of the dignity of their state.

ARTICLE V. These festivals shall be named after the glorious events of our Revolution, the virtues which are most dear to men, and most useful, and the chief blessings of nature.

ARTICLE VII. It shall celebrate, on successive *decadis* (there are 36 of them, one for every 'tenth day' in the Republican Calendar), the following festivals: The Supreme Being, and Nature; the human race; the French people; the benefactors of mankind; the martyrs of freedom; liberty and equality; the Republic; the liberty of the world; patriotism; hatred of tyrants and traitors; truth; justice; modesty; glory and immortality; friendship; temperance; courage; good faith; heroism; impartiality; Stoicism; love; conjugal fidelity; fatherly affection; mother-love; filial piety; childhood; youth; manhood; old age; misfortune; agriculture; industry; our ancestors; posterity; happiness. [Intervening articles lay out details of these festivals, invite everybody to submit hymns, civic songs, and other things to contribute, etc.]

ARTICLE XII. In the event of troubles caused by or arising out of any form of public worship, all those who excited them by fanatical preaching or counter-revolutionary suggestions, and all those who provoked them by unjust or uncalled for acts of violence, shall be equally punished with all the rigor of the law.

ARTICLE XV. There shall be celebrated, upon the 20th next, a national festival in honor of the Supreme Being.[5]

Robespierre's mounting persecution mania frightened some Convention members, but his Festival of the Supreme Being was saved by two timely assassination attempts. On May 23, 1794, a man waited all day for Robespierre himself, then fired twice at one of his friends. The next evening a half-witted girl called at his residence, asked for him, and remarked that it was his duty as a public official to see people because under the old régime it was easy to see the king. Arrested, she was found with two knives. Hysteria swept the Jacobin Club. Robespierre, playing the paranoid martyr, had for three years talked about himself as a man marked for murder by nebulous enemies. Now he vented a harangue:

> Let us rejoice that we have served our country so well as to be judged worthy of the tyrants' dagger. My mind turns more than ever to the unmasking of traitors. We swear by the blood of the martyrs of the Revolution, we will exterminate to the last man the villains who would rob us of happiness and freedom!

So insane was Robespierre's supicion that when a hapless Jacobin proposed civic honors for the locksmith who got the bullet meant for Robespierre's friend, the Incorruptible suspected an attempt to ridicule him and had the member promptly expelled. His dragnet caught not only assassins but friends, relatives, a schoolmaster who had criticized him, a man who had criticized the arrests, a woman who failed to report the critic, a lady gambler, four policemen, bankers, a mistress of one of the Hébertists and her little servant-girl, Nicolle. In all, 54 persons were beheaded. When Nicolle was strapped to the plank, some spectators cried, "NO CHILDREN!" This innocent soul politely asked the executioner, "Am I holding my head right, M'sieur?" The blade fell.

Amidst this hysteria, the Convention elected Robespierre its monthly president by the largest vote ever cast, and so he pontificated at the Festival of the Supreme Being on June 8, 1794. Almost all of Paris—500,000 people—turned out for this weird ceremony. The city was decked out in bunting and foliage. A painter had been appointed to design the celebration. The Convention filed out, each member wearing the new officials dress of blue with tricolor sashes, bedecked in swords, ribbons and plumed hats, and carrying bouquets of flowers, fruit, and corn. Robespierre, a handsome dandy in yellow breeches and a blue coat, delivered an oration praising theism. Amid strains of music, he ceremoniously put a torch to a tall cardboard idol labeled Atheism, and from its falling fabric emerged another effigy tagged Wisdom. Robespierre made another speech, the crowd sang a hymn, and then he led the huge procession to the parade ground. There stood an artificial hill, symbolizing the "Mountain" (as the Jacobins were sometimes called) topped by a "tree of liberty." An immense choir sang a long hymn to the Supreme Being, the crowd joined with patriotic songs, swords were waved, guns fired, and people swooned crying, "Vive lá Republique!" The procession returned to the Tuileries Gardens, and the day concluded with athletic events.

How on earth can we account for so strange a turn?

First of all, Robespierre was an idealist. His ideals and reality clashed harshly and fiercely; this of course taxed his capacity to adjust and threatened his dreamworld. Political expediency required the sacrifice of old friends like Desmoulins and Danton, but his heart exacted a heavy price. And, by this time, Robespierre held absolute power. Yet black marketing, boarding, and disrespect for the revolutionary regime's decrees increased daily. He despaired of man's spontaneous goodness. Robespierre became more than disillusioned; he harbored desperate fears.

A SUPREME ACT OF TYRANNY   After the Festival of the Supreme Being, Robespierre presided in the Convention while his friends Georges Couthon, a paralytic cripple, presented the infamous Law of 22 Prairial.[6] This incredible law, drawn up by Robespierre and Couthon without Committee of Public Safety approval, permitted the Revolutionary Tribunal to dispense with witnesses. It allowed no sentence except acquittal or death, and defined crimes against the state so vaguely that almost any indiscretion could send a person to the guillotine. Even the expression of counter-revolutionary ideas by a prisoner in the dock could not be tolerated. Professional jurors, guided by a mystic intensity of faith, would know and ferret out the "enemies of the people." Robespierre assumed that these rabble would detect error and judge the accused with an infallible people's intuition. Constitutional immunity for the national representatives was nullified.

The Law of 22 Prairial was Robespierre's supreme act of tyranny. He was determined to make men virtuous, even if he had to chop their heads off to do it. And now he set about it with a grim, deadly determination. Between April 1, 1793, and June 10, 1794, the day the Law of 22 Prairial passed, the Revolutionary Tribunal condemned 1,254 people to death.[7] In the next seven weeks between June 10 and Robespierre's own downfall on July 27, 1,376 people were guillotined—more than in all the previous months of the Reign of Terror.[8]

A shocked Convention, fearing this man ravaged by a cancerous idealism, tried to avoid a vote. But Robespierre insisted, and won. The next day, before members of the Committee of Public Safety arrived, Convention members hurriedly passed a timid motion reasserting its "exclusive privilege of the National representation to impeach and try its own members." Robespierre considered this a provocation and insult. Denying any evil motive, he castigated— ominously without naming names—"a few intriguers" who still tried "to make a new faction." This was a tremendous mistake. Each man now felt himself marked by Robespierre. An underground opposition headed by representatives like Fouché—the machiavellian, "the psychologist of genius," the unfrocked monk, who later became Napoleon's chief of secret police—developed within the previously overshadowed Committee of General Security, which governed police, courts, and prisons. These counter-revolutionaries chose this moment to deliver a stroke of psychopolitical warfare as shrewd as any ever aimed against a totalitarian ruler.

THE PHILOSOPHER-TYRANT STUMBLES   In an obscure corner of Paris lived an 88-year-old religious crackpot named Catherine Theot, who styled herself the Mother of God and conducted queer ceremonies in which she issued prophesies. Before the Revolution, she announced that she was "the Virgin who would receive the child Jesus, who was coming to earth, carried by an angel, to bring peace to the world, and to receive all the nations." For such nonsense, she was confined as a lunatic for three years. Now, enjoying a new popularity in the revolutionary turmoil, she announced that the succession of "Moses, Solomon, the Prophets, and the Apostles" would climax with "the mother of the Savior" who—his plans slightly revised—would come down, amid lightning flashes, near the Pantheon and end the reign of the anti-Christ. Her house became a center for seances and of a popular cult that held weird initiation ceremonies involving liturgical kissing and the sign of the cross.

Just as Robespierre started his campaign for worship of the Supreme Being, agents of his opponents visited the old woman and gently steered her thoughts to Robespierre. Her ex-monk promoter was found to have a certificate of patriotism signed by Robespierre, whom he had been badgering for an appointment. With these ingredients to manufacture an effective scandal, the Committee of General Security on May 12, two days after the Festival of the Supreme Being, raided Mme. Theot's establishment. Later, they produced a letter "found" under Mme. Theot's bed addressing Robespierre as the "Son of the Supreme Being, Eternal Verb, Redeemer of Mankind, Messiah," calling him her "dear minister," and claiming that his mission was foretold by the prophet Ezekiel. She praised him for the honor he had rendered to her "son," the Supreme Being.

Writing was not among Mme. Theot's claims and accomplishments. Nevertheless, the document proved a devastating weapon against Robespierre. Five days after the Law of 22 Prairial became official, three days after Robespierre's shotgun blast of suspicion, and two days before the 54 victims were guillotined for complicity in the assassination attempt, the Committee delivered to the Convention its report on the Theot affair. It was a masterpiece of propaganda. Robespierre, still president of the Convention, had to sit and listen while his opponents presented the most mortifying details of every absurd, unsavory element in the affair. They appropriately changed Mme. Theot's name to Theos for the occasion.

Robespierre was furious and thoroughly embarrassed. The case put him in a ridiculous dilemma. If he allowed Mme. Theos and her followers to be tried and executed, he would seem to have let them die because they made him look silly. If he saved them, he would be acknowledging them as supporters, or at least charged with having basked in their adulation. Choosing the more humane course for once, he had the cases quashed and became the man who protected those who called him the Son of God.

Stung, the philosopher-tyrant now withdrew into a shell. His alarmed supporters urged him to seize the occasion and once more strike down the conspirators. This time they were real, and gathering strength. But Robespierre sulked at his residence, in almost complete seclusion. After June 19, the last day of his presidency, he took no part in the Convention's debates until the showdown on 8 Thermidor (July 26), two days before his death. He spoke only twice at the Jacobin Club. Undoubtedly, he was motivated partly by the need to reconsider his position and to contemplate the future. But could this withdrawal also have been a subconscious influence of his martyr complex? Was it an act of subconscious suicide, a sublimal step to allow his enemies to end the frustration and disappointment he felt over the unideal world that refused to conform to his ideals?

THE TYRANT'S END   For a month the factions grappled for advantage. On July 23, Robespierre's friends and compromise-minded opposition elements arranged a joint meeting of the two Committees and invited Robespierre to address them. But Robespierre blundered. He allowed the bitterness within him to spew out. Pacing to and fro as his anger soared, he glared sneeringly at his enemies while denouncing them. He appealed to the Convention. Meanwhile, the girding factions each compiled their guillotine lists. All the leaders knew that their lives depended upon this battle.

The Robespierre here is a mixture of defiance and despair. With a sad voice, he declared his own purity, faith and dedication to high ideals.

> There do exist pure and sensitive souls. There does exist a tender, but imperious and irresistible passion, which is at once the torment and the delight of magnanimous minds—a profound horror of tyranny, a compassionate zeal for the oppressed, a sacred love of one's country, and a love of humanity still more holy and sublime, without which a great revolution is no more than the destruction of a lesser by a greater crime. There does exist a generous emotion to found on earth the first republic in the world—an enlightened egoism, which finds pleasure in the quiet of a pure conscience, and in the ravishing spectacle of public happiness. You can feel it, at this moment, burning in your hearts. I can feel it in my own.[9]

Robespierre revealed the torment within him and the melancholia that must have consumed him during his self-exile:

> My mind, though not my heart, is beginning to despair of that Republic of Virtue whose plan I had traced out . . .
> What patriot would care to go on living, when he has no more opportunity of serving and defending oppressed innocence? What motive for survival is there under a regime in which intrigue is forever victorious over truth, in which justice is a lie, and in which the sacred interests of mankind are ousted from men's hearts by the vilest passions and the most fantastic fears?[10]

Robespierre wearily repeated the old refrain: there is a conspiracy against freedom and "to unify the whole government" traitors must be punished. But Robespierre's zeal and convictions were gone. He sadly ended:

But I was not made to govern—only to combat crime, and the time has not yet arrived when men of good will can serve their country without suffering for it.[11]

In the debate, when called upon to name names, Robespierre would only reply, "I dare not name them at this moment and in this place . . . I stand by what I have said." And he refused to participate further in the debate, leaving every member in such fear and uncertainty that some dared not sleep in their own homes that night. Fouché and his colleagues worked furiously to exploit the opportunity. Robespierre's supporters too met most of the night at the Jacobin Club. Many urged an appeal to force and an insurrectionary triumvirate to be headed by Robespierre, or even a personal dictatorship. But Robespierre himself, always a man of words and not acts, shrank from violence. "The mass of the assembly will listen to me," he maintained.

"Don't be alarmed," Robespierre told a friend the next morning as he left home for the last time. "The mass of the Convention is pure. I have nothing to fear." But so doubtful was the outcome that an anti-Robespierre leader entered the house with two speeches in his pocket—one for and one against Robespierre.

When Louis de Saint-Just, one of Robespierre's aides, began to speak in behalf of the philosopher-tyrant, he was interrupted and his right to speak was challenged. Wild applause erupted. A member then proceeded to indict Robespierre with a long list of charges. Several times Robespierre tried to defend himself, but was met with the prearranged cry of "Down with the tyrant!" He was shouted down repeatedly. His opponents moved cautiously, first winning the arrest of a Robespierrist general, then lesser lieutenants. Robespierre looked angrily to the Mountain—the high bank of benches where many of his supporters sat. Some turned their heads, while others returned his looks defiantly. He now addressed the main body of the house. "It is to you that I address myself, for you are honest men, and not brigands. . . ."

But the shouting swelled. Robespierre screamed at the chair: "For the last time, President of Assassins, I demand the right to speak!" A thunderous uproar drowned him out. At this crucial moment Robespierre's voice failed him. *"It's Danton's blood that's choking him!"* screamed one of his opponents.

A motion for Robespierre's arrest was made. At first, only a few voices supported it, then the massed body sniffed the drift, and cries of "Vote! Vote!" spread. Soon it was ordered, and with his principal associates, Robespierre was led away.

Paris Commune radicals sounded the tocsin, the usual prelude to insurrection, and called upon the people to overthrow the "criminals" persecuting Robespierre. The Jacobin Club sent deputations to the Commune declaring its determination to conquer or die. Three thousand Commune militiamen gathered at the City Hall square. But a fatal indecision afflicted the radicals. Even Robespierre seemed to doubt his dreamed Republic of Virtue; when supporters came to free him he hesitated to leave his prison cell to join the anti-government revolt, consenting only after a delegation arrived to remind him: "You do not belong to yourself, but to the country, and to the people." Robespierre joined the Commune leaders at the City Hall, and far into the night they dispatched appeals for support, drew up arrest warrants for Convention leaders, and prepared for the showdown they thought would come the next day.

But the Paris crowds did not respond with the enthusiasm of yore, for the Committee of Public Safety's inability to enforce price ceilings while controlling wages had caused much hardship. At midnight, a heavy rain began and the tired and hungry communal militiamen, disheartened by their leaders' inaction, began to disperse.

Then at 2 A.M. the Convention leaders decided to strike swiftly. Using the Commune's password and shouting "Vive Robespierre!" a small spearhead slipped into the City Hall and swooped down on the plotting insurrectionaries. In the scuffle Robespierre turned a pistol upon himself to blow his own brains out, but his aim was deflected, and he only shattered his jaw.[12]

The next day, white from bleeding, he was carried on a stretcher to the guillotine while crowds jeered and taunted. For half an hour, he lay on the ground while the blade thudded down upon 22 of his colleagues. At last, half conscious, he was strapped to the board. The executioner to bare his neck ripped away the bandage from his jaw, and Robespierre's last utterance was an irrepressible cry of pain. It was the scream of an anguished idealist against the pain of a perversely unideal world.

EPILOGUE   The Tragedy of Robespierre is that *he was the first man in history who mass-murdered in the name of liberal idealism.*

If man is to have any hope, we must condemn Robespierre. We cannot excuse him; we cannot even forgive him. But, being idealists ourselves, and like him, humanitarians sharing a dream for a better world, we can sympathize with him, and most important of all, we can *understand* him—hoping that someday, his type will become extinct.

We must emphasize, before leaving Robespierre, that he was not simply a product of Rousseau's philosophical ideas on the Virtue of "the people" and the nature of "the General Will." Nor was Robespierre merely an emotional type brimming with messianic notions of world-saving, paranoid delusions of persecution and neurotic needs for self-justification. *He was a unique compound of both these streams of human development,* cast into the furnace of urbanization, social instability, revolution and power seizure and transformed into a new element. Now the world had a new kind of man, an emotional personality type combined with an intellectual heresy of Western humanism. Social historians have wasted much time debating communism's origins. Are they psychological, philosophical—or what? How can we separate the elements?

Robespierre is important in the history of modern revolutionary radicalism because he developed words and justified genocide against all persons who stood in the way of achieving his Golden Dream. Robespierre articulated forms of logic that have since been employed by latter-day extremists justifying hate and slaughter of "imperialists," "capitalist exploiters," Jews, and Negroes. As Walter Lippmann has summed it up:

> Rousseau and the Jacobins, Marx and the nineteenth century socialists, did not introduce new impulses and passions into men. They exploited and aggravated impulses and passions that are always there. In the traditions of civility, man's second and more rational nature must master his first and more elemental.
>
> The Jacobins and their successors made a political religion founded upon the reversal of civility. Instead of ruling the elemental impulses, they stimulated and armed them. Instead of treating the pretension to being a god as the mortal sin original, they proclaimed it to be the glory and destiny of man. Upon this gospel they founded a popular religion of the rise of the masses to power. Lenin, Hitler and Stalin, the hard totalitarian Jacobins of the twentieth century, carried this movement and the logical implications of this gospel further and further towards the very bitter end.
>
> And what is that bitter end? It is an everlasting war with the human

condition: war with the finitude of man and with the moral ends of finite men, and, therefore, war against freedom, against justice, against the laws and against the order of the good society—as they are conserved in the traditions of civility, as they are articulated in the public philosophy.[13]

Chapter 5
BABEUF: THE RISE OF HATE MEDIA

The hallmark of the agitator is the high value which he places on the response of the public. As a class the agitators are strongly narcissistic types . . . The oratorical agitator, in contradistinction to the publicist, seems to show a long history of successful impostership in dealing with his environment.

—Harold Lasswell,
Psychopathology and Politics

WHY BABEUF IS IMPORTANT   Revolutionary radicalism's first combat party started in the smelly prisons of Paris in the autumn of 1795 after Robespierre's fall. Ultimately it crystallized around a peculiar type of journal whose virulent editor made it a veritable hate magnet for all the disaffected, unrelenting messianic radicals whose thirst for blood had not been quenched by the Reign of Terror. How this formation occurred shows many of the dynamics in messianic extremism as an endemic phenomenon of urban man and the mass media. For only in the large urban agglomerations with their mass audiences and their frustrating complexities do we usually get the "critical mass" of outcasts and hot-eyed haters and disgruntled intellectuals to form the amalgam that is the modern revolutionary movement. Paris in 1795 offers a uniquely documented case study.

The people of France were jaded by the terror and counter-terror that had filled the River Rhone with corpses of Jacobins and Robespierrists. They wanted a rest from utopia-building. The Committee of General Security packed the jails with a flotsam and jetsam of persistent radicals, and the Convention went about the business of trying to resurrect some order out of the wreckage of France's political and social institutions.

One of these random agitators was François-Noel Gracchus Babeuf, a compulsive quarreller and ne'er-do-well whose careers included domestic servant, clerk, accountant, feudal tax collector, petty bureaucrat, political journalist, agitator, and finally conspirator. In him blended many of the psychological and philosophical elements that became modern revolutionary radicalism. He was jailed in February 1795 for incendiary attacks on the government in his newspaper, *Tribune of the People.*

THE BABEUVIST DECISION FOR VIOLENCE   In their cells, the political prisoners watched and wrangled over the new constitution the Convention was debating. They quickly split into two camps. One we might call the moderates, or due process party. These "flattered themselves that from the latitude of the Constitutional Order might result some favorable change for the people,"[1] in the words of Philippe Buonarroti, one of the prisoners who lived to write the story of these events.

In the other camp, polarizing around Babeuf and Buonarroti, were the irreconcilables. Their vision of apocalyptic violence was too dear. They spurned the path of peace and due process offered by the Constitution of 1795. "*To preserve opulence and misery*—such is the spirit which pervades every sentence of it!"[2] That was their instantaneous judgment. They ridiculed the other prisoners who viewed the new constitution hopefully as "persons of timid character of indifferent principles who purchased their liberty by a base submission to the pleasures of the aristocracy; these accepted the new Constitution." Such emotional rejection of people with differing ideas is, of course, characteristic of "the closed mind."[3]

The Babeuvists chose instead the alternative of conspiratorial subversion and violence, plotting to seize power and wage genocidal war on all dissenters. Buonarroti in his history of Babeuvism made no bones about that: "With such enemies to deal with, the question was not whether they should be punished, but *how they were to be exterminated.*"[4] The Babeuvists thought that *"It is extremely probable that a single additional act of severity in France, at that period, would have secured to the human race a complete and everlasting victory over its enemies."* So they resolved to strike that one last bloody blow. This was the Babeuvist choice: to spurn the path of patience, cooperation and peaceful persuasion for the way of conflict, disruption, and destruction. They rejected the Jeffersonian concept of a free marketplace of ideas and the evolving strategy for social change embodied in the American Constitution of parliamentary due process. Instead of open persuasion they chose deception, hate propaganda, and timely application of violence.

The issue embedded in the Babeuvist choice has plagued the socialist movement throughout its history. In fact, it divides every social and reform movement seeking change in the name of justice. Shall those desiring change seek it through impatient violence, or through peaceful reform obtained by persuasion through parliamentary due process? The Babeuvists made the decision for violence.

HOW BABEUF CAUGHT FIRE   François-Noël "Gracchus" Babeuf was born in 1760, when Rousseau was writing his two most famous books, the *Social Contract* and *Émile, or On Education.*

His father had been a major in the French and Austrian armies but in 1738 he deserted and fled France, to return only in 1755 when Louis XV pardoned him. He got a job collecting the infamous *gabelle,* or salt tax, for which he received a commission. At the age of 44, he married a girl of twenty, who promptly bore him a son, François-Noël. Later in his more messianic stage, Babeuf was to claim that he was born on Christmas night, December 25, 1760, "in a hut . . . like the Redeemer"; this, he alleged, was why he was named "Noël."[5] He also claimed his father had tutored Emperor Joseph II of Austria; all this was part of his efforts to create a mystique, thereby enhancing his role of revolutionary leader.

The father lost his job as tax-collector and was reduced to working on the military fortifications at Saint-Quentin. Four more children in rapid succession pressed the family into abject poverty. Such education as the children got was done by the major. From him, François-Noël learned mathematics, Latin, and German.

At 16, the boy went to work as a junior clerk and apprentice to a *commissaire a terrier,* a job peculiar to semifeudal France. His main duties were surveying land, maintaining feudal archives, and exacting the full quota of dues and services owed by tenants on the estate to their lord of the manor. He was helping support his brothers and sisters, and when his father died in 1781 he had to support his mother as well. In 1782 he married a housemaid, Marie-Anne-Victoire Langlet, nearly four years his senior. She was practically illiterate and of very poor parentage.

When their first daughter arrived a year later, François-Noël was living in Roye, a small town of 3,000 souls 65 miles north of Paris, and acting as a *commissaire a terrier* in his own right. The couple had six more children, only three of whom survived childhood. Thus, at 25 Babeuf had at least a moderately lucrative position in society, the equivalent of a white-collar worker in the petty bureaucracy, and he could take pride in having raised himself from deep poverty.

In 1785 he began a long, rambling philosophical correspondence with Dubois de Fosseux, secretary of the nearby Academy at Arras and a figure of provincial importance. The unequal correspondence stimulated young Babeuf's thinking on politics and economics. Babeuf was quickly enveloped by the Rousseauist and radical-utopian ideas that were sweeping France in these years. He wrote Dubois that he hoped to raise his eldest son, Robert, on Rousseau's educational principles, even to the point of rechristening him Émile in homage to Jean-Jacques' book. In 1787 Babeuf sent Dubois a little booklet on "The Constitution of the Military Corps," which Dubois politely commended but called too dangerously "against the Government" to be sponsored and published. That same month, Babeuf suggested an essay topic which revealed his developing interest in communistic ideas:

> Given all present knowledge, what would be the state of people whose social institutions were such that there would prevail among its individual members, without any distinctions, the most perfect equality; that the soil they would live on belonged to no one but to all; that everything would be held in common, including the product of every kind of industry? Would such institutions be authorized by natural law? And, further, would there be practicable means of securing absolutely equal distribution?

He also advocated abolishing the right of inheritance:

> Each citizen on death would make the whole of Society the heir of all his property, and no one would any longer want to see his next of kin die in order that he might have the double advantage of enjoying what they would have possessed, and of putting other aspirants in the position of acquiring the same desires.

Babeuf's distinction in this age was that he insisted, from the outset, that attention be paid not merely to political forms and new republican constitutions but also to the problems of economics, the organization of society, production and labor, land tenure, and the distribution of wealth within the community. Most of his contemporaries maintained that political reforms came first; that the social and economic problems would remedy themselves; and that social and economic equality would automatically follow political equality.

At the same time, Babeuf expressed his impatience with the *form* of political reforms favored in his day. He was *impatient* with democracy. As early as 1786 Babeuf had voiced grave doubts about the "mania of plurality of voices," complaining about the preponderance of "stupid" majorities. He saw an innate indolence of the people that leads them to prefer the things they know and to which they are accustomed. Every change means an effort and a disturbance.

> The majority is always the party of routine and immobility; always it is unenlightened, encrusted, apathetic . . . Those who don't want to progress are always the enemies of those who run in advance, and, unhappily, it is the majority who obstinately persists in not budging.[6]

From this fundamental distrust of the people grew—in 1795 at the crucial last planning session of Babeuf's Insurrectional Committee—the recognition of the need for a *revolutionary dictatorship* to *force* people to be free and equal in the Republic of Virtue.

In 1786 Babeuf published two professional booklets on land titles and fief management. He built up a good practice among the nobility and clergy of his province. But he soon encountered the tendency of nobility to behave arrogantly and dishonestly toward the middle-class professional and service folk. In 1787 the Count de Casteja quarreled with Babeuf over whether the latter should dine with the Count's other employees, and wrote him a haughty rebuke. Babeuf, though stung, replied with dignity. The Prior of Saint Taurin settled for a six-month job only upon threat of litigation. The Marquis of Soyecourt refused to pay Babeuf's bill for 12,000 livres. Unable to afford a costly lawsuit against so powerful a noble, Babeuf was forced to settle for only 2,400, less than a fourth his due. All this ruined him financially, so that in 1787 he had to move his family into Roye's poorer working-class district. The experience galled him and instilled a deep hatred for France's social order and bitterness in his political thinking.

Thus it is not surprising in 1789 to find Babeuf leading the preparation of Roye's petition of grievances to the new estates general. As attacks on castles spread through Picardy, Babeuf helped burn the seignorial archives: this was the utlimate act of rebellion, the destruction of the materials of his own profession—like a lawyer burning lawbooks. He cut loose and went to Paris following the fall of the Bastille. The great surrender of noble privileges on August 4, combined with destruction of the archives, left him a man whose only useful skill was his pen. He wrote his affectionate and apologetic wife about his plans for earning more money. The Revolution had inflamed his mind with a new vision and *endowed him with a new self-image—the world's first professional revolutionary and mass media hate propagandist.* He wrote:

> Electrified by the intervention of an unexpected disposition of things, we conceived the reasonable possibility of contemplating the application of the theories which only a little time before we did not flatter ourselves to have been treating in relation to our own time.
>
> Our soul, from that time inflamed with all the courage necessary, showed them to be practicable the project of overwhelming criminal hands with the elements of perfect justice.

This messianic vision had reoriented Babeuf's life. In an autobiographical note written in 1794 he commented on his profession: "before the Revolution archivist and surveyor. After the Revolution, propagandist of liberty and defender of the oppressed." The Revolution had "spoiled him furiously," he said, and rendered him incapable of pursuing any profession except "publicism" and "matters concerning legislation." Politics and the true principles of law were so irresistible that he regarded them as his "unique vocation." He claimed that a "fault inherent in our nature," a "sort of inmost vanity," told him and those sharing his vision that they were *better than many of their brethren,"* and were to proselytize for the "terrible mystery" and to regenerate the world.[7]

THE UNIVERSAL TENDENCY TOWARD TYRANNY   Here in Babeuf we see one of human history's most corrupting forces: The egomania and arrogance of the intellectual that leads him to believe that he is chosen to direct the lives of his fellow men as a puppeteer maneuvers his stringed dummies.

As one scholar notes: Here we have it all—

> . . . that disposition, the quality of mind—a complex mixture of ideas, mystical faith, volition, passion, emotion, messianic hope and error— that has for a hundred and fifty years been among the most important factors in the destinies of mankind; the faith in a single and final cause of and answer to all evils the world over; the belief that the secret has at last been found, that humanity is heading in an irresistible march for some denouement, a violent breakthough to a preordained, perfect and ultimate scheme of things.[8]

As a matter of fact, it is only human (and therefore a universal tendency) to think that we are, each of us, honest, and that in our own beliefs and convictions we are *correct.* Therefore anybody who disagrees with us must be *wrong;* ergo, he must be stupid or *dishonest,* either with himself, with the world, or with us. Since each of us has this trait, each of us, therefore, is a potential totalitarian. This trait is the Deadly Sin of Pride.

Babeuf attacked every single French régime within a five-year period—Bourbon, Mirabeau moderates, Girondins, Jacobins, Thermidorians—even Robespierre's rule. Opposing Mirabeau's efforts to compromise for a constitutional monarchy, he produced a pamphlet called "The New Distinction of the Order, by M. de. Mirabeau." He founded a journal called *Le Correspondent Picard* that produced forty numbers and 200 lawsuits in six months, plus a short jail term, but little money. For the next two years he lived at Roye, writing pamphlets and participating in stormings of castles and burnings of government offices. He organized protest strikes, boycotts, petitions, and collective refusals to pay the feudal dues that remained. He saw himself as the defender of the oppressed, one of those "men exaggerated, morose, extravagant, by nature destined to trouble the public order and tranquility" with an "air tortured and savage . . . like Rousseau." His "revolutionizing" earned him several prison terms.

When the citizens of Roye refused to pay local taxes Babeuf was accused of fomenting the agitation. In 1790 he was elected by a 15 vote margin to the town council, but before the year was out the government ejected him, declaring him ineligible. Babeuf was elected a commissioner for his district charged with investigating and determining the rights of the commune. After a violent clash with the mayor, he was arrested on government orders. By now he was developing a paranoia and persecution mania.

> There is a powerful horde of detractors who look upon me as one of the greatest menaces to the mass of abuses on which they and their like continue to fatten themselves [he wrote on August 20, 1791]. This class of parasites on society never miss a chance to launch attacks against me . . . They have treacherously struck at all my sources of income, diminishing them one by one, inciting and encouraging my debtors not to pay me, my creditors to pursue me, persuading those who had commissioned my services to withdraw their commission.

At the same time, Babeuf liked the combativeness of revolutionary politics, because it allowed him to discharge the bitterness stored deep in his soul and impelled him to build a world modeled after the ideas of Rousseau, Mably, and Morelly:

> Politics, and meditation on the true principles of laws and their executions hold so irresistible an attraction for me that I am inclined to think that there lies my true vocation.

In 1792 Babeuf settled in Amiens, becoming archivist and administrator for the department of the Somme. Quarreling bitterly with the local representative, he left and landed a similar post in the Montdidier district. Here, too, he quarreled with the district president, an extreme royalist and an aristrocrat, who brought a forgery charge against him. Babeuf fled to Paris where in 1794 he obtained another minor bureaucratic post which advanced his career: secretary in the Bureau of Subsistences under the Paris Commune. Finding much thievery and graft in this municipal department, he concluded the authorities were planning an artificial famine and publicly denounced them. This hate-targeting got him cashiered.

Babeuf then took the name of "Gracchus," after the great Roman reformers and tribunes, and started a newspaper, the *Journal of Liberty of the Press*. His fiery attacks soon caused the Committee of General Security to proscribe him. Babeuf went into hiding, clandestinely publishing his journal under a new title—*Tribune of the People*. Eventually he was caught and jailed, but managed to get a "Manifesto" smuggled out to his "Fellow Citizens."

One of his prison cellmates tells us Babeuf had to work himself into a frenzy before writing one of his inflammatory tirades. He would nervously pace the room until his eyes blazed and he snarled phrases through clenched teeth. He would kick the furniture and cry "To Arms! Insurrection!" Then, seizing his pen, he would write furiously until his whole body, bathed in sweat, trembled and quaked with rage. Knowing this about his psychological composure, then Babeuf's rejection of conciliation and due process upon release from jail, and preference for violence and conspiracy, seem quite natural. His personal magnetism, his mastery of mass media hate propaganda, his flair for leadership and demagoguery crystallized like-minded and disturbed individuals into modern history's first urban revolutionary radical cabal.

EARLY ORGANIZATIONAL EFFORTS   The division between the radical prisoners and the moderates was so surprisingly sharp that we must look to psychology for an explanation. Even in prison they divided into tight parties—Equals (as the Babeuvists called themselves) and the self-styled Patriots of 1789. Nothing could change the Equals' attitudes toward the new government—not the suppression of the royalist insurrection of 13 Vendémiaire (October 5, 1795) against the Convention and new Constitution by a young artillery officer named Bonaparte and his "whiff of grapeshot"; not the election of two Jacobin generals to the new five-man Directory; not even the Convention's last act (October 26, 1795) of freeing all the political prisoners, including the Babeuvists who had attacked the new constitution. Their minds were hopelessly closed. They were committed to an apocalyptic struggle and to an instant idealism.

But once free, the Equals soon faced the frustrating fact that the people of Paris and France wanted no more of their shrill cries. So they were forced to adopt, for the first time in the history of modern urban revolutionism, the tactic of secretly organizing, agitating, and awaiting what the Leninist would come to call the "revolutionary upsurge." In November 1795, a select group—Buonarroti names 17 but omits Babeuf—met at the house of one Buoin and "all swore to remain in union, and to make equality triumph." The revolutionaries resolved to form a "new popular society," and organized as the Society of the Pantheon. They began meeting in the crypt of an ancient convent near the Pantheon. This, the "Cave of Brigands," was an ideal setting for conspiracy.

> The dim flicker of torchlight, the hollow echoes of voices, and the cramped positions of the members sitting or standing on the ground and leaning against the pillars, impressed everyone with the grandeur and the danger of the whole enterprise, as well as the courage and prudence it called for.[9]

To avoid any resemblance to the old Jacobin clubs, the Society kept no minutes, had no rules or officers, raised money by passing a hat, and admitted anyone presented by two of its members. This proved to be its undoing. Many of the moderate Patriots of 1789 who favored working with the existing government got in and soon rammed through a resolution swearing fidelity to the Constitution of 1795 and, adds the disgusted Buonarroti, "filled with a thousand base flatteries."[10]

So on the sly, Buonarroti, Darthe, and other Equals tried to form a secret insurrectionary committee. Only after lengthy ideological and political discussions did they get down to the business of overthrowing the government.

To counter police surveillance, the Equals, for the first time in the history of modern revolution, created the cell structure of conspiracy. According to Buonarroti, the project was devised by

> distributing all the patriots into small obscure clubs, chosen delegates from which were to form district societies, subject to a central committee, which was to have been composed of a small number of tried Democrats, charged with imparting to the whole a uniform impulse.[11]

Marxists and Leninists took their modern Communist Party structure right out of Buonarroti's book.

THE NEWSPAPER CRYSTALLIZER   Meanwhile, Babeuf published his journal again as soon as he had got out of jail. His first issue on November 5, 1795, haughtily cried: *"The Tribune of the People* is free. The government has been so clumsy as to let it go. Now we must see where this imprudence will lead it." He then returned to his incendiary methods. The dynamism of his appeal lay, like that of Marx later, in presenting the communist utopia as an immediately practicable and attainable system.

He had always believed in communist ideas, borrowing early in life from Morelley's *Code of Nature* (1755) the principle he was to transmit to Marx: "From each according to his ability, to each according to his needs." Earlier Babeuf had written in his first journal, the *Correspondant Picard:*

> The constitution must be a national patrimony, where there is bread both of the spirit and of the body for the people as a whole, where a guarantee of complete intellectual, and material life is not only made clear, precise and positive, but also is immediately sanctioned by the placing in common of all resources which have indefinably multiplied and accumulated through an organization intelligently contrived and general labor wisely directed.

Late in 1795 Babeuf for the first time committed himself wholly to communist theories. The next few issues of the *Tribune* carried his outline of a naïve communism: There must be no privation of those goods which Nature gave for the enjoyment of all. Where, by the inevitable accidents of nature, a natural shortage developed the consequent hardship must be borne by all. The only road to justice and equality is to establish an *administration commune* to suppress private property, to allocate to each man the work for which he is best fitted (for all work essential to the community is equally honorable), and to oblige him to deposit the product of his labors in a common pool. Then all that is needed is a simple agency to divide up the national wealth. This agency, "keeping a register of all individuals and of all goods, will partition these goods according to the strictest principles of equality and deliver them to the home of each individual." Under such a government, locked doors, crime and punishment, lawsuits and prisons, envy and hate will vanish, and the golden age will appear.

Babeuf's doctrine relied heavily on Rousseau's *Discourse on Inequality.* He saw all history as the story of avarice. He identified the "haves" with idlers, never admitting that their wealth might have been a reward for merit or industry. The oppressed poor are romanticized—they are always righteous and good! Manual labor is the only real source of wealth. Managers and entrepreneurs are immoral. "Society is a cavern. The harmony which reigns there is a crime," he wrote in No. 34 of the *Tribune.* "What does one mean to speak of laws and of properties? Property is the dividends of usurpers, and the laws the work of the strongest," he exclaimed. *Society is thus a permanent civil war among the classes.*

While elaborating on these messianic communist ideas, Babeuf also stepped up his attacks on the existing government. Soon enough, the Directory ordered his arrest. So Babeuf went underground in February 1796. He demonstrated pure genius at printing and distributing his newspaper clandestinely.

Infuriated, the Directory threw Babeuf's wife into prison on a charge of clandestinely distributing his paper. This was a godsend to the embattled Equals in the Society of the Pantheon, for Babeuf's writings had been taboo there and members had maintained a "rigorous silence" toward him. But the Equals turned Mme. Babeuf's case into a *cause célèbre,* collecting petitions and money for her. Babeuf, his writings and radicalism were in vogue again.

Police agents in the Pantheon Society soon obtained the evidence they needed: Darthe read to the assemblage some numbers of Babeuf's *Tribune of the People* that attacked the Directors and certain deputies. The reading evoked bursts of applause. In February 1796, the government sent General Bonaparte to silence the society, and that grand officer had his soldiers ceremoniously present him with the key to the old convent.

"THE CONSPIRACY OF THE EQUALS" Babeuf's incendiarism mounted. Each line he wrote was a call to revolution. "Alas! Everybody is poor under this regime except the handful of speculators and rascals it protects. The people die of hunger. They perish successively from all sorts of privations!" he cried. "In a crisis so extreme, half cures won't do. We must have an emetic, mercury, castor oil, the infernal stone. Yes, yes, we will administer them." "It is no longer a question merely of reestablishing the death penalty, but of cutting the throats of the oppressors."[12]

The Equals, riven by their own personality clashes and dogmatic theoretic quibbles, turned more and more to Babeuf for leadership.

"I believe that we are approaching a very critical moment," wrote Charles Germain on March 16.

> Will it be decisive for democracy? Your role of Tribune of the People imposes on you the obligation of tracing for the people the plan, the scheme of attack. You are the actual chief of the democrats who wish, at your command, to establish equality. You are the recognized leader by them, and it is therefore you who should—you alone who can—show the way, or show them what must be done.[13]

Soon after, editor Babeuf hatched his "Conspiracy of the Equals." For several weeks while hiding from police in the homes of his former jailmates, he had been plotting with two of his fellow publicists, Felix Lepelletien, the only well-to-do Equal, and Silvain Marechal, orator and professional demagogue, to harmonize the subjects and tone of their political works. But Babeuf schemed to "direct all the democratic movements to a common center." He engineered the dissolution of the cell structure his fellow Equals built around the Pantheon Society. Then about March 21, 1796, Babeuf, his two fellow writers and an obscure person named Antonelle constituted themselves into a "Secret Directory of Public Safety." Their aim:

> To bind to a single point the scattered threads of the democracy, for the purpose of directing them towards the reestablishment of the popular sovereignty . . . to rally and place at its immediate disposal all the friends of liberty—to calculate their forces, and to give them an impulse favorable to instruction and to the general deliverance, without at the same time exposing either the conspiracy or its partisans to be compromised by treachery or indiscretion.

For the first time since the general amnesty, of all the attempts to organize, this conspiracy clicked—for it had what the others lacked: Babeuf's newspaper and leadership.[14]

Babeuf and his three colleagues drew up a special act of self constitution:

EQUALITY   LIBERTY

Creation of an Insurrectional Directory

The democrats of France, grievously affected, profoundly indignant, justly revolted at the unheard-of state of misery and oppression of which their unhappy country presents the spectacle;

Ardently remembering that when a Democratic Constitution was given to the people, and by it accepted, the preservation of that Constitution was placed under the safeguard of all the virtues;

Considering, therefore, that to the purest, most courageous virtues; belongs the initiative of undertaking to avenge the people whenever, as now, its rights are usurped . . .

Believing that the reproach is an unjust one which accuses the people of cowardice . . .

Recognizing that the overflowing measure of the crimes of an usurped authority has ripened the inclinations of every virtuous soul in favor of a revolutionary explosion . . . have resolved as follows:

1. They constitute themselves, from this moment, an Insurrectional Directory, under the name of the "Secret Directory of Public Safety." In this capacity they assume the initiative of all movements intended to lead the people to the recovery of its sovereignty.

2. This Directory consists of four members.

3. This Directory shall be secret; the names of its members shall be unknown to even its chief agents. Between these and the members of the Directory there shall be an intermediary agent to carry communications from one to the other.

4. The Secret Directory of Public Safety pledges itself to discharge the immense range of duties which that great title imposes on it.

5. A distinctive mark shall be affixed to such written instructions, as it may be indispensable to give to the principal agents . . . it shall be a guarantee to them, notwithstanding the default of signatures, for the authenticity of the Acts to be communicated by the Secret Directory.[15]

Chapter 6
BABEUF: FOUNDING THE TECHNOLOGY OF SOCIAL DEMOLITION

> Arise, ye prisoners of starvation,
> Arise, ye wretched of the earth,
> For justice thunders condemnation—
> A better world's in birth
>
> —The Internationale

> The ruling principle of Hate . . .
> For its pleasure doth create
> The things it may annihilate.
>
> —Byron, "Prometheus"

MASS MEDIA AND ORGANIZATIONAL DEPLOYMENT   Babeuf operated in Paris, then a metropolis of 600,000. Save only for London and Imperial Rome, no city of such size had ever existed in human history. And Imperial Rome never had printing presses which agitators could employ for systematic hate propaganda. So Babeuf was pioneering in the unexplored fields of urban sociology and dynamics, experimenting with mass audiences on an unprecedented scale, employing new techniques of mass organization, mass manipulation, mass propaganda and hate targeting. He was the first man ever to use a newspaper as an instrument of mass conspiracy, propaganda preconditioning, and urban insurrection. Thus, his innovations in 1796 earn him the right to be ranked as a founder (if not *the* founder) of a new field of human endeavor: *the technology of social demolition.*[1]

Babeuf's conspiracy reached its climax in just six weeks of frenzied agitation. His plan was simple. The Secret Directory—the central committee—selected a "chief revolutionary agent" for each of Paris's 12 precincts. He had to be proposed by one of the Secret Directory. As with most revolutionary organizations, the agents Babeuf recruited were no more "proletarian" in origin than the central committeemen themselves. They were all of the petit bourgeoisie and artisan class—petty bureaucrats, professional men, policemen and soldiers, architects, and small tradesmen such as tailors and printers. Their sole connecting link to the central committee was to be one Didier, a locksmith. He was supposed to know neither the Directory members nor their operations, but they had such confidence in him this rule was not strictly respected. In fact, they allowed him to propose and add to the central committee both Darthe and Buonarroti himself. By April 1, a seven-man central committee was meeting regularly in Babeuf's hideout, the apartment of one Clerex, a tailor. And the committee's agents had already established dozens of little secret cells of five or six persons.[2]

The Secret Directory's first duty was *"to convince the multitude, and to make proselytes,"* says Buonarroti. He thus underscored the two most basic functions of any political ideological organization—propaganda and recruitment:

> To this end, the Secret Directory spared neither discourses nor writings; and to circulate them with more effect, it instituted in Paris a great number of small associations, mutually unknown to each other, but all under the direction of the Democrats, who themselves received their cue and instructions from the twelve revolutionary agents.
>
> It is worth observing in the instructions given to these agents the precautions by which the Directory of Public Safety endeavored to guard the Democrats from the consequences of imprudence and perfidy. From the outset the Revolutionary agents were designed to become the levers by which the people of Paris was to dart upon its tyrants. Meanwhile they formed associations, directed popular discussions, circulated writings, and reported to the Secret Directory the progress of opinion, the intrigues of the aristocracy, and the number, capacity, and energy of the Democrats.[3]

Aside from its agents the Secret Directory had certain active sympathizers who had knowledge, though imperfect, of the conspiracy. A leather merchant, Monnier, appears to have steered possible recruits along. Several shopkeepers and innkeepers furnished meeting places. A printer, Lamberte, printed their materials without question. None of these were fully initiated. In addition, two police commissioners had an indeterminable connection with the conspiracy and extended a degree of protection. A General Ganier tried to affiliate, but evasive replies to requests for intelligence made him suspect. A police captain, Peche, offered 300 guns. There were many other such vaguely defined knowledgeable sympathizers, and of course thousands more who knew nothing of a conspiracy but sympathized with Babeuf's propaganda.

In addition, Buonarroti speaks of receiving "240 francs in specie" from "the Minister of an allied Republic,"[4] almost certainly the Dutch ambassador, Jacques Blauw. Buonarroti was in close touch with the Dutch Jacobins, and Blauw actually participated in an insurrection in Amsterdam on May 8, 1796, obviously timed to coincide.[5]

The Secret Directory set up a table of organization delineating the duties of the 12 revolutionary agents in their wards:

> Each of these is charged to organize, in his arrondisement, one or more unions of patriots; to foster and direct the public mind in those unions by the reading of popular journals, and by discussions on the rights of the people, and respecting its present situation.
>
> These agents shall take note of the daily thermometer of public opinion. They shall render account in those notes of the dispositions more or less favorable, of the patriots; they shall signify the individuals they may observe most capable of seconding the progress of the movement designed to be brought about; they shall indicate the description of employment, or revolutionary enterprise, to which they may suppose each of these individuals suited. They shall, in like manner, take note of the intriguers—of such imposters who may try to insinuate themselves into the meetings; and they shall moreover, render account of the impediments and opposition which the latter may offer to the development of energy, to the inspiration of sound principles and regenerating ideas . . .
>
> The intermediary agents shall apply successively for these notes of daily observations every day, or every second day, to each of the principal agents, at their residences, if necessary.[6]

A subsequent instruction ordered: 1. Agents must submit a list of all depots and stores of food, arms and munitions in their respective precincts. 2. They will report on "the workshops there, the number of workers employed in each, the type of work they do, and their known opinions." 3. They will make "a census of patriots with means who could receive and lodge in their dwellings brothers and departments which the Secret Directory will establish to aid the Parisians in overthrowing the tyrants." 4. They will engage these patriots "to raise a fund to help defray the great expenses of printing which the revolutionaries are obliged to make." 5. They will furnish a "list of police agents and informers." 6. They will organize "companies of crowd collectors" (*groupeurs*) who must daily go to the Tuilleries and other places where people gather to "talk there about the meaning of the most recent numbers of the popular journals." 7. They will organize "companies of bill-posters" who will at the same time "tear down the writings of the royalists and patricians."

Students of modern communism will recognize instantly that this was quite an advanced organizational concept for intelligence collection, command and control channels. The Communist Party organization in Paris today is probably not much more sophisticated. The primary organizational functions were present: *propaganda, recruiting, financing, intelligence,* and *chain of command.* The only fundamental improvement Lenin was to add was *training,* a combination of psychological moulding to create the organization man, and formal schooling to equip him with the knowledge of tactics and organizational skills for efficiency as a conflict manager and social demolitionist.

BUILDING THE OPERATIONAL CODE   The Babeuvists even had the typical communist manipulatory attitude toward the public. The Secret Directory's instructions to the 12 revolutionary agents declared:

> When we invite you to organize in your arrondisement one or more patriotic reunions, we need not suggest the expediency of doing the thing quietly and unostentatiously; and it is possible for you to form such reunions, and even to identify their spirit with yours, *without appearing to be either their founder or leader.* Let us sacrifice the vanity of appearing to advantage to the glory of being really useful. *There is no stronger guarantee of grand and substantial success, nothing which confers more real self-satisfaction, than the internal consciousness that one is the invisible instrument by which great springs of action are moved* ... It will be time enough to receive the applause of our brethren when we shall have saved them.
>
> Thus, then, *it appears to us perfectly practicable for the principal agents, to institute, organize, and direct the clubs we seek without appearing to institute, organize, or direct anything.* (Emphasis added.)[7]

The Secret Directory preferred to infiltrate and capture existing organizations and clubs. It pointed out that the "patriots" were in the habit of assembling at several coffee houses, and instructed the agents to seek to increase the number of gatherings at each; and to multiply the number of meeting places rather than to build up crowds, which might attract police. "Visit each of those places in turn; even prefer private residences to coffee houses for holding your meetings, if practicable . . .

> In general, avoid giving a public or external importance to those assemblings; do not call them clubs, societies, or unions; avoid all pompous denominations; say simply *such* a coffee house; *such* a dwelling; and the action of going there call *taking a stroll—visiting,* etc. Let the *things* be but not the *words.*[8]

Spoken like a true Leninoid! Is it any wonder that Marx and Lenin both imbibed Buonarroti's book with these spicy details of conspiratorial *modus operandi?* Or, that modern revolutionary agents seek always to act under the names of "nationalist," "liberal," "progressive," "pacifist," or "reformer"?

The agents were directed to read the "popular journals" in their coffee house circles and use them to "foster and direct public spirit . . . Mind! *Above all, the reading of popular journals.*"[9] Of course, the Secret Directory meant those publications through which Babeuf promulgated his line: The leader contributed regularly to the *Enlightener of the People,* edited by S. Lalande: Antonelle, a Secret Directory member, edited the *Journal of Free Men,* whose pages he opened to Babeuf.[10] "The choice of such journals will not be difficult. You will easily know them. They will serve you as a mariner's compass, guide your movements, and serve instead of general instructions," said the Secret Directory.

The plotters planned to neutralize the royalist forces by deception and mobilize and direct popular indignation against the government by the careful selection of slogans:

> Convinced how important it is to completely baffle the Royalists and to deceive them respecting our real intentions in the movement which is preparing, in order to prevent both them and the Government from employing against us, during the movement, their old proscriptive epithets of *terrorists, jacobins, seditionists, men of Prairial,* etc. I think we should all, from the outset, have chalked upon our hats—*Army of the people; down with the tyrants.*
>
> Also, there shall be borne three sorts of banners, upon which will be the following inscriptions—*Army of the people; down with the tyrants; vengeance of the people.* This appears to me a capital expedient to make our very enemies subserve our designs. You may judge of it by the applause given at the theaters to the words, "Tremble tyrants," etc . . . It will be necessary to make a theatrical display of banners, as if descending from the clouds, and bearing

the inscriptions, *Constitution of 1793; general happiness; victory of the people, etc.*"[11]

Babeuf laid down a basic rule for crowd management which all revolutionary planners have since followed. *"From the start, force the people to commit acts which will prevent them from deserting the revolutionaries and retreating. All reflection on the part of the people is to be prevented."* For this purpose he listed among his first objectives to be taken by the crowds "les caves," the wine and brandy cellars.

BABEUF'S HATE MAGNET. The *Tribune of the People* drew many discontented people to Babeuf's standard. One scholar analyzed the list of 642 subscribers, and comparing it to that of the *Constitutional Orator*, a conservative pro-government organ, found the *Tribune*'s only a sixth as large. Both contained precisely the same social classes: businessmen, manufacturers, civil servants of all grades, small tradesmen, and professional men such as lawyers and doctors.

Tribune subscribers included many of the old Jacobins, the Robespierreists, and the professional army. They lived all over France except the west, and—noteworthy—most heavily in those areas where the White Terror had been strongest. Widows of guillotined revolutionaries and former agents of the Terror who had been imprisoned by the Directory dotted the subscription lists. Babeuf's conspiracy mobilized not people who wanted a communist order in France, but drew from the discontented middle and artisan class those who were oppressed by inflation and economic dislocation and were eager for revenge against the moderate post-Thermidor regime. They were motivated chiefly by a hatred for the government, by feelings of largely personal grievance and vengeance. The letters Babeuf received from many of his supporters confirm this diagnosis: they expressed disagreement or plain bewilderment with his talk of equality, but applauded his invective against the Directory.[12]

Babeuf's *Tribune of the People* was thus a primitive ancestor of today's communist and radical revolutionary mass publications such as the *Daily World, The Guardian,* or *The Militant,* which, carefully avoiding all the complexities and abstractions of Marxist theology, concentrate on invective against the whole of existing society. Such publications are magnets for the Lee Harvey Oswald types—the malcontents, misanthropes, and embittered idealists who are the basic human raw material of revolutionary movements.

REVOLUTIONARY ANTI-MILITARISM   The Secret Directory realized that military force against their coup or "even the bare contemplation by the people of such resistance"[13] might prove fatal. So the Babeuvists recruited agents in all the battalions around Paris. They even used prostitutes to carry their ponderous appeals to the troops.

Darthe recruited as chief military agent one Georges Grisel, a young captain of a battalion encamped near Paris. To prove his ardor Grisel wrote an insurrectionary pamphlet designed to provoke insubordination, and the Babeuvists realized they had a veritable hate propaganda genius on their hands. Grisel wrote tracts such as a dialog between "Jambe-de-bois," or "Wooden-leg," a grizzled, disabled veteran, and a young soldier in the Paris garrison, "Franc-Libre," comparing the soldier's lot in 1792 with his contemporary degradation and misery. Another was from Franc-Libre to a friend in the Army of the Rhine, filled with slang phrases and subtle appeals, and very effective. "We are p____ upon, my poor friend. Yes, we are p____ upon, and without resource if we swallow the crap that has been crammed into our mouth," it began, turning eventually from the soldier's lot to the corrupt government officials who fattened upon his misery.

With his brilliant propaganda tracts Grisel began turning in regular reports. His recommendations to the Secret Directory were a masterpiece of psychological-warfare target analysis that served as a model for the Leninists. Appeal to the crudest mass emotions and most material, concrete motives, he advised. Forget the high-flown theory and idealism of your communist political tracts. Grisel was a century ahead of his time. Not until Lenin began to perfect the bolshevik science of sloganeering did the revolutionary art surpass this Babeuvist.

Babeuf himself was so impressed he followed Grisel's advice in a general directive for all the Equals' propaganda:

> It is a long recognized truth that men make decisive moves only for their own interests. It is necessary to speak to them of immediate and material advantages.
> There are two principal references by which one can and must speak to the interest and the soul of men who have protected their country:

their interest in regard to the present situation, and their interest in regard to the future situation.[14]

Babeuf cites the example of a soldier returning from active duty. The propagandist approaches him with questions. What is his pay? "Why that is more paltry than the pay of the meanest German soldier." With a salary of two *sous* a day, he cannot help but die of hunger. Badly clothed, undernourished, undermined by sickness, he will return home. "What will they find there?" That is what the propagandist must know how to present most eloquently, says Babeuf:

> Deep misery, a thousand times deeper than that which their unfortunate fathers underwent, awaits them. The Republic promised to provide them enough land to guarantee subsistence. What has become of this land? It has been returned to the traitors from whom it had been justly confiscated. The defender of the nation, returning to his humble hut, ought no longer to find it lorded over by the castle of the insolent gentry who made his father work in slavery. But this is not the case. He will find this devouring monster more furious, more pitiless than ever. The former defender of freedom will pass his old age in frightful slavery and misery.
>
> Then tell them that their only hope is to follow those who still can alter this frightful perspective. You can even assure them that from the very day when they will have sided with the people in regaining their rights, they will no longer want for anything; they will be overwhelmed with everything man needs. Tell them moreover that from the morrow of the revolution henceforth, abundance and a most happy fate will be guaranteed to all soldiers for the rest of their lives.[15]

In the attention the Babeuvists devoted to infiltrating the ranks of the army and promoting disaffection and mutiny, they pioneered the techniques the bolsheviks were to develop into a practical art during their work in the Czarist army. This is the branch of social demolition technology known as "revolutionary antimilitarism," the isolation, undermining and disorganization of the organized defense forces of the state to remove them as an obstacle to the revolutionary forces.[16]

FIRING THE POPULACE   During April 1796, the Secret Directory bombarded the Paris populace almost daily with incendiary broadsides that created great excitement. Two of these formulated the basic philosophy of the *Equals*, and reflect their apocalyptic visions. The *Analysis of the Doctrine of Babeuf* was a masterpiece of propaganda. It followed several tried-and-true propaganda rules: clarity of expression, simplicity of ideas, and appeal to the material interests of the target audience. Generally it embodied the principles of the Constitution of '93. To the lower classes of Paris, harassed by famine and unemployment, it was a counsel of despair, presenting the solution of destruction as the simplest means of building a better order. Like all powerful social revolutionary movements, it preached the utopian escapist doctrine of the Phoenix, the beautiful world rising from the burning ashes of the old.

ANALYSIS OF THE DOCTRINE OF BABEUF*

*Proscribed by the Executive Directory for Having Told
The Truth!

ARTICLE I

Nature has given to each individual an equal right to the enjoyment of all the goods of life.

ARTICLE II

The end of society is to defend this equality, often assailed by the strong and wicked in the state of nature; and to augment, by the cooperation of all, the common enjoyments of all.

ARTICLE III

Nature has imposed on each person the obligation to work; nobody could, without crime, evade his share of the common labor.

ARTICLE IV

Labor and enjoyments ought to be in common. That is to say, all ought to bear an equal portion of labor, and derive from it an equal quantity of enjoyments.

ARTICLE V

There is oppression wherever one part of society is exhausted by labor, and in want of everything, while the other part wallows in abundance without doing any work at all.

ARTICLE VI

Nobody could, without crime, exclusively appropriate to himself the goods of the earth or of industry.

ARTICLE VII

In a veritable society there ought to be neither rich nor poor.

ARTICLE VIII

The rich who will not renounce their superfluities to help the needy are enemies of the people.

ARTICLE IX

No one should be able, by monopolizing the means, to deprive another of the education necessary for this happiness; education ought to be in common.

ARTICLE X

The aim of the French Revolution is to destroy inequality, and to establish the common happiness.

ARTICLE XI

The Revolution is not finished, because, the rich absorb all wealth, and rule exclusively; while the poor work like veritable slaves, languish in poverty, and count for nothing in the State.

ARTICLE XII

The Constitution of 1793 is the true law of Frenchmen, because the people have solemnly accepted it . . . [The remaining three articles proclaimed the duty of each citizen to re-establish and defend the Constitution of 1793, and anathematized as "counter-revolutionary" all who supported the Constitution of 1795. Each article continued with prolix "proofs" and "explanations".]

The Secret Directory's revolutionary agents displayed genius in getting these propaganda broadsides before the people despite efforts by police and antagonists to tear them down. Juste Moroy, agent of the 12th ward, reported:

I posted the placards not in the night but at 8 o'clock in the morning, so the workers, having breakfast at 9 o'clock, might read them. Because the patriots had seen the royalists and speculators tear down the placards at night, I said, 'They don't want the truth to penetrate; how can we make sure that the people will be enlightened?' I decided to post them not at night, but between 4 and 5 o'clock in the morning. The workers go to their work at six o'clock; at this hour the royalists and the speculators are not up yet. The people while going to work read the posters, and the royalists then can tear them down whenever they wanted.[17]

He also reported:

> With the aid of some true republicans, I have already formed little clubs of five or six persons . . . I have gotten issues of Babeuf's paper into two barracks. I am waiting for news of the effect they produce . . . I have now recruited crowd collectors.

Bodson, one of the conspirators, suggested using women and children to post notices and distribute pamphlets because they were relatively immune to arrest and would work for a pittance. Once he reported that several "patriots" in one of the groups assembled around a poster were arrested: "Exaggerate the number of them," he advised; "Carry indignation to a high pitch."

Baudemann, another member of the conspiracy, specialized in propagandizing the barracks, and was fairly successful at fund-raising. In one day four of his "sans-culottes" collected over 400 livres. Ficquet, still another conspirator, improved the crowd collector system by enlisting workers who could read and discuss the organization's journal right in the shops during work hours.[17]

The "Manifesto of the Equals" foreshadowed Marx's "Communist Manifesto" in both tone and particulars:

> PEOPLE OF FRANCE!—For fifteen centuries you have lived as slaves and therefore in misery. For six years you have stood breathless, waiting for independence, happiness and equality.
>
> EQUALITY! ! The first desire of nature, and the first need of man, chief bond of all legitimate society! People of France! From time immemorial we have been told—hypocritically—that men are equal; and from time immemorial inequality of the most degrading and most monstrous kind has insolently weighed on mankind . . .
>
> We claim hence forth to live and die, as we are born, equals: we want true equality or death. And we will have it whatever the price. Woe to those who stand in our way!
>
> The French Revolution is but the forerunner of another revolution far greater, far more solemn, *which will be the last* . . .
>
> "What do we want," you ask, "more than equality of rights?" We want equality not merely written in the "Declaration of the Rights of Man". We want it in our very midst, in our hearths and homes. And we will pay any price for it, to make a clean sweep so that we can cherish it alone. *If need be let all the arts perish so long as true equality remains!*
>
> We aspire to THE COMMON GOOD OR THE COMMUNITY OF GOODS! No more individual ownership of land, the land belongs to nobody. We lay claim to, we demand, the common enjoyment of the fruits of the earth; these fruits exist for all . . . *Let there be no differences*

*between human beings other than age and sex. Since all have the same
needs and the faculties, let there be one education, one fare for all.
They are satisfied with one sun, one air, why should not the same
quantity and quality of food suffice for each?*

PEOPLE OF FRANCE!

Never was a more vast design ever conceived and put in execution.

The moment for great measures has arrived. Evil is at its height; it
has reached its maximum, covers the face of the earth . . . The moment
has come to found the REPUBLIC OF EQUALS, that great hospice
open to all men. The days of general restitution are come. Weeping
families come and seat yourselves at the common table set by nature
for all her children . . .

What can avail a few thousand malcontents against such a mass of
human beings, all happy, and astonished at having been so long in
quest of a felicity which they had within hands' reach. On the morrow
of this true revelation, men will say to each other in amazement:
"What! Was universal happiness to be had for so little? We had but to
will it. Ah! Why did we not will it sooner? Why had we to be told so
many times? Without doubt while there is still a single man in the
whole world who is richer and more powerful than his fellows or
equals, he destroys the equilibrium, and crime and misfortune come
on the world . . .

PEOPLE OF FRANCE!

Open your eyes and hearts to full felicity; recognize and proclaim
with us the

REPUBLIC OF EQUALS!

The very idea that all persons "have the same needs and faculties"
and therefore should have identical education and quantity and quality of food is so far out of contact with reality that it stamps the
Babeuvists as hopeless ideological psychopaths. The willingness to
"let all the arts perish so long as true equality remains" shows a
fixation on the overvalued idea of "equality."

To popularize their doctrines the Babeuvists also used the pretty,
red-haired Sophie Lapierre, a singer at the popular Cafe of the Chinese Baths and reputedly Darthe's mistress. Darthe or Marechal
would compose political verses which she would sing, and soon they
were hummed and sung all over Paris. "Dying of hunger, dying of
cold . . ." ran one baleful tune. Another had an inspirational refrain:

> Awake! When liberty's trumpets sound
> March out of your night profound,
> People! Reclaim your rights,
> For everyone does the sun shine its light.

This flood of antigovernment propaganda rolled in with food shortages and inflation that were producing frightful distress. By mid-April both police and Babeuvists were alarmed by their agents' reports—the former fearing an insurrection, the latter a premature unplanned outburst. On April 14 a police agent described crowds gathering to read Babeuvist propaganda:

> At the entrance of the Faubourg Antoine some women assembled complaining that their husbands were not working and that nevertheless they had to buy bread and pay taxes which seemed higher than before the Revolution.

They protested that the government had "taken their arms from their husbands, but their bare hands would do and they were not afraid to die."[18] Murmured snarls from the populace were pouring in among the reports.

> The softness of which the people accuse the government leads many exalted leaders to express regrets over the regime of Robespierre; when one points out to them that this would cause much bloodshed, they answer, "That's very bad, but today people die of hunger and malnutrition,' or 'I'd rather die of a bayonet thrust than of hunger and languor."

Ugly crowds were gathering on the bridges, parks and streets of Paris around Babeuvist placards and "crowd collectors."

The Executive Directory declared public gatherings illegal. This severe repression alienated the moderate forces who despaired of peaceful reform and flocked to the Babeuvist banner: their rage complicated the Secret Directory's task of restraining events. Its revolutionary antimilitary propaganda provoked a surprise crisis. The Government Directory found so much disaffection in the "Legion of Police" that in alarm on April 28 it ordered the battalions removed from Paris. This action violated the law constituting the Legion, which stated it should never be engaged in service outside the city. At that the Babeuvist clandestine apparatus shrewdly switched to spreading fear among these troops that they were about to be sent to the fighting fronts where the Republican Army was still engaged with the hostile forces of Europe's monarchs. Open mutiny followed, and all Paris crackled with the tension of imminent revolt.

If the Babeuvists had struck at this moment they might have gained power. Most certainly they could have produced a sizable bloodbath. But the unexpected submission of the two mutinous battalions compelled an instant suspension for fear of ill-prepared action. The government disbanded the two units and smothered the insurrection in its cradle. The Babeuvists embraced the disbanded troops as they straggled into the city and took them into their homes to form cadres of their future "popular army."

On May 1 the Secret Directory set up a five-man Military Committee, including Grisel. The Secret Directory met them face-to-face, along with the trusted Didier and one or two other key plotters. In so doing, the Babeuvists made a fatal mistake: they violated their own constitutional rule that none of the plotters were to know the central committeemen except through reliable intermediaries.

THE DICTATORSHIP OF THE REVOLUTION   In its last meetings the Insurrectional Committee discussed a "very delicate" point: once power was seized, who was to wield it?[19] The conspirators reached no conclusive decision, but clearly they were grappling with a basic problem that was to lead Marx and his successors to proclaim the necessity for a "dictatorship of the proletariat." Buonarroti led the faction favoring this answer; his reasoning was the classic apologia for the intellectual and "general staff" revolutionary who profoundly distrusts the very people in whose name he proposed revolution and a new era:

> *A people whose opinions have been formed under a regime of inequality and of despotism is little fitted, at the commencement of a regenerating Revolution, to distinguish wisely (by voting) the men most capable to direct and consummate it with success.* This difficult task can belong only *to certain wise and courageous citizens,* who, strongly impregnated with the love of country, and of humanity, have long before fathomed the sources of public calamity—have disenthralled themselves from the common prejudices and vices of their age —have shot ahead of contemporary intellects, and who, despising money and vulgar greatness, have found their happiness in rendering themselves immortal by insuring the triumph of Equality. Perhaps, therefore, in the beginning of a Revolution, it is of less consequence, even as regards (and for the sake of) the real popular sovereignty itself, the busy ourselves in collecting the votes of a nation, than *to make the supreme authority fall by the least arbitrary means possible into hands that are wisely and vigorously revolutionary.*[20]

Here we see the arrogant intellectual who is so convinced of his own rightness that he thinks he knows what is good for people—even better than the people themselves. Once in power, this creature's democratic pretensions twist to explain via Orwellian doublethink how democracy is really not necessary to run a democracy—one does not need to consult the people about their own good, one need only consult the philosopher-king.

To make the judgment that a people freed from a tradition of oppression would not be capable of selecting its leaders implies all the evils of totalitarianism: the new class, the terror, the purges, and all else that follows in the history of the revolutionary vanguard concept.

To understand the source of this concept—egocentrism and intellectual arrogance—we need only ask, "Why do the advocates of this dictatorship by 'certain wise and courageous citizens' always choose themselves?"

ORGANIZING THE PEOPLE'S ARMY   The plotters planned for the sudden creation of a popular army. The 12 precincts of Paris were to be organized into an army of three divisions, each comprised of four precincts and headed by a general. These were to be under the orders of a general-in-chief, who was in turn under the Secret Directory's Insurrectional Committee. Under the division commanders were placed the chiefs of precincts, then chiefs of sections, which were divided into platoons with appropriate leaders. The first platoon in each was to be formed out of the most ardent "democrats." The Insurrectional Committee actually selected section chiefs and platoon commanders and its generals were Fion, Germain, Massart and ex-general Rossignol, "conqueror" of the Bastille. The latter, crusty soul, declared he would have nothing to do with the insurrection if "heads do not fall like hail" and inspire a terror that would shake the universe.

At the sound of the alarm bell and proclamation of the Insurrectional Act, these commanders were to present themselves to the people to form them into proper ranks. The plotters believed they would get a mass rising of all the working class at the call of their revolutionary agents. The Secret Directory counted on having 17,-000 men in Paris ready to begin the insurrection, not counting the many workers whose discontent was growing.[21]

The Army's columns were to march on the legislative body, the

Executive Directory, the general staff of the Army of the Interior, and the government ministries, in support of agents appointed to arrest members of the government. The best disciplined sections and those least armed were to march toward the depots of arms and ammunition, and particularly toward the camps of Grenelle and Vincennes, where the plotters believed 8,000 soldiers stood ready to join the insurrection.

To insure this military mutiny the Secret Directory planned to augment persuasion with force. "Orators were to remind the soldiers of the crimes of the government, and of their duties toward their country," recalled Buonarroti. "Women were to present them with garlands and refreshments. The Invalides (disabled soldiers of the revolutionary wars) were to invite them to follow their example."

If the worst happened, the Military Committee prepared to barricade the streets and shower the troops with stones, slates, tiles bricks and torrents of boiling water mixed with sulphuric acid.

The rest of the popular army was to guard the entrance to Paris, to maintain communications between the different bodies, to protect the provisions entering the city, to prevent "antipopular gatherings," to intercept all "aristocratic" correspondence, to put to death anyone attempting to exercise any governmental authority, to check all pillaging and to execute the orders of the Secret Directory.

The Insurrectional Committee remembered well the lessons of previous attempted uprisings when crowds called out to revolt grew hungry and melted away. Accordingly it carefully mapped food depots and arranged to provision abundantly all assembly points. Bakers who refused to give up their bread or liquor merchants who refused the brandy needed to inflame the populace to violence, or the armorers who refused to give up their muskets and powder, were to be hanged from the nearest lamp post.

BLUEPRINTING "THE REPUBLIC OF VIRTUE"   As soon as the insurrection succeeded, a "great national community of wealth" was to be established in the Republic of Virtue. All citizens would be invited to give their wealth voluntarily to this community. Those who refused would be disqualified from full citizenship and civil or military office, and upon death all private property would revert to the community. Thus in one generation private property would wither away. The poor, destitute, and all over sixty would automatically become citizens.

The national community would guarantee all full citizens an equal and adequate livelihood. In return, each would have to pledge himself to perform all labor of which he was capable in agriculture or industry. Citizens would be grouped according to occupation, and each group would elect its own officials to organize production and supervise its equal distribution. Territorially there were to be local communal authorities responsible for local administration and for executing the laws made by the central authority. These local authorities would organize communal meals and supervise the occupational groups within their territory.

This was, of course, a naive program—but Lenin and his Bolsheviks had not advanced far beyond it when they actually seized power in Russia in 1917.

To give the masses an idea of what was in store for them in the new communist utopia, the Insurrectional Committee decided that under its two decrees the "unhappy poor" should be immediately clothed during the insurrection at the expense of the Republic and on the same day lodged in the houses of "the rich," who would be left to scrounge for themselves or hunt up the hovels vacated by the poor. The commissary agents in each precinct were to make good on the spot the first demonstrations of this "kindly relief."

Also planned for the big day was the "grand example" of the public executions of the members of the Executive Directory and the two Councils. "According to some opinions in the Insurrectional Committee," says Buonarrotti, "the condemned were to be buried under the ruins of their palaces, which were to be left in that state as a monument to posterity of the just punishment inflicted on the enemies of equality."[22]

THE PLOT THICKENS   The next night, May 2, 1796 the 13 top conspirators met at the house of Droust. The Military Committee reported and, before deciding on the moment of insurrection, asked for fresh information on the number of "democrats" and of the capacity of some individuals. They also wanted more details on the arms and ammunition they would have to seize at the start of the action—the deposits available at shops of armorers and gunsmiths, the connivance of the guards at the magazines and other key military locations.[23]

The "Assembly" then resolved to "accelerate the dénouement of the conspiracy," meet again in two days to hear a final report, and fix the day of action.

The plotters had hardly dispersed when the Minister of Police clattered up with a detachment of infantry and cavalry and broke down the door. He found only Darthe, plus the householder Droust whom he didn't consider worth arresting.

Captain Grisel reassured everybody that both the previous governmental inactivity and this obvious blunder were reasons for confidence that the police had no solid knowledge of what was going on.

Babeuf and Buonarroti spent the next night at 21 Rue de la Grande Truanderie, home of the tailor Tissot, "meditating and preparing for the insurrection and subsequent reforms." The next morning, the police burst in upon them, their papers laid out about the room, and arrested them. Simultaneously, at Dufour's house a raid netted Darthe, Germain, and other chief plotters who had met there to fix the day of the coup. The police cleverly covered the commotion by explaining to spectators they were only hauling off some robbers.

TRIAL AND EXECUTION   The plotters produced their own downfall by violating the rules of internal security adopted in their constitution. For after they met face to face with the Military Committee on May 1, none other than the ardent and trusted Capt. Grisel decided to turn police agent, and from May 4 on he kept the government informed of everything he learned.

The trial of the Babeuvists took three full months. It opened on February 20, 1797 with 47 defendants. Setting the classic defense and tactics for such trials, the conspirators turned it into a trial of the régime by arguing that the government was a usurpation and therefore the conspiracy wholly justifiable. They also converted the trial into a platform for propagandizing their doctrines before the public and before history. The audience was packed with sympathizers who loudly applauded. At critical moments the prisoners would burst forth with the *Marseillaise*, led by Sophie Lapierre, the songstress of the Cafe of the Chinese Baths. The prisoners conspired in their cells and even in the courtroom. They apportioned duties—one to heckle witnesses, one to arrange interjections in the speeches of the prosecution, and so on. When Grisel appeared to testify they turned the courtroom into a virtual riot of snarling recriminations. Each day's sessions they ended with republican hymns. These tactics, this gasconade, won public sympathy.[24]

The prosecution aided the defense by an error that was also to become a classic pattern of régimes opposing radical revolutionaries: overstating the case against them, accusing them of every crime committed since the downfall of Robespierre, and painting them as such inhuman monsters that the whole case sounded like a fairytale.

Still, the evidence against Babeuf personally was damning. Of the 500 documentations—almost all seized with Babeuf and containing the organization, plan, acts and correspondence of the Insurrectional Committee—more than a hundred were in his own handwriting. The information throughout was against him.[25]

On May 27, 1797 the jury rendered a verdict of guilty. The death sentence was passed on Darthe—who had made a speech refusing to recognize the court's jurisdiction and refused further defense—and Babeuf. Upon hearing the sentence, the condemned pair stabbed themselves with clumsy homemade daggers, but botched the job. After a night of agony in their cells, they were carted dying to the guillotine and beheaded.

SOCIOLOGICAL SIGNIFICANCE   Though the "Babeuvist Plot" became little more than a historical footnote to most modern readers, it had a tremendous impact on the nineteenth-century revolutionaries, on Marx, on Lenin, and on our own century. The sociological significance of the Babeuf conspiracy is that *it presented for the first time in modern history the spontaneous, automatic coalescence of frustrated, hate-filled persons into a cohesive political grouping around a mass communications medium for the purpose of propagating messianic doctrine and waging apocalyptic struggle through a combat party form of organizational weapon.* Like the "random" accident in the primeval sea that with inevitable probability produced the first reproductive cells, this 1796 coalescence was to exhibit powers of recreation. By its very example, the Babeuvist plot stimulated the formation of clandestine revolutionary organizations in nineteenth- and twentieth-century Europe.

SUMMARY   Babeuf's distinctive contributions to the growth of revolutionary radicalism were as follows:

1. The Babeuvists for the first time in modern Europe advanced the concept of *power seizure* by a small minority elite.

2. They introduced the *organizational weapon* of systematic clandestine infiltrations and manipulation of alien organizations, creation of secret front groups, etc. by hidden agents under the discipline of a central revolutionary command.

3. They adopted *violence* as a prime tactic and glorified it.

4. They adopted *deception* and *hate propaganda* as additional characteristic tactics.

5. They used a mass media *journal* broadcasting their virulent

revolutionary hate themes to *attract* the discontented and frustrated throughout society.

6. While acting in the name of humanism the Babeuvists *dehumanized their opponents*, denying them the most ordinary human compassion, sympathy, and human rights. (There was nothing new about this in a Europe accustomed to religious wars and inquisitions; what was new was transplanting this dehumanization into secular conflicts over social and political organization.)

7. The Babeuvists, being struggle-minded, adopted a crass *manipulatory attitude* toward the masses they claimed to love and serve. They sought actively to deceive and mislead the masses and secretly manipulate them with all the devices of conspiratorial maneuver.

8. To win the struggle at hand the Babeuvists cast aside morality and aimed at only one goal: the seizure of power. In short, in the name of social concern, they adopted *Machiavellianism.*

9. They developed new techniques of *mass propaganda*, including a rudimentary form of *motivational research* and *sloganeering.*

10. They developed the logic and rationalization of the *revolutionary dictatorship* during which the enemies of the revolution would be exterminated and the ideal society imposed.

11. The Babeuvist choice of violence and disruption over due process and evolution was influenced more by psychopathic *emotional compulsions* than by a rational analysis of the situation. These compulsions were the product of random historical circumstances and the endemic social stresses and cross-cultural incongruities in the transition from authoritarian and aristocratic feudalism to the modern industrial social structure.

Chapter 7
BUONARROTI: THE ORGANIZATIONAL SPIDER

About forty years ago a good woman, who kept the boarding house where I took my meals, related an anecdote about her father, a simple workingman of Nantes, which greatly impressed me. This man was very young when the Revolution broke out. He accepted it with enthusiasm; took part in the struggle of the Jacobins against the Vendeeans; witnessed with regret the imperial *régime* destroy the democratic liberties so dearly bought; and at each revolution, in 1814, in 1830, and in 1848, believed that the ideal republic, dreamed of in 1793, was about to reborn. He died during the second Empire, more than ninety years old, and at the moment of death, raising to heaven a look of ecstacy, was heard to murmur: 'O sun of '93, I shall die at last without having seen the rays again.' This man, like the first Christians, lived in the hope of the millennium.

—Gabriel Monod

HANDING DOWN THE LEGEND OF BABEUF   Without chroniclers and organizers, the great charismatic figures of history would have disappeared in history's shadows. Without Plato's record, Socrates would be forgotten. Without Mark, Matthew, Luke and Paul, Jesus Christ would have faded into the footnotes of the Roman Empire. And without Philippe Buonarroti, Babueuf would be unknown in the history of revolutionary utopianism. For Buonarroti was one of the plot's chief conspirators, and he lived to write its story. His book became the bible of conspiracy for the nineteenth-century revolutionary movement.

Europe's utopian communists, radicals, reformers, and revolutionaries of the 1830s and 1840s passed Buonarroti's book from hand to hand. An obscure Russian poet-philosopher named V.S. Pecherin recorded that a Polish friend showed it to him and he anxiously searched all over Zurich for a copy, without success; then one day, trembling with excitement, he found it in a second-hand bookshop in Liege.[1]

Moreover, Buonarroti developed the techniques of clandestine recruiting and organizing which Babeuf in his haste had slurred over; and he created the international organization which kept alive the legend and methodology of Babeuf in the post-Napoleonic reaction.

Buonarroti brought to Babeuf's group powerful talents and experience of his own in the arts of conspiracy, agitation, and revolutionary ideology. He had *charisma*, a quality of magnetic attraction that inspired and converted younger men in the nineteenth century who knew him. He lived to be 76 years old—until 1837—and was a living archive and apostle of the Babeuvist choice for conspiratorial violence as the prime tool for social change.

The red thread running through the lives of Rousseau, Robespierre, and Babeuf has been *frustration* arising from difficult childhoods, family circumstances, or stations in life. But in Buonarroti we encounter a new and different thread, an equally important part of revolutionary radicalism. It is *pure idealism*.

In fact, Buonarroti apparently had little of the standard causes for frustration. He was born in Pisa, Italy in 1761, in fair comfort and of noble lineage (a descendant of Michelangelo's brother). His father, a Tuscan nobleman, had good connections with the Archduke of Tuscany, the future Emperor Leopold II, and got his son a position as page at court. At 17 he became a law student at the University of Pisa, and there through a particularly "enlightened" professor met Rousseau's ideology. The introduction produced a virtual religious conversion—to an other-world dream of perfection so vividly experienced that it was akin to opium-smoking hallucinations. Buonarroti henceforth developed a new kind of frustration, the frustration of idealism with the existing imperfect world that produces an unalterable hostility—*hate*.

"Rousseau was my master," Buonarroti said later:

> From then on I had the deep conviction that it was the duty of a man of means to work towards the overthrow of the social system which oppresses civilized Europe in order to substitute an order which would conserve the dignity and happiness of all.

At his trial before the High Court at Vendome Buonarroti ended his defense with a remarkable prayer to his god, Jean-Jacques Rousseau:

> God of liberty, divine Jean-Jacques, thou who madest me disdain the delights of my paternal home, thou who hast initiated me into the mysteries of philosophy, thou who *has torn* me from my country, from my family, from my friends . . . thou who has enflamed me with the sacred love of virtue, redouble my courage and give my accents the force to destroy the sophisms of the enemies of a country whose foundations thou hast laid.

It remained for Babeuf to blend hate and revolutionary conspiracy, so that his plot alone is identifiable as the first clear revolutionary combat party prototype. But Europe had previous plots and secret societies built around the new religion of Rousseauism, and Buonarroti may have been a part of one of them. This was the Illuminati, a quasi-Masonic secret order founded in Bavaria in 1776 by Adam Weishaupt, a professor from Ingolstadt and a renegade Jesuit. Weishaupt heartily hated the Jesuits and aimed to replace Christianity with a secular religion of reason based on Rousseau's doctrines. Weishaupt consciously modeled his order on the Society of Jesus with the expressed intention "of using for good ends the means which the Jesuit order has employed for bad."[2] The means consisted mainly in organizational structure and techniques: A. The obligation of unconditional obedience along military lines of command reminiscent of Loyola's *Constitutions*; B. A far-reaching mutual surveillance among the members of the order; C. A kind of person-to-person confession which every inferior had to make to his superior. These same organizational devices, of course, appear in the modern Communist Party under the new labels of Party loyalty and discipline, democratic centralism, and "criticism and self-criticism."

During the 1770s and 1780s freemasonry was spreading all over Europe and America. It first developed in England as a secret fraternity of freethinkers opposed to organized religion and authoritarian institutions, either secular or religious. Benjamin Franklin, in fact, as American ambassador to Paris used his own Masonic lodge, the *Neuf Souers*, as a major transmission belt for propaganda and agitation to tug the French government into the American Revolutionary War. Franklin used the devices of infiltration and front groups with an effectiveness that would move the most modern communist propagandist to admiration.

The Illuminati were operating in the Freemasonry environment. From 1778 onward they began to make contact with various Masonic lodges and in many they managed to gain a commanding position. In 1785 the Bavarian government banned the movement.* It is possi-

*The Illuminati had a ghostly resurrection in the United States in 1798. The new nation was fighting an undeclared sea war with revolutionary France, and people were alarmed by real and fancied machinations by "Jacobin agents." Whereupon a New York publisher issued a book published the year before in England by a Scottish scientist, John Robison, *PROOFS Of a CONSPIRACY against all the RELIGIONS and GOVERNMENTS of Europe, carried on IN THE SECRET MEETINGS OF FREEMASONS, ILLUMINATI AND READING SOCIETIES.* Robison sketched a paranoid web of universal conspiracy woven with contradictory threats of popery and atheism and

ble that about 1786 Buonarroti joined a Florentine lodge where, under the guise of practicing the Scottish rites of the Masonic Order, the Illuminati may have been propagating their radical interpretation of Rousseau's *Discours sur L'Inegalite* and the *Contract Social.* In any case, Buonarroti later was quite familiar with both Weishaupt's ideology and organizational methodology,[3] for in 1797, after Babeuf's conspiracy, the Illuminati were publicized in a four-volume work on the history of Jacobinism.[4]

In 1776 the Florentine government raided Buonarroti's library and confiscated a number of French works containing anticlerical and masonic propaganda. Spared punishment by his father's intervention, he took up editing a radical journal. In 1789 he hailed the French Revolution as the dawning of heaven-on-earth:

> I devoured the news from France. I compared the discourses of the patriots of the Constituent Assembly with the precepts of Jean-Jacques and asked myself: *Is all in earnest for the beginning of the reign of justice?* I had been waiting a long time for the signal. It was given. The *Declaration of the Rights of Man* confirmed my hopes and succeeded in inflaming me . . . I needed no more to convince me that all who sensed the obligations that tied them to humanity were being called upon to work collectively for its enfranchisement. I swore to defend liberty.[5]

In 1793 after a stay in Corsica, Buonarroti went to Paris and was naturalized as a French citizen by decree of the Convention. He attended Jacobin Club meetings and paid homage to Robespierre at the Duplays' house, where legend has it he frequently dropped by in the evenings to give music lessons to the Duplay daughters, and play on the clavichord while "The Incorruptible" hummed tunes.[6]

Buonarroti was named national commissioner for the tiny area known as Oneglia near Nice on the Italian Riviera, which he tried to transform into a base for revolutionizing Italy. After Robespierre's overthrow, he was recalled to Paris and eventually imprisoned in Plessis in March 1795. There he became a part of the Babeuvist

Jacobin radicalism against constitutional democracy and all moderate government. Yale's President Timothy Dwight delivered a Fourth of July oration asking: "Shall our sons become the disciples of Voltaire, and the dragoons of Marat; or our daughters the concubines of the Illuminati?" The fantasy of a grand Illuminati conspiracy spread and helped fuel the hysteria that produced the Alien and Sedition Acts of 1798. In the 1820s it provided the hate-target for the short-lived Anti-Masonic Party. As late as June 1964 *American Opinion*, the John Birch Society's magazine, offered an exact reproduction of the "very rare 1798 edition" of Robison's book.

conspiracy, which landed him back in jail after seven months of freedom. Though lengthy, his imprisonment was not very disagreeable; he was placed in an island fortress near Cherbourg, and allowed to share his quarters with Teresa Poggi, the mistress he picked up in Corsica after abandoning his Italian wife of noble birth. He even continued to ply his revolutionary trade, with Teresa's help, conducting a clandestine correspondence with remnants of the neo-Jacobin organization in Paris. Characteristically, even as a prisoner he concentrated not on extricating himself but on exploiting his predicament for revolutionary purposes. He urged friends to turn the Babeuvists' conviction into an insurrectional *cause célèbre*, and to intensify unrest by publicizing conditions at Cherbourg. After the triumph of Napoleon, whose family Buonarroti had befriended in Corsica, he was transferred to Sospello in the Maritime Alps, where he was able to begin plotting anew. "However closely I was watched by the police, I never lost sight of the sacred end to which I had committed myself when I left Florence."[7] Finally, in 1806 his pleas to be allowed to go to Geneva, the home of his beloved Jean-Jacques, were granted, much to the disgust of the prefect there who, already harassed by the presence of many Jacobins and troublesome foreigners, regarded this new one as "the craziest" of all.

THE FIRST INTERNATIONAL REVOLUTIONARY ORGANIZATION   Buonarroti now resumed in full his chosen profession of revolutionary. He was involved in a military conspiracy known as the *Philadelphes* that sought to assassinate Napoleon in 1812. Meanwhile, probably about 1809 Buonarroti had organized his own personal secret society, the *Sublime Maitres Parfaits*, which aimed far beyond opposing Napoleon in France and Italy. The Parfaits' objective was no less than to republicanize Europe. It worked indirectly by attempting to direct, control, and influence other secret societies for its aims, or sometimes merely to counteract their policies and neutralize them. In Buonarroti's mind it was to be a directing committee for the revolution akin to the " general staff" concept of the Leninist party, acting as the central core organization, or vanguard, with a solar system of satellite societies, fronts, and infiltrating member-agents. From this central committee Buonarroti would exercise command ranging from absolute control to the capacity merely to disorganize and deflect target organizations through concealed agents. Buonarroti improved on the Babeuvist techniques of infiltration and "front" creations. For example, every candidate for the "supreme command" had to go through the masonic hierarchy and acquire a key position in a lodge in his own country.[8]

In a Europe that during the Restoration forced all liberals, all republicans, in fact all opposition, to work underground, Buonarroti's idea of an organizational nerve center was a powerful concept. Indeed, historians credit Buonarroti with forging "the first link in the chain of international organizations which led three decades later to the foundations of Marx's First International." A "general law" of his society was "to link to a common center all the friends of equality, whatever their country or religion may be." This closely resembles Article One of the Statutes of the First International: "To obtain a central point of communication and cooperation among the workers of different countries who aspire to the same end." Indeed, the First International merely combined the fragmented descendants of the secret societies which Buonarroti sought to tie together. In 1835, Buonarroti was able to boast in a circular, "Our institution embraces all nations."[9]

Buonarroti was, therefore, the founder of the first international political party and revolutionary organization.

ORGANIZATIONAL STRUCTURE   Buonarroti organized his *Parfaits* along the lines of freemasonry. Its essential character was compartmentalization: certain aspects of the organization, leadership, and methods and ultimate aims were only known to a few of the members belonging to the inner circle. In short, he followed the essence of the secret society as defined by Adam Weishaupt of the Illuminati. All of Buonarroti's societies show the same structure: they were divided into different grades; the highest grade, composed of the elite, controls and directs the other grades who do not know the men composing it nor the place of its residence. The rules, oaths, and table of organization were reduced to the smallest possible size on the very thinnest papers, so that in case of surprise the document could be burned or swallowed. The credos of the lower grades gave their communicants no hint of the communist credos or insurrectionary aims of the higher grades; any good republican or liberal desiring universal suffrage under a constitutional monarchy might take the first two credos without reservation and without suspecting the society's true purpose. But the doctrine got more radical as he lockstepped up.

In a notebook of the *Monde,* the name Buonarroti used in the late 1820s, he first grappled with the conflict between his democratic ideology and the tactical necessity for autocratic command in the combat party, a conflict which Lenin was to resolve with his doctrine of "democratic centralism," and Hitler with his "leader principle." Wrote Buonarroti:

> The Secret society . . . is a democratic institution in its principles and in its end; but its forms and its organization cannot be those of a democracy.
>
> With respect to doctrines, which one assumes are held in a pure form by the leaders, they would be better preserved and transmitted by them than by the crowd of initiated whose opinions, whatever one does, will never be altogether fixed nor uniform. With respect to action, whether preparatory or definitive, it is absolutely necessary that the impulse come from above and that all the rest obey. This society is nothing else but a secret army, destined to fight a powerful enemy.[10]

In the same notebook, Buonarroti clearly shows the influence of Weishaupt and his Illuminati. Buonarroti conceived of himself as a kind of secular Ignatius Loyola. He wrote:

> Amid the collapse of free institutions, amid the general corruption of sentiments, one cannot find . . . future regeneration *save in a secret corps guided by a pure and dictatorial authority;* what the Jesuits did to mislead and enslave men, the Monde has attempted to do in order to enlighten and deliver them. Good and evil can be operated by the same mechanism; if the end is just and wise, what difference does it make if the means have been used in other circumstances for a contrary end!
>
> The Jesuitical congregation can be compared to an army full of enthusiasm and submissive by conviction to a homogenous and absolute authority. It is precisely an equivalent army that the Monde has attempted to establish against tyranny."

Buonarroti realized that Europe had moved too far from Robespierre for him to operate on the previous tactical assumption of a lightning power seizure on a single "great day." From a simple conspiratorial organization aiming at a single violent blow to jolt humanity back onto the path toward a "Republic of Virtue," he now began to think of a secret "order" which, as a purified community within a corrupt society, would gradually save the world by erosive "capillary" action. It was a notion precisely foreshadowing the "Woodstock Nation" and "alternative culture" ideologies of American Radicalism Vintage 1970.

[125]

In one form or another, under some name, Buonarroti kept his society functioning as long as he lived. In the underground world that honeycombed Europe during the 1820s and 1830s, the name of Buonarroti was if not omnipotent at least omnipresent. Bakunin, Marx's great rival in the First International, who knew what he was talking about, called Buonarroti, "the greatest conspirator of his age," and that was no exaggeration.

RECRUITING But Buonarroti's most important role was not in further developing and handing down the organizational forms of conspiracy per se. It was in *recruiting*. As one of the few surviving "true believers" of '93, he set about converting the youth of a whole new generation. Through his eyes they saw the Babeuvist dream and in his presence they imbibed the legend. And here we encounter another vital element of revolutionary radicalism: *personal evangelism*. Without face-to-face propagandizing, the faith would soon die. Buonarroti realized this, and like any evangelist he developed very careful conversion techniques, including criteria for screening potential recruits. After all, was it not lax recruiting procedures and failure to size up properly the character of Grisel that destroyed the Babeuvists?

To identify the properly predisposed "organization man" for his organizational machine, Buonarroti set forth these "signs by which one may recognize whether a man is worthy of initiation":

> Devotion to the principles of the order and willingness to sacrifice to them personal interests and pleasure.
> Courage; that is to say, scorn of danger, of work and hardships.
> Reflection, gravity, prudence.
> Respect for the forms, for the allegories, for the hierarchy and for the scale of grades.
> Patience and perseverance.
> Scorn for wealth, position, men, and power.
> A modest, sober, and regulated life.
> Inviolable respect for the word, the promise, and the vow.
> Willingness to overlook personal wrongs.
> Moderation in the use of intoxicating liquors.
> The habit of speaking little and to the point.
> No wish to make an impression, to shine to impose oneself.
> Caution in gambling, in love, in anger and in the opening of one's heart.
> Exquisite sensibility concerning the wrongs that weigh on humanity.

Only by carefully applying these selection criteria could the *Parfaits* form "an elite corps capable of realizing the great goal of its organization and its efforts."[12]

Buonarroti's livelihood as a teacher gave him an excellent opportunity and "cover" for recruiting. He would tutor his students first in Italian or music, then in conspiracy. His personal magnetism and powers of persuasion were near irresistible. A Genevan writer has left in his unpublished memoirs a vivid account of his experience with the old conspirator:

> I came to this town at the end of November 1813 to study law and had an idea of taking Italian lessons. I was referred to Buonarroti who spoke, with the expression of a genius, the most pure Tuscan. As a teacher he was impossible; always transported by his imagination and his fantasy, without caring in the least for the progress of his student . . . His instinctive destination lay rather in music. When I arrived at his home, I always found him at his piano, his long gray hair, shaggy and flowing, his shirt collar open, showing off to advantage a superb and truly inspired head. He improvised, striking fireworks from his instrument with long agile and powerful fingers, launching into songs without words which seemed to be the explosion of mysterious thoughts. I made a point of tearing him away to give his Italian lesson. The result was that soon he persuaded me to take singing lessons. It was no good my telling him I had a deaf ear and a poor voice. Buonarroti was persuaded that he could teach me to sing. I think he would have succeeded thanks to his indomitable energy and the contagious power of his musical ardor.
>
> But alas! I only had six lessons, thanks to the approach of the Austrians. After that, I never again tried to continue this experiment that had been interrupted. Buonarroti's sacred fire was alone capable of lighting in me some sparks of musical talent. As for Buonarroti himself, I never knew what became of him. His figure is still in front of me as one of the most brilliant types of the Italian race and genius. He was a worthy descendant of Michelangelo.[13]

THE ANDRYANE PHENOMENON   This lion of a man who could persuade a tone-deaf law student to take singing lessons also persuaded many who had no such natural inclination to take up conspiracy. In fact, it was probably only the Austrian army's approach that saved this young man. Another, Alexander Andryane, was not so lucky. When Andryane came to Buonarroti to study first Italian, then music, and finally conspiracy, he was "far from sharing his ultra-republican ideas," as he himself recorded in October 1820. In fact, his letters to his parents before meeting the maestro were colored with repugnance for the "blood-drinkers" of '93. But Andryane, too, soon found himself under the spell:

> A broad-brimmed hat covers his white hair; his forehead is wide and arched; his eyes, under bushy eyebrows, are lively and shine frequently behind his eyeglasses. In summer as in winter he wears the same suit, the same waistcoat *à la Robespierre*, the same black trousers which don't quite reach his short topboots—a strange enough attire in itself and one which alone would suffice to make him stand out if something proud and unique did not also force you to stare at this sexagenarian whose path crosses yours constantly in the narrow streets of Geneva, passing near you, holding sheets of music under his arm, with a grave, preoccupied and mysterious air.[14]

Of course the odd attire and air of mystery were carefully cultivated for their impact on just such young men. Buonarroti fascinated him at first as a pure curiosity: "Strange character! wherein one finds united all the virtues of a Greek sage with all the exaggerations of a Jacobin of '93." Like many of his fellows he was amazed by the persistence and energy of this old man working at what seemed so obviously a lost cause "for thirty years without ever stopping, like a spider in his hole, spinning the threads of a conspiracy that all the governments have broken, each in turn, and that he never tires of renewing." The awe of this first meeting grew with familiarity. Within eleven months, by August 1821, Andryane was drawn into the web despite his own inclinations:

> Although I am far from sharing Buonarroti's exaggerated opinions, I respect him too much, however, not to be flattered by the proposition he has just made me; and I admit I am impatient, waiting for the day when I will become part of the association of which he has spoken to me with so much enthusiasm.[15]

Here is surely one of the first fully documented examples of the recruitment not of a member of Buonarroti's new profession of revolutionary but of a full-fledged and witting "fellow traveler." Andryane's "novitiate" ended on October 10, 1821, with the initiation into the Society. From then on he ran numerous missions for his master.

Before one such trip to Lyons to an assembly, Andryane paused to

reflect on *"the irresistible influence that he exerts on all who approach him and of whom I am myself at this moment such a striking
example . . . since nothing was further from my desire and my will
than to attend this assembly."*

The Buonarroti-Andryane case illustrates a basic principle on
which revolutionary utopianism came to operate: even a bad
ideology can be sold by the power of personal persuasion and organizational envelopment. From Babeuf to the Bolshevik power-seizure
in 1917, the communist movement was denied access to the ordinary
mass media—large circulation newspapers, mass organization, etc.
And so inevitably it was forced to rely on *personal proselytization.*
Face to face salesmanship predominated. The columnists sold their
doctrine the way Fuller Brush salesmen sell brushes. The operated
in the way of the early Christian apostles or the early Methodist
circuit rider, through personal evangelism. Today in the noncommunist world where most communist parties are still unwelcome, if not
unlawful, communists still operate fundamentally by this principle.
And the ideology of communism conveyed by a dynamic professor
of journalism at the Central University of Caracas will always win
against the ideology of democracy purveyed through a U.S. Information Service library or a Voice of America shortwave broadcast.
Hence the importance of Buonarroti's meticulous attention to the
principle of personal proselytization and the technology of recruitment and conversion.

Andryane was a prototype of the individual who fits into the radical machine as a fellow traveler or collaborator, drawn in by the
compelling force of associations and personal persuasion rather than
by conviction. Before he knows what is happening, he is trapped—
and if he wakes up, it is too late. In Andryane's case, the result was
tragic, for it landed this earnest, likeable young man in prison for a
long term. With insurrection crackling in the air, Buonarroti sent
him to Milan in 1823 stuffed with documents, including the *Rules
and Statutes of the Sublime Maitres Parfaits* and the names of countless conspirators, "a mass of papers, one more useless and dangerous
than another, sufficient to compromise half of Italy," according to a
fellow conspirator.[16] And the police pounced on him and seized the
lot.

Since the police of Europe, like the revolutionaries, cooperated
across international boundaries, Andryane's arrest and the incrimi-
nating documents enabled them to unravel a good deal of Buonar-

roti's web. Expulsions in Switzerland and France and arrests in Germany wrecked the society's leadership. Buonarroti himself fled to Brussels in 1824, where he set about the painful task of mending his web.

But more important, he used the next four years to produce the book that is his lasting claim to fame and influence on the modern world. In 1828 he published his account of the Babeuvist plot, *The Conspiracy for Equality, with Justificatory Documents.* This book became the text, virtually the bible, of a whole new generation of European revolutionaries. A French edition was published in 1830, and in 1836 the English Chartist Leader, Bronterre O'Brien, brought out an English translation in London.

LAUNCHING THE BABEUVIST LEGEND   Buonarroti's book landed at a critical moment in French and European political thought. Of course the Jacobin tradition was strong in France; many of the young men coming of age in the 1820s were sons of Republican revolutionaries, the Men of '93. But the Men of '93 were not so well remembered. The Babeuvist choice was an obscure current while the Republican due process concept dominated the mainstream of radical thought. Opponents of the reactionary Bourbon monarchy tended to favor a republic, liberal constitutional democracy—though at this time of reactionary absolutism working for constitutional democracy in Europe meant being revolutionaries.

Then came Buonarroti's book, vividly recreating the romance of Babeuf, with its messianic mentality, its utopian vision, its communist ideology, and its action blueprint. By virtue of its detailed account of the organization and methods of the conspiracy of '96, it became the handbook of the radical revolutionary movement in the 1830s and 1840s in France, and the basic source for its ideology. In fact Buonarroti's *Conspiracy* started the whole Jacobin trend in European socialism.

Buonarroti's book and his magnetic personal presence in Paris where he moved after the July Revolution of 1830 was enough to tilt many young men over the Babeuvist choice into the radical revolutionary camp of opposition. To them Buonarroti seemed almost a supernatural apparition; they worshipped him like a god. He gathered them into a reorganized version of the *Parfaits*, this time calling it the *Charbonnerie Democratique Universelle.* One of Buonarroti's friends of these years was Theodore Schuster, a former law instructor at the University of Göttingen. In 1834 Schuster founded the "Society of Exiles" in Paris, the first among the German refugees there.[17] This society became the "League of the Just," which Karl Marx later converted into the world's first Communist Party. But Buonarroti's most promising recruit was a young firebrand liberal named Auguste Blanqui. He was 23 in 1828, teetering between the ideologies and terminologies of constitutional liberalism and something more radical when Buonarroti's book and personal magnetism caught him.[18]

This was a momentous connection. Blanqui was to become a colleague in conspiracy—and teacher—of Karl Marx, and later, through his writings on the methodology of conspiracy and insurrection, an example for Lenin. In fact, some scholars argue that Blanqui's influence on Lenin and Leninism outweigh Marx's. Certainly Blanqui and Buonarroti formed the direct link between modern communism and the Babeuvist plot, the prototype of all that followed.

II. KARL MARX: THE IDEALIST WHO SAW RED

Chapter 8
"NEW GODS FOR THE VACANT SHRINE"

It was only towards the middle of the 20th Century that the inhabitants of many European countries came, in general unpleasantly, to realize that their fate could be influenced directly by intricate and abstruse books of philosophy.

> —*The Captive Mind*
> Czeslaw Milosz

So long as man remains free he strives for nothing so incessantly and so painfully as to find someone to worship. But man seeks to worship what is established beyond dispute, so that all men would agree at once to worship it. For these pitiful creatures are concerned not only to find what one or the other can worship, but to find something that all would believe in and worship; what is essential is that all may be *together* in it. This craving for *community* of worship is the chief misery of every man individually and of all humanity from the beginning of time. For the sake of common worship they've slain each other with the sword. They have set up gods and challenged one another: "Put away your gods and come and worship ours, or we will kill you and your gods!" And so it will be to the end of the world, even when gods disappear from the earth; they will fall down before idols just the same.

> —The Grand Inquisitor
> *The Brothers Karamazov*
> Fyodor Dostoyevsky

MARX TODAY   America's campus radicals today acknowledge but one god—Karl Marx. His writings rank among the campus bookstore bestsellers. The most widely quoted teacher in America is a self-proclaimed Marxist philosophy professor. His star pupil, a Communist Party member, was indicted and tried for complicity in the kidnap-murder of a California judge, a hate target of the "power structure" designated by Marxian philosophy. Another self-proclaimed Marxist murdered a President of the United States, John F. Kennedy, and a third killed his brother Robert F. Kennedy, a senator and presidential candidate. The terrorists whose bombs maim and kill across the nation proclaim their justifications through the news media in Marxist terms. Around the world Marxist guerrillas attack governments in a score of nations, and a billion human beings—a third of mankind—live under regimes professing fealty to Marxian concepts.

Yet who among prophets or critics know the revealing life story of this German philosopher who died obscurely in London nearly a century ago? Such knowledge can help us understand and cope with his followers today.

To find out "what Marx really meant" scholars have expended tremendous energy pouring over Marx's early manuscripts, combing his correspondence, and comparing Friedrich Engels's later retrospections of their joint ventures. Yet such effort is relatively fruitless for the simple reason that it assumes Marx had any discoverable rational meaning and empirical synthesis at all.

In fact, as we shall see, Marx's entire thought structure was largely an emotional reaction and a rationalization and ventilation of personal passions, not an objective analysis of nineteenth-century European capitalist society. Marx dressed this compulsive reaction in rational and even scientific costume because he admired the authority of science, coveted the respect men had for it, and sought to arrogate its certainty for his own writings. Therefore, Marx's writings are the worst place to begin, in order to understand him. We must begin with his life and his passions to find what he was reacting to when, for example, he wrote as a youthful radical that "the weapon of criticism must not replace the criticism of weapons."

THE STUDENT REBEL   As the Congress of Vienna's cloak of reaction and authoritarianism spread across Europe after 1815, intellectuals, reformers, and constitutionalists were further than ever from the levers of power. They had no opportunity to learn to manipulate them or appreciate the complexities of statecraft. So simple solutions seemed practical. It was easy to imagine inside one's head ideal social arrangements, like Plato's "forms," so long as one did not have to stuff reality into them. So the intellectual *avant garde* succumbed to fads like that started by Saint-Simon, the French nobleman whose valet was instructed to awaken him every day with the cry, "Arise, Monsieur le Comte, you have great things to do today!" Saint-Simon claimed (and too many believed) that the Emperor Charlemagne appeared to him in a dream and annointed him a "philosopher" with the duty of saving the world from want, misery, and injustice. He thereupon founded a sect with a semimystical, amorphous doctrine, a sort of industrial religion of protest against a society of "idle rich" and underpaid working classes. His "Priesthood of Humanity" was a sort of transmogrified band of platonic guardian sociologists who were supposed to guide the development of industrial society.

Just across the border in Germany was the little town of Trier, population 11,400, on the Mosel River. There an old gentleman named Ludwig von Westphalen, the Royal Prussian Privy Counsellor (the King's representative to the town government), an educated and liberal aristocrat, would go for long walks in the surrounding fields and hills. Tagging along at his heels would go the teen-age son of Westphalen's neighbor, an apostate Jewish lawyer he had befriended. The old man would lecture, like Plato strolling through the groves of Academe. Years later, the youngster would recall how he drank in dreams of a better world through the old Privy Counsellor's talks about Saint-Simon and the utopian socialists. Even when he finished college, he dedicated his doctoral dissertation to Westphalen with this moving inscription:

> May all who are in doubt have the good fortune that I have had and be able to look up with admiration to an old man who retains his youthful vigor and welcomes every advance of the times with enthusiasm and passion for truth and an idealism which, bright as sunshine and proceeding from deep conviction, recognizes only the word of truth . . . You, my paternal friend, provided me always with a living *argumentum ad oculos* that idealism is not a figment of the imagination but a truth.

This idealistic lad entered Trier high school just as Berlin, frightened by the Paris revolution of 1830, cracked down on the borderlands west of the Rhine that had tasted liberal French rule during the Revolution and Napoleonic Era. Frederick William III established a commission "for the suppression of politically dangerous groups," and its agent in Trier complained of the Trier school, whose students in 1834 were found writing political poems; one was imprisoned for months. Shortly before our young man graduated in 1835 the Prussian authorities, alarmed by dozens of critical police reports, thoroughly investigated his school. They did not remove the headmaster, but saddled him with a joint headmaster, the Latin teacher, Loers. Custom required young men to call on their old headmasters for goodbyes before leaving for the universities in the fall. The young idealist visited every one except Loers. "Herr Loers took it very much amiss," a fretful father wrote him at the University of Bonn. "You and Clemens were the only ones." The father, knowing the authorities were not blind to such acts, tried to cover up by lying to Loers that his son had gone to call but did not find him in. Though it was an innocuous demonstration, it was the first sign of open revolt history records of young Karl Marx.

Ideals can be very corrupting in a world that stubbornly refuses to conform to every romantic whim. And young Karl's world balked more than most.

The family and community Karl Marx was born into on May 5, 1818, could hardly have been better designed to foster revolt. His father Hirschel was a ne'er-do-well Jewish lawyer who projected his own ambitions onto this "fortune child." Hirschel Marx was twelve years old when the French revolutionary armies swept into Trier, and for the next 20 years, until Napoleon arrived at Waterloo, Hirschel Marx was a Frenchman. Trier even had its own Jacobin Club, and when Karl was in high school the town's most outstanding citizens still looked back in pride on their own Jacobin past. Hirschel himself, a neighborhood friend recalled, was "a real eighteenth-century Frenchman who knew his Voltaire and Rousseau inside and out."

Hirschel genuinely admired the Prussian heritage of Frederick the Great, philosopher-king who attracted Voltaire and D'Alembert to his court. So he felt no grudge when the return of Prussian rule with its anti-Jewish laws forced him in 1816 to choose between continuing his law practice or his religion. He merely abjured his Jewish faith, notwithstanding that his brother was the rabbi of Trier's Hebrew flock and his ancestors included many distinguished rabbinical scholars. Hirschel was baptized "Heinrich Marx" in the national Evangelical Church (Trier had 11,000 Catholics and only 330 Protestants). And when Karl was born on May 5, 1818, he, too, was baptized.

Karl felt keenly the handicap of being a Jew in a gentile world. When he was a boy an agricultural crisis produced a virulent reaction against Jewish "usurers" in the agricultural Moselle Valley. In his high school essay "on choosing a career" young Karl tempered effervescent expression of idealistic duty to serve mankind by noting, "But we cannot always follow the profession to which we feel called; our relationships in society have already to some extent been formed before we are in a position to determine them. Already our physical nature threateningly bars the way." His own swarthy features prompted someone to nickname him "the Moor," and it stuck even with his own father.

Heinrich Marx noted very early that his first-born son was endowed with "splendid natural gifts." But he also encountered such stubbornness and harsh defiance that he and his wife would speak of "the demon" in this boy. In high school Karl developed a romantic passion to be a poet. But practical Heinrich wanted him to pursue a legal career. The two quarreled bitterly. But in October 1835 when Karl went to the University of Bonn, a provincial school of 700 students, against his own wishes and to appease his nagging father he registered to study law.

That Heinrich Marx projected his own ambitions and sought compensation through his son for his own thwarted, ineffectual life is evident in a letter of March 1837:

It is wonderful how I, by nature a lazy writer, become quite inexhaustible when I begin to write to you. I cannot, and would not, conceal from you my weakness for you. My heart often revels in thoughts about you and your future. And yet at times I cannot free myself from gloomy apprehensive, terrifying ideas, when like a lightning flash there breaks the thought: Is your heart equal to your head, to your capacities? Has it room for those tender, earthly feelings which bring so much consolation in this vale of tears to the man of feelings? I cannot help but wonder if you are not ruled by a terrible demon who so often destroys men, no matter whether he is of heavenly or hellish nature . . .

Your first successes, the flattering hope of seeing your name in high renown, are not only, like your earthly welfare, dear to my heart; they are illusions which I have long nursed and which are deeply implanted in my being. At bottom however these are the feelings of a weak man, and are not free from alloy of all kinds: pride, vanity, egoism, etc. etc. etc. I can assure you that the realization of these illusions would not suffice to make me happy. Only if your heart remains pure and beats with pure human love, and no demon of evil had power to estrange it from its better feelings—only then can I find the happiness which for long years I have dreamt of through you. Otherwise I should see the fairest purpose of my life shattered.

In college young Karl rebelled against his father and all that he stood for. His first year he spent wrecking his father's ambitions and finances. He participated in fraternity street fights, fought a duel (receiving a thrust over the eye), spent a day in the campus jail for a rowdy drunk, and dawdled over his poetry instead of his book. Father Marx decided to transfer his son to a more austere school.

In October 1836, 18-year-old Karl Marx arrived for his first year at the University of Berlin. He paused at No. 1 Leipziger Street, the quaint row house where the immortal German poet-critic Gotthold Lessing lived in the previous century. A room was for rent! Karl snapped it eagerly, for he was determined to become a great poet himself. He would conquer fame, fortune and position with the brilliant poetry he would write here! And then he would return to Trier to marry the fairest young belle of the town—Jenny von Westphalen, next door neighbor, favorite playmate of Karl's older sister, and daughter of his own beloved mentor Baron von Westphalen. Jenny, though four years older, had promised to wait for him while he finished his education.

During this crucial year Karl's father pelted him with advice and urgings, constantly reiterating his desire for Karl to succeed. He begged, pleaded, wheedled. He tried every approach he could dream up. Karl had to face his obligations toward his future bride, especially providing her with the material comforts to which her family position entitled her. The father's ambitions for the son bubbled over: "The wish to see your name rise high in the world as well as the wish to see you well fixed in the world's material goods are not the only wishes I cherish for you, though they are longtime dreams for you." Heinrich even tried to guide the boy in his infatuation with poetry. After all, he reasoned, many a poet had won fame at 19, but a lawyer must wait many years. So he harangued his son "to take soon a decisive step in the world." Write a patriotic ode that would make him the nation's hero! Would not "an episode from Prussian history" fit the need? Perhaps the Battle of Waterloo will do, or any "honorable one for Prussia." "Such an ode, if it were patriotic, full of feeling, and worked out in a genuine German spirit, would be enough to make you famous."

From first to last money was a constant contention between father and son. Karl spent it like a drunk sailor, with no conception of what he was doing to his family. Heinrich's health was failing. He had seven other children to support. In his final letter, Heinrich rebuked Karl for spending "more in three months than I have earned all winter. . . . I cannot drive away the thought that in your place I should have treated my parents with greater consideration, with more unselfish love . . ."

A few weeks later Heinrich Marx died. Karl, just past his twentieth birthday, did not make it home from Berlin in time for the funeral. Soon his mother complained that her son had become a stranger to his family and "renounced everything which had formerly been valuable and dear to him."

For Karl in the winter of his first Berlin year experienced a psychological earthquake and joined Germany's "new left."

"NEW GODS FOR THE VACANT SHRINE"   Karl hardly left his room in the Lessing House for six months. He wrote four volumes of poetry and a 300-page work on "jurisprudence," trying to work out a philosophy of law. In the process he found himself face to face with the cosmic conundrum that always confronts young post-adolescent collegians first learning to exercise their newly-developed powers of abstract thought: *"I was greatly disturbed by the conflict between what actually is and what ought to be which is peculiar to idealism,"* Karl wrote his father.

And one afternoon after Christmas he faced an even more personal conflict between "what is and what ought to be." He laid out his own volumes of verse alongside the works of the German masters and made a soul-wrenching discovery. His poetry was impossibly dull. He was no poet—and never would be!

> Suddenly, as if by the wave of a magician's wand, the riches of true poetry dazzled me like a distant fairy palace, and turned all my hopes to naught . . . The experience was shattering. All my creations were shivered to fragments.

This moment of thwarted romantic idealism fueled Karl Marx with the fierce hatred of a balky world, setting him on a course that even today shakes our world. The realization wounded him so deeply he actually suffered excruciating migraine attacks. He visited a doctor, who sent him to the suburb of Stralau for some fresh air and scenery. He went, as he wrote home, seeking *"new gods for the vacant shrine."*

> My holy of holies had been shattered, and new gods had to be found for the vacant shrine. Setting out from idealism . . . I proceeded to seek for the idea in the real world itself. If in earlier days the gods had dwelt above the earth, they had now become its center.

"To seek for the idea in the real world itself—gods come to its center . . . new gods for the vacant shrine!" This was the 18 year old's self-assigned task. And he created the new gods themselves, in his next dozen years as a student, "underground press" editor, political pamphleteer and organizer, fashioning a compound of romantic rage and poetic idealism that has dominated our century and shaped the lives of us all.

In Stralau Karl *found* his new gods for the vacant shrine. Meeting there were Germany's "Young Hegelians," a circle of instructors, students and young graduates who were propounding a "God-is-dead" philosophy of total revolt and rationalized hatred and contempt for the whole of existing society.

Hegel, like Roberspierre whom he admired, in his youth had a vision of a perfect world. He declared that the God of traditional religion was but Man's deification of his own ideal qualities as Creator and guiding genius of the Universe. Hegel viewed history as the painful process of Man realizing himself as God, striving in reality toward the ideal he had created for himself in the concept of God. Philosophical thought, Hegel declared, is Man's highest activity, guiding the historical world process—and therefore the Philosopher is God incarnate. And Hegel deified himself as the philosopher who had achieved the highest insight and wisdom; he actually felt driven to recognize God in his own person. But from the ardent young admirer of the French Revolution Hegel became the old and honored professor of philosophy at the University of Berlin. He identified the Prussian monarchy, not himself, as the real bearer of human progress, the hope of the bourgeoisie and constitutionalism. He published ten fat volumes explaining himself in obtuse abstraction, then complained, "Only one man understands me—and even he does not." It was probably just as well—for his early adolescent messianic complex was so puerile that the mature Hegel sought to destroy all his early essays and manuscripts to hide the truth. He died in 1831.

THE CANCER OF IDEALISM   The "Young Hegelians" Karl Marx joined in the winter of 1837 in Stralau were rediscovering the young messianic Hegel. "God is dead," they proclaimed. "Man is God." It was up to philosophers to bring about a realization of the ideal world their vision had brought them. They must remake the world according to their vision—or stuff the world into the iron mold of their ideals. "Philosophy revolts against the world!" is the way young Marx formulated their movement. And they came to choose a slogan: *"The Realization of Philosophy!"*

"It is a psychological law," Marx wrote in 1839 at age 20, "that the theoretical spirit turns against the earthly reality existing apart from itself . . . Just as Prometheus, having stolen fire from heaven, begins to build houses and establish himself on the earth, *so philosophy, having embraced the whole world, revolts against the world of phenomena.*[1] So now with Hegelian philosophy."

Thus the historical record is clear: the founder of modern revolutionary radical thought developed a *will to revolt* against a world not yet shaped in his dream of utopia, with himself as Philosopher-King, long before he knew or cared a jot about its economic or social particulars. At the time Marx arrived at this radical stance, he had never paid the slightest attention to the real conditions of life in early urban and industrial society, nor displayed the slightest trace of social concern or sympathy for anybody but himself. He was simply a brilliant but spoiled middle-class youngster with strong neurotic symptoms and beset by deep guilt and resentment over the ambitions his father pressed upon him and his own inadequacies.

Between 1839 and 1841 Marx made copious notes for a doctoral dissertation explaining that the Young Hegelians wanted to "liberate" the "earthly reality" from its present "unphilosophical condition." Humanity was now on the verge of an "iron epoch" calling for "integral commanders" who will never accept a "peace treaty with real needs." Marx spoke the language of warfare and toyed with military concepts like the "general staff." For he had declared unlimited war, no less, against the existing world—a philosopher-king seeking to conquer his kingdom!

The young radicals soon saw in Karl a "young lion" whose demonic obsession they spoofed in a poem: "Who's this charging on who so rants and raves? 'Tis the wild fury, black-maned Marx, his fists clenched in raging, desperate air as though ten thousand devils had him by the hair."

The chief devil gnawing him was the world's unphilosophical demand that he support himself. After six years in college building his romantic utopias, drinking beer and hiding from the real world, Karl's widowed mother demanded that he get out and earn a living. Karl complained that he and his fiancée had fought "more unnecessary and exhausting conflicts than many three times as old as we" with their families; their parents "prate continually of their 'experience of life,' one of the favorite expressions in our home circle." Ultimately, his mother cut off his allowance.

But it was the carrot and stick wielded by one of his Young Hegelian elders that dislodged him from college. Bruno Bauer, who had become a theology professor at the University of Bonn, held out the promise of an instructorship and publication of a new "Journal of Atheism." "Do stop your shilly-shallying and end this wearisome vacillation about a piece of nonsense and pure farce like an examination," Bauer wrote. Marx attended only two courses in his last three years at the university; altogether in five years he took thirteen courses, which a normally industrious student could do in a year and a half. Afraid to take the doctoral exams at Berlin, Marx sent a dissertation off to Europe's mail-order diploma factory, the University of Jena. Its preface chose an appropriate quote from Aeschylus: "I harbor hate 'gainst all the gods!" His doctorate arrived in a few weeks.

Marx went to Bonn in July 1841 to join Bauer just in time to see his radical big brother expelled from his post for indiscreet atheistic lectures. So young "Dr." Marx went to Cologne, to join some fellow New Left radicals on a new newspaper, the *Rhenish Gazette.* Soon after, the editor antagonized Prussia's censor, was dumped by the owners, and Marx found himself editor with the assignment of placating the government. On October 15, 1842, at twenty-four, Karl Marx had his first, and last, fulltime job.

Marx's editorship was a revealing episode. Ensconced as prestigious director of one of Germany's leading papers, he became the perfect establishmentarian. He scorned the notions of "communism" spreading among the utopian socialists: "The undeniable collision between the have-nots and the middle class will be solved peacefully." Communism is a pipe dream. Manuscripts from Berlin friends brought scoldings to stop sending such "vaporings full of world revolution and void of sense." To one author who attacked compromise, Marx replied that such extremism was absurd because all progress depends upon the "liberal-minded, practical men who have undertaken the troublesome role of struggling step-by-step for freedom within constitutional limits." Such a statement we would sooner expect from a Speaker of the U.S. House of Representatives!

Even Berlin's censor was amazed to find Marx's *Gazette* "much calmer." But Marx's young assistant noticed "a malicious fire" in his eye and found him "swayed almost more by envy of others' achievements than by his own ambition—an untrustworthy egotist and lying intriguer who wants only to exploit others." Each evening, as they drank and debated, Marx would focus his scorn on some hapless companion and repeat, "I am going to annihilate you!" Naturally, he soon exploded in print with a denunciation of the Berlin regime, and Wilhelm IV ordered the probationary newspaper suppressed. Marx paused only long enough to plant in another paper a ghosted article placing full blame—and credit—for the *Gazette's* policies on the "rare many-sided talent" and "sharp, incisive mind" of Dr. Marx. Then he resigned the only job he ever held in a front-page editorial and left Cologne, in a friend's words, "possessed by hatred and mad with rage."

Only twenty-five and a minor national hero, Karl married Jenny von Westphalen on June 19, 1843, and moved in on her newly-widowed mother. Surveying his wrecked dream for "the realization of philosophy," he concluded that his journalistic disaster occurred because the autocratic Prussian dictatorship had an army while "philosophy" had none. He scribbled in his notebook: "Philosophers heretofore have only *interpreted* the world; henceforth they must strive to *change* it. The weapon of criticism can never substitute for the criticism of weapons."

But where could a philosopher find an army that would empower him to redesign civilization to fit his dream?

GENERAL MARX FINDS HIS ARMY One afternoon while strolling about Kreuznach, Marx opened a new book he had laid aside some months before when a favorable Rhenish *Gazette* review pricked his interest. Ironically, the book was written by a German police agent sent to Paris to report on exiled German workers and the new-fangled ideas of "socialism" and "communism" stirring them so. Marx read, and became excited. He saw phrases he was to make immortal in his famous *Communist Manifesto:* "The poor class, toiling and suffering, transforms itself into a powerful organization, negative and menacing: the proletariat. *Communism looms as a somber and menacing specter.*"[2] Here, at last, was the weapon Marx was looking for—a secular political power strong enough to smash the Prussian dictatorship!

The general had found his army, the knight errant his sword. Marx began writing the famous essay in which he brushed aside forever questions of theology: "Religion is the opiate of the people . . . ," his swift pen scrawled. The true reformer must concern himself with the condition that needs an opiate: society in general. Henceforth, Marx decided this day, politics, not theology, not philosohpy, must be his calling. He must marshal the secular forces of the proletariat and through its power *reshape* society, so that people will no longer need the illusion of religion.

LORENZ VON STEIN It is one of the enduring ironies of history that the book which so inspired Marx was instigated by the Prussian secret police. Nineteenth-century governments were in one respect at least much wiser than the twentieth-century democracies. They recognized that ideas are powerful weapons, that their creation and propagation as well as diversion and destruction may be systematized, and that such weaponry may determine the rise and fall of such governments. Accordingly in October 1841 the Prussian government commissioned Lorenz von Stein, a young doctor of laws recently graduated from Kiel University, to make an on-the-spot survey of the disturbing new-fangled French radicalisms called "socialism" and "communism."

Von Stein was a conservative Hegelian and a staunch monarchist. While in Paris he was to observe and report any communist connections of migratory German workers to the minister of police, Von Rochow. Out of his experience Von Stein wrote a history of French radical thought, presented within a framework of Hegelian theorizing about society. He called the book *Socialism and Communism in Today's France—A contribution in Contemporary History*, and published it in Leipzig in September 1842.

Von Stein's book read "like a fairy tale from afar" to Germany's intellectuals, as one contemporary declared. Before it appeared in September 1842 only a handful of brief articles reporting the latest curiosities in Paris were available to the German public. Even the word "socialism" was barely known, to say nothing of the term "proletariat."

Von Stein began with Babeuf in the 1790s. He treated French communism and socialism as ideologies expressing the interest of the "proletariat." In his view, an entirely new class had emerged during the great French Revolution when the workers of Paris first took events into their own hands. This overzealous mass had an imperious tendency to universalize its condition of propertylessness by creating a "community of goods." Consequently, warned von Stein (for he disapproved), the proletariat contained the seeds of the total overthrow and dissolution of historic European society founded on the principles of monarchy and property. Wittingly or unwittingly, said von Stein, communist and socialist theorists were elaborating an ideology for this new class in its "battle of labor-power with capital." Thus he produced the first significant formulation of the class struggle theme which Marx made the heart of his grand strategy for "the realization of philosophy."[3]

Von Stein wrote:

The entire mass of people is divided into possessors and nonpossessors, between those who join the strength of their labor with capital and those who are only workers. The first are necessarily victors in the domain of profit, whereas the others succumb. The result of the struggle, on the plane of property, is the division between Capital and labor power. The representatives of the first constitute the bourgeois class, the bourgeoisie; the people, itself, has as sole wealth its labor power, and this is what characterizes it. (p. 73)

One cannot postulate the principle of absolute liberty and equality without recognizing with it as a necessary consequence the absolute liberty of industry. This very law of free competition nevertheless produces as a consequence the contrary of what the principle requires; in effect as an inescapable consequence of free industrial right it dictates the triumph of capital over the human person and his enslavement, in the most intolerable and hardest manner. (p. 120)

Where free competition has been introduced, far from having produced the general good, it has had as an effect the enrichment of many people, but also the impoverishment of a still more considerable number. From this is born the sharp conflict between the bourgeoisie and the people in real life. Those who possess only their power of labor are not in a position to gain property which is the absolute condition of independence and concrete equality. (pp. 84–85)

The relationship of these two classes (bourgeoisie and proletariat) is not one of independent coexistence but of dependence of the latter on the former. The suzerainty which formerly existed in the agrarian domain exists now in the industrial domain. This explains the opposition and the struggle between factory proprietors and the workers. (p. 85)

The result of the July Revolution has been to raise again the idea of absolute political equality of all individuals; the result of its triumph has been the absolute difference between possessors and non-possessors. (p. 99)

Through the July Revolution the influence of private property has attained its high point, so much so that the possessor class has seized the power of the state. But the more this power affirms itself, the more it sees its irreducible enemy rise resolutely against it . . . The proletariat at once awakens to the consciousness of class, rises little by little against the enemy which holds it inflexibly in its position of subordination, against the regime of private property. (pp. 100–101)

For the first time one sees rising the idea which seemed to have disappeared, that the true good of the people can be obtained only by the abolition of private property. (p. 102)

[The proletariat say]: "Now we have recourse to the means which permitted you to destroy the crowns of the princes and which you have celebrated so much." (p. 103)

"Without recognizing the right of property, we recognize your right to defend it; on the other hand, we require that you recognize our right to attack property everywhere we can do so and by all means." (p. 104)

The thinker [for socialism] ought to be able to conceive a form of society in which property could be maintained without constituting an absolute obstacle to the full development of the personality. (p. 26)

The organization of labor that socialism would like to establish ought not only to permit the acquisition of private property, but also to open the way to the realization of the supreme terrestrial destiny of man. (p. 132)

Von Stein's report set forth clearly the destructive power potential of the proletariat as a class. His very words already foreshadow by six years those celebrated cadences of Marx in the *Communist Manifesto:*

> The question of whether the human personality can reconcile itself with private property begins to gain currency among the propertyless class, and little by little augments among it the number of those who respond to this question with a fanatical negative. The conviction of the impossibility of legally resolving this question emerges, the mass organizes itself around principles which support these claims, and the poor class, toiling and suffering, transforms itself into a powerful organization, negative and menacing: the proletariat . . . Besides Saint-Simonism and Fourierism *communism looms as a somber and menacing specter* whose reality no one wishes to believe, but which everyone nevertheless sees even while they doubt its existence.[4]

Finally, von Stein observed a crucial emotional distinction between socialism and communism—which endures to this day:

> Socialism is essentially different from communism, which has a purely negative character vis-à-vis the present state of things, or which aspires in a confused and unconscious manner to realize the idea of a new social order which it conceives vaguely. This difference is essential; socialism is positive, whereas communism is negative, socialism wishes to create a new society, whereas communism wishes to destroy the present society . . . Socialism wishes to realize its ends by the power of the truth, *whereas communism wished to do it by the violence of the crowd, by revolution and by crime.*[5]

Marx virtually swallowed von Stein's book whole. From this police agent's analysis of the revolutionary ideology and class struggle growing in France Marx lifted the heart of what was to become Marxism. But he imparted to it the *élan* of rage and bitterness he brought with him out of Germany. This hate, rather than shrewd theoretical or sociological observation, was what gave the borrowed von Stein analysis immortality.

Chapter 9
PROCRUSTEAN PHILOSOPHY ORGANIZES THE WORLD

Man is the only creature who refuses to be what he is. The problem is to know whether this refusal can only lead to the destruction of himself and of others, whether all rebellion must end in the justification of universal murder.

Metaphysical rebellion is the movement by which man protests against his condition and against the whole of creation. It is metaphysical because it contests the end of man and of creation. . . . The metaphysical rebel declares that he is frustrated by the universe. . . . We find a value judgement in the name of which the rebel refuses to approve the condition in which he finds himself. . . . Metaphysical rebellion is a claim, motivated by the concept of a complete unity, against the suffering of life and death and a protest against the human condition both for its incompleteness, due to death, and its wastefulness, due to evil. . . . At the same time that he rejects his mortality, the rebel refuses to recognize the power that compels him to live in this condition . . . Quite simply, he blasphemes primarily in the name of order, denouncing God as the father of death and as the supreme outrage.

When the throne of God is overturned, the rebel realizes that it is now his own responsibility to create the justice, order and unity that he sought in vain within his own condition, and in this way to justify the fall of God. Then begins the desperate effort to create, at the price of crime and murder if necessary, the dominion of man. This will not come about without terrible consequences, of which we are so far only aware of a few. . . .

* * *

Whatever we may do, excess will always keep its place in the heart of man, in the place where solitude is found. We all carry within us our places of exile, our crimes and our ravages. But our task is not to unleash them on the world; it is to fight them in ourselves and in others.

—Albert Camus, *The Rebel*

THE PROLETARIAT: TOOL OF PROCRUSTEAN PHILOSOPHY

Von Stein convinced Marx that the "proletariat" was the only segment of society that showed promise as a sufficient secular force for his philosophical revolution. In fact, von Stein had noted in his study of the post-Babeuvist communists that emotions and violence had motivated them. Marx quite soundly—for his revolutionary purpose —decided to place himself at their head. So he had to build his theory around this given tactical necessity of recruiting the proletariat and riding them to a power seizure.

Marx began this task at Kreuznach in a short essay on Hegel,

[146]

completed after he and his wife Jenny moved to Paris in November 1843. Then only 25, Marx announced his "discovery" of a weapon that could revolutionize Germany and achieve "the realization of philosophy"; in so doing he set the course for everything that was to come not only for him but for communists for a century. By simple fiat he divided humanity into a "chosen" class of the future destined to rule mankind, and all others whom he scorned as "exploiters" unworthy of ordinary human rights, who must be crushed from the body politic at the first opportunity. It was a classic plan of in group-out group identification for mass manipulation through hate propaganda.

Discussing Feuerbach's critique of religion, Marx's essay quickly dismisses religion as a central concern for the practical man who wanted to influence the world. "Religion is the sigh of the oppressed creature, the feelings of a heartless world, and the spirit of unspiritual conditions," he said. "Religion is the opiate of the people."

The real concern must be the condition of life which needs an opiate, Marx wrote. The immediate mission of history—and of the philosopher as its brain—is to *reshape society* so that man will no longer need the illusion of religion and instead can become truly human, the master of his world and fate.

> Thus the criticism of heaven is transformed into a criticism of earth, the criticism of religion into a criticism of law, the criticism of theology into a criticism of *politics*.[1]

Finally Marx arrived at the fundamental problem which had nagged him since Cologne: Where can the philosopher get his army for world-changing?

In one paragraph above all others he expressed the heart and soul of modern revolutionary radicalism as it developed in the twentieth century:

> The weapon of criticism cannot replace the criticism of weapons. Physical force must be overthrown by physical force; theory, too, becomes a physical force as soon as it takes possession of the masses . . . *A radical revolution needs a material basis*.

And how does "theory take possession of the masses"? As Marx's actions later elaborated, by teaching and preaching, by recruiting and organizing, like every evangelist in history from Paul the Apostle to the Wesley brothers with their "method." Once the philosopher converts the masses to his militancy, he will march to power at their head, and remake the world.

> *It is not enough that the Idea should press forward to realization; Reality must urge itself toward the Idea* . . . Philosophy finds its *material* weapons in the proletariat, and the proletariat can find its *intellectual* weapons in philosophy . . . *Philosophy* is the *head* of this emancipation of man and the *proletariat* is its *heart.* Philosophy cannot be realized without the uprising of the proletariat, and the proletariat cannot rise without the realization of philosophy.

THE STRATEGY OF HATE PROPAGANDA   Marx's essay clearly outlines that this mobilization of the masses—"philosophy taking possession of the masses"—should be accomplished by a deliberate preachment of hate—"the reckless criticism of all that exists."

> But *war* upon the state of affairs in Germany! By all means! This state of affairs . . . remains a target of criticism just as the criminal who is beneath humanity remains a target of the *executioner.* In its struggle against this state of affairs criticism is not a passion of the head, but the head of passion. It is not a lancet but a weapon. Its target is an *enemy* which it aims not to refute but to *destroy* . . . Criticism is no longer an end in itself, but simply a means; *indignation* is its essential mode of feeling, and *denunciation* is its principal task.[2]

Here is where radicalism begins to develop its unique *vocabulary of hate* that Lenin later perfected and Hitler aped. Marx invented it; Marx—who as a little boy loved to lacerate his playmates with epithets and satire and in his later alcoholic euphorias loved to boast, "I am going to annihilate you . . . I am going to annihilate you."

> If the revolution of a nation is to coincide with the emancipation of a particular class of bourgeois society, if one particular class is to represent the whole of society, then conversely, *all the evils of society must be concentrated in another class, one particular class must sustain the general attack,* must embody the limitations and represent an obstacle; *one particular social class must be regarded as the scapegoat* for all the sins of society, so that emancipation from this class appears a general emancipation. For *one* class to be the liberating class *par excellence,* another class must be openly the oppressing class. (Emphasis added.)

This is, simply, a grand strategy for selecting hate-targets with which to mobilize the masses for social demolition. As Marx and his Leninist adapters worked it out in later operations, the scheme consists of disintegrating the target society through hate propaganda, polarizing the factions and progressively isolating the government's support into every narrower circles, until the revolutionary forces can seize power. Marx declared that the revolutionary must provide the masses with a *hate target,* and manipulate them with it.

At this point, we see the Babeuvist path diverge more sharply from the constitutional due process path. For Marx converted words into weapons in a war of annihilation. Is a nation to be a free community for reasoned democratic dialog and discussion of common problems, as Jefferson planned? Or an arena for gladiatorial combat-to-the-death with the insurgent faction through hatemongering and social fission establishing a new dictatorship of the philosophers, as Marx planned?

Lenin himself regarded Marx's class struggle theory as "the main-spring of events . . . what actually lies at the bottom of events,"[3] and clearly understood that Marx's choice of the "proletariat" for the chosen class of his hate-the-government philosophy was an expedient. The proletariat was simply the most available secular force the philosopher-king could harness to procrusteanize society. In 1913 Lenin wrote:

> The genius of Marx lies in the fact that he was able before anybody else to draw from and apply consistently the lesson that world history teaches. The deduction he made is the doctrine of *class struggle.*
>
> People always were and always will be the stupid victims of deceit and self-deceit in politics until they learn to discover the *interests* of some class behind all moral, religious, political and social phrases, declarations and promises. The supporters of reforms and improvements will always be fooled by the defenders of the old order until they realize that every old institution, however barbarous and rotten it may appear to be, is maintained by the forces of some ruling classes. And there is only *one way* of smashing the resistance of these classes, and that is *to find, in the very society which surrounds us, the forces which can—and owing to their social position MUST—constitute the power capable of sweeping away the old and creating the new, and to enlighten and organize those forces for the struggle.*[4]

To Marx and Lenin, then, hate propaganda was an emotional tool to "organize forces for the struggle," the hook by which "philosophy takes possession of the masses." Hate propaganda could "sharpen the class conflict" and galvanize them into an army for Procrustean philosophy and the "general staff of the revolution."

Thus, it was a disgruntled intellectual's quest for a constituency powerful enough to install himself in power, and not compassion for the poor, the worker, and the child laborer, that moved Marx. Western liberals erroneously credit communism with arising out of concern for social conditions when it really arose out of the frustrated powerlessness of the cloistered intellectual class. When Marx mounted the proletarian horse he had never had any contact with the proletariat in the flesh, never observed their working and living conditions, never explored their feelings. He had never cracked an economics text or peeked into sociology so far as the historical record shows. ("I began my research into economics in Paris," he wrote years later in the preface to his *Critique of Political Economy.)* Only after he reached Paris did he visit some of the workingmen's associations and observe them first-hand. There was nothing "scientific" or empirical or compassionate about his selection of the working class as the philosopher's revolutionary weapon of salvation.

BUILDING THE ORGANIZATION AND HARNESSING THE PROLETARIAT   The Franco-German *Yearbook* appeared in February with Marx's essays on the Jews and Hegel, only to meet instant disaster. Prussian border police seized it, knocking Ruge out of German sales and Marx out of his job. By now he was a father. He sent Jenny and the baby back to Kreuznach and joined the Paris bohemians, notably Heine, the German poet, and Michael Bakunin, the Russian anarchist. He launched a massive reading program that included Buonarroti's history of the Babeuvist plot and Machiavelli's *The Prince.* He filled notebooks with extracts from Adam Smith, David Ricardo, and Jean-Baptiste Say. And in his "Economic and Philosophical Manuscripts of 1844," he began working out his ideology of dialectical materialism and class struggle.[5]

According to reports of the Prussian secret agents who swarmed Paris in the summer of 1844, Marx often visited worker meetings at the Barriere du Trone, Rue de Vincennes. He studied the workers closely—the first he had ever known. He noted somewhat romantically:

> At the communist workers' meetings the purpose of their conversation is instruction, propaganda . . . Smoking, drink, food are not the purpose of sociality—not even aids to it. Company, society, conversation for the sake of good company—these are enough. The Brotherhood of men is here no phrase but a reality, and a true spirit of nobility shines out from these workworn faces.

He admired "their studiousness, their thirst for knowledge, their moral energy, their restless urge for development." Marx had found men to lead.

Soon the Procrustean philosopher began trying to "teach" them, to make them "class conscious," make them "understand" the nature of the class struggle and their role of saving mankind for him and other philosopher-kings. He was taking the first halting steps toward building the revolutionary combat party: proselyting, trying to win converts to the ideology forming in his mind, to recruit soldiers for the political army he wanted to lead to power. Marx dimly apprehended the essential elements of the process: propaganda, recruiting, training, indoctrination, hierarchical command, and social demolition operations.

MARX AND ENGLES FIND EACH OTHER   In September 1844 Frederick Engels passed through Paris. The Franco-German *Yearbook* contained articles by both men that revealed an astonishing similarity in thought, so Engels stopped to spend ten days with the remarkable Dr. Marx, two years his elder.

Engels was the oldest of eight children of a wealthy German textile manufacturer, who also owned a mill at Manchester, England. With Engels, too, the projection of familial rebellion against iron discipline into compulsive revolution against society at large is fairly transparent. His father, a man of strict orthodox beliefs, tried to raise his children to regard the Bible as the specific Word of God. But when Frederick Jr. was but 14, the father wrote his wife:

> Frederick brought home middling reports for last week. As you know, his manners have improved. But in spite of severe punishment in the past, he does not seem to be learning implicit obedience even from the fear of chastisement. Today I was once more vexed by finding in his desk a dirty book from a lending library, a romance of the thirteenth century. May God guard the boy's heart, for I am often troubled over this son of ours, who is otherwise so full of promise.

When the boy left school at 17, he went into his father's business for appearance's sake. Reading Strauss' *Life of Jesus*, an epochal young Hegelian work, shattered what religious faith he had and further strained his ties with his father. He left the family business and joined the Prussian Army in October 1841 just before his 21st birthday. Returning home in October 1842, Engels stopped in Cologne and spent an afternoon with Moses Hess, then 30, who was known as "the communist rabbi" for his missionary zeal in proselyting for French utopian ideas. Hess later wrote a friend: "He, an embryonic revolutionary, parted from me the most enthusiastic communist." Engels himself credited his conversion to Dr. Hess, and a year later expressly declared that the latter was "the first to make communism plausible to me and my circle."

Engels spent two years in his father's plant at Manchester and wrote the two *Yearbook* articles which appealed so to Marx. In fact, Engels was far ahead of Marx in his direct observation of contemporary society, and Marx realized it. This is why he was so eager to talk to the young manufacturer's son. Engels wrote of "the unreasoning, unfeeling mechanism of competition" which added more machinery and cut wages while workers would not buy the products they made. He wrote of the ever-increasing momentum of capitalist production, the recurrent commercial crises, the law of wages, the scientific progress which he maintained was being perverted into a means for consolidating the slavery of mankind, and so on. In 1844 Engels gave, and Marx received, and aimed to exploit, "target intelligence" in economics and sociology of modern industry as well as the conditions of the working class that Marx aimed to propagandize and mobilize.

Marx and Engels planned to publish a German edition of Buonarroti's *Conspiration Pour L'Egalite*, translated by Moses Hess, but the project never materialized. Buonarroti was so influential in Marx's Paris circle that one leading communist, William Weitling, even named a son after "the Great Conspirator." (Weitling was the first communist to proclaim openly that one of the items of his program was "to shoot without mercy all enemies of communism.") Marx's extensive collection of books on the French Revolution contained a copy of Buonarroti's *Conspiration.*

BUILDING THE IDEOLOGY   Expelled from France in late 1844, Marx spent the next three years in Brussels, and devoted himself to two fundamental tasks: building his ideology of self-righteous hatred, and building his organization. He plunged into a new reading binge and began clarifying his views and boiling them down into a magnificent *Reader's Digest*-style condensation for popular consumption. The distilled essence of these years burst forth on the eve of the revolutionary upheavals of 1848 like a cock crowing before a fiery dawn. That work was the *Communist Manifesto.* Marx's life after this pronouncement was devoted mainly to winnowing out facts that would serve as "evidence" to "prove" his "scientific" theory; the result he presented, twenty years later, as *Das Kapital*.

In the process of writing *The Holy Family* and *The German Ideology* Marx sharpened further the idea taking form in his brain: that it was not the state that shaped society, but the reverse—that society, and specifically economic relationships, dictated the nature of government. This was his "materialist interpretation of history," or "historical materialism." This process, Marx decreed, renders inevitable capitalism's destruction by history's chosen class, the proletariat. Marx was only building a theoretical superstructure atop the "categorical imperative" announced in the Hegel essay of finding and mobilizing a "material force" capable of seizing power. His theory of economic determinism gave the underprivileged worker and frustrated intellectual exactly what Christianity offered the same social strata in Christianity's embryonic stage as a radical social movement: certainty of salvation and triumph. It also camouflaged the crass opportunism and machiavellianism that led Marx to adopt the proletariat as the chosen class.

In *The Holy Family* and *The German Ideology* Marx included a few ideas about the nature of man and the Marxian vision of his future that reveal much. What little he did say about the new communist society was hopelessly visionary and utopian, a simple reflection of Rousseauism swallowed whole from his father. Marx repeats the cant that "man is naturally good"; his words might have been penned by Rousseau—or by a twentieth-century social worker:

> The materialist doctrines of original goodness, equal intellectual endowments of men, and the all-importance of experience, custom, education, and environmental conditions are necessarily connected to communism and socialism. If man derives all his knowledge, and his perceptions, etc., from the world of the senses and from experience in the world of the senses, it is our business to so order the empirical world that man shall have truly human experiences in it, shall experience himself to be a human being. If self-interest rightly understood is the basic principle of morality, it behooves us to make sure that the private interest of the individual shall coincide with the general human interest. If man is unfree in the materialist sense (this meaning that he is free, not through the negative power of avoiding this or that, but through the positive power of fulfilling his own true inidividuality), it behooves us, not to punish individual offences, but to destroy the anti-social foci of crime, and to give every one social space for the manifestation of his life activities. If man is formed by circumstances, *we must make the circumstances human.* If man is social by nature, he

can only develop his true nature in society, and we must measure the power of his nature, not by the power of the isolated individual, but by the power of society.

To get a perfect man, you build a perfect society ruled by the philosopher-king, the "general staff of the revolution," the intellectual elite. Put man in this perfected environment, and he will become a perfect being. This made good ideology and revolutionary propaganda, but not very good sociology or anthropology. Indeed, many years later Engels openly declared in his *Anti-Dühring* essay that Marxism was but a modification and elaboration of Rousseau's "Essay on the Origin of Inequality." Marx was merely propounding a semantically complex Germanic and Hegelianized version of Rousseauism.

In developing his concept of "alienation" in the 1844 manuscripts Marx merely revamped his essay equating Jewish emancipation and human emancipation with emancipation from "commercialism" and "huckstering." (See Chapter 11, page 173.) He took the term "alienation" over from the Hegelians—Hegel borrowed the concept from Rousseau—and gave it his own meaning and mood. Basically, Marx in the 1844 manuscripts forced himself through incredible contortions to arrive at the conclusion—and protest the fact—that the necessity of earning subsistence forces man to violate his "fundamental nature" (essence or "species-being") which in Marx's opinion is to reason and to create ("free conscious activity"). Throughout his life this problem of how man makes a living haunted Marx. Says one scholar, "Marx never abandoned this conception of occupational specialization as slavery. Indeed, it becomes an almost obsessive theme of his own later writings and also those of Engels."[6] And as Fromm points out, "The concept [of alienation], although not the word, remains of central significance throughout his whole later main work, including *Das Kapital*,"[7] and it was bad anthropology and bad psychology.

There Marx contended:

In handicraft and manufacture, the workman makes use of a tool; in the factory the machine makes use of him. There the movement of the instruments of labor proceed from him; here it is the movement of the machines that he must follow. In manufacture, the workmen are a part of a living mechanism; in the factory, we have a lifeless mechanism, independent of the workman, who becomes its mere living appendage.[8]

In the *Economic and Philosophical Manuscripts,* written in the April-August 1844 period in Paris, Marx wrote:

> What constitutes the alienation of labor? First, that the work is *external* to the worker, that it is not part of his nature; and that, consequently, he does not fulfill himself in his work but denies himself, has a feeling of misery rather than well being, does not develop freely his mental and physical energies but is physically exhausted and mentally debased. The worker therefore feels homeless. His work is not voluntary but imposed, *forced labor.* It is not the satisfaction of a need, but only a *means* for satisfying other needs. Its alien character is clearly shown by the fact that as soon as there is no physical or other compulsion it is avoided like the plague. External labor, labor in which man alienates himself, is a labor of self-sacrifice, of mortification. Finally, the external character of work for the worker is shown by the fact that it is not his own work but work for someone else, that in work he does not belong to himself but to another person.[9]

In both passages we can almost hear the romantic young poet arguing with his father over parental urgings about a career and the father denouncing his son's spendthrift ways at college. Anything that keeps a man from doing what he *wants,* argues Marx, is *alien* to his nature and is *forced labor.* If he wants to stay in his room and compose poems all day, why shouldn't he? Would not that be the ideal society? Would it not be paradise if none of us had to work? A psychoanalyst would quickly declare these writings an example of the displacement of the college youth's rebellion against the nagging father's pressure to abandon his flights of poetry for the dusty law-books and make a "position" for himself in the community. Certainly Marx's rebelliousness far antedated any concern with the factory worker's wretched condition.

The thought of a man working at one profession his whole life repelled Marx. In a revealing passage he declared:

> As soon as labor is distributed, each man has a particular, exclusive sphere of activity, which is forced upon him and from which he cannot escape. He is a hunter, a fisherman, a shepherd, or a critical critic, and must remain so if he does not want to lose his means of livelihood; while in communist society, where nobody has one exclusive sphere of activity but each can become accomplished in any branch he wishes, society regulates the general production and thus makes it possible for me to do one thing today and another tomorrow, to hunt in the morning, fish in the afternoon, rear cattle in the evening, criticize after

dinner, just as I have a mind, without ever becoming hunter, fisherman, shepherd or critic.[10]

This is really a *reductio ad absurdum*. Can we imagine being a barber this morning, a space scientist this afternoon, and an opera singer tonight? Who is going to carry out the garbage in the communist utopia? Tomorrow's opera singer or yesterday's space scientist? Marx's mistake was in blaming a particular organization of society, i.e., capitalism, for what is really an objective and inherent condition of life itself: that certain work must be done, and that division of labor is inherent in any organization of society above nomadic existence. The simple truth behind Marx's theory of "alienation" is that he rejected the mundane facts of life such as the necessity of making a living and doing some unpleasant things in this vale of tears. He would not admit that there are such things as necessary chores, however unpleasant, inherent in life. Years later in London, even when his own child was dying of malnutrition, this visionary would not bestir himself from his books to go out upon the London streets to get work and earn some money for the poor baby.

BUILDING THE ORGANIZATION   The two world-changers had not only to write their Gospel: they had to create—or capture —their own evangelical organization to spread it.

Surveying the scene of organized political activity in Europe, Marx and Engels saw only one logical candidate for capture—the "League of the Just." Marx had attended a few meetings while in Paris but never joined. Following the Babeuvist and Blanquist secret conspiratorial models, a Buonarroti disciple started this secret society in Paris in the 1830s among exiles and German workers. After the Blanquist uprising in 1839, the League's members scattered to the winds, founding units wherever they went. Most of them settled in London. In 1840 the London unit founded a "front" group as a legal organization—"the London German Workers Union." Propaganda was their chief purpose, though they provided benefits for sick workers. All units maintained committees of correspondence to exchange reports on political conditions in their respective countries. By the late 1840s, the London front group numbered between 400 and 500 workers, and the still-secret League had 70 to 80 members, twice the strength of the Paris branch. So in 1846 League headquarters moved from Paris to London.

As their first step, Marx and Engels one day merely began to call

[156   ]

themselves "The Communist Party."[11] They asked socialist friends in Brussels to join "the Party," and recruited seventeen, counting themselves. Fifteen of the seventeen were writers; the other two were typesetters and hence almost genuine "workers." Fourteen of the seventeen were of "bourgeois" origins. Thus the world's first "Communist Party" had a distinct middle-class and élitist cast, and was embarrassingly short of true workingmen in this, the workingman's party. Likewise, its emotional tone was one of frustrated *déclassé* intellectuals with more ambition than ability. The average age was 28—the oldest 37 and the youngest 21.

"EXCOMMUNICATIONS AND ANATHEMAS"   Marx and Engel's second step was to form in the spring of 1846 a front group of their own, a "communist corresponding committee," which they used as a stalking horse to subvert the League of the Just's correspondence apparatus. They persuaded the London League to respond, and enlisted other socialist-communist individuals or groups in Cologne, Paris, Silesia, Wuppertal, Kiel, and elsewhere. Into this circuit Marx and Engels poured a steady charge of pamphlets, circulars, and propaganda tracts. They expounded "scientific" socialism and attacked the old "sentimental" socialism of the utopian schools.

But the world changers had more in mind than merely making propaganda. As Marx's exchange of letters with Proudhon reveals, they were thinking of no less than an international revolutionary organization—and Proudhon, just as clearly, so understood them. On Mary 5, 1846, Marx wrote from Brussels asking Proudhon to act as the French correspondent of his "International Correspondence Committee": The Committee "will concern itself both with the discussion of scientific questions, *with the exercise of supervision over the writings of popularization and with socialist propaganda* which, by this method, can be disseminated in Germany,"[2] Marx wrote. *"And in time of action it is certainly of great importance for each one to be informed of the state of affairs abroad as well as in his own country. . . .* This correspondence demands the utmost secrecy on your part."

Thus Marx already, in 1846, rendered obsolescent the classic view of nation-states, sovereignty, "noninterference," and international relations. For he was laying the foundation of an international political movement, commanded and coordinated with more or less common operational doctrine, strategy, and tactics. Lenin only developed and refined. Proudhon's remarkably prescient response shows he clearly sensed that Marx was already far along toward creating a new totalitarian machine. Professing what he called his "economic antidogmatism," Proudhon wrote:

> For God's sake, after having abolished all dogmatism in the first place, do not let us in our turn dream of indoctrinating the people ourselves. Do not let us fall into the contradiction of your compatriot Martin Luther, who after having overthrown Catholic theology set about immediately with all the apparatus of excommunications and anathemas to found a Protestant one. I applaud with all my heart your idea of presenting all opinions. Let us have a good and honest discussion; let us give the world the example of a wise and far-seeing tolerance; but simply because we are at the forefront of a new movement, let us not become the leaders of a new intolerance. *Let us not appear as the apostles of a new religion.*[13] (Emphasis added.)

Proudhon took specific exception to Marx's phrase "in time of action." Revolutionary action as a means of social reform was not necessary, he contended, because he opposed any appeal to force. Proudhon declared the goal should be to have property burned under a small flame rather than to strengthen it through a "St. Bartholomew [massacre] of its owners." Proudhon was stating the case for evolution versus revolution, due process versus destruction, that later split the Marxist Second International over Edward Bernstein's revisionism versus Lenin's Bolshevism. Whereupon Marx turned his terrible vocabulary of hate full-force on Monsieur Proudhon.

The Marx-Proudhon duel might be ranked as the first head-on clash between Europe's Social Democrats and the Communists, the peaceful reformers and the incendiary revolutionaries, the Babeuvists and the Constitutionalists.

Marx and Engels used the correspondence device to propagandize for their theory of "scientific socialism" and to attack the "sentimentalism" of William Weitling, Proudhon, and other utopian socialists. Where the utopians used the moral "ought," Marx used the scientific certitude of "will." Results were astounding.

The leaders of the League in London saw an economic depression approaching. According to the words of one of their circulars, they believed that a serious downturn would "probably settle the fate of the world for centuries." The leaders had no grand strategy, no plan of campaign, no theory of the contemporary era. Marx did—he had all the answers. He had only to tap the "scientific" socialism in his own dogmatic brain. So in the summer of 1846 the London group proposed a congress to found a party program and set tactics, and sent Joseph Moll, a watchmaker, as a special emissary to invite the renowned Dr. Marx to be their philosophical and dialectical leader.

Moll arrived in Brussels in early February 1847. He explained that his London cohorts were convinced Marx was right—that they must jettison the old conspiratorial forms and traditions, reorient themselves theoretically and organizationally into a party of the working class. They would become a general staff for the proletarian army which Marx's theory declared was chosen of God, renamed "history," to lead mankind to the Promised Land. Now: would Dr. Marx do them the honor? He would or he *did*. But first he and Engels stipulated that "everything conducive to superstitious authoritarianism be struck out of the rules."

The congress met in June 1847 and obliged. It completely recast the League of the Just into the Marxian image, renaming it "The Communist League." Engels as the Paris delegate dictated the terms. (Marx, either for reasons of finances or tactics, stayed in Brussels.) With this congress, the semieducated ex-workingmen accepted as their spiritual leader the one-time philosopher.

The League was reorganized into cells of not less than three and no more than ten members, pyramiding up to the central authority and the congress. Thus the familiar pyramided Babeuvist-Blanquist cell structure appeared from the first. The new organization declared its aims to be overthrowing the bourgeoisie, establishing proletarian rule, abolishing the old society based on class contradictions, and building a new classless and propertyless one.

At least for ordinary peacetime purposes, the League became a straightforward mass propaganda organization. It had to remain a secret society, of course, because it could not register with the police. But it was rather an association of workingmen for propaganda among the masses on a democratic basis. Open propaganda was to replace conspiratorial plotting, because "the communists scorn to keep their views and intentions secret," as Marx's *Manifesto* later declared. All officers were to be elected. The June congress sent the new statutes to all branches to be discussed, and scheduled a second congress for December 1847 to ratify the new structure.

Engels, back in Paris, went to work drafting a party program. Significantly, Engles cast this first statement of communist principles in the form of a catechism, 25 questions and answers, appropriately called a "confession of faith." He saw it as a religious document, despite all the talk about "scientific socialism."

A month later Engels wrote Marx on the eve of the December congress,

> Think over the confession of faith a bit. I think it would be better to drop the catechism form and call the thing: Communist *Manifesto*. As a certain amount of history will have to be brought in I think the present form is unsuitable. I am bringing along what I have done here. It is in simple narrative form, but miserably edited and done in a terrible hurry.[14]

He then suggests an outline, to be concluded with a description of "the Party policy of the Communists, *in so far as it can be made public.*" This last note shows the *Manifesto* was not as candid as the authors would have had the world believe.

The London congress appointed Marx and Engels to draft a "profession of faith". Marx delivered it on February 1848. The *Manifesto of the Communist Party* brilliantly packaged Marx's rationalization of his hate worked out over the preceding five years. It became a classic of history, abounding with slogans that Marx's followers, through the years, have hurled from thousands of platforms and packed into thousands of editorials. This package of ideology, plus the Babeuvist organizational forms with which Marx and his predecessors were experimenting, provided the crucial catalyst that shaped the revolutionary movement of the rest of the nineteenth century. The manifesto foreshadowed the remarkable power of the new science of sloganeering Lenin later developed. Its massive simplicity in dealing with incomprehensibly complex problems give it universal appeal. The government "is but a committee" of the exploiter class, Marx declares. "Law, morality, religion are to the worker so many bourgeois prejudices, behind which lurk in ambush just as many capitalist interests." Millions chose as their watchwords such sentences as these: "The workers have no country!" "The history of all previous existing society is the history of class struggles." "The Communists disdain to conceal their views and aims. They openly declare that their ends can be attained only by the forcible overthrow of all existing social conditions. Let the ruling class tremble at a Communist revolution. The workers have nothing to lose but their chains—they have a world to win. Workers of the world, unite!"

The *Manifesto* capsulized the fundamental concepts of Marxist ideology: 1) The in group-out group identification of the class struggle; 2) The idea of a chosen class; 3) Economic determinism (historical or dialectical materialism); 4) Inevitability of proletarian triumph; 5) Obsessive future orientation (fixation on a seductive future that devalues the present); 6) The commitment to violence.

Lenin himself cited the *Communist Manifesto*'s description of the class struggle as the heart of Marxist ideology and "the mainspring of events":

> The history of all hitherto existing society is the history of class struggles. Freeman and slave, patrician and plebeian, lord and serf, guild-master and journeyman, in a word, oppressor and oppressed, stood in constant opposition to one another, carried on an uninterrupted, now hidden, now open, fight, a fight that each time ended either in a revolutionary re-constitution of society at large, or in the common ruin of the contending classes . . . Society as a whole is more and more splitting up into two great hostile camps, into two great classes directly facing each other: Bourgeoisie and Proletariat.[15]

Marx devoted the rest of his life to hunting evidence to prove the "theory" he had already declared true, the economic interpretation of history and its corollary, class struggle. Repeatedly in his letters, Engels kept demanding and urging proof—and only then did Marx give belated attention to the fields of economics and history and to what was actually on record. *Das Kapital* was but an attempt to prove the sociological correctness of "our theory" by compiling every trace of evidence that could be bent to his purpose.

Chapter 10
PHILOSOPHY ON THE BARRICADES—AND IN EXILE

The revolutionary heart of Communism is . . . a simple statement of Karl Marx: "Philosophers have explained the world; it is necessary to change the world." Communists are bound together by no secret oath. The tie that binds them across the frontiers of nations, across barriers of language and differences of class and education, in defiance of religion, morality, truth, law, honor, the weaknesses of the body and the irresolutions of the mind, even unto death, is a simple conviction: It is necessary to change the world. Their power, whose nature baffles the rest of the world, because in a large measure the rest of the world has lost that power, is the power to hold convictions and to act on them. It is the same power that moves mountains; it is also an unfailing power to move men. Communists are that part of mankind which has recovered the power to live or die—to bear witness—for its faith. And it is a simple, rational faith that inspires men to live or die for it.

—Whittaker Chambers, *Witness*

Love cannot redeem, love cannot save us . . .
Pronounce, O Hate, the Last Judgement;
Break thou, O Hate, the chains . . .
We've tried love long enough;
Now at last we mean to hate.
—George Herwegh, German poet
and friend of young Marx,
"Song of Hate," 1841

THE "MAD YEAR" OF 1848: PHILOSOPHY TAKES TO THE BARRICADES   Marx finished *The Communist Manifesto* not a moment too soon. Within a month revolution flared in Paris, and as he predicted, all Europe responded to the crow of the Gallic cock. A grain crop failure and the Irish potato blight had produced skyrocketing prices, food riots, and actual starvation. The railroad boom of the early 1840s collapsed by 1847, producing a wave of unemployment. Petty larceny cases jumped from 25,000 to 41,000 in a year. A mob attacked Prime Minister Guizot's residence on February 23, 1848, and soldiers killed or wonded fifty people. Too late, Guizot resigned and King Louis Philippe offered concessions. The revolt spread, the king abdicated, and socialist and republican deputies formed a provisional government.

Of course, Europe's radicals thought their day had come. In London, the Communist League's central committee dissolved itself, pausing only long enough to transfer executive authority to Marx with instructions to form a new central leadership in Paris. Marx, honored by an invitation from the new government in Paris, arrived March 4. That very night, Marx joined one of the many Paris "clubs" —the government listed no less than 147 in March 1848.[1] There were communists, Jacobins, Robespierrists, deists, and Babeuvist-Blanquists. Marx chose the Society of the Rights of Man, presided over by one Villain, a Blanqui sympathizer. Blanqui himself, freed from banishment, had arrived in Paris on February 25. Marx called him and his comrades "the real leaders of the proletarian party" and their doctrine "revolutionary socialism" or "communism."[2] The Blanquist club was an armed association organized along military lines. It was one of the largest, with members all over Paris, many of them tried revolutionists. That Marx chose to join them shows his thinking on organization technology.

Marx spoke at the central club on the evening of March 4. "I am a revolutionist," he is reputed to have said.

> I want to march in the shadow of the Great Robespierre. Well, here is what this virtuous citizen would say to you if he were still alive today: When an overcrowded vessel is caught at sea in a violent storm, a part of the crew is thrown overboard to save the rest.[3]

In other words, exterminate the bourgeoisie to save society from catastrophe. He was offering the masses a hate target for their frustrations.

PREPARING CADRES FOR INFILTRATION   Among the 100,-000 Germans in Paris Marx had a few dozen communists at his disposal. He found that George Herwegh and other romantic radicals had devised a plan to invade the Fatherland for democracy. To combat this "German Legion" notion, Marx organized his own "German Workers Club" using Babeuf's tactics and Parisian communists as agitators. Marx's agents advertised his club as a new meeting place for democratic German workers, attracting several hundred tailors, bootmakers, and such. Marx proposed individual infiltration into

Germany, in place of the military invasion planned by Herwegh.

Meanwhile, Marx was steadily reinforced by arrivals from Brussels and London, until soon their number reached about 300. With the hierarchy assembled now in Paris, the central committee was duly reconstituted, and elected Marx its president.

Ten days after Marx's arrival in Paris, democratic upheavals erupted in Budapest and Vienna. Within another week, bloody fighting broke out in Berlin, and Frederick William IV, paralyzed, ordered all troops out of the city.

Marx quickly drafted a new plan. Each of his 300 communists, rightly placed, could organize a communist chapter, or cell, in Marx's own native city in Germany, à la Babeuf. Marx and Engels jettisoned the name "Communist League" and in its place hoisted the banner of the "Communist Party of Germany." They wrote a pamphlet of 17 "Demands of the Communist Party of Germany," and handed bundles of them to each of the 300 agent-organizers. Marx outlined a clear strategy of deliberate hate-targeting to rouse the masses:

> It is obvious that in the bloody fighting that lies ahead, as in the fighting of the past, the workers will be victorious chiefly through their own courage, determination and self-sacrifice . . . Far from opposing the so-called excesses, those examples of popular vengeance against hated individuals or public buildings which have acquired hateful memories, we must not only condone these examples but lend them a guiding hand.

THE CREEPING RED FOG   In late March, with some financial aid from Prime Minister Flocon, who wanted to be rid of the Germans, Marx's infiltrators began to filter across the border. On April 5, Marx himself went back along with the general staff of the League. All carried copies of the *Communist Manifesto* (a thousand of which had arrived that week from London freshly printed) and the "Demands of the Communist Party in Germany." Coincidentally, the leaders left Paris the same day as the German Legion, but without bands and banners. A young Legionnaire later to become famous as a Marxist agent himself, Wilhelm Liebknecht, then 22, sent a report about the departure to some German newspapers:

> The German communists left Paris too. Unlike the German Democrats they did not depart fraternally and sociably, in closed ranks, but each man went to a different point on his own initiative—travelers each carrying the salvation of the world in his own breast.

In Cologne, two communist agents, with the support of German democrats in Cologne, proceeded to organize a newspaper, reporting all the while to Marx in Paris. All members of the editorial board and staff were members of the original party in Brussels—Marxian communists from the start. No sooner had Marx arrived than they offered him the editorship. The first issue appeared on June 1, 1848 —the *Neue Rheinische Zeitung,* in honor of Marx's previous journalistic venture.

To his dismay, Marx found the Germans to be hostile to communism and radicalism. The revolutionary impetus came from middle-class and bourgeois republicans and liberal democrats who favored a consitutional monarcy but wanted no tampering with property rights. Even before Marx left Paris, he received his Cologne agents' report that "communism" was a word people shuddered at, and anyone who espoused it openly would be stoned. Engels wrote from Barmen, "If a single copy of our 17 points were distributed here, everything would be lost. The mood prevailing among the bourgeois is really infamous." Years later, Engels explained,

> When we returned to Germany in the spring of 1848 we joined the democratic paty as the only possible means of getting the ear of the working class. The only possible banner for us to take our stand under was the banner of democracy. Had we been unwilling to do this ... we should have had no choice but to content ourselves with preaching the doctrines of Communism in some obscure hole-in-the-wall local paper and founding a small sect instead of a great party of action. The time had passed for us to be preachers in the wilderness.

Thus, Marx and Engels endorsed the use of tactical deception by democratic masquerade for advancing communist programs. What had happened to the famous cry that "the communists disdain to conceal their views"? No sooner had *The Communist Manifesto* been published than Marx and Engels sacrificed ideology to the tactical requirements of the power quest. That the two fathers of communism should have reasoned this way at the outset reveals volumes about the movement's psychological mainspring: *For the communist, nothing is fixed save the goal of power conquest, and all that advances the struggle becomes moral.*

WAGING SECRET "WAR ON DEMOCRACY!"   Soon after receiving Engels' warning from Barmen, Marx warned the other communists through the *Neue Rheinische Zeiting.* His very language foreshadows the vague Aesopian jargon of modern communist pronouncements: "We do not at the outset make the Utopian demand for a single indivisible German republic," he declared, jettisoning the very first of his 17 demands.

> But we demand of the so-called Radical-Democratic Party that it do not confound the point of departure of the struggle and of the revolutionary movement with its final aims. It is not now a matter of realizing this or that point of view, this or that political idea, but of insight into the course of development. The National Assembly [in Frankfurt] has only to perform the immediate and practically possible steps.

These were thinly veiled instructions to communist agents all over Germany who—again following Buonarroti's tactical handbook on Babeuf—were instructed to read the party press for the latest guides to action and propaganda lines. The communist, Marx declares, "has only to perform the immediate and practically possible steps." He must not make Utopian demands; that is, he should not disclose himself as a communist and demand the full communist program.

So zealously did Marx execute this grand strategy that he even forbade the use of the words "communism" and "socialism" in his paper. When his and Engels' articles were collected into a ponderous volume eighty years later, the words "communist" and "communistic" did not appear.

According to Marx's plan, he and his general staff—the cadres from his Brussels group, now in Cologne—constituted the high command of the proletarian army. His agitators in the field had only to read the paper every morning to get the catchwords, ideas, accusations, and disclosures to guide them in their organizational work.

Before leaving Paris, the field commanders had been instructed to keep a sharp eye on the workers in their future districts. They were to screen and recruit the likeliest leaders, cautiously leading those properly predisposed to communism and ultimately introducing them to the *Communist Manifesto* and the *Communist Demands.* Thus, they were instructed to form communist cells in every city, to remain invisible, and to anticipate the proletarian revolution. Meanwhile, spreading outward from these cells the communists were to infiltrate and create a great public organization. The 300 secret communists were to establish themselves in their own towns as zealous democrats, join the democratic clubs, establish rapport with the members, and then declare themselves dissatisfied with the existing spirit. They were to demand a more active prosecution of the demo-

[166]

cratic revolution. Using this subterfuge they were either to capture the existing democratic clubs or form new ones with their committees, staffs, and organizational machinery firmly in the control of the communist cells. Then they were to await further instructions from Cologne.

Engels called this the "Plan of Campaign against Democracy." "It was at bottom nothing but a plan of war against democracy," Marx said several years later. It failed for two reasons. First, their organization was not prepared for the test of 1848. Their "Communist party" was less than two years old when it began. They had not had the time to complete their training and develop their cadres. The League's agents reported inadequacies from every direction. No organization existed in Berlin. Some 20 sympathizers had virtually no contact with each other. Weeks of effort in cities like Breslau, Hanau, Cassel, and Mainz produced not a single member. In Frankfurt there were two, in Coblenz four.[4] Marx wrote his agitators inciting letters that fumed at the failures.

The second cause of failure was the wave of reaction that swept Europe in June 1848. A general economic improvement had put masses of people back to work—and hence back into their normal political lethargy.

But the coup de grace was a bloody insurrection in Paris. Elections were held after Marx's departure, despite the radical effort to substitute an elite revolutionary "dictatorship" to "educate" the people. Every male Frenchman over 21 was ruled eligible, increasing the electorate from 200,000 to 9,000,000. Eight million voted for the new National Assembly to draw up a new constitution. The radicals and socialists won only 100 out of 876 seats. The massiveness of their defeat intensified their hatred. They had expected to lead a new crusade across Europe, using Paris as their power base. So now the Blanquists and other radical clubs on June 23, with 40,000 men, set out to destroy the infant democratic government, throwing up barricades at strategic points.

But a surprising thing happened. For once, a liberal government, duly elected, did not flinch before the paralyzing idea of using armed force against a radical-led army of compatriots. The National Assembly sent out the army. At least 1,500 insurgents were killed in four days of fighting, and 4,000 more subsequently deported.

This was the first revolutionary civil war on the European continent. The specter of bloody social revolution, for the moment a grim reality, terrified the moderate bourgeois liberals and propertied classes throughout Europe. Everywhere they recoiled from the prospect of radical bloodletting.

THE RED SCARECROW   Marx made the fatal tactical blunder of lowering his false banner of "democracy" for one fleeting moment during the Paris insurrection. For the *Neue Rheinische Zeitung*, the 40,000 rebels became "the people"; the 8,000,000 French voters who backed the new government became "the bourgeoisie." Marx vented his rage on the workers' battalions that helped to quell the uprising. These heroes of the February barricades became "the organized tatterdemalion-proletariat"—"recruited for the most part from the riffraff of Paris," "one-time beggars, tramps, swindlers, street-urchins and thieves," "bribed vagabonds" who "let themselves be hired to butcher their brothers for thirty *sous* a day."[5]

But the reports from Paris were too clear. One Berlin paper called Marx's version a "chimborazo of insolence." Other critical articles appeared, and people began to accuse Marx of being—horrendous thought!—a disguised "red." Many of Marx's stockholders either demanded their money back or refused further payments. Marx's three-week-old journal was thoroughly isolated; its circulation never exceeded 6,000.

Europe's revolutionary tide was receding. In Prussia, King Frederick William IV, sensing the changing atmosphere, slowly began to reassert his authority. This move drove Marx to even more radical flag-waving. This suited the regime's purposes, however, for the authorities were content to use Marx as a strawman in their counter-revolutionary plan. The regime noted that Marx, though ineffectual politically, scared many persons and represented the "red peril." The authorities let him confuse and frighten democrats with his harmless clamor, thus making them all the more willing to accept the reimposition of royal authority.

By November, the king felt strong enough to send troops to scatter the National Assembly. All the while Marx in Cologne fanned the fires of revolution. On the New Year, the great pope of "scientific" socialism prophesied another upheaval: "Our table of contents for 1849: a new uprising of the French working class—and world war."[1] Not until the last fires of insurrection in the Rhineland died did the government of His Majesty the King of Prussia speak to Marx in Cologne. On May 11 the police issued an order for his expulsion.

Marx closed down the *Neue Rheinische Zeitung* with a final blast at the government:

> Why bother with your foolish lies and formal phrases? We are ruthless ourselves and we ask no consideration from you. *When our turn arrives we shall make no apologies for our terrorism* . . .

EXPECTATION AND FRUSTRATION   Defeated, Marx retreated to London. There he passed the next 35 years constantly anticipating "the revolution," and detecting harbingers in every border dispute and economic crisis in Europe. "A new colossal outbreak of the revolutionary volcano was never more imminent," he wrote Engels in 1849. To his restless Communist League followers he promised the great upheaval by "August 1850 at the latest." All the *Manifesto*'s expectations "have been completely fulfilled!" he argued. But they were fed up: they expelled Dr. Marx. A discerning comrade wrote:

> In order to supplant the aristocracy he needs a strength he can find only among the workers. So he has built his system around them. But he laughs at the fools who join in his proletarian litany.

To win back their deserting army, Engels urged, Marx must provide "proof" of "this theory of ours." A book—"a really fat volume" —was the answer. "What will become of all the gossip and scandal that the emigrant mob can bring up when you can retaliate with the book?" From Germany followers wrote that they were "starving" for the book. From Germany his most gifted follower, Ferdinand Lasalle, an eloquent lawyer, wrote that he was "starving" for the book that would provide the "proof" of the truths proclaimed in the *Manifesto*. A Cologne cell member wrote that the German communists "could not wait" for it because it would have "very great propaganda value."

So Marx went to work in the British Museum Library, burrowing through what he termed in his letters to Engels "the economic shit." Indeed, his whole project was not to discover objective truth in economics and social science, but to build a powerful ideological and propaganda weapon that would mobilize a mighty political movement and promote him to its head as philosopher-king.

Yet weeks became years—crammed with feverish work and expectation. Marx and Engels kept postponing "the day." In 1854 Marx, earning a few dollars as a London correspondent, assured New York *Tribune* readers that the European revolution was about to "step forth in shining armor, sword in hand." In 1857 Engels, with his youthful military experience and as the self-designated future commander-in-chief of the revolutionary armies, began cramming on military books and fox-hunting so he would be in physical shape to "throw myself at once into the existing organization of the Prussian, Austrian, Bavarian and French armies." From London, Marx wrote, "I am working like mad, day and night, putting my economic studies together so that I may at least have the outlines clear before the deluge comes." Ten more years passed, with yearly forecasts of imminent revolution, before Marx published *Das Kapital*.

The work bitterly disappointed his panting followers. "Where does this get you? What good is it?" one asked. In Germany the founder of the Marxist party responded almost in tears, "I have never been so disappointed in any book." Despite Engels' ghosted reviews, both praising and denouncing it, *Das Kapital* sold only 200 copies in its first year.

As economics, Marx's work was simply a farce. Increasing pauperization of the masses? Europe's prosperity increased, and mostly in those countries whose capitalist economies had developed best. Longer work hours imposed by greedy capitalists? Even as Marx tried documenting his prediction, legislation dropped the workday maximum almost everywhere from 14 and 16 hours to 10. (The British did it in 1847, one year before the *Manifesto!*) Was the state merely "the organization of the exploiting class," and legislatures and laws their committees and instruments? Those same "committees of capitalists," the governments and legislatures, consistently narrowed the limits of exploitation as Marx wrote. The very documents he used to prove the misery of workers and factory conditions were official British Government factory inspectors' reports that produced public outcry and regulatory laws. Suffrage laws in Germany, France and England made the factory worker's vote equal to the millionaire's. The "Iron Chancellor" Bismarck, who created the world's first social security pension system for workers, with tragic prophecy twitted the tiny Marxist party in Germany's Parliament:

If only I could find out what the future state would be in line! We can only catch glimpses through the cracks. If every man has to have his share allotted from above, we come to a prison existence where everyone is at the mercy of keepers. In our modern prisons the warden is at least a recognized official against whom one can lodge a complaint. But who will be the keepers in the socialist prison? There will be no possibility of complaints. They will be the most merciless tyrants ever seen, and the rest will be their slaves.

Poor Marx! As he worked away in the British Museum Library, the world simply ignored him.

In 1883 Karl Marx died a lonely exile in London. He was still waiting for "the realization of philosophy" and the resolution between "what is and what ought to be" that he had envisioned as a youthful collegian. Engels lived twelve years longer and saw democracy progress much further. "History has shown us to have been wrong," he wrote shortly before death. "The mode of struggle of 1848 is today obsolete in every respect. We, the 'revolutionists' and subverters', are striving far better on legal methods."

Chapter 11
WHAT MADE MARXISM TICK?

Political prejudices, preferences, and creeds are often formulated in highly rational form, but they are grown in highly irrational ways. When they are seen against the developmental history of the person, they take on meanings which are quite different from the phrases in which they are put.

The prominence of hate in politics suggests that we may find that the most important private motive is a repressed and powerful hatred of authority, a hatred which has come to partial expression and repression in relation to the father.

—Harold Lasswell, 1930
Psychopathology and Politics

THE EMOTIONAL ENGINE　　How can we understand the extraordinary picture of pathology and philosophy we have traced in the origins of "Marxism"?

Even as a child, Karl Marx's first recorded response to human society revealed an underlying hostility. His outstanding trait was a fierce hate. As with so many young radicals in our day, Marx's language of hate appeals to them more than his logic. Marx's sister Sophie recalled that Karl was "a terrible little tyrant" who turned to his remarkable gift of words into a fearsome weapon, fashioning cruelly cutting lampoons and satirical verses with which he would bully playmates. Repeatedly his imperious and volcanic hostility struck others who knew him. The Russian liberal, Paul Annenkov, found Marx at 27 "haughty, almost contemptuous. His sharp voice rang like metal, remarkably suited to the radical judgements he habitually delivered on men and things. His tone expressed his own firm conviction that his destiny was to reign over men's minds, dominate their wills and dictate their laws. Before my eyes stood the personification of a democratic dictator." A few months later during Germany's 1848 revolution Marx similarly impressed the Cologne democratic congress. "Never have I seen a man of such offensive, insupportable arrogance," recorded 19-year-old fellow delegate Carl Schurz, who later emigrated to America and became a noted journalist and political leader. Moreover, "Marx would not give even a moment's condescending consideration to any opinion that differed

[172]

from his own." In London exile a young Prussian officer saw in Marx, then 30—

an insolence worthy of Napoleon . . . He laughs at the fools who join in his proletarian litany. If he had as much heart as intelligence, if he could love as intensely as he can hate, I would go through fire for him. But personal ambition in its most dangerous form has eaten away anything that was good in him. Everything he does is aimed at the acquisition of personal power.

Marx's capacity for hate impressed even his closest family. To his own parents the natural brilliance of their "fortune child" seemed flawed by a strange "demon" of defiance and rage within. After Marx's death his daughter in an affectionate, worshipful portrait for followers felt compelled to beg understanding "that he could hate so fiercely only because he was so true and tender." A century later, a French historian studying notebooks the 26-year-old Marx kept in Paris on the economics of Adam Smith, Ricardo, and Mill found leaping forth from every page a *"colere vindictive."* Marx called for a "reckless criticism of all that exists, reckless in that it shrinks neither from its own conclusions nor conflict with the powers-that-be," what our own radicals would today call "the establishment." Says a distinguished American scholar:

The fiery spirit of revolt that breathes in this passage never abated as long as Marx was alive, and it remained one of the few most essential elements of Marxist ideology, pervading everything the man wrote.[1]

More than any philosophical precept or economic reality, this passionate hate is the enduring power and appeal that Karl Marx imparted to the system that bears his name. To the modern psychiatrist his life from early childhood to maturity, from the philosophy that sprang from his brain to the agonizing migraine headaches and boils that tortured his body, provides compelling signs of deep compulsive hositility and aggressive emotions born of overreaching ambitions and parental prodding. It is one of history's ripe ironies that Karl Marx was the opposite of what he tried to appear—a dispassionate philosopher rationally blueprinting a "scientific" world transformation. Instead he was a "compulsive revolutionary," condemned by his own frustrations and failures to see the world in terms of struggle, bloodshed, and hate. That the so-called ruling class will have to be overthrown by violent revolution is an article of faith and a prediction, not a scientific observation. It tells us more about the personality of the prognosticator than about any objective reality.

How this fierce volcano began to burn in Marx's inner being is lost in the mists of his childhood. We can only conjecture at its origin and marvel at its ferocity. But in the young man we can see how the fierce collision of his romantic idealism and poetic aspirations with the harsh limits of his own world and talent stoked the furnace of hatred.

"EXPULSION FROM EDEN"   During the Cologne-Kreuznach interlude, Karl Marx wrote two essays that offer lightning-like flashes of insight into his inner being. The first he wrote just after he moved from the University of Berlin into the real world. As a free-lancer he contributed an essay to the *Rheinische Gazette* on the Rhenish Diet's debates on press freedom. Except for a couple of poems, it was his first published work. He dissected the Prussian king's censorship policies. But the true threat to press freedom, he concluded, was not so much the government as the reality of economic necessity. "Is a press which degrades itself to a trade free?" he asked. A writer must certainly earn money in order to live and write, but he should not exist and write in order to earn money. The first freedom of the press must consist of its *emancipation from commerce.*

The second essay Marx wrote at 25, after his expulsion from his Cologne editorship. He entitled it "On the Jewish Question." It was intended to answer two treatises by Bruno Bauer on the political emancipation of the Jews. He had not yet read von Stein or begun to study economics or adopted the concepts of "capitalism" and "proletariat." Just as he had argued about the press a year earlier, Marx argues that Jews can be free only when they are freed from the necessities of making a living. Throughout, he identifies Jewry with what he later termed "capitalism." What is it that makes a Jew a Jew? His commercialism, his talent for business and moneymaking. "What is the basis of Judaism? *Practical* need, self-interest. What is the worldly cult of the Jews? *Buying and selling.* What is their worldly god? *Money.*" They are slaves to the necessity of earning money, just as the press and the writer are slaves to the same necessity. "Very well then: emancipation from buying and selling and from money— that is to say, from practical, real Judaism—would be the self-emancipation of our age. An organization of society which abolished the preconditions and thus the very possibility for buying and selling would make the Jew impossible," claims Marx. He rails against "the indignity of buying and selling" and "hucksterism" and equates freedom for Jews with freedom from all mankind in "the emancipation from commercialism and money, and consequently from practical real Jewry . . . The emancipation of the Jews is the emancipation of society from Jewry."

In short, the young intellectual seems to equate human freedom with emancipation from the practical necessity of having to earn a living! He is rebelling against the "expulsion from Eden" that accompanies passage from childhood and adolesence to mature adulthood and independence! He is rebelling against his father's demand that he "make a place for himself in the world," that he submit to the necessity of earning a living by studying law! He is raving neurotically and trying desperately to escape from the condition into which he was born: his Jewishness and the detested necessity of earning a living. His identification of salvation for all mankind as "the emancipation from commercialism and money" reflects the rebellious young poet's battles with his father over choosing a profession and applying the self-discipline required to succeed in it!

"The more we want to change others, the less we feel the need to change ourselves," observes one twentieth-century psychiatrist.[2]

THE MORBID MARX   When Marx was 30, at the start of his London exile when he was drinking heavily, he suffered the first of a series of ill-defined liver attacks that he was to experience the rest of his life. They returned regularly each spring, lasting up to three months. He complained of jaundice, found himself "yellower than a quince," and suffered frequent vomiting attacks. He also complained of a nervous derangement, blaming it on the liver, "which causes more suffering than the liver itself."[3] He thought his ailment hereditary—a liver attack was blamed for his father's death. At least one doctor told him flatly the source of his ailment was of a nervous nature.[4]

Marx also had frequent migraine attacks. He would have such sudden pains that he would be forced to set aside his book; a black veil would cover his eyes and he had difficulty breathing. Once he experienced paralysis—a common migraine symptom.

Modern behavioral scientists have identified a characteristic personality constellation in migraine patients.[5] Typically, during childhood the migrainoid has been pushed to perform beyond his capacity, thus engendering feelings of inadequacy and frustration. He has been prevented from expressing normal aggressive feelings constructively by the rigid attitudes of the adults in his environment. He tends to be a perfectionist, and is generally rigid in his thinking and excessively aggressive toward his environment. The personality picture is usually one of *chronically repressed rage.*[6]

At 45 Marx suffered a new plague—boils which occasionally had to be lanced and dressed. But during a trip home to Trier after his mother's death to settle the estate, he suffered massive furunculosis —successive generations of boils. He ran a fever and suffered much pain. Two months passed before he was able to return to London, but the "disgusting and perfidious" disease recurred for years in the fall and winter.

"The world will have cause to regret my carbuncles," Marx remarked upon completing *Das Kapital.* It is not altogether absurd to accept the comment at face value. For both the book and the boils seem to have been common symptoms of a deep repressed rage within this tortured human being.[7] All his life, he warred with the universe. He created a myth of a divided Manichean world, with himself leading the Forces of Light. "Capital," in his mind, personified greed, acquisitiveness, commercialism, the "practical Jewry" and social climbing which he rebelled against in his father. "Labor"—the workers—was the personification of man's creative spirit, the poet in us wanting to be free to pursue a vision. It personified the romantic young sophomore struggling to express himself poetically, wanting to be free of the father's urging to "make a place for yourself in the world." The rage within emerged in both his physical ailments and his philosophical structure.

Biographer Ruhle cites two major sources of neurosis in Marx's background.

One was his position as first-born son in a family with a high tradition of intellectual achievement and with a doting father who regarded him as a "wonder child." *"The urge to be godlike shapes his plans in life and guides all his activities,"* says Ruhle. Like many parents today the father's voice constantly called after him: "Show what you can do! Climb! Have a brilliant career! Do something extraordinary! Be first!" This will-to-conquer and urge to superiority were noted by many acquaintances and biographers; they are manifestations of an inferiority complex.

The second source of Marx's neurosis was his Jewish origin. He initially identified "capitalism," which became the passionate hate of his life, with "practical Jewishness . . . the empirical essence of Judaism, huckstering, self-interest, money." Reading this essay, Ruhle says,

> The reader cannot escape the feeling that he is ostentatiously showing his opposition to Judaism, is demonstratively severing himself from his own race, and by emphasizing his anticapitalist tendencies is declaring himself before all the world not to be a Jew. But one who takes so much trouble to declare that he is not a Jew must have reason for being afraid of being regarded as a Jew. I think there can be no doubt that this social factor of Marx's Jewish origin intensified his sense of inferiority, and must have increased his urge toward compensatory achievements.[8]

On virtually every point where we can check the known facts of Karl Marx's life and personality, he fits the personality profile of the authoritarian personality as it has been mapped by contemporary social scientists. The congruence suggests the conclusion that his personality and world view reflected a deep tension in early parent-child relations that commonly produces a compulsive intolerance of ambiguity and a compulsion to render dogmatic value judgments in terms of good and bad, tossing people into neat pigeonholes of "we" and "they." Another trait common to such authoritarian personalities is a preoccupation with power; this develops from a flawed parent-child relationship in which conformity to parental values arises not from love and healthy identification and internalization but from fear of deprivation or punishment.[9]

Typically this personality distortion is born of the parents' marginality and *exaggerated concern with social status*. Such people posit a rigid and externalized set of values. They consider "good" what is socially accepted and helpful in social climbing, and "bad" whatever deviates and is socially inferior. According to Dr. Else Frenkel-Brunswik: "The less the parents can accept their marginality, the more urgent becomes the wish to belong to the privileged groups. With this narrow and set path in mind such parents are likely to be intolerant of any manifestation on the part of the children which seems to deter from, or to oppose, the goal decided upon. The more urgent the social needs of the parents the more they are apt to view the child's behavior in terms of their own instead of the child's needs."[10]

The dogmatic child of such parents exhibits three closely related traits: a deprecation of the present, a premonition of catastrophic upheaval, and a longing for sweeping change. The tendency to wish for hazy, all-out change rather than for methodical progress shows how poorly the dogmatic child is rooted in the daily task of living. He harbors a deep fascination with the thought of chaos and destruction, and thus is attracted to leaders or ideologies that justify such license. Ideas that do not agree with the rigid, simplistic prescribed solutions of his ideal world threaten his psychological survival, because they jeopardize his method of handling repressed anxieties and his suppressed reservoir of hate and resentment toward parental authority figures. The fact that these feelings against parents have to be excluded from the consciousness contributes to a general lack of introspection and insight, a rigidity of defense and a "narrowness of the ego." In fact, this repression becomes a gigantic barrier that not only inhibits the psyche's inner vision but hinders the subject's entire relationship with outside reality. It produces a personality rigidity in even such basic functions as perception, cognition, problem-solving and in fields far removed from social or emotional involvement. Such a personality becomes a creature viewing the outside world through cracked windowpanes.

This parent-child profile might well have been drawn of Hirschel Marx and the young Karl.

The evidence is thus compelling that Marx was a victim of deep emotional disorder that produced not only his grave psychosomatic symptoms—his migraine attacks and other bodily ills—but his ideological "ism." We might almost declare that his repressed volcanic passions produced both the eruptions on his body and the fierce red boils he left on the politics of humanity. Obviously Marx was motivated by something other than humanitarian compassion. We see in him a primeval destructive revolutionary urge grafted onto a humanitarian reform movement under a cloak of liberal and utopian terminology. The resulting confusion is such that many liberals even in our own day have not fully sorted out the distinction between violence and reform, nor have they rooted from their ranks all the compulsive revolutionaries.

WHY MARXISM SPREAD   Marx's contribution to the birth of revolutionary radicalism was by 1848 virtually complete. The intellectual power of this movement was produced in the years 1838–48. These were the years of Marx's life that influenced Lenin and his successors. Bolshevik theorists of the early Soviet republic such as Bukharin said they preferred the writings of the "younger Marx." *Das Kapital* they recognized implicitly or explicitly was only an attempt to marshall factual evidence to "prove" the preconceived apocalyptic theory they all accepted anyway for the same nonrational, nonempirical reasons that the young Marx concocted it in the first place. Many realized, upon sampling Marxism, that its violence and dogmatism were out of tune with the realities of late nineteenth-century Europe. Thus revisionism began, and Engels, outliving Marx by twelve years, endorsed it. But many did not see the divergence. It was a blindness induced by compulsive self-interest.

Marx was the first major thinker of the Industrial Revolution to advance a strategy of social change that was "scientific" and "certain." Seeking a blueprint for the rational reconstruction of society, intellectuals and reformers of all emotional inclinations, nonviolent as well as revolutionary, embraced his thought. Many dogmatic personalities and closed minds were attracted to his simplified thought package because it provided an outlet for self-righteous, messianic hate, and because it satisfied their struggle for significance and their quest for a messianic role. Many political opportunists found in the Marxist package the organizing constitutive ideology they needed to mobilize the industrial workers into political parties and labor unions and make themselves economic and political powerbrokers. And so Marx's individual pathology proved to be an epidemic philosophical-psychological mutation—a cancerous idealism that would become infectious to all radicals.

Marx converted the comforting, protecting, and escape-providing Jewish tribal doctrine of "God's Chosen People" to a non-Jewish generic form that could be marketed to gentiles much as Jesus's doctrine was marketed in the first century. Marxism spread for much the same reason among the same sort of rootless urban people in the new industrial era: railway worker, peasant, college professor—all could become God's elite and obtain salvation, escape, and comfort by the simple act of profession. "I believe. I am History's Chosen, the vanguard of humanity and the New Jerusalem." It proved a marketable package around the world. A railroad worker in Sudan, a dockworker in Singapore, a village schoolteacher in Central America—each could elevate himself above his fellows simply by believing and professing. Marx furnished "new gods for the vacant shrine" to a new self-anointed priesthood.

The ironic tragedy of Marx's theory of change through economic class struggle was that he, the romantic idealist, ruled out common humanity, compassion, mutual respect, compromise, and selflessness. His great crime was that he dethroned man's civilizing emotion—love and the spirit of cooperation—for his more primitive, monstrous emotion, hate. By emphasizing the baser emotion in man's ambivalent Jekyll-Hyde nature, Marx erected a throwback philosophy, anti-civilization and anti-*homo sapiens*. His philosophy was profoundly reactionary, for it returned men to the jungle law of a might-makes-right struggle and a "divine right" rule by a "new class" revolutionary elite.

The power and durability of Marx's doctrine is not in its sociological soundness, but in the fact that it rationalizes and justifies hate, and provides visible and accessible hate targets to satisfy one's frustrations with an imperfect and un-ideal world.

That is why Marx's ideas appeal so to angry young men; and why so many young Marxists become ex-Marxists as they grow older and understand more. The mature man knows that man is far too varied —and far too wicked—to become the Superman of the postrevolutionary dream; far too complex, in short, to be forced into Rousseau's or Marx's intellectual iron maiden.

There are many young Marxists, but relatively few old Marxists. Marx's doctrine is a young man's delight and an old man's poison.

Thus Marx's ideology was destined to survive. It abounded with hate-targets and slogans. Eager politicians of the embryonic European labor movement soon discovered weapons in his ideological framework they could use to mobilize the growing masses of industrial workers for wresting political power from the craftsmen, shopkeepers, landowners and industrialists in the parliaments and chanceries. A young Russian radical lawyer named Lenin found the propaganda and organizational weapons that he and his Bolsheviks needed to batter the czarist autocracy with strikes, riots, and urban insurrections. From Marx's romantic poet's dream of a utopian world, more ruthless power seekers from Lenin and Stalin to Mao and Castro fashioned intellectual mortar for the deadliest tyranny the world has ever known. Its victims in the twentieth century are estimated at upwards of 50 million dead.

Hate is a mighty engine, and the apocalyptic rages of the young Dr. Marx lived on, engulfing succeeding generations of young radicals. And each generation since has had to fight its own battle with the cancerous, corrupting compound of idealism and hate he created. In each, like Marx, some have not waked up to the wondrous reality of continuing human revolution until they have already missed it. They, too, become idealists who see red.

III. THE RUSSIAN JACOBINS

Chapter 12
CHERNYSHEVSKY: THE GREAT PREDECESSOR

The appearance of strong personalities has a decisive influence in history. They impose their character on the direction of events, speed up their course, impart regularity to the chaotic agitation of the forces produced by the movement of the masses. The new type has been born and is multiplying fast. We did not see these people six years ago. Three years ago, they were despised and held in contempt. But it does not matter what one thinks of them now. In a few years, in a very few years, people will appeal to them: Save us! And whatever they say *will be obeyed by all.*

—Chernyshevsky,
What Is To Be Done?

DESTINY CALLING   Lenin is the founding titan of twentieth-century totalitarianism. In him, radicalism came full flower, reaching the zenith of its evolution from Adam Weishaupt's Illuminati, with their concept of a secular priesthood preaching a secular religion, Robespierre's "Republic of Virtue," and Buonarroti's network of secret Jacobinic societies. Lenin developed the concept of "the professional revolutionary" and the design of a system of mass organizations dominated by a central cartel of professional organization men. He devised a formal technology of mass manipulation, hate propaganda, and social demolition. Moreover, he improved upon Robespierre's notion of a revolutionary dictatorship by adding another dimension to the "Reign of Terror"—the concentration camp, which Stalin and Hitler perfected to genocidal proportions.

But Lenin synthesized more than he invented. He pulled together elements that were "in the air" in late nineteenth-century Russia, and only by considering his Russian progenitors can we understand the roots of Leninism.

Soviet historians themselves award the title of "the Great Predecessor" to Nicholas Gavrilovich Chernyshevsky. Born ten years after Marx, he was the son of a Russian Orthodox priest. Because family tradition had predestined Chernyshevsky for the priesthood, he spent his youth in a seminary.

From earliest youth Chernyshevsky had considered himself destined to eminence. Even his seminary peers and teachers regarded him as a future star of the Orthodox Church. At 16 he knew Latin,

Greek, Hebrew, French, German, English, and Polish. The Bible, the gospels, the legends of the saints, and the other theological tracts left a peculiar stamp on his mind. Always exuding a chiliastic outlook, he was convinced that the day would soon come for those who had abided by the "true faith"—when, in the words of the Prophet Amos, "the mountains will flow with wine."[1]

A TOUCH OF MEGALOMANIA   All this training and experience left him with a strong touch of megalomania. Abandoning the clerical career, in 1846, at 18, he went to St. Petersburg University, and then became briefly a high school teacher. When only 20, in his diary he described himself as a future leader, "a leader and one of the main personalities of the extreme Left." Already he was a determined Jacobin "Montagnard," "a supporter of socialists and communists," and an advocate of "dictatorship." He recorded "an irresistible longing for the imminent revolution" and dreamed of a secret printing press and of writing appeals for revolt. Three years later, he considered his knowledge so great that he could write "an encyclopedia of knowledge and life." "Since the time of Aristotle, no one has done what I want to do; I will be a good teacher to the people for centuries."

This young self-annointed messiah was soon attracted to Russia's leading literary journal, *The Contemporary*. Founded by the poet Pushkin shortly before his death in 1837, *The Contemporary* had risen by the late 1850s to the then-huge circulation of over 6,000. Edited by the radical poet Nekrasov, it featured Turgenev, the young Tolstoy, and many other leading lights of this flowering period of Russian literature. In 1853 Nekrasov recruited Chernyshevsky, who at 25 began contributing critiques, essays and articles. Chernyshevsky changed the direction and significance of the magazine, making it the beacon of radicalism. Soon he found himself, still in his twenties, Russia's most influential social and literary critic, the intellectual guide of the new intelligentsia. Though muffled by czarist censorship, *The Contemporary*, under Chernyshevsky's guidance, soon passed Alexander Herzen's London-based and uncensored *The Bell* in influence.

Chernyshevsky dodged the censors by the simple device often employed by revolutionary radicals: the coded Aesopian jargon of fables, veiled allusions, allegories, and cryptic language. To a censor lacking the code key, Chernyshevsky's writings, brimming with great revolutionary ideas, seemed obtuse, dull, empty. As Vera Ivanova Zasulich—a young firebrand of the following generation of "People's Freedom (or Will)" and a future colleague of Lenin—explained to a young Bolshevik:

When Chernyshevsky introduced some mysterious hieroglyph into his articles, he always explained what he meant to his friends and to the chief contributors of *The Contemporary*. These explanations got through to revolutionary circles, and were eagerly passed on by word of mouth. Even after Chernyshevsky had been exiled to Siberia and could no longer explain his articles, there circulated for a long time a sort of key for the clear understanding of things he was compelled to put only in a very veiled and opaque form.[2]

Thus, in an article on the organization of communist agricultural associations in Russia, Chernyshevsky hinted that the great number of "ancient buildings" scattered all over the country would become quite useful. Though he inserted obscure and obtuse sentences to throw off the censor, his radical readers knew that he was referring to monasteries and churches and meant that they were to be abolished and their properties used to organize Fourier-like "phalansteries."

Chernyshevsky's writings seethed with a fierce hatred and sarcastic scorn of liberalism. For example, the liberal factions in Italy "imagine that political revolutions can be carried out without any incidences of disturbing the peace in the streets." Or, an Italian liberal "as is customary among the liberals idealistically [has] held two equally dreamy ideas in his head which contradicted each other: that the people are wild beasts which must not be let out of the cage, and that the people are capable of imperturbable gentleness and persistent observation of all good forms." Although the czar's censor —for whom liberals were a problem—saw nothing wrong with such commentary, Chernyshevsky's readers easily understood the radical message.

Chernyshevsky sought only absolute solutions to social problems. "Either-or: there is no middle"—such was his psychology. A materialist similar to Ludwig Feuerbach, a positivist like Auguste Comte, and a determinist, he fashioned his models of socialist institutions and private cooperatives after the schematic ideas of Charles Fourier, Owen, Robert Dale, and Louis Blanc. He worshipped Robespierre and Blanqui. Personally, he was turbulent and difficult to get along with. K.D. Kavelin, a *Contemporary* collaborator, said of Chernyshevsky:

Such a cantankerous fellow, such a bully, such a quarrelsome fellow sowing discord and strife, such a tactless and self-assured individual I have never seen before in my life.[3]

"TAKE UP THE AXE!" In 1860 Chernyshevsky wrote an anonymous letter, signed simply "A Russian," to *The Bell*, Herzen's revolutionary journal in London. For the first time, through the uncensored pages of *The Bell* of March 1, 1860 he was able to express himself freely, and his radical formulation shook the young Russians to their foundations. He urged Herzen to cease his panegyrics to the czar and to abandon hope for revolution from above. He lumped the "liberal landowners, liberal professors, liberal authors" with the hated czarist monarchy. He mourned Nicholas I, the reactionary autocrat, because "under him the needed work could be carried through to the ultimate end," whereas the more liberal Alexander, who was freeing the serfs, raised hopes for peaceful reforms, filled people's minds with nonsensical pleas for patience and moderation, and prolonged the idiotic faith in the good intentions of the czar-autocrat. Thus, peaceful progress delayed the day of revolution; only violence could cleanse the national life. In striking the psychological chord that links Buonarroti and Lenin, Chernyshevsky formulated the classical position of the true revolutionary, so often quoted by Lenin: *"The worse things are, the better for us."* His peroration is a bloody-minded Babeuvist call:

> Our situation is intolerable . . . Only the axe can save us, and nothing but the axe! Change your tune and let your *Bell* not call to prayer, but let it sound the alarm! Summon Russia to take up the axe!

Chernyshevsky's letter inspired a young student-apostle named P.G. Zaychnevsky to produce a "proclamation" summarizing the mentor's social and political program. He published it in the name of the "Central Revolutionary Committee" in May 1862 under the title "Young Russia." It was one of the most bloodthirsty proclamations ever circulated in Russia:

> Soon the day will come when we shall unfurl the great banner of the future, the red banner, and with the battle cry, "Long live the Social and Democratic Republic in Russia," march upon the Winter Palace to exterminate everyone there. It is quite possible that the affair will end with the extirpation of the Imperial family alone, i.e., some one hundred people in all. But it is also possible that the entire Imperial Party will arise as one to defend its Emperor. In that case, fully confident of ourselves, of our strength, of the sympathy of the people with our cause, and the glorious future of Russia thus destined to be the first to realize the great ideal of Socialism, we shall utter the cry, "Use the

axe," and then crush the Imperial Party, dealing with it as mercilessly as it is now dealing with us. . . .

We are convinced that the revolutionary party which is to assume power must maintain its present centralized organization so that it may build the foundation for a new social-economic order in the shortest possible time. This organization must usurp government through a dictatorship and must stop at nothing. Elections to the National Assembly must be directed by the government which shall immediately make certain that its members include none of those who are in favor of the present order, should any such persons still be found alive.[4]

We shall be more consistent than the great terrorists of 1792. We shall not draw back if we see that the overthrow of the existing system demands the shedding of twice as much blood as was shed by the Jacobins in the 1790s. . . . With full faith in ourselves, in the people's sympathy, and in the glorious future of Russia, to whose lot it has fallen to be the first to bring about the triumph of socialism, we will shout as one man: "Take up your axes!" and then we will attack the supporters of the throne with no more mercy than they show us; we will kill them in the squares, if these low swine dare to appear on them, kill them in their houses, kill them in the narrow streets of the towns, in the broad avenues of the capitals, kill them in the villages and hamlets. Remember, who is not with us is against us, and who is against us is an enemy, and enemies must be destroyed by all possible means. Long live the Russian social and democratic republic.[5]

This rhetorical bomb circulating among the radical student circles of Moscow and St. Petersburg exploded amid a wave of hysteria over the "nihilists." Ivan Turgenev coined the term in his novel, *Fathers and Sons,* published in 1861. The work reads like a portrait of America's "New Left" hippies and radicals of the 1960s. The central character, Bazarov, is a hippie type, a professed nihilist scorning the simple values of the countryside in which the novel is set. The book created a sensation. Radicals accused Turgenev of turning reactionary and of defaming the young. Even Russia's conservatives were reluctant to accept the validity of Turgenev's portrait of nihilistic youth as contemptuous of everything from God and marriage to the art of Raphael. But the Chernyvshevsky-Zaychnevsky proclamation convinced the doubters. It demanded "the abolition of that most immoral institution—marriage," among other things, as a hindrance to "human progress and the family." (Its authors admitted they intended "to make all the liberal and reactionary swine sick.") Moreover, in the spring of 1862 large-scale fires plagued St. Petersburg, possibly arson or simply the result of deplorable safety practices amid sprawling wooden buildings. The reactionary press blamed the "nihilists," and the radicals blamed right-wing *agents-provocateurs* bent on sabotaging the emancipation of the peasants scheduled for the coming year. Regardless, the czarist secret police seized the opportunity for a wholesale repression. *The Contemporary* was suspended for eight months. Chernyshevsky himself was jailed in July 1862.

"WHAT IS TO BE DONE?"   In the forbidding Peter and Paul Fortress, Chernyshevsky began a novel to answer Turgenev, who the younger generation felt had slandered and misrepresented their ideas. Entitled *What Is To Be Done? Tales About New People*, the work appeared anonymously in 1863 in numbers 3–5 of the revived *Contemporary*.

Russian radicalism—indeed the world radical movement—has never been the same. Chernyshevsky's novel thrilled and inspired three generations of Russian radicals. *What Is To Be Done?* recruited hundreds into the new priesthood of revolution. Memoirs or statements to police interrogators contain such declarations as, "I became a revolutionary at the age of ＿＿＿ after reading Chernyshevsky." He was far more influential than Marx in the Russian revolutionary movement and, indirectly as we will see, in world radicalism. As literature, *What Is To Be Done?* was the same ponderous and dull allegory Chernyshevsky had always written. But as a prescription and vision of apocalyptic revolution, it was miraculously moving to those who knew the "key" to deciphering it. To the discerning reader, the novel delineated a new personality type and role on the world stage—the "new people" or "professional revolutionary." It shaped a pattern and cast a die that was to stamp hundreds—and one day literally millions—of True Believer revolutionaries.

What Is To Be Done? was the first work in Russian literature to develop a picture of life in the ideal society of the future—the first Russian utopia. And Chernyshevsky's "new people" were the revolutionaries who would usher in the dream.

"MOVERS OF THE MOVERS"   Chernyshevsky always used a euphemism for his revolutionary. A "decent," "real," or "new" man finds his highest interest and most satisfying sensual pleasure in serving the cause of society. His "ideal men" are those able to *"realize the correct principles."*

Such persons are few in number but through them the general life blossoms and without them, the people would suffocate. They are the quintessence of things, they are like the distinctive fragrance of rare wine. From them comes strength and originality: they constitute the flower of the best people. They are the mover of the movers, the salt of the earth. Honest men and good men exist aplenty, but those of whom I am thinking are rare specimens.

"The appearance of strong personalities" has a decisive influence in history. They impose their character on the "direction of events, speed up their course, *impart regularity to the chaotic agitation of the forces produced by the movement of the masses.*" Never using the term "revolutionary," Chernyshevsky described his élitist vanguard theory with all the force at his command. He borrowed from the Bible. His work is a hymn to his "new type":

Every one of them is a courageous individual who does not hesitate or retreat, who is capable of dedicating himself to the cause and, once he elects to do so, takes it up with such force that it does not slip out of his hand.

Through yet rare,

the new type has been born and is multiplying fast. It is a product of the times and is a sign of the times. We did not see these people six years ago. Three years ago, they were despised and held in contempt. But it does not matter what one thinks of them now. In a few years, in a very few years, people will appeal to them: Save us! And whatever they say *will be carried out by all.*

The Aesopian disguise is obvious—and it was to the young people who read Chernyshevsky. "New Men!" An elite of rare leaders who, like Moses, would lead the Chosen People out of the Wilderness into the Promised Land! Modern messiahs! Men like Robespierre and Blanqui, whom Chernyshevsky idolized.

THE ASCETIC WORLD-SAVER A chief character in *What Is To Be Done?* was Rakhmetev, who lived the pure ascetic life and subjected himself to intense privations in preparing for a higher goal. Chernyshevsky left this "goal" vague, to fool the czarist censors, but his followers knew what it was: namely, the revolution, and the new society in which everyone would be totally free. We see this fierce janissary of the future, for example, reading 82 hours straight, keeping himself awake the first two nights by sheer willpower, fortifying himself in the third with eight cups of strong coffee. Rakhmetev sleeps on nails to harden himself. He lives by the clock: so much time for reading, so much for helping others. He keeps strict rules over his physical, moral, and intellectual life—breaking them only in order to study people. He lives chiefly on raw beefsteak, and is powerfully built. (Here Chernyshevsky drew on Feuerbach, who summed up his exaggerated materialism in the epigram, "Man is what man eats!" and proclaimed the aristocrats ruled because they ate beef and workers would grow strong only when they quit eating potatoes.) Rakhmetev wanders like a nomad as a farm laborer, a carpenter, joining a bank of Volga boat haulers who hold him in awe and make him a legend after he vanishes. He appears at the house of a great European thinker: "I have thirty thousand thalers, I need but five thousand. I beg you to accept the rest." The philosopher, living in poverty, is startled, and asks why. "For the publication of your works," answers Rakhmetev.

Chernyshevsky clings to that article of faith of Rousseau, the natural goodness of man, and yet a thoroughly antidemocratic snobbery comes through his professed belief in democracy and equality. At the death of a virtuous prostitute, her lover-reformer Kirsanov's feelings are described thusly:

> His old love for her had been no more than a youth's desire to love someone, no matter whom. Needless to say Nastenka was never a match for him, for they were not equals in intellectual development. As he matured, he could do no more than pity her . . .

Chernyshevsky's "new men" are certain that they are above the vulgar multitude and are its destined rulers.

What Is To Be Done? became the bible of Russia's young radicals. It became a must in all underground libraries and reading programs. The names of Chernyshevsky's heroes became literary pseudonyms. Their sayings became moral rules. For example, "I will not eat anything that is never available to the simple people. I need to do this in order to feel—even if only in a small way—how limited and hampered their life is in comparison with mine."

The megalomanic and élitist stamp of Chernyshevsky's early seminary experience was strongly imprinted on his novel. On the eve of his long exile to Siberia he wrote his wife: "Our life belongs to history. Hundreds of years will pass, and our names will still be dear to the people. They will think of us with gratitude when our comtemporaries are long dead." He proudly told a police official that his name would live in Russian literature along with Pushkin, Gogol, and Lermontov. He wrote in his novel the role he imagined for himself as an agent of salvation—and the ruler of the Kingdom Come—for all mankind.

THE UNANSWERED LETTER   Chernyshevsky himself was through when he put down his pen in the Peter and Paul Fortress. In 1864 he was subjected to the "civil execution" reserved for important prisoners. Wearing chains, he was driven to a scaffold and exhibited before hundreds of spectators wearing a placard that proclaimed him a "State Criminal." His sentence read seven years hard labor. He was forced to kneel, and a sword was broken over his head. Then he was driven away.

Chernyshevsky was not allowed to return to European Russia until 1883. Near his death in 1889, he was unable to answer a worshipful "fan" letter from an 18-year-old lad who had read his novel and was moved to choose as his lifelong profession that of "revolutionary." The boy was bitterly disappointed that he did not receive an answer. But he was not deterred in his choice of career; the world knows him today by his revolutionary name—Lenin.

Chapter 13
NECHAYEV: "THE REVOLUTIONARY CATECHISM"

> Tiger! Tiger! burning bright
> In the forests of the night,
> What immortal hand or eye
> Could frame thy fearful symmetry?
> . . .
>
> What the hammer? What the chain?
> In what furnace was thy brain?
> What the anvil? What dread grasp
> Dare its deadly terrors clasp?
>
> When the stars threw down their spears,
> And water'd heaven with their tears,
> Did he smile his work to see?
> Did he who made the Lamb make thee?
> . . . .
>
> —William Blake, "The Tiger."

> These deceivers are very clever and have studied particularly carefully the generous side of the human soul, very often of the soul of a youngster, in order to be able to play on it as on a musical instrument . . . Without doubt I could never have been a Nechayev; that is not in my nature. But perhaps, in the early days of my youth, I could have become a Nechayevist . . .
>
> —Dostoyevsky, *Diary of a Writer*, 1873

"THE NECHAYEV MONSTER"   In the fall of 1868, from groaning Russia sprang a monster of revolutionary fanaticism such as the world had never seen before. He studied Buonarroti's book on the Babeuvist Conspiracy, read what he could find on Blanqui's development of the technique of conspiratorial insurrection, and added to their formulas an awesome and incendiary ingredient of his own: *The Catechism of the Revolutionary*. The modern revolutionary movement reflects more strongly the influence of this work than it does of Marx and Engels' *Communist Manifesto*.

The author—that monster of revolutionary fanaticism—was Sergei Nechayev.

We know little of Nechayev's early life. He was born in 1847, at

Ivanovo, a little provincial capital of 40,000 people, 150 miles northeast of Moscow. His father was a sign painter and carpenter. His mother, a seamstress, had been a serf until his father bought her freedom and married her. She died when little Sergei was six. At nine, Sergei apprenticed in a factory, but on his eighth day he went to deliver an envelope, lost his way in a sudden snowstorm, lost the envelope,and was fired. His father, hot with anger, flogged him with a birch rod—his first corporal punishment. Years later, a childhood friend recalled the incident as a turning point that left Nechayev with a core of bitterness—but nothing we know about Nechayev's early life can explain the terrible hate that generated this fiery revolutionary.

Nechayev supposedly was 16 when he learned to read from a private instructor. By the time he was 17 he had struck up a correspondence with a writer about ten years older than he, F. D. Nefedov, the son of a comparatively prosperous serf who had been able to study in Moscow. Nefedov sent him books, and Nechayev asked for more and more. Their correspondence reveals Nechayev's passionate determination to escape at whatever cost the world into which he had been born. His hostility is striking; the three words he uses most often to describe his environment are "deserted," "dirty" and "boring." In 1864, Sergei, then 17, wrote Nefedov: "Reality without any refinement hits me so hard I have to leap into the air."

In August 1865 he went to Moscow, wanting to become a schoolmaster, but he failed his examinations. He finally passed when he was 19. There is a story that he drank heavily for a while, but gave it up. In any case, in April 1866, he went to St. Petersburg and landed a job teaching in a parochial school.

REVOLUTION AMONG THE STUDENTS   Russia's universities bubbled with ferment throughout the 1860s. The Third Department of His Majesty's Chancellery, the political police, kept a close watch —but not close enough to prevent an unbalanced student named Dmitri Karakozov from taking an ill-aimed shot at the czar in 1866. Karakozov was hanged, and 35 of his fellow students were sent to jail. The experience caused liberal Alexander II to turn reactionary. To inculcate respect for authority, students were required to salute the faculty, and all corporate organizations such as fraternities, mutual aid societies, reading rooms and cooperative eating places were forbidden.

In September 1868, an agent from one of the underground student cells in St. Petersburg returned from Switzerland with a newspaper article by that old Russian nobleman-turned-anarchist, Mikhail Bakunin. St. Petersburg's students copied and read this paper, because in it Bakunin defined the role he thought students should play in the revolutionary movement. Following the novelist Herzen, Bakunin admonished the intellectual youth to "go to the people." But he added:

> It is not by founding schools that we will arrive at our goal. A single way is open to us: revolution. Let our people conquer liberty to start with, and they will desire and know how to educate themselves. Our task is to prepare, by propaganda, the uprising of the people.[1]

"TIGER, TIGER, BURNING BRIGHT"   St. Petersburg's most radical students met at the lodgings of a young journalist named Peter Tkachev. At the age of 17 he had been expelled from the university, jailed briefly in student disturbances, and now eked out a living writing. Bakunin's exhortation electrified his circle, and though most still had not the slightest idea of the necessities of revolutionary organization, they declared themselves ready to follow Bakunin's strictures.

In their midst one evening in October 1868 as they sat debating around a smoking samovar, an unknown face appeared. Though he had large shoulders, the newcomer seemed puny. With closely cropped hair and a round face, his eyes alone drew attention: Little and black, their stare seemed to pierce everything. He followed the discussion attentively, showed not the least desire to participate himself, and left without anyone so much as hearing him speak. Tkachev told them a student had recommended him as a "real revolutionist, a peasant who had preserved all the serf's hatred against the masters." Hardly had the door shut, however, than this visitor returned and approached a schoolteacher named Orlov with a rolling fire of impatient questions.

"His name is Nechayev," Orlov told them later, "I believe he is the son of a simple muzhik and that he learned to read only at the age of 16. He did his studying while traveling as a house painter."

This story of a "child of the people," the son of a worker, produced a strong impression, for the students came mostly from the bourgeoisie or *petit noblesse,* and they immediately accorded Nechayev immense prestige. He cultivated this aura by his behavior. He would sit quietly in the corner, and in the midst of the students' abstract theoretical wrangles jump up suddenly as if jabbed with a hot iron, and shout "Remember Karakazov!," thereby invoking the name of the one student who had dared to act instead of talk. In abrupt, machine-gun-like words he would demand a break in all relations with "bourgeois society." He would recite by heart Chemkughikov's celebrated poem on Karakozov's death. Or, as if exhorting soldiers in the midst of a bloody civil war, he would call upon the students to kill as many enemies as possible, that is, government officials and army officers. This wild fanaticism and primitive oratory attracted the wilder sorts and altogether subjected them to the will of his powerful personality. His ferocity entranced the radicals he met. Soon he founded a new group that met in his own room at the parish school where he taught.

They discussed Buonarroti's *Conspiracy of the Equals,* and began to talk about forming a political organization. Nechayev's group was tremendously impressed by Buonarroti's account of the Babeuvist conspiracy and the techniques developed there for propagandizing, organizing, and manipulating the masses. Nechayev himself was enthralled by this concept of a powerful secret paramilitary organization, commanded by a tiny nucleus. Though the ideas of Bakunin and Marx later influenced him, he remained at heart a Babeuvist.[2]

Nechayev convinced himself that the revolution would begin precisely on February 19, 1870, the ninth anniversary of the liberation of the serfs, on which date the serfs would have to decide whether to return a portion of their lands to their former landlords or continue buying it in installments. Nechayev and Tkachev collaborated on *A Program of Revolutionary Action.* They made a giant stride beyond the usual apocalyptic rhetoric—they stressed the necessity "to create the largest number of *revolutionary prototypes* and to develop in society the consciousness of an eventual and inevitable revolution as a way of achieving a better order of things."[3]

It is all there in that sentence—the training of professional revolutionaries, the deployment for mass propaganda and preconditioning, the in group-out group hate targeting process, and the cataclysmic showdown between the Forces of Light and the Forces of Darkness. Nechayev and Tkachev each in his own way elaborated vital elements of this formula, and three decades later Lenin would put them together again in a mighty mold to mass-produce those "revolutionary prototypes."

"THE NECHAYEV TRICK"   In January 1869, many students weary of empty talk decided to organize a series of student assemblies. They found a liberal noblewoman who agreed to let them meet in her ballroom. Secret police were posted to watch each entrance and quietly count arrivals. Nechayev's group wanted to address a petition to the government or the crown prince, and to organize a grand demonstration in front of the czar's Winter Palace. Others resisted, and more arguments followed. Finally one night Nechayev mounted a chair. With a gesture, he ordered silence. "Enough talk!" he cried in a cutting voice. "Let those who are not afraid separate themselves from the cowards! I have prepared a petition and I ask you to sign it immediately!"

At first, Nechayev's friends advanced. After a brief hesitation, most of the others came, one by one, to add their name while Nechayev, a slight smile on his lips, watched the operation. After 97 had signed, suddenly from the hall a voice arose. "Stop! Don't sign! If this list falls into the hands of the police, we'll all be lost!" From all sides, cries arose. "Destroy the list!" But when they looked, it was no longer on the table—and Nechayev had also disappeared. The meeting dissolved in pandemonium.

That night, Nechayev met Vera Zasulich, a 17-year-old girl whose revolutionary career was to span beyond the 1917 revolution to Lenin's rule.

"This very morning I was ordered to police headquarters, and they told me that if the meetings do not stop immediately, I will be arrested,"[4] Nechayev declared.

"In that case, it would be better to renounce them," cried Vera.

"On the contrary," replied Nechayev. "They absolutely must continue. In any case, my arrest is inevitable. Not that I attach the least importance to the demands of the students—but if they are arrested, then sent home to the provinces, that would cause them to serve a revolutionary apprenticeship. They will be filled with resentment against the regime and will make common cause with the people."[5]

The idea revolted Vera: "He does not have the right to doubt the devotion of these young men," she thought. But Nechayev was thinking of a passage he read in Buonarroti's book about Babeuf: "All reflection on the part of the people is to be prevented. . . . It is essential that they should first commit acts which would prevent any retreat." Nechayev had had enough of the students' interminable talk.

The next day Nechayev disappeared. (The petition with 97 names mysteriously turned up 60 years later, after the czar's fall, in the police archives.)[6] A few days later, Vera received by mail an evelope containing two letters. She read the first:

While I was walking today on the bridge to Vassilievsky Island a police wagon passed me loaded with prisoners. A hand reached out through the barred window and dropped a note. At the same time I heard a voice say, "If you are a student, send this on to the address written on it." I am a student and consider it my duty to comply with the request. Please destroy my note immediately so that my handwriting cannot give me away.

A Student

The other note, scribbled in pencil, clearly was in Nechayev's handwriting. It declared:

They are taking me to a fortress, I don't know which. Let the comrades know about it. Do what you can for me. Do not lose courage and continue our work. God willing, we shall see each other again.

NECHAYEV

This word spread like wildfire among the St. Petersburg student community. They took the reference to "a fortress" to mean the forbidding Peter and Paul Fortress which stood on a small island facing St. Petersburg. Nechayev became the first martyr of the student revolt, and the remaining leaders called a mass meeting to demand his release.

The police were puzzled, for they knew he was not in the fortress. In fact, while the students protested and the police searched, Nechayev slipped out of the country to Switzerland.

Nechayev's egotistical, scheming mind designed this brilliant deception to create a legend around himself as a revolutionary leader. He reasoned that a revolution must have a heroic leader, a near-myth with an aura of mystery, and superhuman character who could inspire instant obedience and terrorize as well. And he nominated himself.

Early in March Nechayev wrote student friends explaining in dramatic detail how he escaped from the Peter and Paul Fortress. He had simply put on the coat of a general and sneaked out, he said. Then fleeing to the border he had been arrested in southern Russia, overpowered one of his guards and outdistanced them. Again this story was believed, and the Nechayev legend grew.

BAKUNIN   In Geneva, Nechayev looked up the famed Old Man of the Russian Revolution, Mikhail Bakunin, a leader in the European revolutionary movement for 30 years. Once a wealthy officer in the czar's imperial guard, he had forfeited his Russian estates and had not seen his native land for nearly two decades. Nechayev announced himself as an agent of the "Russian Revolutionary Committee," and Bakunin, now 54 years old, fat, toothless, and leading the despairing life of the exile, listened enthralled as Nechayev spun the wild yarns about his exploits with the police and his great revolutionary organization inside Russia. The old revolutionary patriarch drew new vigor and inspiration from "the tiger cub," "the young savage," or just plain "boy," as he called his new partner. They began to plan a new revolution in Russia, issue manifestoes, and write pamphlets. Bakunin even dieted and lost fifty pounds. The Russian writer Alexander Herzen visited him in May and wrote that he was "charging forward like a locomotive that has got too much steam up and has run off the rails."

During Nechayev's six months in Switzerland, the St. Petersburg post office alone seized 560 mail items he sent involving 387 persons. Of course the czar's police arrested or questioned many of them—exactly as Nechayev ruthlessly calculated. This was the very sort of contempt for other human beings and utter disregard of fairness and decency that went down into Russian revolutionary history as "Nechayevism."

THE CATECHISM OF THE REVOLUTIONARY   Nechayev and Bakunin published several pamphlets in Geneva. One entitled "Principles of Revolution" proclaimed:

> We recognize no other activity but the work of extermination, but we admit that the forms in which this activity will show itself will be extremely varied—poison, the knife, the rope, etc. In this struggle revolution sanctifies everything alike.

However, the ultimate was *The Catechism of the Revolutionary,* one of the most portentous documents in history. It cast the mold for the professional revolutionary which Lenin later would use later for mass-production. As historian E. H. Carr wrote:

> Before Nechayev, none of these young men had been bold enough to press negation to its logical and ultimate conclusion, to reject and defy moral as well as political obligation. Nechayev took the final step. He raised revolution to the status of an absolute good; and he recognized no other kind of moral obligation. He made unscrupulousness a fine art.[7]

When he returned to Russia in 1869, Nechayev had carried along a coded copy of the *Catechism*. Showing it only to his most trusted conspirators, he claimed it was written by the mythical "central committee." Later that year the police found the encoded text on one of his followers, deciphered it, and published it as shocking proof of the savage ferocity of the revolutionaries. It had the desired effect.

THE CATECHISM OF THE REVOLUTIONIST

The Revolutionist's Duties Toward Himself

1. The revolutionist is a doomed man. He has no personal interests of his own—no business affairs, sentiments, attachments, property, not even a name of his own. Everything in him is subordinated to one exclusive interest, one thought, one passion—the revolution.

2. In the very depth of his being not merely in word but in deed, he has broken every bond which ties him to the social order and to the whole civilized world, with all the laws, morals and generally accepted conventions and ethics of that world which he considers his ruthless foe. If he continues to live in it, it will be solely to destroy it the more quickly.

3. The revolutionist despises every sort of dogma and has renounced the peaceful scientific pursuits, leaving them to future generations. He knows only one science, the science of destruction. For this and only for this purpose he will study mechanics, physics, chemistry, and possibly medicine. But every day and night he studies the living science of human beings, their characters, circumstances and all the phenomena of the present social order in its various strata. The object is the same: the quickest possible destruction of this whole filthy order.

4. The revolutionary despises public opinion. He despises and hates the existing social order and code of morals with all its motivations and manifestations. For him morality is everything which contributes to the triumph of the revolution. Immoral and criminal is everything that stands in his way.

5. The revolutionist is a dedicated man. He is merciless toward the State and toward the entire system of educated classes; he can in turn expect no mercy from them. Between him and them there is a continuous and irreconcilable war to the bitter end—whether it be waged openly or secretly. He must be ready to die at any moment. He must train himself to stand torture.

6. Tyrannical toward himself, he must also be tyrannical towards others. All soft and tender affections arising from kinship, friendship, love gratitude, and even honor itself must be obliterated, and in their place there must be the cold and single passion for the revolution. For him there is only one pleasure, consolation and reward—the success of

[197]

the revolution. Day and night he must have one thought, one aim—inexorable destruction. Striving coldbloodedly and indefatigably toward this aim, he must be ready to destroy himself and to destroy with his own hands everyone who stands in his way.

7. The nature of the true revolutionary excludes all romanticism, all sentimentality, all exaltations and enthusiasms. He must also exclude personal hatred and revenge. The revolutionary passion, practiced in every moment of the day until it becomes a habit, must be combined with cold calculation. At all times and all places the revolutionary must refuse to allow himself to be guided by his personal impulses, but only by whatever the general interests of the revolution demand.

The Relations of the Revolutionist Toward His Comrades in the Cause

8. A revolutionist can have no feeling of friendship or attachment to anyone unless, like him, they have proven themselves by their actions to be revolutionists like himself. The measure of friendship, devotion and other obligations towards such a comrade is determined solely by the degree of his usefulness in the practical work of the all-destructive revolution.

9. Solidarity of the revolutionists goes wthout saying. The whole strength of the revolutionary cause is based on it. The fellow revolutionists who stand on the same plane of revolutionary understanding and ardor should as far as possible, discuss all important matters jointly and decide them unanimously. But in accomplishing whatever plan is finally decided upon, the revolutionist must rely altogether upon himself. The contract of revolutionary destruction execution demands that no comrades should come running up with advice and assistance if this detracts from the success of the plan.

10. Each comrade should have under him several revolutionaries of the second or third rank, that is, comrades who are not completely initiated. These he must regard as portions of a common fund of revolutionary capital, to be expended as he thinks fit. He should expend them as economically as possible always attempting to derive the utmost possible use from them. He is to consider himself as capital, fated to be spent for the triumph of the revolutionary cause; however, he has no right personally and alone to dispose of that capital without the consent of the aggregate of the fully initiated.

11. When a comrade is caught in a dangerous extremity, in deciding the question whether or not to save him, the revolutionist must take into consideraton not his personal feelings but solely the interests of the revolutionary cause. Therefore, he must weigh on the one hand the usefulness of the comrade, and, on the other, the expenditure of revolutionary forces necessary to rescue him, and he is to decide according to which side outweighs the other.

The Revolutionist's Relation to Society

12. Whether a new member, after giving proof of loyalty by word and deed, is to be accepted into the organizations is a matter to be decided only by unanimous agreement.

13. The revolutionist enters the world of the State and of the educated privileged classes and lives in it only for the purpose of its fullest and quickest destruction. He is not a revolutionist if he is attached to anything in this world. He must not hesitate to destroy any position, any place, any man—he must hate everything and everybody in it with an equal hate. All the worse for him if he has parents, friends or loved ones; he is not a revolutionist if they can stay his hand.

14. For the purpose of ruthless destruction, the revolutionist can and frequently must live in society while pretending to be something entirely different from what he is. For the revolutionist must penetrate everywhere, into all of the higher and middle classes, the merchant's store, the churches, the nobleman's homes, the bureaucratic world and military circles, into literature, into the Third Department (Secret Police) and even into the Tsar's Winter Palace.

15. All the members of this filthy society can be split up into several categories. In the first category are those who are condemned to death without delay. The organization should draw up a list of persons thus condemned in the order of their relative harmfulness to the success of the cause, and the executions should be carried out according to the prepared order.

16. In making up these lists and for the purpose of establishing the order of execution, one should by no means be guided by the personal villainy of the individual, nor even by the hatred which he calls forth in the organization or among the people. This villainy and this hatred may even be useful insofar as they help to arouse the masses to revolt. It is necessary to be guided only by the measure of usefulness of these executions for the revolutionary cause. Thus, first of all, those men must be destroyed who are particularly harmful to the revolutionary organization and also those whose sudden and violent death may fill the government with the greatest fear and shake its power by depriving it of its most intelligent and energetic men.

17. The second category must consist of persons whom we spare only temporarily so that their bestial behavior may drive the people to inevitable revolt.

18. To the third category belong a great many brutes in high positions distinguished by neither intellect or energy, but due to their position—enjoying riches, connections, influence and power. The revolutionary must exploit them in every possible way; entrap them, confuse them, and, getting hold of their dirty secrets as far as possible, turn them into one's slaves. Their power influence, connections, riches and strength will thus become the inexhaustible treasury and support of various revolutionary enterprises.

19. The fourth category is composed of ambitious politicians and liberals of various shades. We shall pretend we are following them blindly, while in fact we take them under our own control, get possession of all their secrets, compromise them to the utmost, so that there will be no way out for them and they can be used as instruments for stirring up disorder in the State.

20. The fifth category consists of doctrinaires, conspirators, revolutionists: all idle word spillers who orate in meetings or on paper. They must be continually pushed and driven forward to make violent neck-breaking statements, the result of which would be the complete destruction of most and the real revolutionary training of a few.

21. The sixth category is expecially important; women. They should be divided into three main groups. First: those empty-headed, frivolous and vapid women, whom we shall use like the third and fourth category of men. Second: women who are ardent, gifted, and devoted, but who do not give themselves to us because they have not yet worked themselves up to a passionless and austere revolutionary understanding: these are to be used like men of the fifth category. Finally, there are the women who are completely ours, that is fully initiated and having completely accepted our program. They are our comrades. We must regard these women as the most valuable of our treasures; without their help it would be impossible to succeed.

The Attitude of Our Organization Toward the People

22. The organization has no aim other than the complete liberation and happiness of the masses, i.e. of the people who live by manual labor. But convinced that this liberation and achievement of this happiness is possible only by means of an all-destroying popular revolution, the organization will by all its means and all its power further develop and intensify those evils and those miseries until the people's patience is at last exhausted and they are driven to a general uprising.

23. By Revolution the organization does not mean a revolution tailored according to the classical Western model—a pattern which is always restrained by the property rights and the traditions of the social orders of so-called civilization and morality. Until now such a civilization has cast down one political form only to sustitute another, thereby attempting to bring about a so-called revolutionary state. The only salutary form of revolution is one which destroys the entire state to the roots and exterminates all imperial traditions, the whole social order and all the existing classes in Russia.

24. With this end in view the Society refuses to impose any new organization from above. Any future organization will no doubt evolve out of the popular movement and out of life itself. But this is a matter for future generations to decide. Our mission is destruction, terrible, total, universal and merciless.

25. Therefore, in getting closer to the people, we must above all join

those elements of the masses which from the very beginning of the imperial power of Muscovy, have never ceased to protest, not only words but in deeds against everything directly or indirectly connected with the State; against the nobility, the bureaucracy, the clergy, business and against the parasitic kulak. We must join hands with the bold gangs of bandits—the only genuine revolutionists in Russia.

26. To weld these people into a single force which is wholly destructive and wholly invincible—such is the sole object of our organization; this is our conspiracy and our task.

Nechayev's strategy of assassination sounds like a piece of bloody-minded nonsense utterly beyond believing. Yet, in fact, communist guerrilla terrorists have followed Nechayev's strategy of selectivity precisely in the preinsurgency and early violent stages of the guerrilla wars in the Phillippines in 1950–54 and South Vietnam in 1958–63. As an American correspondent in Vietnam in the early 1960s noted:

The Viet Cong never knock off the government official who is either corrupt or a knuckle-head who makes enemies among the people; they go after the able democratic servant who wins loyalty for the government by looking after people's problems.[8]

And when the Black Panther Party launched its campaign of bombings and police assassinations in 1967–71, Nechayev's *Revolutionary Catechism** became one of their favorite propaganda tracts.

---

*For many years historians hotly disputed whether Nechayev or Bakunin wrote the *Catechism*. It was published about the time Bakunin antagonized Marx by trying to take over the First International, and the Marxists tried to pin the blame on Bakunin to discredit him. Some of the phrases are clearly Bakunin's and no doubt he collaborated with Nechayev on it. But the evidence and weight of authority favor Nechayev's primacy in the authorship. The probable truth is that the ideas in the *Catechism* were mostly those of the semiliterate Nechayev who persuaded Bakunin to write them down in coherent form. Regardless of whose hand put it on paper, it reflects Nechayev's energy and ruthless fanaticism, not that of the old man. The *Catechism* may have been a product of the pen of Bakunin; but it was certainly a product of the mind and personality of Nechayev. All authorities agree that Bakunin was deeply under the spell of Nechayev's powerful personality during this period. Most of the support for Bakunin's authorship, apart from the Marxists eager to smear him, hinges on the testimony of one individual: Michael Sazhin, who was a friend of Bakunin in the years 1872–74. He stated in reminiscences published in 1925 that he had seen the original manuscript on the *Catechism* in Bakunin's handwriting. But he was 80 years old in 1925, describing events more than fifty years previously. Moreover, Sazhin was not a trustworthy or unprejudiced witness. The Russian anarchist Lermontov who knew him well described him as "treacherous, vain and selfish." E. H. Carr notes that Sazhin gave contradictory accounts of an unfriendly interview he had with Antonia Bakunin (Carr, p. 471). Bakunin himself had a quarrel with Sazhin that was bitter and lasting, and after this quarrel Bakunin in his diary most frequently used the term "blackguard" to describe Sazhin. Bakunin spoke of his "profound baseness" and wrote a bitter personal letter (Oct. 21, 1874) accusing him of having "done everything possible to kill me physically, morally, socially." This, then, is the man whose testimony is used to support the belief that Bakunin wrote the *Catechism*. See K. J. Kenaflick, *Michael Bakunin and Karl Marx* (London: Freedom Press, 1948), pp. 130–131n.

We find in the *Catechism*, says Cannac (p. 45), the personal mark of Bakunin: the cadence of his style. "But the principal articles of this revolutionary credo, which make a veritable code of duplicity and cynicism, bear indubitably the stamp of Nechayev's personality and proceed in a straight line from his scorn for the individual. It remains that, if Bakunin let Nechayev thus express himself through him, there was between them not merely collusion, but profound accord."

Max Nettlau, who probably knew Bakunin best, his biographer James Guillaume, and Dragomanov, editor of his correspondence, have all maintained the *Catechism* was not his work. To have written it would have been entirely out of character for Bakunin. He was not a man of violent disposition, he was not bloodthirsty, and the idea of instituting a Reign of Terror on the morrow of a victorious revolution was so repugnant he expressly disavowed it more than once in his writings. For instance, in the "Letter Composed at Marseilles," he wrote: "It is not necessary to kill these people. The guillotine does not kill reaction. It only makes it revive. Besides, as the immense majority of the bourgeois are reactionary, where would you stop? When one is carrying out a revolution for the liberation of humanity, one should respect the life and liberty of men; but there is no need why one should respect purses filled with plunder. It is much more humane than cutting throats, and a thousand times more harmful. By cutting off the most criminal heads, one makes them more interesting, and produces a reaction in their favor; while in cutting open criminal purses, one stops reaction at its source, one destroys its means." In "The Knouto-Germanic Empire," Bakunin says: "The Revolution is neither vindictive nor bloodthirsty. It does not demand the death, nor even the transportation in mass, or even individually, of all this Bonapartist Rabble . . . The people are not at all cruel; it is the privileged classes who are that . . . They suffer too much themselves not to be compassionate to suffering." Long before, in "The Confession," Bakunin declared concerning the revolution he was projecting in Bohemia: "It was my intention to destroy all castles, to burn all administrative records and all titles of the feudal lords, to declare null and void all mortgages, as well as other debts not exceeding a certain amount. In short, the revolution which I planned was to be directed against institutions rather than against human beings." (Max Nomad, *Apostles of Revolution*, New York: Collier Books edition, 1961, p. 159) In short, it is evident that Bakunin would have found it congenitally impossible to write "The Revolutionary Catechism" alone, uninspired and unaided by his "tiger." See Kenaflick, pp. 124–125. Kenaflick declares it is surprising that the *Catechism* "should ever have been accepted as a product of Bakunin. Psychologically speaking, Bakunin could no more have written this document than Francis Bacon could have written the plays of Shakespeare." (p. 197) But of course there are those who cling to belief in Bacon's authorship—and so it is with many who still attribute the *Catechism* to Bakunin.

Chapter 14
NECHAYEV: "THE POSSESSED"

My conclusion is in direct contradiction to the original idea with which I started. Starting from unlimited freedom, I arrive at unlimited despotism. I will add, however, that there can be no solution of the social problem but mine . . . What I propose is paradise, an earthly paradise, and there can be no others on earth.

—"Shigalev," member of the
"Central Committee"

People are ashamed of all independent thinking. Do you know how many converts we shall make by trite and ready-made ideas?

—"Verkhovensky,"
The Possessed
by Fyodor Dostoyevsky

BUILDING "THE ORGANIZATION"   Returning to Moscow in September 1869, Nechayev moved to forge a revolutionary machine by applying his *Catechism's* ruthless principles. He worked under an assumed identity—for example, as "the engineer Pavlov," or "Ivan Petrovich," names as common in Russia as Smith or Jones in the United States. He would introduce himself as an emissary of Bakunin who, entering his "tiger cub's" game, armed him with a document declaring:

The bearer of this certificate is one of the accredited representatives of the Russian Section of the World Revolutionary Alliance. No. 2771.

/s/ *Mikhail Bakunin*

The document bore a seal, in French, containing the words "European Revolutionary Alliance—Central Committee." The number 2771, of course, implied to hopeful apocalyptics that at least 2770 other agents like Nechayev were carrying out the Central Committee's orders in Europe and Russia. The name of the world body suggested that this was the famous International Workingmen's Association, the "First International" of Karl Marx, about which most Russians had only dim notions and sketchy information.

[203   ]

Nechayev continued weaving his legend to provide gullible recruits with a revolutionary model. He would, for instance, lament "the famous and melancholy occasion when our Nechayev was shot by the police on the road from Tambov to Perm." Or he would declare that Nechayev was living as a worker somewhere in the Ural Mountains. On one occasion he promised to give a member of his group the "posthumous memoirs" of Nechayev who had "died in a Siberian prison." He told those he permitted to know his real name tall stories about his important role in Geneva in the worldwide revolutionary movement headed by Bakunin. He would suddenly appear at meetings with "sealed orders" from the "Central Committee."

Nechayev formed the "Great Russian Section, Moscow" and imposed the "General Rules of the Organization" which commanded conspiratorial discipline and complete obedience to "the organizer" —namely, himself. Each central group member was to form his own cell, ad infinitum. At the top of this pyramid reigned "the Committee," whose will Nechayev transmitted; not even his closest central group associates were allowed to know about this committee. And of course "the Committee" existed only in Nechayev's mind. He not only liked the glamour, but found the aura of authority useful.

Surprisingly Nechayev recruited many members with this hocus pocus. Yet so many of them wanted to be deceived, to believe in "the Organization," and above all to be instructed in ways to help "the Revolution." Nechayev impressed better-educated and intellectually superior persons not with a program of ideas but with his immense energy and dedication. He lured them into a whirlpool of feverish and intoxicating activism. He persuaded one recruit to help smuggle literature from Switzerland, saying:

> This is not the time to work out theories. You talked enough in 1862 without doing anything. Times have changed. It is your business now not to talk but *to do*, and to do as you are told by men who are more competent than you are in this matter. Your duty is to obey and not to argue.

One of Nechayev's followers, A. Kuznetzov, described his methods to police in his deposition of January 7, 1870:

> He used various methods to recruit his followers, and dominated those who did not submit to his will in this way: he surrounded them,

without their realizing, with people who tried to persuade them by explaining that all had to serve the common cause. This was necessary, they said, even from their personal point of view, as otherwise when the people revolted they, too, would be exterminated. In this way, those who at first did not want to end by submitting or at least offering him money, and then they found themselves bound by this action. In general Nechayev was extraordinarily efficient at inducing people to join his society. But he used persuasion only when this was necessary to win their allegiance. When he had obtained this, his attitude changed completely: then he gave orders and demanded submission.

To get money for his escapades, Nechayev concocted a characteristic plot. He ordered a follower to decoy a wealthy young liberal named Kalatchevsky into his apartment and give him some pamphlets. Kalatchevsky accepted the papers out of curiosity, and hardly got into the street when a "secret police agent" accosted him. "I know you are carrying seditious proclamations," the stranger said. Mere possession of such literature was enough to send a man to prison. The mysterious agent motioned Kalatchevsky into a carriage and offered to set him loose on the spot if he signed a draft for 6,000 rubles. Faced with this or Siberia, Kalatchevsky signed. Of course, the "police agent" was Nechayev.[1]

"THE DEVILS"   Nechayev claimed 150 members in his conspiratorial apparatus in Moscow. In the Petrovsky Agricultural College he had a clandestine study cell of eight "students." One day—a conspirator later testified he thought it was November 4, 1869—the "organizer" brusquely ordered a student named Ivan Ivanovich to post some inflammatory leaflets in the dining halls. Ivanov refused, saying that the leaflets inciting students to rebellion would only provoke police reprisals and the closing of the dining halls—actions Nechayev may have wanted. White with rage, Nechayev demanded obedience "in the name of the Committee." Ivanov refused, hinting some doubt about its existence. Most likely he was wise to Nechayev's game. Nechayev held long discussions with cell members at the Agricultural College about Ivanov's "act of treason." He persuaded or terrorized his conspirators into accepting the necessity for "liquidation." They told Ivanov that Nechayev had obtained a new printing press and intended to put him in charge of it. The press was supposedly hidden in a cave in the expansive grounds of a semideserted park on the outskirts of Moscow, Petrovsky Park. Ivanov went there on the appointed night with a cell member. Nechayev and the three members were waiting with a knife and gun. Nechayev and a comrade were to enter the cave with Ivanov to see the fictitious press, then Nechayev himself would strangle Ivanov.

Nechayev botched it. In the darkness of the cave he grabbed the wrong victim, who immediately filled the night with screams. Nechayev's colleagues outside thought the death sentence was completed. They were startled when the intended victim came hurtling out of the grotto. Nechayev caught him, threw him to the ground, sat on him, and shouted for the gun. Ivanov fought wildly, and in the struggle bit off Nechayev's thumb, but Nechayev finally put a bullet in his head. Weighting the corpse with stones, Nechayev and cohorts dumped it through the thin ice covering the park lake. Some hours later, Nechayev showed several persons the revolver which had accidentally fired, almost killing Pryzhov, one of the participants in the murder. Nechayev blithely remarked that if Pryzhov had been killed the murder could have been pinned on him.

That eerie night became one of the most celebrated scenes in literature, for the ensuing trial fascinated Fyodor Dostoyevsky, who immortalized it in his novel, *The Possessed* (or *The Devils*). The novel's character Verkhovensky was the real-life Nechayev.

Five days later, newspapers reported the discovery of Ivanov's body, which floated to the surface. The police in no time unraveled the mystery. They smashed "the Organization," arrested 300, and finally placed 87 on trial for conspiracy to overthrow the government. Disguising himself as a woman, Nechayev fled Russia, leaving his colleagues to stand trial for murder.

Bakunin, ignorant of the Ivanov murder, was so delighted to learn that "Boy" was back in Geneva that he "jumped for joy so that he nearly broke his head on the ceiling," as he wrote a friend. He listened raptly to tales of the vast organization operated by "The Committee" back in Russia. Then rumors began to spread among the revolutionary exiles that Nechayev had murdered Ivanov. Nechayev denied them at first. Later he blandly excused the murder in a publication entitled "The People's Vengeance No. 2," declaring that "connection with us [the revolution] is eternal, inviolable, inseparable." Thus, any deviation from the policy laid down by "us" would require that the person defying the revolutionary leader must be "cast out of midst like a decaying limb":

Is it necessary to add that such expulsion from our ranks in the present situation when the entire course of our activity and the entire mechanism and composition of our forces is an impenetrable secret to the outside world—that such an expulsion is at the same time an expulsion from the ranks of the living?

BAKUNIN DISCOVERS THE TRUTH Gradually, Bakunin became aware of the real "boy." When a revolutionary named Lopatin who had seen Nechayev operate in both Switzerland and Russia exposed Nechayev's lies, it dawned on Bakunin that he himself was a victim of the manipulatory code of the *Catechism of the Revolutionary*, Rules 19 and 20 for dealing with "liberals" and "doctrinaires." Nechayev had bilked Bakunin of part of a 10,000 franc fund a wealthy and idealistic Russian landowner turned over to the revolutionary exiles for the cause, had stolen a box of Bakunin's vast correspondence with the international revolutionary groups all over Western Europe, and had left for London. Undoubtedly, the Nechayev's words in the *Catechism* sobered Bakunin:

One may conspire with them [Liberals of various shades] in accordance with their programs, making them believe that one follows them blindly and at the same time one should get possession of all their secrets, compromise them to the utmost, so that no avenue of escape may be left to them, and use them as instruments for stirring up disturbances in the State.

Horrified, the old man wrote his London friends:

. . . If it seems strange to you that we are warning you against a man to whom we have given letters of introduction, letters written in the warmest terms, then remember that these letters were written in May, and since then we have been confronted with some grave incidents— incidents which have made us break off all relations with N. At the risk of appearing to be out of our minds, we believe we have the sacred duty to warn warn you against him. And now I shall try to tell you very briefly the reasons why we have changed our opinion of him.

It is perfectly true that N. is the one man most persecuted by the Russian government, which has covered the whole continent of Europe with a cloud of spies determined to find him in whatever country he can be found. It is true too that the Russian government has demanded his extradition from Germany as well as Switzerland. Yet it remains true that he is one of the most active and energetic men whom I have ever met. When it is a question of serving what he calls "the cause," he does not hesitate or stop at anything and is as pitiless with himself as with everyone else. That is the exceptional quality that attracted me and for a long time drove me to try and keep in touch with him. Some say that he is just an adventurer. That is not true! He is a fanatic, full of dedication, and at the same time an extremely dangerous fanatic. To join with him can only lead to results that are ruinous for all; and this is why: there was a time when he joined a clandestine Organization which really existed in Russia but now this organization no longer exists, as all its members have been arrested. At the moment only Nechayev has remained, and he himself constitutes what he calls the committee. When the organization was destroyed, he tried to create a new one abroad. All this would be absolutely natural and normal as well as extremely useful; but the methods he has used for this purpose deserve every censure. He was terribly affected by the catastrophe of the clandestine organization in Russia, and has gradually convinced himself that, to found a serious and indestructible society, it is essential to build it on Machiavelli's policies and adopt the Jesuit system. For the body—only violence; for the soul —lies.

Truth and mutual trust, real solidarity exist only among a dozen people who make up the holy of holies of the society. All the rest serve as a blind soulless weapon in the hands of these dozen men who are bound together by the sternest oaths. It is allowed, indeed it is even a duty to cheat underlings, to compromise them, and in cases of necessity to have them killed. He is wholly the conspirator. And so, now that you have received N. because we sent our own letter of recommendation, and you have given him your confidence and recommended him to your friends . . . what will happen when he has entered your world? Let me tell you. First, he will tell a host of lies in order to increase your sympathy and confidence in him, but this is not all. The sympathies of lukewarm men, by which I mean men who are not wholly dedicated to the revolution, men who have other interests, men with family ties and love affairs and friendship and social relations—such men he regards as unworthy, and he will do everything he can to submit them wholly to the cause, and quite without your knowing it, he will try to take over your whole life. To do this, he will spy on you and attempt to get possession of all your secrets, and if left alone in a room in your absence, he will open all your drawers, read all your correspondence and if he finds a letter which in some way compromises you or your friends, he will steal it and guard it carefully for his own purposes of intimidation. He has done this with other friends, and when we faced him with the charge, he dared to say: "So I did it? Well, that's our system. That is how we treat enemies—we have to compromise everyone who is not completely with us." By this he means all those who are not completely convinced of the complete validity of his system and have not promised to apply it themselves.

Then, too, if you introduce him to a friend, his first aim will be to sow dissension, scandal, and intrigue between you. If your friend has a wife or a daughter, he will attempt to seduce her and get her with child, forcing her beyond the limits of conventional morality and so place her that she is compelled to make a revolutionary protest against society.

Every personal tie, every friendship, everything . . . all these he will regard as evil, and he will do his best to destroy them, and he will do this because these things weaken the effectiveness of his secret organization. Do not, I beg of you, cry out that this is an exaggeration! All this has happened and can be proved. When he is unmasked, this poor N. is so childlike, so simple in spite of his systematic perversity—he even thought he could convert me and begged me to develop this theory in a Russian journal which he wanted me to publish. He has betrayed the confidence of us all, stolen our letters, horribly compromised us— in a word, he has behaved like a villain. His only excuse lies in his fanaticism! Without knowing it, he is terribly ambitious, because he has come finally to the conclusion that the revolutionary cause can be identified with his own person, and so leads the life of a martyr, full of privations and unbelievable hard work; therefore you cannot call him an egoist in the worst sense of the word. He is a fanatic, and fanaticism has led him into becoming an accomplished Jesuit—there are moments when he is no more than a beast. Most of his lies are white lies. He plays the Jesuit game as others play the game of revolution. But in spite of his naivete, he is extremely dangerous, because every day he commits crimes, abuses confidence, acts treacherously; and it is all the more difficult to prevent these things from happening because one hardly suspects their possibility. In spite of all this he is a force to be reckoned with, because he has immense energy. And so it was with immense sorrow that I broke with him. I thought of how service to our cause demands immense reserves of energy, and how rarely we come upon anyone so richly endowed with pure energy. But after thinking the matter out, I came to the conclusion that no other course was open to me, and now that we are apart, I must keep fighting him to the bitter end. Believe it or not, his last project was to form a group of thieves and bandits on Swiss territory, evidently with the intention of bringing about a revolution. I have prevented that by making him leave Switzerland, and it is quite certain that if he had continued with his project, this group of bandits would have been captured within the space of a few weeks—he would have been lost, and everyone else would have been lost with him. His friend and Companion S. is an outright scoundrel, a brazen liar, without the excuse of the saving grace of fanaticism.

CAPTURE AND TRIAL   For two years after his break with Bakunin, Nechayev wandered about Europe fleeing extradition. On August 14, 1872, a paid spy lured Nechayev into a police trap. The Swiss police turned him over within hours to the czar's officers, and he was spirited away under heavy guard to stand trial.

When Bakunin heard of Nechayev's extradition, he wrote a friend (November 2, 1872):

> I pity him deeply. Nobody ever did me, and intentionally, as much harm as he did, but I pity him all the same. He was a man of rare energy, and when we met him, there was burning in him a very ardent and very pure flame of love for our poor oppressed people; our historic and national misery caused him to feel a real suffering. At that time his exterior was unsavory enough, but his inner self was not soiled. It was his authoritarianism and his unbridled self-will which, very unfortunately and through his ignorance, working together with the method called Machiavellianism and Jesuitism, definitely plunged him in the mire.
>
> However, an inner voice tells me that Nechayev, who is lost forever —and who certainly knows that he is lost—on this occasion will call forth from the depths of his being, warped and soiled, but far from being vulgar, all his primitive energy and courage. He will perish like a hero and this time he will betray nothing and no one. Such is my belief. We will see if I am right.[2]

Right he was. For Nechayev's conduct in prison, however sordid his prior life, can only inspire awe—even admiration—for so fierce, so courageous, so powerful a personality. He emerged from the illiterate brutishness of czarist Russia with a frustration-charged fury so powerful that it fueled the entire Russian revolutionary movement, building what ultimately became Lenin's revolutionary machine. Lenin was, after all, but a systematic Nechayevist who established a school for producing professional revolutionaries according to the *Cathechism.*

Nechayev's trial opened on January 8, 1873. His haughtiness and defiance stunned the court. The murder of Ivanov had been merely "a purely political matter," Nechayev icily informed the tribunal, and therefore the court of criminal jurisdiction had no right to try him. He screamed defiance at the judges. To the prosecutor's questions, he shouted denunciations of the czar. Throughout the trial, he insulted and ridiculed the court and the monarchy. At last, after the sentencing, he was dragged from the court screaming, "Down with despotism!"

"THE PRISONER IN CELL NO. 5"   Nechayev's years in prison are one of the most bewitching human epics in history. For the legend grew. To the guards he was nameless, save as "The prisoner in Cell Number 5 of the Alexis Ravelin," the maximum security section of the Peter and Paul Fortress whose very existence was known only by rumor. By order of the czar weekly reports on the prisoner and his condition were sent to the Imperial Palace. Nechayev was allowed reading matter and writing materials.

The Third Department intently studied and carefully analyzed Nechayev's prison scribblings. There were drafts of his two letters to the czar; some treatises on the student movement at the end of the '60s (in which Nechayev depicted himself as the driving force); a couple of literary sketches on students and émigré life; and a draft for a novel in the French genre, dealing with a love affair between a little seamstress (like his mother) in Paris and a communist leader who was also the lover of a noble lady. This sentimental and pompous rigmarole dealt with whether a revolutionary has the right to waste time in satisfying his lower instincts when all his energy is needed for the social struggle. (Nechayev's answer: erotic pleasures do not weaken an energetic man.) As the official police analysis noted, Nechayev displayed particular relish in describing the brutalities of the revolutionaries and the low morals of noble ladies. Judging Nechayev's writings worthless, the Third Department destroyed them, and only the official report remains—but it offers a remarkable analysis of Nechayev's character and views:

Nechayev cannot be called an average personality. The deficiency of his original education is continually evident, but it is covered over by an astonishing pertinacity and will-power manifesting themselves in the mass of knowledge that he acquired afterwards. This knowledge and the effort that was necessary to acquire it have developed in him all the advantages of the self-taught man in the highest degree: energy, habitual self-reliance, complete command of the subjects with which he deals. At the same time they have also developed in him all the disadvantageous traits of the self-taught: contempt for everything that he does not know, complete lack of critical evaluation of his knowledge, envy and relentless hatred of all who received by their good fortune the education which cost him such an effort, recklessness. He is unable to distinguish sophistry from logic and *deliberately ignores any facts which do not accord with his views.* He is full of suspicion, contempt and enmity against all who, by their means, their social position, or their education gain nothing in his eyes. Only men of equal upbringing and of the same views as his are for him real servants of the people and deserve trust and sympathy. All others who stand out of the masses are regarded as enemies of the people, and peaceful, fruitful and manifold development can only ensue after their liquidation. Although he several times rejected violent overthrow, because that would be only a reaction without creating anything positive, he considers violence necessary, because the upper classes must be liquidated at any price. *Hatred is for him one of the most important driving forces of social development.* Often persons in the position of the author deserve to be respected by their adversaries, but this author does not produce such a feeling of esteem. *He finds satisfaction in cherishing his hatred for all higher placed persons. With egoistic pleasure he describes himself as a revolutionary not by conviction but by temperment . . .* (emphasis added)[3]

After eight years the fierce revolutionary, by the sheer force of his personality, finally captivated his captors. When a guard brought food or cleaned his cell, he told about his sufferings and the evils of the world. Nechayev received no answer, he would address the man directly:

> Yes, you do not answer. You are forbidden to speak to me, but do you know why I am imprisoned here? This is the fate awaiting a man who sacrifices his life for such people as you, your fathers and brothers. They catch him and put on a chain, and then such a fool as you is ordered to watch him, more closely than a dog. You do not deserve to be called human beings, but thoughtless animals. . . .

Goading forth remarks about obedience, he would cite scriptures, speak of the deception and oppression of the peasants. By winning little favors, he compromised and then blackmailed guard after guard, until he virtually commanded them all. Nechayev gained enough power to communicate with neighboring cells and learned of the growing organization on the outside, modeled after his very own principles.

A VOICE FROM THE DEAD   In December 1880, Nechayev's seventh year in prison, the Narodnaya Volya or "People's Will" plotted to assassinate Czar Alexander II by digging shafts and storing dynamite under streets he traveled near the Winter Palace. One evening, as the tiny "Central Committee" met, a member came in and announced: "A letter from Nechayev!"

"The letter came like a bombshell, like a message from another world!" said Vera Figner, a member of the little circle. Indeed it was, coming from a legendary figure long presumed dead. As Figner recalled it:

> It was completely objective in character: no effusions, not the slightest sentimentality, not a word about the past, not a word about what Nechayev must have gone through or was suffering at present. He

simply and clearly put the question of his escape. He wrote as a revolutionary who had just fallen out of the ranks to his comrades who were still free. The letter created an astonishing impression: all the black spots that had darkened the picture we had of Nechayev, all the fog of dishonesty and trickery that had been hanging round his revolutionary figure cleared away. What remained was only the mind which could not be dimmed in the long years of solitary confinement. There remained a spirit which had not been broken, however great the weight of the punishment brought to bear against it; an energy which all the calamities of life had not been able to crush.[4]

For months, Nechayev corresponded with the revolutionaries, advising, inspiring, exhorting, and always demanding destruction of the regime. And always his letters were splotched with his own blood. In return, the organization sent him long reports in code, money, even food.

The czar's police smelled the plot. By placing an informant in the prison, they learned that their "prisoner in Cell No. 5" had compromised more than fourscore guards and warders. In December 1881 four officers and 35 guards were imprisoned or sent to Siberia. Nechayev was chained to the wall and placed on a starvation diet. Scurvy and rot set in. Nechayev wrote his last letter to the czar, for the most part still haughty, still protesting, reviewing the "gross injustice" of his trial and imprisonment, but ending in pitiful despair. The letter was written in blood, with a nail. Sometime in November 1882, Nechayev died quietly in his cell.

THE NECHAYEV LEGEND   Nechayev was, says a distinguished historian of the nineteenth-century Russian revolutionary movements, *"the first Russian professional revolutionary, a man who gave to the cause not his spare evening* but the whole of his life."[5] His *Cathechism of the Revolutionary* had a more profound and fundamental role in setting the cast of the modern revolutionary radical organization than even Marx and Engels' *Communist Manifesto.* Nechayev contributed little to revolutionary political thought, or to the techniques of revolution and political organization. But he gave the movement a code for revolutionary activities and unrestrained Machiavellianism in the pursuit of power. As such, he supplied the very model of the twentieth-century bolshevik revolutionary. Though he bilked a great deal of money out of Bakunin, Nechayev did not spend a penny on himself, even though starving.

"All who knew Nechayev are unanimous in acknowledging him as a man for whom, always and in all circumstances the cause of revolution stood first," declares Russian historian Boris Kuzmin. "He had no private life of his own and no private attachments of any kind."[6] One contemporary was overpowered by his "colossal energy, his fanatical devotion to the revolutionary cause, his character of steel, and an indefatigable capacity for work."[7] Said another: "I have lived for forty years and I have met many people, but I have never met anyone with Nechayev's energy, nor can I imagine that anyone like him exists."[8] Those members of the "People's Will" who escaped Russia after their successful assassination of Alexander II in March 1881 published a report on their clandestine links with Nechayev and his incredible prison exploits. And so the legend grew.

> The *Cathechism* was to become the Koran of those fanatical and unscrupulous elements who tried to combine individual terrorism with certain forms of banditism. Many among them actually knew those 26 articles by heart. Among the most harmful and dangerous in effect were articles 19 and 20. They present the scriptural sanction, as it were, of what was to become known and generally condemned in the Russian revolutionary movement as "Nechayevism"—the method of Machiavellian and Jesuitic deception and double-crossing applied to everyone with whom a revolutionist comes into contact.[9]

Since 1917, the Bolsheviks have honored Nechayev the legend. Prefacing a collection of famous revolutionary trials, a Soviet historian calls him a "super-revolutionist" whose stamp of genius impresses itself upon the whole of the Russian revolutionary movement," and questions the revolutionary ardor of those who opposed his methods—presumably including Marx. In 1926 another Bolshevik writer proclaimed him as "the first pioneer" of Lenin's revolution and the model of the Bolshevists:

> Everything that Naychev envisaged at that far-off time has found its deepest and most complete realization in the methods and tactics of the political battle of the Russian Communist Party throughout its history . . . He took as the basis of his program precisely that form of political struggle which found its crystal-clear accomplishment in Russian Bolshevism. Neither before Nechayev nor after him has anything similar existed in our movement. In him we find the elements of Bolshevist tactics . . .
> He was no theoretician. He was above all a practitioner of the revolutionary cause. He used the right means to achieve the triumph of the socialist revolution, and the goal that he could not achieve in his own

time was reached many years later by the Bolshevists who were able to put into practice the tactical rules which Nechayev first laid down . . . every "Professional Revolutionary," every Bolshevist can only put his signature to the paragraphs of the *Cathechism* . . .

If one substitutes contemporary terminology for Nechayev's one can recognize in the scheme of "People's Retribution" the model of the present party apparatus . . .

In his basic assumptions Nechayev was first and foremost a communist.[10]

Lenin praised Nechayev. Bonch-Bruyevich, whose job it was to develop the Bolshevik's special library of revolutionary literature in Geneva, records that Lenin emphasized Nechayev's importance:

People completely forget that Nechayev possessed unique organizational talent, an ability to establish the special techniques of conspiratorial work everywhere, an ability to give his thoughts such startling formulations that they were forever imprinted on one's memory.

Lenin cited a leaflet that asked the question many terrorists posed —"Which members of the reigning house must be destroyed?" And Nechayev's succinct answer was: "The whole great responsory," the entire Romanov dynasty. "This is simple to the point of genius!" exclaimed Lenin.[11]

"All of Nechayev should be published," Lenin urged Bonch-Bruyevich. "We must seek out everything he wrote, decipher all his pseudonyms, and collect and print everything he wrote." Lenin called him a "titanic revolutionary."

Chapter 15
TKACHEV: THE JACOBIN

Supported by the destructive power of the people and skilfully directing it toward the elimination of the enemies of the revolution, the revolutionary minority demolishes the bulwarks of the old government and deprives it of its means of defense and counteraction. Then the revolutionary minority introduces new, progressive and communist ideas into life. In its work of reformation, the revolutionary minority need not rely upon the active support of the people. The revolutionary role of the people ends the instant they have destroyed the institutions which oppressed them.

—Tkachev, 1875

"KILL EVERYONE OVER 25!"   Among the 87 alleged Nechaye-vists the czarist police netted and tried in 1871 was 27-year-old Peter Tkachev. His crime: issuing a proclamation during the March 1869 student revolt, a few days after Nechayev skipped west with "the Nechayev trick." Though a second offender—first jailed for two months after student demonstrations in 1861—Tkachev drew only sixteen months' exile, and that to his mother's estate. Abandoning his wife, he ran away to Geneva to join other émigré journalists in December 1873.

Tkachev and Nechayev closely associated with each other in Petrograd's tiny student radical circle, although only briefly. In fact in 1868 Tkachev published an antecedent of Nechayev's *Catechism*. It appeared in *The Cause*, Nos. 4 and 5, under the title "The People of the Future," and contained virtually identical rules on many points. At the time Tkachev also anticipated the American "New Left" cry a century later of: "Don't trust anyone over 30." Tkachev proclaimed: "We should kill everyone over 25 and make a new start."[1] His choice of age of liquidation was undoubtedly influenced by the fact that he was 24 himself at the time.

Tkachev joined Lavrov's populist *Forward!* in Geneva, which preached the "to the people" line of peaceful progress through enlightenment. Tkachev, a convinced élitist, proudly claimed the title of "Jacobin," often quoted and praised Robespierre, and so he quickly quarreled with the "populist" line. He joined a Russian Blanquist circle and helped translate works of the old French conspirator and disciple of Buonarroti on the technique of *coup d'état*. In late

1875 the group launched its own publication, *Alarm*, with Tkachev as editor.

A JOURNAL FOR REVOLUTIONARIES   Tkachev's philosophy of journalism reflected his élitist view that revolution must be made and directed by a militant, intelligent minority. "I had no thought of distributing *Alarm* inside Russia," he wrote.

> *Alarm* was not intended to be an agitation-type publication. Its task consisted merely of swaying revolutionaries . . . It was enough that merely a handful of revolutionaries would become familiar with its program and basic principles, that it would provoke a lot of talk among the revolutionaries. It would be sufficient to . . . prove the rationality and practicability of these ideas and disseminate them among the majority of revolutionaries.[2]

Tkachev's approach proved to be shrewd and sound. Within two years an avowedly Tkachevist "Society for the Liberation of the People" appeared inside Russia. Its members comprised most of the Russian Jacobins, those who espoused a one-party seizure of power and postrevolutionary dictatorship by a radical minority through terror. Reflecting the Babeuvist influence, the Society's bylaws provided: "A member of the Society is compelled to hold secret its very existence, as well as the identity of anyone belonging to it." Under the Central Committee's direction its agents would be ordered secretly to penetrate other revolutionary organizations and work clandestinely to bring them under its control.[3]

In 1879 Tkachev's staff at *Alarm* turned against the master on the issue of terror. They, sympathizing with the Nechayevists and *People's Will* terrorists inside Russia, wanted to endorse the widest use of violence, both mass and individual. Tkachev regarded this tactic as ineffectual and harmful, though he did not rule out terror against spies and informers or mob violence under selected circumstances. Tkachev moved to Paris in 1880 and joined the French Blanquist journal, *Ni Dieu, Ni Maitre*. The same year his old *Alarm* colleagues tried to move their headquarters to St. Petersburg, and their press and matrices for a forthcoming issue were all seized by police on arrival. *Sic transit gloria mundi!*

Tkachev himself in 1883 fell horribly ill with what was diagnosed as a "paralysis of the brain." Hospitalized, he degenerated into a "living corpse," and died on January 5, 1886. He was probably a victim of ataxia, a sometimes hereditary disease that attacks the spinal column and brain stem, causing shrinkage of the cerebellum and a slow death; the onset usually occurs around the fortieth year, as with Tkachev. His own father died when Tkachev was young of an unrecorded ailment, possibly the same.

"THE FIRST BOLSHEVIK"   In the 1920s, before Stalin installed the Lenin cult which required the myth that Bolshevism sprang from the founder's brain like Minerva from the head of Zeus, Soviet historians briefly hailed Tkachev as "the first Bolshevik." Lenin obviously considered him so. In 1904 he told Bonch-Bruyevich that Tkachev "was unquestionably closer than others to our point of view." Lenin considered the latter's work so important that the Geneva bolsheviks searched the journals of the 1870s for all of his writings. Lenin read all of Tkachev's work and recommended that his comrades do likewise. In fact, Lenin would instruct newly arrived bolsheviks from Russia to study the illegal literature, telling them: "Begin by reading familiarizing yourself with Tkachev's *Alarm*. This is basic and will give you tremendous knowledge."[4]

It was good advice. For here is what the bolshevik neophytes read:

> Successful organization depends on the formation and unification of scattered revolutionary elements into a *living organism* which is able to act according to a single common plan and is subordinated to a single common leadership—an organization based on the centralization of power and decentralization of function.[5]
>
> If organization is necessary for any large or strong party, it is without question even more necessary for a weak or small party, for a party which is only at the beginning of its formation. Such is the position of our social-revolutionary party. For it, the problem of unity and organization is a matter of life and death."[6]
>
> Neither now nor in the future will the common people by its own power bring on a social revolution. We alone, the revolutionary minority, can and should do that as soon as possible.
>
> We should not deceive ourselves that the people by its own might can make a social revolution and organize its life on a better foundation. The people, of course, is necessary for a social revolution. *But only when the revolutionary minority assumes the leadership is this revolution.*[7]
>
> Neither in the present nor in the future can the people, left to their own resources, bring into existence the social revolution. Only we revolutionaries can accomplish this . . . Social ideals are alien to the people; they belong to the social philosophy of the revolutionary minority.[8]

"PROPAGANDA" AND "AGITATION"   One of Tkachev's seminal essays was his 1874 "Tasks of Revolutionary Propaganda in Russia." Here he made the crucial distinction between "propaganda" and "agitation"—which he frequently repeated and which Lenin adopted (via Plekhanov who used it in an 1880 essay). According to one historian of the Leninist movement, "The implications of this distinction constitute the history of Bolshevism."[9] It was the distinction between the professional propagandist and his target audience: "Propaganda" explains many and complex ideas, i.e., the totality of revolutionary principles, to future revolutionaries, while the agitator tries to exploit a few ideas to incite the many. Tkachev wrote:

1. *Propaganda addressed to the majority of the educated and to the privileged stratum:* the same relationship as with the people—exploit the tactic of agitation. Feelings of dissatisfaction and contempt for the existing regime must be stirred up, at the same time giving great attention to whatever facts may exist which would best kindle these feelings. In the selection of these facts, revolutionary propaganda must interpret the facts not so much in the light of the principles governing the present regime as in the degree they bring about the suffering of the people in this or that stratum.

2. *Propaganda addressed to the revolutionary youth and their party.* They must pay particular attention to organizational questions in carrying out their goals. The youth must be convinced of the present necessity for immediate, practical revolutionary activity. It must be explained to the youth that the principal condition for the success of this activity depends on the lasting organization of its revolutionary forces, on the unification of particular, individual acts into a single whole, a disciplined, orchestrated whole. Our revolutionary practice has worked out a number of roads of revolutionary action: the avenue of *coup d'état* conspiracy; the avenue of popular propaganda (what your journal *Forward!* calls "development in the people of consciousness of their rights and demands"); the avenue of direct, popular agitation (that is, direct incitement of the people to rebellion). This is not the place to argue about which of the three types of action is most expedient and useful. All three avenues are equally expedient for the speediest realization of a national revolution. Let each choose whatever kind of action best suits the conditions. Whoever wishes to employ all three at the same time, let him—whatever is best for him. And whoever does not know which course of action he wants to follow, let him not waste time and energy in preliminary self enlightenment and reeducation of people . . .
As to the question, "What is to be done?"—let us not preoccupy

ourselves with that any longer. That has been settled long ago. Make a revolution. How? However you may, however you are able to. Given a rational organization of forces, no single attempt, no single application of force can prove useless. Therefore, the question of organization is the most pressing problem to be conveyed by revolutionary propaganda addressed to our youth. Because of its extraordinary importance, no other question should be given more attention, especially in the case of practical revolutionary activity in the present; no attention should be given those questions which have no direct connection with practical revolutionary action or which are concerned mainly with the future—questions which can only lead to further divisions and disunity among our revolutionary youth . . . For now, the present must occupy our attention.[10]

"UTILIZE THE PEOPLE!"   In 1875 Tkachev synthesized the revolutionary ideas which had accumulated since the French Revolution in a way that left little for Lenin and his Bolsheviks to do but fill in details:

A real revolution can be brought about only in one way: through the seizure of power by revolutionists. In other words, the immediate and most important task of revolution must be solely the overthrow of the government and the transformation of the present conservative state into a revolutionary state. *The capture of a government power in itself does not yet constitute a revolution.* It is only a prelude. The revolution is brought about by the revolutionary government, which, on the one hand, eradicates all the conservative and reactionary elements of society, eliminating all those institutions which hinder the establishment of equality and brotherhood among men, and, on the other hand, introduces such institutions as favor the development of these principles.

The revolutionary minority, having freed the people from the yoke of fear and terror, *provides an opportunity for the people to manifest their revolutionary destructive power.* Supported by this power and skilfully directing it toward the elimination of the enemies of the revolution, *the minority demolishes the bulwarks of the old government and deprives the latter of its means of defense and counteraction.* Then, utilizing its authority, the minority introduces new progressive and communist ideas into life. In its work of reformation, *the revolutionary minority need not rely upon the active support of the people. The revolutionary role of the people ends the instant they have destroyed the institutions which oppressed them,* the instant they have overthrown the tyrants and exploiters who ruled over them. By utilizing the revolutionary destructive power of the people, by eliminating the enemies of the revolution, and by basing its constructive acts upon the character and urgency of the people's wants (that is to say, upon the conservative forces of the people), the revolutionary minority will lay the foundation of a new and more sensible social order.[11]

Here was simon-pure Leninism a generation before Lenin. Tkachev enunciated a *divine right of revolutionaries* theory of the minority vanguard, self-appointed to rule. Lenin merely had to work out the tactics of organization for power seizure—no small feat, of course.

Tkachev zeroed in on a mushy contradiction in the Marxian construct: the contradiction between Marx's doctrine of the inevitability of the revolutionary cataclysm and proletarian triumph through economic determinism, and the need of young revolutionaries to organize and act and play a meaningful role rather than simply to ride passively on "the wave of the future." Tkachev scorned Marx's dialectical materialism and the assumption Marx and Engels generally made that a feudal society such as Russia would have to pass through a capitalist stage before the necessary conditions for proletarian revolution could exist. Tkachev would have heartily agreed with the 1844 Marx's Tenth Thesis on Feuerbach—that philosophers have talked enough about the world, and it's now time for them to change it:

> Although a person and individual and individual actions play an extremely important role in these historic changes, which are called historical progress, and although individual actions may destroy that which has existed for centuries and lay out a new road for the future development of mankind—despite all this, individual action must be based upon certain real social elements. It must find support and justification in the given conditions of the economic life of the people. Without this support and without this firm soil under its feet, it is completely powerless and whatever individual action is carried out will only be of ephemeral importance . . . Nobody takes issue with this basic truth at present and soon it will be copied into children's notebooks.[12]

Paul Axelrod, the Grand Old Man of Russian Marxism, recounted in his memoirs a dispute he had once with a Tkachevist of the *Alarm* circle, or "Jacobin," as they were also called:

> I asked him, "Do you, as the member of a minority, consider it right that you force the people to be happy?"
> The question greatly amused my co-debater. "Why, of course!" he answered. "Since the people themselves do not understand their own good, thus what is truly good for them must be forced upon them!"[13]

Tkachevism, or Russian Jacobinism, was thus pure Rousseauism—"People must be *forced* to be free."

"FORCE CONSCIOUSNESS!" Tkachev himself once wrote a slightly different formulation—significant in that it closely resembled Lenin's own later formula for "injecting" consciousness into the masses:

> The very difference between a violent revolution and a so-called "gradual evolution" lies precisely in the fact that the revolutionary minority is no longer willing tò wait, but takes upon itself the task of forcing consciousness upon the people.[14]

Tkachev was acquainted with Saint-Just, Mably, and the Babeuvists, and his writings are studded with references to Robespierre, whose failures he urged revolutionaries never to repeat. Their "collective dictatorship" would not hesitate in its reign of terror. It must hold in its hands total power over both material and spiritual aspects of social life—not only the economy and lawmaking, but press, education, even family life. A socialist "Committee of Public Safety," following the French Convention's term, must be established to root out hostile elements among the older generation. The Russian initials —KOB, for Kommisiya Obshchestvennoi Bezopasnosti—foreshadow the dread Soviet KGB of today, the Committee for State Security. Other phrases prophetic of future communist debates tumble forth in Tkachev's prose: the "permanently revolutionary" workers state, led by the "people of the future," "the articulate minority," "the new intelligentsia," "the best folk in our midst."

It is hardly surprising that one young neophyte Bolshevik who broke with Lenin in 1904, lived through the Bolshevik Revolution and became a close scholar of Lenin's life and roots concluded that *Lenin's Bolshevik theory and practice would have looked essentially the same even without mixing in the Marxist ideology.*[15]

Chernyshevsky, Nechayev and Tkachev thus created a distinctive mold, entirely new in history: a new type for a priesthood of messianic revolution. They were drawing together, elaborating and sophisticating the relatively primitive and artless Babeuvist technology of social demolition toward an advanced Twentieth Century state. Into their epic mold events soon rammed one of the most powerful and singular minds of the age, shaping it uniquely.

IV. LENIN: THE MAN WHO HARNESSED HATE

Chapter 16
THE DIE IS CAST

"What kind of people are they, to go on raving with this never cooling, feverish ardor, year in, year out, on nonexistent, long-vanished subjects, and to know nothing, to see nothing around them?"

—"Dr. Zhivago,"
Boris Pasternak

Better than anyone, Lenin knew how to be silent about the secret storms of his soul.
—Maxim Gorki

A TERRORIST HANGS   The sun was just rising, chasing away the cool mists from the waters of Lake Ladoga around the island near St. Petersburg on which stood the forbidding old Schlusselburg prison-fortress. It was May 8, 1887. As the sun's first rays touched the seventeenth-century walls and towers, guards led two young men toward the shadowed gallows in the courtyard. A priest walked to them, holding forth a cross. Alexander Ulyanov, 21-years-old, kissed it dutifully. His companion pushed it roughly away. They mounted the scaffold. Moments later, the trap sprang and the two plummeted with the deadly jerk at the end of their ropes. In the fragrant dawn of a clear, warm spring day, guards cut down their bodies and laid them beside their three colleagues hanged in the predawn darkness. It was the sickening end to their plot to destroy the czarist autocracy by throwing a bomb at His Imperial Majesty Alexander III.

But from that moment another bomb began ticking, a bomb of powerful hate, in the sleepy provincial capital of Simbirsk 600 miles away on the banks of the Volga. Alexander Ulyanov's 17-year-old brother Vladimir wondered in cold rage: What had turned "Sasha" from the brilliant budding scientist he knew, always cutting up worms and studying them under his microscope, into a bomb-making chemist and plotter? When Chebotarev, a classmate at St. Petersburg University, came home in June, Vladimir quizzed him intently. He wanted to know about Sasha's last days, about the police interrogations, and "especially about the impression Alexander

[223   ]

made on me when he sat in the dock," Chebotarev recorded. "He questioned me quietly, even too methodically, but apparently not merely out of simple curiosity. He was especially interested in the revolutionary outlook and orientation of his brother."

Indeed he was. As a child Vladimir had always modelled himself on Sasha. "Volodya, how do you want your cereal?" their mother would ask. "Like Sasha." When Alexander returned from school wearing his new student uniform, Vladimir wanted one too. Now Sasha was dead. And Vladimir realized he hardly knew this young man, four years his senior, who was now gone forever. Yet Sasha was a heroic martyr to many of Russia's liberals and intellectuals, for at his trial he gave defiant and courageous voice to their highest dreams of political liberty and a democratic constitution for suffering Russia. What made Sasha a terrorist?

Vladimir walked into Sasha's room and got down his favorite book: Chernyshevsky's novel, *What Is To Be Done?* He read the "Tales of New People," of the "Movers of the Movers," of the ascetic Rakhmetev, who slept on nails, lived on beefsteak, and worked without sleep for days on end by sheer willpower; of these "strong personalities" who guide history, impart direction to the chaotic agitation of the forces, whose number is multiplying and to whom the people will soon appeal and whose commands "will be carried out by all."

In that single summer, pencil and notepad in hand, Vladimir Ulyanov read this book through five times. He spent weeks scribbling notes on every page. It "plowed me over deeply," he told friends years later.

> Each time I found new and potent ideas in it. Chernyshevsky captivated my brother. And he captivated me! He completely transformed my outlook! It is great literature, because it teaches, guides and inspires you. *It is a work which gives one a charge for a whole life.*

The impressionable high school senior, Vladimir Ilich Ulyanov, was well on his way to becoming one of the most potent, systematic minds of the twentieth century—the man we know as Lenin. He would create a design for a new type of tyrant, personify that design, and in turn impress the stamp onto millions more in the Twentieth Century Megamedia Age. He would mass produce "rock hard" revolutionary radicals and professional engineers of social demolition. With his single will, Lenin would create "the direst affliction the world today has to contend with, the totalitarian, one-party state," as Max Eastman expressed it:

Up to Lenin's time tyrants ruled by personal force. Lenin, however, invented rule through a "party," which combines the attributes of a political party in the usual sense with those of a church, an army, a consecrated brotherhood and an advertising monopoly. The design was copied from him by Mussolini, from Mussolini by Hitler, and from the three of them by every little demagogue with brains and a thirst for power. There is no "if" in history more certain than that if there had been no Lenin there would have been no communist revolution in Russia.[1]

CRADLE OF HATE   Vladimir Ilyich Ulyanov was born April 22, 1870. The name they gave him meant "Lord of the World." His world was a sleepy river town, Simbirsk, with a population of 30,000, in which his father was a substantial pillar. Ilya Ulyanov was a school teacher and administrator, "a strong man of firm character who was very stern in his relations with his subordinates," a friend recorded. His family relationships reflected this sternness. His wife Maria was the daughter of an Army doctor-turned-farmer, of Jewish origin. Maria and Ilya had six children. Ann was born in 1864, and Alexander born March 31, 1866. Maria became pregnant soon after marriage. She kept the baby with her and from then on did not regularly share a bedroom with Ilya. She thought him weak and had little affection for him. Ilya, moody and preoccupied with problem pupils and his increasing administrative duties, was soon bored with Maria and the family. Her sister Anna, her first-born's namesake, criticized Ilya for "negligence" and lack of interest in "togetherness."

In 1874 Ilya became superintendent of schools for all of Simbirsk province. That meant only twenty schools, in poor condition, for a population of about a million. Russia, however, was then undergoing governmental administrative modernization and reform. Ilya at 43 had but 12 years to live, and yet he left a mighty monument: 434 small primary schools with 20,000 pupils and several excellent high schools with several hundred students. In his tenth year as superintendent he was made Actual State Counsellor, a hereditary title among the nobility and fourth among 14 ranks on the table of protocol, the equivalent of a major general. When he died in 1886, at age 54 of a cerebral hemorrhage, his widow received an annual pension of 2,200 rubles, perhaps $10,000 in 1970 dollars—enough for Madame Ulyanov to finance her son's revolutionary career until she herself died at 82 in 1916, just a few months before he returned to Russia to become its ruler.

The two oldest boys were eight and four when their father went on the road as provincial administrator, traveling constantly by train, carriage, sleigh, steamboat. He was away for weeks, sometimes months at a time. His homecomings were probably experienced as unsettling and stressful events. The family atmosphere was such that it worth noting that one time Maria greeted him tenderly. "What's the matter?" Ilya asked. "You're so nice to me tonight."

Even when Ilya was home, to the boys he appeared formidable and distant, harsh and forbidding. They experienced none of the warmth and affection required for healthy identification, internalization, and psychological integration. Emotionally they were raised as "half orphans," a biographer notes.[2] To modern Americans, this picture of an emotionally absent pyramid-climbing careerist father whose sons stray into alienation, political extremism or worse will seem drearily familiar.

THE MAKING OF A MISANTHROPE   The very first recorded behavior we learn of Vladimir Ulyanov is a symptom of hostility toward his world. He did not walk until he was three years old. He took his first steps at the same time as his sister Olga, 18 months younger. Even so, these first ventures were experienced as pain and hostility. He would often fall on his head, his screams raising the household. "Probably his head was heavier than his body," Anna remembered the family speculating. "Mother was always afraid he might fracture his skull." One particularly bad fall was serious enough to produce fears of brain damage and defective development. Late walking—say, six months beyond the norm—is no cause for concern, and indeed may be an indicator of extraordinary brightness. But to a modern child psychiatrist such extreme regressive behavior indicates much stress, anxiety, and antagonism in a child's environment. It could result from parental pressure to perform precociously, sibling rivalry, or other pathogenic stresses.

Indeed, a malicious streak soon developed in Vladimir's soul: quick at repartee, sharp of tongue, he loved to display his growing intellect with railleries at the expense of his younger siblings, cousins, and playmates. His mockery and sense of superiority created a wall between him and his peers. "He had no very close friends," Anna recalled. He was habitually silent, reserved, rarely spoke unless addressed. He was a loner, even to his mother and sister Anna. Whenever a brother, sister or school chum interrupted his concentrations, he would speak with icy politeness: "Will you kindly favor me with your absence?" The father, who as a teacher was no mean judge of such matters, once characterized his children, calling Volodya "choleric"—bilious in temperament, easily angered, quick-tempered. He was wild, unruly, boisterous, and terribly destructive of toys. For a birthday a nurse gave him a papier-maché troika. He ran off, hid behind a door, and with quiet concentration twisted off the legs of the three horses. His sister Anna gave him a ruler when he was five. He ran off, broke it, and showed her the pieces.

As a young man Lenin once asked a companion to remember that Dimitri Pisarev, the foremost nihilist writer of an earlier generation, had cried, "Break everything! Beat everybody! Beat and destroy! What goes under is old stuff which has no right to exist. What remains whole, be blessed!" Repeating that passage, Lenin began to laugh hysterically, declaring "We shall pulverize the bourgeoisie!"

Astonished, his friends objected that the purpose was not destruction for destruction's sake. Lenin replied that what existed was decadent: "Consider the bourgeoisie, or democracy if you prefer. It is doomed. By destroying it, we only fulfill the inevitable historical process."

Or fulfill instead the savage penchants of the little lord-of-the-flies? Lenin learned to read at five. (Brother Sasha learned at four.) He breezed through school. He headed his class perennially, and was notably conscious of intellectual superiority over his peers. Alexander went in for science. He was always busy with his microscope and experiments. Vladimir followed Latin, history, and literature. Maria, too, excelled. All three won the gold medals awarded the outstanding student upon graduation.

Vladimir demonstrated very early both the urge to lead and the ability to impose his will, by violence if necessary. But usually he used his gift for cutting words and his manipulative cleverness. He would devise strange games, varying the rules to suit his whims and moods and to show his mastery and superiority. His imperiousness was so rigid even as a youngster that his brother Dimitri, four years junior did not like to play chess with him. Volodya began at nine with his father and Sasha. "He was my teacher, and a very strict one, and that's why I preferred to play with father who let me take moves back," Dimitri recorded. Volodya was emphatic: "Under no circumstances take back a move. Once you've touched a piece you have to move it." Letting a player touch a figure and then another spoiled the game, he insisted. Better to think out the move and be sure what you are going to do.

Vasili Starkov, a fellow Marxist who knew Lenin at age 23 in St. Petersburg, recalled the same sort of rigidity:

> His undeviating and uncompromising attitude toward principles amounted to, as we soon began to say, "rock-hard." Very unyielding in formulating general principles, he showed himself relatively flexible on questions of day-to-day tactics; in such matters he manifested no excessive rigor.

On January 12, 1886, Ilya Ulyanov died unexpectedly at 54 of a cerebral stroke—the same age his famous son would be when he died of the same ailment. That winter Vladimir, then fifteen, and his sister Anna, six years older, took many long walks. "Volodya was in a hostile mood toward the school, the directorate, school studies, and to religion too, and did not object to abuse the teachers. [In some of these tricks I too participated.] In a word, he was in a period of throwing off authority." Indeed, he was rebelling more, as many youngsters do at such a stage. Replying to a 1922 census questionnaire Lenin wrote: Nonbeliever since the age of sixteen," which he reached four months after his father's death.

"How do you like Volodya?" Anna asked Sasha one day late in 1886 after they both returned to St. Petersburg to the university. "He is undoubtedly a very gifted person, but we don't get along at all," Sasha answered. Why? Sasha evaded. Anna guessed:

> Sasha did not like those traits in Volodya's character which, to a lesser extent, also irritated me: his strong tendency to mock, to wound; his rudeness and his arrogance—especially when they were directed at Mother to whom he would at times talk back in a way he never dared when father was alive. I remember Sasha's disapproving look when he heard such backtalk.

Anna recalled that mockery was "absolutely foreign" to Sasha's nature, but "mockery came natural to Volodya at all times and in this transitional period (summer 1886) in particular." The compulsive need to strike at persons verbally was obviously but a manifestation of deep subterranean turmoil.

His entire life reflected the hostility and antagonism toward the universe he expressed once as an adult while listening to a friend playing a Beethoven sonata:

I can't listen to music too often. It affects your nerves, makes you want to say stupid nice things and stroke the heads of people who could create such beauty while living in this vile hell. And now you mustn't stroke anyone's head—you might get your hand bitten off. You have to hit them on the head without any mercy.

A TURN TOWARD TERROR   Sasha, a sensitive soul, was experiencing a turmoil of his own. Neither he nor Anna made it home for their father's funeral. Sasha was so anguished with grief he contemplated suicide, and Anna and their friends feared for him. "He was a rare individual," his schoolmate Orest Govorukhin recorded three years later.

> He had equal respect for his own dignity and the dignity of others. He was a morally delicate personality. He avoided all sharp words and was incapable of them. *I never once saw him carefree and gay; he was forever lost in his thoughts*, given to reverie, and in a melancholy mood.

Since entering St. Petersburg University in 1883, Alexander had totally immersed himself in chemistry and biology. He seemed destined to be a great scientist, and was already thinking about a professorship. But his intelligence, moral superiority, and chemical skill made him an attractive asset for a trio of radicals plotting big things. They coveted Alexander's chemistry expertise: He could become a fine bombmaker.

Scientist and moralist that he was, Alexander was wooed with the promise that "Marxism" provided a "scientific solution" to a whole series of social and economic questions which should concern any "progressive" young man concerned about Russian reality. The radical trio met in Alexander's apartment for prolonged debates over several months.

Marxism was a new ideological wind in Russia. The czar's censor allowed publication of a *Das Kapital* translation in 1872, but the book had little influence. The "People's Freedom" movement— *Narodnaya Volya* (significantly, in Russian the word for "freedom" and "will" is the same)—dominated Russian revolutionary thinking. In 1881 Narodnaya Volya terrorists killed Alexander II. Ironically, unknown to his assassins, that very day the czar had signed a decree to bring elected representatives into the highest councils of state. Vera Figner, an executive committee member, recorded in 1918

that the committee wrote his son and successor, Emperor Alexander
III:

> While demanding the formation of a Constituent Assembly the execu-
> tive committee promises to abide by the will of the people which was
> to be expressed through chosen representatives. Should the people's
> representatives favor some measure that is directly opposed to the
> demands of the revolutionary party, this party would under no circum-
> stances resort to acts of violence and terrorism to enforce its program,
> but would limit itself to peaceful propaganda.

The flavor of their idealism was apparent in the message of sympathy
the executive committee addressed to the American people a few
months later when the anarchist Guiteau assassinated President
James Garfield:

> In a country in which individual freedom makes possible every honest
> ideological combat, in which the free popular will determines not only
> laws, but also the personality of the Executive—in such a country a
> political murder as a means of combat is an expression of exactly the
> same spirit of despotism which we seek to abolish in Russia. Personal
> despotism is as abominable as party despotism, and violence is only
> justified when directed against violence.

After Alexander II's assassination, police smashed the Narodnaya
Volya, driving its leaders into exile. At its peak, the party numbered
probably only 500 including sympathizers.* From Switzerland the
Russian émigrés added the ideological death blow. Sparked by such
former populist revolutionaries as George Plekhanov, Paul Axelrod,
and Vera Zasulich, they replaced populist ideology with Marxism. In
1883 and 1884 Plekhanov published his epoch-making essays, *Socialism and the Political Struggle* and *Our Differences*, which attacked
the basic populist views.

These were the works that led Alexander Ulyanov—and ultimately
Lenin—to study Marx. Until now Chernyshevsky's *What Is To Be
Done?* had been Alexander's favorite book. As he grew more intimate with his three new radical friends, he took up *Our Differences*,
and then carefully studied volume one of *Das Kapital*.

Ultimately Alexander had the job of drafting a program for their

---

*Trotsky later reported that the Executive Committee consisted of 28 persons, while
the general membership up to March 1881, never all active at once, comprised 37
persons. See *The Young Lenin* (New York: Doubleday, 1972), p. 36.

group—the "Terrorist Fraction of the People's Freedom Party." The program's theses embodied economic determinism, the inevitable apocalyptic clash of classes, and the ultimate triumph of "the revolution" and the Forces of Light over the Forces of Darkness—the typical young Karl Marx formulation. In his preparations, Alexander borrowed a copy of the young Marx's 1844 *Franco-German Yearbook* from a classmate, V.V. Vodovozov, and with his coconspirator, Govorukhin, translated the 1843 essay on "Hegel's Philosophy of Right," the Marxist cornerstone strategy of mass hate propaganda. In February 1887 Govorukhin inexplicably fled abroad, carrying the translation. He had it published in Geneva later that year.

Alexander's circle planned to kill the czar on March 1, 1887, the sixth anniversary of the murder of the czar's father. The conspirators now numbered seven, ranging in age from 20 to 26; four, including Alexander, had just turned 21. Alexander sold his gold high school outstanding graduate medal for 100 rubles, perhaps $250, to buy chemicals, and manufactured six bombs in his room. He carefully briefed the one who was to hurl the deadly weapon.

Unknown to his companions, a conspirator in early February wrote an indiscreet letter to a friend in Kharkov—a hymn to terror. "To enumerate the qualities and advantages of the red terror I shall not attempt, for I would have enough of them to take centuries," he scrawled among his more purple passages. Police in Kharkov intercepted the letter, and on February 27, St. Petersburg detectives identified the sender. They began watching the Nevsky Prospect, and at once noticed their suspect and two others loitering suspiciously. They stayed out for five hours. The czar did not go out that day. Or the next. But police saw the same trio, one with a large book, a "Dictionary of Medicine." The other two had bulky objects under their overcoats. Police arrested them; two drew pistols, which misfired. The book was hollow with a crude bomb inside, and the other two carried bombs also.

Police quickly rounded up 74 suspects, including Alexander and Anna. Fifty were soon released. Ultimately fifteen were tried by a court of senators appointed by the czar. An artillery general testified that the two pistols found on the prisoners were incapable of firing and that the dynamite bombs would not have exploded with the crude triggers Alexander fashioned.

Alexander's behavior at the trial was characteristically upright, idealistic, independent, and not a little suicidal. Of the fifteen defendants he alone refused to have an attorney. At the first session, he squeezed the hand of a fellow defendant, Lukashevich, and whispered, "If you need to, put all the blame on me!" "I read in his eyes the irrevocable resolution to die," Lukashevich later wrote. It was obvious to others, too. The chief prosecutor noted sympathetically: "Probably Ulyanov admits his guilt even in regard to crimes which he did not commit." When asked why he had not fled, as some did, Alexander answered: "I didn't want to escape. I wished to die for my country."

Alexander's last request was that his family replace for Vodovozov the rare *Franco-German Yearbook* the police had seized from his room.

LENIN FINDS HIS ROLE   Lenin himself ranked Alexander's martyrdom as the most important event of his youthful life. Upon his return to Russia in April 1917, asked to write a sketch of himself, he wrote an eight-line "unfinished autobiography":

> My name is Vladimir Ilyich Ulyanov. I was born in Smibirsk April 10, 1870. In the spring of 1887, my older brother Alexander was sentenced to death by Alexander III for an attempt (March 1, 1887) on his life . . .

The first night he met his future wife in St. Petersburg, he walked her home from a revolutionary meeting and began their courtship along the banks of the Neva by telling her about his brother's execution. At 18, jailed for two days after a protest demonstration at Kazan University, he answered a cellmate's question on what he would do after release: "What is there for me to think? My path has been blazed by my older brother."

Perhaps only someone who has experienced it can understand the deep impact the death of a close role-model, a father or brother, can leave on a 17-year-old. Regardless of the *reality* of the dead model's personality and performance, the youth's idolized *perception* of his identity and purpose imprints itself upon the inner consciousness. That identity imprint becomes his map and guidance system through life just as the North Star becomes the sailor's guide on his voyage through chartless, churning waters. It is a constant, a stabilizing inner gyroscope locked onto an ultimate aim, value, or dream.

Vladimir immediately plunged into Chernyshevsky. There he learned, as he later said, that "every thinking, decent person must be a revolutionary," and more—"*what the revolutionary must be like, what his rules must be, how he must go about attaining his goals, and by what methods and means he can bring about their realization.*"[3] This was Lenin's reply in 1904 to a questioner. During the summer of 1887, as we have seen, he went through the book five times, "with pencil and note pad in hand." Years later his wife noted: "I was surprised how attentively he read this novel and how many subtle and fine points he had noticed it it."

In the usual adolescent search for significance, young Lenin found his identity in Chernyshevsky's fierce apocalyptic and messianic scheme, the scheme of a renegade theology student who nevertheless had the deep traces of Revelation and Manicheanism and Christian gnosticism and megalomania etched in his mind. The impressionable youth hurled himself into this mold, and emerged with his identity established for life. Chernyshevsky "plowed me over," he exclaimed at 34. And so he did. He established the framework of Lenin's mind. Lenin's contribution, product of this frame of mind, was to develop the technology for mass producing more "new people" of this mind set, and for teaching them to be the "movers of the movers." How to impose their will on "the direction of events, speed up their course, and impart regularity to the . . . movement of the masses"? Lenin developed the answers in his technology of mass propaganda and apocalyptic orchestration. One who knew him intimately in his thirty-fourth year and later studied his early life in detail concluded:

> *He subconsciously never deviated from the political worldview of Chernyshevsky, which left a deep mark on his brain.*[4] The whole being of Vladimir Ulyanov clung to and, as if under a spell, was drawn to the idea of the "finale," the hour when the "expropriators will be expropriated." This revolutionary chiliasm . . . possessed him like a fever.[5]

The 17-year-old had found his model. *He was already a Leninist before he became a Marxist!*

Far more than the chiliastic vision, young Ulyanov found in Chernyshevsky an expression and ventilation of the subterranean rage he felt toward his world. Chernyshevsky gave him words to express it, and targets toward which to aim it. Above all, Chernyshevsky fixed the young man's rage on "liberals."

When the news of his brother's arrest reached Simbrisk, Volodya went forth to find someone to accompany his mother on the coach

[233]

ride to Syzran 120 miles away, the nearest railroad station, for her trip to St. Petersburg. Even an older teacher-friend who visited almost every evening to play chess with Vladimir stopped calling. Years later, Lenin recalled the experience:

> At the age of seventeen I began to hate and despise the liberals. Not one rascal of a liberal in Simbirsk had the courage to express his sympathy in even one word to my mother after the execution of my brother. In order not to meet her, they crossed to the other side of the street.[5]

Vladimir's college career lasted exactly three months. The University of Kazan had 918 students, most of them sons of government officials, like Vladimir Ulyanov. In Moscow a student slapped an inspector during a public concert and was sent to an army penal battalion for three years. The wave of protests spread to Kazan. On December 16 a crowd gathered to demand changes in university administration, Vladimir among them. The students passed resolutions that might have come from Columbia or Harvard in the 1960s —demands that the universities be run by the professional senate with no government interference; that students be freed of supervision of their private lives; that scholarships to be distributed by elected representatives; that students have the rights to assemble and petition; that officials responsible for "police brutality" at Moscow be punished. Vladimir Ulynaov, brother of the notorious executed assassin, was reported seen running up and down a hallway in the front row of protestors clenching his fists.

Ultimately a hundred students were expelled or asked to resign. Ulyanov was arrested that night, spent two days in jail, and was among the first 45 expelled outright. He went to Kokushkino, where his mother had taken the family to the estate she inherited from her father. Again he lost himself in Chernyshevsky. Later he confessed he never read as much or as passionately as during his forced stay in Kokushkino.

> I read every word of Chernyshevsky's magnificent comments about esthetics, art and literature. . . I was conquered by Chernyshevsky's encyclopedic knowledge, the clarity of his revolutionary views, and his unyielding polemical talent.[7]

What the 18-year-old read in Chernyshevsky's essays sounds sometimes like a cross between Horatio Alger and a Boy Scout Patrol

Leader's Handbook, and it had at least as powerful a molding effect. Chernyshevsky knew how "to expound purely revolutionary ideas in the legal press which was subject to censorship," Lenin wrote in 1894. Let us examine some of the precepts Vladimir studied:

A political leader must be resolute and determined, and once he has set himself to a definite goal, he must *ruthlessly pursue it to the end.*

Whoever is afraid of being covered with dirt and dust and soiling his boots is not acceptable for social activity . . . but *the profession is not at all a neat one.* However, moral cleanness can be understood in various ways.

A man [a revolutionary] who aspires to do something useful, must be convinced that *he cannot expect support from anyone except from people who sympathize with his intentions.*

Honesty and integrity alone are not enough in order to be correct and useful. Consistency in ideas is also necessary. If you have accepted a principle, *do not retreat before its consequences.*

Whoever takes up the cause must know where it will lead him, and if he does not want its inevitable attending circumstances, he must not want the cause itself. *Political revolutions have never been accomplished without cases of arbitrariness*, which have destroyed the forms of legal justice observed during quiet times. Revolutions excite and stir up the feeling of the people, and excited feeling forgets about forms. Whoever does not know this does not understand the character of the forces by which history is moved; he does not know the human heart. The person who takes part in a political revolution and imagines that in doing this he will not *many times violate* the legal principles of quiet times must be called an idealist.

A person is guilty before history if he takes up a cause whose character he does not understand. He is guilty because through his mistakes he brings too much harm to the cause and to all whom it concerns . . . You must weigh good and evil, and *if it seems to you that in essence the cause is good, do not be confused or embarrassed by the fact that it contains aspects of evil;* . . .

Whoever does not want to agitate and arouse the people, whoever finds detestable the scenes that are inseparably connected with the stimulation of popular passions, must not take it upon himself to direct the cause, whose support can only be the animation of the mass.

Great people [leaders of the revolution] are great people not just because they *hasten to strike while the iron is hot and know not to lose days while the circumstances are favorable to the cause.* However, it is well-known that he *cannot strike the iron who is afraid of the noise disturbing people who are asleep.* Only energy can lead to success, and energy consists of *not hesitating to take those measures which are necessary for success* . . . but make up your mind *not to spare people* before you begin the war . . . If *you are afraid* or shun those *measures which the cause requires*, then *do not get involved in it* and do not take the responsibility upon yourself to direct it—you only spoil the cause. There is nothing worse than when a man who accepts the leadership of a cause yields to self-delusions regarding the phenomena which may be evoked by these means. Nothing is worse than this, with the possible exception of his not understanding how people must act who consider [the cause] as good.[8]

In 1904 in a Geneva sidewalk cafe Lenin, then 34, was musing inattentively as three fellow Bolsheviks discussed Russian literature. One fellow remarked that, objectively laying aside revolutionary messages, they would certainly have to admit Chernyshevsky's *What Is To Be Done?* was poorly written and untalented. With a start Lenin sat bolt upright. His cheeks "turned crimson with indignation" and he "threw himself literally like a tiger on the speaker," reports Nikolai Valentinov who, as the hapless offender, had good reason to remember the astonishing reaction.

"Do you realize what you are saying?" Lenin flared. "How could such a monstrous and absurd idea come into your head—to describe Chernyshevsky's work as crude and untalented! He was the greatest and most talented spokeman of socialism before Marx! Marx himself called Chernyshevsky a great Russian writer . . . I declare it is *impermissible* to call him crude and untalented!"

Thus Lenin launched into a long, detailed rhapsody to Chernyshevsky and his influence on The Master's development—so ecstatic that his whole circle of followers was utterly flabbergasted. Lenin did not often show such emotion, after all. After his conquest of Russia made him a giant of history those present wrote down and compared their recollections, and the revealing substance of his remarks has been preserved.[9]

Chapter 17
CREATING THE SOCIOLOGY OF DISCONTENT

The rebel turns his indignation now against this injustice, now against another; the revolutionary is a consistent hater who has invisited all his power of hatred in one object. The rebel always has a touch of the Quixotic; the revolutionary is a bureaucrat of Utopia. The rebel is an enthusiast; the revolutionary, a fanatic.

—*Arrow in the Blue,*
Arthur Koestler

LENIN, MEET MARX   At 18 Vladimir Ulyanov was thus already a committed "professional revolutionary," guided by a strong Jacobin vision and tradition as well as committed to destroying Russia's *ancien régime* and installing Kingdom Come with himself and his "new people" at the helm. Only thereafter did he begin to explore Marxism. He first picked up Plekhanov's *Our Differences.* In 1904, asked when he first read Karl Marx's *Das Kapital,* he replied firmly: "At the beginning of 1889."[1]

At this point (18 months after his brother's execution and his own immersion in Chernyshevsky, and a year after his college expulsion), he had swallowed the entire messianic package of hate. Young Lenin set outside his consciousness all concern with the underlying romantic Roberspierrist-Babeuvist assumptions of postrevolutionary utopia and concentrated solely on the technology of revolution. He was open-minded only on the methods his new class should use in their task of demolition. Neither Marx nor Chernyshevsky had written that handbook.

We do not know when Lenin read his brother's translation of Marx's 1843 essay, with the keystone strategy of mass-hate propaganda. But it was in print a few months after his brother's execution. And with the stress Alexander put upon replacing Vodovozov's copy of the original *Franco-German Yearbook,* we may be sure young Vladimir read the essay early and with intense interest. (He cited it in his 1894 book, *What the "Friends Of the People" Are.*[2]) Moreover, his mind fastened on the crucial passages like a bear trap. Scholars have wondered where Lenin got his doctrine for the use of language as a weapon of destruction and annihilation.[3] It came from his penchant as a youth for "mockery." He was uniquely equipped by temperament, taste, talent, and experience to understand as few others have Marx's meaning in its full implications, and to apply the doctrine: the use of hate propaganda as a weapon of mass manipulation and social demolition in the increasing social complexity of industrial society.

Both Chernyshevsky and Marx intellectually enflamed the young Lenin's sense of apartness and destiny; their doctrine of historic destiny of the "new people" (whom he renamed "professional revolutionaries") became part of his soul. Lenin firmly believed in the triumph of certain hegemonic powers and forces in history—ultimately in himself and his own destiny as dictator of the world. His very name proclaimed so. How could a teen-ager resist such a seductive ideology?

In fact, what we see in Lenin is nothing short of what Bonaro Overstreet calls "arrested adolescent development," i.e., young persons succumbing to radicalism by being "bribed with the idea that they are agents of salvation." They find their own sense of significance and self-esteem in the radical world view. Chernyshevsky and Marx and their doctrine of messianic "new people" became the keystone of Lenin's own personality integration.

This trait struck many observers throughout his career. Once and only once did he ever criticize his idol Karl Marx. His commitment was slavish and total. He was compulsively intolerant of any ambiguity, a salient trait of the "authoritarian personality" and the "closed mind" so thoroughly documented by twentieth-century behavioral scientists.[4] Vodovozov, Alexander's book-lending friend, became intimately acquainted with Vladimir Ulyanov in 1891 in Samara:

> It seems to me that it would be more correct if I said that Marxism for him was not a conviction but a religion. Although he was very much interested in objections to Marxism, he made the presumption that there are and cannot be any valid arguments against Marxism, and he studied them, not with the aim of searching for the truth, but with the aim of finding at their base an error, of whose existence he was convinced beforehand. . . . In him one sensed that degree of certainty which is incompatible with truly scientific knowledge.[5]

Nikolai Valentinov adds the weighty testimony of one who debated Lenin at great length and knew him intimately:

> His brain, obeying some inexplicable power, seized and grasped every letter of Marx and swallowed as absolute truth all of his statements, words, and utterances. Thus, at the beginning with his earliest

years, at the time when he lived in Kazan and Samara [1888–1893] his brain became the despository for the labor theory of value, the theory of land rent, the conviction of the homogeneity of the development of industry and agriculture, the schemes of the second volume of *Das Kapital* concerning the "conversion of all social capital," and a great deal more. Throughout his whole life, Lenin never dared to approach with the least bit of criticism or doubt anything he had taken from the doctrine of Marx. He accepted the doctrine of Marx *purely religiously* . . .

In the presence of such convictions there is no place for searching, inquiring, critical, nonossified thought which follows and keeps up with the rapid changes of life, especially in our epoch, with the new discoveries, with the feverish accumulation of an enormous amount of new knowledge. Here we stand on the threshold of the transformation of Marxism into a monolithic, totalitarian conception, any criticism of which is *ipso facto* considered to be a crime. Not a step further than that which is found in the writings of the fathers of the Marxist church!

Marx became for Lenin what Christ is for those who believe in him, that is, a teacher and guardian of eternal truth, the highest example, an all-wise counsellor . . . But if Marx was Christ for Lenin, then Chernyshevsky was his John the Baptist, and he was equally unable to endure blasphemous remarks about him.[6]

Maxim Gorky, the brilliant and discerning novelist, knew Lenin intimately from his thirty-fifth year until death and backed him with thousands of dollars of his royalties.[7] In a moment of irritation and anger Gorky compared Lenin to the celebrated seventeenth-century Archpriest of the Old Believers, Avvakum, a sort of Russian Savonarola, who preached:

As it is written in the old books, so will I hold and believe, and with that I will die. Until my death I will keep what I have received and accepted. Before our time it was prescribed; and thus it will endure for all time. If someone will make only small changes, let him be damned.[8]

The comparison to Lenin's fanaticism was apt.

Lenin himself wrote Inessa Armand, his mistress, "I cannot quietly endure blasphemous remarks directed at Marx." In his 1908 essay, *Materialism and Empiro-Criticism*— a polemic against the heretical Russian Marxists following the Austrian scientist Mach's views on philosophical idealism—he asserted:

The theory of Marx is objective truth. If we follow Marx's theory we will come closer and closer to objective truth. If we go *any other way*, we will not come to anything—except confusion and lies . . . From Marxism, which is molded out of one piece of steel, it is impossible to extract even one basic premise or one essential part without deviating from the objective truth, without falling into the arms of bourgeois-reactionary lies.[9]

Max Eastman, an American radical journalist, spent 1922–1924 in Russia just before and after Lenin's death, and was allowed to study several volumes of Marx and Engels in which the Great Man had pencilled marginal comments. Reported Eastman:

I never found one question mark, one word in opposition, one mildly critical phrase. Their mood was adulation. They were the comments of a schoolboy learning his "lesson," of a seminary student studying the Scripture. Marx took the place of Sasha in Lenin's mind, and he took the place of God.[10]

So many witnesses at so many stages of Vladimir Ulyanov's life present overwhelming proof that the Marxian belief system played a compulsive-defensive role in his personality integration. They had seen him, argued with him, lived with him. Valentinov saw Lenin bristle, redden, and snap in response to his own criticism of Chernyshevsky and Marx. Lenin's own ego, his self-esteem and confidence in his messianic role, rested on his faith in Chernyshevsky and Marx. Thus, before turning 21, he had become a slavish and fanatical addict dependent on the Marxian doctrine of hate.

FARMER, LAWYER, REVOLUTIONARY   Early in 1889 Maria Ulyanova sold the family home in Simbirsk and bought a farm for 7,500 rubles for her 18-year-old son, hoping he would become a gentleman-farmer. On May 3 they moved to the place at Alakayeva, a village of 84 families and 300 souls some 35 miles from Samara. The place had 225 acres, a mill and manor house. Vladimir was unable to manage the peasants; after six months he quit farming and the family moved into Samara, spending summers on the farm for the next five years.

Located on the Volga, Samara had a population of 100,000 and no university. It was a place where old Narodyaya Volya exiles were permitted to live after serving out their prison terms. Vladimir sought them out, and began in earnest to study revolutionary operations and conspiratorial techniques. He spent long nights questioning the masters in minute detail. He learned how they came into the movement, how they won new recruits, what their program was and how they expounded it, how they circulated it and how the masses responded. He stored up all they could tell about chemical inks, secret codes, signals, false passports, jailbreaks, and escapes from exile. He absorbed the history of nearly a century of revolutionary plots, struggles, and failures in Russia. Anna records that he also studied the trial records of old revolutionaries, probably including Nechayev.[11] The old veterans, pleased to have a young listener, told him how the Narodnaya Volya had organized, who chose the executive committee, what authority it had, how it admitted and instructed members and limited their knowledge of each other to a minimum to frustrate czarist spies.

One veteran was Maria Yasneva, nine years older than Lenin. She was a personal pupil of Zaychnevsky, Chernyshevsky's great Jacobin apostle, and an ardent exponent of the Russian "Jacobin" school of radicals. It was this association that produced her exile in Samara under police supervision. She found Lenin "already conceived of the dictatorship of the proletariat. He often dwelt on the subject of the seizure of power, one of the points of *our Jacobin* program."

Ultimately she became an equally ardent Bolshevik, finding a logical extension of her Russian Jacobin tradition. She married V.S. Golubev, who became a terrorist "judge" in the Bolshevik Cheka, forerunner of the KGB. Valentinov, who watched Lenin revert to Jacobinism in his 1904 duel with the Mensheviks, held that Lenin's Bolshevik theory and practice would have looked the same *even without mixing in the Marxist ideology.* Marxism provided the ideological cement for holding together the amalgam of messianic radicals with a little extra promise of certainty. This very attraction made it for Lenin a highly practical tool of target-audience analysis in fashioning his hate propaganda. For his interest was turning now strongly to the manipulative and organization-building problems of propaganda. Thus his questions to Yasneva. "He did not question either the possibility or the desirability of the seizure of power, but he was quite unable to understand what sort of 'masses' we wanted to get support from," she recorded.[12]

Obviously Lenin, systematic genius that he was, was impatient with the older radical idealists' notions of "the masses." *Which* masses? *Who?* Where will they come from? How will we "movers of the movers" connect them to the revolutionary organization? At 21, Lenin was like the young Karl Marx of 1843, a general in search of an army. He wanted details about where to recruit and how to command!

The Jacobinism-Tkachevism Lenin learned through Yasneva and others led him to piece together the answers over the next 13 years. Yasneva also supplied the solution to how to organize. She told him of Zaychnevsky's Jacobin rule: "To be able to seize power, we must have a strictly centralized organization." She explained Zaychnevsky's demand for "unquestioning" obedience to party orders and how he cut short even "the slightest suggestion" of deviation. She gave him Zaychnevsky's favorite saying: "Jump into the water and don't splutter." "When I say frog, you hop—and ask how high on the way up," goes the contemporary American colloquial version. Lenin in 1904 remembered Yasneva's advice when he was conducting his terrible polemic with Plekhanov, Martov and Trotsky over his demand for a militarized combat party. They called him "Jacobin." "Yes!" Lenin proudly proclaimed. And he wrote another of his basic treatises on organization, one of the books of the Bolshevik bible— *One Step Forward, Two Steps Back.*[13]

In May 1890 Maria Ulyanova journeyed to St. Petersburg and won permission for her problem-son to take the law examinations at St. Petersburg University the next year. That fall Lenin himself went there to talk with the professors and prepare. His younger sister Olga, a student, introduced him to V.V. Vodovozov, Alexander's old schoolmate and lender of the 1844 *Franco-German Yearbook.* Vodovozov acted as Lenin's informant and guide around the university. Lenin spent two months there in 1890 and two each in the spring and fall of 1891. In January 1892 he received his law diploma and was admitted to the Samara Circuit Court junior bar, and in August 1892 he was granted his full legal license. Passing his legal exams based on the four-year university course in but a year's time was a tour de force. But Lenin only dabbled in law, assisting a couple of barristers for appearance's sake. His mother's income provided amply for him. His real heart was in becoming a revolutionary. Meantime, late in 1891 Vodovozov moved to Samara and in the next year often visited the Ulyanov family. His testimony is revealing.

Vodovozov found Lenin surrounded by an atmosphere of worship and remarked that the "incense" of his family had already turned his head. The Ulyanov family regarded him not merely as a talented person but as a *genius.* Mama listened to his passionate speeches and dogmatic declarations indulgently. His older sister Anna regarded him an oracle; her husband, too, and the rest of the family ultimately became Marxists. The younger brothers and sisters idolized him. A "presentiment" of his greatness dominated all and the family catered to his every whim. Vodovozov found that the family's "incense" had also ultimately wafted to a circle of naïve admirers outside among Samara's young radicals, including Yasneva. They accepted him as an authority, too, and by his 1893 stay on the farm they made frequent pilgrimages to Alakayeva. Another member of the Samara circle, Semenov, wrote: "In his presence all of us restrained ourselves. A frivolous conversation, a dirty jest, were impossible in his presence."

Vodovozov found the 21-year-old Lenin in 1891 already shaped, and rigidly so: "A profound faith in his righteousness showed through all his conversations." He had swallowed whole his self-constructed package containing Marx and Chernyshevsky. He declared himself completely satisfied with Marx on all points and felt that he had completely mastered the doctrine. Vodovozov found him deliberately narrowed, almost obsessed, excluding all knowledge outside his own immediate interest. He was ignorant in the fields of natural science, philosophy, arts and *belles-lettres*. But in history, political economy, social and revolutionary movements "his knowledge was striking because of its profound nature and versatility, especially if one considered his age," Vodovozov wrote in 1925.

> At this time he already knew *Das Kapital* very well and was also thoroughly acquainted with the extensive [German] literature of Marxism. *He gave the impression of a person who is completely finished and shaped in the realm of politics.*[14]

Heaven save the world from any man whose thought is finished at age 21!

Lenin would not tolerate anyone near him who stood up to him, disagreed, or maintained the slightest independence of thought. He would soon break off all personal relations with anyone who did not burn incense before him. Such was Vodovozov's fate. "I will not sit at the same table with philistines!" Lenin spat. After Vodovozov stood up to him, Lenin hardly shook hands, and when they met later in St. Petersburg he pointedly snubbed his old benefactor. The other members of Lenin's circle, both family and comrades, also "developed an almost hostile attitude" toward Vodovozov. There was no room in the circle for anyone but worshippers and blind followers.

It was a hate commune, and those who did not share the hate were not admitted.

In the light of Vodovozov's independence and rejection, therefore, his testimony is especially valuable. It is extremely significant that even he, judging the young man of 1892, began to feel that "Ulyanov's role will be great." He repeated this estimate eleven years later in Kiev in 1903 every time Lenin's name came up, Valentinov recalled.[15]

Vodovozov was particularly struck by Lenin's passion, duplicating Chernyshevsky, in arguing that for the sake of the triumph of their ideas the revolutionaries must not hestiate to use any and all means. Lenin incessantly insisted on a kind of superman antinomianism. "He did not admit any doubts about the permissibility of using any means —if only they led to the goal."[16] Vodovozov began calling his young antagonist "Marat," after the most extreme terrorist of the French Revolution.

So dominating was this obsession with instrumentalities that Lenin in his entire adult life never let into his consciousness any question about the goal itself: whether the Marxian prophecy of a human flowering instantly on the morrow of the revolution would in fact occur. Not until *after* the rebellion and massacre of 18,000 soldiers and workers demanding free elections at Kronstadt in 1921, until Lenin was practically on his deathbed, did he consider the problem. But by then his brain was disintegrating.

The source of his quarrel with Vodovozov illuminates this obsession. In 1891 a famine swept Russia and peasants began to flood the cities begging bread and work. Alone among Samara's radicals, Lenin and Yasneva scorned the famine relief efforts as fundamentally reactionary plots. "Obviously he thought the revolutionary should take another path," Yasneva remembered. No doubt they both recalled Chernyshevsky's 1860 cry: "The worse, the better for us." Soon they won the others over, but Vodovozov argued with Lenin at length. The 21-year-old's response was pure "Leninism":

> The famine is the direct result of a definite social order, and as long as this order exists, such hunger strikes are inevitable; one can eliminate them only be destroying this order. Although it is in this sense inevitable, the famine at the present time also plays the role of a progressive factor. Destroying the peasant farm, driving the peasant from the country into the city, the famine creates a proletariat and contributes to the industrialization of the country; this is a phenome-

non of a progressive character. But the famine can and must be a progressive factor not only in the economic sphere. It compels the peasant to think about the foundations of the capitalist order, destroys his faith in the tsar and tsarism, and consequently, in due course, will facilitate the victory of the revolution. The aspirations of society, so-called, to come to the aid of the famine-stricken, to ease their suffering are understandable . . . The famine threatens this social order with shock and perhaps destruction; the urge to alleviate the consequences of the famine, therefore, is completely natural. Basically, this is an urge to weaken the inevitable future shocks, to save the foundations of bourgeois society, and, consequently, to save themselves. Psychologically, all the talk about feeding the hungry is the expression of the usual sugar and honey sentimentalism which is peculiar to our intelligentsia.[17]

THE GESTATION OF LENINIST POWEROLOGY   In March 1893 via remote control Lenin came under the influence of a brilliant young Marxist, Nikolai F. Fodosseyev (1871–1898). A year younger than Lenin, he was expelled from Kazan high school in 1887 for participating in a People's Freedom self-education circle and reading subversive literature. A prodigious reader and organizer, he turned to Marxism and began actively organizing and propagandizing in 1888. Fedosseyev thus encountered the practical problems in mass-marketing Marxist ideology. His quick mind snapped on them masterfully.

Self-education was the fashion in Russian revolutionary circles. So reading lists, bibliographies and other study aids were necessary tools; Alexander Ulyanov's circle in St. Petersburg had undertaken to produce some in 1887. Fedosseyev collected press clippings on Marx and Marxism, set up a clandestine printing press and reproduced rare books and articles. Maxim Gorky, who saw his "catalog" in 1889, years later told Lenin "no one could have put together a better guide." Filled with radical books, synopses and reviews and articles, it was a "font of wisdom."

Lenin did not meet Fedosseyev before leaving Kazan in 1889. Even so, he probably would have been caught in the net had he been there in June when police discovered Fedosseyev's illegal printing press and arrested his ring. Fedosseyev divided his program into three parts: ideology, organizational technique, and propaganda. He was already engaged in audience target analysis. He divided audiences into cultured classes, peasants, workers, soldiers, and "the people." He stressed the importance of print media, and of organizing for both propaganda and paramilitary combat. He was developing a scheme for the Marxist party's "inner organization"—for what ultimately became "Leninism."[18] Lenin himself paid Fedosseyev the supreme compliment in 1908 when he told Gorky the young man "would have become a Bolshevik."

Released from prison in January 1892, Fedosseyev settled at Vladimir, a little town 105 miles from Moscow, and began building an action program for organized, concerted, and sustained operations among industrial workers: an orchestration of propaganda. He began advocating a Marxist propaganda effort among the Russian proletariat—the first Russian Marxist to move beyond the stage of self-education circles. This landed him back in prison in September 1892.

The police allowed a Fedosseyev disciple from the Kazan circle, Isaac C. Lalayants, to go to Samara in exile in March 1893. Lenin met him immediately at the home of an old People's Freedom exile. Soon they and Aleksey Popov (alias Sklyarenko) formed a fast circle. During Lenin's summer on the farm the other two frequently journeyed the 35 miles to visit. They shared letters and manuscripts from Fedosseyev. Lenin himself wrote to Fedosseyev in the Vladimir prison. From his cell Fedosseyev became Lenin's mentor and prod in solving the question Yasneva could not answer: *Which* masses?

That summer Lenin resolved it was time for a serious professional revolutionary to do market research on the question. And that meant going where the "masses" were—St. Petersburg.

Before leaving, he conducted a pioneering experiment. He paid for the printing of 200–250 questionnaires and commissioned an idealistic friend who had founded an agricultural commune to collect replies from Volga villagers. They were sent along to him later.[19] It was a milestone in the development of Leninism and the sociology of discontent, a power-oriented social analysis which we may label Leninist *powerology*. Lenin was a full generation ahead of Madison Avenue in mass marketing "motivational research."

This survey marked the young Lenin's first attempts to apply his Marxian class struggle concepts to the realities of Russian life and the changing rural-urban economic scene. That summer, to his fellow Samara radicals visiting him on the farm at Alakayeva, he read his first work written for publication. It was a "book review" that was a small booklet itself, 46 closely printed pages, 23,000 words, taking three hours to read aloud. Possibly because of its length, the editor of a liberal populist magazine rejected it, thereby bruising young

Vladimir Ulyanov's pride and earning a few choice Leninist words of scorn.[20] In his article, possibly because he aimed at public consumption through a liberal magazine and had to pass both the editor and the czarist censor, Lenin did not quote Marx a single time, a remarkable omission. But he clearly was seeking to apply Marxist "class analysis" and find "exploitation," or some grounds for charging it, so he could thereby mobilize one group against another for his revolutionary army.

Lenin was reviewing a populist economist's study of changes in farming in southern Russia. He quoted copiously from the author's statistical tables and research, paraphrased, and added only a few paragraphs of his own analysis. But obviously, he was excited by the radical change underway—the capitalist revolution Marx wrote about in *The Manifesto* was already shaking the Russian grassroots! In some areas as many as half the farms had acquired mechanical harvesters in the past ten years! New, more efficient plows and drills and threshers were being introduced; savings-and-loan associations were forming to provide credit. Some peasant families were prospering, buying more land and machinery, creating a mass market for the growing urban factories. On these larger units, labor productivity rose dramatically. Inefficient smaller units were squeezed; their owners sold out and became laborers. But inexorably, mechanization and the trend to larger units released—forced—people from the farm economy and toward the cities and their factories. The famine in 1891 only hastened the process. Here was class war in progress in the countryside! Small wonder that Vladimir Ulyanov sought intelligence on the peasant economy and began to chart the contours of the peasant attitude structure.

URBANIZING RUSSIA   The nation Lenin surveyed was already in the midst of a social revolution. The ancient neolithic peasant agriculture was shifting to urban industrial capitalism. Until the late nineteenth century, Russia had a feudal slave economy based largely on subsistence farming. The czarist government followed the 1861 emancipation of 22,500,000 serfs with administrative and judicial reforms streamlined along Western models. These changes promoted industrialization, the development of the money economy, and urbanization. Coal mines, railroads, and factories grew apace.

Marx in the *Communist Manifesto* wrote that industrial development transforms workers from incoherent masses scattered over the whole country into concentrated masses. Thus it creates improved communication, worker associations, and the "contact that was needed to centralize the numerous local struggles, all of the same class struggle character, into one national struggle between classes." Many read him to mean that the process would occur spontaneously.

Indeed, the process was occuring before young Vladimir Ulyanov's eyes. New methods of farming were shattering a basic people-to-land ratio of "forty acres and a mule" that had held roughly constant since before the Mongol hordes, before Christ, from the time mankind's earliest cities of Babylon and Ninevah grew just below Russia's southern borders in the Tigris-Euphrates valleys. Railroads and steamships made travel possible. The telegraph permitted communications instantly across Russian vastnesses. By telephone, capitalist entrepreneurs even predicted, people would soon be able to talk from St. Petersburg to Moscow—a distance of 400 miles! One could distribute a newspaper to more people at a factory gate in St. Petersburg in a single afternoon than he could reach in the average Russian village or town in a whole month a half century previously.

When Lenin was born Russia had not a single city of a million. When he arrived in St. Petersburg, the nation had *two* genuine megalopolises. In 1863 the combined populations of Moscow and St. Petersburg barely counted 1,056,000. In the 1897 census they numbered 2,552,000. During the year Lenin arrived, Russia experienced its first serious outbreaks of labor violence. The Yaroslav strike of 1894 was the most violent of many in 1893–1895.

But a Marxist "plowed over by Chernyshevsky" would not and could not trust spontaneity and magic social processes. As a "new type," Lenin knew that his duty was to "impart regularity to the chaotic agitation of the movement of the masses." *He had to learn how to be a "mover of the movers."*

LINKING THE REVOLUTIONARIES   Arriving in the capital city in September, Lenin brought with him from Samara letters of introduction and the beginnings of a reputation as a bright young revolutionary. After all, he was the kid brother of one of Russia's genuine revolutionary martyrs. Ostensibly he joined a prominent liberal law firm, but his real job was apprentice revolutionary. He promptly linked up with a two-year-old Marxist club of ten or a dozen young men, mostly students at the St. Petersburg Technological Institution. Stephan I. Radchenko, the organizing leader, gave young Ulyanov an important piece of the puzzle he was working with: Like the Jacobins, Radchenko rejected the notion that "the workers" would automatically lead the movement and instead argued for a "small highly conspiratorial party of revolutionaries recruited exclusively from the intelligentsia."[11]

The circle also supplied recruits for the revolutionary general staff, names that were to loom large in Bolshevism's history. Leonid B. Krassin became a top Lenin lieutenant in charge of bank robberies. Gleb M. Krzhizhanovsky rose to become chairman of the USSR's Supreme Council of National Economy in the 1920s, chairman of the Committee on Higher Education and a vice president of the Academy of Sciences; a real "old Bolshevik," he died in 1959 at age 87.

The importance Lenin placed on linking up with Fedosseyev is demonstrated by the trouble he took to meet him. Three weeks after arriving in St. Petersburg, Lenin traveled the 400 miles back to Moscow and the 105 miles out to Vladimir. He did not see the brilliant young revolutionary, for he was again in prison, but established contact through a girlfriend and received a manuscript from him. Fedosseyev recognized a grave threat to Russia's young Marxists in the populist attacks on their attitude toward the 1891 famine and their lust for violent revolution. Possibly he asked Lenin to tackle the problem of answering the populist argument for peaceful change. At any rate, Lenin went to work on it.

LENIN'S SOCIOLOGY OF DISCONTENT   We come to a crucial bit of evidence for understanding Lenin's life and his "ism." In April 1894, just as he reached his twenty-fourth birthday, Lenin completed the first part of his first book. Before the summer ended he added two more parts. They constitute conclusive proof that Lenin had developed the heart of Leninism shortly before his 24th birthday—just as Karl Marx developed the core of his strategy of hate propaganda in 1843 when he was but 25.

Lenin's manuscripts were duplicated in June, July and September by a priest in Vladimir, a part of Fedosseyev's organization, and by other Marxist circles which circulated them illegally. Young Lenin became nationally known among radicals. In his book, *What The "Friends of the People" Are and How They Fight the Social-Democrats*, he answered the attacks on Marxism that were published in *Russian Wealth*, a monthly magazine of the populists—the old "People's Freedom" democrats whose progeny, the Socialist Revolutionaries, were to outpoll Lenin's Bolsheviks in Russia's only free election in November 1917 by 16 million to 10 million out of 41 million votes cast.

[249   ]

With pyrotechnics, Lenin unveiled his childhood talent for "mockery" and arrogant invective. He tears his adversaries apart, accusing them of misunderstanding and distorting Marx, then making his own selections and giving the Pure Gospel according to Lenin the True Apostle. It was to become his standard polemical format.

Viewing Marx's life and writings objectively, we must say that Lenin was essentially right. *He truly did understand Marx as no one else had*—and Marx probably would have agreed with Lenin's interpretation, though perhaps he might have balked at some of the later inferences Lenin drew from these starting premises. In his "Friends of the People" essay Lenin for the first time quotes Marx's 1843 essay on Hegel, where the Master worked out his grand strategy of hate propaganda. Lenin also quotes Marx's revealing 1843 correspondence with Ruge. Lenin brought to these works a personality perfectly attuned to receive the heart and soul of Marx's doctrine, his ideas on mass hate propaganda as an organizing and mobilizing weapon. In their basic emotional cores, the 25-year-old Marx and the 24-year-old author of *What the "Friends of the People" Are* were true-life brothers. The kinship shows in their penchants for invective and sarcasm as well as their rational elaboration of hate strategies. Young Lenin's mind and soul fastened on young Marx's basic insight and made it a part of himself.

After verbally pommeling Marx's critics, he proceeds to preach to his fellow Marxists on what they must do to bring the revolution. Lenin cites Marx on "the unifying significance of capitalism." "Rural Russia constitutes a system of small, scattered markets," he points out. Its "mass of small rural exploiters represents a terrible force, especially terrible because they oppress the isolated, single toiler," and given "the absence of communications," there is no hope of mass organization and revolution; the "material conditons" are absent. This is

> why Social-Democrats regard the work of our capitalism as progressive when it draws these small, scattered markets together into one nationwide market, when, in place of the legion of small well-meaning bloodsuckers, it creates a handful of big "pillars of the fatherland," when it socializes labor and raises its productivity, when it shatters the subordination of the working people to the local blood-suckers and subordinates them to large-scale *capital*. This subordination is progressive compared with the former . . . because it **AWAKENS THE MIND OF**

THE WORKER, converts dumb and incoherent discontent into conscious protest, converts scattered, petty senseless revolt into an organized class struggle . . . a struggle which undoubtedly therefore can count upon CERTAIN SUCCESS.[22]

Lenin quotes Marx's 1843 essay:

> Cristicism has plucked the imaginary flowers which adorned the chains, not that man should wear his fetters denuded of fanciful embellishment, but that he should throw off the chain and reach for the living flower.[23]

And he also quotes Marx's September 1843 letter to Ruge:

> We do not say to the world: "Cease struggling—your whole struggle is senseless. All we do is to provide it with a true slogan of struggle.[24]

Lenin continues:

> It remains an indisputable fact that the working class movement spreads and develops precisely where and to the extent that large-scale capitalist machine industry develops; the socialist doctrine is successful precisely when it stops arguing about social conditions that conform to human nature and sets about making a materialist analysis of contemporary social relations and explaining the necessity for the present regime of exploitation.[25]

Capitalism is "progressive" precisely because it provides visible and accessible hate targets for mobilizing the masses, because it offers opportunities for hatemongering in its specialization and division of labor. This is the "unifying significance of capitalism" for the Marxist "movers of the movers!"

Marxist revolutionaries must rid themselves of all paralyzing notions of peaceful reform and progress and of democratic, constitutional organization and restraints. Class cooperation is impossible for the simple reason that it will prevent the apocalyptic cataclysm. Lenin thus casts out the devils of liberalism:

> Today, the theories of these democratic ideologies, when they come forward as the spokesmen of the interests of the working people, are positively reactionary. They obscure the antagonism of contemporary Russian social-economic relations and argue as if

things could be improved by general measures, applicable to all, for "raising," improving," etc., and *as if it were possible to reconcile and unite.* [Emphasis added—E. H. M.] They are reactionary in depicting our state as something standing above classes and therefore fit and capable of rendering serious and honest aid to the exploited population. They are reactionary, lastly, because they simply cannot understand the necessity for struggle, a desperate struggle. . . . Socialists must make a **DECISIVE** and **FINAL** break with the ideas and theories of the democrats.[26]

Here Lenin joins an epoch-making and civilization-splitting debate. On the other side were such men as James Madison, "The Father of the Constitution," and Samuel Gompers, "The Statesman of American Labor," who fought harsh battles against the proto-Leninists of their own day and realm for the notion that government may be a neutral referee in a pluralistic society, governing for the general good among a diversity of competing interest groups. In the Twentieth Century the Leninists and the Madisonians were to wage what Adlai Stevenson at the time of the 1962 Cuba missile crisis aptly called "the world civil war" over these conflicting ideologies. Lenin continued:

The socialist intelligentsia can expect to perform fruitful work only when they abandon their illusions . . . Their **THEORETICAL** work must be directed towards *the concrete study of all forms of economic antagonism in Russia, the study of their connections and successive development;* they must *reveal this antagonism wherever it has been concealed by political history, by the peculiarities of legal systems or by established theoretical prejudice.* They must *present an integral picture of our realities as a definite system of production relations, show that the exploitation and expropriation of the working people are under this system, and show the way out of this system that is indicated by economic development.*

This theory . . . if it satisfies the requirements of science, then every awakening of the protesting thought of the proletariat will inevitably guide this thought into the channels of Social-Democracy. The greater the progress made in elaborating this theory, the more rapidly will Social-Democracy grow . . .

In thus emphasizing the necessity, importance and immensity of the theoretical work of the Social-Democrats, I by no means want to say that this work should take precedence over **PRACTICAL** work. On the contrary, the practical work of propaganda and agitation must always take precedence . . .[27]

Behind his turgid Marxese here Lenin is saying: *we do not study society as scientists seeking to understand it but as revolutionaries seeking to explode it!* Regardless of reality, we must force it into our theory. We must have our Armageddon! For Lenin, as for the 25-year-old Marx himself, Marxism was not a tool of inquiry for studying society, but a propaganda strategy for conquering it. The end precedes and dictates the means! We must scavenge every conflict and frustration and hook it to our quest for political power.

Under these circumstances, theoretical and practical work merge into one aptly described by the veteran German Social-Democrat, Liebknecht, as:

Study, Propaganda, Organization.

You cannot be an ideological leader without the above-mentioned theoretical work, *just as you cannot be one without directing this work to meet the needs of the cause* . . .

The political mission of the Social-Democrats lies in promoting the development and organization of the working-class movement in Russia, in *transforming this movement from its present state of sporadic attempts at protest, "riots" and strikes devoid of a guiding idea, into an organized struggle* of the **WHOLE** Russian working **CLASS** directed against the bourgeois regime and working for the expropriation of the expropriators . . .[28]

Already Lenin's mind is hurtling past the problem of increasing every friction and directing every protest in the industrial economy toward the orchestrating of social conflicts into an overwhelming crescendo. *Discontent is everywhere;* everywhere it is found it must be linked to the party through propaganda:

The exploitation of the working people in Russia *is everywhere* capitalist in nature . . . The worker cannot fail to see that he is oppressed by *capital,* that his struggle has to be waged against the bourgeois *class.* . . . All that is needed is simply *to make him understand his position,* to make him understand the political and economic structure of the system that oppresses him, and the necessity and inevitability of class antagonisms under this system . . .

Large-scale capitalism . . . inevitably severs all the workers' ties with the old society, with a particular locality and particular exploiter; it unites them, compels them to think and places them in conditions which enable them to commence an organized struggle. Accordingly it is on the working class that the Social-Democrats concentrate all their attention and all their activities. When its advanced representatives have mastered the ideas of scientific socialism, the idea of the historical mission of the Russian worker, when these ideas become widespread, and when enduring organizations have been established among the workers to transform the worker's present sporadic economic war into conscious class struggle—then the Russian **WORKER,** rising at the head of all the democratic elements, will overthrow absolutism and lead the **RUSSIAN PROLETARIAT** (side by side with the proletariat of **ALL COUNTRIES**) *along the straight road of open political struggle to* **THE VICTORIOUS COMMUNIST REVOLUTION.**[29]

The End

1894

Leninism—the sociology of discontent and technology of social demolition—was thus born in St. Petersburg in 1894. The messiah-general had found his army and the essential sales pitch and outlined the campaign strategy for waging his war at Armageddon. Lenin was 24 when he became the world's first full-fledged Leninist, a powerful mould that would stamp millions of replicas.

In an appendix he added crucial afterthoughts:

We are still doing too little in the matter of organization and propaganda among the workers. . . . Our socialists must set to work with the utmost energy; they must work out in greater detail the Marxist conception of history and present position of Russia, and make a more concrete investigation of all forms of the class struggle and exploitation, which are particularly complex and masked in Russia. They must, furthermore, popularize this theory and make it known to the worker; they must help the worker to assimilate it and devise *the form of organization most* **SUITABLE** *under our conditions for disseminating Social-Democratic ideas and welding the workers into a political force.*[30]

Marx considered the whole value of his theory to lie in the fact that it is "in its essence critical and revolutionary." Marxism . . . directly sets itself the task of *disclosing* all the forms of antagonism and exploitation in modern society, tracing their evolution, demonstrating their transitory character, the inevitability of their transformation into a different form, and *thus serving the proletariat as a means of ending all exploitation as quickly and easily as possible . . .*

"We do not say to the world: Cease struggling—your whole struggle is senseless. All we do is to provide it with a true slogan of struggle."

Hence, the direct task of science according to Marx is to provide a true slogan of struggle . . . It is impossible to provide a "slogan of struggle" unless we study every separate form of the struggle minutely, unless we trace every stage of the struggle during the transition from one form to another, so that we can define the situation at any given moment, without losing sight of the general character of the struggle and its general aim, namely, the complete and final abolition of all exploitation and all oppression.[31]

"The direct task of science is to provide a true slogan for the struggle." That task alone dominated Lenin for the rest of his adult life. It obsessed him. He thought beyond it only fleetingly and falteringly in bitter disillusionment and despair in the waning months of his thinking days.

Chapter 18
BUILDING HATE MEDIA

Every revolution was first a thought in one man's mind.

—On History,
Ralph Waldo Emerson

Revolutions are made by fanatical men of action with one-track minds, geniuses in their ability to confine themselves to a limited field. They overturn the old order in a few hours or days, the whole upheaval takes a few weeks or at most years, but the fanatical spirit that inspired the upheavals is worshipped for decades thereafter, or centuries.

—Dr. Zhivago,
Boris Pasternak

GENERAL ULYANOV SURVEYS HIS ARMY   Eighty-thousand workers lived in the slummy factory suburbs ringing St. Petersburg. Lenin had never until this time—age 24—met any. He had only read about them in Marx, and written a book about the role they must play in the grand plan of apocalyptic revolution. Wasn't it high time for the Generalissimo to review his troops and begin assuming command for the campaign ahead?

The St. Petersburg circle held a meeting in February, disguised as a traditional Shrove Tuesday pre-Lenten pancake party to fool the police. There Lenin met a young teacher, Nadezhda K. Krupskaya. A year his senior, she had been in Radchenko's cell from the start, and she was a rather fanatical, cold person. ("She looks like a herring," Lenin's sister Anna wrote when they met.) Krupskaya had heard of Lenin; in the fall he had written a 15,000-word essay "On the Market Question" that cell members were passing about eagerly because it proved that capitalism was coming to Russia, and hence revolution. Krupskaya recalled that at the time most of them had never seen the *Communist Manifesto,* though they had muddled through the readily available volume of *Das Kapital;* and so they were mystified as to just *how* the revolution would come, according to Marx. It seemed to be supposed to happen by some mechanistic and automatic fashion. This "certain learned Marxist from the Volga" obviously had some of the answers, because he had read the earlier holy scriptures of the young Marx. So the pancake party was arranged to let the other cell members meet and question him.

Somebody suggested that one urgent task was work on the Illiteracy Committee, a liberal do-good program to teach workers to read. Krupskaya recalled: "Vladimir Ilyich laughed, and somehow his laughter sounded so wicked and dry. I never heard him laugh that way again."

"Well," he said, "If anyone wants to save the country by working in the Illiteracy Committee, let him go ahead, we shall not interfere."

Obviously, Krupskaya understood perfectly—Lenin had another strategy.

Krupskaya was teaching workers to read in the Smolenskaya Sunday Evening School for Adults, in a suburban factory district. After the pancake party, Lenin walked her home. At first he saw in her only an intelligence source and an intermediary for meeting workers. On Sunday evenings Lenin would seek her out for long walks after her classes during which he would interrogate her profusely about the conditions, interests, attitudes, and life of the workers. As Krupskaya recalled, "Vladimir Ilyich was interested in every detail that could help him to piece together a picture of the life and conditions of the workers, *to find some sort of avenue of approach to them in the matter of revolutionary propaganda.*"[1] He gave her elaborate questionnaires to guide her in eliciting information from her pupils. He made her bring trusted individuals home with her for questioning, and he made them sweat under his systematic, pressing interrogations. Lenin was in the midst of writing his *Friends of the People* book: "All we do is provide a true slogan for the struggle." And so he had to start by pioneering in-depth interviews, sampling techniques and motivational research.

Up to this point St. Petersburg's Marxist party of the workers had no workers at all; it was an isolated gaggle of intellectuals. But by autumn 1894 Lenin formed a worker class of his own from Krupskaya's pupils, trusted recruits, and used them as guinea pigs for teaching Marxism. He learned more than his pupils from these classes: how to adapt *Das Kapital* to everyday Russian life; how to simplify the Marxian terminology; how to articulate the class struggle dogma in simple terms; how to lead workers to identify "exploitation" in their concrete everyday lives, to see the visible and accessible hate targets of "capitalism"; how to identify the Forces of Light and Forces of Darkness struggling in their own midst.

One worker Lenin recruited through Krupskaya was Ivan Babushkin. Converted to Marxism, he became a resourceful smuggler of illegal Bolshevik newspapers, was caught rushing a trainload of arms to a Bolshevik unit in Siberia following the Moscow 1905 insurrection, and summarily shot. His memoir, therefore, reflects not the later Lenin glorification cult but the true 24-year-old Babushkin saw in 1894:

> He never consulted any notes, and he was continually pausing to provoke us to speak or arouse us to start a discussion. And then he would urge us on, always making us justify our positions. Thus our lectures were always lively and interesting, and we began to get accustomed to speaking in public. All of us greatly enjoyed these lectures and were constantly amazed by our lecturer's power of intellect. It was a standing joke among us that he had so many brains they had pushed his hair out. These lectures trained us to do independent organizing and research. The lecturer would hand us lists of questions which required detailed knowledge and observation of life in the factory and workshop.

Indeed, Babushkin complained that Lenin handed him so many assignments he had almost no time to do his own work, and his toolbox was crammed with little notes about wages and working conditions for reports to his teacher. For his part, Lenin saw in these workers "the future Bebels," after the model of the great German socialist leader who rose from worker ranks. "The role of the intellectuals is to make special leaders from among the intelligentsia unnecessary," Lenin wrote in one of his illegally circulated essays.

Another worker who recorded his memories of Lenin's classes was Vladimir Kniazev, a dockworker. Lenin would masquerade with cap drawn over his eyes and collar turned up; his pupils knew him only as "Nikolay Petrovich."

> He spoke seriously, precisely, carefully reflecting on each word. He spoke as though he admitted no counterarguments. The workers listened attentively and answered his questions about their work, the factories, labor conditions, their comrades, what interested them most and what they read and whether they were capable of understanding and assimilating socialist ideas, and so on.
>
> The principal idea of Nikolay Petrovich, as we understood it, was that the working class was not sufficiently conscious of its own interests and did not yet know how to make profitable use of its own strength. Workmen failed to realize that once they were united, they could break all their fetters. By continually developing their consciousness, they could improve their situation and ultimately free themselves from slavery.
>
> Nikolay Petrovich spoke for more than two hours. He was easy to

listen to, for he explained everything precisely and simply. Comparing his talk with those of other intellectuals, we decided he was altogether different because more convincing; and when he left after setting the date of the next meeting, the comrades turned to one another and said, "Well, there's a fellow who knows what he is talking about."

Krupskaya recalled that Lenin would devote the second half of his two-hour classes to questioning the workers about conditions, showing them how their problems and experiences connected with the whole class structure of society, and telling them how the existing order could be changed.

LAUNCHING HATE MEDIA   In January 1895 Lenin collaborated with Babushkin on a project that should go down in the history of mass communications and mass organization alongside Gutenburg's Bible, KDKA-Pittsburgh's 1920 first newscast, and America's first transcontinental telecast. *He produced the first Russian Marxist leaflet for the workers of the Semyannikov factory, designed to agitate the unrest a worker-pupil had reported there.*[2] At the time the Petersburg Marxists had no printing facilities. So they copied four leaflets by hand and Babushkin distributed them; plant foremen confiscated two, and the other two circulated from hand to hand. A fragment is preserved in Moscow's holy of holies.[3] Lenin, as journalist, was building hate media for the megamedia frontier of the twentieth century.

Very quickly Lenin had the other Marxists in St. Petersburg taking notice. Here was a leader, this new fellow from the Volga. He knew what he was doing. He had real workers organized! Like Lenin they went disguised with pencils and notebooks into the factory districts. He sent Krupskaya and her girlfriend Yakubova with shawls over their heads to make them look like millworkers to visit the Thornton hostel, both the single and married quarters. Krupskaya wrote:

It was only from information gathered in this way that Vladimir Ilyich wrote his correspondence and leaflets. And what a schooling this was for all the comrades who worked at that time! That was when we really learned to give attention to detail!

All copy for leaflets passed through Lenin's hands before going to the underground printshop. Once when Krolikov, one of Krupskaya's pupils, came in with a completed survey protocol Lenin had given him Vladimir Ilyich fairly pounced on it. A Marxist intellectual came in chortling about material he had collected at a boot factory in the Moskovskaya Zastava suburb. "They fine you there for everything!" he babbled. "If you set a heel on crooked you get fined right away!" Lenin laughed: "Well, if you set a heel on crooked then you're asking to be fined."[4]

Lenin's Marxists distributed his leaflets in restrooms, marketplaces, anywhere that they could get them to workers. Two female comrades went to the Laferme Tobacco Factory on Vasilyevsky Island with leaflets for the women workers rolled up and tucked under their aprons so they could peel them off one by one. When the whistle blew they walked toward the workers pouring through the gates, thrusting leaflets into their hands almost at a run.

THE MALIGNANT OBSESSION   At a meeting in a St. Petersburg suburb on Christmas in 1894, Lenin read a paper, praising recent works by Plekhanov, and denouncing an essay by Peter Struve, a young moderate Marxist of their circle whose distaste for apocalyptic violence had made him one of Lenin's favorite devils for exorcism. Present that day was Alexander N. Potresov, a year older than Lenin and Struve, son of an army officer, who was to become Lenin's colleague on the future board of *ISKRA*, Lenin's first revolutionary newspaper. "I remember to this day the vigor and sharpness of Ulyanov's criticism," Potresov recorded years later. "My opinion was that he undoubtedly represented a great force . . . His face was worn; his entire head bald, except for some thin hair at the temples, and he had a scanty reddish beard. His squinting eyes peered slyly from under his brows." Potresov also noted Lenin's "hypnotic power" over people. At 24 Ulyanov was already known as "the old man," and "his voice sounded old and hoarse . . . *There must have been an inner reason, springing from his emotional make up, that was responsible for the complete suppression of youthfulness in the man,"* Potresov concluded.

To Peter Struve, Lenin's seething hatred for "the liberals" and "bourgeoisie" was a spectacle to behold: "That hatred had something terrible and repulsive in it . . . animal emotions and repulsions . . . abstract and cold, like Lenin's whole being." Struve, just Lenin's age, was a westerner of broad background, grandson of a famed German astronomer and son of a governor of Astrakhan province. For him, everything Lenin did showed a compulsive "aiming at the final destruction and extermination of the enemy."[5]

Not only Ulyanov's fellow revolutionaries were thusly impressed.

Lenin, then 23, stood up at a meeting and engaged an older and respected populist leader in sharp debate. One comrade, Victor Chernov, remembered it vividly as an unusually vehement and destructive onslaught. Lenin had taken copious notes and dissected the speaker cruelly, even maliciously, and with obvious effect. They had a cat-and-dog debate. As a secret police report dated January 20, 1894, put it: "A certain Ulyanov, almost certainly the brother of the Ulyanov who was hanged, made a spirited attack." Even to the police observer, young Lenin was impressive—and all tooth and claw.

Buonarroti heaped astonishing scorn and hatred upon the young United States, its Constitution, and its example of peaceful progress and reform. Chernyshevsky manifested the same attitude. Such spleen can well only from deep irrational compulsions. So it was with Lenin. Liberals, with their doctrines of reconciliation and peaceful progress, constituted a grave threat to his sense of identity and self-esteem. *They endangered his apocalyptic lusting.*

In May 1895 the St. Petersburg Marxists sent Lenin on a mission to western Europe, his first trip abroad, to establish contact with the great exiles, Axelrod and Plekhanov, the founding fathers of Russian Marxism, and with the formidable German social democrats and other political allies. Lenin went first to see Plekhanov in Geneva, then Axelrod in Zurich, presenting each with a book of collected essays his cell had published. Axelrod read them overnight. One, signed K. Tulin, "made an excellent impression. It was not very well constructed, perhaps even careless. But one felt in it a temperament and the fire of the spirit of battle. One felt that *for the author Marxism was not an absolute doctrine but a weapon in the revolutionary struggle. . . .*"

Next morning Lenin returned and asked about the symposium. "The essay by Tulin made a particularly good impression," Axelrod answered. "At last there has awakened in Russia real revolutionary social democratic thought."

"That is my pseudonym," Lenin owned proudly.

The piece was his long denunciation of Peter Struve's "legal Marxism" or "revisionism" or "reformism."[6] Struve had written that Marx had "at times" thought of the collapse of capitalism as coming abruptly and catastrophically, but declared "modern Marxists" saw it rather as a gradual transition through a series of reforms. "Let us confess our lack of culture, and turn to capitalism for instruction," Struve concluded.

[261]

Such heresy infuriated Lenin:

Reforms are not to be contrasted to revolution. The struggle for reforms is but a means of marshalling the forces of the proletariat for a final revolutionary overthrow!

This esprit de corps appealed to Axelrod, but he undertook to moderate Lenin's attitude toward the liberals. He urged an alliance, arguing that "Both [i.e., "modern Marxists" and liberals] face the same urgent problem—the overthrow of absolutism."

Lenin smiled. "You know, Plekhanov made exactly the same remarks about my articles. He expressed his thought in picturesque fashion: 'We turn our face to the liberals,' he said, 'But you turn your behind.' "

Plekhanov recalled their discussion:

He all the time tried to convince me that the liberals and democrats belong to the bourgeois species. But I had known this at the time when Lenin did not yet know how to blow his nose in a handkerchief. I also knew something else—about which he had no idea and conception. . . . He did not understand that in Russia there are no political, legal, and cultural forms or any customs and usages which would give her the right to call herself a capitalist country. Those things which bourgeois liberalism must bring to a country and everywhere in Europe had already brought, never occurred to Lenin, and therefore, instead of attracting and enlisting the liberals as allies in the fight against absolutism and the old, antediluvian order, he saw in them only the bitterest enemies.[7]

Axelrod spent a week with young Ulyanov in Geneva, mostly debating this harsh attitude toward liberals. Lenin ultimately deferred—for the moment. Axelrod and Plekhanov were deeply impressed. Until then their movement had produced no one who combined Marxist theory with practical organizing ability.

As Axelrod wrote Plekhanov, "Now we have that man. He is Ulyanov, future leader of the labor movement."

Lenin journeyed on to Paris to meet Paul Lafargue, Marx's son-in-law, a leader of the French socialists. He reported great enthusiasm among Russian workers for Marx's teachings.

"They study Marx! But do they understand him?" Lafargue asked.

"Yes," answered Lenin.

"Pooh! They understand nothing. No one here understands him and our movement is twenty years old."

But Lenin understood. He understood even better than Marx did himself what must be done to make the Master's hate strategy a practical reality.

THE VILNA INVENTION   All over Russia Marxist circles, comprised exclusively of intellectuals, were puzzling over how to bridge the gap between their abstruse theories and the workers' limited interest and attention. In Vilna, the Lithuanian capital, a young socialist named Arkady Kremer devised a fiendishly simple solution. Labor unions were illegal, and Russian workers were almost totally unprotected by law. Kremer told his comrades: Forget about the abstract writings of Marx, Chernyshevsky, and the theoreticians. Concentrate instead on helping the workers gain concessions from the bosses—temporarily at least. Kremer dug out a forgotten but never repealed statute of Catherine the Great providing a twelve-hour day for apprentices, with a two-hour lunch break. This law formed the basis of a campaign for shorter hours. Soon the Vilna socialists were the only ones in Russia who actually had any real mass of workers in their midst and under their leadership.

So Kremer wrote a brilliant little pamphlet describing his invention—revolutionary sloganeering, issue-linking and issue-broadening. Calling for "continual agitation based on existing minor demands and needs,"[8] he also argued that "class consciousness" came through actual conflict with visible hate targets, the "class enemy." Thus workers would be moved imperceptibly into a generalized hostility to the state and its capitalist bosses. It was a grand strategy for mass emotional engineering.

Kremer's circle included Julius Martov, an old friend of Radchenko's who had been exiled to Vilna. Martov also was under Fedosseyev's influence, through a mutual friend. Martov edited and wrote a foreword for Kremer's pamphlet thus summarizing the strategy:

Agitation must proceed on the basis of everyday economic needs that lead to a clash between proletarian and employer.... Once drawn into the social struggle on the basis of these everyday craft interests the masses will in this process be prepared for the acquisition of broader socio-political aspirations.

Krupskaya later recalled the impact of Kremer's Vilna invention and contrasted it with the practical ignorance of the French socialists:

> The method of agitation based on the workers' everyday needs struck deep root in our Party work. I did not fully appreciate how efficacious this method was until years later, when, living in France as a political emigrant, I observed how, during the great strike of the postal workers in Paris, the French Socialist Party stood completely aloof from it. It was the business of trade unions, they said. In their opinion the business of a party was only political struggle. They had no clear idea whatever about the necessity of combining the economic with the political struggle.[9]

Martov returned from exile to St. Petersburg in October 1895, with Kremer's pamphlet in hand. He met Lenin right away. Lenin found that Martov's Vilna experience in sloganeering meshed perfectly with his own thinking, and so the two made common cause. (Lenin paid his debt to Kremer's pamphlet later in his booklet, "What Is To Be Done?" "Truly useful," he called it.[10]) Lenin and Martov agreed to merge their two Marxist cells, making 22 members.

Since his return to Russia in September Lenin had been planning a newspaper. He established relations with the hated People's Freedom group because they had an underground printshop, the Lahta Press. He and Martov soon brought St. Petersburg's three remaining Marxist groups under their leadership. Lenin was the key figure in the "central group," and subgroups included a strike group for worker operations, and a "literary group" in charge of intelligence and secret operations.

Soon men and women in the Thornton textile factory, the metal workers in the Putilov plant, the Semmyanikov workers, and others distributed leaflets that demonstrated an intimate knowledge of their needs and expressed their grievances in simple terms, linking both of them with a grander, more abstract struggle for "socialism and freedom."

The first great wave of strikes hit St. Petersburg that fall, and Lenin and his fellow Marxists were excited, as they wanted to launch their newspaper so they could be in the middle of it. In November Gleb Krzhizhanovsky wrote a leaflet on weavers' demands in the Thornton textile plant, where workers were angry over an arbitrary and deceitfully explained wage cut. On November 18 some 500 weavers walked out. The next day Lenin wrote a pamphlet that magnificently summarized their complaints, called on the dye workers and others to join and stand solidly "to the end," and dealt knowingly with rent, housing, wages and working conditions.[11] It was a magnificent expression of his "mockery." And it never mentioned Marxism, revolution, class struggle, or the Kingdom Come.

By now Lenin was the recognized leader-teacher of revolution among all his comrades, not only in propaganda and mass manipulation but in clandestine organization and operational techniques. He designated Krupskaya, who was relatively unknown, to be the emergency contact if police arrested the key leaders. He taught her secret codes, invisible writing, and smuggling techniques he had learned from the old exiles in Samara. He even instructed Axelrod in a letter to Geneva: "Write with *Chinese ink*. Better still, add a small crystal of *potassium dichromate* ($K_2Cr_2O_7$): then it won't wash off. *Use the thinnest paper possible.*"[12]

By early December the St. Petersburg Marxists were ready to go with their newspaper, *The Workers' Cause*. They named their organization the "Petersburg Combat Party for Working Class Liberation," a name and probably a concept Axelrod had suggested to Lenin. On December 20 Lenin and some comrades met at Krupskaya's apartment to go over the two sets of page proofs.

That night police arrested Lenin, Martov, Krzhizhanovsky, and many other key members in the new combat party.

DEVELOPING A CALCULUS OF MASS IRRATIONALITY

Lenin had four years to ponder the successes and mistakes of his first venture into mass propaganda and social demolition. In *What Is To Be Done?* written in 1902 he frankly and coldly dissected that experience:

> We, the ideologists, the leaders, lacked sufficient training . . . In order to profit from the experience of that movement, and to draw practical lessons from it, we must thoroughly understand the causes and significance of this or that shortcoming . . . Revolutionary experience and organizational skill are things that can be acquired, provided the desire is there to acquire them, provided shortcomings are recognized, which in revolutionary activity is more than half-way towards their removal.[13]

Here was the cold, clinical tactician talking!

Lenin spent fourteen months in prison in Leningrad. He was a political prisoner, not a common criminal. And unlike what was to come in Russia later under his own rule, the political prisoner's lot under the czar in this day was not uncivilized. He was allowed books —his jailers trundled virtually whole libraries to him—and visitors. He kept his sister Anna trotting all over St. Petersburg seeking books, smuggling out pamphlets and leaflets, delivering coded messages, and performing other organizational chores. He began writing a 632-page tome tracing the "growth of capitalism in Russia." "I have a plan that has occupied my mind considerably ever since I was arrested," he wrote on January 2, 1896, his first letter from prison. The task took three years. He totally immersed himself in the statistics and sociology of Russia's growing urbanization, ingesting a large data base from the first national census in 1897. In the process, he formulated an even grander design: the plan for a gigantic communications monopoly to propagandize and tap every pool of discontent in the new modern industrialized, urban society.

While Lenin labored in his Petersburg cell, in Vienna a young physician named Sigmund Freud was discovering a vast subterranean sea of irrationality in man. Together Freud and Lenin destroyed the Enlightenment model of rational man that had dominated eighteenth- and nineteenth-century political thinkers. While Freud mapped the subsurface emotional currents, Lenin in prison was designing a structure to harness the irrational energies of those currents—a calculus of mass irrationality.

Lenin had carefully studied some of the key early Marxist writings. He pondered such Marxisms as:

> It is not sufficient that the idea strive for realization; reality itself must strive toward the idea.
> This dualism (of *spirit* and *matter, God* and the *world*) expresses itself within history, within the world of man itself, so that a few chosen *individuals* as *active* spirit confront the remainder of mankind as the *spiritless mass,* as matter.
> We must make the actual pressure even more pressing by adding to it the consciousness of pressure; the shame even more shameful by making it public . . . We have to make the ossified conditions dance by singing them their own melody! We have to cause the people to be *frightened* by their own image, in order to give them courage.

What *was* the man talking about? He was but dimly understood by the European socialists who read only *Das Kapital* and the *Mani-*

festo, both undertaken at Engels' urging precisely as propaganda tracts, both preaching an inevitability in the class struggle process. Were they mere imagemaking exercises to give the masses courage? And not scientific predictions? The evidence indicates that Marx himself regarded them so, although as with all con men he appeared at times to believe in the powers of his own propaganda.

And Lenin was restoring Marxism's original meaning. He had read the 1843 Hegel essay very early in his study of Marxism simply because his older brother Alexander had cherished it enough to translate it into Russian. The young Marx's position coincided perfectly with that of Tkachev and other Russian Jacobins: "Consciousness" must be "injected" into the masses from without, from "philosophers" or "revolutionaries" of the intellectual class.

As a result of these theoretical orientations, Lenin came to grips with the problem of harnessing, by means of organization, the most irrational, spontaneous forces to be guided by "reason," by the "consciousness" of the philosopher-king. He recognized the irrational, unreasoning forces as a given that he, the "mover of the movers," must place in a rationalized scheme of revolution. Finally, he recognized the element of spontaneity in a "revolutionary upsurge," and devised a strategy for agitation that assumes unpredictability. In the revolutionary situation, initiative almost inevitably goes to the masses, at least temporarily, as Chernyshevsky preached, and the revolutionary must expect to get dirty. It is the test of the revolutionary leader that he learns how to use these elemental forces and ride to power on the waves of spontaneity like an agile surf rider. He must develop a calculus of the irrational, a scientific sociological analysis of the irrational-emotional forces among the masses.

This was the problem to which 26-year-old Vladimir Ulyanov riveted his entire consciousness. He left himself no mental energy to question the Marxian prediction of post-revolutionary "blossoming" of human culture. He was the total social demolition engineer with no thought of a design for construction. This is how the coldest rationalism and wildest utopianism could exist side by side within him.

After 600 pages of painful descriptive detail of "the development of capitalism in Russia," Lenin summarizes capitalism's "mission" and "progressive character." And what are its chief virtues? Capitalism "increases the number of large industrial centers." It "increases the population's need for association, for organization . . . Capitalism *at the same time splits the whole of society into different groups of persons occupying different positions in production,* and gives a tremendous impetus to organization within each group." Moreover, it leads also "to a change in the mentality of the population . . . The disappearance of all forms of personal dependence and patriarchalism in relationships, the mobility of the population, the influence of the big industrial centers, etc.—all this cannot but lead to a profound change in the very character of the producers."[14]

We can see clearly here the mass propagandist at work on target-audience analysis, preparing his campaign strategy. Lenin is not indulging in abstract ideological fancy. He is a careful social scientist at work for manipulative ends.

Marx and Lenin both noted that *the growth of cities made mass incitement, mass propaganda, mass insurrection and mass revolution possible.* Urbanization, the concentration of population, produced mass audiences on a scale that simply had never before existed in human history. The Paris of Babeuf offered an audience of 600,-000. Marx was twelve years old when London became the first city in the history of mankind of reach the million mark. The Paris he knew, the Paris of the 1848 revolution with its mass demonstrations, riots, and armed insurrection, was just approaching a million, the second city ever to present such a mass audience.

Lenin's Russia had just entered the industrial and urban age. The Russia he was born into was a rural nation of peasants, without a single megalopolis. The fourteen largest towns in 1863 numbered only 1,741,900, but by 1897 they grew to 4,266,300—growth of 153 percent. Towns of 50,000 or more increased from 13 to 44; those over 200,000 from two to five. Russia in 1897 counted 128,924,289 inhabitants, with 16,785,212 in cities and towns. Lenin made careful studies of census statistics on the number of workers (and their families) in each of these urban centers. He documented every phase of the growth of mass production, transportation, and industry, and the movement of people from rural to agrarian subsistence economy into the money economy of the industrialized society. And all led to one conclusion: These population concentrations, and their divisions of labor and competing interests, offered ripe opportunities for the radical hate propagandist. He was debating the "populists" and "legal Marxists" and "revisionists" over strategy for Russia's revolutionists, seeking throughout, in every cipher and footnote, to prove: *Yes, we CAN make a revolution in Russia. The industrializing and urban-*

izing nation offers mass audiences we can mobilize IF we organize correctly, project the right messages and raise the correct slogans.

"You will not find in Lenin a single purely theoretical work; each has a propaganda aspect," a noted Soviet historian wrote in 1924. Yes! Everywhere Lenin looked, he looked with the eye of the master mass mediatician, measuring his audiences, his slogans, and his targets of opportunity! In 1843 Marx saw salvation arising from "the workers," who would be the target audience for his elitist hate propaganda. He thought industrial society could be destroyed simply by polarizing the workers and their employers.

Lenin had a more sophisticated tactical analysis, although strategically and essentially identical to Marx's. Like Freud in his *Civilization and Its Discontents,* Lenin saw that the complexities of the industrial urban culture produced frictions and "pressure points" that would generate frustration and discontent in all segments of the populace. "Every trace of even the most rudimentary discontent" and protest could be harnessed by the revolutionary hate propagandist, he declared.[15] Like a complex machine, society could be tuned to new levels of production, prosperity and happiness if one lubricated the bearings and joints with oil; this is what the "legal Marxists" wanted. But if the revolutionaries put sand in the bearings instead, the machine could be overheated and blown apart—with the revolutionary collecting the pieces. Then under his dictatorship, a Jacobin terror, no further sanding will be possible, and he can put the machine back together according to his own design notions, and without submitting to the independent will of anyone—judiciary, legislature, or voter.

The 26-year-old Lenin was charting the pools of frustration and discontent.

That Karl Marx chose the undifferentiated "proletariat" as his chief target audience was—and Lenin so came to regard it—merely an accident of time and circumstance. The industrialized, urbanized society of the twentieth century offered a greater array of target audiences—students, bourgeois *déclassé* intellectuals, lumpenproletariat, even disaffected capitalists, *ad infinitum.* All could be sloganeered and exploited as reservoirs of recruits for the officer corps of the revolution, and cannon fodder for its army come the messianic apocalypse.

The corpus of Marxism-Leninism thus is the applied sociology of analyzing and sloganeering and mobilizing various target audiences within modern urban society, orchestrating them harmoniously into a grand strategy of revolutionary violence programmed by the general staff of self-annointed "movers of the movers."

DESIGNING THE MEDIA MONOPOLY   In February 1897 Lenin was released from prison and sent to exile for three years in Siberia. "Exile" meant simply living free as any soul in a small town. Shushenskoye, where he was sent, had 1,300 inhabitants, a church, and three large taverns. The local constable, nominally his supervisor, was an old retired noncommissioned officer who became Lenin's fond hunting companion and chess partner. He could with permission (or without) slip away to visit comrades exiled in nearby villages and entertain them in his own home. He got mail twice a week, including all the books he ordered. Lenin was a good athlete and enjoyed winter and summer sports. In fact, his years in Siberia were his happiest: He had it much better than many comrades who were sent above the Arctic Circle. A year later Krupskaya, arrested during the 1896 strikes, was allowed to join Lenin, and they were married.

In March 1898 ten delegates met in Minsk as a "founding congress" for the Russian Social Democratic Labor Party. They included Struve, Radchenko, and Arkady Kremer. Within three days they had given their party a name, fashioned a structure and a central committee, drafted a program and manifesto, and decided to launch a party publication. Struve, later to become a member of the Duma and defender of constitutional monarchy, wrote the program, much to Lenin's utter outrage. The Congress split over "spontaneity," emphasizing economic struggle and peaceful reform, and "consciousness," emphasizing organization. It was the Babeuvist decision for violence all over again. But to this day the Soviet Communist Party congresses number from the tiny Minsk meeting. Lenin was able to convene a bigger congress among the Siberian exiles. He got 17 together in Yermakovskoye to approve his draft of a *Protest of the Russian Social Democrats,* which denounced the revisionist doctrines of conciliation and peaceful progress and pointed out that their heresy would deprive Russian Marxism of its most vital element, the class struggle.

In this last year, his head full of the early Marx's writings, his own two-years' experience in leaflet-writing, agitation, and mass organizing in St. Petersburg, and his gargantuan survey of "the growth of capitalism in Russia," Lenin conceived his grand design for an organizational and mass-media monopoly—the twentieth-century totalitarian party. He later unveiled and developed the design in three major essays written between May 1901 and September 1902, and elaborated on them in subsequent works.[16] But in Siberia he saw "where to begin"—with a newspaper, located in the sanctuary of West Europe. It would be more than a medium of communications, however. *It would be "a collective organizer," creating an organization of professional propagandists and political organizers to carry out his grand design.* "Vladimir Ilich hardly slept at all, and grew terribly thin," Krupskaya records.

> He sat up all night, working out his plan in fullest detail. He discussed it with Krzhizhanovsky and with me, and corresponded with Martov and Potresov about it, and made arrangements with them for going abroad. He grew more and more impatient as time went on, eager to throw himslf into the work.[17]

LENIN'S INVENTION   On January 29, 1900, the day his term ended, Lenin left Shushenskoye. Seasoned by study, experience, and reflection, he was now ready for *action*.

He spent six months inside Russia contacting Marxist circles, converting people to his idea, adding them to his organization, setting up a distribution net. Then he headed west. The exiles formed an editorial board: Lenin, Potresov, Martov, Axelrod, Plekhanov, and Vera Zasulich (the Grand Dame of People's Will terrorists who had known Nechayev personally and in 1878 shot a czarist official, won acquittal by a jury, and fled into exile).

Not by accident Lenin persuaded his colleagues to accept the name *Iskra (The Spark)* for the newspaper. He took it from Chernyshevsky's satirical magazine, published from 1859 to 1873, which had been quite popular in the Ulyanov home. The newspaper was to be printed in Leipzig, courtesy of the German Social Democratic Party, and while Lenin's coeditors remained in Switzerland, he would dominate the product. Since Krupskaya functioned as corresponding secretary, he also controlled the Russian underground organization.

Eight thousand of *Iskra's* first issue rolled off the press on Christmas Eve 1900. Lenin wrote the inaugural editorial, "The Urgent Tasks of our Movement."

There, for the first time, the world saw the first hint of Lenin's invention:

> We must train people who will devote not only their spare evenings but the whole of their lives to the revolution; we must build up an organization large enough to permit the introduction of a strict division of labor in the various forms of our work. . . . If we have a strongly organized party, a single strike may turn into a political demonstration, into a political victory over the government. If we have a strongly organized party, a revolt in a single locality may grow into a victorious revolution.[18]

Train professional revolutionaries! A strict division of labor! A single strike may turn into a victorious revolution! (The 1905 Revolution happened just that way.) Lenin's plan was nothing more than an organized assembly line for producing the professional revolutionaries.

So, we will have professional revolutionaries. What will they do? How will they organize and operate? Lenin showed them *how.* He began to recruit the apprentices, to build the organization, and to teach them how to orchestrate mass propaganda into a mass movement.

Every inventor builds on previous technology. So did Lenin. He was the synthesizer and catalyzer. He put together components that were already "in the air." Bakunin had developed the plan of an international conspiratorial society consisting of fully dedicated militants, highly centralized in organization, inspiring and leading the masses by revolutionary deed and example. He was following the pattern of Babeuvist and Buonarrotist web-spinning. Nechayev in his *Revolutionary Catechism* created the embryonic conception of the "real old Bolshevik," stating in uncoded, blunt language the image of Chernyshevsky's "mover of the movers." Tkachev's conception of the revolutionary party and reign of terror was pure Jacobinism and Babeuvism—a highly centralized, disciplined fighting formation, organized to seize power from established authority. He emphasized the post-revolutionary dictatorship—a monopoly of all power, all organization, all communications media, to enforce the utopian dream. To all this, Lenin added the exploitation of mass media and mass propaganda as weapons of social demolition and as a baton of conflict orchestration.

Nothing like Lenin's trilogy unveiling his grand design exists in all political literature before him. No political figure ever wrote in such organizational and propaganda terms. His concern with "links" and "division of labor" and newspaper circulation and mass audiences was a quantum leap ahead into a totally new human epoch, the age of mass marketing and mass manipulation and what sociologist Kenneth Boulding aptly termed "the organizational revolution." The kind of thinking and calculating Lenin was doing—about a nationwide organization and communications network—simply was not possible before the railroad age. In 1776 news of the American Declaration of Independence required a month to cover the 750 miles from Philadelphia to Savannah. In 1812 Napoleon traveled from Vilna to Paris with the news of his Russian defeat in 13 days. With the best of horse relays, he averaged only 5 miles per hour, about the same maximum speed of communication Caesar enjoyed between Gaul and Rome. Yet by Lenin's time regular mail or smuggling moved in half the time, and telegraph transmission was instantaneous. Man's technology for creating and managing a continental-scale organization was light years ahead. And Lenin's political terminology and technology represented a leap at least as far ahead of all previous political writing.

Chapter 19
THE AT&T OF HATE

Our fighting method is organization. We must organize everything, take everything into our own hands. . . .

> —V.I. Lenin
> July 5, 1918
> *27 Collected Works 517*

A large-scale mass motivation campaign must be opened . . . Nationalism must be promoted, sufferings pointed out, national and class hatred provoked . . .

> —Resolution of the "Central
> Office for South Vietnam"
> (North Vietnamese Communist
> Party), March 1966.

"CONCILIATION" VS. "COMBAT"   Lenin emblazoned the frontispiece of his "What Is To Be Done?" with a quote from Ferdinand Lassalle: "The greatest proof of a party's weakness is its diffuseness and the blurring of clear demarcation; a party becomes stronger by purging itself." Henceforth Lenin made this his slogan: *Purge the Party, Strengthen the Party.* It must be "an exclusive group" united into a revolutionary army by a common will to revolution, men who have consciously "chosen the path of struggle instead of the path of conciliation." Those wishing to join his grand design had to conform to it. And let us stop debating over violent revolution and start making it. Let the Bernsteins, Struves, revisionists, economists, and other conciliators begone. You who wish to wander in that swamp, go—and let us be about our business!

> In fact we think that the swamp is your proper place, and we are prepared to render you every help in getting there. Only let go of our hands, don't clutch at us and don't besmirch the grand word freedom, for we too are "free" to go where we please, free to fight not only against the swamp, but also against all those who are turning toward the swamp![1]

Lenin's essay was, in short, a prospectus on a vast new revolutionary enterprise, a guild of professional engineers of social demolition running a cartel of mass hate propaganda organizations. He announced he would sell stock in the future revolution to all who wished to join his enterprise—in exchange for their cooperation. Through his new mass media, he would call the signals and wave the baton; the orchestra or team must carry out their orders, "the line." Lenin's plan was for a wide-open, overt conspiracy for political conquest. Anyone who wished could become a "professional revolutionary," and join "the regular army of tried fighters," and take his place "at the head of the mobilized army."[2] The ultimate product would be "revolution," and a piece of the future "revolutionary dictatorship." *The AT&T of hate would be a joint-stock venture open to all collaborators.* (To one prospective buyer who asked in 1901 how long until the revolution, when she might hope to collect dividends, Lenin answered: "About thirty years.")[3]

"THERE IS SPONTANEITY AND SPONTANEITY"   Lenin was writing under the influence of a spontaneous "revolutionary upsurge" of "the masses" inside Russia. In the spring of 1901, students and workers staged several demonstrations, strikes, and riots. On January 11, the Ministry of Education drafted 183 Kiev University students into the army in punishment for their rebellious demonstrations. Mass meetings and clashes with police and the mounted Cossacks took place in St. Petersburg, Moscow, and other cities. On March 17 in St. Petersburg's Kazan Square thousands of students fought the police, and some were killed. Ultimately 30,000 students took part in a strike in the winter of 1901-02. On May Day 1901 police in Tiflis fired on a street march of students and workers, wounding 14 and arresting 50. (One of the key organizers was Joseph Dzhugashvili, a radical theology school dropout who took the revolutionary pseudonym "Stalin.") In May 1901 strikers at the Obukhov steel works near St. Petersburg fought police, who killed two and wounded seven. Similar clashes erupted over Russia in these two years. Such spontaneous movement of the workers posed major challenges and opportunities for the "wise men" and "mover of the movers." "That the mass movement is a most important phenomenon is a fact not to be disputed. The mass movement places before us *new* theoretical, political, and organizational tasks, far more complicated than those that might have satisfied us in the period before the rise of the mass movement."[4]

The foremost task was to reconcile the "spontaneity" of the masses with "consciousness"—the Marxist minority's will to violent revolution. Lenin probed the problem that nagged and harried Americans about the mass riots on campuses and in congested urban slums in the 1960s. Were they "spontaneous"?

"There is spontaneity and spontaneity," says Lenin. Certainly there is a "spontaneous element," he concedes, but:

> The "spontaneous element," in essence, represents nothing more not less than Marxist political class consciousness [revolutionary will] in an *embryonic form* . . . This was, nevertheless, more in the nature of outbursts of desperation and vengeance than of struggle.[5]

The famous 1896 "St. Petersburg industrial war" haunted Lenin. The workers had achieved major economic gains—but no revolution. While he was in jail and the decimated remainder of the "Combat Party" cranked out leaflets, some 30,000 workers struck. Ultimately they won a law reducing the workday from 14¼ to 11½ hours; they had demanded a 10½-hour day, but this was progress enough to excite the "legal Marxists" and "conciliationists," Lenin's hated antagonists. In Siberia he and Krupskaya translated a book by Sidney and Beatrice Webb on English trade unions. Obviously, Lenin concluded, if left to their own devices, there was danger that his revolutionary armies would desert for the comforts of constitutionalism, peaceful progress, and bourgeois enslavement! That would deprive the messianic Marxists of their Army of the Apocalypse! There would be no glory in that for the young man who yearns to be a "mover of the movers!"

Thus "subservience to spontaneity" becomes a cardinal Leninist sin:

> There is much talk of spontaneity. But the *spontaneous* development of the working-class movement leads to its subordination to bourgeois ideology: For the spontaneous working-class movement is trade-unionism, *only* trade-unionism, and trade-unionism means the ideological enslavement of the workers by the bourgeoisie. Hence, our task, the task of revolutionary Marxism, is *to combat spontaneity, to divert* the working class movement from this spontaneous, trade-unionist striving . . . to bring it under the wing of revolutionary Marxism[6]

In short, we must rob the labor movement to reach our own messianic revolutionary goal! We, the movers of the movers! We, the general staff, must not let our proletarian army desert! So we must

[276]

be done with this "slavish cringing before spontaneity." *"A fierce struggle against spontaneity is necessary."*

How?

The workers movement must be captured!

As I have stated repeatedly, by "wise men," in connection with organization, I mean *professional revolutionaries*, irrespective of whether they have developed from among students or working men I assert: (1) that no revolutionary movement can endure without a stable organisation of leaders maintaining continuity; (2) that the broader the popular mass drawn spontaneously into the struggle, which forms the basis of the movement and participates in it, the more urgent the need for such an organisation, and the more solid this organisation must be (for it is much easier for all sorts of demagogues to side-track the more backward sections of the masses); (3) that such an organisation must consist chiefly of people professionally engaged in revolutionary activity; (4) that in an autocratic state, the more we *confine* the membership of such an organisation to people who are professionally engaged in revolutionary activity and who have been professionally trained in the art of combating the political police, the more difficult it will be to unearth the organisation; and (5) the *greater* will be the number of people from the working class and from the other social classes who will be able to join the movement and perform active work in it.[7]

LENIN'S LAW   Lenin erected his plan on empirical observations: *Discontent and frustration in modern life exists everywhere. It knows no class limitation. It lies there, a raw material waiting to be collected and processed into a Marxian "political consciousness"— revolutionary will.*

Indeed, is there a single social class in which there are no individuals, groups, or circles that are discontented with the lack of rights and with tyranny and, therefore, accessible to the propaganda of the Marxists as the spokesman of the most pressing general democratic needs?[8]

"GO AMONG ALL CLASSES"   Thus Lenin's Law gives rise to the great Leninist Corollary.

Our task is to utilize *every manifestation of discontent,* and to *gather and turn to the best account every protest, however small. . . . Concentrate all droplets of popular resentment. Combine all these streamlets into a single gigantic torrent!*[9]

[277]

Therefore, Marxist revolutionaries "must *go among all* classes of the population; they must dispatch units of their army *in all directions.*"[10] Here Lenin innovated on Comrade Marx:

> The theoretical work of revolutionaries should aim at studying all the specific features of the social and political condition of the various classes . . . The principal thing, of course, is *propaganda* and *agitation* among all strata of the people . . . He is no revolutionary who forgets in practice that "the Communists support every revolutionary movement."[11]

"POLITICAL EXPOSURES"   And how to create this "torrent of discontent"? It must be done through "political exposures," a label Lenin attaches to propaganda techniques we have come to call hate-targeting, sloganeering, issue promotion and preconditioning.[12] *The agitator must exploit every social conflict, every clash between interest groups or between groups and authority, every abuse and blunder and outrage, real or fancied. He must spotlight each "pressure point" and connect it to the revolutionary cause. The ultimate aim is to program the minds of the masses into a preconditioned in-group out-group identification, "the people" versus "the exploiters":*

> *Any and every* manifestation of police tyranny and autocratic outrage, not only in connection with the economic struggle, is not one whit less "widely applicable" as a means of "drawing in" the masses. The rural superintendents and the flogging of peasants, the corruption of the officials and the police treatment of the "common people" in the cities, the fight against the famine-stricken and the suppression of the popular striving towards enlightenment and knowledge, the extortion of taxes and the persecution of the religious sects, the humiliating treatment of soldiers and the barrack methods in the treatment of the students and liberal intellectuals—do all these and a thousand other similar manifestations of tyranny, though not directly connected with the "economic" struggle, represent, in general, *less* "widely applicable" means and occasions for political agitation and for drawing the masses into the political struggle? The very opposite is true.

Lenin invokes Tkachev's definition—he diplomatically attributes it to Plekahnov, his editorial board chairman, who copied it: "A propagandist presents many ideas to one or a few persons; an agitator represents only one or a few ideas, but he presents them to a mass of people." Lenin explains:

The agitator, . . . speaking on the same subject [as distinquished from the propagandist], will take as an illustration a fact that is most glaring and most widely known to his audience, say, the death of an unemployed worker's family from starvation, the growing impoverishment, etc., and, utilising this fact, known to all, will direct his efforts to presenting *a single idea* to the "masses", e.g., the senselessness of the contradiction between the increase of wealth and the increase of poverty; he will strive *to rouse* discontent and indignation among the masses against this crying injustice, leaving a more complete explanation of this contradiction to the propagandist. Consequently, the propagandist operates chiefly by means of the *printed* word; the agitator by means of the *spoken* word. The propagandist requires qualities different from those of the agitator.

Throughout, Lenin maintains this distinction between "propaganda" and "agitation." Workers are not to be educated, they are to be "trained"—preconditioned:

A basic condition for the necessary expansion of political agitation is the organisation of *comprehensive* political exposure. *In no way* except by means of such exposures *can* the masses be trained in political consciousness and revolutionary activity. . . . Working-class consciousness [read: "revolutionary will"] cannot be genuine political consciousness unless the workers are trained to respond to *all* cases of tyranny, oppression, violence, and abuse, no matter *what class* is affected— unless they are trained, moreover, to respond from a revolutionary Marxist point of view and no other. The consciousness of the working masses cannot be genuine class-consciousness, unless the workers learn, from concrete, and above all from topical, political facts and events to observe *every* other social class in *all* the manifestations of its intellectual, ethical, and political life; unless they learn to apply in practice the materialist [i.e. Marxist-Manichean] analysis and the materialist estimate of *all* aspects of the life and activity of *all* classes, strata, and groups of the population.[15]

The masses will never learn to conduct the political struggle until we help *to train* leaders for this struggle, both from among the enlightened workers and from among the intellectuals. Such leaders can acquire training *solely* by systematically evaluating *all* the everyday aspects of our political life, *all attempts* at protest and struggle on the part of the various classes and on various grounds. . . .[16]

Not only must Social-Democrats not confine themselves exclusively to the economic struggle, but that they must not allow the organisation of economic exposures to become the predominant part of their activities. We must take up actively the political education of the working class and the development of its political consciousness . . .

The question arises, what should political education consist in? Can

it be confined to the propaganda of working-class hostility to the autocracy? Of course not. It is not enough *to explain* to the workers that they
are politically oppressed (any more than it is *to explain* to them that
their interests are antagonistic to the interests of the employers). Agitation must be conducted with regard to every concrete example of this
oppression (as we have begun to carry on agitation round concrete
examples of economic oppression). Inasmuch as *this* oppression affects
the most diverse classes of society, inasmuch as it manifests itself in the
most varied spheres of life and activity—vocational, civic, personal,
family, religious, scientific, etc., etc.—is it not evident that *we shall not
be fulfilling our task* of developing the political consciousness of the
workers if we do not *undertake* the organisation of the *political exposure* of the autocracy *in all its aspects?* In order to carry on agitation
round concrete instances of oppression, these instances must be exposed (as it is necessary to expose factory abuses in order to carry on
economic agitation).[17]

"AN IRRESISTIBLE DESIRE TO REACT"   The properly
"trained" worker will see reality through Marxist-colored glasses, his
entire world shaped—distorted—by the preconditioning:

> He himself will be filled with an irresistible desire to react, and he
> will know how to hoot the censors one day, on another day to demon-
> strate outside the house of a governor who has brutally suppressed a
> peasant uprising, on still another day to teach a lesson to the gen-
> darmes . . .
> As for calling the masses to action, that will come of itself as soon as
> energetic political agitation, live and striking exposures come into
> play. To catch some criminal red-handed and immediately to brand
> him publicly in all places is of itself far more effective than any number
> of "calls." the effect very often is such as will make it impossible to tell
> exactly who it was that "called" upon the masses and who suggested
> this or that plan of demonstration, etc.[18]

In this last paragraph Lenin has just depicted the ultimate aim and
result of the most sophisticated and subtle strategy for mass preconditioning and planned inducement of mass violence ever devised.
Once the "political exposures" have preconditioned large masses of
people to the flaring point, violence will begin to erupt "spontaneously" so that *the effect very often is such as will make it impossible
to tell exactly who it was that 'called' upon the masses and who
suggested this or that plan of demonstration.* Such was the accomplishment of Lenin's modern American apostles in "police brutality"
sloganeering that ultimately produced the 1964 Harlem eruption,

the 1967 Newark and Detroit riots, and others that followed in U.S. cities and campuses in the mid-1960s.[19]

Political exposures are as much a declaration of war against the government as economic exposures are a declaration of war against the factory owners. The moral significance of this declaration of war will be all the greater, the wider and more powerful the campaign of exposure will be and the more numerous and determined the social *class* that has *declared war in order to begin the war.* Hence, political exposures in themselves serve as a powerful instrument for *disintegrating* the system we oppose, as a means of diverting from the enemy his casual or temporary allies, as a means for spreading hostility and distrust among the permanent partners of the autocracy. . . .

We revolutionary Marxists will organize these nationwide exposures; all questions raised by the agitation will be explained in a consistently revolutionary Marxist spirit, without any concessions to deliberate or undeliberate distortions of Marxism; the all-round political agitation will be conducted by a party which unites into one inseparable whole the assault on the government in the name of the entire people, the revolutionary training of the proletariat . . . and the utilization of all the working class's spontaneous conflicts with its exploiters which rouse and bring into our camp increasing numbers of the proletariat.[20]

Here, obviously, is a grand strategy for programing mass emotions on a scale never before dreamed of. "The most backward worker will understand, *or will feel* . . . Feeling that, he himself will be filled with an irresistible desire to react . . . to hoot . . . to demonstrate. . . ." Lenin was far ahead of Freud or Pavlov in understanding the irrational bases of much human behavior, and in planning to exploit it far ahead of Madison Avenue's "image makers," motivational researchers, and "hidden persuaders."

"A GIGANTIC BELLOWS"   Lenin asks, "What type of organization do we require?" His answer: "The character of any organization is naturally and inevitably determined by the content of its activity."[21] His professional revolutionaries—"these systematically organized troops"—will be "engaged exclusively in all-sided and all-embracing political agitation, i.e., precisely in work that that *brings into closer proximity and merges into a single whole* the elemental destructive force of the crowd with the conscious destructive force of the organization of revolutionaries."[22] Ergo, they must have "such an organization as will combine, in one general assault, all the manifestations of political opposition, protest, and indignation."[23]

Therefore his organization must be, first and foremost, a *communications* company. *A newspaper!*

> *A newspaper is not only a collective propagandist and a collective agitator. It is also a collective organizer. This newspaper would become part of an enormous bellows that would blow every spark of the class struggle and of popular indignation into a general conflagration . . . Around it a regular army of tried fighters would systematically gather and receive their training.*[24]

The revolutionaries' newspaper would be like "the scaffolding around a building under construction, which marks the contours of the structure and facilitates communication between the builders, enabling them to distribute the work and to view the common results achieved by their organized labor." Like an American jazz combo, they would improvise, harmonize, and syncopate; one member taking the lead, then the other, as the situation developed. *The revolutionary movement would be a media-managed mass movement. Its reporters would be gatherers of target intelligence, slogan-makers, issue-raisers, political agitators, and ultimately, orchestrators of the final movement in the Revolutionary Symphony.*

Only with such an organization, in place at all times and functioning with a ready reserve of prepared people, could the professional revolutionaries be ready to perform the peculiar tasks of revolution —just as a news organization or fire department as Americans know them are in-place organizations ready to respond to unforeseen contingencies.

> It would be a grievous error indeed to build the Party organization in anticipation only of outbreaks and street fighting, or only upon the "forward march of the drab everyday struggle." We must *always* conduct our everyday work and always be prepared for every situation, because very frequently it is almost impossible to foresee when a period of outbreaks will give way to a period of calm. . . . *The revolution itself must not by any means be regarded as a single act, but as a series of more or less powerful outbreaks rapidly alternating with periods of more or less complete calm.*[25]

Therefore, the nature of the task dictates the nature of the organization. And Lenin's definition of revolution—a quiet, objective, and coldly clinical sociological analysis—shapes the design.

"AN ARMY OF ONMISCIENT PEOPLE"   A national newspaper would coordinate the "political exposures," but other media would supplement it. Leaflets, for example, would continue to be the chief local medium "for catching the enemy red-handed." "That is quite beyond the ability of an illegal paper generally. It can be done only by a leaflet, because the time limit for exposures of that nature can be a day or two at most (e.g., the usual brief strikes, violent factory clashes, demonstrations, etc.)" Through this medium the worker would get his "local factory exposures," would learn "who had been 'picked for a lambasting' and who had been 'flayed.' "

Working for the newspaper would teach the professional revolutionaries to master fully "the task of comprehensive exposure and comprehensive agitation."[26] Moreover,

> There is no other way of training strong political organizations except through the medium of a nationwide newspaper . . . a revolutionary organization capable of uniting all forces and guiding the movement in actual practice and not in name alone, that is, an organization ready at any time to support every protest and every outbreak and use it to build up and consolidate the fighting forces suitable for the decisive struggle.[27]

They would perforce become a gigantic communications net over the nation, catching every discontent and every conflict, "inducing people to think about all these things, to summarize and generalize all the divers signs of ferment and active struggle."[28]

> The masses will never learn to conduct the political struggle until we help to train leaders for this struggle, both from among the enlightened workers and from among the intellectuals. Such leaders can acquire training solely by systematically evaluating all the everyday aspects of our political life, all attempts at protest and struggle on the part of the various classes and on various grounds.[29]
>
> To be able to write in newspapers (not in popular pamphlets) about municipal and state affairs, one must have fresh and varied material gathered and written up by able people. And in order to be able to gather and write up such material, we must have something more than the "primitive democracy" of a primitive circle, in which everybody does everything and all entertain themselves by playing at referendums. It is necessary to have a staff of expert writers and correspondents, an army of Social-Democratic reporters who establish contacts far and wide, who are able to fathom all sorts of "state secrets" (the knowledge of which makes the Russian government official so puffed up, but the blabbing of which is such an easy matter to him), who are able to penetrate "behind the scenes"—an army of people who must, as their

[283   ]

"official duty" be ubiquitous and omniscient. And we, the Party that fights against *all* economic, political, social, and national oppression, can and must find, gather, train, mobilise, and set into motion such an army of omniscient people.[30]

Elsewhere Lenin further described the role he envisioned for these journalist-ideologists:

> The "ideologist" is worthy of the name only when he *precedes* the spontaneous movement, points out the road, and is able ahead of all others to solve all the theoretical, political, tactical, and organizational questions which the "material elements" of the movement spontaneously encounter. In order truly to give "consideration to the material elements of the movement," one must view them critically, one must be able to point out the dangers and defects of spontaneity, and *to elevate* it to the level of consciousness.[31]

In short, the ideologist is a pragmatic and empirical sociologist-propagandist whose duty it is to quarterback the mass movement!

DEVELOPING THE TECHNOLOGY AND PERSONNEL OF SOCIAL DEMOLITION   While in his St. Petersburg prison cell, Lenin had reflected on his two years of experience as a "mover of the movers" and on his own and his little band's shortcomings. Why had he failed and gotten himself and his followers arrested? Lenin concluded that they were *amateurs*, when they needed to be seasoned *professionals*; that their knowledge of the art of mass organization was terribly backward: "We were unable to meet the immediate requirements of the time owing to our lack of revolutionary experience and practical training."[32] Therefore, they needed training, professional development, division of labor and specialization, and the organizational sophistication that goes with it.

A professional organization of organizers such as would form around his nationwide newspaper, Lenin declared, would stimulate the development of both the *technology* and the *engineers* of social demolition. In fact, only by such broad experience, contacts and interchange can revolutionaries truly become professional.

> We strive "to stretch a line" through the countryside too, where there are hardly any bricklayers anywhere, and we are *obliged* to encourage *everyone* who reports to us even the most common facts, in the hope that this will increase the number of our correspondents in the given field and will ultimately *train us all* to select facts that are really the most outstanding.[33]

Then we will begin to find out what issues and what slogans and what "exposures" really work. A national newspaper, summarizing the results of the most varied activities, will

> *stimulate* people to march forward untiringly along *all* the innumerable paths leading to revolution, in the same way as all roads lead to Rome. . . . Communication would become the rule and would secure (what is more important) an exchange of experience, of material, of forces, and of resources. . . . The success of one locality would serve as a standing encouragement to further perfection. It would arouse the desire to utilize the experience gained by comrades working in other parts of the country. . . . Every outbreak, every demonstration, would be weighed and discussed in its every aspect in all parts of Russia and would thus stimulate a desire to keep up with, and even surpass, the others.[34]

The nationwide organization could compile special handbooks for agitators in each industry and craft, summarizing experience from scores of case studies of conflicts "which now literally gets lost in a mass of leaflets and fragmentary correspondence." Such handbooks would contain carefully researched data on working conditions, lists of demands advanced in successful agitations elsewhere, grievance censuses, data on needed legislation, and such. Armed with such industry-wide data, a professional agitator attacking a local factory would not have to waste weeks compiling information scattered among workers from each department, the office staff, inspectors, doctors, and myriad petty reports.

> I vividly recall my "first experiment" which I would never like to repeat. I spent many weeks "examining" a worker, who would often visit me, regarding every aspect of the conditions prevailing in his enormous factory. After great effort, I managed to obtain material for a description of one single factory! At the end of the interview the worker would wipe the sweat from his brow, and say to me smilingly: "I find it easier to work overtime than to answer your questions."
>
> A compilation of such demands and needs might serve for years as an excellent handbook for agitators on economic questions in backward localities or among the backward strata of the workers. Examples of successful strikes in a given region, information on higher living standards, of improved working conditions in one locality, would encourage the workers in other localities to take up the fight again and again.[35]

THE MASS MEDIA PYRAMID   Lenin thought of his organization of mass media specialists as a guild of professional organizers. To Lenin all organizations were forms of mass communications media. It is as if the American Society of Association Executives decided to convert itself into a revolutionary military body whose members would respond on command to divert their myriad organizations and their mass memberships to the quest for political power. The members of the revolutionary organization must be disciplined and devoted to the revolutionary vision. The organization developing around the newspaper would form a gigantic *mass media pyramid*, embracing the entire nation's populace as its ultimate target audience. At the apex will be a "Party Center" consisting of a "Central Organ" (the newspaper *Iskra*) and "Central Committee." This Party Center will exist outside the target nation in a safe sanctuary:

> The newspaper can and should be the *ideological* leader of the Party, evolving theoretical truths, tactical principles, general organizational ideas, and the general tasks of the whole Party at any given moment.[36]
>
> But only the Central Committee can be the direct *practical* leader of the movement, maintaining *personal* connections with all the committees, embracing all the best revolutionary forces, and *managing* all the general affairs of the Party such as the distribution of literature, the issuing of leaflets, the allocation of forces, the appointment of individuals and groups to take charge of special undertakings, the preparation of demonstrations and an uprising on a nationwide scale, etc.[37]

From this Party Center the lines of feedback and command run out to each major urban center, such as St. Petersburg, to a metropolitan central committee. That communications node's lines run in turn to *factory committees* and *district committees*—blanketing both the places of work and residences of the target audiences.

The metropolitan C.C.'s "special work" task forces include printing, transport, agitational tours, a passport bureau, combat squads to deal with spies and *agents provocateurs*, groups in the army, and other clandestine paramilitary units for terrorism, mass manipulation, and the like. Especially important is the propaganda unit. It must be area-wide "owing to the scarcity of our propaganda forces" and simply because it is not desirable to have separate district propaganda units. "Propaganda must be carried on in one and the same spirit by the whole committee, and it should be strictly centralized." Therefore it must be a branch of the committee or one of its specialized institutions.[38]

"A POSTAL SERVICE OF OUR OWN" "Every factory must be our fortress," Lenin declares. The St. Petersburg Central Committee must name agent-organizers for every plant. Beginning with whatever contacts and recruits they can gather, they must build an internal paramilitary command. The ultimate goal is to build a factory committee and concentric circles and planetary systems of specialized task forces for every mission.

The most important task force is a network "for delivering and distributing literature." It must provide the central committee "with a real postal service of our own, so as to possess tried and tested methods, not only for distributing literature, but also for delivering it to the homes, and so as to provide a definite knowledge of all the workers' addresses and ways of reaching them."[39]

Other task forces shall read illegal literature; track down and expose spies (don't kill them—use them as propaganda targets to "educate the working class masses"); give special guidance to the trade union movement and economic struggle; etc. A special circle must develop "agitators and propagandists who know how to initiate and to carry on long talks in an *absolutely legal* way (on machinery, foremen, etc.) and so be able to speak safely and publicly, to get to know people and see how the land lies, etc." "We also need combat groups, in which workers who have had military training or who are particularly strong and agile should be enrolled, to act in the event of demonstrations, in arranging escapes from prison, etc." Through this "network of all kinds of circles" the factory committee must "embrace the whole factory, the largest possible number of the workers."[40]

These circles and task forces will vary widely in the strictness of their organizational form and their degree of secrecy, depending on their nature and functions. They will range "from the 'strictest,' narrowest, and most restricted type of organization to the 'freest,' broadest, most loosely constituted, and open type." Some will maintain strictest secrecy and military discipline—for example, the distributing groups. They will belong to the Party and know a certain number of its members and functionaries. Some will be mixed groups of Party members and nonmembers performing commonly understood tasks—the economic research groups studying labor conditions and drawing up trade-union demands. And some will be open propaganda fronts whose members will not necessarily know that the people running their organization are Party members. But in every case, the Party members in the group must execute the Party's commands and report in full on his group's work and status.[41] And he must be the organizational quarterback:

> The whole art of running a secret organisation should consist in making use of *everything possible*, in "giving everyone something to do," at the same time retaining *leadership* of the whole movement, not by virtue of having the power, of course, but by virtue of authority, energy, greater experience, greater versatility, and greater talent.[42]

"THE DISTRIBUTIVE MACHINE"   A crucial orchestrating role is assigned to the *district committees:*

> If we secure regular contact between a special district group of distributors *and all the factories* in that district, as well as the largest possible number of *workers' homes* in that district, it will be of enormous value, both for demonstrations and for an uprising. Arranging for and organising the speedy and proper delivery of literature, leaflets, proclamations, etc., training a network of agents for this purpose, means performing the *greater* part of the work of preparing for the future demonstrations or an uprising. It is too late to start organising the distribution of literature at a time of unrest, a strike, or turmoil; this work can be built up only gradually, by making distributions *obligatory* twice or three times a month. If no newspapers are available, leaflets may and should be distributed, but the distributive machine must in no case be allowed to remain idle. This machine should be brought to such a degree of perfection as to make it possible to inform and mobilise, so to speak, the whole working-class population of St. Petersburg overnight.[43]

Lenin defined five levels of individual affiliation with his cartel:

1. *Unwitting prospects.* "Groups of students, officers, or office employees engaged in self-education *in conjunction with* one or two Party members should in some cases not even be aware that these belong to the Party, etc."[44]

2. *Collaborating Circle Associates.* Members of the many special-

ized task forces and front groups will not necessarily be Party members, although their organizations "should enjoy the status of committee institutions or branches" of the local Party committee. They "will not join the Party, and will have the status of circles formed by Party members, or associated with one Party group or another, etc." "In *internal* matters members of *all* these circles are of course on an equal footing, as are all members of a committee." But only the person appointed by the local committee will have the right of personal contact with the committee, the Central Committee and the central organ.[45]

3. *Party Members.* "Some will openly declare their wish to join the Party, and if endorsed by the Committee, will join the Party, and will assume definite functions (on the instructions of, or in agreement with, the committee), will undertake to obey the orders of the Party organs, receive the same rights as all Party members,"[46] etc. The essential condition of Party membership:

> In one respect we must *absolutely* demand the *maximum degree of organization* in all these branch groups, namely, that every Party member belonging to such a group is formally responsible for the conduct of work in the group and is obliged to take *every* measure in order that the composition of each of these groups, the whole *mechanism* of its work, and the content of that work should be *known as fully as possible* to the C.C. and the C.O. That is necessary in order that the Center may have a *complete* picture of the whole movement, that the selection for various Party posts may be made from the widest possible circle of people; that all groups of a similar nature throughout Russia may learn from one another (through the medium of the Center), and that warning may be given in the event of the appearance of *agents provocateurs* or suspicious characters).[47]

4. *Local Committee Members.* The factory or district committee "should consist of a very small number of *revolutionaries*, who take their instructions and receive their authority to carry on all Social-Democratic work in the factory *directly from the committee*. Every member of the factory committee should regard himself as an agent (!) of the committee, obliged to submit to all its orders and to observe all the 'laws and customs' of the 'army in the field' which he has joined and from which in time of war he has no right to absent himself without official leave."[48]

5. *Central Committee Members, Central Organ Members, Executive Committee Members.* These are of course the army high command and general staff, the most experienced, disciplined revolutionaries. They are experienced organizers, executives, editors, propagandists, intelligence analysts, guerrilla leaders, company and field grade commanders.

CLOSING THE FEEDBACK LOOP   Lenin stresses complete command feedback and control for making the Party organization function. *"The greatest possible centralization* is necessary with regard to the ideological and practical *leadership* of the movement and the revolutionary struggle."* But this requires *"the greatest possible decentralization* with regard to keeping the Party center (and therefore the Party as a whole) *informed* about the movement, and with regard to *responsibility* to the Party . . . This decentralization is nothing but the reverse side of the *division of labor* which is generally recognized to be one of the most urgent practical needs of our movement."[49] In short, "decentralization" means the business of all the bricklayers is to *report* and *obey*. They are automata. The thinking, dreaming, line-drawing architectural brain is at the Party Center.

> The leadership of the movement should be entrusted to the smallest possible number of the most homogeneous possible groups of professional revolutionaries with great practical experience. Participation in the movement should extend to the greatest possible number of the most diverse and heterogeneous groups of the most varied sections of the proletariat (and other classes of the people). The Party centre should always have before it, not only exact information regarding the activities of each of these groups, but also the *fullest possible information regarding their composition*. We must centralise the leadership of the movement![50]

As for democracy within the Party ranks:

> The application of the elective principle and decentralization is absolutely impermissible to any wide degree, and even altogether detrimental to revolutionary work carried on under an autocracy. . . . The possible and usual objection [is] that strict centralization may all to easily ruin the movement if the center *happens* to include an *incapable* person invested with tremendous power. This is, of course, possible.

But no rules can provide against it. The only answer must be "measures of 'comradely influence,' beginning with the resolutions of each and every subgroup, followed up by their appeals to the C.O. and the C.C. and ending (if worst comes to worst) with the *removal* of the persons in authority who are absolutely incapable."[51]

But what if the person at the center is not incompetent but unscrupulous, talented and mad—like Stalin? Lenin never imagined the possibility. Nor did he question his own assumption of his own—or Marx's—infallibility.

THE ORCHESTRATION OF HATE   The existing situation is a cacophonous barnyard, Lenin declares. The Party center is cut off from the direct practical work of the local committees. These committees are "a regular jumble of persons, each of whom carried on all and every kind of work, without devoting himself to some definite type of revolutionary work, without assuming responsibility for some special duty, without carrying through a piece of work to the end, wasting an enormous amount of time and energy in radicalist noise-making." Meanwhile a great mass of students' and workers' circles are altogether unknown to the central committee, while others are "just as cumbersome, just as lacking in specialization, just as little given to acquiring the experience of professional revolutionaries or to benefiting from the experience of others, just as taken up with endless conferences 'about everything,' with elections and with drafting rules, as the *committee* itself."[52]

If the center is to work properly these local committees "*must reorganize themselves*, must become more 'business-like' organizations, achieving real 'perfection' in one or another practical sphere.

> For the centre not only to advise, persuade, and argue (as has been the case hitherto), but really conduct the orchestra, it is necessary to know exactly who is playing which fiddle, and where and how; where and how instruction has been or is being received in playing each instrument; who is playing out of tune (when the music begins to jar on the ear), and where and why; and who should be transferred, and how and where to, so that the discord may be remedied, etc.[53]

"Inner Party publicity"—a widespread understanding among the real Party professionals of the overall situation and tasks at hand—will create automatically the responsibility and coordination and discipline necessary to a functioning unit. Only then can a national organization really function as a team. "Inner Party publicity" can only come under the autocracy by feeding intelligence to the Center, which in turn through the Central Organ keeps the cadres informed and in step. The Party must constitute itself as a perfect feedback loop to all members, who will through experience understand the tasks at hand and perform the necessary functions. They must become like a well-drilled professional football team, with perfect timing, instant reaction, total information and understanding of the field position and game plan. Lenin's design was nothing less than a plan for using mass media and mass agitation to program the consciousness and emotions of the nation's entire populace, and to create and orchestrate tidal waves of emotion—"a single gigantic torrent"—that would batter and sweep away the government.

THE DYNAMO OF TOTALITARIANISM   Lenin bared the emotional soul of his Grand Design in the midst of a rage against Struve and the constitutionalists in 1901. This 16,000-word tract has been relatively ignored, far less celebrated than his others. One feels like grabbing mankind by the lapels and saying: "Don't you see? Look—here! See what this man is telling us!" It is the essence of his plan for harnessing hate energy, a force more potent than all the atoms being unlocked by Mr. Einstein in Zurich.

We've heard Lenin's litany against the "revisionists" and constitutional reformers before—ever since Christmas Day 1894 when "the old man" first trounced "Bobo" Struve. So what's new?

It is what the true Marxist must do.

"WE MUST AROUSE HATRED!"   "You talk about *future* sacrifices in order to frighten people away from the struggle," Lenin wrote. "My good gentlemen! It would be far better for you to refrain altogether from talking about the 'revolutionary outbreak' than to ruin your reasoning with such a finale. Apparently you do not wish *to create* 'great events,' you merely want to talk about 'the shadow of great events.'"

To create *revolution*—an apocalyptic cataclysm! Only *that* will satisfy the deep yearning of Lenin's soul; his goal is not the postrevolutionary "good society," but the cataclysm itself, a deep, compulsive craving for violence, bloodshed, firing squads, and terror. What should be the correct course, which he excoriates the liberals for spurning?

Show the "horrible price" the people have paid and are still paying to absolutism, in order to arouse their hatred and indignation and instill in them a readiness and a passion for battle.[54]

Arouse hatred! Instill passion for battle! *We must arouse hatred—create* revolution! That must be the revolutionary's correct mission!*

Here we have the curious blending of compulsive hatred and coldly rational calculation that characterizes Leninoid radicalism. The motive springs from deep volcanic passion, the method from objective empirical analysis. It is an arrested adolescent fixation veneered with an adult capacity for means-end logic. If the end is to satisfy and adolescent appetite for violence, the means must be mass hate propaganda orchestrated toward the cataclysmic "great events."

MASS MEDIA AS "MADD MEDIA"   Such was Lenin's grand design for a massive monopoly of hostility and protest. It was almost as if he committed a Freudian typographical error, transforming *mass media* into "madd media." For that is exactly the type of media enterprise he proposed to build—*an AT&T of hate.* It was to be a gigantic communications corporation designed to locate every social friction and interest conflict, to identify every reservoir of discontent, to generate more, to create social cleavages, and to orchestrate all into a boiling tidal wave of emotion. This human communications cartel would collect target audience feedback and deliver audience stimuli in measured doses to generate, collect, synchronize, and direct the hate energies of the populace. It would be a fire department with alarm boxes on every corner, and giant bellows and gasoline hoses to blow and fuel every spark into a five-alarm blaze. Every time Mrs. O'Leary's cow kicked, the bellows-blowers and gasoline sprayers would come running to burn Russia down. It would be the pyromaniac's delight! Is it any wonder that Lenin, contemplating the splendid practicality of his dream, exclaimed: "Give us an army of professional revolutionaries and we will turn Russia upside down! Once we have an army of specially trained worker-revolutionaries

*Compare this statement: "A revolutionist must be able to do everything—to unchain volcanic passions, to arouse outbreaks of fury, to set masses of men on the march, *to organize hate and suspicion with ice-cold calculation*, so to speak with legal methods." The speaker? He was 31-year-old Paul Joseph Goebbels, the frustrated, crippled Ph.D. Bolshevik sympathizer who had by this time become a rising star in Hitler's young Nazi movement. In *Der Angriff*, February 18, 1929. Hitler had just named him Nazi Party propaganda chief a few months earlier. Goebbels was an ardent admirer of the Bolsheviks and student of Lenin.

[293   ]

who have passed through a long course of schooling, no police in the world will be able to cope with them!"

We do not and cannot know which spark—of the innumerable sparks that are flying about in all countries as a result of the world economic and political crisis—will kindle the conflagration, in the sense of raising up the masses. We must therefore, with our new and communist principles, set to work to *stir up all the sundry, even the oldest, mustiest and seemingly hopeless spheres,* for otherwise we shall not be able to cope with our tasks.[55]

Blow, bellows, blow!

Chapter 20
THE MAGNETISM OF THE DREAM

WESTERN SOCIALIST (delegate to 1910 international socialist conference, Copenhagen): "Do you mean to say that all these splits and quarrels and scandals are the work of one man? But how can one man be so ineffective and so dangerous?"

AXELROD: "Because there is not another man who for 24 hours of the day is absorbed by the revolution, who has no other thoughts but revolution, and who even when he sleeps dreams of nothing but revolution. Just try and handle such a fellow."

THE DREAMER AND THE BRICKLAYERS   On the night of February 24, 1956, First Secretary Nikita Khrushchev of the Communist Party of the Soviet Union rose to address the Twentieth Party Congress. He delivered one of the most explosive and consequential speeches of the twentieth century: a report on the crimes of Joseph V. Stalin.

Khrushchev spoke until 4 A.M. He reportedly broke down in tears four times while describing the tortures and murders of dedicated "Old Bolsheviks," many of them personal comrades of Lenin. Thirty delegates fainted or had seizures. Outraged, Khrushchev told of the savage techniques by which the Stalinist secret police tortured confessions out of hardened revolutionaries who had withstood even the Nazi Gestapo. Even after they were released and "rehabilitated," after eight, ten, fifteen years in Siberian prisons, some of these old Leninists had to be convinced that their confessions were false, that they were indeed innocent—*that it was the Party of the Great Lenin, and not they themselves, that had been wrong!*

What kind of madness is this?

We find a clue near the end of "What Is To Be Done?" Lenin pauses in an uncharacteristic break from his concern with his Design to quote the Russian radical poet Dimitri Pisarev on "the rift between dreams and reality." "There are rifts and rifts," wrote Pisarev, and "my dream may run ahead of the natural march of events or may fly off at a tangent in a direction in which reality will never proceed." A dream that only runs ahead of reality will cause no harm, and it may spur men to greater heights.

The rift between dreams and reality causes no harm if only the person dreaming believes seriously in his dream, if he attentively observes life, compares his observations with his castles in the air, and if he works conscientiously to achieve his fantasies. If there is some connection between dreams and life then all is well.[1]

Just so, Lenin responded to his critics who argued that his design for a party machine created an autocratic, suffocating bureaucracy. It is not "suffocating bureaucracy" when masons lay bricks in various sections of an enormous, unprecedentedly large building, to use a line to help them find the correct place for their bricklaying, and to show them the ultimate goal of their common labors.

> Are we not now passing through precisely such a period in our Party life when we have bricks and bricklayers, but lack the guideline for all to see and follow? Let [my critics] shout that in stretching out the line, we want to command. . . .[2]

Thus Lenin in proclaiming himself the master architect of the New Jerusalem invited all who would put their faith in him to join his grand design.

PRISONERS OF THE DREAM   "Many have left testimony of their sudden sense of the bigness of Lenin's simple, practical-sounding plans, and the potency of his concentrated will," writes noted scholar Bertram Wolfe. "As with a Loyola, as with all outstanding organizers of parties of action, the force of Ulyanov's personality, no less than his ideas, was beginning to bind men to him by ties that resembled those of disciple and master."[3] Krupskaya, who served as corresponding secretary in the early organizing days and saw intimately how Lenin bound men to himself, pinpointed his program's key appeal:

> It put forward a complete organizational plan in which everybody could find a place, could become a cog in the revolutionary machine . . . It called for plodding, tireless work to build that foundation so necessary for the Party in the conditions then prevailing, if it was to exist not in words but in deeds.

Not even Lenin could foresee what would happen when all the bricklayer mentalities were plugged into his "line" and became cogs in his machine. Many souls have what psychologist Else Frenkel-Brunswik calls "an intolerance of ambiguity": they cannot stand the very uncertainty of life and death; they crave certainty and salvation, and flee reality. They seek refuge in a church or a secular faith that assures them salvation and peace. Lenin himself was such a mentality. He found his faith—in his own destiny as "ruler of the world" and "mover of the movers"—in the Marxian apocalyptic-messianic world view.

Lenin offered a Grand Design for a New Temple, naming himself as the great priest-architect and issuing an invitation to all who would become bricklayers in building the New Jerusalem. An almost magic magnetism took over. Lenin did not himself understand the power he let loose when he energized his mass media machine with the simile of "the line," a mason's line to guide in laying their bricks. He did not understand how many bricklayer mentalities lived out there in the world, or how unquestioning they could be. Yet the magnetism of his dream took over, drawing to him and his party all the bricklayer mentalities craving a certain share in the Salvation among the Chosen People—bricklayer mentalities who would follow unquestioningly "the line" laid down by Comrade Lenin, saved from all sin and uncertainty by their faith that whatever crimes they were compelled to commit, they were building the New Temple for all Mankind. Lenin drew them together, and they laid bricks endlessly—not for a temple but for a torture chamber.

Their craving for certainty and salvation proved so strong that they ultimately carried out The Leader's will, suppressing all questions, even when The Leader was Stalin and The Line required torturing their fellow Party members to extort confessions. They followed even when The Line required *their own* torture and confession in the name of the New Jerusalem. They did not question that the Party was all-wise and all-good. For to do so would mean to question self, and such questioning would be more painful than the physical torture and brainwashing of their interrogators. Even as Lenin wrote about bricklayers and dreams, he expressed the mind of a 17-year-old, living inside the body of the man of 32. Violating Pisarev's warning, he did not recognize the difference between dreams and reality. He did not "attentively observe life, comparing his observations with his castles in the air." He expected to apply revolutionary terror; he expected terrible injustices to happen. He expected to kill the czar and slaughter the bourgeois liberal intellectuals—he even relished it. But he did not expect to have to kill 21,000 soldiers and workers at Kronstadt in 1921. The scale of terror that would be required to press humanity into the procrustean design was beyond his imagination; and when the facts rebelled, when the reality confronted him, he palled, began to retreat, sickened and died.[4]

But too many bricklayers abounded, eager to lay their bricks as part of a master plan, and to be told they were building a utopia for mass salvation. And waiting in the wings was Stalin, a terrible sick mind, the mind of the theology student lusting for Apocalypse. So the bricklayers kept laying, assured they were building a temple for mankind; they *had* to believe, for what other plan could exalt their talents, and them? They could not believe, could not face, could not accept, that they were building a mausoleum. But they were.

Both Lenin and the minion-mentalities who followed his line needed their delusion. All were held together by their hate for reality and their lust for significance. They were prisoners of the malignant dream.

BUILDING THE ENGINE OF RIGHTEOUSNESS   As we have seen, even in 1891 at 21 the young Lenin had as an integral part of his personality a kind of automatic screening device that rejected from his circle every person who, like Vodovozov, would not worshipfully and obeisantly accept his dominance and infallibility. This personality trait figured greatly in Lenin's life in the founding years of Bolshevism, 1902–1905. Inevitably, the personality of the leader determined and shaped the movement into one of followers arrayed in a mechanism for obedience.

In his associations with his fellow *Iskra* board members, Lenin was confronting a new experience for the first time in his life: dealing with men his age or older who were his intellectual peers—established revolutionaries not accustomed to bowing and scraping.

By mid-1902 Lenin was already splitting the *Iskra* board. He kept it in constant turmoil, his erstwhile ally Alexander Potresov wrote, by his "great cunning and his readiness to do anything to make his opinion prevail . . . Frequently my editorial colleagues and I felt out of place in our own newspaper office." Though Potresov often sided with Lenin, he recorded:

> At first it seemed to us that we were a group of comrades: that not just ideas united us, but also friendship and complete mutual trust . . . But the quiet friendship and calm that had reigned in our ranks had disappeared quickly. The person responsible for the change was Lenin. As time went on, his despotic character became more and more

evident. He could not bear any opinion different from his own. It was foreign to his nature to be just to someone with whom he was in serious disagreement. His opponent would then become a personal enemy, in the struggle with whom all tactics were permissible. Vera Zasulich was the first to notice this characteristic in Lenin. At first she detected it in his attitude towards people with different ideas—the liberals, for example. But gradually it began to appear also in his attitude towards his closest comrades . . . At first we had been a united family, a group of people who had committed themselves to the Revolution. But we had gradually turned into an executive organ in the hands of a strong man with a dictatorial character.

Potresov had met Lenin in 1894 in St. Petersburg, and had recorded his first impression: "A great force. But at the same time with a quality of one-sidedness, a king of single-note simplification, a quality of oversimplifying the complexities of life." By early 1903 Martov and Potresov began to feel uneasily that Lenin was returning to the rigid sectarianism Potresov had noted nearly a decade earlier. Lenin sharply divided all his associates according to who was for and who against him. "For him there existed no personal or social relationship outside these two classes." Early in 1903 Lenin stubbornly resisted an editorial board investigation of a victim's accusation against one of his appointees among the *Iskra* agents. The squabble, Potresov wrote, "opened Martov's eyes to the amoralism in Lenin's makeup." He discovered that Lenin was "uncompromisingly severe with 'strangers'" but was "prepared to defend 'his own' agents with characteristic subbornness, consciously closing his eyes to their personal misconduct." Nikolai Valentinov, Angelica Balabanoff, and many others who were to collaborate with Lenin at various stages of his career were likewise to split with him over this same trait.

A PARTY WITHIN A PARTY   Unwilling to accept the meddling interference and free dissent of his colleagues, Lenin began secretly building his own organization of 100 percent disciples. Krupskaya, the corresponding secretary, stopped showing the others all of her correspondence with the local circles inside Russia. Lenin supervised the *Iskra* representatives and made sure the corresponding secretaries were people of his choice. He personally read every letter and answered in person or through Krupskaya. He picked promising people out of local work to use as traveling national agents, just as he had forecast in "What Is To Be Done?" He invited released exiles to come stay with him while abroad, so he could evaluate their potential

and bind them firmly to himself by briefing them with "inside information" on all the groups and feuds, interpreted in his own light.

Lenin's *Iskra* organization inside Russia functioned in 13 cities for
the most part, with a few traveling agents shuttling among them. His
chief *Iskra* agent was Gleb Krzhizhanovsky, the engineer, his trusted
old friend from the Samara days. Lenin's agents agitated and recruited by ingenious methods. "Sowing" was a favorite; leaflets
would be passed out or scattered about factories and residential areas
at night or thrown from theater balconies. A trained recruiter would
read a perfectly legal newspaper to a circle of his fellow workers,
injecting veiled comments and watching for any listeners who
showed promise. These the recruiter would supply "legal" books,
then illegal propaganda. Clandestine discussion groups and schooling
sessions were usually held outdoors, in the woods, on picnics, and
such. Circles were organized for a standard *Iskra* indoctrination
curriculum of between six and ten lectures.

By the end of 1902 most Social Democratic Party cells had fused
into the *Iskra* network. Russia was fermenting. Strikes generated
student walkouts, street demonstrations, peasant riots, In 1903 the
disorders were intensifying, and Lenin was learning to gauge such
phenomena as "mass movement" and "revolutionary upsurge" and
to manage a strategy and organization that assume unpredictability,
requiring perpetual readiness, quick responses and tactical switches.
He was also practicing the practical art of mass organization and
leadership. In *Iskra* for the first time Vladimir Ilyich Ulyanov
dropped all other pseudonyms (he had used at least 18 in the previous 6 years) and used a single underground name—Lenin. He used
it on all his signed articles, and began signing it to personal letters
to his followers like a king or commander: "Lenin writing to . . ." or
"Lenin speaking . . ." The change discloses Lenin's new conception
of his task: building an image, playing a role, creating a concept and
providing a ready label for a package of systematic views on ideology,
organization and tactics. "Leninism" became the tag for his new
monopolistic company, and a powerful psychological molding tool.
Ultimately, Potresov wrote, "In Lenin's organization, discipline
reached the point of almost military obedience."

THE "SPLIT"   The Second Congress of the Russian Social Democratic Labor Party opened July 30, 1903, in an abandoned, rat-
infested warehouse. Belgian and Russian secret police agents lurked
around the neighborhood. Plekhanov delivered a moving keynote

address from a stage draped in red bunting. The delegates, many with tears in eyes, stood and sang "The International."

Lenin could count 33 delegates and possibly as many as 39 of the 51 votes for *Iskra*, and many of them directly under his control. For example, his own brother Dimitri and three women Krupskaya appointed, and a number of *Iskra* smugglers, represented Lenin and only Lenin. Others were trusted agents who had created little groups for the purpose of electing themselves delegates.

Lenin made a quick reach for dominance that antagonized his fellow Iskrists, especially Martov. He maneuvered to get Plekhanov elected chairman and himself vice-chairman. And he called the *Iskra* supporters into four secret caucuses, acting as if he were the party boss of bosses.

Antagonized by the Belgian police, the convention adjourned August 5th and moved to London, where 24 of the 37 sessions were held. After the London opening, the *Iskra* majority was disintegrating. By the twenty-second meeting, when the Party rules were discussed, Martov was leading open rebellion against Lenin. The issue: defining Party membership. In "What Is To Be Done?" Lenin had prescribed his definition of the Party:

> *The organization of the revolutionaries must consist first and foremost of people who make revolutionary activity their profession . . . Such an organization must perforce not be very extensive and must be as secret as possible . . . A broad organization cannot apply methods of strict secrecy.*[5]

Nor can a broad organization be easily dominated—and domination was what Martov feared.

So Martov offered an amendment. Lenin's draft held that one should become a member *"by personal participation in one of the party organizations."* Martov proposed to define membership *"by regular personal assistance under the direction of one of the party organizations."*

What is the difference? So many of the delegates themselves wondered as the two factions wrangled and ranted. Lenin's vesuvian eruption was far disproportionate to the substance, and so was Martov's dogged resistance. It was a power struggle pure and simple: who would run things?

To Lenin's surprise, his trusted young Trotsky sided with Martov.

So did Axelrod: "Is not Lenin dreaming of the administrative subordination of an entire party to a few guardians of doctrine?" Trotsky later echoed this line in his famous critique, written in 1904 and wished forgotten in 1917: *"The organization of the Party takes the place of the Party itself; the Central Committee takes the place of the organization: and finally the dictator takes the place of the Central Committee."*

Martov won, 28 to 23. The defeat touched off an emotional explosion from Volodya Ulyanov the petulant adolescent, not Lenin the professional revolutionary. He went wild with rage, as he himself said somewhat sheepishly as he later contemplated the shambles his reaction created and sought to puzzle through the consequences and reassemble a strategy for building his Grand Design.

Determined to rule or ruin, Lenin called a caucus of "Iskrists"— the last ever. Of the six-member editorial board only Plekhanov sided with him; the caucus divided seven for Martov, nine for Lenin. Lenin stalked out, slammed the door, and ordered a meeting of his nine "Leninists." He posted a guard outside with orders keep out any of those who voted against him. As he himself later confessed: "Lenin conducted himself like a madman. Right. He banged the door, that is correct . . . If there had been no 'rudeness' perhaps more than nine would have been on my side . . ."

"THE MAJORITY"   Lenin later admitted, "Beaten in the question of Article I, I could not help but try to get even in all the other questions which were left." Others, bored, skipped sessions to see the London sights and relax. Only Lenin attended every single session. He spoke 120 times and clearly dominated the convention. All alignments were either for or against Lenin and his "Leninists." Watching him hammer and rage, the admiring Plekhanov exclaimed to Axelrod: *"Of such stuff are Robespierres made."*

Defending his view of a monolithic party, Lenin defeated the Jewish Bund's demand for autonomy in Jewish affairs—and the Bund's five delegates walked out. Two "economists" quit as time went on. The departures wrecked Martov's majority and left Lenin with a solid 24 votes to Martov's 20. Determined—as he later said— to rule with "an iron fist," Lenin moved to purge the *Iskra* editorial board of Potresov, Zasulich, and Axelrod, leaving Martov, Plekhanov and himself. The delegates reacted in pandemonium. Dotting the Congress minutes are notes of "universal disorder," "threatening shouts," and "cries of 'lies,' 'shame.' " Trotsky tried to substitute a motion affirming all six, and lost by two votes. Thereupon the Martovists declared they would participate no further, and Martov himself declared he would not serve on the board since Lenin and Plekhanov could gang up and control everything.

Lenin, with his instinct for the propaganda jugular, insisted that the delegates continue in rump session as "the majority." In the ballot Plekhanov got 23 votes, Martov 22, and Lenin 20. Henceforth Lenin claimed he and his faction represented "the majority" in the Russian Social Democratic Labor Party, while the Martovists were "the minority." His group assumed the name of "majoritarians," or "bolsheviks," and forevermore called their opponents "the minority," or "mensheviks." The Leninists were to repeat this word warfare coup many times, creating a propaganda facade to hide their own weakness.

Historians have tried to plumb the causes of the Lenin-Martov split, and to explain the ideological and psychological variations between the Bolsheviks and Mensheviks. Yet most such ruminations lose sight of the obvious—all the more obvious when one has studied the development of Lenin's personality. The cause of the split was, simply, Lenin's petulant *will to dominate,* and the refusal by Martov and the many others to be so dominated. The key to the split was the quote Lenin chose for the frontispiece of "What Is To Be Done?" It was the slogan translated from the Lassalle quote: "Purge the Party, Strengthen the Party." He was going to build his company, his cartel, his monopoly—and its members had to accept his design and rule or get out. That was what the fight was all about.

IN THE WILDERNESS   Though he carefully nurtured his mythical facade of dominance, claiming *à la* Nechayev to represent a powerful Party "majority," Lenin left London with only half a loaf. Still, it *was* half a loaf. He had his own faction, a faithful few tested bricklayers he knew he could count on to follow his Leninist "line." And he still controlled *Iskra.*

He soon lost that. Back in Switzerland he and Plekhanov had long arguments. Plekhanov voted with Martov to reinstate the other three editorial board members. At that Lenin himself resigned, an action he later considered hasty. *Iskra* passed to Menshevik control. So within months the results of the 1903 Congress were totally reversed, and Lenin was an isolated exile in the Party, though he still retained his Party posts.

Plekhanov exhulted: "Robespierre has fallen!" The "new" *Iskra,* as

Lenin henceforth called it, directed all its fire on the old editor. Plekhanov accused him of creating a "new edition" of the Nechayev dictatorship, and on May 1, 1904, prophetically dissected Lenin's organizational principles:

Imagine that the Central Committee possesses the still debated right of liquidation. Before an approaching congress the Central Committee everywhere liquidates the elements with which it is dissatisfied, everywhere seats its own creatures and, filling all the committees with these creatures, without difficulty guarantees itself a fully submissive majority at the congress. The congress, constituted of the creatures of the Central Committee, amiably cries, "Hurrah!" and approves all its successful and unsuccessful actions, and applauds all its plans and initiatives. Then, in reality, there would be in the party neither a majority nor a minority, because we would then have realized the ideal of the Persian Shah.

Plekhanov's paragraph is equal to a college course covering fifty years in the history of the Soviet government.

Chapter 21
BUILDING THE AT&T OF HATE

A revolutionary Social Democrat must be, cannot but be a Jacobin. You ask me what Jacobinism means. First of all, the Jacobinism of today demands recognition of the need for the dictatorship of the proletariat, since the victory of the proletariat cannot be consolidated without it. Secondly, Jacobinism calls for a centralized Party structure in order that this dictatorship be brought about. Rejection of this truth leads to organizational opportunism, which, in its turn, leads steadily, little by little, to the rejection of the dictatorship of the proletariat: all opponents of orthodox Marxism see eye to eye on this.Thirdly, Jacobinism demands real, strong discipline in the party in order to further the struggle. The Menshevik outcries about "blind subordination" and "barrack discipline" reveal their love of anarchistic phrases, their slackness—typical of intellectuals—and their view of themselves as chosen spirits who stand outside and above the party laws drawn up by the party congress. If we take away discipline and frustrate centralism, where will the dictatorship find its supporters then? Dictatorship, centralism, strict and strong discipline—all these are connected logically, each complements the other. All this taken together is the Jacobinism which is being fought against . . . A revolutionary Social Democrat—this has to be grasped once and for all —must be and cannot but be a Jacobin.

—Lenin, 1904

THE CHARISMATIC PERSONALITY   From Lenin's Slough of Despond the Bolshevik party was born. Beaten in the exile maneuvering, Lenin still had an ace: his and Krupskaya's monopolization of the organizational contact inside Russia. He procured resolutions, written in suspiciously identical language, excoriating the Mensheviks and demanding they submit to his mythical "majority." He would draft the resolutions himself, smuggle them to trusted agents, and coach them in bullying, hectoring, and cajoling the local "committees" to ratify them, whereupon he would cite them as proof that the "masses" backed the Bolsheviks. In July 1904 he answered Plekhanov:

> We have no party, but we have a new party coming into being, and no subterfuges and delays, no senile malicious vituperation from *Iskra* can hold back the final and decisive victory of this party.[1]

Was this mere bravado and desperate defiance?
Lenin's resoluteness attracted those persons who craved certainty

[305]

and a destiny. For above all, Lenin impressed both friend and foe as a Man of Destiny. Potresov, who split with him finally in 1905, after ten years of exile from Soviet Russia described the man's growing charismatic powers:

> Neither Plekhanov nor Martov nor anyone else possessed the secret of the directly hypnotic influence Lenin exercised on others, I should say his power to dominate them. Plekhanov was respected, Martov was loved, but only Lenin was followed unquestioningly as if he were the sole undisputed leader. For only Lenin represented that rare phenomenon, rare especially for Russia: that of being a man of iron will, of indomitable energy, who combined a fanatical faith in the movement and the cause with no less faith in himself. . . . Without wasting any superfluous words on it, Lenin always felt that the Party was he, that he was the will of the movement concentrated in one man. . . .

Change some names, and the same might be said of another radical movement and leader that formed in Germany in 1921–24.

Lenin was also developing his power as an orator. Maxim Gorky recorded his first exposure to a Lenin speech at the 1907 London Congress:

> "Comrades" Lenin said in a gutteral voice, and at first I thought he was speaking badly, but after a minute I and everyone else were "devoured" by his speech. *For the first time I heard complicated political questions discussed simply. He made no effort to produce eloquent phrases, but every word was uttered distinctly, and the exact thought was made amazingly clear.* It is very difficult to explain the unusual effect he had on us. . . .

The year 1904, after his resignation from *Iskra*, was Lenin's darkest. He was without any real organization, bereft of his dreamchild newspaper, and forlorn. Yet the very fanaticism that enabled him to fight on alone was what made him a winner in 1917, impelling him to call for a coup d'état in the crucial hour when all others were seized by doubts. This very self assurance drew action-oriented revolutionaries to him.When victory seemed distant, Lenin could make it seem sure and near. In 1907 a follower asked what would happen when it came. Lenin declared quickly that people would be asked whether they favored or opposed the revolution. Those opposed would be lined up against a wall and shot; those in favor would be invited to work with the Bolsheviks. In her only recorded dissent,

Krupskaya objected that this would penalize people for having the courage to express their convictions. But in the event Lenin's jest— if it was that—turned out to be too close to reality.

THE TRICKLE OF RECRUITS   A steady trickle of prospective recruits and admirers came through underground channels. One who came in January 1904 was a young man fresh from the Kiev prison, where he had gone on a hunger strike to intimidate the authorities into freeing him. Though he came as a worshipful admirer, 24-year-old Nikolai Valentinov was also a strong personality and independent thinker. Had he not imposed his will on his jailers? And thus he was destined not to last in the Leninist circle where total submissiveness was the primary qualification. Lenin's internal automatic screening mechanism functioned unfailingly to select as "Bolsheviks" those persons willing to submit to the dictates of the Great Architect's Grand Design. The slightest independent tendency, whim, or dissent, as Valentinov discovered quickly enough, brought anathema and excommunication. Lenin's circle admitted only complete "organization men." Nowhere is Lenin's systematic administration of the automatic selection process and his quick banishment of dissenters more clearly demonstrated than in his nine-month flirtation with and ultimate rejection of Valentinov.

Valentinov listened submissively enough for several months. Ultimately he engaged Lenin in a philosophical dialogue on the metaphysical and epistemological bases of Marxism. For Valentinov the philosophical conversations were the beginning of his de-Leninization. He saw at once Lenin's total commitment to the propagandistic value of philosophy. The ultimate test of "truth" was utility in propagandizing and building the Bolshevik organization!

During an ideological argument Valentinov reproached Lenin for his indifference to the conduct of a Bolshevik comrade who had been given a passport and funds for a mission to Russia but squandered his money in a brothel and never reached his destination. Lenin's answer was characteristic:

> You very probably would never have gone to that brothel, and certainly you would never spend party money on drink; so far as I know you have no weakness for liquor. But you are apt to do things that are much worse. You are capable of intriguing with the Menshevik Martinov, an inveterate enemy of our orthodox, revolutionary old *Iskra.*
> You are capable of approving the reactionary bourgeois theory of Mach, a foe of materialism. You are capable of admiring the alleged

"quest for truth" of Bulgakov. All this adds up to a brothel many times worse than the whorehouse with the naked tarts visited by X. Your brothel poisons and obscures the class consciousness of the workers; and if we are to judge your conduct and that of X from this point of view, the only correct one for a Social Democrat, we shall arrive at different conclusions. You deserve to be held up to shame for trying to substitute an obscure theory for Marxism, while the offence of X may be easily condoned. As a party man, X is a steadfast, seasoned revolutionary; he has proved himself a staunch *Iskra* man before the congress, during the congress, after the congress, and that is of primary importance . . .

You're right in this, you're absolutely right. All those who give up Marxism are my enemies. I refuse to shake hands with them, and I do not sit down at the same table with the Philistines.

The faithful Bogdanov, who ultimately spent some years estranged from his leader over the same issue, visited Valentinov to try to bring the promising young recruit back into the fold. They spent two days discussing empirocriticism and materialism. Bogdanov had read his way through this school of philosophy and agreed with its critique of philosophical materialism, and he and Lenin had nearly quarrelled over it. But Bogdanov pushed it aside, demonstrating the capacity of Bolsheviks to surrender their individual autonomy to the point of self-extinction to the dream. Bogdanov was a good "bricklayer" and a party-liner:

> Lenin's rather bear-like handling of philosophical doctrines does not for one moment detract from his authority—the authority of an outstanding organizer, economist, and politician, the greatest man in our Party. It's probably no secret to you that we have decided to break off party relations with the Mensheviks, to have our own organization, our own central committee and local committees . . . We shall win. The majority of the Party will follow us. In the coming struggle we must all, as one man, rally around Lenin, help him in every way, give him the maximum support although for some of us not all sides of his character are acceptable. . . . There must be greater respect for Lenin among us Bolsheviks! We must defend him and not attack him, particularly in such a rude manner. You must make up this quarrel.[2]

Philosophy and truth must depend on Party unity, utility, and tactical expedience in the power struggle! Lenin is a great quarterback, and so all must accept and obey him in everything! Here was a "leadership principle" Adolph Hitler would understand. In fact, Bogdanov's attitude mirrors exactly the spirit we see at the analogous stage in the formation of the Nazi Party in 1921–23 among the little band of "true believers" forming around Adolph Hitler.[3]

Valentinov could not swallow this "leadership principle." Finally Lenin told him:

> There is only one answer to revisionism: smash its face in! Whoever joins the Party must follow its ideas, must share them instead of trying to undermine them. If you don't like them, there's the door. You are free to leave.

Valentinov did so, on September 16, 1904. "It was impossible to be a disobedient follower of Lenin. One could avoid submission only by breaking with him," he explained. Stalinism, he argued, was inherent in Leninism.[4]

DEFINING THE LENINIST   In his long walks with Valentinov around Geneva, Lenin snarled at Mensheviks and other Russian radicals who found him too dictatorial and bloody-minded. "Don't lose sight of the wood for the trees!" he ranted and raged, half to himself and half to his young neophyte Bolshevik:

> Ask yourself the general question, and answer it clearly: *What, in fact, does it mean to be a real Marxist?* Being a Marxist does not mean learning Marxist formulae by heart. A parrot can do that. Marxism without appropriate deeds is nothing—only words, words, and more words. But for deeds, the right mentality is needed. The words of the minority (i.e., Mensheviks) are Marxist in outward appearance, but they have the mentality of wishy-washy intellectuals, individualists who have rebelled against proletarian discipline, against clear organizational forms, against firm party rules, against centralism, against everything that they can regard as a restriction on their "psyche." Their mentality is that of bourgeois democrats, not of socialists.

Here we see Lenin defining the role and personality type of the real professional revolutionary—the organization man of the social demolition corporation he had blueprinted and was beginning to recruit staff to form. He was defining the true "Leninist."

> The bourgeois spinelessness of the minority and the whole incompatibility of their outlook with what revolutionary Marxism demands are best shown by their cries about "conspiracy," "Blanquism," "Jacobinism." How does Trotsky try to run me down? By calling me a Jacobin, a Robespierre. What does Axelrod try to frighten us with? With the warning that our movement might fall under the influence

of a "Jacobin club." What did Martov say about the Jacobins at a meeting of the Mensheviks recently? That there could not be anything in common between Social Democracy and Jacobinism. . . .

How then, Lenin's young recruit asked, shall we define what we mean by Jacobinism?

> Take the history of the French Revolution and you'll see what Jacobinism is. *It is a struggle to achieve the end in view, with no shying away from drastic plebian measures, a struggle without kid gloves, without tenderness, without fear of resorting to the guillotine.*
> People like Bernstein and Company [i.e., the Marxist revisionists]—who think that democratic principles have absolute value—cannot be Jacobins, of course. Rejection of the Jacobin method of struggle leads quite logically to rejection of the dictatorship of the proletariat, that is *of the coercion which is necessary and obligatory, which is indispensable for the smashing and annihilation of the enemies of the proletariat and for securing the victory of the socialist revolution. It requires a dictatorship, and the dictatorship of the proletariat requires a Jacobin mentality in the people who set it up.*
> Everything is interconnected here. The dictatorship of the proletariat *is an absolutely meaningless expression without Jacobin coercion.* When today's Girondins of the minority (Mensheviks) mouth their phrases about Jacobinism, they are stealthily *undermining the idea of the dictatorship of the proletariat, which is the most fundamental point of orthodox revolutionary Marxism . . . It is precisely the attitude toward Jacobinism which divides the socialist world movement into two camps—the revolutionary and the reformist.*[5]

Here we meet the ancient Babeuvist choice again—for violence, terror, and totalitarian tyranny, against democratic socialism, reform, constitutionalism, peaceful parliamentary process. Lenin accurately defined the choice and the personality type needed for building an organization of radical tyrannists!

AN ADMIRER FROM JAPAN   Prospective Bolshevik recruits were not the only ones who came to Geneva to see Lenin. An extraordinary visitor was Colonel Motojiri Akashi, a top intelligence operative of the Japanese imperial army. To reduce the rising unrest on Russia's homefront, the czar's advisers felt a small and victorious foreign war would be a healthy diversion. Accordingly, in February 1904 the Russians went to war against the Japanese over Far East expansion. Therefore Colonel Akashi's mission was that of canvassing the Russian revolutionaries in Europe and deciding which merited support.

Akashi, Japan's prewar military attaché in St. Petersburg, met Lenin in July 1904, when the war was in its sixth month. They later met a second time in 1904. Akashi reported to Tokyo:

> Lenin is considered by other socialists to be a rascal who uses all kinds of methods to reach his objectives. On the contrary, he is a sincere man and lacks egoism. He gives everything to his doctrine. *Lenin is the person who can accomplish the revolution.*[6]

About the time of his first meeting with Akashi, Lenin judged the time ripe for a new start because "We have revolutionaries, and their number is steadily growing, who prize the operational code of the old *Iskra* that schooled them above any editorial circle of former leaders." His Japanese contact set him loose with renewed energy—and resources—to build his design. In August he called a conference of his followers at Lac de Bre, near Geneva. He was able to muster a grand total of 22 Bolsheviks, including himself and his wife. There they decided to organize their own central committee within the Russian Socialist Democratic Labor Party (RSDLP), dominate the larger party if they could and if not, build their own from scratch. Within 13 years this tiny apostolic circle would number 17,000 and conquer Russia; within 60 years some 45 million organized Leninists in 105 political parties around the world would control the governments of a third of all mankind—the first truly global political party. Lenin financed this portentous beginning with Japanese cash. Akashi's estimate was not as lavish as it may have seemed in Tokyo in 1904.[7]

Nearly penniless before, Lenin soon after Akashi's visit suddenly had the money to launch a new newspaper, representing his Bolshevik faction and embryonic organization within the Russian Marxist party. On November 27, 1904, from Berlin the Okhrana—the czarist secret police—reported that Lenin was organizing to launch the new journal. The first issue named *Forward* (*Vperyod*), appeared in January 1905.[8]

Having launched it, Lenin then wrote S. I. Gusev, secretary of the St. Petersburg Bolshevik committee:

> Do not forget that the strength of a revolutionary organization lies in the number of its contacts. So far not one of the Petersburg people (shame on them!) has given us a single new contact. . . . It is a scandal, it is murder, it is ruin. . . . You have read *Forward* to young people, haven't you? Then why haven't you linked us up with any of these

young people? Find us *ten* new, young and loyal friends of *Forward* who know how to work, who know how to establish links, who will then manage to correspond without you. Remember this![9]

For Lenin *Forward* was a second beginning; it was the propaganda tool so vital for building the kind of organizational weapon that he had envisioned during his Siberian sabbatical. But this time he had a clearer vision of his task. He had a newly steeled determination to be ruthless and intolerant—and his *Forward* mirrored it. The new beginning happened not a moment too soon.

"BURN EUROPE!"   On January 22, 1905, just as his third issue went to press, a watershed event in Russian history occurred— "Bloody Sunday." Some 200,000 St. Petersburg workers marched on the Winter Palace to present their grievance petitions to the czar. Troops fired into the crowds, killing an estimated 300 and wounding 1,500 or more.

News of the massacre threw Lenin into a frenzy. In a *Forward* editorial, he thundered "The prestige of the czarist name has been ruined forever!" and then asked: "Can the Marxist revolutionaries seize this spontaneous movement? . . . to rally and organize better and popularize their *general armed uprising of the people.*"[10]

In the same issue he prescribed the role of the revolutionary propagandist in a time of mass revolutionary upsurge:

> We must make it the constant job of publicists to write the history of the present day, and to try to write it in such a way that our chronicles will give the greatest possible help to the direct participants in the movement and to the heroic proletarians there, on the scene of action —to write it in such a way as to promote the spread of the movement, the conscious selection of the means, ways, and methods of struggle that, with the least expenditure of effort, will yield the most substantial and permanent results.[11]

Lenin certainly followed his own advice. He rushed to the Geneva library and began translating the classic writings on street fighting by the French Gen. Gustave-Paul Cluseret, a veteran of U.S. Civil War and the Paris Commune. He bombarded his agents inside Russia with exhortations and instructions. A classic example was his bloody-minded letter of October 16, 1905, to the Military Committee of the St. Petersburg RSDLR. It was simply a design for using his tiny band of Bolsheviks as Typhoid Marys for spreading apocalyptic hysteria and violence:

> I am appalled, truly appalled, to find that there has been talk about bombs for *over six months*, yet not one has been made!
>
> Go to the youth! That is the only remedy! Or else, by God, you will find youselves left with learned memoranda, plans, blueprints, schemes, excellent prescriptions, but without an organization, without a living cause. Go to the youth. Form fighting squads *at once* everywhere . . . Let groups be organized immediately of 3, 10, 30 persons. Let them arm themselves at once as best they can, be it with a revolver, a knife, a rag soaked in kerosene for starting fires, etc.
>
> Do not make membership in the party an absolute condition—that would be an absurd demand for an armed uprising. Do not fail to contact any group, even if it consists of only three persons; make your one sole condition that it should be reliable as far as police spying is concerned and prepared to fight the troops . . .
>
> You must proceed to propagandize on a wide scale. Let five or ten people make the round of *hundreds* of students' and workers' study circles in a week, penetrate wherever they can, and everywhere propose a clear, brief, direct, and simple plan: organize combat groups immediately, arm yourselves as best you can, and work with all your might; we will help you in every way we can, but *do not wait for our help;* act for yourselves . . .
>
> The propagandists must supply each group with brief and simple recipes for making bombs, give them an elementary explanation of the type of work, and then leave it all to them. Squads must *at once* begin military training by launching operations immediately, at once. Some may at once undertake to kill a spy or blow up a police station, others to raid a bank to confiscate funds for the insurrection, others again may drill or prepare plans of localities, etc. But the essential thing is to begin at once to learn from actual practice: have no fear of these trial attacks . . . Let every group learn, if it is only by beating up policemen: a score or so casualties will be more than repaid by the fact that we will train hundreds of experienced fighters, who tomorrow will be leading hundreds of thousands.[12]

And if the armed uprising succeeded, what should be the revolutionary government's objective? Lenin wrote it in two words: "BURN EUROPE."

After Bloody Sunday the Japanese gave money to the Russian revolutionary groups to finance gun-running, with the aim of a summer uprising. Lenin put his newspaper's director of circulation, Maxim M. Litvinov (later Soviet People's Commissar for Foreign Affairs), to work smuggling guns along with copies of *Forward*.

He also had enough money to call his own Bolshevik party congress in London, April 25, May 10. He called it the "Third Congress," claiming to represent the whole RSDLP. This was the real founding congress of what was to become the Bolshevik Party, later the Russian Communist Party and the global Comintern network. Here Lenin had assembled the real "rock hards," as they came to call themselves—men he had satisfied himself would follow his uncompromising line of violent revolution unswervingly through tactical and ideological battles. The selection process was no one-way situation, however. The "hards" had also picked Lenin as the leader they would follow through all fire and feuding in the certain faith he could lead them as the Chosen People into the New Jerusalem.

FROM COMMA STRIKE TO ARMAGEDDON   After disastrous military defeats, the czarist regime signed a peace treaty with Japan in September 1905. Like an avalanche of snow triggered by the mere snap of a twig, Russia's Revolution of 1905 occurred over a trivial matter: a printer's comma. That October Moscow's printers went on strike. Paid on a piecework basis, so much per 1,000 letters set, they demanded a few more kopeks for punctuation marks, too. Their "comma strike" sparked sympathy strikes in other trades. The bakers, even the *corps de ballet*, struck. Some 120 cities were paralyzed in one of the most complete general strikes in history. On October 30 the czar issued his famous "October Manifesto," which granted basic civil liberties to all, regardless of religion or nationality, even legalized political parties, and created an elected legislative body, the Imperial Duma.

All this while Lenin had remained in Geneva, for he wanted no more of jail. During the summer he supervised Litvinov in smuggling 15,000 rifles, 3,000 revolvers, and several tons of dynamite and revolutionary literature. When the "Days of Freedom" and the accompanying amnesty had been well-tested, he returned to St. Petersburg about November 20. On November 9 the Bolsheviks had launched a new, *legal* daily, *New Life*. Its circulation reached 80,000 and ran for 28 issues, 15 of which were confiscated despite the new free press guarantees. Lenin's first article appeared on November 23. Characteristically, he told the Bolsheviks to keep their secret apparatus intact while exploiting the new freedoms "to create many new legal and semilegal Party organizations."

Meantime, the Menshevik-dominated strike committee pressed new demands, especially for an eight-hour day, testing both its and the government's mass support. On December 9 the government, groping toward restoring order, arrested the Soviet (strike committee) president. On December 10 the Bolshevik Central Committee discussed the armed uprising Lenin had been urging since January. In anticipation of it, Lenin had ordered Leonid Krassin, an engineer and old St. Petersburg comrade, to set up a special Bolshevik "Combat Bureau" and bomb factory. On December 13, insurrections erupted in several cities. Lenin proposed (and on December 18 the Moscow Bolsheviks endorsed) a plan for turning a general strike into a general uprising. The St. Petersburg Bolsheviks were to support their Moscow comrades by destroying the railroad tracks between the two capitals to prevent troop movements.[13]

The strike began on December 20. Next day it shifted to larger-scale demonstrations, with sporadic gunfire. The following day Bolshevik paramilitary units led the masses in throwing up barricades and fighting government troops and police. Street fighting also erupted in Rostov, Saratov, Vilna. Eventually the government was able to reinforce via the St. Petersburg railroad and thoroughly crush the Moscow uprising by December 30.

BOLSHEVIK BANDITS AND GIGOLOS   Since Japanese support had ended with the war, Lenin resolved to resort to "expropriations" of banks, customs houses, ticket offices, and payroll trains. Krassin's "Combat Bureau" went to work, and the Bolsheviks used both their own members and common criminals, who collaborated for shares. The Leninists were not the only political thieves. The Social Revolutionaries, after the October Manifesto had granted them a constitution and representative assembly consonant with their populist principles, renounced terror. But some extremist "Maximalist" members bolted and formed their own "exes";* they, too, collaborated and divided the booty with Krassin's Bolshevik Combat Bureau, for, after all, he furnished first-rate bombs and other useful engineering devices. Over 200 "expropriations" occurred in early 1906. In March twenty Maximalists robbed the Bank for Mutual Mercantile Credit in Moscow of 875,000 rubles. At the Stockholm Congress Lenin openly defended this robbery and other "exes" activities by hinting that the Bolsheviks had shared the loot.

The greatest Bolshevik robberies were masterminded by Stalin and his boyhood buddy, "Kamo." The latter, young cross-eyed Ar-

*The term used euphemistically by the revolutionaries to denote "expropriations"—i.e., robberies.

menian whose real name was Semyon A. Ter-Petrossian, had entered the Bolshevik pantheon under his revolutionary name for feigning insanity for three years to escape punishment after his arrest in a counterfeiting scheme. Kamo hijacked 200,000 rubles in early 1906 on the Georgian Military Highway, and under Stalin's supervision in June 1907 executed the most famous of all revolutionary "expropriations." Tipped off by spies, Kamo's Bolsheviks ambushed two State Bank messengers in a crowded Tiflis square, hurling bombs at the cossack guards. Forty people were killed, and the marauders got away with the huge sum of 341,000 gold rubles.

Lenin also oversaw operations, such as the assignment of a comrade to seduce a wealthy Moscow dame. When a professor, a party member, objected that their comrade seducer Victor Taratuta was a scoundrel, Lenin laughed:

> That is exactly why he is useful to us. Precisely because he will stop at nothing. Would you agree to be a gigolo? To live with a Moscow heiress for her money? No! And neither would I. But Victor did. And so he is a very useful man who cannot be replaced!

To another Bolshevik intellectual Lenin explained:

> Revolution is difficult business. It cannot be made with gloves or manicured nails. A party is no girl's dormitory. Party members should not be measured by the narrow standard of petit-bourgeois morality.

Within a year, Lenin spent as much as a million rubles from his robberies to publish three newspapers, print pamphlets, pay Bolshevik salaries and travel expenses, and above all, to launch in Kiev an institution unprecedented in human history: the revolutionary combat training school.[14] This formal schooling was probably Lenin's single greatest innovation in the rise of revolutionary radicalism— and it was made possible by armed robberies.

Marxist capitalist-haters though they were, the Mensheviks opposed such criminality because of possible public revulsion, and because it gave Lenin too much organizational muscle. In May 1906 the RSDLP tried a "unity congress" at Stockholm and the Mensheviks pushed through a resolution forbidding "expropriations" and ordering dissolution of all units engaged in them and expulsion of all expropriators. Lenin was astonished to find strong opposition in his own camp. In disgust he withdrew his own substitute motion, and the prohibition passed 64 to 4, with 20 abstentions, Lenin's diehards. Lenin himself stayed away from the session at which the vote was taken!

He did win an amendment sanctioning "defensive" actions against governmental terror and the Black Hundreds, who were reactionary vigilantes fostered and often armed by the czarist police. When the new RSDLP Central Committee with a Menshevik majority established a "military-technical" bureau to handle these matters, Lenin easily gained control of it. He used this body as his own extralegal Bolshevik Center, and formed a secret finance-military affairs committee of himself, Krassin, and Alexander A. Bogdanov. They continued their robberies, complying with the Menshevik prohibition by having the robbers "resign" from the party in advance. The "resignations" were mere charades, for the robbers, in fact, were under Lenin's command.

As Lenin explained to Anatoli Lunacharsky (future Societ Commissar of Education) before the Stockholm unity congress: "If we have a majority in the Central Committee, we will demand the strictest discipline. We shall insist that the Mensheviks submit to party unity. . . . "

"And what happens if we are in the minority?" asked Lunacharsky.

"Whatever happens, we shall never permit the idea of unity to be a noose around our necks. We shall never permit them to lead us by a leash."

As it happened, the Bolsheviks got only three of ten Central Committee seats. The congress drew 150 Social Democrats; of 112 voting delegates Lenin could count on about 46, his opponents 62. Thanks to the October Manifesto, the RSDLP had become by this time a real party; its ranks numbered around 100,000. While the Mensheviks represented an estimated 18,000, Lenin could count perhaps 13,000 Bolsheviks. When the second elected Duma assembled in February 1907, 65 Social Democrats took seats with 36 of them Mensheviks to 18 Bolsheviks.

With his "expropriated" booty, and all the organizational muscle it supplied him, Lenin at the next Congress (held in London in April 1907) was able to seize the party. Since he could pay delegates' transportation, he had enough to dominate the congress. The Congress proudly noted that there were 116 worker delegates and 196 intellectuals and professional revolutionaries, 118 of whom were living at the Party's expense. Lenin controlled about a hundred dele-

[317]

gates, to perhaps a dozen fewer for the Mensheviks. He got himself elected chairman over Plekhanov by a few votes, and went home with seven to nine votes on the 13-member Central Committee under his control.

"A TROOP OF JUVENILE DELINQUENTS"   The 1907 Congress was an achievement for Lenin. *He had largely built his design for an AT&T of hate!* His flaming exhortations to violence in 1905 had set him apart—a veritable hate magnet to all predisposed to terrorism. His willingness to organize "expropriations" attracted outright criminals and all the pathotypes of the twilight underworld of intrigue and conspiracy. The hoodlum element joined now the Black Hundreds, now the Leninist "fighting bands" or "fighters," finding ideological and moral cloaks for their jungle savagery. Ordinary brawlers could and did, as Rosa Luxemburg vehemently protested, by professing revolutionary faith become crusading knights.[15] As a noted scholar aptly put it, Lenin "commanded a troop of overage juvenile delinquents."[16]

He had still more grandiose plans, of course. But he had a real paramilitary party in being, with thousands of professional propagandists and organizers schooled in mass manipulation and hardened by hundreds of strikes and street battles. Lenin's Bolsheviks amounted to a sizable bloc of representatives in Russia's embryonic constitutional legislature, a network of agents and publications in factories and cities across the nation, and a ready force for massive protest marches and street demonstrations. He was forging the grand apocalyptic army about which he had dreamed about in Siberia and detailed in "What Is To Be Done?"

Little wonder, then, that Lenin was cocky enough to present the London Congress with a pamphlet answering Menshevik objections to his incendiary rhetoric that was at once a breath-taking declaration of his totalitarian mentality and a blood-curdling demonstration of his ruthless tactical and propaganda genius:

> My wording is calculated to evoke in the reader hatred, disgust, and contempt . . . That tone is calculated not to convince, but to break up the ranks of the opponent, not to correct a mistake but to annihilate him, to wipe him and his organization off the face of the earth. The wording is indeed of such a nature as to evoke the worst thoughts, the worst suspicions about the opponent and indeed, as contrasted with the wording that convinces and corrects, it "carries confusion into the ranks of the proletariat."

I shall always act in that way . . . shall always conduct—a fight of exterminatio.[17]

It was a fitting confirmation sermon by the high priest for his young revolutionary hate party. Now that the party was a going concern, Lenin, fearing arrest, fled Russia in 1907, to live in exile again. He would not return for ten years. When he did, in April 1917, it was to organize and lead the armed insurrection he had so long advocated. Unlike 1895 and 1905, this time he had a living, breathing combat party. And he won.

The Russian "masses" are still waiting for the promised Kingdom to Come.

V. GLOBALIZING HATE MEDIA

Chapter 22
COLONIZING LENINIST HATE MEDIA CARTELS

All over the world the association of Communists is growing. In a number of countries Soviet power has already triumphed. The victory of the communist revolution is assured. The comrades present in this hall saw the founding of the first Soviet republic. Now they see the founding of the Third—Communist—International. And they will all see the founding of the World Federative Republic of Soviets.
—Lenin, Speech on the Founding of the Comintern, March 6, 1919.[1]

Revolutionaries who take the law into their own hands are horrifying not because they are criminals, but because they are like machines that have got out of control, like runaway trains. . . . There are limits to everything. In all this time something definite should have been achieved. But it turns out that those who inspired the revolution aren't at home in anything except change and turmoil, they aren't happy with anything that's on less than a world scale. For them transitional periods, worlds in the making, are an end in themselves. They aren't trained for anything else, they don't know anything except that. And do you know why these never-ending preparations are so futile? It's because these men haven't any real capacities, they are incompetent. Man is born to live, not to prepare for life. Life itself, the phenomenon of life, the gift of life, is so breathtakingly serious! So why substitute this childish harlequinade of immature fantasies, these schoolboy escapades?

—Boris Pasternak,
Dr. Zhivago

"I SPIT ON RUSSIA"   Lenin and his Bolsheviks seized power from the war-weary, irresolute Social Democratic Kerensky regime in a lightning coup d'état on November 7, 1917. But in the Leninist vision, installing his media monopoly in Russia was only a step toward establishing a global media monopoly. *"It isn't a question of Russia at all, Gentlemen,"* Lenin told a visiting radical delegation a few days after his coup. "I spit on Russia . . . *This is merely one phase through which we must pass on the way to a world revolution."*[2]

Lenin's concept of "media" included far more than the press. Professional revolutionaries "should use all media to which they have access," he declared in 1920, specifying the press, public meetings, trade unions, and cooperative societies.[3] To him, communications embraced every form of human organization, whether tiny cells or vast crowds. And global organization through Leninist hate-targeting and mass propaganda was clearly a practical proposition.

Having successfully established a media monopoly in Russia per his design, Lenin thereupon set about expanding it globally. But while using the newly-won Russian base and resources for extending it, he had to elaborate the ideology and organization for entrenching it at home. Innate in Lenin's concept of the press and every other form of organization as both media and as weapon was his idea of Jacobin revolutionary tyranny—of "revolutionary dictatorship" by the Bolshevik media monopolists. In a 1920 speech[5] he declared:

> Why should freedom of speech and freedom of the press be allowed? Why should a government which is doing what it believes is right allow itself to be criticized? It would not allow opposition by lethal weapons. Ideas are much more fatal things than guns.

The Supreme Editor claimed the right to cut all copy he disagreed with—and the throats of all dissenting writers and organizers, too.

He was brazenly open about this prescription of raw terror for maintaining his media monopoly. He decreed the death penalty not only for "propaganda or agitation" against the Soviet regime but for people *who might possibly indulge in agitation or propaganda that might "objectively" affect state security!* This was not an emergency civil war measure, but was written on May 17, 1922,[4] more than two years after Lenin had been boasting for propaganda purposes about renouncing capital punishment.[6] It was part of his outline on drafting a criminal code for the post-civil war period:

> The courts must not ban terror . . . but must formulate the motives underlying it, legalize it as a principle, plainly, without any make-believe or embellishment. It must be formulated in the broadest possible manner. . . .

Again on October 10 Lenin asserted that "The scientific term *'dictatorship' has no other meaning but this.*"[7] Even George III or Nicholas II, those proponents of divine right rule, would have hardly uttered such a claim. This is the political philosophy of a Pharoah, not of a "progressive vanguard" of humanity.[8]

Of course in globalizing his hate media company Lenin had an unprecedented technical and human base to build on. Let us consider some of the forerunners.

EARLY REVOLUTIONARY INTERNATIONALISM   Rousseau's ideology, with its universal aspirations and new modes of thought about the nature of man and society and their relationships, was inevitably destined to give rise to international organization. Rousseau provided what sociologists call a "constitutive ideology," or what the communist organizational warriors call an "orientation theory"—a grouping of ideas that attracts and welds individuals together with common goals, hate targets, and outlooks.

The first attempt began even before Rousseau died. This was Weishaupt's "Illuminati" in Bavaria, a Rousseauist secular religion international in scope and patterned after that other model of international organizational efficiency, the Jesuit Society (see discussion in Chapter 1). The ideological seeds developed further in Robespierre's time. Robespierre criticized the authors of the Declaration of the Rights of Man for thinking of the French nation as "a human herd planted down in a corner of the globe" and not as one of a family of nations, "all of whom have a duty to help and a *right to be helped* by one another." He proposed to add to the Declaration four more articles:

> Article 1. Men of all countries are brothers, and the different peoples ought to help one another according to their ability, like citizens of a single state.
> Article 2. He who oppresses a single nation declares himself the enemy of all.
> Article 3. Those who make war on a people to arrest the progress of liberty, and to destroy the rights of man, deserve to be attacked by all, not as ordinary enemies, but as brigands, rebels and assassins.
> Article 4. All kings, aristocrats, and tyrants, of whatever kind, are slaves in rebellion against the human race, which is the sovereign of the world, and against nature, which is the legislator of the universe.[9]

Article 4 is an open proclamation of war and "permanent revolution" against all the existing governments of Europe, a design for world rule, and declaration of universal civil war.

The Babeuvists took the next obvious step of organizing to extend the revolution. Buonarroti dabbled in diplomacy, fomented revolt in Italy, and coordinated a simultaneous uprising in Holland that occurred on schedule despite the Babeuvist failure. Buonarroti's "Charbonnerie Democratique Universelle" created elements Marx later used for his First International.

MARX'S FIRST INTERNATIONAL   Marx was living the quiet exile's life in London, working on his book about capitalism, when one day in 1864, a French music teacher named Le Lubez knocked on his door. He asked if Marx knew a German worker living in London who could make a short speech in English? Yes, Marx did, but why? Oh, two English unions had sent a protest to Paris inviting common action on the suppression of the Polish rebels. Liberal elements in all West European countries were organizing demonstrations in their favor, and the French were sending over a delegation for a London rally, Le Lubez said. So Marx rounded up one Eccarius, a tailor and old member of the Communist League who though now a British subject would do for a German.[10]

Marx's tailor "came off splendidly" and so did the meeting, which was packed. British, German, French, Italian, Swiss, and Polish socialists there decided to form a "Workingman's International Association." And Marx, tagging along to watch his tailor perform, got himself appointed to the committee to draft a declaration of principles and provisional statutes. Here Marx pulled a wily stunt. He let the others—unschooled workmen, the unsophisticated music teacher, an old Owenite manufacturer, and similar political neophytes—wallow in confusion, and with the deadline pressing, just when they had a rough, rambling draft ready, Marx filibustered. They met at his home for the supposed final session. With "mild opposition" and "a lot of talking backwards and forwards" Marx kept them tangled up in a dialectical knot until one o'clock in the morning. By this hour, they had only "discussed" the first of 40 proposed rules. As Marx later boasted, at this point "Cremer said *(and this was what I had aimed at)* 'We have nothing to put before the committee. . . .'" And so the meeting broke up, agreeing that the "papers" should be "left behind" for Dr. Marx's "opinion."[11] Discarding the whole mess, he then wrote his own principles and statutes. The committee meekly accepted them.

At the committee meeting, Marx also delivered "An Address to the Working Class." He surveyed the post-1848 situation, quoting a mass of statistical data about worker living conditions. Sixteen years before when he wrote the *Communist Manifesto*, he had not the slightest interest in social reforms. Now, however, he faced a different situation: He wanted to win the existing moderate British trade union movement as an organizational base for propaganda purposes. Before him were the labor lords of London, realistic, no-nonsense fellows who were not likely to take kindly to hot-eyed revolutionary fire-breathing. They wanted—and had proved they could attain— better conditions without tearing up and reorganizing society. So this time Marx praised the introduction of the ten-hour day legislation as one of the great achievements of the British working class, "the victory of a principle—for the first time the bourgeoisie capitulated to the working class." He also dropped his original indifference to the wage strike. In short, Marx accepted the trade-union weapon as a legitimate weapon in the class struggle—a radical departure from the contemptuous attitude of all socialist revolutionary schools to the everyday demands of the working masses. In this speech Marx planted the seeds of "revisionism," "legal Marxism," and "reformism" that were to bedevil all radical hate-filled Marxists from Lenin to Mao Tse-tung who have been hell-bent on revolution. The workers' economic struggles, reasoned Marx, must be combined with the political movement for broader democracy as a means of winning worker support for the political ambitions of the procrustean intellectuals.

In Marx's 1864 address we cannot find such words as "socialism," "communism," or "revolution," which dot the *Communist Manifesto*. Rather, he used generalities like the Delphic oracle or so many Bible verses, which can mean different things to different men. "The emancipation of the working class must be the work of the working class itself," he intoned. Moderates understood that to mean workers should vote the Socialist or Labor ticket. The ultra-radicals interpreted it as encouragement to seize power by violence. Trade unionists took it to mean work harder, produce a bigger pie, then through such direct actions as sabotage and the general strike, get a bigger slice. Marx declared, "It is the duty of the working classes to conquer political power." Radicals thought he meant with cannon, barricades, blood and guts. And the moderates thought he meant with ballots, handbills, and the peaceful attainment of a parliamentary majority, which was the contemporary notion of the various socialist movements.

This virtuoso performance persuaded many people who would not otherwise have followed Marx. Even modern U.S. communists point to Marx's management of the opening congress of the First International as a splendid example of how communists should exploit the practical everyday demands of noncommunist workers and build "united front" movements.[12] Marx, too, was quite pleased with himself. The council, including England's leading trade unions, asked just two little changes in his proposed constitutional documents. "I was obliged to insert in the preamble two phrases about 'duty and

[324   ]

right', ditto 'truth, morality and justice,' " he chortled to Engels. But, he boasted, he saw to it that truth, morality and justice *"were placed in such a way that they can do no harm."*[13]

Thus Marx converted the new International into his own instrument, even as he had done the League of the Just in 1847. He had other persons translate his address into French and Italian and send it to labor publications throughout Europe. An emissary was dispatched to Naples to persuade the Congress of the Italian Workingmen's Association to sign up. Marx and Engels found they could control the Association so well through its general council in London that they usually did not even bother to attend its annual congresses.

Though its elements were too diverse to work harmoniously, the International gave Marx entrée to union newspapers and publications in many countries. This became exceedingly valuable after publication of his *Das Kapital* in 1867. At its zenith around 1870, the International had a dues-paying membership of about 800,000.[14] Marx was delighted with its progress. In September 1867 in a letter to Engels he slipped the mask off the secret springs which kept him running through his years of hardship and exile: "Things are marching on. And in the next revolution which is perhaps closer at hand than it seems, *we* (that is you and I) will have this powerful *engine* [English, in the German original] in *our hands."*[15]

THE INTERNATIONAL DISINTEGRATES　　After Napoleon III's military defeat and abdication in the Franco-Prussian War, the Paris National Guard joined the city's radicals in setting up a city government after the 1793 pattern and defying the national government. The National Assembly, chased away to Bordeaux, required three months to raise troops and take the city, at a cost of an estimated 20,000 dead. The radicals were not real communists, but basically resurrected Jacobins who wanted a constitutional republic of small independent shopkeepers, not the abolition of private property.

Yet Marx was so eager for a sight of his apocalyptic vision that in the name of the International he hailed the Commune and interpreted its policies as identical with his own principles. That blew it. The British trade unions couldn't stomach the violent rabble that Marx praised, so they walked out. Bakunin's anarchists tried to take over the International and ended up splitting it at the 1872 Hague Congress. Marx and Engels beat them back and moved the executive office to New York to keep it out of Bakunin's reach, then let the organization die quietly in 1876.

But the First International had served a vital role in the creation of the modern revolutionary radical movement: It spread Marx's more moderate, diluted socialist ideas to a number of trade unions and allied political groups. Within its institutional framework, the social democratic parties, the future recruits of Lenin's revolutionary combat parties, the colonizers, were incubated.

In the late nineteenth century, throughout the broad march of liberalism, reformism, trade unionism, and socialism, Marxian class-hate ideology floated and filtered like a poison gas, infecting the vulnerable and the frustrated. Whether they were attracted to reformism and "legal" Marxism or radical revolutionism depended more on their own personality and emotional predisposition than on objective circumstances.

The unifications of both Germany and Italy in the 1870s under parliamentary institutions permitted socialist parties to operate and, consequently, paved the way for the growth of powerful social democratic parties, Edward Bernstein's "revision" of Marx, and "legal" Marxism. Marx himself opened the day by moderating his frustrated violence of 1848–50 as he saw parliamentary and nonviolent changes occur. In 1872 in Amsterdam he uttered those words that twentieth-century communists have tried so hard to bury in their dusty libraries:

We do not deny that there exist countries like America, England, and if I knew your institutions better, I would add Holland, where the workers may be able to attain their ends by peaceful means.

Marx qualified this statement, however:

If that is true, we must also recognize that in *most* of the countries of the Continent force must be the lever to which it will be necessary to resort *for a time* in order to attain the dominion of labor.

Engels outlived Marx by 12 years, to 1895, and saw more of the growth of parliamentary institutions and peaceful social change. He mellowed even more, introducing a new edition of Marx's work by hinting that new methods might be needed in the socialist struggle under changed conditions. Edward Bernstein, living in London in exile from 1880 to 1901, closely befriended Engels during his last seven years. In 1899 with Engels' blessing, Bernstein published a work entitled *Evolutionary Socialism* in which he repudiated orthodox Marxist doctrine of violent revolution, theories of impoverishment, capitalist collapse from inherent contradictions, and the labor theory of value. Noting that these theories had not been borne out by events, he called on social democrats to free themselves from stale revolutionary phraseology and to acknowledge themselves to be a party of reform—"which in these days they in fact are."

LENIN LAUNCHES A NEW INTERNATIONAL   Twice before World War I Lenin tried to form a radical revolutionary caucus within the Second International, a loose alliance of socialist parties formed in 1889. At the 1907 Stuttgart Congress he headed the 63-man Russian Social Democratic Labor Party delegation, and again at Copenhagen in 1910, led 39 delegates under tight Bolshevik control. Both times he tried, illegally under International rules, to form a fraction of Marxists sharing his minority revolutionary views. *"There proved to be only a few of that kind within the Second International,"* Zinoviev noted in his memoirs. At Copenhagen, the most Lenin could round up was ten followers, and "even half of these had cold feet," Zinoviev recalled. "Comrade Lenin was regarded with a great degree of mistrust. . . . The Copenhagen attempt to form a Left Wing within the International was a fiasco."[16] By 1914 Lenin had become so isolated that the International was on the verge of expelling him for his violent factionalism within the Russian socialist branch.

Lenin was not surprised when World War I broke. He was living in Cracow, just across the border from Russia, where the Austrian general staff had perhaps arranged for him to live in expectant deployment for political warfare purposes.[17] But when the socialists in the French Assembly and German Reichstag voted *yes* on their governments' requests for war credits, he was stunned. He had always thought, in event of war, his supposedly revolutionary comrades would join in exploiting the opportunity to overthrow the capitalist regimes. Indeed, in 1907, he, Martov and Rosa Luxemburg won the Second International Congress over to a resolution favoring just this strategy. Yet here in August 1914 were headlines in the German Social Democrats' newspaper, *Vorwärts:* "WAR! GERMAN ARMY MARCHES ON FRANCE!" The story said the entire 110 members of the mighty German Social Democratic Reichstag faction voted war credits like all the rest of the mad patriots! The whole newspaper, Lenin concluded, was a German General Staff fake to sow confusion in socialist ranks.

As soon as the awful reality dawned, Lenin developed a new plan. Time and again he had split with Europe's socialist leaders, split his own party, and stood alone. Now he must have his Gideon's army of disciplined professionals in his new art of political-organizational warfare. Only *his* army would fight wearing the civilian's clothes as camouflage.

In September 1914 Lenin gathered all the Bolsheviks in Berne, Switzerland to hear his new design. He announced the epitaph of the German, Belgian, and French Social Democratic Party leaders "of the Second International (1889–1914)." They had directly betrayed socialism, whose fundamental cause was "the actual prevalence of petty bourgeois opportunism . . . substituting bourgeois reformism, rejecting class struggle in its inevitable conversion at certain moments into civil war, and preaching class collaboration."[18] Labelling them "opportunists" and "social chauvinists," he accused them of yielding to governmental bribes "either with ministerial posts [in France and Britain], or with a monopoly of unhindered legal existence [in Germany and Russia]." These "traitors" had transformed their parties into "a national-liberal *counterrevolutionary* party."[19]

> We find that the socialist and labor organizations are now split into two big camps in all countries of the world. The smaller section, the leaders, functionaries and officials, have betrayed socialism and have sided with their governments. The other section, to which the mass of class-conscious workers belong, continues to gather its forces and to fight against the war and for the proletarian revolution.[20]

This was Marxist hokum, of course. The "masses" of every socialist party in Europe supported their governments in August 1914. Lenin simply hoped that as frustration and war weariness developed, he could drive a wedge between other socialist leaders and their followers and hijack their mass base. (And on Russia's moderates, this strategy worked!)

And so, cried Lenin, the true revolutionaries, the real Bolsheviks, must create a new International of revolutionary parties. "Down with mawkishly sanctimonious and fatuous appeals for 'peace at any price'! Let us raise high the banner of civil war!"

> The Second International is dead, overcome by opportunism. Down with opportunism, and long live the Third International, purged not only of "turncoats" . . . but also of opportunism! The Third International is confronted with the task of organizing the forces of the prole-

tariat for a revolutionary onslaught on the capitalist government, for civil war against the bourgeoisie of all countries, for political power, for the victory of Socialism![21]

The German Foreign Office, anticipating war, had closely watched the Bolsheviks and other European revolutionaries. The Germans were perfectly happy to support covertly Lenin's strategy; they felt secure at home and knew Lenin would direct his own revolutionary energies in Russia, where trouble would be helpful.

MISSIONARY WORK IN SWITZERLAND Lenin plunged into recruiting for his new scheme in 1915. The Italian Socialist Party called an antiwar conference, and Lenin sent Zinoviev to represent the Russian Social Democrats at the Berne planning session with instructions to fight for restricting invitations only to known revolutionary "Lefts." (He was outvoted.) Lenin "was very excited" during the next two months, Krupskaya recalls. He urged friends everywhere to get invitations for reliable Lefts, to propagandize them with the Bolshevik position, and to assign their proxies to Lenin if they couldn't attend.

Lenin arrived at Berne a day early to campaign among the delegates. "As soon as we arrived at Berne," said one French delegate, "the Russian comrades whom Lenin had sent to the station met us. They conducted us to a room in the People's Hall and there, for eight hours on end, Lenin and I discussed, toe to toe, the attitude which we should observe at the Zimmerwald Conference." Lenin didn't win him over, however.[22]

The 38 delegates—British Socialists, Russians, Poles, Swedes, Bulgarians, Dutch, French, Swiss, and Germans—rode to the little village of Zimmerwald ten kilometers away. Lenin wanted them to endorse in the name of international socialism his strategy of converting the World War into a world revolution and class war. Raising the slogan of peace, Lenin argued, was "superconfused, pacifist, Philistine, and an aid to the governments (who wish to hold out one hand for peace in order to extricate themselves) and an impediment to the revolutionary struggle."[23]

The Zimmerwald delegates split three ways, 19 or 20 voting against Lenin to demonstrate for peace against the warring imperialist governments. These were most of the Germans, the French, some Italians and Poles, and the Russian Mensheviks; they shunned Lenin's civil war strategy "like fire."[24]

To Lenin their Zimmerwald Manifesto was just a lot of arm-waving. It instructed no one, he disgustedly pointed out. Moreover, the pacifist socialists were wringing their hands over the war with no plans for exploiting it for the revolution. *Only five* delegates joined Lenin in signing a minority declaration: Karl Radek, a radical Polish socialist dissident who had his own small band in Bremen, Germany; a tiny Dutch band under the astronomer Pannekoek and poet Gorter; and a Swedish group under Socialist Youth Movement chieftain Hoglund.[25]

But Lenin proved his case. By taking over Russia, he provided in the eyes of influence-starved radical and socialist idealists everywhere the most powerful argument for his bolshevist combat party of a professional revolutionary officer corps: *Success*. What Lenin could not sell in 1915, he found plenty of buyers for in 1919.

EARLY COLONIZING EFFORTS   Lenin and his "Zimmerwald Left" colleagues had 100 francs among them. (He had not yet begun to receive the subsidies from the German General Staff to finance revolutionary activity inside Russia.) Nevertheless, Lenin kept fighting. He sought contact with radical socialists in Switzerland, France, Scandinavia, and the United States, always with the same objective: to rally the radicals who favored his position, to spread his ideas on revolutionary strategy, to create an organized revolutionary vanguard within each socialist party. To this end, Lenin ordered members of the Bolshevik Paris section to join the French Socialist Party and disseminate Bolshevik ideas through speeches and translated articles. In January 1916 he sent his mistress, Inessa Armand, to Paris to spread Zimmerwald Left propaganda.[26]

Angelica Balabanoff, the petite Italian socialist and humanitarian idealist who became secretary of the Zimmerwald Left and later of the Communist International, noted "Lenin's habit of selecting his collaborators and trusted men precisely because of their weaknesses and shortcomings and also for their checkered past."[27] Typical of those Lenin was recruiting for his revolutionary machine was a young Frenchman named Guilbeaux. When he showed up among the political exiles in Switzerland following the outbreak of World War I, the Bolsheviks noted quickly how he "ostentatiously showed hostility toward his country." As Balabanoff recalled:

> At close range it became clear that his behavior was by no means a reflection of Socialist or Internationalist principles. He gave vent to his opposition to the war in an exaggerated, stupid, vulgar manner. He

shouted insults against France and her representatives. I was greatly
surprised to find that the Bolsheviks seemed to take him seriously.
They elevated him to the position of French deputy to the International meetings. In this post he revealed his total ignorance of the most
elementary precepts of socialism, but he had the occasion to evince the
greatest zeal in carrying out the orders of the Bolsheviks.[28]

Guilbeaux underwent a transformation under the Bolshevik influence. At first he had been respectful to his seniors in the socialist
community. Soon he became "arrogant and cynical." Balabanoff objected to his taking money secretly from a German industrialist for
a socialist periodical he was editing. He responded: "What's wrong
with it? To succeed in our intent, we would unite even with the
devil." Balabanoff protested to Lenin. "Lenin gave me a look of tacit
commiseration and said, 'Why get excited over so little?' I remained
speechless."[29]

Lenin's correspondence was a steady barrage of instructions for
ferreting out, persuading, and organizing other radicals. To Aleksan-
dra Kollontay, a Russian socialist visiting in the United States in 1915,
Lenin sketched his plan to create an international revolutionary
party. He told her that within a few days his "group" in Switzerland
would publish a pamphlet that would be the "first demonstration of
the nucleus of the Left Social Democrats *of all countries who have
a clear, exact and full answer to the question of what to do and where
to go."* Since Lenin wrote every important Bolshevik document published in Switzerland, the "group" meant himself. He further urged
Kollantay to "endeavor to see (for five minutes at least) the local
Bolsheviks everywhere: 'freshen' them up and *connect them with
us.'*[30] Lenin always stressed personal evangelism and face-to-face
persuasion in building an organization. Bukharin, another Lenin
agent, arrived in New York in November 1916.[31] Lenin urged him
to gather a small group of Russian Bolsheviks and Lefts in America
to send interesting literature to him, to translate and publish Bolshevik propaganda sent from Europe, and then smuggle it into England.

In November 1915 through Russian party channels, Lenin received a leaflet of a U.S. "Socialist Propaganda League." It called for
revolutionary socialism instead of opportunism, resistance to military
preparedness and army enlistment, and immediate steps to organize
a new International. The American organization turned out to be the
creation of Boston Latvian immigrants whose foreign language fed-

eration was affiliated with the U.S. Socialist Party while maintaining its ties to the Russian Social Democratic Labor Party in the old country. And as luck would have it, the Bolsheviks were dominant in Latvia's socialist party. In 1915 radical Lefts in Boston steamed into the Massachusetts Socialist convention intent on taking over, even though they had only 16 delegates out of 276. They could muster only a third of the total for their revolutionary resolutions; possibly 1,500 of the 4,550 Massachusetts Socialist Party members supported their position. So they set up the Socialist Propaganda League, a party within a party, to plot a power struggle for the next convention. Their inaugural proclamation was the leaflet Lenin received. With the usual combination found in the American radical movement, the immigrant backers provided the ideological ammunition while native spokesmen signed the leaflet with names like Fitzgerald, Williams, Gibbs, Swift, and Edwards.[32]

Lenin liked what he read. He wrote back "an *enormous* English letter," complimenting their manifesto and urging them to adopt his doctrines and keep in touch with him.[33] He also wrote Bukharin to get in touch with the League and develop it as a Bolshevik organizational base. "There must be a base in the United States for struggle against the English bourgeoisie which has carried the censorship to absurdity," he wrote. It worked. The League adopted Lenin's views, becoming a fragment of what later became the Communist Party of the United States of America.

THE ARMED DOCTRINE   After the February 1917 revolution in Russia had toppled the czar, the German General Staff shipped Lenin and a mere dozen[34] of his fellow Bolshevik professional revolutionaries back to Russia in the famous "sealed train." In seven short months Lenin repaid them by destroying Kerensky's Social Democratic government and taking Russia out of the war. Lenin analyzed well his own mistakes in 1905, and the moment he touched Russian soil he dropped all bashfulness about the "peace NOW" slogan he had derided so fiercely at Zimmerwald. Embracing this magic siren, Lenin and his professional vanguard of a mere 5,000 to 10,000 Bolsheviks[35] rode to power on the crest of a wave of convulsive warweariness that swept all Europe.

One of the Bolshevik regime's first acts was to provide for the global colonization of Bolshevik revolutionary parties. Though barely six weeks old, the Soviet Government on December 24, 1917, allocated two million rubles to "foreign representatives of the Commissariat of Foreign Affairs for the needs of the international revolutionary movement." Trotsky promised "our entire support to the whole working class of every nation which rises up against their own imperialists, against the chauvinists, against the militarists."[36] Lenin and Trotsky, in *Izvestia* on December 26, 1917, announcing this cash allocation for foreign revolutionary parties declared their intention "to come to the aid of the Left Internationalist wing of the working-class movements of all countries with all possible resources, including money, quite irrespective of whether these countries are at war or in alliance with Russia, or whether they occupy a neutral position."[37]

In January 1918 gigantic mass strikes for immediate peace with Russia swept Hungary, Austria, and Germany, only to be crushed by the governments. Lenin could only tremble at the thought of what could have been achieved if Bolshevik organizations had existed to manage and expand this discontent. Though his own regime was insecure and the task of organizing his government was immense, he found time to launch the first Bolshevik colonization project: training recruited German, Austrian, and Hungarian prisoners of war to found revolutionary parties in their home countries.

After the German peace treaty in March 1918 Lenin sent Bolshevik ambassadors to Vienna and Berlin with orders to build up tight parties in the Bolshevik organizational mould. He sent Bukharin and Radek to Berlin as liaison officers to Rosa Luxemburg's radical Spartacist League. On December 31, 1918, Radek talked the Spartacists into converting themselves into a Communist Party of Germany and appealed to the antiwar Independent Socialists to join in a radical revolution, promising that Russia would join them on the Rhine and declare a new revolutionary war on "the imperialist Allies." Moscow even instructed Radek to conclude a secret pact with Karl Liebknecht, cofounder of the Spartacists and son of Karl Marx's agent-founder of the German Social Democratic Party. Radek promised Liebknecht that the Russian Government would recognize him as president of the German Soviet Republic and furnish funds and weapons.[38]

The Bolsheviks, controlling whole armies now, naturally thought primarily of advancing their revolution through armed force. In the winter of 1918–19, they expected communist revolutions by Leibknecht and the returning converted war prisoners in the defeated and chaotic German and Hungarian capitals, and actually sent military orders for conquest of Europe in the spring of 1919.[39]

In March 1919 a Hungarian Bolshevik outlined this plan of conquest:

> Within three weeks we shall have an army of 150,000 well-drilled men, fully equipped. We are surrounded on all sides by discontented people. We shall begin in Czechoslovakia. Then will come Rumania, then Yugoslavia. Three months later Italy will join us. On the eighth of April there will be a meeting of the Soviet of Workers' and Soldiers' Deputies in Berlin. We have absolutely trustworthy information that Germany is going Bolshevik. Under the circumstances, how will France be able to stay out much longer? Then England's turn will come. Everything is in readiness as far as Czechoslovakia, Rumania, Bulgaria, Italy, France and England are concerned, up to the last piece of paper. No country will be able to resist us."[40]

Returning Austrian POWs, their way paved by Lenin's embassies in Zurich and Vienna, established an Austrian Communist Party on November 4, 1918, beating the Hungarian returnees by two weeks and the German Spartacists by eight to become the first Leninist Communist Party outside Russia. Party Card No. 1 went to Ruth Fischer, one of Vienna's radical students, daughter of a noted professor and author of several works on philosophy and sociology.[41]

THE 133-DAY DICTATORSHIP IN HUNGARY Among the Hungarian POW recruits was a 32-year-old Hungarian named Bela Kun. The son of a village notary public in Transylvania, Rumania, he had graduated from college in law, switched to journalism, then politics. Kun joined the Hungarian Social Democratic Party in Kolozsvar and became secretary of the workers' sick benefit society there. He promptly embezzled funds, was kicked out in disgrace, and found an obscure job in a socialist paper in Budapest. Drafted when war began and captured by the Russians in 1916, Kun was put in a POW camp at Tomsk in Siberia. Bolshevik agents spotted him by virtue of his fervent socialist propaganda and anti-Habsburg attitude.[42] They brought Kun and other former socialists to Moscow for training as cadres to take the Bolshevik faith home with them.

Lenin himself took an interest in Kun and his fellow Hungarians. Always alert to signs of popular discontent for possible exploitation, Lenin was intrigued in January 1918 when the Hungarian Social Democrats called strikes to protest the harsh peace of Brest-Litovsk which the Central Powers, including their own government, had imposed on the Russian comrades. Shattering battlefield defeats forced Austria-Hungary to surrender to the Allies in October 1918. In Budapest on October 31 a Republic was proclaimed with a government headed by a pacifist-leftist aristocrat, Count Karolyi, and staffed with nondescript radicals from the aristocracy, the bourgeoisie, and the Social Democrats. Lenin knew the time was ripe to strike.

Kun and the other ex-POWs were working in Moscow on a newspaper called *Social Revolution* designed for Hungarian consumption. Now in early November Lenin sent Kun at the head of the trained Bolshevik cadre back to Budapest with a large bankroll and masquerading as a Red Cross doctor carrying a fake passport. Operating with the assistance of the Russian Red Cross mission in Budapest, Kun and his comrades founded the Hungarian Communist Party on November 21, 1918.[43] Two weeks later they started a newspaper with Moscow's money. Called *Red News*, it blared the usual virulent Marxist class hatred. "Organize your Red Guard!" it cried to the people.

> The most urgent task before us is the equipment of the proletariat with proper serviceable weapons. The communist organizations must be developed so that at any moment they may be ready to take over power.[44]

Kun made a wild stab at recruiting soldiers for an armed revolt, and it landed him in jail. But in March 1919, the Versailles Peace Conference demanded huge territorial surrenders. Hungary's shaky Social Democratic regime, with economic disasters accumulating, turned to Kun in jail: Would he, a known Leninist agent, take power and seek the mighty Red Army's help against the imperialist Western powers?

Would he! Kun, released from jail at 9 P.M. on March 21, seized the reigns of government. Armed Bolshevik bands took up positions in Budapest, and the government announced the cession of power.

Kun's bloody and chaotic "Dictatorship of the Proletariat" lasted 133 days. For a time his hastily organized "Red Guard" beat back invading Czechs and Rumanians. But as Fidel Castro did a generation later, Kun promptly wrecked what was left of his country's agriculture and economy. Despite daily telephone and radio consultations with Lenin in Moscow, Kun's situation grew more desperate daily. So did his measures. The "struggle mentality" dominated more and more. On May 3 Kun proclaimed the very essence of Bolshevism:

> I know of no difference between moral and immoral acts; I recognize only one standpoint—whether a thing is good or bad for the Proletariat. Comrades, I should have no hesitation whatever in cramming an imperialist with lies barefaced enough to raise a blush in my own cheeks; for I hold it infamous to tell the truth to a bourgeois if that truth is disadvantageous to the Proletariat.[45]

Nor did he wince at more barbaric means. He named one of his fellow Moscow-trained comrades to organize a reign of red terror against all opposition. From the jails he formed a corps of 200 thugs recruited from the dregs of society, dubbing them "Lenin boys" on the model of Lenin's own Cheka. They tortured and murdered thousands. One woman suspected of counterrevolutionary sentiments, for example, had all her teeth dug out with a chisel. Several hundred persons were forced to dig their own graves and then were shot, or simply shot and dumped in the Danube.[46]

But anti-Bolshevik sentiment grew so much worse that Kun's poorly schooled cadres were not prepared to cope with it. A railway strike and peasant uprising developed. Finally a plot in the Hungarian high command enabled the Rumanians to march into Budapest by surprise. On August 1 Kun fled to Vienna with leading Bolshevik cohorts, and thence to Moscow where he became a sycophantic servant of Lenin and roving agent of the Comintern.

It was an inglorious end to this first episode in the campaign to Leninize the world. Still, Lenin had succeeded in implanting embryonic organizations of professional revolutionaries in three countries —with many more to come.

Chapter 23
THE FIRST GLOBAL MEDIA CONGLOMERATE

Only hypocrites or simpletons can fail to understand that the particularly rapid successes of the revolution in Russia are due to the many years' work by the revolutionary party in the ways indicated; for years illegal machinery was systematically built up to direct demonstrations and strikes, to conduct work among the troops; a detailed study was made of methods; illegal literature was issued summing up experience acquired and educating the whole Party in the idea that revolution was necessary; leaders of the masses were trained for such events, etc., etc., . . . inculcating upon the masses the idea of the inevitability and the necessity of *defeating* the bourgeoisie in civil war, of pursuing a policy wholly dedicated to this aim, of elucidating, raising and solving all problems from this, and only from this, point of view. That is why our sole aim should be once and for all to push the incorrigible reformists into the cesspool of the hirelings of the bourgeoisie.

> —Lenin, "The Tasks of the Third
> International," July 14, 1919.[1]

The principal tasks of the Communist Parties at present is to unite the scattered communist forces, to form in every country a united Communist Party (or to reinforce or revive already existing parties) in order to increase tenfold the work of preparing the proletariat for the conquest of political power.

> —Lenin, *Thesis on the Fundamental Tasks
> of the Second Comintern Congress*, July 4, 1920[2]

FOUNDING THE COMINTERN   The first global political machine in history was Lenin's Third Communist International ("the Comintern"). It was not only the first truly global political party, but the first truly global communications medium and communications cartel. Backed by captive Russia's resources, the Comintern expanded the "Communist Party" from what had been in 1900 an idea inside Lenin's head and in 1904 a minority fragment of a party in Czarist Russia consisting of Lenin, his wife and 20 comrades to 105 Communist parties around the world with 42 million members by 1960. Although a major fissioning process has since developed, today the international communist movement—which Lenin himself always noted was part of a broader "world revolutionary movement" —is a whole system of mature totalitarian organizations, in some cases wholly dependent of the mother Soviet Communist Party.

Undoubtedly, Lenin's and the Comintern's accomplishment con-

stitutes the most successful record of political foreign aid and technological transfer and diffusion in history. Today colonies of cartelized
engineer-practioners of the Leninist hate media and social demolition technology are at work in every nation. To understand the
global plight of constitutional democracy—of "the open society and
its enemies"—we must know how this technological diffusion and
colonization occurred.

Two events convinced Lenin that he must crash ahead with a
Third International. First, late in December 1918 he learned that
Britain's Ramsay MacDonald, Germany's Karl Kautsky, and other
moderate democratic socialists were organizing a conference to
resurrect the Second International. Second, on January 15 the new
Communist Party in Berlin, inspired by Lenin's example and abetted
by his agent Radek, staged an insurrection that failed, and Rosa
Luxemburg and Karl Liebknecht were killed by militia officers in
suppressing the revolt that neither had planned or endorsed. The
abortive insurrection temporarily shattered Lenin's hopes for an immediate German revolution. He soon realized that, regardless of the
existing European chaos, world revolution required massive efforts
at stationing professionalized cadres and assembling revolutionary
organizations as "vanguards." Moreover, the failure did provide one
dividend: Luxemburg's death removed a rival to Lenin for leadership of revolutionary socialists. She had bitterly criticized his concept
of party manipulatory mastery over the masses, favoring instead
educating the workers and a more democratic, less authoritarian and
militaristic organizational structure. She had opposed him in creating a new international before the masses were properly prepared.
Now she was out of the way.

On January 18, 1918, *Pravda* carried a dramatic and emotional
account of the murders, and on January 23 Lenin declared that the
creation of the German Communist Party meant "the truly
proletarian, truly international, truly revolutionary Third International—the Communist International, became a fact."[3]

That night Lenin called three men to the Kremlin: his foreign
minister, Chicherin; the Finnish communist, Y. Sirola; and the Rus-
sian-British communist, J. Fineberg. They met in Czar Nicholas II's
royal bedchamber. In it was an opulently emblazoned canopied bed,
and on the wall, a painting—a young girl reclining at the mouth of
a cave reading a book resting on a skull. A screen partitioned off the
bed, and the four men gathered around a table with only a single
electric light on it, forming a tiny bright circle in the shadows of the
cavernous room.[4]

Lenin revealed a draft of a manifesto naming 39 left-wing parties
and radical conglomerations all over the world that he knew a little

about and considered suitable material for his purpose. He proposed inviting them to send delegates to a founding Congress of the Third International in Moscow. The other three agreed. Chicherin sent out the message by radio the next day over the names of nine men purporting to sign in behalf of left-wing groups or communist parties representing Russia, Poland, Hungary, Germany, Austria, Latvia, Finland, the Balkans, and the United States. In fact, the only signers who really represented anyone were Lenin and Trotsky, who signed for the Central Committee of the Russian Communist Party. The U.S. "representative" was Boris Reinstein, a Russian who was chased out of the country by the czar's police, did a jail term in Paris for revolutionary conspiracy, and made his way to America in 1901 at the age of 33. He opened a drug store in Buffalo, New York, joined the Socialist Labor Party, and left the country in 1917 without a passport to represent the SLP at a socialist conference in Stockholm. After Lenin's triumph in Russia, a group of Bolshevik sympathizers won him over and persuaded him to go to Moscow, where he became the official guide for visiting American journalists.[5]

Lenin's invitation openly proclaimed that its purpose was to create a competing international revolutionary organization to struggle against that capitalist counterrevolutionary alliance, the League of Nations, and the "social traitors," the democratic socialists, who helped the capitalists to deceive the working class. The manifesto proclaimed that the new Comintern would be a common command center for permanent coordination and systematic leadership of the movement, "subordinating the interests of the movement in each country to the common interest of the international revolution."[6]

Lenin openly avowed that he was going to found the first global political party in history.

A few days later Angelica Balabanoff learned that Radek was back in Moscow from his Berlin misadventure organizing "foreign sections" of the "Communist Party" in the Commissariat of Foreign Affairs. She "found that this widely heralded achievement was a fake." The members of these "sections," practically all war prisoners, had joined the party only to get favors and privileges. Practically none had ever had any connection with the revolutionary or labor movements in their own country or knew anything of socialism. Two of these prisoners, Italians from Trieste, were about to be sent to Italy with a large sum of money and special credentials from Lenin. Balabanoff had only to talk with them in Italian to discover that they knew nothing about the Italian socialist movement, not even the elementary terminology of socialism. She protested to Lenin in person.

"Vladimir Ilyitch," she said, "Get back your money and your credentials. These men are merely profiteers of the Revolution. They will damage us seriously in Italy." But Lenin was thinking only of shattering the existing democratic socialist organizations so that he could pick up the pieces for combat party construction. He waved her off: "For the destruction of Turati's party, they are quite good enough."[7]

A few weeks later, the Italian Bolsheviks complained to Moscow that this pair of POWs had squandered the money entrusted to them in the cafes and brothels of Milan.

THE COMINTERN "CONGRESS"   Six weeks after Lenin's call, the heralded day of the founding arrived, March 3, 1919. The First Congress met in the Kremlin, in a small hall in the old Courts of Justice near Lenin's apartment. "There was a make-believe side to the whole affair," wrote British journalist Arthur Ransome, himself a Bolshevik sympathizer:

> The meeting was in a smallish room, with a dais at one end, in the old Courts of Justice built in the time of Catherine the Second, who would certainly have turned in her grave if she had known the use to which it was being put. Two very smart soldiers of the Red Army were guarding the doors. The whole room, including the floor, was decorated in red. There were banners with "Long Live the Third International" inscribed in many languages. The Presidium was on the raised dais at the end of the room, Lenin sitting in the middle behind a long red-covered table with Albrecht, a young German Spartacist, on the right and Platten, the Swiss, on the left. The auditorium sloped down to the foot of the dais. Chairs were arranged on each side of an alleyway down the middle, and the four or five front rows had little tables for convenience in writing.[8]

Unfortunately, only one bona fide delegate answered Lenin's invitation. With the Allied blockade and tenuous communications, Lenin had fully foreseen a shortage of legitimate foreign delegates and the need of a little magic to put on a good show. But he was surprised to draw only one person. So he staged a hoax: He called in members of the parties in Russian states such as Latvia, Lithuania, the Ukraine, and Finland who were already formal Russian Communist Party members without the slightest autonomy. He hauled in the war prisoners, who had not for years had any contact with their native lands. And especially valuable were the foreign radicals who happened to be in Russia at the time, and could speak with some coloring of authenticity for radicals in their own nations. Such was one S. J. Rutgers, Dutch engineer, revolutionary socialist, and friend of Lenin's Zimmerwald allies Pannekoek and Gorter. He "represented" Holland, the United States, and Japan—*all three*. His qualifications were that he had lived in New York a couple of years, where he knew Trotsky and Bukharin and had become acquainted with the Socialist Propaganda League of Boston. And he had passed through Japan hurriedly in 1918 on his way to throw in his lot with Lenin and Trotsky. "Representing" Hungary was a prisoner of war who later made away with a pile of Bolshevik cash. England's "representative" was a Russian émigré named Feinberg on the Soviet Foreign Ministry's staff. The Bolsheviks were so desperate for "votes" that when word came that Guilbeaux—the hot-eyed young man Lenin picked up in Switzerland despite Balabanoff's objections—was on his way from France, they sent a special train to the border to rush him in; and they granted him five votes as a "representative plenipotentiary" of the entire French "left wing." Boris Reinstein, despite the use of his name on the original Congress invitation, had to decline to act for the American Socialist Labor Party on grounds he had received no credentials.

Hugo Eberlin, the only real foreigner of the 35 "delegates" with the political right to represent anybody and vote for anything, hindered more than he helped. He came from the Spartacist League. As fate would have it, he had talked with Rosa Luxemburg before her death, and she instructed him to oppose Lenin's idea of a Third International. She wanted to wait until further mass parties were ready to join, so that Lenin's personal influence and elitist party doctrine could be stifled by the democratic traditions of the Western labor movement.[9] Eberlin quickly saw through Lenin's hoax and publicly declared that the gathering could not be considered a constituent assembly for anyone or anything, let alone a new international. So the Bolsheviks hurriedly decided the meeting should be labeled merely "an exchange of ideas."

The next day, however, the Bolsheviks announced grandly that the situation had changed completely. They discovered a German printer who lived in Russia during the Revolution and became an ardent Bolshevik; Radek had taken him to Germany for propaganda action on his late lamented mission, and called him back for the Comintern Congress. Because of disrupted transportation, he arrived a day late, after the vote Eberlin disrupted. Partly out of naïveté and partly under Radek's instructions, the printer gave a glowing account of what he had seen and heard on his trip.

Breathlessly, he claimed that every country he had visited vibrated with enthusiasm for the Bolshevik revolution, and that the workers were eager to follow its example and the new International. Everyone got so excited—wanted so to believe—that Lenin, Trotsky, Bukharin, and Zinoviev engineered a new vote for forming a new international immediately. They ran roughshod over Eberlin.[10]

Lenin needed support so badly that amid the speeches he scribbled a note to Balabanoff: "Please take the floor and announce the affiliation of the Italian Socialist Party to the Third International."

Balabanoff, always the incorrigible idealist, blinked and scribbled back: "I can't do it. I am not in touch with them. There is no question of their loyalty, but they must speak for themselves."

Lenin fired back another note: "You have to. You are their official representative for Zimmerwald. You read *Avanti!* [the Italian socialist newspaper] and you know what is going on in Italy."

So reading an Italian newspaper qualified one to be a "delegate" at this Congress! This time Balabanoff merely shook her head at Lenin.[11]

Immediately after this meeting, Trotsky informed Balabanoff that the Central Committee had named her secretary of the new International. She objected, but as secretary of the old Zimmerwald conference her reputation among Europe's socialists made her a useful choice notwithstanding her idealistic scruples. She took her protest straight to Lenin, who told her coldly, "Comrade Balabanoff, discipline must exist for you also. . . ."

Even Balabanoff's objections withered in the fervor of the mass meeting the Bolsheviks staged that night to hail the proclamation of the Third International. It was held in one of the largest Moscow theaters, with the participation of the "foreign delegates." "One can hardly imagine the state of mind of the masses streaming to that convocation," wrote Balabanoff, who was there to translate speeches:

> Isolated from the world for so long, they thought they could finally see that promised ray of light, finally hear that long-awaited voice of solidarity that would bring them the liberation promised by their leaders. This joyful anticipation was in the air, one sensed it in the people's eagerness to get seats in the hall, in the outcries of joy over the possibility of seeing the representatives of the hoped-for world revolution. I admit, this euphoria was transmitted to me to the extent that I identified myself with some of the speakers in translating their addresses. I felt that my words struck the listeners' conscience, creating a re-

sponse that transformed the hall. I too was transformed. I seemed to see before me the protagonist of that epic revolution that was destined to create a new world. I was almost grateful to Lenin and Trotsky for having obliged me to accept the assignment.[12]

TALENT SCOUTING THE WORLD'S RADICALS   Lenin and his comrades were sorely irritated at their First Congress' dearth of foreign delegates. So they sent out talent scouts all over the world to recruit likely foreign radicals. One such was Rutgers the Dutchman. Lenin sent him to Amsterdam in November 1919 with instructions to open a Comintern bureau for western Europe and rally what comrades he could before the next Comintern congress. In February 1920 Rutgers rounded up 16 delegates from Germany, England, Switzerland, Belgium, Holland, and the United States for an Amsterdam conference. A few others took part without voting privileges from Hungary, China, and Dutch Indonesia. Rutgers, rich with Kremlin cash and feeling quite free in tolerant Holland, wanted to impress his recruits with the benefits of cooperating with Moscow, so he put them up in one of the best hotels. They ate in a well-known restaurant, where they roared out radical songs. Rutgers had not the slightest inkling that one of the delegates, Nosovitsky, was faithfully sending reports back to Scotland Yard and the U.S. Justice Department, or that the Dutch police had a recording machine on in the next room to their secret conclave. On the fourth day the canny Russian Michael Borodin spotted the police tap, whereupon the delegates scattered. The Dutch police netted many, but Borodin and a few comrades managed to hide out at Rutgers' home and continue the discussions.[13] Such episodes were repeated in Asia, Latin America, and the United States.

THE MAGNETISM OF MONEY   The Bolshevik seizure of power in Russia gave Lenin two mighty tools with global reach for his project of colonizing revolutionary hate media cartels around the world. One was Russia's resources, a persuasive attraction to revolutionaries used to scraping out threadbare existence as exiles by doing translations, working at mundane jobs, begging and borrowing. To them money meant printing equipment, leaflets, newspapers, travel, party congresses and training schools, and freedom from grubbing out a living so they could devote full time to revolutionary organization, recruiting, training and agitation. To get Moscow's support and approval, many radicals suddenly found it awfully easy to swallow

[343   ]

the Lenin doctrine and squeeze into the approved organizational mould and tactical pattern. The idealistic Balabanoff was appalled at the effect of Russia's gold:

I was most disturbed to find how many of our agents and representatives were individuals long discredited in the labor movement abroad. They were chosen because they had nothing in common with the labor movement and could, therefore, obey the most contradictory and outrageous orders quite mechanically and with no sense of responsibility. Adventurers, opportunists, even former Red-baiters, all were grist to Zinoviev's mill. . . . They departed on secret missions, supplied with enormous sums—and as emissaries of Moscow to the revolutionary workers abroad, they moved in the reflected glory of the October Revolution. If the prestige of their mission impressed thousands of the faithful, the power and money which emanated from them attracted new opportunists on every hand. The arbitrary creation of new parties had behind it the facilities and resources which only the control of a governmental apparatus can provide. Expensive new agencies with numerous personnel were established overnight. The International became a bureaucratic apparatus before a real Communist movement was born[14]

The American Socialist Labor Party sent two emissaries to the Third Comintern Congress in 1921, without Moscow's encouragement, to see what they might glean from this mighty new International. The delegates reported sadly back to New York that they learned "that the CPUSA [Communist Party of the United States of America] is financed from Russia and that the SLP might have been, or should have been, the leader of that movement here." But, the Comintern had decided the SLP was "too inactive, too slow and antiquated to perform the revolutionary mission in this country . . . too timid, too pacific, and too anxious to sidestep political and personal danger." Forlorn and almost green with envy, they added, "Financial support, valuable things such as diamonds, etc., were in readiness to help us here, but we had failed and were found wanting. . . . Out of approximately 2,000 delegates and invited guests, there were only two whose trip was financed by the organization which they represented and these were the representatives of the SLP of the U.S.A."[15]

THE MAGNETISM OF SUCCESS   Lenin's second globe-girdling tool was the compelling psychological attraction of his own success as a model for other radicals of all stripes. Beyond money and facilities, the world's revolutionaries needed the prestige of the first Soviet state. Because Lenin was a professed Marxist, a socialist, and recognized member of the Second International, other Marxists everywhere indentified with him. He was the first of their number ever to seize power anywhere, and he seemed to be fulfilling their own dreams and ideals. Regardless of what was actually happening in Russia, they did not see the Bolshevik Revolution as it really was. Each thought Lenin was actually building in Russia the utopia he wanted to build in his own country. They all projected their own wish fulfillment onto Lenin. (We have already seen how Balabanoff herself behaved under this intoxicating influence.)

At this time in far off Peru, Eudocia Ravines, who was to become the founder of the Peruvian Communist Party, was minding a store in the town of Cajamarca. A studious young intellectual whose father had been killed in a border dispute, Ravines had finished high school but was too poor to attend the university. Nietzsche and Renan's *Life of Jesus* destroyed the faith he had learned at his mother's knee. His conversion to communism developed logically:

> The city where nothing ever happened and there seemed no future for anyone, depressed me more and more. I left accordingly for Lima, the coastal capital, to look for work and more money with which to help my family.
> It was 1917 when I came to Lima, hungry for some faith and doubting my own destiny. Work was hard to find; time passed slowly, and so I devoured the news.
> A bloody revolution had broken out in Russia. The Czar has been dethroned and the socialist Alexander Kerensky, is the head of the government of the Russian Republic.
> The French revolution has reached Russia, I thought, pleased by the downfall of Russian czarism whose tyranny was familiar to me from my wide reading of Russian literature. I walked the streets looking for work, little guessing that this revolution which was shaking the world would shape my entire future.
> More names appeared in the news about Russia—Lenin, the Bolsheviks, the communist party, Trotsky, the Red Army, Zinoviev, Bukharin, Kamenev, Dzershinsky. All the events taking place in Russia went straight to my heart. Every morning I read the news avidly, and in it *I saw gradually a possibility of believing in something again, of constructing for myself a new faith. It was the possibility of believing in Man, in his rise, and in the creation of a better world for everyone.*
> As I read about it in classic literature, Russian life had seemed to me grievous, similar to that of my own highland country, and that of the

dusty seacoast towns. I could find genuine analogies between the Indian and what I imagined the Russian *muzhik* to be; the bloody Russian insurrection and the mute protest of my own people—who were born, lived and died on the ground—seemed parallel expressions. Gradually I began to believe that the Russian revolution would show us, too, a way out. The Bolsheviks said they were ushering in the dawn of a new day.[16]

It was like young Karl Marx all over again: "Seeking new gods for the vacant shrine."

The radicals flocking to Moscow to share the glory and wealth all became the human raw material for the mechanics of a global political machine colonization. The Bolsheviks set up careful procedures for grading and using everyone. Balabanoff writes:

> Many approached "the fatherland of the revolution" out of a more or less idealistic impulse, to satisfy their curiosity or to prove their solidarity with a suffering and rebelling people. As soon as they arrived in Moscow they were classified as superficial, naive, ambitious or venal. Then they were used according to this classification. All, without exception, were given confidential assignments and often even sent to their own countries with great sums of money for propaganda purposes, which frequently amounted to simple corruption. Very few were able to resist so much flattery. Those who had come to Russia as revolutionists or conscientious sympathizers left, broken-hearted and pained, but many others, in particular the naive and the ambitious, remained imprisoned in the trap into which they had fallen and ended by getting used to their despicable function of corrupters.
>
> Others became cynics and, having lost all faith in the revolutionists, went over to the enemy, fired by inextinguishable rancor against those who had abused their credulity, good faith, and naivete. The largest category was formed by those men who, having been corrupted, had become corruptors themselves. In the beginning of the regime, these were the only emissaires the Bolsheviks sent to the Western countries.
>
> Step by step this employment became a lucrative profession. Men without home or occupation—adventurers, smugglers, gamblers with life—put themselves at the service of the Bolsheviks. Their mission consisted in corrupting, slandering, and dividing the working men's Socialist movement.[17]

Ironically the very idealism many souls carried to Moscow became the hook that fastened them—after they were frustrated and embittered by the reality they found—to the Leninist hate-media company. In some cases they slung off and hooked onto the fascist hate-media cartels being constructed by Hitler and Mussolini.

To help hold together this mass of human raw material and sprawling new organizational structures, Lenin started a periodical as he had done in 1901. On May 1, 1919, the first number of the *Communist International* appeared in Moscow, a magazine whose frontispiece avowed its purpose with a drawing of a worker breaking the chains encircling the globe. It was published in half a dozen languages so that young Leninist groups and leaders in all lands could pick up the latest Moscow line. *This magazine was the first global political publication in history, a milestone in the development of the technology of propaganda, communications media and organizational science.*

In the first issue Comintern President Zinoviev chortled:

> Old Europe is dashing at mad speed toward the proletarian revolution. . . . The movement is proceeding at such terrific speed that we may say with full confidence, within a year we shall already begin to forget that there was a struggle for communism in Europe, because in a year the whole of Europe will be communist. And the struggle for communism will be transferred to America, perhaps to Asia, and to other parts of the world.[18]

DESIGN FOR A GLOBAL POLITICAL ARMY   Lenin worked furiously to get his plan for a world-wide Bolshevik organization ready for the Comintern's Second Congress in July 1920. He knew he could count on plenty of delegates from all sorts of political organizations to show up at the promise of the price of transportation to Russia and an expense-paid tour of the world's first socialist republic, all with time out for revolutionary plotting in Moscow. At first Lenin opened the Kremlin door wide, bringing in all kinds of messianics and world-changers. Some were so radical that they resisted participating in "bourgeois" parliaments and trade unions. Others, too democratic, rejected Lenin's demand for absolute conformity to his design. It suited his purpose to draw these in too, for the present— because it sabotaged the "reconstructionists" trying to rebuild the old Second International. Once when his "Comrep" from France reported the conversion of a radical socialist who had been hostile to the Bolsheviks before their Russian victory, Lenin grimaced, then laughed cynically and responded: "Ha! In a good menagerie, you've got to have all sorts of animals!"[19]

THE 21 CONDITIONS   But the winnowing began at the Second

Congress. Lenin's famous "21 Conditions," which became the standard table of organization of the revolutionary "combat party," would make sure that all hate-media corporations would fit his standard Bolshevik mould. All parties had to meet these tests to be acceptable to the Comintern—and to its paymaster. Lenin devised them to screen out all but the most suitable prototypes. To avoid disruption he designed Point 7: "The Communist International cannot put up with notorious opportunists," listing by name the moderate socialist leaders in Europe and America. He wanted no "menshevik mentalities," no democratic reformers, in his way. Fresh raw material that could be pressed into the mould of the Bolshevik "organization man" would do better—young men who had risen in the antiwar movement, and old and corrupt men. Lenin hoped they could go over the heads of established socialist leaders and hijack their mass support.

Lenin's other conditions aimed to give his global political army the cohesion and unity of a trained military unit in battle. "The Bolsheviks could not have maintained themselves in power for two and a half years, not even for two and a half months, without the strictest discipline, truly iron discipline," he said.

> Victory over the bourgeoisie is impossible without a long, stubborn and desperate war of life and death, which requires perseverance, discipline, firmness, indomitableness, and *unity of will.*[20]

Any party that met Lenin's 21 conditions would not be a political party in any conventional sense. It would be an *army of political guerrilla warriors, moving incognito among the peoples of the world, soldiers without uniforms, unidentifiable but always functioning with military discipline as engineers of social demolition, under a high command with a grand strategy mapped at the top. In fact, Lenin called the Comintern "the world army of the revolutionary proletariat."*

Lenin's struggle mentality always shaped his thoughts on organizational structure. He demanded a wholly military chain-of-command structure. All affiliates *must* confirm all decisions of the Comintern Congresses and must schedule their own Party congresses *after* the Comintern's. Their Party press *must* publish all important documents of the Moscow Executive Committee. In between Comintern congresses the Executive Committee would exercise supreme command and each affiliating Party's central committee would be but a

Comintern "section," hence as subject to its high command as any Army division is subject to supreme headquarters. These central committees, in turn, rule absolutely over all party elements—in the unions, the armed forces, parliaments or press. According to Condition 12, every Party member is subject to "iron discipline bordering on military discipline."[21] "What would the International be like," Lenin asked the Second Congress, "if every little faction came in and said: Some of us are in favor of one thing and some of us are opposed —let us decide the question ourselves? What would be the use, then, of having an International?" "Must we always agree with the majority? Not at all."[22] If the Comintern made a decision, the affiliate must obey even if a majority felt otherwise. This is the doctrine of "democratic centralism."

Chapter 24
LENINIZING THE BOLSHEVIK MEDIA AFFILIATES

It is now absolutely indispensable for every Communist Party to systematically combine legal and illegal work, legal and illegal organizations . . . All legal Communist parties must immediately from illegal organizations for the systematic conduct of illegal work and for complete preparations for the moment the bourgeoisie resorts to persecution. Illegal work is most necessary in the army, the navy and the police . . . The parties should not restrict themselves to illegal work, but should conduct legal work as well, overcoming all obstacles, starting legal publications, and forming legal organizations under the most varied names, which could be frequently changed if necessary . . . The Communist parties must create a new type of periodical press for mass distribution among the workers: first, legal publications, which without calling themselves communist and without publicizing their links with the Party, must learn to make use of any legal opportunity, however slight . . . Secondly, illegal leaflets, even the briefest and published at irregular intervals . . . providing the proletariat with outspoken revolutionary information and revolutionary slogans.

—Lenin, July 4, 1920
"Theses on Comintern Fundamental Tasks"[1]

Third International supporters should use all media to which they have access—the press, public meetings, trade unions, and cooperative societies—to expose systematically and relentlessly, not only the bourgeoisie but also its accomplices—the reformists of every shade.

—Lenin, No. 1 of "The 21 Conditions,"
terms of admission into the Comintern
July 1920

It is possible that even a small party, after it has thoroughly studied the course of political development and become acquainted with the life and customs of the nonparty masses, will at a favorable moment evoke a revolutionary movement. You will have a mass movement if such a party comes forward with its slogans at such a moment and succeeds in getting millions of workers to follow it. A revolution can be started by a very small party and brought to a victorious conclusion. . . . At certain times there is no necessity for big organizations."

—Lenin, speech, July 1, 1921
Third Comintern Congress[2]

THE TACTICAL HANDBOOK   Not since 1902 when he wrote "What Is To Be Done?" had Lenin undertaken to write a detailed explanation of his concept of mass media, mass organization, and propaganda for neophytes. He devoted the fifteen years following

[350   ]

publication of "What Is To Be Done?" to the nuts-and-bolts work of executing that Grand Design, building his AT&T of hate, and establishing its monopoly in Russia. Now in the summer of 1919 Lenin, though the busy chief of the Soviet state, took time again to instruct neophytes in Leninist social demolition technology. He wrote a booklet called "Left-Wing Communism: An Infantile Disease." It was prompted by the problem presented by some British and German radicals who wanted to shun legal election campaigns and labor unions in their countries as "capitalist devices for enslaving the masses." But it became Lenin's "Sermon on the Mount"—still a basic handbook and bible of Bolshevism, quoted alike by Peking and Moscow and taught in all Red schools of social demolition along with "What Is To Be Done?" and "Letter to a Comrade On Our Organizational Problem."

Lenin completed the long evolution of revolutionary ideology from theoretical Marxism to utter power-seeking pragmatism by grounding theory squarely on tactical necessity. He reduced Marxism to one simple principle: *Theory means to do what must be done to achieve power.*

> It is stupidity, not revolutionism, to tie one's hands beforehand, openly to tell the enemy, who is at present better armed than we, whether we will fight him, and when.To accept battle at a time when it is obviously advantageous to the enemy and not to us is a crime. And those political leaders of the revolutionary class who are unable to 'tack, to maneuver, to compromise' in order to avoid an obviously disadvantageous battle, are good for nothing.[3]

All that Mao Tse-tung added in his guerrilla warfare writings was mere military elaboration of these words. Lenin proceeded to lay out a grand strategy for mass manipulation and "peacetime" social demolition.

> The more powerful enemy can be vanquished only by exerting the utmost effort, and by the most thorough, careful attentive, skillful and *obligatory* use of any, even the smallest rift between the enemies, any conflict of interests among the bourgeoisie of the various countries and among the various groups or types of bourgeoisie within the various countries, and also be taking advantage of any, even the smallest, opportunity of winning a mass ally, even though this ally is temporary, vacillating, unstable, unreliable and conditional. Those who do not understand this reveal a failure to understand even the smallest grain of Marxism, of modern scientific socialism *in general* . . .
> It is necessary to link the strictest devotion to the ideas of commu-

nism with the ability to effect all the necessary practical compromises, tacks, conciliatory maneuvers, zigzags, retreats, and so on . . . to accelerate the inevitable friction, quarrels, conflicts and complete disintegration among the Mensheviks, Socialist-Revolutionaries, Constitutional Democrats, monarchists and bourgeoisie; to select the proper moment when the discord among these "pillars of sacrosanct private property" is at its height, so that a decisive offensive will defeat them all . . . The ruling classes should be going through a governmental crisis which draws even the most backward masses into politics. *Symptomatic of any genuine revolution is a rapid, tenfold and even hundredfold increase in the size of the working and oppressed masses— hitherto apathetic—who are capable of waging the political struggle . . .*

In order to accomplish its task the revolutionary class must be able to master *all* forms or aspects of social struggle without exceptions; second, that the revolutionary class must be prepared for the most rapid and brusque replacement of one form by another.

Everyone will agree that an army which does not train itself to wield all weapons, all means and methods of warfare that the enemy possesses, is behaving in an unwise and even criminal manner. *This applies to politics even more than it does to war.* In politics it is even harder to forecast what methods of struggle will be applicable and to our advantage under certain future conditions. Unless we master and are able to apply all means of struggle, we stand the risk of suffering great and sometimes decisive defeat, if changes beyond our control bring to the forefront a form of activity in which we are especially weak . . . Revolutionaries who are incapable of combining illegal forms of struggle with *every* form of legal struggle are poor revolutionaries indeed. It is not difficult to be a revolutionary when revolution has already broken out and is in spate, when all people are joining the revolution just because they are carried away, because it is the vogue, and sometimes even from careerist motives. . . . It is far more difficult —and far more valuable—to be a revolutionary when the conditions for direct, open, really mass and really revolutionary struggle *do not yet exist,* to be able to champion the interests of the revolution by propaganda, agitation and organization in non-revolutionary bodies, in a non-revolutionary situation, among the masses who are incapable of immediately appreciating the need for revolutionary methods of action. To be able to seek, find, and correctly determine the specific path or particular turn of events that will *lead* the masses to the real, decisive and final revolutionary struggle—such is the main objective of communism in Western Europe and America today.

We cannot tell—no one can tell in advance—how soon a real

*Emphasis added. Note that Lenin here makes a perfectly objective, scientifically verifiable sociological observation, completely unclouded by dogmatic distortion. This capacity for mixing objective sociological analysis with dogmatically-guided manipulation is the hallmark of Leninism, the most dangerous facet of his evil genius.

proletarian revolution will flare up, and *what immediate cause* will most serve to rouse, kindle, and impel into the struggle the broad masses, who are still dormant. Hence, it is our duty to carry on all our preparatory work so as to be "well shod on all four feet."

We do not and cannot know which spark—of the innumerable sparks that are flying about in all countries as a result of the world economic and political crisis—will kindle the conflagration, in the sense of mobilizing the masses; we must, therefore, with our new and communist principles, *set to work to stir up all and sundry, even the oldest, mustiest and seemingly hopeless spheres,* for otherwise we shall not be able to cope with our tasks, shall not be comprehensively prepared . . .

Only one thing is lacking to enable us to march forward more confidently and surely to victory, namely, the full and completely thought-out awareness by all Communists in all countries of the necessity of displaying the utmost *flexibility* in their tactics.[4]

Lenin urged communists to recognize *"the definite peculiar features"* which their struggle must assume in each country in order to adapt to "the peculiar features of its economics, politics, culture, national composition (Ireland, etc.), religious divisions, etc." Communists are thus enjoined to make *a dispassionate sociological analysis of their own societies,* to locate the weak spots, and to drive into them with shattering aggressive power, using whatever political weapon fits, just as a dentist selects his drill to suit the tooth and cavity. Copying Nechayev, Lenin commanded communists to infiltrate all sectors of society:

In all organizations without exception (political, industrial, military, cooperative, educational, sports, etc., etc.) groups of nuclei of communists should be formed—mainly open groups but also secret groups. And these nuclei, closely connected with each other and with the Party Central Committee, interchanging their experiences, carrying on work of agitation, propaganda and organization, adapting themselves absolutely to all spheres of public life . . . must systematically train themselves and the Party, and the class, and the masses, by means of this diversified work.[5]

Thus did Lenin plant the first seed of the united front and massive infiltration by his global cartel of mass media monopolizers.

THE "SPLIT" STRATEGY   When the Second Congress convened in the Kremlin's Great Hall on July 19, 1920, the dangled resources and prestige of the first Soviet state attracted radical factions from America and from virtually every existing social democratic party of Europe. And most important, there was a sprinkling of "delegates" from Asia, though they had few organizations back home to represent as yet.

Lenin's grand strategy was simple: to split off from Europe's social democratic parties all the radicals he could, hijacking with them as many members and as much of the party organizations and trade union strength as possible. Lenin and his colleagues knew this split was only the first step. They would still have to drill the opportunists, idealists, and emotional radicals they would thus collect into obedient Bolsheviks, revolutionary professionals, proper Bolshevik "organization men." Or purge them. Through the splitting action of his 21 conditions and a rigorous program of training schools in the Soviet Union for professional party cadres, Lenin would shape this raw material into his new revolutionary media cartels. (This process continued throughout the 1920s.)

Just before the Second Congress met, border fighting on the Polish-Russian border erupted into a full-scale war, and by July the Soviet Army had launched an all-out offensive deep into Poland. Lenin declared he was waging a "war of liberation" whose dual purpose was to revolutionize Poland, Hungary, and Germany and to "probe Europe with the bayonet of the Red Army." Zinoviev set up a large map of the Russo-Polish front in the Comintern congress hall, and each advance of Red troops was marked on it. Every morning the delegates crowded excitedly in front of the map. They were regaled with victory communiqués, most of which Zinoviev fabricated in order to create a suitable atmosphere. Lenin consented to this charade to create enthusiasm among the delegates for the international Communist movement that he was trying to launch.[6] Boasted Zinoviev:

> The best representatives of the international proletariat, with halting pulses, followed every advance of our troops, and all clearly understood that the fulfillment of the military task would mean the speeding up of the international revolution. All knew that the fate of the international proletarian revolution literally depended at that time on every forward move of our Red Army.[7]

But Lenin was in a more sober attitude. His Bolshevik regime was by now relatively secure—but so, he realized, were the imperialist regimes of the West. Lenin believed in historical cycles such as that which elapsed between Russia's revolutions of 1905 and 1917. And clearly, the postwar revolutionary tide had receded. The Bolsheviks faced a long period of what Stalin later called "socialism in one country," during which they would have to maintain their power base and build up revolutionary organizations outside Russia for the struggle ahead. Lenin told the Congress delegates they would have to perform the same organizational tasks the Russian Bolsheviks had between 1905 and 1917 if they were to learn how to lead the masses to revolt—such tasks as building their own numbers and operational expertise, and training and probing. To the dismay of the British extremists, he told them to get into the mass organizations and election campaigns, on conditions that they be permitted to carry on "free and independent communist activity." The Congress hotly debated this question, but of course Lenin prevailed.

The Second Congress established, at long last, the dream of Buonarroti, Marx, and Bakunin: a permanent organization, military in the broadest Clausewitzian sense of continuity between peace and war as "politics by other means." And part of that dream was to have great resources and a geographical base which would allow the revolutionary combat parties to exist during times of stability in full readiness to emerge whenever crises occurred.

Despite the Zinoviev's Polish circus sideshow, the "split" strategy came as a jolt even to the more radical social democrats who showed up in Moscow. It took many of them a long time to realize that the Bolsheviks meant what they said: namely, that a split on an international scale in the socialist movement was inevitable. Lenin and his fellow fanatics would hear nothing of letting them have their cake and eat it too. To get Russian support the social democrats either became full-fledged communists, or became the declared enemies of the Comintern.

Filippe Serrati, the Italian socialist leader, left Moscow in 1920 disheartened and disgusted. So did many others who had not understood the fierceness of Bolshevism when they journeyed to Moscow. But many returned home, too, determined to execute their instructions for splitting their parties.

The Comintern sent representatives to the Social Democratic Party congresses in western Europe to supervise the splitting operation. Zinoviev appeared personally at the German Congress held at Halle in October 1920. The Italian Social Democratic Party met in Leghorn; there, too, Comintern emissaries quarterbacked the pro-Bolshevik fraction that proclaimed themselves the Italian Communist Party. The French Socialist Party met at Tours in December 1920. Comintern supporters won surprising majorities at both the Tours and Halle congresses, but only a minority of the members of each mass party actually joined the new communist parties that emerged. The Swedish Social Democratic Party split in 1920, again in 1924, thereby eliminating even Lenin's Zimmerwald ally Hoglund, and still again in 1929.

THE UNITED FRONT   The Second Congress had hardly ended when the battered Red Army retreated from Warsaw. By the Third Congress in July 1921, even Trotsky admitted (in his report on "The World Situation and the New Tasks of the International") that while the Bolsheviks in 1919 had expected world revolution to break out within a few months, now it had turned out that some years might elapse. Radek hammered home the theme of bolshevization of the young parties in the long period of organizational work and drill ahead: "Revolutionary agitation is struggle, revolutionary propaganda is struggle, and so are underground organizations, the military training of the proletariat, party schools, demonstrations, uprisings."[8] Lenin spoke to the delegates of the task of careful preparation, recruitment and organizational work that they must execute while waiting for the next wave, and he propounded the "united front" stratagem, which they must use to infiltrate and manipulate mass organizations. "But after we have won over the masses through our tactics of moderation, then comes the use of the tactics of offense, offense in the strict meaning of the word,"[9] Lenin declared. The delegates duly passed "theses" accepting the new situation estimate and strategy based on it.

Thus, after rigidly insisting at the 1920 Congress that the West European communists "split" their socialist parties, Moscow in 1921 ordered a "united front" in which the communists were to court and snuggle up to the socialists again in order to have access to the masses. Lenin's advice to the British communists became global policy. The British seed sprouted into a worldwide "strategic maneuver," as Zinoviev called it.

This was one of those abrupt about-faces that mark the history of Leninism. Such switches result from its utter pragmatism about power-seeking. As the prospect of the Western revolution faded, the splitting tactics of 1920 backfired. The Communists of West Europe found themselves on the defensive for disrupting the existing working-class organizations, and increasingly isolated. So, when the wind shifted, the skipper ordered a new set for the sails. New conditions require new tactics. It was as simple as that. (After the October 1962 missile crisis, the resurrection of the "peaceful coexistence" line and the signing of the limited nuclear test ban treaty was just such a strategic maneuver to buy time, reorganize, and mount a new cycle of advanced weapons development.)

All the adversities notwithstanding, by the time the Third Comintern Congress convened in June 1921, it represented a truly global political party and conglommerate of mass hate media cartels of apprentice professional social demolition engineers. It drew 605 delegates representing 103 organizations from 52 countries, including the 72-man Russian delegation headed by Lenin. They came from 48 communist parties, 8 socialist parties, 28 youth leagues, 4 syndicalist organizations, 2 opposition communist parties (from Germany and Spain), and 13 other organizations. It was, for the space of two short years, a marvelous accomplishment of global recruitment, organization, and technological and ideological diffusion.

BOLSHEVIK COLONIZING IN THE EAST   The Russian Bolsheviks actually started proselytizing and organizing foreign communist parties in Asia before they set up the Comintern. They convened the "First Congress of the Communist Organizations of the East" in Moscow in November 1918, with about 40 participants, drawn primarily from the Central Asian peoples on Russia's borders. These were enough, however, to create a suitable facade of internationalism behind which the Soviet government could operate. The "delegates" approved a resolution for a "Department of International Propaganda," thereby legitimatizing the establishment of a Soviet Government political warfare organization. The new department opened twelve divisions, one of which was to be devoted solely to Japan. As the only independent and industrialized power in the Far East, Japan occupied a special place in Lenin's grand strategy.

A Second Congress of the Communist Organizations of the East opened in Moscow on November 22, 1919, with Joseph Stalin, Commissar of Nationalities, as chairman. Lenin—always propagandizing, always proselytizing, always seeking to spread the Marxist dogma of hate and conflict and organize its carriers—addressed them. He made a stirring appeal to "see to it that communist propaganda is conducted in each country in a tongue which your people can understand."[10] The colonies of Africa and Asia were the keystone of the world imperialist structure, said Lenin: Yank it out, and the whole mess would come tumbling down.[11]

The Comintern therefore staged a gigantic "Congress of the Peoples of the East" later in 1920 in the Moslem city of Baku, on the Caspian Sea near Iran. It attracted (at Russian expense) 1,891 delegates from 37 nationalities who responded to the dangling prospect of Soviet support for their varied political schemes. Comintern President Zinoviev was elected president, and proclaimed:

> The Soviet Union was surrounded by enemies, but now she can produce weapons with which to arm all the oppressed and lead them into the common battle and to victory! The Communist International turns today to the people of the East and says to them, "Brothers, we summon you to a Holy War, first of all against British imperialism."[12]

Instantly every man in the hall leaped to his feet. They waved curved daggers, Damascan swords and pistols on high, shouting, "Jehad, Jehad. We swear, we swear."

Many of these delegates, of course were honest nationalists who went home empty-handed and promptly forgot about communism. But many promising recruits were gleaned. And to train them and the other selected young Asians flocking to Moscow in the arts of Bolshevik organization and political warfare, Lenin in 1921 established the "University of the Toilers of the East," also known as Far East University. Its job: to turn out the cadres of the future colonies of Leninist organizations in Asia. A year later a special school called Sun Yat-sen University after the great Chinese nationalist leader was set up to train Chinese comrades. As a recruiting aid, the Comintern had going for it one of the most powerful of human motivations: escape from boredom.

By November 1922 President Zinoviev was able to tell the Fourth Comintern Congress:

> Organized Communist Parties and groups have been established during these fifteen months in such countries as Japan, China, India, Turkey, Egypt, and Persia—countries where at the time of the Third Congress, we had only a few loosely organized groups. Numerically, these parties are still very weak, but the nuclei have been formed.[13]

STALIN COMPLETES "BOLSHEVIZATION"   After the fourth Comintern Congress in November 1922, Lenin's grip on the levers of power slipped sharply, and he died on January 21, 1924. Stalin quickly stepped in and forged ahead with "bolshevization."

His first step was to replace Trotsky as commissar of war with Mikhail V. Frunze in 1924. Frunze promptly established a complex system of advanced colleges to train foreign communists as professional revolutionaries.

This formalization of revolutionary training in schools of social demolition marked the most radical new departure in warfare and the strategy of international conflict since the invention of gunpowder. The faculty staffs included the highest-ranking Russian officers and politicians, such figures as Marshal Tukhachevsky, Bukharin, and occasionally Stalin himself[14] The students learned the traditional arts and techniques of the communist agitator and propagandist from writing leaflets and managing street demonstrations to instigating riots, launching guerrilla warfare and waging full-scale civil wars. They learned the tricks of sabotage, espionage, infiltrating and running labor unions, and setting up front organizations. Frequently, selected students got military training at the regular Red Army schools and even attended classes and discussions at the Frunze Academy, the top Soviet war college. But above all they learned the techniques of secret infiltration and organizational colonization, the *sine qua non* of mass manipulation.

The Far Eastern University had opened in 1921, attached to the Soviet Government's Commissariat of Nationalities. Though intended for students from Soviet Asia and the colonial countries, in 1925 it admitted four American Negroes (considered colonials, too) and one African Negro who had been studying in the United States. That spring, Bela Kun, chief of the Comintern's Agit-Prop Department, reported plans to found a Comintern school to train a maximum of 60 to 70 qualified "students" in both theoretical subjects and the practical methodology of revolutionary social engineering. In May 1926 the Lenin School opened in Moscow, serving primarily Western Europe and North America.

Later its student body grew to 900 from all over the world. The Lenin School offered a full course of *three years,* and a short course of *one year.* The first U.S. quota was seven, and that increased to 40 to 50 a year. In the 1920s and 30s, the Lenin School turned out thousands of trained leaders; its graduates include most of the chief non-Russian Communist Party leaders who rose to prominence after World War II—men such as Chou En-lai of China, Harry Pollitt of Great Britain, L. L. Sharkey of Australia, Sanzo Nosaka of Japan, Ernst Thaelmann of Germany, and Maurice Thorez of France.[15] Gus

Hall, boss of the United States Communist Party, was there in 1932 and 1933.[16] Joseph Z. Kornfeder, a top Comintern aide, estimated that nearly 600 American Communist leaders and "activists" were trained in the Lenin School and other Soviet schools, and that the total trained worldwide by 1959 was 120,000.[17]

In Leningrad, the OGPU (the Soviet secret police) ran a mysterious school of sabotage, espionage, and other black arts. Communists there learned how to fight the police during demonstrations, how to develop the militancy and courage of demonstrators, how to spearhead street brawls, riots, strikes, and armed uprising, and all the techniques of espionage, counterespionage and party security. At the Frunze Military Academy, the Soviet Union's combination of West Point and the War College, a third of the students were from foreign countries; one of them was a Yugoslav named Josip Broz, better known as Marshal Tito, whose World War II guerrilla expertise made him the dictator of his country.

Like Lenin, Stalin recognized that the postwar revolutionary wave had receded. The colonized communist parties must be prepared for the next revolutionary wave. In May 1929, addressing the American supervisory commission of the presidium of the ECCI (Executive Committee of the Communist International) Stalin said:

> I think the moment is not far off when a revolutionary crisis will develop in America. It is essential that the American Communist Party should be capable of meeting that historical moment fully prepared and of assuming the leadership of the impending class struggle in America. Every effort and every means must be employed in preparing for that, Comrades. For that objective the American Communist Party must be improved and bolshevized.

Lenin differed from Stalin in that while he insisted that his media-monopoly colonies be centralized under Comintern command, he also gave the individual parties considerable freedom of action in local tactics and strategy much as an army commander allows a brigade or division commander to decide how he shall take an assigned hill. Between 1918 and 1924, communist parties in eight European countries made 14 serious attempts to seize power. Efforts in Bavaria, Hungary, Finland and Germany nearly succeeded. The ones in Bulgaria and Estonia became mere abortive putsches. Moscow supported them all with money and advice, but the local parties laid most of the plans and executed them.[18] (This, basically, was the strategy to which Khrushchev returned, especially after Castro's Cuban triumph in 1958.)

The German uprising of 1923 was the last serious effort at independent insurrection. It was concocted by the German Red chiefs and a few die-hards in the Comintern in Moscow who still believed in Trotsky's immediate "permanent revolution." The Fifth Comintern Congress in June 1924, eight months after the German failure, was a sober post-mortem. Virtually all grimly accepted Stalin's "socialism in one country" strategy—the strategy of pausing and consolidating the Soviet base.

Stalin crushed all independence and individuality out of the young colonized revolutionary cartels around the world. Just as Lenin had insisted on a "split" of the European socialist parties to purify his fledgling organizations, Stalin resorted to purges for the same purpose. He expelled early founders of colonized parties such as M. N. Roy of India, Zinoviev, Radek, Bukharin and Manuilsky of Russia, and Jay Lovestone and later Earl Browder of the United States. The significance of these purges was simply that the Bolshevik cartel was pushing out all leaders with vestiges of dissent and nationalism after they had served their purpose, and developing new leaders who were flexible, tactically oriented, and obedient to Stalin. The purges were the global monopoly's way of insuring unity and "iron discipline" at all echelons.

THE COMINTERN ORGANIZATION   Lenin, Stalin, and their Comintern high command developed their global organizational machinery pragmatically and experimentally. They improvised as conditions required. The Comintern established four major executive departments at its Moscow headquarters: The Organization Bureau (Orgburo); Agitation and Propaganda Bureau (Agit-Prop); Statistics and Information; and an Eastern Bureau. In addition there was a Technical Information Bureau, an International Control Commission to audit finances and administer discipline, and various other functional agencies. These handled such activites as running global propaganda campaigns, collecting intelligence on the status of foreign communist parties and general conditions abroad, and organizing the training courses for foreign communists. Action departments provided such things as forged passports and special weapons, a basic network of clandestine travel and communications, covert control and operations.

The Moscow headquarters staff also contained "sections," each of which secretly established overseas "secretariats" or "bureaus" in central cities in each world region. The Latin American Secretariat, for instance, was in Buenos Aires; the Far East Bureau in Shanghai, China. In each case Comintern headquarters sent out battle-tested Bolshevik veterans like Mikhail Borodin, M. N. Roy, and Palmiro Togliatti as "Comintern Representatives"—"Comreps" for short—to open up the bureaus and organize and supervise the fledging foreign conflict corporations.

The Orgburo (Organization Bureau) was "the heart of the Comintern," according to General Walter Krivitsky, the former Stalinist secret police officer. Its boss was Ossip Piatnitsky, a Bolshevik who before 1905 had smuggled Lenin's *Iskra* into Russia from Switzerland.[19] Started in January 1924, the Orgburo led the worldwide drive to "bolshevize" the polygot hate-media colonies and to insure that they followed Leninist organizational principles. Piatnitsky immediately stepped up the Comintern's pressure demanding more party schools, more foreign party functionaries assigned to the Lenin Institute and other professional training schools in Moscow, and more attention to organizational skills and tactics.[20] He gathered a talented staff of organizers, practical behavioral scientists and trouble shooters who would go anywhere at a moment's notice to do anything from solving a factional feud to instructing on the arts of organizing factory nucleui, women's clubs, sports clubs, peasant leagues, or "anti-imperialist" fronts. Messages poured in from the world over informing the Orgburo of problems and progress; another stream of messages left it with criticisms and suggestions. The Orgburo would send instructors to represent it within the foreign parties. It held two organizational conferences in Moscow in 1925 and 1926 to direct their reorganization. And it continually brought party organizers in for special training schools and apprenticeship within the Orgburo itself. Some were assigned to work for a year or so in the "more advanced" parties—usually the German Communist Party—for further training, observation, and practical experience. Kornfeder, the American Communist, after completing the Lenin School's three-year course, even served as Stalin's aide before being sent off to Latin America to set up the communist parties of Colombia and Venezuela.[21]

A key Comintern operation was the Orgburo's Cadre Section, a gigantic central file of *all communists and all sympathizers in the world.* Each man had a dossier which had every detail about him—

his weaknesses, likes and dislikes, personality traits, and, in the case of sympathizers and fellow travelers, the issues on which he could be counted to help the Party and the ones on which he was unreliable. These dossiers also contained information for blackmail purposes.[22] For the OGPU, Stalin's secret police, these files were a mine for picking party members and allies who might be useful as secret agents.

Chapter 25
CASE STUDIES IN LENINIST COLONIZATION

Everywhere we have proletarian armies, although poorly organized and requiring reorganization. We can organize these into a single detachment, a single force. If you will help us to accomplish this, then no one can prevent us from accomplishing our task, and this task will be that of leading on to the victory of the world revolution and the establishment of an international proletarian Soviet Republic.

—Lenin, speech of July 19, 1920
Second Comintern Congress

Rebellion, forgetful of its generous origins, allows itself to be contaminated by resentment; it denies life, dashes toward destruction, and raises up the grimacing cohorts of petty rebels, embryo slaves all of them, who end by offering themselves for sale, today, in all the marketplaces of Europe, to no matter what form of servitude. It is no longer either revolution or rebellion, but rancor, malice, and tyranny.

—Albert Camus, 1951
The Rebel

ORGANIZING THE WORLD'S "TRUE BELIEVERS" Moscow's hate-media colonies developed from three sources: 1) Radical groups that grew up independently of Russian genes; attracted to Lenin's example and Russia's resources, they accepted Bolshevik tutelage, dominance, and direction. 2) Socialist groups that Lenin split from the radical wing of European socialism and labor movements. 3) Groups that Moscow organized from scratch.

Moscow organized these creations in four waves. Prisoners of war recruited inside Russia during World War I established the parties in Hungary and Austria and tried vainly in Turkey and Italy. Later the Comintern sent agents out to recruit whatever idealists and ambitious radicals they could as prototype "organization men." Invariably the Soviet embassies acted as talent scouts. The second wave of revolutionary cartel colonization, 1919–1925, established parties in most of Asia and the Middle East. The third wave, 1928–1935, covered Latin America. The fourth, from 1945 to about 1965, covered most of Africa. Many of the Asian and African parties were organized in colonial dependencies by the communist parties in the mother countries. (Indeed, this was one of the duties Lenin laid down in his "21 Demands.") After World War II, the French Communist Party set up welcoming committees, social clubs, even free dormitories and boarding houses, for African students, the future leaders of independent nations. The American and British communist parties sent "technical advisers" to Ghana, which in 1958 became the first African colony to win independence. These Reds assisted Kwame Nkrumah, who had been a secret communist party member while studying at the London School of Economics, in converting his nationalist Convention Peoples Party to a Bolshevik totalitarian structure.

Comintern agents in the early organizing days went with unerring instinct to the social groups of frustrated and disgruntled intellectuals and middle-class "bourgeoisie." The pattern is repetitive.

GERMANY   Germany provides the best example of a communist party growing largely without Bolshevik initiative. The first real translation of Marx's hate strategy into a mass movement occurred in Germany even as Marx was organizing the First International in the 1860s.

Marx was incapable of accomplishing this kind of thing, though he tried persistently from the very moment he read Lorenz von Stein and decided that the proletarian masses were the tool and he and his fellow philosophers would have to use to "change the world." In Paris Marx had attended the club meetings of German workers, conducted classes in his new philosophy of class warfare, and made a few converts.

But only when Marx's theories soared via the golden oratory and *charisma* of Ferdinand Lassalle did his vision of a working-class combat party for revolutionizing the world become real. Lassalle, a Dusseldorf lawyer, met Marx and Engels during the 1848 struggles. He embraced Marx's ideas and memorized the *Communist Manifesto*. Lassalle waged a hefty correspondence with Marx in London. His eloquence and its impact on his contemporaries rank him with Mirabeau or Danton. According to the joke of the day, Marx lisped and Engels stammered in twenty languages, but Lasalle's eloquence had no equal. He fascinated everybody who came under the spell of his conversation even for a moment. His personal magnetism was similar to Buonarroti's.

For a time he wrote books—three of them—but in 1862 he saw another opportunity to crusade. Prussia's liberals were at loggerheads with Bismarck, the prince of the feudal Junker class, over constitutional changes. Lassalle plunged into politics. Seeking to realize his youthful revolutionary democratic ideals, he published "The Working Man's Program," which called on the German workers to form their own political party and fight for their political and economic emancipation. He founded a new party in 1863 and called it the "General German Workers' Union." From this embryo the German Social Democratic Party grew.

Lassalle, only 37 years old, traveled from city to city preaching his Marxist gospel of class struggle. His eloquence attracted great crowds of workers. He effected mass conversions like an American evangelist at a revival meeting. Never before had Marxist hate been preached so openly and undisguisedly. The government tried frantically to silence him, charging all possible crimes from high treason down. He won a prison term—and more notoriety. Mammoth mobs turned out to meet the great secular evangelist.

Marx watched all this from London with malicious eyes and bruised ego. From his gutter watching the great messianic procession march by in his own homeland, behind another leader using his own phrases, he wrote bitterly to Engels that Lassalle "apparently thinks he is the man to step into our shoes." In no time at all he split with his disciple, who never stopped trying to please him. Though ostensibly arising over tactics, the feud seems to have resulted from personal jealousy and Marx's endless capacity for hate and envy. Lassalle after 1848 had served a six-month jail sentence—but he still lived in Germany, was winning acclaim, and even had the audacity to publish a bulky two-volume, 1,200-page work on Greek philosophy at a time when Dr. Marx was a relatively unknown and unpublished exile. Lassalle rushed a copy to Marx, his idol, who praised it but behind Lassalle's back told Engels the work was "a bad piece of bungling." In the following years, Marx and Engels stretched for superlatives of invective in their mutual correspondence to express their contempt for Lassalle. He became "the little Jew," "the little Kike," "Jew Braun," "Ephraim Smart," "His Excellency Ephraim Smart," "Baron Itzig," "Izzy the Bounder," and that "Jew-nigger Lassalle."

Marx visited Berlin for a month in 1861 after the German government declared a general amnesty. Lassalle met him at the train and would not hear of him staying in a hotel. He stayed in Lassalle's house. Lassalle also found Marx a job as London correspondent for a Vienna newspaper, the *Presse*. Only after Lassalle returned Marx's visit in London during the Great Exposition of 1862 did he come to grasp his mentor's deep jealousy and hatred for him.

Marx had an agent in Berlin he hoped to use to steal "Baron Izzy's" thunder—Wilhelm Liebknecht, one of the idealistic German rebels who had in 1848 tried to organize a revolutionary corps to invade Germany while Marx was plotting to infiltrate. At that time Liebknecht was 22 and Marx 30. For 13 years Liebknecht lived in exile in London in close contact with Marx, becoming a faithful disciple. But after the 1861 amnesty, he returned home. "It is of utmost importance for us," Marx wrote Engels in 1864, "to keep Liebknecht in Berlin, so that he can steal a march on Izzy, and so that he can also, at a given moment, spread information among the workers as to our attitude towards Lassalle. We must keep him there and to a certain extent support him. If you will send him some money it will give him a lot of encouragement."[1]

Three months later Lassalle was killed in a duel over a love affair. The shocking news caused but an instant of pause in London. "He was after all an enemy of our enemies," growled Marx. But he shed no tears. "It is hard to believe that such a noisy, restless, pushing fellow is dead as a doornail, and from now on has to keep his mouth shut forever."[2]

But the movement Lassalle founded—the world's first truly Marxist mass party—marched on. Only hereafter it marched under Liebknecht, "our governor-general in Germany," as Engels called him.[3] Liebknecht became the prime agent for spreading the influence of Marx's new International. His influence triumphed in the union of German Socialists in 1874 at the Congress at Gotha, and from that time he was regarded as founder and leader. From 1874 until his death in 1900 he was a member of the German Reichstag.

The German Social Democratic Party became by far the largest political labor group in Europe. It was the pride of the Second International. In the Reichstag elections of 1890 it polled nearly a million and a half votes. The German party was always the foremost proponent in the Second International of resorting to the general strike in case Europe's governments went to war. But in August 1914 the Social Democrats could not resist the old radical cry of 1848 that Germany was being attacked by czarist Russia. When the party caucused, a minority led by Karl Liebknecht, son of Marx's faithful disciple, violently opposed voting war credits, but the majority invoked party discipline and when the Reichstag met the entire Socialist contingent voted *for*, the event which so stunned Lenin.

Rosa Luxemburg was jailed for inciting insubordination in the army, and Liebknecht was sent to prison in 1916 for shouting "Down with the War!" at a column of troops marching through Berlin's Potzdamer Platz. As the war dragged on, antiwar sentiment rose and on March 24, 1916 the pacifist elements split away, forming the "Independent Social Democratic Party."

In September 1916 Rosa Luxemburg began writing from her prison cell a series of political letters signed with the *nom de plume* "Spartacus," after the leader of the 73 B.C. slave revolt against Rome. These letters were read eagerly in party circles and won Rosa a following which formed a left wing of the Independent Socialists under the name of the Spartacist League. The German government promptly took the leading Spartacists into "protective custody" to prevent them from fomenting antiwar strikes and mutinies.

In October 1918, the smashing allied assaults forced the German High Command to recognize the war was lost, and to move to transform Germany into a constitutional monarchy and seek an armistice. Political prisoners were released. But antiwar fever spread too fast and on November 3 a mutiny broke out in the fleet at Kiel, sparked by one of those absurd and utterly nonpolitical "concrete grievances" the Leninists had learned to exploit so well: the officers ordered a cut in the soap ration. The revolt soon spread to Berlin, with Lenin's ambassador Adolf Joffe financing part of it; he was expelled on November 5. On November 9, two days before the Armistice, Liebknecht, leaving jail like an avenging angel, moved to proclaim a Soviet republic. The cabinet tried to head this off by proclaiming the Kaiser's abdication and turning the government over to Friedrich Ebert, one of the two Social Democratic ministers. Imitating Lenin's 1917 Petersburg example, workers' and soldiers' councils sprang up in Berlin and gave their revolutionary blessing to Ebert, who proclaimed a republic.

On December 19, Ebert persuaded the Congress of Soldiers' and Workers' Councils to fix elections for a constituent assembly for one month ahead. Revolutionary sailors intervened on December 23, occupying the chancellery and taking Ebert prisoner. Loyal troops rescued him the next day. Another majority socialist, Gustav Noske, organized a volunteer corps to defend the Social Democratic government, declaring, "Someone must play the bloodhound; I am not afraid of the responsibility."

Lenin had his own plans for Germany, however. As early as November 12, Karl Radek, a top lieutenant, sent a radiogram from Moscow to Berlin suggesting a common struggle on the Rhine against the capitalist Allies. On December 5 Lenin sent Joffe, Bukharin, Rakovsky and Radek to Berlin. The Ebert government refused them admission, but Radek disguised himself as a returning Austrian war prisoner and slipped through.[4]

On New Year's Day, 1919, the Spartacists met in Berlin. Radek, Luxemburg and Liebknecht were present. Radek spoke briefly about a new International and a German-Russian working class league. The members voted to proclaim themselves a German Communist Party. The communists wanted an immediate power seizure. Why should they not do what Lenin had done two years earlier in Russia and oust a shaky social democratic regime that wanted to govern democratically? Luxemburg argued against it. More preparation was needed, she argued, and besides, Lenin's concept of an elite "dictatorship" was undemocratic and tyrannical. Why not participate in the elections three weeks hence? She won the wavering, hot-headed Liebknecht. But the delegates decided upon immediate revolution.

Several thousand people turned out into the streets, many of them armed. They moved into the building of the SPD paper, *Vorwärts*, an odd revolutionary target. On the afternoon of January 5, the communists proclaimed the overthrow of the Ebert government. But the Social Democrats answered that they would no longer be "terrorized by lunatics," and on January 11 Noske's volunteers entered Berlin. Fierce street fighting lasted four days, but by the 15th the volunteers were in control. During the roundup of Sparticists, political gangsters murdered Liebknecht and Luxemburg and threw their bodies into a canal.

The elections were duly held on January 19. Radek was arrested and jailed on February 12. But, the German Communist Party survived, and sent its delegate to the Comintern congress, so that Lenin had his organizational base in Germany.

BULGARIA   Socialists in every country divided on the issue of violence-versus-reform. But outside Russia, only in Germany, Holland, and Bulgaria did formal organizational splits develop before the Comintern came along.

Bulgaria's chief prophet of violence was one Dimiter Blagoyev. Son of a poor Macedonian family, he studied shoemaking in Constantinople, attended school in Bulgaria, and helped fight and expel the Turks in 1879. Then, reading Marx and Lassalle, he became a convert to the Marxist class-hate doctrine. In Odessa and St. Petersburg, Blagoyev became active among student revolutionaries and the "People's Will" movement. In 1883 he started Russia's first Marxist study circle, called the "Blagoyev group," and even undertook to publish a propaganda paper called *The Worker*. Thus, he had the distinction of bringing Marx's constitutive ideology of class hate to Russia and, indirectly, to Lenin himself.

Expelled in 1885, Blagoyev went back to Sofia, continued studying Marxism, and in 1891 helped found the Bulgarian Social Democratic Party. As in every other country where intellectuals and labor leaders were groping for new institutional forms and new strategies of change to manage changing social and economic conditions, the new party polarized around the radical revolutionaries and the reformists.

Around the turn of the century Blagoyev linked up with a youthful, precocious firebrand, Georgi Dimitrov, destined years later to become Comintern president. Son of a hat shop owner, the lad was enrolled in an American missionary school at ten, was expelled, then became a printer's apprentice at 12 and a printer's union functionary in Sofia at 16. In 1903, then only 18, he and Blagoyev split the Social Democrats and with their "narrow-minded ones" formed close ties with Lenin and his Bolsheviks. Lenin's "What Is To Be Done?" became their bible.

Dimitrov and his radicals developed considerable experience in agitation and organization independently of Lenin. They played an important role in the more than 600 strikes that rocked Bulgaria between 1908 and 1912, recruiting and organizing strike committees and training leaders. Dimitrov and Blagoyev shaped their party hierarchy along Bolshevik lines of command and control.

And so, on January 15, 1919, even before Lenin issued a call for a new International, the Bulgarian "narrows" announced their willingness to join. They were unable to send delegates to Moscow, so a Bulgar member already there represented them. Dimitrov led the Bulgarian party and unions to endorse the Comintern in their May congresses, to affiliate, and to adopt the required title of "Bulgarian Communist Party." They were the only party besides the Bolsheviks themselves that deserved the name. Of all the assorted groups which adhered in 1919 to the Comintern, the Bulgarians were the only ones who wanted to become what Lenin and his comrades thought was a real "Bolshevik" party. They were the only ones whose leaders who had anything close to a true understanding of Lenin's concept of the "combat party."

GREAT BRITAIN   So many radical sects knocked on the doors of the Kremlin that Lenin's problem often was not finding suitable cadres, but selecting from or combining the competing volunteers. Such was the case in England and the United States. Four fuzzy fringe groups clustered on the British Labor Party's left wing. 1) The 2,500-member Socialist Party, oldest socialist organization in Britain, with an extreme Marxist orientation, admirer of Lenin and the Bolsheviks; in 1919, it began to define its attitude on the relationship between its revolutionary objectives and traditional institutions such as parliament, arriving independently at the same conclusions as Lenin—good revolutionaries must exploit "all forms of struggle." 2) The thousand-member Socialist Labor Party, a tiny Scottish revolutionary band on the Clydeside that kept its membership small by admitting only those who belonged to no other political organization; its leaders gained wartime prominence in industrial agitation in the Clydeside shop stewards' movement. 3) The Workers' Socialist Federation, and East London group run by a free-floating female crusader, Sylvia Pankhurst, a famous suffragette who until the Bolshevik revolution engaged in pacifist agitation and distributed eggs and milk to needy mothers and babies. When Lenin crushed the Constituent Assembly in St. Petersburg on January 18, 1918, Pankhurst made Robespierre-like excuses despite the rape of her suffragette principles. 4) The South Wales Socialist Society, with only a few hundred actives and no regular publication. Of the four, only the British Socialist Party belonged to the Labor Party under its peculiar confederate structure; the rest regarded such "bourgeois" institutions as legal parliamentary elections and boycotted them.

Lenin named the British Socialist Party among the 39 organizations in his call to the first Comintern Congress. But the BSP hesitated to leap without the "fringe" groups. In June the four parties met in a "Unity Committee." Sylvia Pankhurst couldn't wait. She decided Britain needed a communist party and needed it now. Quitting negotiations, she renamed her group the "Communist Party" and issued a manifesto posing as the Third International's official representative, proclaiming grandly:

> The Communist Party, refusing to take part in parliamentary and local government elections, knowing the futility of parliamentary action, and the confused and artificial character of the Labor Party, instructs such branches as may be affiliated to the Labor Party immediately to withdraw, and to agree to support and encourage the formation of Workers' Committees and Soviets.

At the same time, she wrote Lenin for advice, complaining that the other parties "still cling to the idea of running parliamentary candidates and this is repugnant to the revolutionary industrial workers." The letter did not reach Russia until August 1919. Lenin, formulating his pamphlet on "Left-wing Communism, an Infantile Disorder," wrote Pankhurst to forget her antiparliamentary nonsense and exploit all "bourgeois" institutions to agitate, recruit, and build the revolutionary organization. But Sylvia was a stubborn old lady, and keeping Lenin's reply to herself she continued to bombard the other three radical groups with charges of un-Bolshevik behavior.

In the autumn of 1919 the British Socialist Party decided by referendum to affiliate with the Comintern. Pankhurst steamed off to Moscow to the Comintern's Second Congress to debate Lenin. Lenin told Pankhurst and the ten other delegates who showed up that his recommendation was predicated on the weakness of the British communists and strength of the Labor Party, whose loose organizational structure the fledgling Bolsheviks could exploit. With disarming logic, he told them to "support" the Labor leadership "in the same way as a rope supports one who is hanged." So all four groups agreed at a unity conference on August 1, 1919, to form the Communist Party of Great Britain, and passed a resolution which was duly quoted in their letter applying for Labor Party membership:

> The Communist Party repudiates the reformist view that a social revolution can be achieved by the ordinary methods of parliamentary democracy, but regards parliamentary and electoral action generally as providing a means of propaganda and agitation toward the revolution. . . .
>
> In all cases representatives must be considered as holding a mandate from the Party and not from the particular constituency for which they happen to sit. In the event of any representative violating the decision of the Party as embodied in the mandate which he or she has accepted, the resignation follows of his or her Membership of Parliament or municipality and also of the Party.[5]

This was an accurate statement of Leninist practice, and remains so to this day. The Labor Party secretary receiving the application happened to be one of the few British socialists who had visited and held no illusions about Bolshevist Russia. To the communists' chagrin, after all their squabbling over whether to join, the Labor Party wouldn't have them.

Lenin was unhappy with this situation. In August 1921 he wrote to Tom Bell, Britain's Communist Party representative in Moscow:

> I am afraid we have till now in England few very feeble propagandist societies for communism (inclusive the British Communist Party) but no really *mass* communist movement.

The important thing was—

> 1. To create a very good, really proletarian mass *Communist Party* —that is such party which will *really* be the LEADING force in *all* Labor movement. (Apply the resolution on organizational work of the party adopted by the Third Congress.)
> 2. To start a daily paper of the working class . . . To start it not as a business (as usually newspapers are started in capitalist countries) not with a big sum of money. . . . But as an *economic* and *political* tool of the *masses* in their struggle.

Lenin emphasized that without daily newspapers "there is no BE-GINNING of the really communist mass movement in your country."[6] Though Moscow's money soon provided the newspaper and though this nascent Communist Party of Great Britain (CPGB) accepted Lenin's 21 conditions, it still was a far cry from Lenin's idea of a revolutionary party. Its 2,300 members still did not know the difference between social democratic and Bolshevik organization. Their 1921 constitution was almost federal in structure, permitting regional differences between component parts by allowing separate district representation on the executive body. But in December 1921, pursuing the "bolshevization" campaign, the Comintern staff released a procedure code for the parties to follow in building their organizations and shaping their tactics. The CPGB called a conference in March 1922 and established a three-man commission to translate these instructions into a reshaped British Party. Moscow even sent the ubiquitous Michael M. Borodin (a participant in the 1905 Russian Revolution who was to achieve fame in China) along as special Comintern representative to supervise, and Britain's hate-media colony was well underway. Traveling under the alias of "George Brown," Borodin fell into police clutches in Glasgow, served a short sentence, and was then deported.[7]

ITALY   After Italy won her nationalist struggle to achieve unity in 1870, her liberal intellectuals were eager for the new secular religion of inevitable progress to answer "the Social Question" of Italy's backwardness and poverty. By the late 1880s Marxism was sweeping the country like a religious revival. The Will of God had given way to the Will of History.

In 1890 a young Milanese lawyer, Filippo Turati, interested in Marxism through his defense of some unionists seeking practical trade union advances for the workers, founded the Milanese Socialist League and a fortnightly review, *Social Critique*, to argue the worker's cause among the intellectuals. Turati shrank from the Babeuvist decision for violence—but as a strategist of social change he wanted to avoid ruling it out as a weapon. His league declared:

> Socialism considers as idle, and leaves open, the question whether the unfolding of the great ends of economic and political evolution will make necessary, as has happened so far in the course of history, a violent and bloody clash between opposing interests and between the classes which represent them.

[373   ]

This was an irreconcilable position. In 1892, 400 delegates from labor unions and every type of progressive political group arrived at a conference in Genoa, and the issue exploded immediately. Violence-worshipping anarchists demanded revolution, and one "legalitarian" screamed back: "You are as honest as us, but there is no doubt there's a quarrel between us because we are following a directly opposite course. There is nothing in common between us, so leave us in peace!" The meeting dissolved in an uproar; the next day the "legalitarians" met in one hall, the "anarchists" in another. The "legalitarians" formed the Italian Socialist Party and set about working through the avenues of change open to them through Italy's parliamentary system. The Babeuvist competitors, lacking both program and practical possibilities of action at the time, dissolved and were absorbed. So the Genoa program remained the official Italian Socialist Party policy until 1919; mildly Marxist, it accepted Marx's analysis of the ills of capitalist society but not the younger Marx's remedy of violent revolution. Instead, it spoke of "the conquest of political power" in a way that suggested without specifying elections, so individuals could read in conquest by force and violence if they wished. Turati's dilemma was concealed until Lenin exposed it in 1919.

By that time, the Italian Socialist Party was the strongest party in the nation, with 300,000 members and three million workers in unions who were more or less committed to its politics. In the November 1919 elections the party polled 1,800,000 votes in an electorate of eight million and elected 156 deputies, more than any other party.

But the Socialist Party remained schizoid over the Babeuvist choice, not knowing whether to think of itself as a revolutionary or reformist party. It had been the only major West European leftist party to oppose its country's entry into the war, and the Russian Bolsheviks had done likewise. Lenin's revolution infected many with the idea that perhaps they should take power through violent means. So, jettisoning all civic responsibility, the party simply refused to form a government after winning the right legally—leaving the job to weaker democratic parties and opening the way for Mussolini's fascist triumph.

The party was polarized three ways in 1919. On the right, Turati and a tiny band of revisionists openly called for democratic methods. Around Giacinto M. Serrati, editor of the party newspaper *Avanti!*, stood the main body, clinging sentimentally to the apocalyptic philosophy of the old Marxist revolutionaries, yet opposing Lenin's harsh and dictatorial discipline. On the left, the radical revolutionaries grouped around Amadeo Bordiga of Naples and two Turin intellectuals, Antonio Gramsci and Palmiro Togliatti. They wanted to expell Turati's right-wingers, purge the vaguely romantic humanitarians in the middle, and begin building utopia systematically. They believed Soviet-style worker and peasant councils would produce "a spontaneous and free flowering of worthy and capable individual energies."

Serrati led an apolitical committee of technicians and trade unionists into the blockaded Soviet Union in 1920 to try to help Lenin's regime and to bring home an impartial report that would settle the bitter controversy raging about what was happening in Russia. In Moscow, they found Comintern President Zinoviev scheming to split their ranks and recruit the radical members as a core for the new Italian revolutionary cartel. And they were hauled into the second Comintern congress, about which they had known nothing before leaving Italy. Serrati maintained they could not commit their party, since they had no instructions. The Bolsheviks moved to remove the independent-minded Serrati because he opposed expelling Turati's reformists. So they launched a smear campaign to discredit him in the eyes of his fellow delegates. They brought Bordiga from Naples to heckle and contradict Serrati whenever he tried to speak. Zinoviev and Lenin lost no chance to interrupt and chide him.

The Italians were not prepared for this shocking treatment, or for Lenin's 21 demands. Serrati, disgusted with the obvious Bolshevik determination to rule or ruin the Western radical movements, returned and published the 21 demands in *Avanti!* with the comment that their author was ignorant of the facts of life in Italy, where socialists were different.

The real test came at the Leghorn party congress in January 1921. The "communists," under Gramsci and Togliatti, had a preconvention caucus with Lenin's Comintern representative, a Bulgarian named Kubakchev, and decided they would purge the "reformists," or split the party and form their own following Lenin's instructions. Turati's "reformists" held out for "freedom of interpretation" of the Comintern's directives. Then Comrep Kubakchev read a haughty message from Moscow signed by Zinoviev, Bela Kun, Bukharin, and Lenin:

Before knowing what will be the majority opinion at your congress we declare that those who refuse to accept the separation from the reformists violate the essential order of the Communist International and by that act place themselves outside it. The Italian Communist Party must, one way or another, be created. To this party will go the Comintern's warm support. Down with reformism! Long live the true Italian Communist Party!

The communists won only a third of the votes. Immediately their spokesman, Bordiga, rose and read the declaration of secession, commanding: "Delegates who voted for the communist motion will leave the hall and meet at 11 o'clock at the San Marco Theater." Thus, the Italian Socialist Party was split, and the Communist Party was formed.

With minor variations, Lenin followed the same pattern in other European socialist parties. For some months, Serrati and his followers persisted in regarding themselves as Comintern members, but with "freedom to interpret" its directives. They were unwilling to admit, even then, the reality of the schism over the Babeuvist decision for violence that always divides radical proponents of social change. They even sent a representative to Moscow, but the Bolsheviks excoriated him and sent him home empty-handed.

MEXICO   The first Communist Party in Latin America was organized in Mexico. Lenin gave the operation priority because he needed a diversionary maneuver in Uncle Sam's backyard and because John Reed, his worshipful American newsman, had connections among Greenwich Village radicals and pacifists hiding out there from the wartime military draft.

Mexico already had a tiny Socialist Party. Even including the wartime colony of American draft dodgers, it numbered at most a hundred fiercely anarchistic rebels. Then late in 1918 a mysterious Indian named Manabendra Nath Roy appeared, claiming to be a Hindu prince fleeing from a British death sentence. Tall, with black eyes that flashed frequent wrath, and with boundless energy and ingenuity at organizing, Roy had money, too—lots of it. Born a Bengal Brahmin in 1893, he joined the anti-British Bengali terrorist movement, and after 1914 became an agent of the "Indian Revolutionary Committee" which Berlin established to harry the British. Roy hired a Chinese mercenary army in Canton, aiming to cross the Himalayas and free India. His plans were upset when China joined the Allies. So he jumped to San Francisco in 1916. Thus far Roy was a rebel without a cause save for Indian nationalism. But on the nearby Stanford University campus he met and married an American, Evelyn Trent, who had socialist sympathies and began his conversion. Roy went to New York, soon met Jay Lovestone, a firebrand young socialist student who later became secretary of the American Communist Party. Roy began going to the New York Public Library to read Marx. When the U.S. entered the war he was arrested on the Columbia University campus for plotting with the Germans to run guns to India. He jumped bail and fled to Mexico. Bearing a letter of introduction from David Starr Jordan, president of Stanford University, he soon established contact with President Carranza, who tacitly blessed his mission, and with the Germans, who gave him at least $30,000 in gold to run guns to India.[8] But with the money in his pocket and the German cause declining, Roy took a cruise down Mexico's Pacific coast and returned to the glittering official society of Mexico City to amuse himself at chess.

Roy fell in with the American draft dodgers, a charming and exciting lot of bohemians, and adopted the Mexican Socialist Party. He dipped into his gold hoard to expand the Party's little publication to an eight-page weekly, wrote several pamphlets, and began recruiting prominent government members. Late in 1918 he got the Party leaders to issue a call for a Latin American socialist conference. The project interested President Carranza, struggling with Washington over nationalizing U.S. oil properties, and with Roy he plotted a big street demonstration protesting the threat of U.S. intervention.

Thanks to the dramatic stage management of the Greenwich Village bohemians, Roy's demonstration was a success. One of the Americans even wrote John Reed, the romantic radical just back in New York from St. Petersburg with his lyrical account of the "Ten Days that Shook the World." Reed sent back a picture of Lenin and a bogus message from the Bolshevik regime hailing the Mexican "proletariat" who were presumably about to seize power. Bubbling with this excitement, the rejuvenated Socialist Party named Roy the new "general secretary."

Reed, serving as an unofficial agent of Lenin in New York, undoubtedly reported on the Mexican "movement." Lenin, his shaky regime beleaguered in civil war and fearing the British and French would persuade the Americans to invade and crush Bolshevism, reasoned that if the United States could be forced into armed intervention in Mexico once more as in 1916 it would be diverted from further European adventure. So he sent one of his ace social-demolition engineers to stir up as much trouble as possible. The agent was Michael Borodin, "one of the most persuasive and fascinating Bolshevik propagandists ever sent out from Moscow to spread the revolution abroad."* Born Michael Gruzenberg in 1884 in Byelorussia, like Karl Marx into a Jewish rabbinical family, Borodin entered the revolutionary movement at 16 through the Jewish Bund, a Social-Democratic group, and joined Lenin's Bolsheviks three years later in 1903. Lenin sent him on a mission to Riga in 1905 and Borodin was arrested. Allowed to choose exile, he came to the United States, studied at Valparaiso University in Indiana, married another Russian student, and with her founded a "progressive preparatory" school in Chicago. Lenin summoned him back to Russia in 1918. Among Borodin's exploits was persuading by ruse a visiting reporter-poet in Oslo, Norway, named Carl Sandburg to transport a $10,000 check and trunkful of Bolshevik propaganda back to New York in 1918. New York customs officials relieved Sandburg of all but a letter to Mrs. Borodin in Chicago—and that's how Lenin's "Letter to American Workingmen" came to be published in America!

Borodin left Russia on his mission to Mexico with half a million dollars worth of czarist crown jewels sewn in the lining of his suitcases. He was supposed to sell them illegally in New York to relieve the Soviet trade delegation in Washington, destitute because of the anti-Bolshevik international banking embargo, and to finance his Mexican mission. But in a scrape with U.S. customs officials in Haiti he left the satchels with an Austrian traveler to be delivered to his wife in Chicago. The Austrian, not knowing what was inside, took his time, delivering the jewels months later,[10] but meanwhile Borodin sweated it out in Mexico in acute financial distress.

Borodin's first step was to look up Roy, about whom John Reed had probably briefed him in New York. Borodin had little difficulty completing Roy's conversion to Leninism. The man was ripe anyway, and highly flattered that this personal friend of the great Lenin and "first

*Richard Sanger, an American Foreign Service officer, knew Borodin in Moscow in 1933 while working in the guise of a fellow traveler on the weekly English language Moscow *News,* where Borodin was then editor with the subsidiary duty of indoctrinating and training foreign radical visitors. "He was the most charming murderer I ever knew," says Sanger. "Without batting an eyelash he would look you straight in the eye and say, 'We have got to sacrifice this generation in order to build the future socialist utopia.' " (Interview with the author.) In 1945 Borodin was arrested in a Stalinist purge and died in Siberia. After 1956 he was "rehabilitated."

emissary of the new Comintern in the New World" should be interested in him. Roy even insisted on lending Borodin enough of the German gold to send $500 to Mrs. Borodin in Chicago and $5,000 to the Bolshevik delegation in Washington. (As one of Roy's American chums wryly remarked, Lenin wasn't the only one to finance revolutions with German gold.) Borodin's prime lever with Roy was the glittering promise that if Roy proved himself by converting the Mexican Socialist Party into a Communist Party, then got himself named delegate to the second Comintern Congress, he could win Moscow's full backing for revolution in India. To Roy, only 26, marooned in the Mexican backwater and politically ambitious, this was a game with stakes worth playing for.

Roy found the Mexican and American comrades too attached to anarcho-syndicalist sentiments. So he once again used his golden war chest. To woo the socialist shoemaker whose house was the socialist meeting place, Roy dug up dozens of pairs of shoes to fix, paying gladly even though the work was botched. Stealthily he packed the meetings with hangers-on, mostly refugee émigrés he kept from starving with odd jobs. Finally one night he succeeded in expelling Linn Gale, the red-bearded American draft dodger who was his chief rival. But Roy continued to encounter opposition to changing the party's name or principles. After a wrangle Roy was expelled himself and with his little clique was obliged to create a Communist party— with "six members and a calico cat," as a friend described it.[11]

In November 1919 Roy set out for Moscow for the 1920 Comintern Congress. As a fellow delegate he recruited a favorite old chum, Charlie Phillips, another draft dodger who organized pacifist demonstrations at Columbia University before running south. Borodin's high recommendation got Roy transferred to the Comintern's machinations on India and the Far East, while Phillips succeeded him as the anointed leader of the Mexican Communist Party. Lenin honored Phillips with a long interview during which they discussed how the nationalist Mexican Revolution of 1911–17 might be diverted to the Bolshevik cause.

Back in Mexico, Phillips and his bohemian comrades recruited several prominent political and military leaders of the Mexican Revolution, including two state governors, and several young artists who were gaining world renown by painting the story of Mexican history and the Mexican Revolution. Foremost among these was David Alfaro Sisqueiros, who in 1940 for Stalin's secret police led a commando raid attempt to kill the exiled Trotsky. Sisqueiros became the MCP's general secretary and a world-wide communist "martyr" after the Mexican government jailed him in 1959 for engineering a bloody strike.

On the strength of Roy and Borodin's reports, the Second Comintern Congress decided to initiate a program of hate-cartel colonization in Central and South America. The Comintern appointed a special American Bureau among the embryonic U.S. communists to survey and supervise, and in March 1921 sent two emissaries down from New York. In 1923 the U.S. Communist Party sent Bertram D. Wolfe, a leading member, down to help bolshevize the Mexican comrades. Wolfe maneuvered them behind General Plutarco Calles, one of Roy's recruits to the old Socialist Party, who won the presidency and rewarded the communists with an official government subsidy which continued for 30 years. With continuing U.S. communist supervision, Comintern hate-media operations in Latin America were firmly established.

Chapter 26
COLONIZING LENINIST CARTELS IN ASIA

In this age of imperialism, the characteristic feature consists in the whole world being divided into a large number of oppressed nations and an insignificant number of oppressor nations, the latter possessing colossal wealth and powerful armed forces. . . . There is practically no industrial proletariat in the backward precapitalist countries. However the practical results of our work in these countries have also shown that despite tremendous difficulties to be surmounted we are in a position to inspire in the masses an urge for independent political thinking and independent political action, even where a proletariat is practically nonexistent. . . . Peasants living in conditions of semifeudal dependence can easily assimilate and give effect to the idea of Soviet organizations. It is also clear that the oppressed masses, those who are exploited, not only by merchant capital but also by the feudalists, and by a state based on feudalism, can apply this weapon, this type of organization, in their conditions too. The idea of Soviet [Leninist] organization is a simple one, and is applicable not only to proletarian but also to peasant feudal and semi-feudal relations. . . . Peasants' Soviets, soviets of the exploited, are a weapon which can be employed not only in the capitalist countries but also in countries with precapitalist relations. It is the absolute duty of Communist parties and of elements prepared to form communist parties everywhere to conduct propaganda in favor of peasants' Soviets or of working people's Soviets, this to include backward and colonial countries. . . . We should create independent contingents of fighters and party organizations in the colonies and the backward countries, at once launch propaganda for the organization of peasants' councils and strive to adapt them to the pre-capitalist conditions. Backward countries can go over to the Soviet system and, through certain stages of development, to communism, without having to pass through the capitalist stage.

—Lenin, Speech of July 26, 1920
Second Comintern Congress

LENIN LOOKS SOUTH AND EAST   By the Second Comintern Congress in 1920 Lenin and his fellow Bolsheviks had acquired enough experience to convince themselves that their technology of social demolition and mass organization could be transplanted with only minor adjustments to the "precapitalist" underdeveloped nations of Asia, Africa, and Latin America. They had already successfully conducted two "Congresses of the Communist Organizations of the East," and recruited more or less suitable cadres from numbers of countries. Attending the Second Comintern Congress in Moscow were such men as India's M. N. Roy and the Dutchman Hendricus

[381]

Sneevliet (alias Maring), fresh from Indonesia with a considerable body of successful organizing experience.

Lenin therefore made the necessary ideological adjustments in order to designate the accessible hate targets for his colonized organizations in the backward countries, building primarily on his 1916 pamphlet, *Imperialism, the Last Stage of Capitalism*. And he set his organizers—backed by unlimited budgets and cash—about establishing Leninist media subsidiaries and diffusing the Leninist social demolition technology in Asia.

INDIA Lenin always looked for signs of the great apocalyptic revolution. During an Indian cotton mill protest strike against the British in 1908, he declared that India's proletariat had "matured sufficiently to carry on a mass political struggle." So highly did the Bolsheviks rate the possibility of provoking a world revolutionary crisis by attacking the "imperialist" colonies that a week *before* they seized power in St. Petersburg, they set up a "League for the Liberation of the East."

The new Bolshevik government immediately urged the Indians to "shake off the tyranny of those who for a hundred years have plundered your land." It issued a "Blue Book" on Russian-Indian relations blaming "the evil exploitative will of the English imperialists who have drunk the blood of this unhappy country" for every flood, pestilence, and famine that had struck India. In May 1918, the Moscow wireless station, Radio Moscow's forerunner, announced an appeal for help from a visiting Indian delegation, and the Kremlin responded with a decision to disseminate Red propaganda in India.

This "Indian delegation" was a singularly strange, most un-Bolshevik fellow named Mahendra Pratep, one of the Indians who worked out of Berlin for the German-financed "Provisional Government of India." Following Germany's defeat and numerous conversations, he bluntly told the stupefied Lenin that he was not interested in communizing India but instead wanted to win it for the "Religion of Love."

Although plainly disgusted with this nonsense, Lenin had seen enough of socialist and utopian idealists to know the breed could be useful despite its eccentricities. So he sent Pratep and a certain Baraktullah, another ex-Berlin agent, with a small group of Red Army soldiers, to Kabul, Afghanistan to join the Soviet ambassador. Since the Afghani Emir was fighting a border war with the British in India, he let them establish another "Provisional Government." The new "Government" was threatened immediately. Archarya, another former Berlin agent sent secretly into India by the Germans, appeared in Kabul. An ardent Bolshevik, he tried to persuade the Soviet ambassador to dump Pratep and his "Religion of Love."

While this comedy of errors unfolded, Lenin in 1919 set up in Russian Tashkent a school to train agents for the Asian countries in all the Bolshevik methods of political organization, unconventional warfare, and social demolition. It drew Indian traders from Central Asia, deserters from the British Indian Army, Indian Moslems who had organized to aid the Caliph in Turkey during the war against the British and Greeks, and the Muhajirin, fanatical Moslems who left India in protest against the British Afghan war. The best prospects were lodged in a center called "India House" at the Tashkent School, where they were indoctrinated in Anglophobia and elementary Marxism. From their ranks came such future leaders of the communist parties of India and Pakistan as Shaukat Usmani and Fazl Qurban.[1]

In January 1920, M. N. Roy arrived in Moscow bearing Comintern talent scout Borodin's sparkling recommendation. The fiery and handsome Indian impressed Lenin with his polished English. Roy devised a scheme for conquering India militarily behind the façade of the Tashkent communists and "President" Pratep's paper government in Kabul. With the help of Afghanistan's Emir, who ignominiously lost his border war with the British, he would march at the head of a Russian army peopled with Indian deserters, inflame the northwest frontier tribesmen, occupy some Indian territory, establish a communist government and call on all Indians to revolt against the British. This was about the time that Lenin thought up his famous slogan that the road to Paris and London lay through Peking and Calcutta. On November 7, 1920, Lenin sent Roy out from Moscow leading two trains each with 27 cars. They were loaded with artillery, machine guns, rifles, pistols, grenades, dismantled airplanes, even a complete air force battalion. Two freight cars carried gold bullion, pound and rupee notes. Commander Roy had his own "saloon car." Also aboard were a military staff to train the international brigade in Russian Turkestan, and two companies of crack Red Army soldiers commanded by an American communist, a physical giant known only as "Wobbly John."

Roy began training Indians as good soldiers and communists. Archarya showed up in Tashkent in the spring of 1921. There, under his leadership, among the hate corporation students in "India House" and inside the borders of the Soviet Union, the Indian Communist Party was formed.

But Roy's military expedition bogged down. The Emir didn't want to let in any Soviet force use his territory for an invasion base. Moreover, on September 26, 1921, London sent a sharp note to Moscow about their intrigues in Afghanistan. Russia, stricken by famine and economic chaos, was plainly in no condition to tangle with Britain. The Emir halted the whole operation, and Roy returned to Moscow.

At the Comintern's Third Congress in June 1921, 14 Indians, remnants of the German "Indian Provisional Government," showed up. They had cooled their heels in Berlin since the war hoping to find a new patron but refusing at first to turn to Soviet Russia. But three years changed their outlook, and encouraged by the Soviet ambassador in Berlin they went to Moscow to talk to Lenin. They urged him to dump Roy and let them revolutionize India without accepting Lenin's atheistic ideology. Lenin listened politely and said no. Many of the Indians left Russia miffed, but two remained, one to work in the Comintern headquarters, the other, Nalini Gupta, to become Roy's valued assistant and an important mover in the Indian Leninist subsidiary's early history.

Roy now helped launch Lenin's "University of the Toilers of the East" in Moscow, to replace the Tashkent school. During the next year Roy helped supervise the new university of revolution. In a large four-story building in Moscow he set up a curriculum in Marxist principles and in the Leninist techniques of political organization and social disruption for 600 students from all parts of Asia. Most of them were Chinese and Koreans. Among his pupils was Ho Chi-Minh, who 40 years later was to defeat the French, set up the People's Republic of North Vietnam, and draw the United States into a long and bloody guerrilla war.

Roy's Indian students were later smuggled back into India through China with large sums of money; eight were jailed for a year or two, and some then resumed communist activity. At least one used Moscow's rupees to build himself a home and live like a capitalist.[2] Still, it was money well spent. Qurban, for example, after a three-year jail term remained active, and served as one of the Pakistani Communist Party's leading lights even after independence and into the 1950s.

Having failed in central Asia, the Comintern decided to work through the Communist Party in the mother country, Great Britain. Roy sent Gupta to India to recruit the more radical nationalists in Gandhi's National Congress liberation movement; Gupta found fertile recruiting especially among young intellectuals discouraged by the collapse of the noncooperation movement. He also received help from England. The Comintern Executive Committee on March 4, 1922, ordered the British Communist Party to "launch a well-organized and continued action of supporting the revolutionary movement in India and Egypt" (another British dependency). Accordingly, the British Reds sent out agents to help establish contacts and scout for revolutionary talent. They shuttled regularly between London, Moscow, and India. Communist parties everywhere helped by recruiting Indian seamen at the ports to carry messages and propaganda. Communist dailies were wrapped in outside pages of the London *Times* or New York *Herald-Tribune.* Jackets of popular novels or religious works covered Leninist books. Letters and memos about party organization were disguised as those between clergymen: Party members became "Methodists" and the CPI was the "YMCA." British communist C. P. Dutt took particular delight in addressing comrades as, "Dear Brother in God."

By late 1922 the Comintern could boast of no fewer than five operational communist hate media centers in India, all manned by native leaders—in Calcutta, Bombay, Cawnpore (in Uttar Pradesh), Madras and Lahore.

INDONESIA   The earliest Bolshevik organization outside Europe developed in the Dutch East Indies. In 1913 Hendricus J. F. M. Sneevliet (also known as Maring) arrived at Semarang on the North Java coast as an employee of a trading association. He was a member of the "Tribunist" faction of the Dutch Social Democratic Labor Party that split off in 1909 to form its own proto-Bolshevik party—the same group that collaborated with Lenin at Zimmerwald. Whether Sneevliet went to Indonesia for political reasons is not known, but he went to work immediately. Rallying a few restless Dutch radical socialists, with three others in 1914 he founded South Asia's first Marxist organization, the Indonesian Social Democratic Union (ISDU). He also launched a magazine, *The Free World,* with himself as editor.

Since the 1905 Japanese defeat of Russia, nationalism simmered among all Asians. In 1911 the Indonesian nationalists formed the Islamic Association. Even in this distant corner of the globe, this slight revolutionary stirring attracted Lenin's notice. In *Pravda* (May 7, 1913), he hailed it as a significant "spread of the revolutionary democratic movement."

Although the tiny revolutionary band seemed impotent, Sneevliet proved to be a master at tactical innovation, and devised a stratagem that all newly emerging nations would employ in later years. He felt that the ISDU had to penetrate the Islamic Association in order to steer the approaching Indonesian nationalist revolution along a Marxist path. In 1916 he invented a novel method of infiltration, the "bloc within" technique of dual party membership. The ISDU would sign up Islamic Association members who would retain their membership and operate within it as a tightly organized and centrally

[385]

guided "bloc within," under ISDU orders. This tactic was a wide departure from the usual two-party alliance which the communists have since labeled the "bloc without."

In 1917 Sneevliet recruited two ambitious and politically shrewd Indonesians for his scheme: Darsono, an aspiring journalist in his twenties; and Semaun, a 19-year-old militant railroad worker and Islamic Association chapter president in Semarang. Both were dedicated to overthrowing the Dutch colonial order. Retaining their Islamic Association membership, they became the first "transmission belt" between western revolutionary Marxism and the Indonesian masses.

The Russian Revolution coincided with and abetted their recruitment of young Indonesian intellectuals. Sneevliet, publicly urging Indonesians to emulate the Bolsheviks, recruited others who like Semaun became prominent in both Indonesian communism and Comintern activity: Tan Malaka, son of a high Sumatran official; Muso, a post office clerk; and Alimin, the adopted son of a Dutch professor —all hardly proletarians.

Sneevliet became so successful that the Dutch Political Intelligence Service expelled him from the colony in December 1919. The next year he went to Moscow where he attended the Conimtern second congress as proxy representative of the Indonesian Communist Party and helped draft the "Theses on the National and Colonial Questions." Then he went to China where his "bloc within" technique, combat-tested in Indonesia, succeeded beyond anyone's wildest dreams.

The Dutch and Indonesian radicals he left behind carried on without him. In May 1920, the ISDU became the "Communist Party of Indonesia" (PKI). As one of Sneevliet's Dutch comrades explained:

> We have long been communists. . . . The name change does not change our goal of communism—the establishment of a dictatorship of the proletariat, the only possible course for building a socialist society.

By 1923, Tan Malaka, whose flair for mass propaganda got him appointed "Comrep," could tell Moscow that the PKI controlled 20 Islamic Association sections claiming 100,000 members, 30,000 of whom "we can count on." The PKI itself claimed 38 sections and a hard-core membership of 1,140, a sizable body when compared with the Chinese Communist Party, for example, which had 900 members at that time. Sneevleit's "bloc within" strategy had successfully created a respectable hate cartel colony in Indonesia.

Soon the PKI's founders, flushed with revolutionary zeal, would provoke through reckless uprisings repressive measures by the Dutch authorities. The leaders then spent long periods in exile. For example, Semaun, four months after his expulsion from the Islamic Association, visited the Comintern representative in Shanghai, China, and was sent on to Moscow in January 1922 for the First Congress of the Toilers of the East. By summer he was back in Indonesia, but in 1923, he was expelled for leading a strike and spent the next 20 years in Europe, attending the Fifth and Sixth Comintern Congresses and participating widely in Comintern operations. Alimin, too, went to the Sixth Congress, staying to study at the Lenin School with such distinguished future Red chieftains as Maurice Thorez of France, Earl Browder of the United States, Lawrence Sharkey of Australia, Chou En-Lai of China, Harry Pollitt of Great Britain, and Samzo Nozaka of Japan.[3] Darsono, chased out of Indonesia in 1925 for strike fomentation, made his way to Moscow by the end of 1926 and spent the years 1929–30 at the Lenin school. These years of schooling and revolutionary apprenticeship enabled them to set up their own party schools and organization after World War II and make the PKI the largest communist party in the world outside the Sino-Soviet nations. In 1965 the CPI came within a hair of success in a coup d'état.

JAPAN   In 1901, Sen Katayama, a Japanese who had graduated from Grinnell College in America and spent two years at Andover and one at Yale, formed a Social Democratic Party in Japan among five of his Westernized, Christianized fellow intellectuals. The same day, the Home Ministry ordered him to disband it.

Japan's socialists, prohibited from engaging in political activism, turned to such "nonpolitical" tasks as disseminating socialist ideas. Katayama and his associates toured the country, meeting liberal intellectuals and workers and speaking of peace and justice. Idealistic young students carted socialist literature to the remotest corners of Japan. These early socialists were humanitarians and progressive liberals, very often Christians, with a shallow Marxist veneer. Common ideals of social justice and international brotherhood, rather than economic theory or political dogma, bound them together. But government repression only increased their radicalism. Some went to America or Europe, or withdrew to their home villages. Police persecution and jail drove many insane, some to suicide, and some simply to change their beliefs.

Katayama got himself jailed briefly and then exiled for opposing the Russo-Japanese War of 1904—05. Thereby he won a minor reputation in world socialist circles. But that did him no good in the United States, where he drifted into obscurity earning his living as a short-order cook in San Francisco. He also published a little monthly magazine, *Heimin*, in Japanese and English.

One day in November, 1916 the aging Katayama (he was nearing 60) received a startling wire from New York City—with money to make a trip there. It was from S. J. Rutgers, a civil engineer and Dutch socialist radical, who regarded Katayama as a tool for an enterprise he had in mind. Rutgers was one of the few hundred extremists who, calling themselves "Tribunists," had broken away from the more moderate Dutch Social Democratic Labor Party in 1909 and formed their own Social Democratic Party. Ardent Bolshevik sympathizers, the Dutch minority had backed Lenin at Zimmerwald, and in 1918 founded had the Dutch Communist Party, becoming charter members of Lenin's Third International. Settling in New York in 1915, Rutgers made a good living in foreign trade, and established contact with Lenin. In 1916 he adopted the ultraradical Socialist Propaganda League of Boston and began using the militant Latvian immigrants as his cadres. Rutgers hoped to use Katayama, well known to many American socialists, to build a base for Leninism within the American Socialist Party. Rutgers also thought Katayama had more connections among Asian socialists than he actually had, and wanted to establish connections for Leninism with them, also. And so, early in 1917, Katayama was installed in a quiet room of the Rutgers home in Brooklyn, and when he was not engaged in writing, conferences or agitation, he served as the family cook.

Actually, Katayama was hardly a Bolshevist. As Rutgers well knew, Katayama opposed World War I as an "imperialist war" because he opposed bloodshed and violence, while Rutgers and Lenin, with no such pacifist qualms, wanted to transform the bloody "imperialist war" into an even bloodier "class war." But because the "Grand Old Man" of Asian socialism was destitute, he was vulnerable. Rutgers began to reshape Katayama's thinking, and quickly introduced him to the New York élite of Russian and American revolutionary radicalism. Katayama met Alexandra M. Kollontay, Lenin's agent, who tried to convert him to the Bolshevik position on war and revolution. But as she reported to Lenin, she had only moved him "in the direction" of Bolshevism. On January 14, 1917, Katayama met Leon Trotsky, less than 24 hours off the boat from Russia.

Katayama struggled briefly. But he was slowly caught up in the revolutionary subculture's web of associations, personal relationships, organizational activities, enthusiasms, and intrigues.

The Socialist Propaganda League headquarters was transferred from Boston to Brooklyn, and Katayama became a charter member of the reorganized group. In May 1917 a monthly revolutionary journal, *Class Struggle*, was launched and Rutgers, the "financial angel," made Katayama a "contributing editor." The honor, the security of new friends, and the exhiliration of involvement in a socialist struggle once again was too much for the old man.

After the March Revolution in Russia in 1917, Trotsky, Kollontay, and Bukharin rushed back to Moscow. After the November Revolution, Rutgers went to join Lenin, traveling through Japan with letters of introduction to Katayama's socialist friends. Left behind, Katayama fell on hard times. He opened a popcorn concession in Coney Island, but failed. He tried to earn a pittance by selling socialist papers on the sidewalks of New York and cooking private homes and restaurants.

But Katayama had dreamed of returning to Japan with the support of Lenin and the resources of mighty Russia as the vanguard of mighty proletarian revolution in his beloved homeland. He now became a Bolshevik "true believer." With evangelical zeal and funds from Rutgers in Moscow, he began recruiting from among the ideologically rootless youth in New York's Japanese community. His tiny apartment became a political club. His disciples read the communications he received from well-known socialist leaders in Japan. Moreover, every recruit knew that old Katayama was a personal friend of the American and Russian chieftains of bolshevism. Did he not know the great Trotsky, hero of the November Revolution and commissar of the Red Guard? And Rutgers, who was gone now to Moscow to join the great Lenin?

Katayma gathered around him a half dozen young converts who were for decades to lead the future Japan Communist Party. Among them was Eizo Kondo, an adventurous youth who came to the United States when he was 19, worked his way through school, and later in New York launched a one-man mail order house devoted to Oriental art supplies.

In 1918 a tremendous upheaval occurred in Japan. The wartime industrial boom had unleashed inflation. In August 1918 angry house-wives touched off a wave of demonstrations that, agitated by under-ground literature, swept more than a hundred villages and cities. Hungry crowds looted stores and warehouses, burned newspaper offices, wrecked businesses. The military killed many and arrested thousands in restoring order. Marxists around the world hailed the "August Rice Riots" as harbingers of glorious socialist revolution in Japan. In far-away New York, Katayama, Kondo, and their followers thought so, and in further-away Moscow so did Lenin and Rutgers.

The New York Japanese socialists jumped for joy when Moscow in 1918 invited Katayama to the founding congress of the new Commu-nist International as the representative of the "socialist groups of Tokyo and Yokohama." Katayama and Kondo agreed that Kondo, being younger and more energetic, should return home and do the spadework among Katayama's socialist friends, while the old man would go to Moscow to get Lenin's help. Kondo sailed from San Francisco in May 1919 aboard the "Korea Maru." Undoubtedly the money came from Moscow, because Katayama frequently met with "Consul General" Ludwig Martens, the Soviet's diplomatic agent in New York.

Katayama did not sail for Moscow, however. He became engrossed in the Comintern's efforts in the United States to forge a suitable Bolshevik party out of the American socialist groups that were vying for Moscow's favor—and money. Then in 1921 the Comintern or-dered him to Mexico on an organizing mission. After eight months he was ordered to Moscow for the various congresses the Comintern had called to discuss plans for penetrating Asia.

When Katayama's train finally pulled into Moscow in December 1921, the 61-year-old Japanese revolutionary received a saint's wel-come to the socialist Promised Land. An honor guard of the Red Army and a throng of well-wishers awaited him in the railroad sta-tion. Many of his Japanese comrades from America and the home-land anticipated his arrival. And—yes, it was so!—there to deliver the official words of welcome was none other than the Number 2 hero of the Bolshevik Revolution, Leon Trotsky, commander-in-chief of the world famous Red Army. It was a standard Comintern "red carpet" welcome, shrewdly designed to influence those deemed use-ful in Bolshevik colonizing.

Katayama lived out his days in Moscow serving on the Comintern staff, supervising the activities of the fledgling Asian communist parties, and making occasional inspection tours. He died in 1933, and was buried with pomp and circumstance in the Kremlin Wall.

In the fall of 1920, Gregor Voitinsky, the Comintern agent in China, called a Far Eastern Socialist Conference in Shanghai, and one of the persons he invited was Sakae Osugi, a leading Japanese radical socialist. Osugi, though an outspoken critic of the Bolshevik regime, apparently melted when he saw Voitinsky's bagful of money. He agreed to take Comintern funds back to Japan to finance a radical newspaper, with the stipulation that he hire a Bolshevik editor. He did just that—taking on none other than Eizo Kondo, Katayama's comrade from New York.

Editor Kondo quietly recruited among the leading Japanese Marxists. By the spring of 1921 he had gathered a small group of sympathizers. They now decided to send him to Shanghai to seek more of Moscow's cash. There a Comintern comittee of 12 Koreans and Chinese, presided over by another Moscow representative, a Korean, thought enough of Kondo's progress report in Japan to give him another installment of $3000 for propaganda and organizational expenses. They also invited Kondo and a comrade of his choice to attend the Third Congress in Moscow in the summer of 1921. The Japanese police had other ideas, however: They jailed him as soon as he set foot on the home islands. Several weeks later, they released him for lack of evidence—and without confiscating the American currency he was carrying. In Moscow, the Third Congress opened without a Japanese delegation.

In August 1921 Kondo raised Moscow's hope by creating a tiny "Dawn People's Communist Party," with 19 members. He circulated more Leninist literature, adopted the title of "secret emissary of the Comintern," and by his contacts with Comintern agents and participation in Soviet-sponsored international conferences demonstrated the likelihood of Russian political support and money. The radical socialists quickly edged toward Bolshevik doctrine. "Like a chaotic, formless nebula condensing into a star of definite shape," said Kondo, "the Dawn People's Communist Party was a product of the confused whirlpool of socialists, anarchists, and social democrats."

His description might well have fit all communist parties that Lenin was developing at this time. And as with all of them, the crystallizing force was Moscow's money. For a month or two later, a member of the Third International showed up secretly in Japan bearing funds and instructions. He was a Chinese named

Chang Tai-lei, a young Shanghai professor Voitinsky recruited to be one of the Chinese Communist Party founders. Tai-lei was on his way home from the Third Comintern Congress. In Tokyo he visited Kondo and leaders of other radical groups urging them to select promising young men for a Japanese delegation to the "First Congress of the Toilers of the East" coming up in January 1922 in Moscow. He collected a motley crowd—socialists, anarchists, one of Kondo's Dawn Peoples Communist Party members, and one from the Wednesday Society, a group of politically minded intellectuals, and sent them to Moscow.

The Congress convened on January 21, 1922. Katayama headed the 16-man Japanese group that included five of his New York circle. To emphasize Japan's importance, Stalin personally greeted the delegation. Zinoviev made a big to-do over them. The Comintern staff gave them a model platform, party regulations, and money. They also picked out several of the most likely candidates and persuaded them—about half the delegation—to stay in Moscow to study the arts of Lenin's new revolutionary profession at the Communist University for the Toilers of the East.

Those delegates who returned home scurried to recruit diverse left-wing leaders for a new organization. With assurances of Comintern financing they got the Wednesday Society leaders to agree to sponsor a new communist party. On July 5, 1922, the Communist Party of Japan was secretly organized in Tokyo. Ten days later, the "First Congress," a clandestine gathering of forty radical intellectuals, elected a seven-man "central committee." They sent a secret emissary six months later to the Fourth Comintern Congress, in November 1922. They won official recognition as the "Communist Party of Japan, Japanese Branch of the Comintern." President Zinoviev now chortled:

> In Japan we have a small party which, with the help of the Executive committee, has united with the best syndicalist elements. It is a young party, but it is an important nucleus, and the Japanese Party should now issue a program.[4]

He saw to it that they had a program to issue. The Japanese delegates left Moscow with a draft of radical political demands, written by the Comintern staff under Nikolai Bukharin's direction. Their Second Congress ratified the program. They were on their way.

Although the Japanese Communist Party during the 1920s never exceeded 1,000 members, the Comintern's leaders had every reason to be satisfied. For as veteran Bolsheviks, they knew that under the Leninist concept of a combat party of professional revolutionaries, they had a respectable organizational base.

Chapter 27
COLONIZING LENINISM IN CHINA

How many urgent tasks
Have arisen one after another!
Heaven and earth revolve,
Time presses,
Ten thousand years is too long,
We must seize the day.
The four seas rise high, the clouds
    and the waters rage,
The five continents tremble, wind and
    thunder are unleashed,
We must sweep away all the harmful insects
Until not a single enemy remains.
        —Mao Tse-tung,
        January 1963

Communism is not love. Communism is a hammer which we use to crush the enemy.
        —*Sayings of Chairman Mao*

All the old and new hatred is graven on our hearts. We won't forget it in a hundred, a thousand or ten thousand years. When the moment comes, we will tear the skin from you, rip out your guts, burn your bodies and throw the ashes to the winds.
    —Red Guard poster hung from the gate of the Soviet Embassy
      during the "struggle against revisionism" demonstration, August 1966

UNORGANIZED RADICAL INTELLECTUALS   As in Russia, China's revolutionary movement originated with the intelligentsia. Characteristically, it had no connection with the labor movement. Chinese intellectuals suffered deeply after the 1900 Boxer uprising over the humiliation of the world's oldest civilization at the hands of the "foreign devils" and "barbarians." In 1911 a military revolt overthrew the decrepit Manchu Dynasty, and Dr. Sun Yat-sen hurried home from America to set up a republic. As Dr. Sun tried to pull his feudal nation into the twentieth century, it fell into anarchy. Military dictators took over fragmented provinces, many naming themselves "emperor." Western powers—the United States alone abstaining—

had long since carved out semicolonial states along the coast. Dr. Sun escaped to Japan and exile again, taking a little band of democratic and nationalist intellectuals with him. With constant appeals for Western help, he would return occasionally to one of the coastal cities with his tiny "party," the Kuomintang (or the Chinese Nationalist Party), whenever a scheming warlord offered haven.

Woodrow Wilson's Fourteen Points and talk of "self-determination" inspired new hope for a truly national democratic regime. But at Versailles, Japan claimed the right to inherit Germany's colonial concessions in Shantung Province, the "cradle of the nation" and "Holy Land of China." The British, under a secret wartime pact, had backed the Japanese claim and Wilson yielded, giving China's young student-intellectuals a terrible shock.

On May 4, 1919, 2,400 students at the National University at Peking organized a mammoth demonstration. Students in other cities followed. Chancellors and professors at colleges all over China resigned in sympathy protests. Workers supported with strikes—and the emotional nationalist militancy boosted trade unionism in the next two years. All China seethed. Her disillusioned professors and students wanted a philosophy and strategy to modernize their suffering feudalist society.

The Comintern kept close watch on the "May Fourth Movement." Into this cauldron Lenin sent a top instructor-agitator-recruiter, Gregory N. Voitinsky, who was director of the Comintern's Far East Bureau located at Irkutsk. His orders to Voitinsky were simple: Find out who the leaders are, which are the best prospects, and convert them to Marxism-Leninism; then organize communist cells, recruit talented young political leaders for training in Moscow, and create a Chinese Communist Party.

TALENT SCOUTING   Voitinsky took along two comrades—an interpreter, Yang Ming-Chai, a Chinese émigré who had spent ten years in Russia and joined the Communist Party; and another Russian, I. K. Mamaev, also an able organizer. He went in March 1920 to Peking, where the Soviet government had a diplomatic representative, M. I. Yurin, sent to negotiate new treaties ending the czarist colonial privileges in China. Voitinsky found a dismaying scene. According to reports sent to Moscow—copies of which were seized in a 1927 raid on the Soviet Embassy in Peking—"it was impossible to find anything that could have served as the foundation of a communist party:

> Even an embryonic organization was lacking, since there was no organized group of comrades for the study of Marxism who could at

some future time serve as the nucleus of a new mass organization. China did not even have an organized Social Democratic Party, from which men most devoted to the revolutionary cause could be detached, as was the case in several European countries and the United States. Of course, there were revolutionaries, but they were ideologically far from Marxist. Most were either followers of Dr. Sun or anarchists. . . .[1]

Voitinsky even found that few Chinese could read foreign languages and that almost none of the writings of Marx or Lenin had been translated. So little was known about either of them that many Chinese writers categorized Bolshevism as a faction of Bakunist anarchism instead of Marxism.[2] Not even Marx's *Communist Manifesto* had been translated in full, a situation Voitinsky immediately remedied.

Voitinsky was at a loss on where to start until diplomat Yurin introduced him to a non-communist Russian citizen teaching the Russian language at Peking University. This man introduced Voitinsky to the chief librarian at the university, one Li Ta-chao, a 32-year-old Japanese-schooled liberal student of history and political science. During the militant May Fourth Movement days, Li coached the demonstrating students, who met in his library office. Li also knew many politically-motivated students and intellectuals. Among Li's acquaintances was a young man who had been his assistant in the library, and had returned to his native Hunan Province, where he was showing great talent organizing intellectuals and labor leaders. Voitinsky told Li he was very interested in meeting and recruiting talented young political leaders such as this one, whose name was Mao Tse-tung.

Li was not a total stranger to Marxism. Typical of intellectuals in backward countries everywhere, he had been tremendously excited by Lenin's triumph in Russia. All looked hungrily for ways to modernize feudal societies. Li had turned library rooms over to student activists and dabbled in their societies, whose very names bespeak the general messianic aspiration—a "New Tide Society" and a "Save the Country Society." Shortly before the May Fourth Movement, Li had published an article entitled, "My Marxist Views." It was largely a summary of some of the concepts of orthodox Marxist theory, drawn from Japanese translations of *The Poverty of Philosophy, Communist Manifesto,* and *Das Kapital.* Li's article was no fervent embrace, however, but a rather cool summary. Marx's claim of "inevitability" turned him away because he thought it encouraged passivity. Li, an activist, wanted a practical guide to action. The only elements of Marxism that he found appealing were those that emphasized the need for political activity and "consciousness" among men and their role as history-makers. The idea that social classes can through "struggle" influence history seemed relevant to China and his own—and his fellow intellectuals'—situation.[3]

So late in 1918 Li had started a "Marxist Study Society" among students, who met in his library office secretly in the evenings. Mao Tse-tung probably joined them occasionally. It was the first such group in China. Li's library office became known as "the red chamber." Later he changed the group's name to the "Society for the Study of Socialism," to attract a broader spectrum of students. Soon it had 110 members from the various colleges in Peking.[4]

Voitinsky was not the first Russian Bolshevik Li had met. He and his student followers, stimulated by Marx's teachings, in the spring of 1919 began agitating among Peking's railroad and dock workers. They encountered two young Russian communists accidentally driven into northern China by the civil war in Siberia. This pair taught their Chinese comrades what they could—introducing them to Lenin's *Imperialism, the Last Stage of Capitalism.* And so Li was of course flattered and eager to be sought out in March 1920 by an emissary of Lenin. He and Voitinsky discussed the formation of a communist party in China.[5]

Li introduced Voitinsky to many of the liberal intellectuals, militant nationalist and ambitious young politicians around Peking. Under Voitinsky's coaching in March 1920 they organized a Society for the Study of Marxism.[6] And as bait for others less theoretical-minded but impressed with the Bolshevik success in Russia, Voitinsky got Li to found a "Society for the Study of Russia."[7]

Satisfied with Li's Peking recruit and spade work, Voitinsky moved on to Shanghai, bearing Li's letters of introduction. He was most eager to meet a man Li had told him about; Ch'en Tu-hsiu, the former dean of the Peking School of Letters and ambitious publisher of an *avant garde* magazine, *New Youth*. On June 11, 1919, Ch'en had been arrested for distributing leaflets demanding freedom of assembly and speech, fundamental reforms, and dismissal of pro-Japanese officials. Ch'en languished in jail for 83 days until a wave of mass protests freed him. Famed as a symbol of modern Chinese nationalism and militance, he fled to the French-controlled section of Shanghai to resume publishing his magazine, *New Youth*. There he organized a "New Youth Society" to rally the intellectuals rebelling against traditionalism.

In Shanghai Voitinsky and his two fellow Comintern recruiter-instructors screened a wide variety of liberals and intellectuals, including Kuomintang followers. But Voitinsky became more and more convinced that Ch'en Tu-Hsiu was the most likely leader for the new Leninist combat party. His writings were a mixture of romanticism and humanitarianism without a trace of Marxism. But Voitinsky also saw an emotionalism and spirit of revolt that could be easily transformed into revolutionary energy and used to power the new organizational machine he was going to build. Ch'en fervently opposed traditionalism and war-lordism—and after the disillusionment with Woodrow Wilson and the Paris Peace Conference, he was ready to hate "imperialism."

The son of a wealthy imperial civil servant, Ch'en had spent long periods of study and exile in Japan and France, and helped lead the 1911 revolt that toppled the ancient Manchu dynasty. Bitter disillusionment followed China's inability to organize and democratize herself. In 1915 Professor Ch'en founded his *New Youth* magazine in Shanghai. The first issue, containing a ringing manifesto, sold out instantly and had to be reprinted several times. Copied out in longhand, posted on walls, passed from hand to hand until each copy was read to shreds, it hit China's younger generation "like a clap of thunder which awakened us in the midst of a restless dream," in the words of one young reader. Ch'en's magazine touched off an explosion of organizing among the liberal and progressive youth who formed scores of new societies to promote all sorts of vague ideas and grand plans for the future. (Between 1917 and 1921, nearly 400 student reviews appeared in China, most of them with the character for "New" appearing in the title—*New Light, New World, New Woman*, even *New Air*.) "Solemn Appeal to Youth" shows clearly the mood of the young intelligentsia in this emerging feudal nation, the mood which made Ch'en and his whole generation so psychologically susceptible to the new near-nihilistic Messianic virus of Bolshevism Voitinsky was spreading. Note carefully Ch'en's emotional *time* orientation—deprecating the present and glorifying the future:

> The Chinese compliment others by saying, "He acts like an old man although still young." Englishmen and Americans encourage one an-

other by saying, "Keep young while growing old." Such is one respect in which the different ways of thought of the East and West are manifested . . .

The function of youth in society is the same as that of a fresh and vital cell in the human body. In the process of metabolism, the old and the rotten are incessantly eliminated to be replaced by the fresh and the living. . . . If metabolism functions properly in a society, it will flourish; *if old and rotten elements fill the society,* then it will cease to exist. According to this standard, then is our society flourishing, or is it about to perish? I cannot bear to answer . . . I merely, with tears, place my plea before the fresh and vital youth, in the hope that *they will achieve self-awareness,* and begin to struggle.

What is the struggle? It is to exert one's intellect, *discard resolutely the old and the rotten, regard them as enemies, keep away from them and refuse to be contaminated by their poisonous germs.* To use to the full the natural intellect of man, and judge and choose among all the thoughts of mankind, distinguishing which are fresh and vital and suitable for the present struggle for survival.

Oh, young men of China! Will you be able to understand me? We must have youth if we are to survive.[8]

The very idealism of this plea created a predisposition to bitterness and hate. It is not hard to understand why Voitinsky quickly saw in Ch'en, then a vigorous 41 years old, a ripe convert to the hate ideology of revolutionary Marxism. All he had to do was to explain Marx's class struggle theories, show that it was really a struggle between the forces of past and future, and point to the social groups that represented the reactionary forces arrayed against Ch'en and other "class-conscious" comrades in his vanguard of the golden future.

Ch'en readily agreed to convene some of his militant nationalist and liberal friends to hear this new missionary from Revolutionary Russia. He actually recruited six to start with, in May 1920. As Kremlin reports showed, Voitinsky found them like all the others he had screened: "While they individually professed interest in ideology, none of them (individually or organized in groups) possessed a concrete program of action or slogans to attract and organize the masses."[9] Even so, Voitinsky decided Ch'en and his tiny "cell" could "plant the seeds of a communist party in Shanghai."[10]

As a result, Voitinsky began secret classes at the home of the editor of Dr. Sun's Nationalist Party newspaper, the *Shanghai Weekly Review*. The Russian began by translating Ch'en's emotions about the "new youth" and the "old and rotten elements" in stagnant Chinese society into Marxist terminology. Then assuring his ambitious recruits that history destined them to triumph on the wave of Marxian inevitability, he promised to show them how to lead the forces of the future in the revolution against the forces of reaction surrounding them, as had the Great Lenin.

It was not the Marxist ideology that really hooked Ch'en and his fellow intellectuals. *It was what they heard about Leninism—the techniques of organization, strategy, and tactics that enabled a minority group of utterly dedicated and disciplined individuals to seize and keep power.*[11] Voitinsky and his colleagues gave them detailed information on the Bolshevik revolutionary know-how and methods of Party organization. The Comintern instructors explained in detail the practice of the "dictatorship of the proletariat" from its earliest origin in Babeuf's conspiracy of 1796 on down through Blanqui and Marx to Lenin. The Chinese were spellbound. As educated intellectuals in a backward society, they found it flattering to believe the Robespierrist notion that the dictatorship of a revolutionary elite is justified because the elite sees what the majority of the people would want if only they were sufficiently mature enough and educated to recognize their true interests.

SCHOOLING REVOLUTIONARIES   Patiently Voitinsky led his pupils through long and tedious days of discussions on party techniques. Picking up a new recruit now and then, they learned that the communist party was essentially a conspiratorial group, very much like the leadership of the Chinese secret societies. In Russia this elite had found the correct combination of organizational skills, strategy and tactics for establishing order out of the postwar chaos. The Comintern teachers showed how Lenin combined organization, propaganda slogans, and mass appeals that worked and enabled him to seize power. They taught the Chinese Lenin's methods of penetrating other political associations, of dividing and whittling down all competing parties and groups; the art of tactical compromise and retreat, of exploiting antagonisms within "enemy groups" and the practice of setting up communist cells and mass organizational deployment into a Leninist solar system.

To Ch'en and his fellow radical intellectuals these Russian communists sounded like supermen. They spoke and acted like master strategists and tacticians of political warfare who could give them the key to modernizing China. In May 1920[12] the new Chinese "comrades"—now numbering ten—secretly founded the Chinese Communist Party: They ratified a constitution, established a provisional central organization in Shanghai, and then elected Ch'en as secretary-general.[13]

THE MONEY MAGNET AGAIN Very quickly Moscow's money —which Voitinsky was carrying in his little black bag—began to talk loudly in China. Ch'en's infant Communist Party began receiving a whopping monthly Comintern subsidy of $12,000 a month,[14] with Voitinsky and later "Comreps" closely supervising the expenditures. The Party membership quickly grew to 70.[15] The CCP immediately established in Shanghai the "Sino-Russian News Agency," and in August added the "Socialist Youth Corps" as a recruiting front. Of course, Ch'en still had his immensely popular magazine *New Youth* and his "New Youth Society," which served now as crypto-communist "transmission belts."[16] On August 15, 1920, the party launched its first official publication, a weekly for workers called *Labor Circles.* And on November 7, appropriately for the third anniversary of Lenin's Bolshevik revolution, the party unveiled a new magazine designed to appeal to the intellectual and clerical workers, *The Communist.*[17]

But the most basic step was the founding of a school to train professional revolutionaries—and political organizers—just as Lenin had done a decade before near Paris for his own Bolshevik movement. To fool the ruling warlords and French colonial administrators in Shanghai, and to mask his recruitment activities, Voitinsky and his fledgling Bolsheviks set it up as the "Foreign Language School." He sent the best graduates on to Moscow to the University of the Toilers of the East for more intensive training. Before 1920 ended this school had more than 60 students. The trained organizers it produced were quickly used for organizing labor unions in Shanghai, where there were none. Under Ch'en's direction they formed a mechanics union, a printers union, and a textile workers union.

Voitinsky's aim was to form communist cells all over China—and fast. In September he coached Li Ta-chao in establishing a second cell in Peking, with a branch of the Socialist Youth Corps as a "halfway house" for party membership. Voitinsky was careful not to insist on ideological purity at first; the Peking group was started with but eight recruits, described in a report to Moscow as "six anarchists and two communists"—one of which was Li himself. To upgrade these tiny cadres ideologically, they set up an evening class in a railway station not far from Peking on the Peking-Hankow Railway. At

Changsha, provincial capital of Hunan, Mao Tse-tung, sold on Bolshevism by his former library chief and the prospect of Comintern financing, established a bookstore and the Changsha Society for the Study of Marxism. He recruited scores of members from the New People's Study Society, which he had started earlier, and from the Hunan Student Union. In September 1920 he set up a regular communist cell, and in October received a charter for a Socialist Youth Corps branch.

In the fall, a new warlord seized power in Canton and invited Ch'en, renowned as both educator and journalist, to come take charge of the province's education. Ch'en's conversion to Bolshevism was not known, and as reports to Moscow said, Ch'en "hurried to Canton with the hope of utilizing the opportunity to plant the seeds of a communist organization there." Once again he set up a newspaper, recruited a motley crew of anarchists, nationalist radicals, and communist novices—and organized a "school of propaganda and agitation in Canton to train personnel for future work."[18]

By the end of 1920, Voitinsky and his two Comintern comrads had cells thriving in Wuhan, Canton, Changsha, Tsinin, Peking and Shanghai, and "weekly discussion groups" in others. Except for Ch'en, 41, and Li, 32, most were university students in their early twenties. A report of the Comintern boasted:

> The three cities of Shanghai, Peking and Canton dominate almost the whole of China. They are the centers of the social and revolutionary movement. Shanghai is the center of the nation's industry and commerce, Peking is the political and university center, and Canton is the center of the national revolutionary movement. With the foundation laid in these three important places, the communist movement continued to develop. Within less than six months, communist nuclei had been established in Hupeh, Hunan and Honan. Furthermore, the communist movement spread to Chinese students studying abroad, who organized small organizations in Tokyo, Paris and other places.*
> The Shanghai organization was composed of approximately 70 persons. There were about ten comrades in Peking and ten in Canton. There were three newspapers, one each in Peking, Shanghai and Canton. In addition, there was the Chinese Socialist Youth Corps, with a

*Probably with letters of introduction from Li Ta-Chao, Comintern agents had contacted Chinese students from Peking University in Paris on the "work-and-study" plan which Mao had failed to pursue. Foremost among these was Chou En-lai, destined to become Red China's foreign minister, who traveled about among Chinese students in Europe, with the Comintern financing him; a Paris student communist organization was formed in 1921.

membership twice as large as that of the organizations. A small number among our comrades had had some experience, and this served as the foundation of their future work.[19]

Ninety comrades with three newspapers in the three leading cities! This was a ratio that *Iskra* editor Lenin in 1902 would have considered a marvelous accomplishment for his nascent mass-media cartel!

THE FIRST CCP CONGRESS   Encouraged by this thriving start in less than a year, Lenin sent other Comintern agents out in the winter of 1921, including Litnovsky, Malin, and above all, Sneevliet. Sneevliet joined Voitinsky in journeying all over China recruiting, organizing, instructing the neophytes in the mechanics of the combat party and its tactics of political and organizational warfare.

By July 1921, they felt ready to convene the "First Congress" of the Chinese Communist Party. They had 60 members of the provisional party cells, and 350 members of the Socialist Youth League.[20] So they brought together 12 members,[21] all in their twenties and thirties, at the Po Win Girl's Academy in the French-ruled quarter of Shanghai. Sneevliet attended as official Comintern delegate. For the occasion, young Mao Tse-tung came up from Changsha, already a distinguished organizer and secretary of eight Hunanese trade unions. The discussions dragged on for a week, and they were stormy. Sneevliet, coaching the fledgling Bolsheviks, had to keep reminding them that "doctrinal disagreements must not affect personal relationships."[22]

Finally on July 8, a hot and steamy night, the group met at one member's home to proclaim the party and ratify its constitution. The 24-year-old acting chairman raised his hand to hush the buzzing delegates and begin the meeting. At that moment a Chinese in a long gown drew aside the curtain at the door and peered in at the startled group. "Oh, I must have come to the wrong house!" he exclaimed, bowing. The curtain fell, and he vanished.

Sneevliet, smelling a rat, jumped up, exclaiming, "I propose that the meeting adjourn immediately, and that everyone leave by separate ways!" At that, the delegates rushed into the night, leaving only two members behind. Three minutes later, a squad of Chinese police under a French officer cordoned off the house. The "blundering" stranger had been a spy sent to investigate the peculiar comings and goings in the normally quiet neighborhood. Though the police carefully interrogated their two captives they did not learn they had interrupted a Bolshevik congress.

A few days later, at eight in the morning, the delegates slipped singly onto a local train of the Shanghai-Hangchow railway. They rode out about two hours to Kasing in Chekiang Province, and feigning a holiday mood rented a houseboat on South Lake. All day long this nucleus of the CCP floated on the still waters of the lake, occasionally dropping anchor but generally letting the boat drift where it would. Despite the usual conflicting opinions of the active extremists on the left and the passive liberals on the right, the delegates generally agreed on a minimum policy of concentrating on organizing the industrial proletariat into militant trade unions. They agreed to set up an Organization Bureau and a Propaganda Bureau and to accept the Comintern financing with all that it entailed. Then as darkness descended on the lake, they elected Ch'en Tu-hsiu, who was absent that day, secretary-general. Peasant organizer Mao Tse-tung said little, since he was just learning the Communist faith.

UNITED FRONTING THE KUOMINTANG   While the Comintern's recruiter-instructors were concentrating on their little CCP cells up north, Dr. Sun was rapidly expanding his Nationalist Party in Canton, in the south. As with all lusty young mass movements, Dr. Sun's had a broad base and very loose organization. Communists, being expert organizers and manipulators, have historically found fertile ground for infiltration and exploitation in such movements with rapid growth, loose organization, and initial lack of discipline and incoherence among the membership.* With this in mind Sneevliet visited Dr. Sun in his headquarters in Kwangsi province in November 1921, and in January 1922 he visited Canton to study the possibilities. This was at the time of a Hong Kong seamen's strike in which Dr. Sun's Nationalists provided considerable material aid and haven for the organizers. Sneevliet was tremendously impressed with Dr. Sun's close relations with the trade unions, which had themselves mushroomed in China since the May Fourth Movement.[23]

As he analyzed the situation, Sneevliet later recounted,[24] he immediately saw that his own Indonesian experience offered a tremendous new opportunity in China. Dr. Sun's movement was made to

*Compare for example, the proliferation of civil rights groups in the U.S. in the early 1960s such as the Student Non-Violent Coordinating Committee, the Congress on Racial Equality, Students for a Democratic Society, etc., many of which developed Red infiltration problems.

order for Sneevliet's Trojan horse "bloc within" united front technique, which had worked so well in Indonesia, where a larger nationalist mass movement agreed to take in the communists as members, *en bloc.* The tightly disciplined Bolsheviks would be able to operate under a cloak of respectability and gain better access to masses. In Indonesia Sneevliet's "Indian Social Democratic Association" had been able through the "Islamic Association" to get into the existing trade unions and organize new units everywhere. Moreover, back in Moscow Lenin was fighting the "revolution now" radicals in the Second Comintern Congress for such a "united front" arrangement within the larger established European social democratic parties, so that his tiny newborn communist parties could recruit within the existing mass organizations.

Sneevliet proposed the "united front" to the CCP central committee meeting in August 1922 in Hangchow. But to his disgust, the five Chinese comrades present objected. Imbued with their new Marxist theories, they opposed compromises with such class enemies as the bourgeois Dr. Sun. Preferring to save China by themselves, they claimed Dr. Sun's Nationalist Party wasn't all that big and influential, and they didn't need him or anybody else. Sneevliet quickly shook the fine comrades to their senses, reprimanding them in the spirit of Lenin's tirade against "Left-Wing Communism: An Infantile Disorder." He pointed out that they were too weak themselves to be downgrading Dr. Sun, whose party had 150,000 members, while their own "party" had at most two or three hundred[25] and hardly deserved the name. Sneevliet invoked his authority as Comintern representative (and paymaster) and ordered them to vote the merger.[26]

That same month Sneevliet met again with Dr. Sun in Shanghai. The Canton warlord had expelled Sun, and he was a refugee once more. His fortunes were at an all-time low, so when Sneevliet dangled the hope of Soviet support, Dr. Sun responded warmly. Though Dr. Sun lacked a firm mass organization and had no military forces whatsoever, he himself was a tremendous national symbol. And his Nationalist Party was ten years old, known and respected by the Chinese masses. All it needed was the organization that the Bolsheviks professionals could provide. And in the process they would trap a lot of game themselves.

So Sneevliet returned to Moscow in September 1922 to report his proposal. Could not the communist wolf adopt the nationalist sheep's clothing—and thereby gobble up a lot of Chinese Riding Hoods?

Moscow not only bought the idea. Lenin sent Dr. Abram Adolph Joffe, the top Soviet diplomat who had been his first ambassador to Berlin, to negotiate with Dr. Sun. On January 12, 1923, the Executive Committee of the Communist International (ECCI) ordered:

> Since the independent working-class movement in the country is weak, since the central task confronting China is to carry out the national revolution against the imperialists and their feudal agents within the country, and since the working class is directly interested in the solution of this National revolutionary problem but is not yet sufficiently differentiated as an absolutely independent force, the ECCI considers that it is necessary to coordinate the activities of the Kuomintang (Chinese Nationalist Party) and of the young Communist Party of China.[27]

But in keeping with Lenin's dictum that communists could join ranks with the bourgeois nationalist leaders in colonial countries so long as they kept working as disciplined communists, the ECCI cautioned the Chinese comrades: While working with and through the Kuomintang, the CCP was "not to merge" nor to "furl its own banner." The Nationalist Party was merely to be infiltrated and used as a "front" and "transmission belt."

AMERICA MISSES A CHANCE   Shortly afer his meeting with Joffe, Dr. Sun made one last fervent appeal to the West for the kind of political "foreign aid" he and his feudal national so desperately needed to modernize Chinese society, a kind of aid that Moscow, with a different objective in mind, was eagerly pressing on him. When American Minister Jacob Gould Schurman visited Canton, Dr. Sun called on him and pleaded that the United States persuade the other foreign powers to undertake a five-year military occupation of all China's provincial capitals. During this time an army of military and civilian experts would rebuild both national and local governments, and foreign administrators would train Chinese to succeed them. Then elections would be held and China would join the ranks of independent free nations. In what history may record as the greatest lost opportunity of the twentieth century, the American diplomat (certainly faithfully reflecting the sentiment of his government and people at the time) cold-shouldered the idea.

American rejection of his last desperate plea for Western help left Dr. Sun no choice but to go along with the Bolsheviks. As he bitterly told the New York *Times* correspondent, "We have lost hope of help from America, England, France or any of the Great Powers. The only country that shows any sign of helping us is the Soviet Government of Russia."[28] In June 1923 the CCP's third congress voted to seek a "national front" with the Kuomintang and instructed its members to join. In August[29] Michael Borodin, fresh from his Mexican success, arrived in Canton as an "adviser to the Kuomintang," representing not the Comintern but the "Russian Communist Party (Bolshevik)" —the official title of Lenin's party at the time. Meantime the CCP took its orders from the Comintern. Moscow resorted to this bit of bureaucratic legerdemain to keep Dr. Sun believing that somehow he was dealing on the international level with a fraternal Russian party, and on the domestic level with a spontaneous native Chinese political movement.

Dr. Sun found to his delight that Borodin was a veritable walking encyclopedia of revolutionary technology and organizational know-how. This wizard from Russia impressed Dr. Sun by the simple device of picking a few shrewd slogans and stirring mass demonstrations that promptly frightened an obstreperous war lord into submissiveness. This success promptly persuaded Dr. Sun that with Leninist methods he could convert his party into a power capable of unifying and governing a free and independent China.

Borodin saw at once that the Nationalist Party's prime need was for organized military forces. So Dr. Sun sent his brightest young aide, Chiang Kai-shek, to Moscow with a military-political mission to study Russian Bolshevik organization, strategy, and tactics. When Chiang returned, he organized the Whampoa Military Academy and became its first commandant over a faculty of Russian and Chinese instructors. A young Chinese who had become a Comintern agent-organizer among Chinese students in France and Germany, Chou En-lai, was named director of the academy's political department and promptly organized a front group, the Military Cadres Association, to recruit military officers for a future Red Army.

In January 1924 the Chinese Nationalist Party held its first national congress at Canton and agreed that the communists could join as individuals while the CCP itself was free to maintain its own independent organization and propagate its own views. The congress also accepted Borodin's recommendations for reorganizing the party along the paramilitary organizational lines of the Bolshevik "combat party." In turn the CCP declared its determination to cooperate in the common fight against "foreign imperialism and native reaction." Communist leaders, notably Mao Tse-tung, were given a third of the Central Committee seats. Thus the Nationalists let the Trojan horse into the gates.

RED RECRUITING SOARS Sneevliet's "bloc within" plan proved to be a magnificent stroke of genius. According to Moscow's own figures,[30] "Party membership, including Communist Youth members, did not total more than two or three hundred" when Joffe began negotiating with Dr. Sun. Within four years—by the time the Chinese communists and nationalists split—CCP membership had grown to 60,000.[31] It had firmly established the organizational power base from which it was able to capture China, one-fourth of the world's population, for Leninist totalitarianism.

In addition, the CCP controlled the Chinese Trade Union Congress, organized by the communists as a branch of Moscow's new Red labor International. With headquarters at Shanghai, it claimed two million members by 1927. They also had the All-China Peasants Union, which boasted more than nine million members. But the Comintern "reps," convinced that the urban "proletariat" must spearhead the revolution, were not too eager for the strategy for rural-based revolution led by peasant uprisings that was urged by the Peasant Union president, Mao Tse-tung.

On May 30, 1925, fate handed the "comreps" one of those incidents that inflames people and produces what Bolsheviks call "a revolutionary surge." In Shanghai the International Settlement police under a British officer fired on a crowd of demonstrators, killing 12 Chinese students. Borodin chortled, "We did not make May 30. It was made for us."[32] Great Britain provided a convenient "imperialist" scapegoat and the communist organizers had the martyrs to the nationalist cause they needed. Riding the new wave of xenophobia, the CCP led a nationwide boycott of British goods and an "indignation" movement over the "May Thirtieth Incident." Within six months party members increased tenfold; by July 1926 they numbered 30,000.[33] The Central Committee continued to push further expansion, hammering away with the slogans, "Expand the Party!" and "Enlist more revolutionary workers, peasants and intellectuals!"

At the same time, the CCP mounted an intensive program of training and education for every member of every cell. "Educational propagandists" were regarded as the key elements of the party cells. Their job was to indoctrinate, to carry out the Party's political and ideological propaganda, help cell members analyze current problems from the "correct" theoretical viewpoint, and improve their political interest and practical political skills. Their usual instructional method was the seminar or guided round-table group discussion of the sort Western psychologists today use in prison "group therapy" sessions for remolding the antisocial personalities. The CCP cautioned its propagandists against "injection-type" lectures.[34]

By 1925–26, the CCP had developed two types of party schools to supplement the regular cell training. Local committees set up general schools to train workers as mass agitators; this course lasted two weeks to a month. The party's directing personnel went to advanced schools set up by regional committees where they got a three-month course, carefully including simultaneous on-the-job training "among the masses." Aside from these two regular types of party schools, there were occasional specialized courses and schools. In July 1926, for example, the party ordered training classes in the big cities for low-level cadres working in the labor movement. Party headquarters at all levels were instructed to establish classes to prepare women members to organize peasant women and female laborers. And always, the most promising organizers were sent to Moscow to the Communist University for the Toilers of the East, and after January 1926 to the new Sun Yat-sen University, whose president was Karl Radek.[35]

THE CANTON COMMUNE   Dr. Sun died of cancer on March 12, 1925. Chiang Kai-shek, his successor as Nationalist Party leader, had no illusions about the communists. He needed Russian military help in bringing the rest of China under his control, but he limited their influence in the army and demanded that CCP agitators among workers and peasants adhere to Dr. Sun's program. In May 1926 they agreed. Then in the spring of 1927, as Chiang's army marched on Shanghai, the communist-led workers in the city rose against the commanding warlord, battling fiercely, and opened the city to his army. Chiang, distrusting the communists, demanded that they deliver all arms to him. On Stalin's orders, they refused, burying their arms instead. So on April 12, 1927, Chiang arrested their leaders, quickly crushed the ensuing rebellion, killing upward of 5,000 communists and labor leaders. He then announced the Nationalist Party's rejection of a "super-government under Borodin," ending further collaboration with Moscow.

Under Stalin's personal supervision, the Comintern now sent its top experts in armed uprising and street fighting to Canton to apply the insurrection methods taught at the Lenin institute. They included Heinz Neumann, author of a text on urban insurrection, Besso Lominadze, Joseph Pogany (alias John Pepper, later "Comrep" in the United States), and Voitinsky. This group installed a "commune" in Canton and for three days, December 11–14, 1927, fought a bloody rebellion. The communists gave and received no quarter. But in the end Chiang's Nationalist Army won out, and from then on fought an open civil war with the communists.

Watching all these events quietly from the wings in his native Hunan was Mao Tse-tung. Now he reached out to grasp the tiller of the combat party machine Stalin's ineptness had run aground.

MAO TSE-TUNG   Life had properly fitted (or misfitted) Mao for the job. He was born in 1893 of peasant stock. His earliest remembered condition in the world was rebellion—against his father, a rebellion later transferred to the whole world. Mao's autobiography calls his father "a severe taskmaster who frequently beat me and my brothers" while his mother was "kind, generous and sympathetic." "There were two parties in our family. One was my father, the Ruling Power, the opposition was made up of myself, my mother, my brother, and sometimes even the laborer."[36]

When Mao was six, his father put him to work on farm chores. At eight he entered the local primary school under a severe teacher. Caught between sternness at home and school, little Mao ran away and wandered about the countryside for three days until found by his family. To his surprise, he escaped a beating; in fact, both father and teacher became more understanding. With a wry smile Mao in later life recalled: "It was a successful 'strike'."

Like young Marx, Mao loved to write poetry. But his penchant for day-dreaming and reading only caused more trouble. His practical father wanted the farm work done. Mao found he could calm his father's rages by quoting classical passages from Confucius, whom Papa Mao admired. The son tried reciting those passages bidding elders to be affectionate with their children, but the beatings and scoldings continued. Once, to get revenge on his father, Mao plotted to burn the Confucian temple in the village.

When Mao was 13 his father excoriated him before some guests as "lazy and useless." The boy ran out of the house to the edge of a nearby lake and threatened to jump in if his father came nearer. After many demands and counterdemands they reached a truce:

My father insisted that I apologize and kowtow. I agreed to give a one-knee kowtow if he would promise not to beat me. That war ended, and from it I learned that when I defended my rights by open rebellion, my father relented, but when I remained meek and submissive, he only cursed and beat me more.

Over his father's strong objections Mao left home to attend the Tung-shan Primary School in the next county, one of the new westernized "foreign schools" so popular in this revolutionary era. Mao led his classmates in cutting off their long pigtails, symbolically repudiating ancient Chinese tradition. Caught in the revolutionary fervor of 1911, Mao went to Changsha and at 18, joined the rebel army for six months. Afterward, he considered a police school, a soapmaking school, a law school, and an economics school. He finally entered the First Normal School, a commercial high school in Changsha. There he spent the years 1912–18, and began demonstrating the organizing skills that were to make him so powerful. In 1914 he helped organize a student study society, the "New People's Study Society," and edited its newspaper.[37] The aim was to "reform China." "My mind was a curious mixture of ideas of liberalism, democratic reformism, and utopian socialism . . . I was definitely anti-militarist and anti-imperialist,"[38] recalled Mao.

Mao's mind, in fact, was just plain "anti" at this stage of his life, as a result of his emotional conditioning. His childhood followed a pattern of mother-protection and father-hate that seems generally to produce poets and military leaders—both of which Mao in adult life became.[39] His flirtation with pyromania—plotting to burn the village temple—likewise denotes a revealing pattern. Psychologists maintain that unrequited parental love is the basis of a large percentage of pyromaniac deeds. Rejection and humiliation, often combined with feelings of inferiority and inadequacy, breed emotions of defiance and hatred which may become directed against authority and society in general. Through the agency of fire the weakling can wreak great devastation and bring disorder to an entire community.[40]

He may likewise channel these emotions through Marxism and revolutionary activity, among many other avenues. But as the communist apparatus has grown, using as it does the device of personal evangelism for recruitment, Marxist incendiarism is a more widely available and likely outlet for an endemic human condition. Because

Marxism justifies and exalts the aggressive emotions bred by whatever feelings of rejection, humiliation, guilt, inferiority, and inadequacy, it has become an increasingly common avenue of expression. Indeed the standardized communist training techniques and the whole Marxist conspiratorial system actually breed these emotions, warping the individual to their own pattern, inculcating in him emotional defiance and hatred of "capitalistic" authority and society.[41]

Mao's rebellion against his father violated one of Chinese culture's greatest taboos. The traditional Chinese family placed paramount value on filial piety and the absolute need of the child to defer completely to parental authority. The ultimate crime was expressing any form of opposition or hostility to familial authority. Yet Mao's Chinese Communist Party ultimately seemed to embody Mao's personal reaction formation and displacement of oedipal hostility. Observes one behavioral scientist:

> No other political culture places as much stress upon the emotion of hate as does the Chinese. Both in extolling hate as a positive virtue and in seeking to tap hostile feelings, the Chinese Communists have carried to new extremes a trend which was already well-established in modern Chinese politics. . . . In describing the "good Communist," the Chinese have emphasized a capacity for passion, for protracted and unfaltering hatred of enemies, both domestic and foreign. . . . A key ingredient in the personality of the effective revolutionary hero, as portrayed by the Chinese Communists, is a deep and essentially blind capacity for prolonged hatred. . . . These are examples of calculated efforts to utilize and nurture the passion of hate. . . . In addition, the process of political recruitment appears to have favored those with strong capacities for hatred. The dynamics of Chinese politics have thus magnified the importance of this emotion and tended to bring about the selection for leadership roles of those with a marked potential for sustained hostility. . . . In large part, the outbursts of student aggression which were taken as examples of the political awakening of young China were fed by the tensions and passions of dissatisfaction with family controls. In expressing hostility toward the rulers of China, these young Chinese were in fact also giving vent to their feelings of aggression within the sharply proscribed limits of family life. . . . There is the pattern of direct confrontation with parental authority and the need for total revolt. Even in muted form this does not seem to have been very common in modern China, except among men who later became professional revolutionaries. . . . Mao seems to have sought to justify his revolt against his father by depicting him not only as a harsh and cruel man but also as a rich peasant and landlord. By identifying his father with what communism holds to be an evil class, Mao was able

both to give legitimacy to his own violation of the deepest rules of Chinese behavior and to give a personal emotional meaning to the abstract evil of the "landlord" and "rich peasant."[42]

In the summer of 1917, stimulated by Ch'en Tu-hsiu's *New Youth*, Mao wrote to students in the various schools of China asking them to contact him for "patriotic work." By correspondence and personal contact he gradually built up a following among students and young intellectuals in his "New People's Study Society."

In the summer of 1918 young Mao, at 25 just finishing his secondary schooling, set out for Peking with nine other Hunanese students who had saved enough money to go on to France on a work-and-study scheme. He found, however, money problems aside, that he was very backward at learning a foreign tongue, and decided to remain in China. Broke, homeless, and hungry, he found a job at eight yuan a month in the library of the National University at Peking, dusting and straightening the books and sweeping the floor. His boss was none other than Li Ta-Chao, who introduced his assistant to Marxist ideas. The library job lasted about four months. Despite his low position Mao met the great Ch'en Tu-hsiu, publisher of the *avant garde* magazine he worshipped, and joined the Philosophy Society and the Society for the Study of Journalism. He also joined the thousands of students who celebrated the World War I armistice in November 1918 in a gigantic victory parade. The next day Mao joined the Peking intellectuals who founded the *New Tide Society* they were sure would guide the intellectual revolution sweeping China and the new unified nation certain to result from the Paris peace conference and the great American President Wilson's doctrine of self-determination.

Mao thought that his talents lay in his knack for organizing people. Six months of this exciting Peking life were enough to convince him that he should return to his native Hunan, to organize the people to be ready for this golden future. Though only 26 and a high school graduate, he had a reputation as a seasoned radical. Penniless, he walked back, trudging through the countryside, to Changsha, the provincial capital. He founded the *Hsiang River Review*, recruited scores of young liberal intellectuals into his New People's Study Society, led demonstrations and a student strike against the local war lord, and sent delegations to both Peking and to Dr. Sun in Canton seeking support. Late in 1919 Mao himself went again to Peking and

Shanghai, this time not as a penniless, hungry student but as the respected radical editor and delegate of his organization, to meet with Ch'en and Li and other militant nationalists. Through them in 1920 he caught the virus of the new Marxist-Leninist ideology Voitinsky was spreading in China; this association converted him, with his organizational skills, to the service of Lenin's newly colonized hate media corporation.

Mao's life up to this point reads almost like a copybook sketch in the psychopathology of politics. Here was a young man, predisposed from the earliest social experiences in his own home to violence and hatred against his world, who embraced Marxism. In it, he found a philosophy that enabled him to intellectualize his prior emotional bias, to justify, and even glorify his compulsive predispositions. Marxism was designed by and for his kind, and he badly needed it as a prop to justify and vent his hostility.

The fledgling Bolshevik hate conglomerate directed Mao to devote his organizational talents to launching a trade-union movement in Hunan, and his local successes earned him a place in the CCP's national leadership. After the Communists "merged" with the Nationalists, Mao served simultaneously on the executive committees of both parties. He went to Shanghai, then to Canton, to serve in the CCP's two biggest headquarters (1923–26). In 1925 he became editor of a Kuomintang weekly newspaper in Canton, and even became chief of the Nationalist propaganda department. But in the summer of 1926, with the split already looming, he went back to Hunan as a peasant organizer, his first and fondest activity. Soon he worked up to the presidency of the nine-million member All-China Peasants Union, and began dabbling in peasant uprisings.

It was from this vantage point that Mao watched Stalin's abortive urban uprising in Canton. After that disaster, Mao decided that the Chinese Communists had tried Stalin's way—revolution by operating in the cities with worker forces—and now they would try his way: revolution by fighting in the countryside with peasant guerrillas. As the world knows, Mao's way worked. And today, Mao's band is bending all Red China's resources to supporting the hate cartels everywhere that agree with his pyromanic brand of Leninism.

Chapter 28
RADICAL FORERUNNERS IN THE UNITED STATES

We hate you! Damn you! Hate you!
    We hate your rotten breed.

We hate your slave religion with
    submission for its creed.

We hate your judges. We hate your
    courts.

We hate that living lie
That you call "justice" and we hate
    with a hate

That shall never die.

We shall keep our hate and cherish
    our hate

And our hate shall ever grow.
      —"Hymn of Hate," IWW poem
      Harry McClintock, 1916

EARLY AMERICAN ANARCHISTS   Radicalism in America is nothing new nor alien. On March 29, 1799, one David Brown proclaimed in a letter to the *Salem Gazette, "The occupation of government is to plunder and steal."* This proto-Marxian view of the state came from a Connecticut Yankee veteran of the Revolutionary Army. Brown went on to declare the federal Congress "a tyrannic association of about five hundred out of five millions" ganged up to steal "all the benefits of public property and live upon the ruins of the rest of the community."

For these words Brown was treated to a trial before a Justice of the U.S. Supreme Court, Samuel Chase, adjudged guilty of violating the Sedition Act of 1798, and sentenced to 18 months in jail. He was one of 25 arrested and ten convicted—and the most severely penalized. (Among the convicted was a hapless Independence Day parade spectator who remarked that he wished the cannon salute's wadding had been aimed at the seat of President Adam's pants!)

Another such firebrand was James Thomson Callender, a Scot chased out of Great Britain for his forked tongue. He became one of Thomas Jefferson's kept journalists since his poison pen was useful in the young Jeffersonian party's war on the Federalists. Callendar proclaimed all government evil, "a contrivance of human villainy" and a collective of thieves and exploiters. "The object of every government always has been, and always will be, to squeeze from the bulk of the people as much money as it can get." The Federalists put this flaming Jeffersonian behind bars for nine months, the peripatetic Justice Chase presiding and sentencing. They may be pardoned for expecting Jefferson's election in 1800 to be followed by a full Jacobin Reign of Terror, complete with guillotine.[1]

Modern American radicalism flowed from two fountainheads: 1) Immigrants who brought with them the Marxist ideology of class conflict, which came closer to fitting the more rigid social structure in Europe than in America. 2) Labor leaders who found themselves engaged in a life-or-death power struggle in the late nineteenth century when the whole field of labor-management relations was an uncharted jungle.

The first Marxian socialists in America were German immigrants who came after the ill-fated revolution of 1848. Marx's International Workingmen's Association established its first American section in 1869. In the 1870s and 1880s a new wave of German immigrants arrived, among them disciples of Marx's apostle, Ferdinand Lassalle. The Lassalleans and Marxists in 1876 formed what became the Socialist Labor Party (SLP) of North America.[2] Between 1881 and 1900 the immigrant tide rose to nine million; most of these immigrants were not socialists, but most of the socialists were immigrants. They banded into foreign language federations which were in turn sections of the SLP. In 1882 the fiery German anarchist Johann Most moved to New York and launched a German-language paper; by 1885 an anarchist federation claimed 80 sections and 8,000 members. Anarchists were involved in the infamous Chicago Haymarket Square bombing of 1886, in which seven policemen were killed.[3]

By 1890, the Socialist Labor Party was little more than a moribund foreign-language sect. That year it was taken over by a brilliant Columbia University law professor Daniel De Leon, an imperious eccentric and magnetic personality. This convert to Marxism quickly became its outstanding American interpreter, and he attracted many young native-born American intellectuals to the new secular faith. Years later a disenchanted disciple, Morris Hillquit, called him "an American Lenin of completely indigenous origins."

INDUSTRIAL WARFARE Meantime, American trade unionism was growing in a jungle climate. Labor organizations were compelled to work as conspiratorial groups in secrecy, to overcome lockouts, blacklists, and forcible resistance of employers. Relations between labor and management in this early stage of the Industrial Revolution in America were unregulated and generally uncontrollable except by force on both sides. The Anglo-Saxon penchant for juridical management of social conflict and clashing interests had not yet had time to operate. Working conditions ranged from the primitive to the abominable. Booms and panics followed with crushing regularity. Court injunctions tied the hands of unions on the mere threat of a strike. Employers fought labor organizations with every possible means, crushing strikes ruthlessly with hired gangs of armed guards, police, sheriffs, and federal troops. Open industrial warfare raged in Colorado and Idaho from 1892 to 1899 between the mine owners and the "hard rock" miners. The American Federation of Labor's craft unionism proved unsuited to western conditions, and so in 1893 the Western Miners Federation was formed with William D. ("Big Bill") Haywood as secretary-treasurer. "My father was of an old American family," Haywood could boast, "so American that if traced back it would probably run to the Puritan bigots or the cavalier pirates."[4] Haywood's innate stormy, pugnacious temperament and the battlefield conditions shaped the Miners Federation into a particularly violence-prone organization.

In 1893 Eugene V. Debs, a railway fireman born in Terre Haute, Indiana, organized the American Railway Union on industrial union lines. The next year Debs led a strike against the Pullman Car Company, which ran a "company town" near Chicago in which workers were held in virtual peonage. Rail transportation from Cincinnati to San Francisco was paralyzed. The railroads got a court injunction so broad it was called "a Gatling gun on paper," and persuaded President Cleveland to send Federal troops into Chicago without request from either governor or mayor to break the strike. Debs went to jail for violating the injunction against "conspiracy," though the court winked at the railroad's "General Managers Association" which maintained illegal agreements to control wages, rates and service, thus eliminating the benefits of the competitive system. The workers' union was broken, and for many years its members were blacklisted. They were forced to change their names and wander over the land looking for work. It was enough to make many hate capitalism and its "establishment;" but though Debs was too much a pacifist for that, he did begin to study socialist literature. He was sympathetic toward the Populist Party, which stood for government ownership of railroad, telegraph and telephone facilities; free coinage of silver (which, being inflationary, would favor all debtors over creditors); and a graduated income tax. When the Populists endorsed the Democratic candidate, Bryan, in 1896, Debs campaigned for him, but following the Republican victory Debs was converted to socialism, and in 1898 started his own Social Democratic Party.

Meanwhile the domineering personal rule of De Leon produced rebellion among moderates in the ranks of the Socialist Labor Party and the rebels joined forces with Debs in 1901 to form the Socialist Party of America. Its members included Christian socialists, Marxists, immigrant workers, native intellectuals, trade union officials, and millionaire social reformers. Only a few of the delegates had more than the haziest intellectual acquaintance with theoretical Marxism. Their anticapitalism was more a reflection of reform sentiment, American idealism and utopian socialist tradition than *Das Kapital* and the hate doctrines of Karl Marx. In fact, anticapitalism in America never was total; it merely reflected the antipathy of the small farmers, property owners, and businessmen against the big ones. They wanted inflationary coinage of free silver to reduce their debts to the wealthy capitalists, and they applauded Teddy Roosevelt's trust-busting to control competition, but they thought not at all of abolishing private property generally. They merely wanted to shift "the system" toward greater opportunity to gain more of it for themselves.

"NO ULTIMATE DEMANDS"   Some of the bloodiest battles were fought by the American Federation of Labor—but its leader, Samuel Gompers, was an ex-socialist sympathizer who moved from trade union socialism to trade unionism "pure and simple." The AFL grew in no small part out of reaction against political socialism; Gompers made a credo out of spurning the messianic goals of socialist "impossiblists." Instead the AFL's strategy was to work for the day-to-day practical aims of the workers and immediate objectives that could be realized in a few years. In politics the Gompers rule was to waste no time on offering vast programmatic schemes for a new society but instead pragmatically "to reward our friends and punish our enemies." He waged ideological war on the radicals in the labor movement with the slogan, "No ultimate demands!"

Nevertheless, the heat of industrial warfare brought many to radical socialism. That this gravitation was more often the result of inner emotional compulsions than the objective situation is demonstrated by the fact that far more labor leaders were repulsed by the Marxist class-hate doctrine. For example, "Big Bill" Haywood and two other Miners Federation officers were jailed in Idaho on trumped-up charges of conspiracy in a dynamite murder; yet after a month in the same cell the other two would not even speak to Haywood, so distasteful did they find the dogmatism and violence of his views.

With the capitalists behaving like characters right out of Marx's copybook, it was enough to create rebellion. This inflammable social climate inevitably produced its share of "struggle mentalities," not due to messianic delusions and apocalyptic visions but simply from the emotional consequences of engagement in very real battle. "Whatever may be said," wrote labor's defender Clarence Darrow of the night he watched railroad cars go up in flames during the Pullman strike of 1894, "the fact is that all strikes and all resistance to strikes take on the psychology of warfare, and all parties in interest must be judged from that standpoint. As I stood on the prairie watching the burning railroad cars I had no feeling of enmity toward either side. I was only sad to realize how little pressure man could stand before he reverted to the primitive."[5]

The surprising thing was that the early American industrial wars produced so few real radicals and violent revolutionaries. Even the great Frederick Engels was so impressed—and disappointed—on his visit to America in 1888. He complained that the American workers were preeminently "practical" and judged everything on the basis of concrete results. Though impressed with their tremendous "energy and vitality," he also found them lamentably backward in "theory," so much so that the *Communist Manifesto* of 1848 was "far too difficult for America" four decades later. Engel's letters on America are studded with phrases like "untheoretical, matter-of-fact Americans," "quite crude, tremendously backward theoretically," "contemptuous of reason and science," "so conceited about its 'practice' and so frightfully dense theoretically," "ahead of everyone else in practice and still in swaddling clothes in theory."[6]

[419]

THE "WOBBLIES"   But gradually the more radical labor leaders and socialists gravitated together to organize independent political action and industrial unionism, as opposed to the nonpartisan, craft-structured AFL. So in 1905 Haywood, Debs, Daniel De Leon and 24 others met secretly in Chicago and formed the Industrial Workers of the World (IWW, or "Wobblies"). They proclaimed the need for "one big union" to wage the "irrepressible conflict between the capitalist class and the working class." With Haywood's 27,000-member Western Federation of Miners as the backbone, the Wobblies grew rapidly at first, reaching 100,000 members by the second convention in 1906. The IWW developed an American brand of anarchosyndicalism whose battle cries were "direct action," "sabotage," and "general strike." The Wobblies accepted violence as a natural and ordinary part of the organizing task, owing less from ideological tradition handed down from the old Bakuninist immigrants and European intellectuals than to the gun-toting tradition of the West. The Wobblies organized mostly in the lumber, agriculture, and construction trades which used unskilled migratory workers. In the East they organized the immigrants in the textile trades. None of these workers voted, and so it was hopeless to talk of winning reforms by ordinary political processes. And the employers ruthlessly resisted the Wobbly organizers, who soon learned that gunfire settled many a strike and ended many an organizing campaign. "Some European theories happened to fit into the IWW's practice," says Theodore Draper, distinguished historian of American communism, "but the practice would have existed without the theories."[7]

In this atmosphere the Wobblies concocted a violent, revolutionary brew of industrial unionism far more potent than most of the doctrinaire American Marxists and radical intellectuals could stomach. Debs, a gentle humanitarian soul with pacifist convictions, quickly dropped out. De Leon was expelled in a radical coup in 1908 by those more sympathetic to anarchism than to socialism.

Typical of these firebrand unionists was William Zebulon Foster, the former hobo who was to run three times for president on the Communist Party ticket. He was born in 1881 at Taunton, Mass. His father was an Irish immigrant, his mother of English-Scottish stock. When Foster was seven the family moved to Philadelphia, where his father washed carriages and plotted against the English while his mother bore 23 children, most of whom died in infancy, and devoted herself fervently to Catholicism. Little Bill earned his first pennies as a paper boy, quit school at ten and began running errands and looking after the studio of a down-at-the-heels sculptor. When he was 15 he was stirred by the great Bryan crusade for the presidency in 1896. He became a Rousseauistic wanderer, unable ever to settle at a trade. He spent three years in a type foundry, then worked in a factory that produced fertilizer from the dead carcasses of horses and other animals. Foster developed tuberculosis after three years of this, then three years of sea air cleared his lungs. As a seaman he hit nearly every major port of the world. After an unhappy turn as a farm worker in Florida, Foster became a streetcar motorman on New York's Third Avenue Line in 1901, was fired for union activity, and joined the Socialist Party. Next he popped up in Echo, Texas, as a cook in a tough railroad yard, homesteaded in the rugged Oregon mountain country, did odd jobs around logging camps and railroads. After the 1907 lambing season he sold his homestead, went to work on a railroad, and in 1909 turned up digging sewers in Spokane. The Socialist Party expelled him for advocating violence, so he turned to the IWW and became an organizer.

Foster never liked mining, but in the spring of 1909 the IWW asked him to organize the Coeur D'Alene mines in Idaho. He was a miner for four weeks—until the company chased him out. In 1910 he went to Budapest as a delegate to an anarchist trade unions secretariat meeting, and became convinced that organizing against the AFL was futile. Better to infiltrate and take it over.

When Foster returned home in 1912 and organized his Trade Union Educational League, he was already a proto-Bolshevik. While working as a canvasman with a tent show of actors playing Indiana and Idaho, he wrote a pamphlet called *Syndicalism* which became the handbook and textbook of his tiny TUEL movement. He clearly exhibited the "struggle mentality" at this time, and six years before the organization of the Comintern, apparently independently of Lenin, was anticipating the "struggle" ethics and the organizational warfare tactics of the Bolsheviks. His TUEL plan was to abandon organizing rival trade unions in favor of planting "nuclei" in the AFL unions to "standardize their policies, instigate strike movements, and organize their attacks on the conservative forces in the unions. A fighting machine is thus built up which enables the syndicalists to act as a unit at all times and to thoroughly exploit their combined power."[8] In choosing weapons, Foster wrote in thoroughly Leninist fashion, the syndicalist "is no more careful to select those that are 'fair,' 'just,' or 'civilized' than is a householder attacked in the night by a burglar. . . . With him the end justifies the means. Whether his tactics be 'legal' and 'moral,' or not, does not concern him as long as they are effective." Some scholars maintain that the anarchist Bakunin actually had more influence on Lenin than Marx. It is a moot point, but here certainly we see the common theme in Foster's anarchosyndicalism and Leninism.

Meanwhile, the Socialist Party grew rapidly. Like their European counterparts, the American socialists paid a modicum of lip service to class struggle, anticapitalism, and violent revolution. But in practice they were more and more merely practical reformist politicians. From 1901 to 1912 dues-paying membership rose from 16,000 to 118,000, and Debs as presidential candidate increased the party's vote from 96,000 to nearly 900,000, a full 6 percent of the total. From zero the Party elected more than 1,000 candidates, including 56 mayors, over 300 aldermen, and numerous state legislators.

VIOLENCE VS. REFORM AGAIN   But as the industrial strife sparked by the IWW grew more bitter, the U.S. socialist movement, like its European counterparts, felt the tug of diverging reformist-revisionists on the right and violent revolutionaries who followed the Babeuvist decision for violence on the left. A crisis developed in 1912. In the midst of bitter strife the Los Angeles *Times* building was dynamited and 21 persons killed. Its publisher, whose vicious hatred of unions had largely created the atmosphere that produced this tragedy, screamed for vengeance. A few months later two AFL labor leaders, brothers, were arrested and charged. It looked like another trumped-up charge based on a manufactured "confession," and once more the great Clarence Darrow went to the defense of labor's cause, with the Socialist candidate for mayor of Los Angeles as his associate counsel. But to his dismay, Darrow discovered his clients were guilty and the evidence overwhelming, so he negotiated a settlement in which they were saved from a death sentence provided they would plead guilty *before* the election. The bright hopes of capturing the Los Angeles mayor's office were dashed. Socialist hopes and labor's cause were dealt a staggering blow nationally. "Force and violence" became an issue which had to be resolved to avoid destroying the party's progress. While they had long disputed over violence as a theoretical issue, the American leftists now had to face the Babeuvist choice as a matter of practical politics.

It was "Big Bill" Haywood who precipitated the final showdown.

At the Cooper Union in New York he blasted forth with a characteristic speech: "We should say that it is our purpose to overthrow the capitalist system by forcible means if necessary!"[9] The next socialist convention, in the spring of 1912, gave him his answer. To avoid public reaction against this open incendiarism the party amended its constitution to expel anyone "who opposes political action or advocates crime, sabotage, or other methods of violence as a weapon of the working class." Haywood's supporters were defeated, 191 to 90, and subsequently Socialist Party members ratified the amendment, 13,000 to 4,000. Later that year, at a rally celebrating court victories arising out of the IWW's stormy Lawrence, Massachusetts textile strike, "Big Bill" again championed sabotage and direct action. And for that he was expelled from the Socialist Party's National Executive Committee. Early in 1913 the party ran a referendum on "Big Bill" and kicked him out by a vote of more than two to one.

Such was the crisis that created the *real* native American revolutionary movement. When Haywood stopped paying dues, about 15 percent of the Socialist Party's membership withdrew. Haywood actually won in Montana, Nevada, Oregon, Tennessee, Texas, Utah, Washington, and West Virginia; the heaviest anti-Haywood majorities were in New York, Massachusetts, Pennsylvania, and Wisconsin. In Kansas City, young Earl Browder quit the party in protest against Haywood's treatment. Benjamin Gitlow, a young clerk in New York, shared Haywood's convictions about violence but voted against him in the belief that to advocate it publicly opened the party to *agents provocateurs* and government persecution.[10]

This unexpectedly sudden and sharp confrontation of the Babeuvist choice threw American radicals into utter confusion, and before they could recover and regroup, World War I broke out in 1914. This savage event utterly disheartened liberals, socialists, and idealists throughout the U.S.

LENINIST MISSIONARIES   As we have seen [Chapter 22], Leninism came to America in this period, via correspondence, party links, and personal emissaries. At the invitation of the German Socialist Federation Mme. Alexandra Kollontay, a Leninist agent, lectured across the nation in 1915, using her meetings to promote Bolshevik propaganda and agitate for a Third International. Formerly a Menshevik, Kollontay joined the Bolsheviks after the war broke out and became one of Lenin's chief collaborators. "We have been building not a few hopes on this journey," Lenin wrote her. He used her to get his tracts published in English among the U.S. socialists, and also to gather intelligence about leaders who might be recruited for a Bolshevik colony in America. "Who is Eugene Debs?" Lenin wrote. "He writes sometimes in a revolutionary manner. Is he only spineless like Kautsky?" Her reports were so informative that three months later Lenin knew all about Debs, even citing him in a speech in Berne to prove that proletarians of the world were uniting and ready to rise.[11] Mme. Kollontay made a second trip to the U.S. late in 1916.

In November Nikolai Bukharin, another Lenin disciple, arrived in New York. Slight, sensitive in appearance, he was a veteran revolutionary with a decade of dangerous activity behind him. After his third arrest and release in Russia in 1911, he fled abroad, moving from country to country as the police or his party demanded. Sweden expelled him for antimilitarist activity. He was arrested again in England, and finally reached the United States. On January 12, 1917 he became editorial secretary of the Russian Socialist Federation's organ *Novy Mir (The New World)* in New York. He quickly turned it into a clarion of Leninist propaganda.[12]

Meanwhile, the Socialist Propaganda League was developing in Boston, and so were Lenin's connections with it. The 1916 presidential election was a shock for the Socialist Party and a boon to the radicals in it, because for the first time the party lost votes. Its percentage of the total dropped from 6 to 3; its vote fell a third, from nearly 900,000 to fewer than 600,000. The Socialist Propaganda League held a postelection meeting in Boston at the Latvian Workers Society headquarters on November 26, 1916. A letter was read from Comrade S.J. Rutgers of Brooklyn, the Dutch civil engineer and Bolshevik sympathizer who had decided the league would be useful for Lenin's new Bolshevik International. Rutgers offered and the League accepted $100 as a starter for a weekly publication.

This was the first step which converted the League into the earliest direct organizational ancestor of the Communist Party, U.S.A. Rutgers was at this time in contact with Lenin through Mme. Kollontay, who was on her second mission to the U.S. As we have seen, Rutgers had brought the noted Japanese socialist Sen Katayama to Brooklyn from San Francisco, and with Mme. Kollontay's help was converting him to Leninism so they could exploit his reputation among American socialists. Rutgers was also in direct contact with the Dutch radicals, including Anton Pannekoek, the famous astronomer, and Herman Gorter, a celebrated poet, who were working with Lenin and Zinoviev to propagandize the Zimmerwald Left position.

The first issue of the League weekly, *The Internationalist*, appeared in January 1917, with a Rutgers article keynoting it, and another he persuaded Pannekoek to contribute from Holland. To promote the League further, Rutgers published an article in the *International Socialist Review* hailing it as the "actual beginning in trying to organize the Left Wing forces in the Socialist Party of America." (He should know!) Two months later the *Review* printed the text of the League's manifesto, which showed Rutger's heavy influence.

TROTSKY IN BROOKLYN   On the evening of January 14, 1917, an extraordinary meeting convened at the Brooklyn home of Ludwig Lore. It was called, as Lore later reported, to discuss "a program of action for Socialists of the Left, for the purpose of organizing the radical forces in the American Socialist movement." Twenty left-wing socialists were there, including Rutgers, Mme. Kollontay, Bukharin, Katayama, and an extraordinary newcomer who had just arrived the day before from Europe, Leon Trotsky.

Meeting with them were John D. Williams, representing the Socialist Propaganda League of Boston, one or two other American radicals, and Louis C. Fraina, the fiery young Italian-born theoretician who grew up in New York's Lower East Side, traditional melting pot of immigrants and a stinking slum that bred many messianic "true believers." Fraina had gone through the Socialist Party and the IWW, and landed in the Socialist Labor Party as a disciple of De Leon. Then he became the guiding editorial light of the radical *New Review* for two years before it expired in the summer of 1916 as a result of its extremism.

Trotsky and Bukharin dominated the proceedings that evening. They waged an intense theoretical discussion lasting far into the night. The two Russians agreed that the first step must be, as Lenin himself always prescribed, to launch a new publication. But they wrangled over whether the American radicals should split from the Socialist Party and form a separate organization, as Bukharin wanted, or stay inside and form a radical caucus, seeking to capture the party. A vote was taken and Trotsky won. Mme. Kollontay, who was going to Europe, was appointed to establish the link between the Americans and Lenin.[13] She immediately got off a letter to him which indicates she and Bukharin had held a series of meetings prior to this recorded occasion: "The Dutch Comrade Rutgers, Katayama, and our group have taken a step toward the Zimmerwald Left," she wrote. "However, Trotsky's arrival strengthened the Right wing at our meetings and by the time of my departure the platform had not yet been adopted."[14]

Before this clique could develop their plans the czar was overthrown and replaced by the world's first social democratic regime. Trotsky and Bukharin scurried back to St. Petersburg to fish in the troubled waters. Rutgers, Fraina, and the Socialist Propaganda League got together on a reorganization. The business and editorial offices were moved to Brooklyn. Fraina became editor of *The Internationalist*, whose name was changed, to *The New International*. Rutgers became the financial "angel" and a chief contributor, and Katayama joined the masthead. They also started a bimonthly magazine called *The Class Struggle*. Fraina, though only 23, became the dominant voice of Leninist-inclined radicalism in America, calling for not merely "everyday struggles but for the *final* struggle against Capitalism."[15]

By summer the Socialist Propaganda League claimed 20 branches in 12 states. But the publication flickered out that fall. Fraina moved to Boston to edit the publication of the left-wing socialists there, about the only organized radical socialists left in the country; in Boston later, Fraina gained the distinction of publishing Lenin's "Letter to the American Workingmen."

DEATH AND TRANSFIGURATION   In 1917 the American radical revolutionary movement virtually died; in fact, the whole socialist movement fell on hard times. The Wilsonian reforms and "New Freedom" robbed it of its emotional élan. The czar's fall removed the symbol of authoritarianism from the side of the Allied powers and made it possible for Wilson to lead the nation into the war to "make the world safe for democracy." And in the next few months the Justice Department suppressed many of the Socialist Party's journals and meetings. The gentle Debs, for making an antiwar speech, was sent to Atlanta penitentiary on a ten-year sentence. Radicalism almost disappeared. But in distant St. Petersburg, the trumpet of the New Day sounded a resurrection.

Chapter 29
THE COMINTERN SUBSIDIARY IN AMERICA

I hate them, Oh!
I hate them well,
I hate them, Christ!
As I hate hell!
If I were God
I'd sound their knell
This day.
—W.E.B. DuBois,
Darkwater, 1920

COVETING LENIN'S MAGIC   The Bolshevik Revolution of November 1917 loosed another age of religious war in the twentieth century, and Americans were not immune to the messianic faith. Was global revolution so far-fetched? Was not Trotsky, now the great revolutionary hero and Commissar of the new Red Army, the same obscure revolutionist New York left-wingers had known but a few months before? And now here he commanded the mighty Russian Army.

Lenin became the new god of revolution. America's utopians wanted fervently to believe that Russia, the most feudal and reactionary state of Europe, was about to become a socialist paradise. Young radicals like Jay Lovestone, 20-year-old leader of the Intercollegiate Socialist Society's chapter at the City College of New York, wanted to believe. Labor leaders like the Wobblies' William Z. Foster wanted to believe. Journalists like Lincoln Steffens, Max Eastman, and John Reed wanted to believe. Lenin was the socialist revolutionary who one moment was an unknown, penniless and friendless refugee, and the next became ruler of the biggest nation in Europe. *What was his secret? What new technology of organization and revolution had the Bolsheviks discovered to make such a transformation possible? One and all, they wanted to know.*
CARTEL TALENT SCOUTING   Early in 1918, just before Rut-

gers left for Moscow and a future career with the Comintern, he and Fraina organized in the name of the Socialist Propaganda League and five Russian immigrant groups an "American Bolshevik Information Bureau" in New York City, with Fraina as director. Fraina immediately brought out a collection of the writings of Lenin and Trotsky, whose Aesopian jargon was such that much of it could appeal to the most idealistic American radical.[1]

Then John Reed, swashbuckling news correspondent who was in St. Petersburg at the time of Lenin's coup and had befriended the master, came back in 1918 to tell a romanticized version of the story in his *Ten Days That Shook the World*. Reed had actually been commissioned Bolshevik Consulate General in New York. But Lenin, reconsidering his American friend's romantic notions and wild revolutionary ideas, revoked the commission at the last moment. Reed worked just as hard for him anyway. In January 1919 he joined with Fraina and Bertram Wolfe, a young pacifist who had joined the Brooklyn local of the Socialist Party, in organizing a left-wing caucus within the New York Socialist Party. From that base they began to organize the far-flung and loose Bolshevik sympathizers across the country. Requests for information and messages of support poured in. To organize in New York State they sent out Benjamin Gitlow, a Russian-born Jew and veteran IWW activist, who had got himself elected assemblyman on the Socialist ticket in the Bronx in 1917.

Through the Allied blockade of the new Soviet regime in Russia came the news of Lenin's new Communist International, whose First Congress in March 1919 called on all socialists to unite in forming the Soviet World Republic. Among the 39 groups the Comintern's manifesto appealed to for support were four American elements:

33. The S.L.P. (U.S.A.)
34. The elements of the Left Wing of the Socialist Party (tendency represented by E.V. Debs and the Socialist Propaganda League)
35. I.W.W. (Industrial Workers of the World, America)
36. The Workers International Industrial Union (U.S.A.)

(By this time, of course, Rutgers was in Moscow attending the Congress and advising on American personalties and organizational groupings.)

As one communist later recalled the general psychological attitude of 1919, "The proletarian world revolution had begun. The workers were on the march. The Revolution would sweep on. In a few years —two, three, perhaps five—the workers of the United States would be marching step by step with the revolutionary workers of Europe."[2] And every American believer saw himself at their head. After all, who was Trotsky in January 1917 but an obscure Russian journalist on *Novy Mir* in New York? And Lenin, but a homeless exile in Switzerland? And now look at them!

"For a brief moment, the founders of American communism were destiny-intoxicated men," writes historian Theodore Draper, "appointed to end misery and oppression, break the chains of war, halt the exploitation of man by man, and create a new social order based on justice, freedom and equality."[3] Contributing to this apocalyptic atmosphere was the postwar U.S. labor strife. In February 1919 three gigantic strikes raged simultaneously. The first general strike in U.S. history closed down the entire city of Seattle, while in Lawrence, Massachusetts, over 30,000 textile workers shut down every mill for 16 weeks. In Butte, Montana, for the third time in three years, the miners walked out in rebellion against a wage cut and set up a Soviet-style "Soldiers', Sailors', and Workers' Council" to control the strike. John Reed's hometown of Portland, Oregon, produced a "Council of Workers, Soldiers, and Sailors" proclaiming its intention to "strike the final blow against the capitalist class." So heady was the atmosphere that the *Soviet World* of Philadelphia predicted the birth within the next two years of the Socialist Soviet Republic of the United States of America.[4]

THE SOCIALIST PARTY SPLITS   In the spring of 1919 it seemed as if the pro-Bolsheviks would sweep the Socialist Party. Local after local endorsed the left-wing program—Boston, Cleveland, Toledo, Akron Buffalo, San Francisco, Oakland, Portland, Philadelphia, Detroit, Seattle, Queens, Bronx, Brooklyn, and many others. Seven of the foreign language federations endorsed it. The left-wing demand to quit the Second International and affiliate with the Third carried a referendum more than ten to one. The left wingers won 12 of the 15 seats in the election of a new National Executive Committee. The best-known figures of the old moderate leadership went down to smashing defeat. According to official figures Fraina was the most popular man in the party. Reed and Fraina were chosen as international delegates. The pro-Bolshevik Socialists could claim almost 70,000 members or sympathizers. By April 1919 the prospect seemed so bright that Fraina and his comrades issued a call for a national conference of left wingers to be held in New York City on June 21, "to formulate a national declaration of Left Wing principles and concentrate our forces to conquer the Party for revolutionary Socialism."[5]

But the moderate Socialists had no intention of standing idly by while the extremists captured their party. The right wing launched a preventive war. Its leaders belittled the pro-Bolshevik election victories with cries of "fraud," pointing out that only a fifth of the total membership had bothered to vote and that the organized leftists and some of the language federations had bloc voted on an agreed-upon slate. In May 1919 the incumbent National Executive Committee met, invalidated the election, and promptly expelled the entire Michigan Socialist Party because a recent convention had amended its constitution to repudiate legislative reforms. Out went 6,000 party members. Next the committee expelled seven foreign language federations for endorsing the pro-Bolshevik program and 20,000 more members went out the window. With this mop-up as a start, the committee called a national emergency convention in Chicago on August 30.[6]

As if this wasn't trouble enough, the Michigan outcasts convened their own emergency state convention in June 1919, only a week before the New York National Left Wing Conference, and announced its intention of going to Chicago on September 1 to organize a U.S. party affiliated with the Comintern. This flew in the face of the announced left-wing strategy of capturing the existing Socialist Party.

The New York convention and subsequent birth of the Bolshevist hate organization in America was a comedy worthy of the Keystone Cops. Ninety-four delegates gathered at the Manhattan Lyceum from 20 states, some coming all the way from California. Fraina served as temporary chairman. In three days of debate the English-speaking delegates, most of them New Yorkers, lined up on one side against the foreign-language delegates and the Michigan group on the other, wanting to convert the conference into a full-fledged constituent assembly of a U.S. Communist Party. This proposal was finally beaten 55 to 38, whereupon the Michiganders and the foreign language delegates (most of them Russians) walked out.

COMPETING FOR THE LENINIST FRANCHISE   This was the beginning of factional power-struggles that kept the U.S. hate cartel largely immobilized for the next ten years. Though the competing factions wrangled in ideological and tactical terms, what they were really fighting about was simple: Who was going to be boss?

The remaining delegates in the New York conference established a National Left Wing Council, while the Michigan-Russian immigrant alliance set up a National Organization Committee. The New Yorkers sent the left-wing candidates who had won in the Socialist Party national committee elections to Chicago to hold a rump session and demand that the national headquarters be turned over to them. Rebuffed, most of the National Left Wing Council caved in and voted to join the Michigan-Russian convention scheduled simultaneously with the Socialist Party Convention in Chicago on September 1. With them went Lovestone and Fraina, but Reed and Gitlow still held out, determined to "capture" the whole Socialist Party. And Reed, Lenin's confidant and a romantic popular hero, swung considerable weight.

The ludicrous result was that Chicago found itself hosting *three* conventions. The official Socialist Party opened its convention on August 30 at Machinist's Hall. Reed and Gitlow led a band of 52 hardly revolutionists in an attempt to storm it. They arrived early, got into the second floor auditorium, and occupied seats. Thereupon the regular Socialists had police haul them out, Reed at the head of the lot screaming indignant propaganda about the use of the capitalist police against fellow proletarians.

The next evening at 6 P.M. on Sunday, August 31, 1919, Reed and Gitlow led their band, now numbering 82 from 21 states, downstairs in the Machinists Hall billiard room. There they solemnly proclaimed themselves the Communist Labor Party of America (CLP), gave three cheers for Eugene Debs in the Atlanta penitentiary, three cheers for the IWW, and then lustily sang the "Internationale." They voted down 37 to 31 a motion to unite with the other communist convention scheduled for the next day. Reed let it be known that the foreign federations could come crawling to his convention if they wanted a joint party.

The Third Convention was even more comical. At noon the next day, September 1, 1919, the Russians, the Michiganders, and the cowtail New Yorkers met at the headquarters of the Russian federation, 137 delegates strong. Their hall was decorated with red bunting, revolutionary placards, and two flower displays of roses on a red background shaped like a flag. Big pictures of Trotsky, Marx, and Lenin faced the audience. As the chairman was about to gavel the

[431   ]

meeting to order a platoon of detectives from the Chicago Police Department's "Anarchist Squad" bolted through the door. They ripped down the bunting, placards and flowers while police photographers snapped the entire assemblage, and a ten-piece brass band boomed forth the "Internationale." Sitting quietly—and no doubt amused—in the gallery taking notes was the agent-in-charge of the Chicago office of the Federal Bureau of Investigation![7]

Once the conventioneers got the police out of their way, they formally proclaimed themselves the "Communist Party of America" (CPA), and voted 75 to 31 not even to bother appointing a committee to talk to the rival convention. The issue that had split the two groups, whether to try to capture the Socialist Party, had now disappeared. Even so, both stoutly refused to unite, rejecting each other's overtures on petty excuses that would amaze even the average woman's club. The real issue: Who was going to control the party? Americans or foreigners? It was the same issue that had caused Lenin so much trouble with that old dreadnaught Sylvia Pankhurst in Britain: Was the Bolshevik party to be an isolated cult of revolutionists worshiping doctrinal purity and scorning mass appeal and political activity? Or was it to be a flexible machine for the pursuit of political power, using every means open to it, including legal activities such as participation in political campaigns and mass organizations?

ARRANGING THE CORPORATE MERGER   The two parties together had about 35,000 members (roughly 10,000 in the CLP and 25,000 in the CPA). But 90 percent of these belonged to the foreign-language federations which enrolled their members *en bloc*. Russian and East European membership accounted for over 75 percent of these—most of them converts to Bolshevism after Lenin's November triumph, but who nevertheless claimed to be the only true interpreters and high priests of their fellow Russian's doctrines. At most the communist movement had only three or four thousand native-born or English-speaking members in America; the situation was so bad that one Red chieftain complained that the CP did not have five speakers "who could present its cause in English and the same was true in regard to writers and editors." Within four months the Michigan group left the CPA and that reduced it even further to a foreign language sect.[8]

The CLP and the CPA set up separate newspapers. Both pledged total and unconditional loyalty to the Comintern, but constantly called each other heretical. The CLP, with a higher percentage of

English-speaking comrades, sneered at the CPA as a gang of isolated and impotent foreigners, while the CPA thundered back, "And this party protests its thorough internationalism!"⁹

This was one too many communist parties in America to suit the perplexed Comintern, which growled that they must combine "in the shortest possible time:

> Unity is not only possible, but absolutely necessary. The Executive Committee categorically insists on its immediate realization.¹⁰

And Moscow sent a Comintern "rep" to crack the whip. Not the Comrep, however, but practical politics brought about the first step. The English-speaking New Yorkers who had split with the Reed-Gitlow faction and remained in the CPA found themselves outvoted at every turn by the Russians who considered themselves the only true spokesmen for Moscow. So in May 1920 they split and held a secret "unity" convention with the CLP at Bridgman, Michigan, producing the "United Communist Party" as a result. After another year of bickering the UCP and the CPA held another secret two-week convention at Woodstock, New York in May 1921 and formed the CPA (Unified). Among other things, this convention endorsed Lenin's 21 demands.

TWO POPES: ONE TOO MANY   The U.S. Communist Party was now united, at least in name. But the factions quickly found something else to fight about. In January 1920 U.S. Attorney General A. Mitchell Palmer launched a series of raids and legal actions against radicals of all brands. Homes, headquarters, and meetings were raided, thousands arrested, and aliens deported by the hundreds. Membership melted away to barely more than 5,000,¹¹ and the Party went underground. This led to another long wrangle that gave Moscow no end of headaches: Whether the communists should remain strictly a "revolutionary" underground party, or whether they should organize an open political party. It took two years to paper over that wrangle.

The factional power struggles within the CPUSA eventually polarized around two figures, Jay Lovestone, the New York CCNY socialist firebrand, and William Z. Foster, the former IWW organizer who ran the explosive 1919 strike of 365,000 steelworkers, one of the major strikes of the decade. After the strike was crushed, Foster was famous, but a man without an organization or ideology, looking for a route to power. In 1921 Louis Fraina returned from Moscow on his way to Mexico with orders to recruit an American delegation to the founding congress of a new Comintern front group, the "Red International of Trade Unions." He recruited Foster, who was given the red carpet treatment and introduced to Lenin. Out of sheer infatuation with Leninist methodology, which he hoped would make him president of a Soviet America, Foster converted to Bolshevism. He was one of the very few Americans of native birth who were attracted to the early Bolshevik colonization. Lovestone and Foster fought for control of the CPUSA like two lovers who wanted to marry the same woman, knowing there could be no "compromise" or "accommodation." They waged their power struggle in the languages of doctrine and tactics, each criticizing the other's position on all sorts of grounds. The intricacies of this and other such pots of verbal spaghetti have bemused historians endlessly. But the ultimate issue was the same: Who was going to win the prize and rule the remade communist world?

Lovestone and his allies controlled the party from 1924 to 1929. Ultimately they lost because they failed to step lively enough to keep on the right side of the internal feuds in the Kremlin and to convince Moscow that they were the most subservient soldiers to run the bolshevized hate corporation in America. Lovestone's troubles began at the Comintern's Sixth World Congress in 1928, which marked the "turn to the left" for the Comintern and its global retinue of subsidiaries.

COMPETING FOR STALIN'S PROXY   The Comintern's first task had been contacting radical elements and establishing organizational bases in the chief nations of the world. The second had been to root out all the "left-wing" communists who had been let in the gates in the first process. This meant expelling the Trotskyites who wanted instant revolution and were not content to bide time, build up the organization, recruit, train, and patiently work and wait for favorable developments for revolution. Now Stalin and the Comintern high command were turning to the third task of expelling all others who, for various reasons, resisted absolute obedience to Stalin and wanted instead to maintain some form of individuality, freedom of action, and adaptability to local conditions. Stalin was completing Lenin's original goal of "bolshevizing" the colonized combat parties, which meant ensuring that they were a global monolith containing only fanatical functionaries absolutely faithful to the Leninist party line who could be counted on to follow loyally every switch in the Moscow dogma and Stalin's course.

Bukharin, by this time president of the Comintern, was selected as the personification of "right-wing" tendencies. And Lovestone had the bad luck to make some favorable remarks about Bukharin at the 1928 congress, not realizing that Stalin had marked him for extinction. Then, too, these Americans known as "Lovestonites" had too much of an independent demeanor about them to please the Stalinists for long. Soon after Lovestone returned to the United States he realized he was in trouble, for critical cables from the Comintern began to come in. That was all his opposition, the Fosterites, needed to start sharpening their knives.

MIDNIGHT SHOWDOWN IN MOSCOW The result was the most dramatic showdown between the parent and one of its fledgling Leninist corporations in Comintern history. The Lovestonites won 95 of 104 delegates to the sixth CPUSA convention that opened on March 1, 1929 in New York. But two "delegates" showed up representing Stalin. They were the "Comreps," British communist Harry Pollitt and Phillip Dengel, a German. And they brought secret orders for Lovestone's replacement by William Z. Foster. Lovestone was to be "reassigned" to the Comintern in Moscow, which could mean anything from physical liquidation to mere political annihilation and limbo. The Comintern order stunned the American communists. After much debate and infighting, the Lovestonites cabled Moscow a denunciation of Bukharin and obsequious praise for "the Bolshevik leadership headed by Comrade Stalin." They appealed to Stalin personally to reverse the Comintern's reorganization "proposals." Stalin relented on his demands that the convention elect Foster secretary general, but stuck to his proscription of Lovestone. The convention then elected Gitlow, Lovestone's top lieutenant, and decided to send a ten-man commission to Moscow to try to settle the dispute.

The Comintern appointed a twelve-man American commission to hear the U. S. comrades and resolve the problem. On the commission were Bela Kun, Walter Ulbricht of Germany, V. M. Molotov, and Stalin personally. Altogether it included eight Russians. The commission took a month to study documents, listen to speeches, cross-examine witnesses, and listen to the proposals from all the interested parties.

The commission's report personally excoriated Lovestone and his majority leaders, accusing them of all sorts of largely mythical ideological deviations such as "misleading honest proletarian Party members." The recommended solution: Complete reorganization of the CPUSA along lines suitable to Moscow, and removal of Lovestone from work in the American party.

The climax occurred the next night, May 14, 1929, when the full Presidium of the Communist International, permanent governing body of the ECCI, met in the Red Hall of Comintern headquarters to hear the report and decide the fate of the American movement. Stalin personally presided. About 150 participants and spectators assembled. U. S. students in the Lenin school had been efficiently mobilized to chime appeals for submission like a Greek chorus and make scolding speeches at dissenters. Speeches by the American delegates and others lasted long past midnight, but the outcome was a foregone conclusion: The vote was unanimous save only for Gitlow, the only American with a vote on the Comintern Presidium.

With that, Stalin rapped his gavel and declared that the decision was now final. Heretofore dissent had been permissible, but now the Presidium had made further opposition impossible. In the dead silence of 3 o'clock in the morning he looked squarely at the ten American comrades, then proceeded to poll them one by one, demanding to know whether they would accept and obey the decision. Seven declared they still stuck to their dissent. Two broke down and proclaimed, one tearfully, that they would not only accept the Comintern decision, but proclaim its "correctness." Gitlow, a pugnacious fellow who had spent two years in Sing Sing for his communist faith, spoke last. He attacked the decision. He repeated his devotion to communism as the true way to economic betterment and freedom, but said the decision was wrong and would deeply damage the cause he loved in America. "Not only do I vote against the decision," proclaimed Gitlow looking straight at Stalin, "But when I return to the United States I will fight against it!"

At that, a long whistle whispered through the crowd, and Stalin colored. He raced to the platform and burst into a tirade against the Americans, screaming:

> Who do you think you are? Trotsky defied me. Where is he? Zinoviev defied me. Where is he? Bukharin defied me. Where is he? And you? When you get back to America nobody will follow you except your sweethearts and wives.[12]

And then he added darkly, "There is plenty of room in our cemeteries!" With that he turned on his heels and started down from the platform, secretaries and guards heeling behind. As he stalked down the aisle he stopped at the American delegation and stuck out his hand to the one Negro among them, Edward Welsh, who was standing next to Lovestone. Welsh turned to Lovestone and asked loudly, "What the hell does this guy want?"[13]

Later the Kremlin published a laundered version of Stalin's speech, setting forth the doctrinal significance of what happened:

> We ought to value the firmness and stubbornness displayed here by eight out of the ten American delegates in their fight against the draft of the Commission. But it is impossible to approve the fact that these eight comrades, after their views have suffered complete defeat, refuse to subordinate their will to the will of the higher collective, the will of the Presidium of the ECCI. True Bolshevik courage does not consist in placing one's individual will above the will of the Comintern. *True courage consists of being strong enough to master and overcome one's self and subordinate one's will to the will of the collective, the will of the higher Party body. Without that there is not, and cannot be, any collective leadership.*[14]

That statement no doubt would have pleased Lenin.

THE LENINIZED SUBSIDIARY   Lovestone, Gitlow, and their cohorts had bet on holding their CPUSA majority together and defy Stalin and the Comintern's assertion of ultimate authority. But they lost. For they found that most communists could not bear the psychological shock of defying the Comintern and cutting themselves off from the emotional and financial support that flowed from being part of the monolithic Moscow-controlled messianic world movement. To their dismay, Lovestone, and Gitlow saw their supporters fade like the morning mists. Stalin was right: No one followed them but their wives and sweethearts. A bare 200 members backed their stand in Moscow, and the party expelled the lot of them. (In the following year, around 2,000 members simply left the party.) Lovestone and Gitlow made a pathetic attempt to rally by forming a "Communist Party (Majority Group)." It took Lovestone four months to gather a conference of 40 supporters and issue a publication, *Revolutionary Age.*[15] Without Moscow's money and the apocalyptic *élan* of international power, his tiny sect faded into obscurity, and its members became stout anti-Stalinists and even anti-communists—but impotent, nevertheless. The lesson was plain and large. With the minor exception of Tito, no other Leninist colony dared to challenge Moscow's absolute command for 30 years. In those three decades the world revolutionary movement was thoroughly Leninized.

VI. THE TECHNOLOGY DIFFUSES

Chapter 30
MUSSOLINI: THE ITALIAN LENINOID

What does it matter to the proletarian to understand socialism as one understands a theorem? And is socialism reducible to a theorem? We want to believe in it; we must believe in it. Humanity needs a *credo*. It is faith that moves mountains because it gives the illusion that mountains move. Illusion is perhaps the only reality of life.

—Benito Mussolini, 1912

Theory becomes physical force as soon as it takes possession of the masses. . . . Reality must urge itself toward the Idea. Philosophy cannot be realized without the uprising.

—Karl Marx, 1843

We have created an Ideal, which we will make a concrete reality.

—Benito Mussolini,
Naples Fascist rally
October 24, 1922, eve
of the "March on Rome"

We have failed to understand fascism because we have not understood it to be a variant of perhaps the most significant political phenomenon of the twentieth century: the totalitarian mass movement. By confining our vision to the sterile dichotomy of "left-wing" and "right-wing" movements and the artificial distinctions on which that classification rests or by making a tendentious categorization of the "progressive" and "reactionary" revolutions, we have lost sight of the most obvious realities. The twentieth century has witnessed the manifestation of a singular political phenomenon: the appearance of the revolutionary mass-mobilizng totalitarian movement. "Fascism," however one chooses to define the term, is simply a subset of that inclusive class.

The effort to find some pervasive distinction between "Leninist" and "fascist" movements, or between "revolutionary" or "conservative" movements is labored and unconvincing, since the similarities among totalitarian mass-mobilizing movements are far more compelling than their differences.[1]

—A. James Gregor,
Professor of Political Science,
University of California, Berkeley

A RADICAL IS A RADICAL   It is a testimonial both to the powers of fantasy of the contemporary leftists, and to the efficacy of their propaganda, that they have made the word "fascist" mean to the average American something distinct, and even opposed to, communism or their own brand of revolutionary radicalism. For twentieth-century fascism sprang full-grown from the radical revolutionary movement like Minerva from the head of Zeus.

In fact, Mussolini's fascism was nothing but a Marxian messianic will-to-power worked out in the particular social, economic, political matrix of the Italy of 1919–22. Mussolini himself was a lifelong romantic revolutionary, a card-carrying member of the Italian Socialist Party from his earliest teenage days until past his thirtieth birthday, and considered himself a good socialist and revolutionary until a short three years before his "March on Rome." He always referred to his seizure of power as "the fascist revolution" much as a Russian Bolshevik might refer to "the soviet revolution," and to Italians the word "fasci" meant about the same as "soviet" to the Russians.

Indeed, the differences between Lenin and Mussolini are ephemeral; the similarities are fundamental. For Mussolini was a pure Marxian and Leninoid messianic journalist who was forced by accident of history to found his garb for power on a different constituency from Marx's beloved "proletariat." Lenin made the change unobtrusively; Mussolini openly. Mussolini imposed a Leninist solution in a different milieu.

Mussolini was a utopian radical who started out from the precisely identical ideological point—a quest for the secular power to procrusteanize the world—as did the young Marx and the young Lenin. As Lenin did in 1898–1902, Mussolini discovered the folly of accepting too rigidly the "proletariat" designated as the prime market by the 24-year-old Marx. Lenin modified Marx by declaring that *all* classes contained discontented persons who would buy revolutionary utopian escapism; Mussolini found his buyers among the returning veterans, urban *petit bourgeoisie,* and industrialists—all alarmed and disgusted by the growing violence of Italy's radical socialist revolutionaries and the increasing incompetence of the democrats. Mussolini's ideology was a Rousseauist-Marxist amalgam; his methodology was Marxist-Leninist; his constituency was Leninist in that he took the discontented wherever he found them, but non-Marxist only in that he found them more among the *lumpenproletariat* and capitalists and *petit bourgeoisie* than among the pure Marxist proletariat.

THE ANARCHIST STRAIN   In 1864 Mikhail Bakunin preached his anarchist-Marxist mutant through Romagna, Mussolini's native province, leaving a trail of enthusiastic followers. They adhered to Marx's First International and the dream of a new social order. Among Bakunin's admirers was Alessandro Mussolini, a prodical who squandered his family's farm and became a blacksmith's apprentice.

At 18 he embraced revolutionary socialism, and always remained his village's romantic radical. He opened his own smithy, promoted the local branch of the International, wrote socialist articles, started a cooperative and introduced the first threshing machine. The police jailed him for six months on a charge that he had a "bent for blood crimes and banditry, and had been accused by popular voice, and was therefore believed dangerous to society and public order." The only evidence: A few Bakunin pamphlets, and letters from other Italian adherents of the International. Ultimately Allessandro became his village's vice mayor and town counsellor, a political career that ended in 1902 (Benito was 18) with his arrest for his part in electoral disorders; he spent five months in jail awaiting his trial and was acquitted.

Allessandro named the son born on July 29, 1803, Benito Amilcare Romagnol Mussolini, after Benito Juárez, leader of the savage revolt against Emperor Maximilian in Mexico; a prominent Italian anarchist; and a founder of the Italian Socialist Party. The baby was destined by name and paternal design to be a revolutionary.

Years later, after his "Fascist Revolution" made him dictator of the nation, Benito Mussolini confessed shamelessly to his official biographer: *"I am obsessed by this wild desire. It inflames, gnaws, consumes me like a disease. I want to make a mark on history with my will, like a lion with his claw! A mark like this!"* And savagely he scratched his chairback from end to end. He had the basic messianic lust for significance that impelled Marx, Lenin, and the rest of the pack. The villagers remembered him as a dreamer who would sit for hours gazing across the valley. "One day I shall astonish the world," he told his mother.

Benito was also an incredibly stormy brawler. Though an atheist and rabidly anti-Catholic, Allessandro admitted the boy at nine was beyond his control and sent him to a Catholic boys' school noted for stern discipline. Benito rode off in their donkey cart, his hand bandaged from having swung at a companion and missed, banging against a wall. Disobedient, quarrelsome, self-willed, moody and quick-tempered, he was expelled from two schools for stabbing schoolmates and leading a strike for better food at one.

He received his diploma at 18, spent six months as a schoolteacher, and began a long, anarchic series of love affairs. Writing a 90-page biography at age 28 while in jail, he named 15 women and wrote of others; after he became Italy's dictator his satyriasis required a steady stream of profligate women. Of his 1902 stint at teaching, Mussolini himself wrote: "I was a Bohemian in those days. I made my own rules and I did not keep even them." He took a

20-year-old mistress, always bullied and abused her, and once even stabbed her—the third stabbing he admitted. In his biography he describes raids on dance halls with other hooligans, fights over girls, numerous rapes of prostitutes, and one case at least, rape of a woman who was not, while her husband was away.

All the while the young Benito drank thirstily of his father's socialist preachments:

> Socialism is open and violent rebellion against our inhuman state of things. It is the knowledge and the light of the world. It is free love taking the place of a legal contract. It is justice coming to an unjust world, a free pact among all men. . . .

Such doctrine of righteous rebellion inevitably fed Benito's rebel soul. He took part in the May Day celebrations and Marxian arguments, and absorbed the platitudes from the Socialist press.

Mussolini early discovered a passion for declamation. Like Demosthenes on the seashore, he would stand on the hills above Predappio, his village, reciting lyrical and patriotic poems in a powerful voice, which grew so deep and sonorous that Lady Oxford would one day describe it as the most beautiful voice she had ever heard. His school teachers tapped him to make the address commemorating Verdi's death.

In July 1902, after six months school-teaching, 18-year-old Benito went to Switzerland with only a medallion of Karl Marx in his pocket. He existed as a tramp, hungry, ill, living in a public lavatory, or in a packing crate under a bridge until police arrested him for vagrancy and he spent three days in jail. But at summer's end, he contacted some Italian socialists, made his debut as a radical journalist by contributing to a Socialist newspaper, and became secretary for propaganda with the Lausanne bricklayers and laborers union.

Mussolini began to read voraciously: Lassalle, Kautsky, Kropotkin, Nietzsche, Schopenhauer, Kant, Spinoza, Hegel, Fichte, Babeuf, Proudhon, Blanqui, Sorel. He never went far into Marx, but found Blanqui's angry life and writings exciting. Significantly, the only book he mentioned in his autobiography was Gustave Lebon's *The Crowd*.

Mussolini spoke almost every Sunday to workers in Berne and Lucerne, spinning oratorical visions of violence, breathing atheism, class warfare, rebellion, and apocalypse. His extremism made him a hero of the crowds—and a target to the police. The Swiss authorities jailed him twice, in 1903 for his verbal arson before his union in

Berne when he proposed a general strike and violence to enforce demands, and again in 1904. Jailed briefly, he was put over the border each time, but returned to a different Swiss canton.

Mussolini spent most of his evenings with the quarrelsome, wild Russian nihilists and bohemians. They called him "Benitouchka." He referred to himself as "an apostle of violence," and asked repeatedly, "When will the day of vengeance come?" No evidence indicates Mussolini and Lenin ever met, though both were in Switzerland at the same time. But on March 18, 1904, Mussolini spoke at the commemoration of the Paris Commune before an audience of Germans, Italians, French, and Russians. Dirty and unshaven, he nevertheless spoke so volcanically and magnetically that Angelica Balabanoff asked to meet him and offered help. They soon developed a close intellectual relationship. Balabanoff ultimately moved to Rome, where she joined the Italian Socialist Party, and continued for ten years to tutor Mussolini in revolutionary ideology and propaganda. In 1904 she found him dirty, neurotic, self-pitying, vengeful, and a sponger who hated to work. He was constantly complaining of his health and boasting of his virility. Balabanoff came to feel his boisterous glorification of strength and violence were covers for weakness and fear, and that his socialism was based not on sympathy but on a compulsive craving for leadership and recognition. In her memoirs, she recalled their first meeting. She had never seen "a more wretched human being. In spite of his large jaw, the bitterness and restlessness in his black eyes, he gave the impression of extreme timidity. Even as he listened, his nervous hands clutching at his big black hat, he seemed more concerned with his own inner turmoil than with what I was saying."

Four weeks later Mussolini was in jail for the second time, and a Geneva correspondent for Rome's *La Tribuna* sent back an item referring to him as "il grand duce" of the local Italian Socialist club. Fighting expulsion, he wrote a Swiss comrade:

> People will tell you that I am an "anarchist." Well, comrade, nothing could be more false . . . I defy any authority to find a single article of mine, a single line or argument that could classify me among the anarchists. I have always been registered, both in Italy and in Switzerland, in the Socialist Party.

Late in 1904 Mussolini went home after the king had granted draft dodgers amnesty, pausing in Lugano to see Balabanoff. "Look!" he

growled, waving toward the hotels and restaurants lining the beautiful lakefront. "People eating, drinking, and enjoying themselves.
And I will travel third class, eat miserable cheap food. Porca
Madonna, how I hate the rich! Why must I suffer this injustice? How
long must we wait?"

Mussolini proved a docile soldier, despite his antimilitarist
ideology. Back in Predappio after twenty months, he promptly
landed in jail for three months for siding with the casual laborers
against their "oppressors" the tenant farmers. After two years teaching grammar school, calling himself "Professor Mussolini," he went
to Trento, in Italian Austria, to take a union post and contribute to
the revolutionary weekly.

THE REVOLUTIONARY JOURNALIST   Mussolini exploded at
a complex range of targets, from the Masons to the landlords to the
militarists, nationalists, and Catholics. He ecstatically reviewed
Georges Sorel's new book, *Reflections on Violence*. This French engineer and bridge-builder, turning to Marx in middle age, found Marx
had paid insufficient attention to the means by which the proletariat
was to achieve and then preserve its power; he thus became a syndicalist, holding that the unions, not the state, should own the means
of production. Sorel exhalted the general strike as the ultimate
weapon, and glorified violence in a passage Mussolini quoted:

> Proletarian violence, actuated as a pure manifestation of the sentiment
> of class warfare, appears therefore very beautiful and very epic. It is
> at the service of fundamental interests of civilization and can save the
> world from barbarism.

Such socialist violence, Mussolini reverberated, in the "permanent
war between bourgeoisie and proletariat will generate new energies,
new moral values, new men who will be close to ancient heroes."
Here was pure Marx, pure Nechayev, Chernyshevsky, Lenin.

In eight months "Professor" Mussolini served five or six three-day
jail sentences for libel and other press-law violations rather than pay
small fines, thus inflating his reputation. "I shall break the 'record' for
trials," he boasted. Finally, a blast at the Catholic Church ("that great
corpse"), the Vatican ("that den of intolerance and gang of robbers"),
and Christianity generally ("humanity's immortal stigma of oppro-
brium") got him expelled from Austria in September 1909.

Returning to Romagna, Mussolini became secretary of the Forli

Socialist Federation and founded and edited a four-page weekly named *The Class Struggle*. In it, Mussolini extolled "the iron necessity of violence," praised bomb-throwers and other terrorists from Russia to Los Angeles, and called Italy's parliament "the parliament of the underworld" and "a vain chimera, the great club of the corrupters and the corrupted." Such vitriol got him quoted often in the great Socialist Party official daily in Milan, *Avanti! (Forward)*. He once spent 15 days in jail for threatening to cane a man he thought a "scab" organizer, and led a march on the town hall threatening to throw the mayor out a window if he did not get a cut in milk prices.

In Forli, as boss of the radical socialist clubs and their propaganda organ, Mussolini flowered as a true proto-Leninist, mastering the theory and art of organizing an elite corps of professional propagandists and managing a mass movement. He built his Forli federation squarely along Leninist lines, and in 1911, when the reform wing gained ascendency in the Socialist Party he actually seceded, just like Lenin in 1903–04.

Biographer Gaudens Megaro says of this period:

> In matters of revolutionary tactics and strategy, he was a thoroughgoing Blanquist and might well have been called a spiritual brother of Lenin. Like Lenin and the Bolsheviks, Mussolini was not as much concerned with the organization of a mass party of workers on a democratic basis as he was with forming a group of ardent, resolute revolutionists who would be prepared to execute a violent revolutionary uprising and to lead, if not to "drag along," the mass of workers to support such an act. Implicit in his tactical considerations is what we should now commonly call the "dictatorship of the proletariat" as a necessary step in the building of a socialist state . . . Mussolini's purpose was to make the Forli federation the nucleus of a nationwide revolutionary socialist party.[2]

Mussolini became a genius in hypnotizing his audiences with his "magnificent bass voice" by hurling "short, staccato sentences" and using rhetorical queries to evoke chanted responses like the great evangelists. He also learned to use the newspaper to gather crowds and generate protests, and to stage-manage street demonstrations with secret internal commands and claques.

In 1911 Italy and Turkey went to war over North African colonies. The labor confederation called a general strike, but in Forli Mussolini urged workers not to strike but to revolt. He led two days of riots, cut telephone and train lines to stop troop movements, and landed in jail again. Toward the end of his five-month term, he mused in his jail autobiography, "What does the future hold in store for me?"

It held much: His very volcanic vocabulary had won him notice, and his extremism thrust him into leadership. He left prison a local hero in March 1912. *Avanti!* hailed him as "our noble idealist" and a banquet was held in his honor. Exploiting his martyrdom, the extreme revolutionaries—including his old friend Balabanoff—chose him to lead a coup at the 1912 Socialist Party convention designed to capture control of the party for its revolutionary wing. To a staged ovation, he rose and moved to expel four Socialist members of parliament who joined others in congratulating the king on escaping an assassination attempt. It was "parliamentary idiocy, that unmistakable disease so acutely diagnosed by Marx, in its most serious and mortifying forms," Mussolini said. The recent vote extending universal suffrage was "oxygen that prolongs the dying." The expelled deputies took many comrades with them and founded a new "reform socialist party." The split's engineers rewarded Mussolini by naming him editor of *Avanti!* He accepted, on the condition that Balabanoff function as his assistant editor. Within ten years one would become aide to the dictator of Russia and secretary of the first global political party, the Communist International, designed to colonize the Bolshevik brand of fascism around the world. And one would become dictator of Italy.

Almost unbelieving, Mussolini at age 29 found himself the leading spokesman for the Italian Socialist Party, and master of the most marvelous machine he had ever touched, its daily newspaper and a truly national newspaper at that. He soon proved he was maestro enough for the apocalyptic orchestra at hand.

Mussolini made *Avanti!* more combative and rigid. He encouraged and supported strikes and sounded an insurrectional tone throughout, and exploited a brash, bold typography. Within months Mussolini doubled the newspaper's circulation; within two years it zoomed from 28,000 to 100,000, numbers round enough to make the onetime editor of *Iskra* envious.

On June 7, 1914, a first Sunday and "Constitution Day," a former Mussolini jailmate from his 1912 sentence agitated a crowd in the Adriatic village of Ancona and police fired, killing three. The Socialist Party and General Confederation of Labor called a general strike in protest, and paralyzed all Italy. Mussolini as *Avanti!* editor quarterbacked the signals: "The answer will arise spontaneously!" he exclaimed in Monday's paper. It happppened almost so: Fierce mobs attacked trains, burned churches and city halls, seized property. Mussolini himself in a sports stadium speech blasted the "policy of carnage," led one crowd into Milan's streets, and got himself proudly bashed by the police—but not so badly as to prevent him returning to the stadium next day for another speech.

After three days the strike subsided, and "Red Week" was over. Mussolini drew a true Leninist conclusion:

> If a movement like the present has been possible with the speed and simultaneity which have terrified bourgeois public opinion, this is due —it is not a sin of pride to affirm it—to our newspaper, which daily brings its words to the exploited of Italy. . . . We openly admit and claim our responsibility in these events and in the political situation forming as a result.

THE BIG SWITCH   World War I exploded just after "Red Week," in August 1914. In *Avanti!* Mussolini instantly hurled the same antimilitary slogans and epithets he had used in 1912 against the Turkish war. But in his heart, just like Lenin in Austria, Mussolini suffered torments of doubt. Clearly, Marx's doctrine of international solidarity was wrong. In France, Germany, Britain, and Austria, socialist parliamentarians voted huge war credits for slaughtering their proletarian brothers across national boundaries. And even though Italy declared neutrality, Mussolini watched the Italian syndicalists and nationalists advocating intervention and winning mass sympathy. Mussolini began to fear that he might lose control of the socialist "masses" and miss the great tide of history. Did not the great Marx himself declare that wars often precede and produce revolutions?

"I want to guide the Party intelligently," Mussolini confided to a fellow journalist. "A general conflict is inevitable. The defeat of France would be a death-blow to liberty in Europe. The Socialist Party should not turn its back on the possibility of intervention on the side of France. . . ." Word reached a Bologna publisher who secretly offered to finance Mussolini in an interventionist paper—possibly acting for the Italian Foreign Ministry, which favored intervention and saw a chance to split the largest antiwar party.

So on October 26 Mussolini abruptly quit *Avanti!* and on November 14 his new daily appeared advocating intervention. Significantly, to replace his 1910 choice of *The Class Struggle,* Mussolini blazoned his new daily *The People of Italy.*

This sudden switch to "imperialist warmongering" stunned Mussolini's Socialist Party comrades. They leaped to the conclusion he had sold out for "French gold." (That did not come until several months later, apparently.) In turn, they dealt Mussolini a stunning blow. On November 24 a called Socialist Party meeting convened at a Milan theater to consider his expulsion. As Mussolini rose to explain his revolutionary analysis and plead his case, the comrades threw coins, paper balls, even chairs. Against the pandemonium, realizing his cause lost, he yelled, "You cannot get rid of me because I am and always will be a Socialist!" In a near-hysterical voice, he screamed, "You will all be forced into the war. . . . Your votes against me mean nothing." Some said later his eyes filled with tears. He walked out, leading a small band of "Mussolinians."

MUSSOLINI'S LENINIST TRAJECTORY   Like Lenin in 1904, Mussolini in 1914 found himself an exile from his own party. Very well, then, like Lenin he would build his own party. Unlike Lenin, he was not weaponless. He had his newspaper, and the magnetic messianic violence and picture of the "New Jerusalem" he projected through that newspaper attracted his party. He discovered the magnetic power of hate media, even as Lenin in 1905 and Babeuf in 1795 had done. As a consequence of his incendiarism, Mussolini soon found himself a pole around which assorted anarchists, syndicalists, socialists, revolutionaries, and nondescript radicals gravitated.

And as he had sensed, the Socialist Party did indeed slump. In 1915 Italy declared war. Mussolini was called up, and served honorably in combat. He turned his tour into a field study in social psychology which he exploited in building his movement: "I found my recreation in the trenches studying the psychology of officers and troops. Later on that practice in observation became invaluable to me." (Mussolini may well have been the first politician in history to speak explicitly of "studying psychology.") In February 1917 he was badly wounded when a mortar exploded, and returned in August to his Milan editorial office on crutches—which he used longer than necessary for dramatic effect.

After the war Mussolini began experimenting with various appeals, seeking to create an ideological-propaganda recipe to mobilize a mass movement and seize power. It did not happen all at once, but eventually he got the mix right—and its chief ingredients were utopianism, violent rhetoric, and violent action.

For both Mussolini and Lenin, the 1914 outbreak forced a fundamental rethinking of theory and tactics. But neither ever deviated from the ultimate radical goal: revolution and a radical remaking of reality into a dream-state, a Kingdom Come. Both Mussolini and Lenin slipped into anarchosyndicalism. Lenin's 1917 *State and Revolution* is utter Rousseau-Bakunin blather, as he and his successors as today's Soviet czars were forced to realize in embarrassed silence. After August 1914 Lenin decided that the best revolutionary course was to convert the international war into a proletarian civil war against the bourgeois and autocratic governments while they were engaged abroad. Mussolini decided that the myth of the nation would better inspire the people of all classes to unite and smash the state in the name of the utopian revolution. The two differed only in detail, not in basic design or aim or world view or motive. For Mussolini the 1914 switch was nothing more than a shift of slogan-selection and target-audience analysis.

Forced to conclude that the International was dead, Mussolini on November 10, 1914, explained his resignation from *Avanti!* and switch to interventionism, in the manipulative terms of propaganda warfare:

> The source of our psychological difficulty is this: we Socialists have never examined the problems of *nations.* The International never occupied itself with them . . . We must find a conciliation between *the nation, which is a historic reality,* and class, which is a living reality. It is certain that the nation represents a stage in human progress that has not yet been transcended . . . *The sentiment of nationality exists,* it cannot be denied!

Here Mussolini was backing up to the point from which Karl Marx departed in the fall of 1843 when, as a young messianic philosopher-general hunting an army to lead to Armageddon, in Kreuznach he stumbled on Lorenz von Stein's work and decided "the proletariat" would be the horse the intellectual tick could ride to glory (see Chapter 8). Mussolini, from the same point, decided that the twentieth century required a revaluation and new conclusion: The revolutionary radical must ride the nationalist masses—and build nationalist "consciousness"—instead. Again: no change in objective, merely in propaganda myths and slogans. He simply substituted the myth of national solidarity for the myth of proletarian solidarity.

Mussolini's 1914 "switch" has been made to seem mysterious by those writers who do not understand the essence of revolutionary radicalism and Leninism, and who therefore depict the change as greater than it was. Actually it was no more nor less amazing than Lenin's 1903 split and subsequent party-building within the Russian Marxist movement. Like Lenin, Mussolini was equally a strong-willed and talented power-questing messianic hunting an army. He split with the Socialist Party just as Lenin split with the Mensheviks —because he saw a greater army elsewhere, and a superior pathway to revolutionary victory. The Karl Marx of 1843 would have approved. Both Mussolini and Lenin, in fact, were engaging in exactly the same myth-making and slogan-seeking experimentation that Marx and Engels launched in 1850 when Marx undertook his "thick book" to provide a myth that would captivate and move the proletarian masses. Both Mussolini and Lenin were casting about for the correct combination of ideology, myth, and slogans to move the masses.

Mussolini was greatly influenced by Sorel, who specifically denounced the Marxian thesis that the revolutionary consciousness of the proletariat could be an inevitable consequence of the maturation of the productive forces.[3] Thus, independently, Mussolini—and Sorel —reached exactly the same conclusion Lenin reached in *What Is To Be Done?* when he wrote:

> The working class, exclusively by its own effort, is able to develop only trade-union consciousness and cannot without the propaganda bombardment designed by an elite of professional revolutionaries raise itself to a revolutionary consciousness. (5 *Collected Works* 375)

Increasingly in Mussolini's writings after 1914 we see the growing conviction that national sentiment is the prime mover for change. The energy for prospective revolution is supplied not by a class, but by a *people,* and to agitate and direct these elemental energies an elite was necessary. "Mussolini's development was surprisingly similar to that followed by Lenin after 1900," notes Professor A. James Gregor, one of the most astute scholars of totalitarian ideologies:

> Both Lenin's and Mussolini's interpretation of classical Marxism divested it of its monofactorial pretenses and assigned significant, if indeterminant, weight to human will and consciousness.[4]

Mussolini also independently adopted Lenin's 1902 modification of Marxism that the revolutionary must seek out *all classes,* not just the proletariat, and seek to combine "every droplet" of discontent "into a raging torrent" (see Chapter 19). Until August 1918 Mussolini kept the subtitle "Socialist Daily" beneath his newspaper's masthead. Then he changed it to "The Daily of Fighters and Producers," thus blazoning Lenin's 1902 injunction to revolutionaries "go among all classes . . . dispatch units in all directions" (see Chapter 19). Producers were not solely laborers because "there is work which does not cause sweat, or the famous calluses on the hands," Mussolini decided. He was removing all boundaries to his propaganda appeals—again a Leninist modification right out of *What Is To Be Done?* It placed him in a position to draw money from the wealthy manufacturers, like the Bolsheviks; and to appeal to the three million veterans, who proved a more powerful constituency than Mussolini could have foreseen in 1918.

Mussolini dramatized this modification of Marx visually in the symbol he adopted in 1919 for his new revolutionary movement: the Roman fasces. Roman magistrates carried as symbols of their authority bundles of elm or birch rods from which the head of an ax projected, fastened together by a red strap or band—"fascia" in modern Italian means band. The Roman fasces represented the consul's sovereignty and power of life and death, and in assemblies were lowered before the people who were the ultimate authority and to whom final appeal was allowed. The symbolism also lay in the fact that any single stick would be frail and easily broken, but bound together they comprised a strong, unbreakable unity. In later years Mussolini wrote: "This historical, political and moral agency is something I have created by a propaganda which runs from the days of intervention until now."[5] He made the symbol mean to Italians something like "solidarity" or "togetherness" or "unity"—including even overtones of "brotherhood" or "communism." Such a choice was shrewd—and Leninist.

In fact, at the very moment when Mussolini was publicizing and creating his *fasci di combattimento,* he did not hesitate to emulate the Bolsheviks even to the point of considering his term "fasci" the equivalent of the Russian term "soviet." In November 1918 socialists in Bavaria had proclaimed a "socialist republic" under Kurt Eisner, and on April 6 a "republic of soviets." In Hungary on March 20, 1919, Bela Kun proclaimed his Bolshevist regime. Ten days later Mussolini in *Il Popolo* vibrated with enthusiasm:

We must introduce something new; this consists in the formation of national councils. This is the method for overcoming the dilemma: either parliament or soviet . . . Kurt Eisner, the major theorist of the German revolution, placed himself upon this road.

Mussolini always remained in his own mind a revolutionary radical. As he cried upon his 1914 expulsion, "Twelve years of my life in the Party should be a sufficient guarantee of my Socialist faith. Socialism is something that takes roots in one's blood." He continued calling himself a socialist and as late as 1920, after he had made his transition to nationalist utopianism and was barely two years away from seizing power, Mussolini could still proclaim in *Il Popolo* that he was among the minority—

in potential revolt against the state, not against this or that state, but against the state in itself. . . . Down with the state in all its forms and incarnations, the bourgeois state, the socialist state. The state of yesterday, today, and tomorrow. There remains for me now nothing but the consoling religion of Anarchism.

As in Lenin's 1917 *State and Revolution* there was the suggestion that the state would wither away and the nation would become a free association of productive syndicates, the "noble savage" living in "the Republic of Virtue." And to his death Mussolini always called his power seizure "the Fascist Revolution."

"The more things change, the more they stay the same."

SEEKING A COMBINATION THAT WOULD CLICK   On Sunday morning, March 23, 1919, Mussolini convened a meeting of perhaps a hundred followers from the curious ragbag of discontented socialists, syndicalists, republicans, anarchists, restless soldiers, and unclassifiable revolutionaries who rallied about his newspaper. For three weeks *Il Popolo* had drummed up the meeting to found a "new force," but at most a hundred showed up, at least half from Milan. They endorsed resolutions swearing undying opposition to neutralism, demanding territorial gains for Italy, supporting the League of Nations and denouncing imperialism, and backing veterans' demands. For the first time Mussolini used his fasces symbol, and called the new political organization *Fasci di Azione Rivoluzionaria*—the Revolutionary Action Groups. "Fascism" was born.

He built his paramilitary force out of returning veterans who could not demobilize psychologically and return to the placid and even dull life of civilian routine. The trench warfare of World War I gave rise to special "storm troop" units recruited to lead the assaults. They were drawn from the toughest, meanest, most reckless of men, for obvious reasons. They wore black uniforms with skull-and-crossbones insignias. In Germany they were called "storm troops" and were antecedents of Hitler's paramilitary units of the same name. The Italians called theirs *arditi*, or literally, "the bold ones." Mussolini spoke to a victory celebration in Milan on November 19, 1918, and as the cheers died he climbed down from the granite monument in the square and walked to a truckload of *arditi*. They made room and swung him aboard for a rousing ride through Milan's streets, then stopped at a sidewalk cafe where they drank champagne and Mussolini delivered a patriotic paen to their will, courage, and power. Next day a band of these blackshirts visited his *Il Popolo* office to present him with their black flag and white skull, which he hung on the wall behind his desk. They became a devoted bodyguard—and the famed fascist "blackshirts" were born. They became "Fasci di Combattimento," or "battle groups." In June 1919 he first put them to work breaking up a Red rally and storming and burning the *Avanti!* offices—the first of many such clashes to come.

Mussolini made a virtue of having no program. Throughout his four-year ascent to power, he experimented with slogans, always seeking the combination that would click. His newspaper approved the first postwar strikes and factory seizures, advocating handing over industrial management to the workers along the traditional anticapitalist, antibourgeois line. His advocacy of territorial gains attracted the veterans. He "fancied himself the Lenin of Italy," one observer noted, and to charges of vagueness in his early fascism he made this thoroughly Leninist proclamation:

> *We allow ourselves the luxury of being aristocratic and democratic, reactionary and revolutionary, legalistic and illegalistic, according to the circumstances of place, time, and environment in which we are compelled to live and act.*

Mussolini argued that "fascism" was not a party but a movement, and hence not bound by programs or formulas. Not until November 1921 did he formally found the Fascist Party, and even then he remained vague about aims. He foreshadowed the American SDS radical Mark Rudd's famous 1968 answer: "First we will make a revolution; then we will find out what for." Mussolini in 1922 answered:

> Our program is simple: we wish to govern Italy. They ask us for programs but there are already too many. It is not programs that are wanting for the salvation of Italy, but men and will power.

In June 1919, readying for fall elections, Mussolini published his first attempt at a mobilizing propaganda combination: a leftist, revolutionary program supporting workers' demands, a share in management of industry, a progressive tax on capital, "a real partial expropriation of all wealth." Vainly he tried to form a bloc of leftist groups, but finally had to put forward 20 candidates on an exclusive fascist ticket. In the November 16 election he polled 4,657 out of 346,000 votes in Milan, while the Socialists won 156 of the 535 Parliament seats, their biggest national victory ever. *Avanti!* proclaimed Mussolini "a political corpse" and the Socialists celebrated his "death" with a mock funeral parade through the streets.

It was a premature burial. In thoroughly Leninist fashion Mussolini analyzed the election result as proof he could not win the workers from their traditional socialist position, and dropped his proletarian language and stance for new slogans. He correctly sensed that Italians were getting fed up with the anarchy that Socialists and proto-Bolshevik radicals were generating. Strikes and riots against inflation were rife; 450,000 workers struck that year. Mobs attacked trains, banks, public buildings. The "communists" were proclaiming "soviets." By September 1920 the workers seizure of factories was widespread, and "Red leagues" of peasants were seizing land. The Christian Democrats, liberal constitutionalists, wallowed, and the Socialist leaders were unable to channel the mass movement. Yet as Mussolini later told Hitler, "At the moment when he undertook the struggle against Bolshevism, he did not know exactly where he was going."[6]

On October 30, 1919, Mussolini wrote: "We are organizing bands of twenty men each with some sort of uniform and weapons . . . in order to insure our freedom of speech." Just as he had used his newspaper during "Red Week" in 1914 to spread violence through propaganda, he now spread his "movement" through *Il Popolo*, "spontaneous" yet organized. His fascist bands sprang like mushrooms in northern Italy in response to the Red violence. Despairing of government protection, industrialists and landowners countered by supporting Mussolini's paramilitary squads. Between April 1919 and September 1920 police, Communists, anarchists and fascists clashed 140 times in strikes and riots, with over 320 deaths. By November 1920 clashes were becoming real warfare. Between October 1920 and the March on Rome in October 1922, an estimated 3,300 fascists and communists, antifascists and anticommunists (not all antifascists were communists, nor all anticommunists fascists) died in virtual civil war. Turin's *La Stampa* poignantly complained:

> Educated at the same school, moved by the same adoration of the principle of violence, fascists and communists no longer have the power to keep themselves in check, and in the mad transport of their passion, excited by blood, hatred, and the spirit of revenge, they throw themselves at each other with guns, pistols, grenades and daggers.

Mussolini fanned the flames astutely, presenting fascism as the only force that could suppress the Bolshevist agitation that was undermining the beloved "nation." To many Mussolini appeared to be the only man with voice and will to embody strong government and restore domestic peace. Everywhere there were communist groups, his *fasci* grew; a retired officer, veterans, and hoodlums would coalesce to fight the Reds who had beaten officers and spat upon uniformed men in their antimilitarist demonstrations. *Il Popolo* cried praise of their magnificent deeds, courage, virtue. Mussolini was masterfully wielding the magic mass-media magnetism of violence that had worked so well for Lenin in 1905–07. The difference between the Reds and the Blacks was that in Italy the Reds lacked a leader with Lenin's will and charisma. Mussolini simply out-Leninized the Italian Leninists at their own game!

The Christian Democrats, with 100 seats to the Socialists' 156, were a minority government (see Chapter 24) and their weak, nearly paralyzed government quickly slid into economic crisis, flooding both the communists and fascists with troubled, frustrated people seeking escape from a very cruel reality: unemployment. From only 100,000 the jobless level rose in little more than twelve months to 600,000 at the start of 1922. Mussolini formed an antisocialist alliance with the aging premier Giolitti for the May 1921 election and at age 37 won a seat in Parliament for himself and 34 other fascists. By November, when he formally constituted the Fascist Party, he had

320,000 members in some 2,200 *fasci* (up from 30 *fasci* with 870 members at the start of 1920).

THE MARCH ON ROME   In August 1922 the Socialists tried a general strike. Mussolini sent his *fasci* into the streets to fight the strikers and to supply essential services—deliver the mail, operate the streetcars, and such. Sensing the climate, he began to emphasize the need for a strong man, a strong will, a strong government—and a March on Rome. "The new generations are not going to let the corpse of democracy block their way into the future," he wrote on August 19. Rumors buzzed for weeks. On October 26, 1922, Mussolini marshalled his *fasci* 40,000-strong for a grand review in Naples, really an assessment of strength. Before the parade at the San Carlo plaza he made the most crucial speech of his career. It is notable for its haunting similarity to the young Marx's essays on "the realization of philosophy" and how "philosophy takes possession of the masses." Mussolini compares his "ideal" with the inferior "idealism of socialism."

> We have created an Ideal, an Ideal that is a Faith, a passion. It does not need to be a reality, it is a stimulus and a hope, belief and courage. Our Ideal is the Nation, the grandeur of the Nation, which we will make a concrete reality.*

"We have created an Ideal . . . which we will make a concrete reality." The 25-year-old Marx would have recognized himself in that statement.

Mussolini moved *forte fortissimo* to the ultimate question:

> Legality or illegality? Parliamentary or revolutionary conquests How is fascism to become the state? For we *mean* to become the state!
> . . . Either the government will be given to us or we shall seize it by marching on Rome!

*The original Italian is: "Noi abbiamo creato il nostro mito." The usual translation of *mito* is *myth,* and the word was used by Sorel, in his development of the thought of Pareto, Mosca and Michels, to represent the belief system by which a ruling elite welds the class, nation or people into a coherent whole. Mussolini had of course studied the Sorelian interpretation and variation of Marxism. But San Severino (*Mussolini Speeches*, 1923) translates *mito* as "ideal." Given Mussolini's background as a socialist newspaper editor, a pupil-companion of the Marxist Balabanoff, and the history of Hegelian philosophy's concern with the ideal, "ideal" is probably a more enlightening, meaningful rendering. Like Marx, Mussolini was concerned with the empirical necessity of "philosophy taking possession of the masses" in the name of a utopian dream. In short, how does the philosopher grab power and make himself king? He sells an ideal, a myth—and then establishes a dictatorship of Platonic Guardians of the revolution and its dream. Clearly, the difference is one of detail, not essence. It is still a matter of the Grand Manipulator's guess as to the marketability of his propaganda.

His claque responded: "ROME! ROME!" And thousands of voices echoed the cry.

The March on Rome began. Mussolini retired to Milan, conferring with his high command by telephone, rallying fascist bands from more cities. On October 27 an estimated 70,000 were camping outside Rome, awaiting word on what to do. Everybody vacillated and bluffed. The army began blowing up bridges and cutting rail lines. In many provinces fascists were commandeering autos, seizing weapons, taking hostages, cutting telephone lines, and occupying public buildings, army depots, railroad stations. The cabinet voted a "state of seige" and resigned to allow the premier to negotiate. Premier Facto tried bartering a few cabinet posts. Mussolini's answer: *ALL*—or civil war. Paralyzed by the specter of mass bloodshed, the king refused to sign the proclamation of siege, and on the 29th asked Mussolini to come to Rome and form a new government—to become the dictator of Italy. His revolution was accomplished, almost.

As a last act before leaving Milan, Mussolini moved to forestall the socialist action he knew would come—a general strike. He did not want to be bothered in his first days in office. So he sent his blackshirts to burn *Avanti!* to the ground, thus depriving his most violent antagonists of the means to publicize the call and direct the strikers. The paper's voice was silenced for two weeks. Mussolini thus remembered well his own words in June 1914, claiming credit for *Avanti!* for organizing the "Red Week" violence. It was a direct step toward establishing his revolutionary communications monopoly—and a thoroughly Leninist move.

Chapter 31
HITLER: THE ELECTRONIC LENINOID

To this day the half-hearted and the lukewarm have remained the curse of Germany
. . . For liberation something more is necessary than an economic policy, something
more than industry: if a people is to become free, it needs pride and will-power,
defiance, hate, hate and once again hate.

—Adolf Hitler,
Munich speech,
April 10, 1923

A revolutionist must be able to do everything—to unchain volcanic passions, to arouse
outbreaks of fury, to set masses of men on the march, to organize hate and suspicion
with ice-cold calculation, with "legal" (so to speak) methods.

—Joseph Goebbels,
Der Angrif, February 18, 1929
(later Nazi Minister of Propaganda)

Hate is a factor in the struggle, intransigent hate for the enemy, which takes one
beyond the natural limitations of a human being and converts one into an effective,
violent, single-minded, cold killing machine. Our soldiers must be like that; a people
without hate cannot triumph over a brutal enemy.

—Ernesto "Che" Guevara
Article from "somewhere in the world"
distributed by Pernsa Latina, April 17, 1967

THE RADICAL WHO BURNED EUROPE   In 1905 Lenin
stated the revolutionary program of his projected revolutionary government in two words: *"Burn Europe!"* The man who actually did
it was Adolf Hitler.

The lean facts of the Hitler movement rank him with the great
movement-mongers of all time, from St. Paul to Mohammed to Lenin. As a plainclothes political intelligence investigator for the German Army in late 1919, 30-year-old Corporal Adolf Hitler joined a
55-member "German Workers Party" in Munich. For months he
walked the city's streets, handing out typewritten meeting notices,
and to each meeting he would deliver volcanic speeches. The atten-
dance rose slowly at first; it took months to reach 30. He astonished
his party colleagues by daring to plan a "mass meeting" for February
24, 1920. With bold advertising he attracted 2,000. He organized a

paramilitary auxiliary, the "storm troopers," and led them in street brawls with the communists to attract publicity. Inspired by Mussolini's Italian example, in 1923 he planned a "March on Berlin," leading 3,000 storm troopers in an attempted coup against the Bavarian state government in Munich. Police and storm troops fired on one another, killing twenty. Now a national figure, a hero to many, Hitler spent eight-and-a-half months in jail, wrote a book which he intended as both a statement of his goals and a training handbook for his followers on how to promote the mass movement. In 1927 he counted 72,590 party members, and in 1932 they numbered 1,414,-975. Aided by the 1929 depression, Corporal Hitler won 12 million votes in the 1932 election and became Germany's chancellor. His conquest of power took twelve years. In ten more, his armies had overrun the continent of Europe, conquering more territory than Napoleon or any other conqueror in history. Three years more, and the Great Führer was dead, his armies annihilated, his nation a smoking graveyard, and Europe and America mourning an estimated 30 million war dead.

It all began with an ambitious romantic dream inside this one man's head.

WHAT MADE HITLER TICK?   Hitler's personality is no great mystery. He fits the classic pattern of the authoritarian personality: the child with an indulgent, weak and overprotective mother and a severe, social-climbing father who imposes rigid discipline through fear and vanity rather than love. As a result, the child develops a compulsive overconformity mixed with underlying destructiveness toward established authority, and he projects his subterranean hatred for authority figures onto weak out-groups, usually Jews and other minorities. A distinctive subtype, which Hitler represents, is highly manipulative, almost schizophrenic. Such personalities have "a kind of compulsive over-realism which treats everyone as an object to be handled, manipulated. Their organizational way of looking at things predisposes them to totalitarian solutions." In the opinion of the team of sociologists, psychologists and anthropologists who first mapped the authoritarian personality this subtype is "potentially the most dangerous."[1]

Adolf Hitler's father Alois was the illegitimate son of a poor servant girl. He bore his mother's maiden name of Schicklgruber until he was 39 years old, when Georg Hiedler, the tramp miller's helper who married his mother when he was five, returned and swore an affidavit that he was the father; even then he may have been lying.[2] Alois's mother died when he was ten, and he was fostered by Johann Hiedler, her brother-in-law, until he ran away at 18 to become a border policeman. Alois rose to be a respected Austrian customs official. He married three times. Adolf was born to the third wife on April 20, 1889, when his mother was 28, his father 52.

Alois, a proud, "self-made man," retired at age 58, when the boy was six. He was by this time rigid, domineering, and stern; Adolf years later claimed the old man once gave him thirty lashes, and he saw his father as a drunken oaf and lecherous brute who beat him and raped his young, beautiful mother. Adolf's life, as he saw it, was a power struggle against the old man in which he had to match brute force by his own wile and craft. When he was twelve they waged a titanic battle over his ambition to be an artist—a choice he seems to have seized upon not from any real ambition but because it infuriated old Alois, who was determined to make of him a respected civil servant just like himself. By his own account Adolf conducted his first great campaign with deep fear, secrecy, and lies. "Of course, I drew the short end," he wrote in *Mein Kampf.* "The old gentleman began the relentless enforcement of his authority. In the future, therefore, I was silent . . . I did not always have to contradict him immediately." Instead, he adopted the simple strategem of failing in school so that he had to transfer to another. One teacher recalled, "He lacked self-discipline, was notoriously cantankerous, wilful, arrogant, bad-tempered. He had obvious difficulty fitting in." His father died suddenly when Adolf was 13. Whether he carried a deep lode of guilt, perhaps of having contributed to his father's death, we cannot know; Adolf did later write wistfully:

> His most ardent desire had been to help his son forge his career, thus preserving him from his own bitter experience. In this, to all appearances, he had not succeeded.

The adolescent Hitler, lacking any rapport with his fearsome and threatening father, developed a fixation and fascination with power: how to cope with it, submit to it, acquire and wield it. He followed the classic pattern in which the power-orientation becomes an integral part of a distorted personality and a bruised ego which, to defend itself, must salve its hurt with megalomania. It cannot brook criticism or introspection, but must compulsively crush all opposition and merge with an in-group whose solidarity is fused with the frail ego and exhalted by its hate targets, out-groups chosen because they are visible, accessible, and unable to hit back effectively.

In this adolescent stage, completely deprived of a warm father figure for identification and role-modelling, and in deep inner turmoil, Hitler came under sway of an anti-Semitic history teacher who passionately preached the Pan-German nationalist ideology then current among the German-speaking peoples of the polyglot Austro-Hungarian Empire. "By the fire of his narratives, he sometimes made us forget the present," Hitler recalled.

> As if by enchantment, he carried us into past times and, out of the millenial veils of mist, molded dry historical memories into living reality. We sat often aflame with enthusiasm, and sometimes even moved to tears . . . *It was then that I became a little revolutionary.*[3]

Hitler's contact with this anti-Semitic history teacher came at a crucial stage in his personality development, and at a time when he was warring with his father and rejecting the old man's Austrian and "bourgeois" conventionality. He filled the void with an obvious "militant enthusiasm" and compulsive identification with the ideal of a German nation, as we will see.[4] Hitler himself later said his history teacher was "perhaps a determining factor for my entire later life. . . . How could anyone study German history under such a teacher without becoming an enemy of the state?"

The first time Hitler saw Wagner's opera *Rienzi*, romanticizing the fifteenth-century Roman messianic revolutionary, he was 18 years old. His young roommate Gustl Kubizek recalled that leaving the theater, Adolf was uncharacteristically silent, holding in his usual gush of comment. He shushed Kubizek, too. Adolf led Kubizek to a hill overlooking Vienna, then gripped him by both hands—as he had never done before—and began to talk feverishly. "In a state of complete ecstasy" he ranted that he, too, would someday receive a call from "the people" and lead them to new glories, just like the Roman tavern-keeper's son. "Many years had to pass before I realized the significance of this enraptured hour," Kubizek wrote. Thirty years later, when Adolf Hitler was Führer, he and Kubizek met at the Bayreuth home of Wagner's son. Hitler described the whole episode to Frau Wagner exactly as Kubizek remembered it, and concluded: *"In that hour it began."*

Kubizek thought he understood his roommate. "He was at odds with the world. I thought he had become unbalanced." It was a natural conclusion, based on listening to Hitler orate, his face livid and tense, eyes fixed with the penetrating stare that became notorious, "choking on his catalog of hates," as Kubizek described him.

Hitler ran away from Vienna—and the Austrian draft—in May 1913 to Munich, but when World War I erupted he immediately enlisted in the German Army. He was a ready-made true believer hunting a cause, and a refuge from a life that thus far had proved a wretched failure. He saw the war "as a deliverance from the distress that had weighed upon me during the days of my youth. I am not ashamed to acknowledge today that I was carried away by the enthusiasm of the moment and that I sank down upon my knees and thanked Heaven."

Among the front-fighters in the trenches he attracted attention as "a peculiar fellow" who "sat in the corner of our mess holding his head between his hands, in deep contemplation," remembered a fellow soldier, Hans Mend. "Suddenly he would leap up and, running about excitedly, say that in spite of our big guns victory would be denied us for the invisible foes of the German people were a greater danger than the biggest cannon of the enemy." Whereupon he would launch into violent attacks on the Marxists and Jews. Recalled another: "We all cursed him and found him intolerable. There was this white crow among us that did not go along with us when we damned the war."

In "Red Munich" in 1919, Corporal Hitler attracted his officers' attention in a startling manner. Bolshevik antimilitarist propaganda was rife and mutinous soldiers everywhere. Most defiantly refrained from saluting at all. But not Adolf. One officer recalled: "The officers all noticed him, because his salutes were so punctilious as to be provocative."

MAESTRO OF THE MASS MOVEMENT   Corporal Hitler, a political intelligence investigator, began to act out his adolescent passion play. He brought a store of shrewd observations on the nature of mass movements, propaganda, and organization from his Vienna days. In its ideological compartment, Hitler's brain was a mishmash of racism and pseudoscientific nonsense. Like Marx, he ultimately saw the world as a manichean struggle, but in place of class struggle he formulated his ideological packet as a pure racist power struggle to survive and dominate, a variant of social Darwinism.[5]

Hitler's prose truly glows when he turns to observing individual and mass responses to propaganda and power plays. He was an ideological savage who knew how to hunt, trap and kill in the jungle power struggle, who elevated to a new plane the technology of social demolition and hate propaganda.

Prewar Vienna, 1907–1913, was his living laboratory. He moved there when he was 18, left when he was 24. The very year Hitler arrived the Marxist Social Democrats had just won the largest number of seats secured by any party in the parliament, 87 in a lower house of 516. Hitler admitted that he "rather liked the activity of Social Democracy" in his first months in Vienna. But he worked—for about a week—at a construction job, and was appalled at the Marxist workers' rejection of "everything" and their contention that the beloved nation he identified with was an invention of the greedy capitalist classes to repress and exploit the workers. To prepare for his arguments with them he took up reading the Marxist press. Ultimately their quarrels became so violent the burly Marxist workmen threatened to throw him off the scaffold—a brief personal exposure to the shattering power of physical terror he never forgot.

Hitler left the job, but he continued to study the Marxist movement in utter fascination. Its program, organization, propaganda, and mass marches enchanted him. While he rejected the workers' arguments he was captivated by the passion with which they held and argued their ideas. Years later he maintained that Marxism and Bolshevism spread not by the writings of Marx, Engels, and Lenin, but by the "tremendous oral propaganda" of an army of agitators, "innumerable small and great orators," who in countless meetings won over the "broad masses" with their visions of struggle and triumph and a Promised Land. In his view, the Marxist movement's use of crowds was also decisive. Vienna Marxists exploited the gigantic "hundred-thousand-man mass meeting and demonstration," with flags, banners, torches, and bands to create the impression of an irresistible mass movement. Probably the single most penetrating analysis ever written of man's craving for communion and the mass meeting's power to satisfy it was this passage of *Mein Kampf*:

> ... the leaflet can only suggest or point to something, and its effect will only appear in combination with a subsequent more thoroughgoing instruction and enlightenment of its readers. *And this is and remains the mass meeting.*
>
> *The mass meeting is also necessary for the reason that in it the individual, who at first, while becoming a supporter of a young movement, feels lonely and easily succumbs to the fear of being alone, for the first time gets the picture of a larger community, which in most people has strengthening, encouraging effect.* The same man, within a company or a battalion, surrounded by all his comrades, would set

out on an attack with a lighter heart than if left entirely on his own. *In the crowd he always feels somewhat sheltered, even if a thousand reasons actually argue against it.*

But *the community of the great demonstration not only strengthens the individual, it also unites and helps to create an* esprit de corps. *The man who is exposed to grave tribulations, as the first advocate of a new doctrine in his factory or workshop, absolutely needs that strengthening which lies in the conviction of being a member and fighter in a great comprehensive body. And he obtains an impression of this body for the first time in the mass demonstration.* When from his little workshop or big factory, in which he feels very small, he steps for the first time into a mass meeting and has thousands and thousands of people of the same opinions around him, when, as a seeker, he is swept *away by three or four thousand others into the mighty effect of suggestive intoxication and enthusiasm, when the visible success and agreement of thousands confirm to him the rightness of the new doctrine and for the first time arouse doubt in the truth of his previous conviction—then he himself has succumbed to the magic influence of what we designate as "mass suggestion."* The will, the longing, and also the power of thousands are accumulated in every individual. The man who enters such a meeting doubting and wavering leaves it inwardly reinforced: he has become a link in the community.

This was an instructional tract for his Nazi Party organizers. Hitler developed it squarely out of his observations of the Viennese Marxists:

The Marxist press is written by agitators, and the bourgeois press would like to carry on agitation by means of writers. The Social Democratic yellow journalist, who almost always goes from the meeting hall to the newspaper office, knows his public like no one else. But the bourgeois scribbler who comes out of his study to confront the great masses is nauseated by their very fumes and faces them hopelessly with the written word.

What has won the millions of workers for Marxism is less the literary style of the Marxist church fathers than the indefatigable and truly enormous propaganda work of tens of thousands of untiring agitators, from the great agitator down to the small trade-union official and the shop steward and discussion speaker; this work consisted of the hundreds of thousands of meetings at which, standing on the table in smoky taverns, these people's orators hammered at the masses *and thus were able to acquire a marvelous knowledge of this human material which really put them in a position to choose the best weapons for attacking the fortress of public opinion.* And it consisted, furthermore, in the gigantic mass demonstrations, *these parades of hundreds of thousands of men, which burned into the small, wretched*

individual the proud conviction that, paltry worm as he was, he was
nevertheless a part of a great dragon, beneath whose burning breath
the hated bourgeois world would some day go up in fire and flame and
the proletarian dictatorship would celebrate its ultimate final victory.

Such propaganda produced the people who were ready and prepared to read a Social Democratic press, however, a press which itself
in turn is not written, but which is spoken. For, while in the bourgeois
camp professors and scholars, theoreticians and writers of all sorts,
occasionally attempt to speak, in the Marxist movement the speakers
occasionally try to write.

Hitler used the phrase "the broad masses" as frequently as orthodox Marxists referred to "the working class." This was his target
audience—the same as Lenin defined in his basic works on propaganda and organization: "All classes, every droplet of discontent."
Hitler looked upon history's great upheavals as the result not of
rational teaching but of fanaticism inspiring the masses, an elite-
created "kind of hysteria urging them to action." Here we have a
perfect parallel to the Chernyshevsky-Lenin assumptions of "What
Is To Be Done?" and to the Leninist strategy of mass conditioning
through "political exposures."

In Munich in 1919 by default the embryonic German Workers
Party leaders agreed that Corporal Hitler could be the director of
propaganda. (He was still actually in the army, and maintained a desk
in the Bavarian Army Command's political intelligence section to
which he was assigned until April 1, 1920.) From the start, he ran the
party as a *promotion group* instead of a political unit. His aim always
and in every way was to build his movement, to promote himself, his
idea, and his dream. He began humbly enough, walking Munich
streets for days handing out typewritten invitations to his meetings.
The first one drew seven; then thirteen, 23, 34; the first newspaper
advertisement drew 111. Several months later he drew 400. He
announced his meetings by glaring placards (the kind he once
painted for Vienna merchants for a living). He used trucks to distribute propaganda in the Munich streets. He made the city aware of his
party by means of distinctive uniforms and badges. He organized
parades and street demonstrations. From Harvard-educated Putzi
Hanfstaengl he learned the techniques of American advertising,
football yells, and pep rallies, which he adapted.

Acutely publicity-conscious, he exploited the general press and
even the opposition press to attract attention—and recruits—by

storming Marxist strongholds, or staging his own meetings in social-ist-controlled districts, thus provoking violence and headlines. "The first necessity was to spread our ideas among as many people as possible," he explained. "Propaganda should go well ahead of organi-zation and gather together the human material for the latter to work up."

The most striking feature of his propaganda, as with Mussolini in 1912 and Lenin in 1905, was its aggressiveness. In speeches, pam-phlets and newspapers he minced no words, showed little concern for facts and logic, shed ordinarily politeness, and hit straight at the emotions. It was clear to Hitler and to the targets of his propaganda just what sort of "human material" he wanted to attract for his organization to "work up."

On February 21, 1920, amid quails and qualms of his party com-rades, he staged his first mass meeting, widely advertised by placards. To their dismay and relief, he drew 2,000. Four years later in *Mein Kampf* he recalled:

> When the hall began to empty, and I saw the masses streaming like a flood through the exit, I knew that the tenets of a never-to-be-forgotten movement were going out among the German people. A spark had been ignited, and from its flame in time must come the sword. . . . Amid the vision of a coming resurrection, I foresaw the inexorable ven-geance to be visited upon the traitors of November 1919. The move-ment was started upon its course.

Hitler not only copied the Marxist movement's variegated meth-ods of propagating its ideology, he wholeheartedly shared the Marx-ist contempt for the "bourgeoisie." In his lexicon "bourgeois" became a hate word spat out with the same sneering contempt that Karl Marx always gave it. Indeed, Hitler's hate was as strong because it was born of the same sort of Freudian displacement, arising from the bitter fight he waged with his civil-servant father over the hated civil service career his father had tried to force upon him, just as Karl Marx's father had done.

In his 1942 reminiscing Hitler did not blush to admit copying the Marxists in their antibourgeois orientation, borrowing their method-ology and pirating their constituency:

> Since the beginning of my political activity, I have made it a rule not to curry favour with the bourgeoisie. The political attitude of that class

is marked by the sign of cowardice. It concerns itself exclusively with order and tranquillity, and we know in what sense to understand *that*. I aimed, instead, to awaken the enthusiasm of the working-class world for my ideas. The first years of my struggle were therefore concentrated on the object: win over the worker to the National Socialist Party. Here's how I set about it:

1. I followed the example of the Marxist parties by putting up posters in the most striking red.

2. I used propaganda trucks that were literally carpeted with posters of a flaming red, equipped with equally red flags and occupied by thundering loud-speakers.

3. I saw to it that all the initiates of the movement came to meetings without stiff collars and without ties, adopting the free-and-easy style so as to get the workers into their confidence.

4. As for the bourgeois elements who, without being real fanatics, wanted to join the ranks of the National Socialist Party, I did everything to put them off—resorting to bawled-out propaganda, dishevelled clothes, etc. My object was to rid myself right from the beginning of the revolutionaries in rabbit's pelts.

5. I ordered our protective service to treat our opponents roughly and chuck them out of our meetings with so little mildness that the enemy press—which otherwise would have ignored our gatherings—used to make much of the blows and wounds they give rise to, and thus called attention to them.

6. I sent a few of our own people to take a course in public speaking in the schools organised by the other parties. Thanks to this, we obtained a good insight into the arguments which would be used by those sent to heckle at our meetings, and we were thus in a position to silence them the moment they opened their mouths. I dealt with the women from the Marxist camp who took part in the discussions by making them look ridiculous, by drawing attention either to the holes in their stockings or to the fact that their children were filthy. To convince women by reasoned argument is always impossible; to have had them roughly handled by the ushers of the meeting would have aroused public indignation, and so our best plan was to have recourse to ridicule, and this produced excellent results.

7. At all my meetings I always spoke extempore. I had, however, a number of Party members in the audience, with orders to interrupt along lines carefully prepared to give the impression of a spontaneous expression of public opinion, and these interruptions greatly strengthened the force of my own arguments.

8. If the police intervened, women of our Party were given the task of drawing their attention either to opponents or to completely unknown people who happened to find themselves near the entrance to the hall. In cases like this, the police invariably go about their job quite blindly, like a pack of hounds, and we found that this method was most

efficacious, both for ridding ourselves of undesirable elements of the audience and for getting rid of the police themselves.

9. I disorganised the meetings of other Parties by sending members of our Party in the guise of ushers to maintain order, but in reality with instructions to riot and break up the meeting.

By judicious use of all the above methods, I succeeded in winning the support of such large numbers of the better elements of the working classes that, in the last elections that took place before our assumption of power, I was able to organise no fewer than a hundred and eighty thousand Party meetings.[6]

A LENINIST REVOLUTIONARY ELITE   In the May 20, 1928 election, the Nazis polled 850,000 votes out of 30 million cast, and took only 12 of the 491 Reichstag seats. It was a crushing defeat. In September Hitler assembled his subleaders in Munich for a working session. His speech to them stamps him as deserving to rank with Lenin as a master of manipulative social psychology and sociology. Be of good cheer, Hitler told his discouraged Nazi elite. They must all "strengthen the individual party comrades' confidence in the victory of the movement." How? Hitler fingered the fundamental social fact that the task of revolutionary social demolition attracts a personality type far different to that fitted for the bureaucratic task of governing a community:

> It does not require much courage to do silent service in an existing organization. It requires more courage to fight against an existing political régime. As soon as a man engages in offensive opposition to an existing régime, he will have to summon up more courage than the man who defends it. The movement requires more courage than naked tenacity. Attack attracts the personalities which possess more courage. Thus a condition containing danger within itself becomes a magnet for men who seek danger. A program with radical ideas will attract radical men, a program with a cowardly tendency will attract cowardly men. And then there is the reaction of the existing order. Furthermore, the resistance of the masses sifts even this small number once again. What remains is a minority of determined, hard men. It is this process which alone makes history explicable: the fact that certain revolutions, emanating from very few men and giving the world a new face, have actually taken place. And now, finally, comes the active resistance of the existing state. All parties, public opinion, take a position against us. But therein lies the unconditional, I might say the mathematical, reason for the future success of our movement. As long as we are the radical movement, as long as public opinion shuns us, as long as the existing factors of the state oppose us—we shall continue

to assemble the most valuable human material around us, even at times when, as they say, all factors of human reason argue against it![7]

We could sloganize this summation into a Leninist-Hitlerite law of social dynamics: *Haters will always congregate and breed—and successfully befuddle bureaucrats.* Whether they will conquer depends largely upon how much competence, imagination and luck the bureaucrats can muster.

A year later at his second Nuremburg Party Day, Hitler held up as an example the German Communist Party, the Leninist Comintern subsidiary:

> Let us glance at the development of Marxism in Germany! Wherever a revolt takes place, it is always against weakness and never against strength. Marxism created a community of force-filled men. . . . Where force, determination, boldness, ruthlessness—where these qualities are harnessed to the service of a bad cause, they can overthrow the state. The presupposition is a demand which itself in turn demands force of the individual. . . . For the individual is eager to prove his strength, quite regardless where he is placed. That is why great movements in world history have been able to conquer despite apparently insuperable obstacles, despite economic interests, despite the pressure of public opinion, even despite reason if it is feebly represented.
>
> . . . .Therein lies the future of our movement . . . that slowly, imperturbably, by this process we assemble the historic minority which in Germany perhaps will constitute six to eight hundred thousand men. If you have these men united as the membership of a movement, you have created the center of gravity of the state. If I regard our development up to now, I note the following: First, our program passes as radical, and weak men are afraid to come to us because of the radicalism of our ideas. Second, the régime oppresses us with all the means at its disposal, for it sees the danger inherent in the fact that the human material assembling with us is the best that Germany possesses. As long as this continues, and only the more courageous espouse our cause, we are on the right track and are marching toward victory with an iron firmness. . . .
>
> If the great mass were to join us with cries of hurrah, we should be in a sad state. That is why we distinguish between members and supporters. The supporters are the entire German people, the members six to eight hundred thousand. That is the number which alone is worth anything. All the others only come along when we line up in march columns. This principle of selection, which takes place through eternal struggle, is the guaranty of the future success of our movement. First we shall draw their valuable men from all the national parties, and finally from the international [Marxist] ones as well. What then remains

is the crowd; not persons but numbers that hand in a ballot. That is the great mass. . . .[8]

Here Hitler was preaching pure Leninism, found in the pages of "What Is To Be Done?" "Give me an army of professional revolutionaries and I will turn Russia upside down." Hitler wanted an elite revolutionary party, a minority, built by the careful management of movement media and mass media—a Leninist combat party of professionals in mass manipulation and hate propaganda. *That is why we distinguish between members and supporters.*" Hitler was making Lenin's basic distinction of 1903.

THE LEADER CULT   Sociologist Max Weber coined the term *charismatic* leader for the leader vested by his followers with "man of destiny" attributes.[9] Such leaders were the classic movers and shakers of messianic mass movements in history. The natural history of the great movements of the past, ranging from the Reformation to Methodism to the French and Russian Revolutions, demonstrates that belief in a "man of destiny" is crucial. He is both planner-organizer and prophet, whose talents inspire deep faith among his followers and devotion to the movement itself. With Lenin and Mussolini and Hitler, their faith in their own mission and destiny was infectious; their determination to lead their own movements, marching to their own drumbeats, led them to splitting actions in the embryonic stages of their parties. Lenin in 1903, Mussolini in 1911, Hitler in 1921—each came to his movement's first adolescent identity crisis and split.

By this time Hitler had established himself so preeminently that he was accorded the title of "Der Führer" within his own leader cult (just as had formed around Lenin in Geneva in 1904–05). Anton Drexler and Karl Harrer, the Nazi Party's founders, had originally conceived of a workers' and lower-middle-class party, radical and anticapitalist as well as nationalist. Hitler was rapidly turning it into a "mass party," and his own personal weapon. While he was away in Berlin the others tried to rush through a merger with some other socialist parties, as a counterweight to Hitler's dominance in their own. Hitler hurried home and by the mere threat of resigning forced them to surrender and cede him dictatorial powers. His personal and oratorical magnetism and his mastery of organizational propaganda were so overwhelming that he was "the indispensable man." So he became president, and Drexler was kicked upstairs to honorary president. Thus Hitler imposed his own split-purge, ridding himself of those who would not accept his leadership and dictation just as Lenin had done in 1903–04, and as Marx did perennially to the point where he split himself off from every other soul save for the devoted, effacing Engels. And the complaints of Hitler's opponents sounded exactly like the Mensheviks against Lenin; party committee members wrote a leaflet defending themselves and accusing Hitler of "a lust for power and personal ambition" and of "bringing dissension and schism into our ranks": "It grows more and more clear that his purpose is simply to use the National Socialist Party as a springboard for his own immoral purposes and to seize the leadership."

The identity crisis resolved, the Nazi Party became truly "the Hitler movement," a radical and messianic leader-cult. Its meetings became a personal veneration for "der Führer" who could articulate all the horrendous frustrations and hates in the defeated German soldier's and burgher's soul. By April 1923 "Hitler's Birthday" was a grand celebration, with thousands flocking to the Zirkus Krone to listen to military bands playing patriotic airs, to watch the storm troopers parade, and to lose themselves in the adulation and responses to Hitler's oratory. Goering presented an honorary sword "to the beloved leader of the German movement for freedom, in the conviction shared today by hundreds of thousands of the most loyal Germans, that Adolf Hitler is the only man who can save Germany."[10]

THE MESSIANIC ORATOR   What kind of man, what power, could inspire such devoted worship?

Hitler's calls to violence bounced through Munich like the thump of tom-toms, stirring such passions that they began to call him the *Trommler*, the drummer, after the fifteenth-century messianic drummer of Niklashausen who stirred mass hysteria and revolution in the valley of the Tauber.[11] (See Chapter 1, page 33.) Konrad Heiden, a student who attended his first Nazi meeting in Munich in 1920 and became one of the original anti-Nazis as a result, described the Hitler he saw:

> In this unlikely looking creature there dwelt a miracle: his voice. It was something unexpected. Between those modest, narrow shoulders, the man had lungs. His voice was the very epitome of power, firmness, command, and will. Even when calm, it was a guttural thunder; when agitated, it howled like a siren betokening inexorable danger. It was

the roar of inanimate nature, yet accompanied by flexible human overtones of friendliness, rage, or scorn . . . Hitler has given speech to the
speechless terror of the modern mass, and to the nameless fear he has
given a name. That makes him the greatest mass orator of the mass
age.[12]

Hitler moreover possessed an astonishing ability to verbalize and
concretize causes of dissatisfaction, to focus people's attention on
plausible sources of trouble. He was a master of the hate-target technique, either discovering or creating enemies for people to blame for
all their troubles. One Nazi recalled that in his first party meeting
"much was touched upon that had long been in my subconscious
mind, and was now called forth into consciousness. I went home
deeply moved, thinking that, if the aims and purposes outlined by
the speaker were capable of achievement, *then life would once more
by worth living.*"[13]
Hitler himself wrote:

> The art of leadership consists of consolidating the attention of people
> against a single adversary and taking care that nothing will fragment
> this attention . . . The leader of genius must have the ability to make
> different opponents appear as if they belonged in one category.

Here is a prescription for hate-targeting and issue-broadening and
linking that summarizes the heart of Leninism.
Hitler also hammered on the importance of sloganeering. No
matter how much arguments may be explained, variegated, or
refined, the propagandist must not alter his main theme. All arguments must end with the basic theme expressed as a slogan. The
slogan is an easily memorized formula for the political goals and
values of the party. The propagandist may and must illustrate the
slogan from many angles—but he must always repeat it as the
conclusion of any argument, the panacea and promise. Indeed,
Hitler foreshadowed the New Left hate-targeting among America's youth in the 1960s in his pure genius of playing upon all the
nebulous grievances of his German audiences and focusing them
on a single cause in simple slogans. After the bands played and
the storm troopers marched, he would take the stage surrounded
by his Party officers in resplendent uniforms. One observer[14] described a typical meeting:

The chairman speaks softly, confidentially, soothingly, like a good neighbor. He dwells on the misfortunes of his auditors. He shouts: "What is the cause of our suffering?" Mighty voices from the audience reply: "THE SYSTEM!"

Hitler, launching his radical-revolutionary cartel of professionals in 1920–28, enjoyed two crucial advantages over the young Lenin of 1896–1905: 1) A superior target-audience analysis based on the revolutionary movement's 1914–1919 experience, including especially Mussolini's synthesis in Italy; and 2) Electronic media based on the post-1900 inventions of Marconi and De Forest, combined with the airplane, phonograph, and cinema.

THE IDEOLOGICAL RECIPE   After Hitler moved to Munich in May 1913 he studied his way through Marxism a second time, evaluating Marx's solution to the problem of bringing the utopian Republic of Virtue. He found wanting Marx's mixture of economic determinism and a chosen economic class that would lead to the Promised Land. Hitler criticized the Marxian solution in detail. Not economics, but "ideals," moves masses of men, he declared! "A man does not die for business, but only for ideals." So to move the masses, to conquer the secular power of the state, and thus to begin building the revolutionary New Jerusalem, the revolutionary must resort to "ideal virtues . . . heroic virtues . . . ideals . . . the essence of the force which can lead men to their death of their own free will and decision."[15]

Like Marx, Hitler in these formative young adult years was fleeing from personal failure and the harpy-like problem of engaging in some regular disciplined activity to earn a living. Marx found his solution in a sour-grapes attack on the capitalist economic system (which he identified, significantly, with "practical Jewishness"), and substituting a dream-state "New Jerusalem" founded along the lines of his dream "philosophy" by philosopher-kings riding the proletarian herd.

Hitler reached a solution similar in psychological structure. Yet with his anti-Semitic and Pan-German conditioning and the experience of 1914 nationalism before him, like Mussolini he nominated a different "Chosen People," holding up a utopian design based not on economic class but racial-national purity.

Both the Marxist and Hitlerite psychoideological systems rejected the economic system of the status quo "bourgeoisie," and they used identical messianic prophecies and technologies of mass organization, social demolition and hate propaganda. Both Marx and Hitler were working out their personal problems, their resistance to making a living and failure to find a place in the world, by opting to break up that hated bourgeois world and denying the worth of its economic system. Hitler's whole career, asserts Werner Maser, was "no more than the attempt of a visionary to force reality to conform to his dream world."[16] But they chose to work through differing constituencies.

In his first visit to the German Workers Party meeting of September 12, 1919, Hitler made a speech affirming his anti-Semitic and Pan-German view. Party founder Anton Drexler was so impressed he sought out Hitler and handed him his own 40-page pamphlet, *My Political Awakening.* It excited Hitler, for in it he saw the ideological recipe to power the "movement" he was planning: *National Socialism.* The Munich railroad mechanic wrote that a "new world order" could be installed by mobilizing the embittered and disillusioned lower middle class, the civil service, and the workers. The workers could be won from the Marxist-internationalist left by combining the socialist position on "the social issue" with nationalism which would appeal to the German burghers and civil servants as well as the workers.

Unite the appeals of nationalism on the one hand with socialism on the other! Build a single party as a vehicle for these powerful ideas! Hitler saw this combination at once as a powerful propaganda recipe, almost unbeatable in the mathematics of German social groupings. He embraced it so wholeheartedly, and preached it to every Nazi proselyte with such eloquence,[17] that most forgot it was not Hitler's own invention. No matter; it was Adolf Hitler who made it a living reality.

> I always knew that the first problem was to settle the social question. . . . As long as social classes existed, it was impossible to set free the forces of the nation. I never stopped telling my supporters that our victory was a mathematical certainty, for, unlike Social Democracy [Marxism] we rejected nobody from the national community.[18]

Drexler and Harrer and the other early founders always referred to their party as a "party of the Left."[19] Hitler in later years always referred to Mussolini's triumph in Italy and his own in Germany as "the two sister revolutions." He remarked that the Nazis had worked out their program in 1919 at a time when he knew nothing of Mussolini, and yet had worked out the same formula. Both arrived at the same solution to the same problem of defining an ideology to appeal to all constituencies because they were trying to "unite every droplet of discontent into a raging torrent," as Lenin expressed it, and sweep away existing institutions to make way for the New Order and the New Man. Both drew, one from studying within and one from without, on Marxist propaganda methodology and combat party organizational forms. For Hitler, the satanic simplicity of Drexler's ideological combination proved to be super-Leninist in its correct calculation of German motivation and mass psychology. One sociologist who studied the Nazi movement wrote:

> The synthesis of what were in Germany opposites—nationalism, on the one hand, regarded as the monopoly of the conservative-aristocratic party, and socialism on the other, as the doctrine of the internationally minded Marxists—was a stroke of genius. It gave to the Hitler movement the broadest possible basis of appeal to the German public.[20]

THE ELECTRONIC LENINOID   Lenin was the first radical revolutionary to recognize the nature and importance of the mass movement and to study the means for mobilizing and minipulating it. Hitler was the first radical revolutionary practitioner to exploit the full power of twentieth-century communications media for a totalitarian mass movement.

Ironically it was a technological determinism, not an economic determinism, that enabled Hitler to surpass Lenin. When Lenin as a young man in St. Petersburg began pondering the lessons of his experience in Siberia, he knew only two means of mass communication—the printing press and word-of-mouth. By 1920, when he turned his thoughts to radio, he was concerned not with the problem of mobilizing masses and conquering political power, but of governing conquered masses. At that time Hitler was still looking at the old task of revolutionary social demolition, but with vast new technological tools. When he was a young man in Vienna it was possible to go to a movie, and to talk by telephone to party cadres hundreds of miles away. In 1920–30 Hitler pioneered the use of loudspeakers to stage mammoth mass meetings never before possible with the unaided human voice—a powerful new means of human communication and mass conditioning. In the election campaigns of 1930–33 Hitler exploited radio and the airplane and the loudspeaker and movies to reach unprecedented millions with a conditioning-stimulus effect of incredible power. All this was beyond Lenin's dreams.

In his *Table Talk* in 1942 Hitler recalled his early experimentations with loudspeakers. Using them he was able to break the limit on human voice communication that had held since the Greeks built their amphitheaters for a maximum audience of 20,000. Daniel Webster, the greatest nineteenth-century American orator, evoked admiration for his 1825 Bunker Hill commemoration address because the entire gathering of 20,000 was able to hear and understand. But with his loudspeakers, Hitler soon learned to reach as many as 200,000 in his mammoth rallies:

> At the beginning of our activity, there were still no loudspeakers. The first ones that existed were the worst imaginable. Once, at the Sports Palace in Berlin, there was such a cacaphony that I had to cut the connection and go on speaking for nearly an hour, forcing my voice. I stopped when I realised that I was about to fall down from exhaustion. Kube was the man who had the most powerful voice of us all, the voice of a rhinoceros. *He* held out for only twenty minutes.
>
> Another time, at Essen, it was an utter flop. The whole population had come to our meeting. Nobody understood a word. I was admired simply for my endurance.
>
> It was only gradually that we learnt the necessity of distributing the loud-speakers through the hall. One needs about a hundred—and not just one, placed behind the platform, which was what we had at the Sports Palace. Every word was heard twice: once from my mouth, and then echoed by the loud-speaker.[21]

Hitler also became the first major twentieth-century politician to exploit the airplane for nationwide barnstorming. His 1932 election campaign introduced a new age of mass audiences and mass propaganda. It used films, phonograph records, vans mounted with loudspeakers. In a single day, combining airplane and radio for the first time, Adolf Hitler spoke to two rallies of 60,000 persons each in different cities and in the evening addressed 120,000 massed in a Berlin stadium, while 100,000 more listened outside via loudspeakers and millions more via radio. He barnstormed 21 towns in six days, and magnified his pioneering exploit with the *double entendre* slogan, "HITLER OVER GERMANY!"

HITLER THE REVOLUTIONARY   Hitler never wavered in his devotion to his utopian "People's State." Once he described his dream citizen of the future:

> In my "citizens" a youth will grow up before which the world will shrink back. . . . Then I shall have in front of me the pure and noble natural material. With that I can create the New Order. . . . In my "citizens" there will stand as a statue for worship the figure of the magnificent, self-ordaining god-man.[22]

It was a paen worthy of Rousseau or Robespierre.

Hitler and the communists felt an affinity because like them, he was a revolutionary. No self-styled "Leftist" would have trouble accepting his views on revolution:

> A revolution as three main objectives. First of all, it's a matter of breaking down the partitions between classes, so as to enable every man to rise. Secondly, it's a matter of creating a standard of living such that the poorest will be assured of a decent existence. Finally, it's a matter of acting in such a way that the benefits of civilization become common property.
>
> The people who call themselves democrats blame us for our social policy as if it were a kind of disloyalty; according to them, it imperils the privileges of the owning classes. They regard it as an attack on liberty; for liberty, in their view, is the right of those who have power to continue to exercise it . . . In virtue of what law, divine or otherwise, should the rich alone have the right to govern? The world is passing at this moment through one of the most important revolutions in human history.[23]

Like the Marxists, Hitler glorified the necessity and beauty of conflict, violence, and war as the mainspring of all progress. In so doing, just like Marx and Lenin he was voicing no rational analysis of reality but opening the floodgates on the deepest storms and emotional reservoirs of his soul. The difference, nonessential, was that he couched his glorification of violence in a social Darwinism instead of a historical dialectical and economic jargon:

> Struggle is the father of all things, as with the individual, also with the fate of nations. Only the stronger can raise himself above the weaker by struggle, and everyone who succumbs in this ever-changing struggle has gotten his due from nature.[24]

[477   ]

This was an *idée fixe* Hitler had as an adolescent; it never left, but led straight to the horrendous Nazi *Götterdämmerung* of 1945, when he followed his belief to the bloody end foreshadowed in his 1944 talk to a group of cadets.

> What seems cruel to us is from Nature's point of view entirely obvious. A people that cannot assert itself must disappear and another must take its place. All creation is subject to this law . . . since life on earth began, struggle has been the very essence of existence.

Thus all human progress comes through a jungle-savage combat. Despite the variation in semantic cloak, here was the heart of Marxian revolutionary radicalism.

"WE BOLSHEVISTS OF THE RIGHT"   So it is not surprising that in Germany the two revolutionary movements should have drawn on the same reservoirs of recruits. Reminiscing in 1941, Hitler recalled the famed Coburg street fight of October 1922 in which he and 800 storm troopers routed the communists:

> Later on the Reds we had beaten up became our best supporters. When the Falange imprisons its opponents, it's committing the gravest of faults. *Wasn't my party at the time of which I'm speaking composed of 90 percent of left-wing elements?* I needed men who could fight.[25]

Hitler consciously recruited these "left-wing elements" right out of the flood of war veterans who were unable to demobilize psychologically and return to earning a living in peaceful civil life: "I specifically looked for people of dishevelled appearance," Hitler declared. "During the war, they'd fought with the bayonet and thrown grenades. They were simple creatures, all of a piece . . . With what blind confidence they followed me! Fundamentally they were just overgrown children. As for their assumed brutality, they were simply somewhat close to nature. . . ." These men formed the "Free Corps" that wandered over postwar Germany in 1919–23. The government encouraged and often financed and armed these groups as a secret army reserve evading the Versailles Treaty disarmament provision. These "Freebooters" became the backbone of Hitler's *Sturmabteilung* (SA), the Storm Troopers. Indeed, his first SA unit was created in August 1921 with the pseudonym of the National Socialist Sports and Gymnastics Division under the supervision of an active-duty Army officer, Captain Ernst Roehm, who was adjutant to the commanding general of the Bavarian army command headquartered in Munich. Roehm himself later became Hitler's No. 2. He was the only Nazi ever close enough to use the familiar Germanic *Du* with Hitler. Roehm and his Storm Troopers constituted the Nazi left wing who agitated, Trotsky-like, for a "Second Revolution" after the 1933 accession to power. "Only he who is without possessions has ideals," Roehm declared—echoing the very note that Karl Marx seized upon to describe his beloved proletariat and nominate them the savior-class of mankind.

The Freebooters fought the communists not because they hated communism but because they liked to fight, and the "Red Peril" gave them both excuse and a visible and accessible target. "These men were certainly not 'instinctively anti-Communist,' " notes an American historian. "Quite to the contrary, the radical nature of the Freebooter mentality favored extremist doctrines. And consequently, it liked a lot of what it saw in communism."[26] For example, Friedrich Wilhelm Heinz, a war volunteer at 16, member of a postwar Free Corps brigade and later supreme Nazi S.A. leader for western Germany, wrote ecstatically: "Russia . . . gave the example: Attack! Attack with arms! Attack by terror and atrocities! Attack to the point of destruction!"[27]

The Freebooters admired the Bolsheviks because they attacked the same things as the Freebooters hated: liberalism, parliamentarianism, and the smug complacency of the *burgerlich* mentality. They hated *"The System,"* using the very phrase that became the prime hate target of American campus radicals of the late 1960s. "The whole system is a racket," growled Moeller van den Bruck in 1923.

> Some are swindlers, others are swindled, but it is always the people who are the victims. . . . Only the fighting parties, whether of the Right or the Left, have any convictions. Only they have power.[28]

Obviously, such a mentality would fit comfortably into any Leninist revolutionary party as easily into a Nazi or fascist version, since it shares the Marxist-Leninist conviction that the real enemy is liberal democracy and reformism via peaceful due process. Such people have no taste or patience for the peaceful process of persuasion and compromise. Manfred von Killinger, a Free Corps leader who later became a prominent Nazi, liked to speak of his men as "we Bolshevists of the Right," and in fact before joining Hitler took his Free Corps Storm Company to Poland and fought side by side with Lenin's Red Army in the Russo-Polish war of 1920.

"RADICALISM IS TRUMPS" Like contemporary American radicals, the Freebooters and proto-Nazis could define their revolution only in terms of what they hated, not what they wanted. They would agree with Mark Rudd, the 1968 Columbia University revolutionary-turned-bombmaker, when pressed on the point: "First we will make a revolution! Then we will find out what for!" SA Boss Roehm rambled to the same conclusion: "Now we revolutionaries can say this: we will not be saved by returning to the old, to reaction. And not by depending on the exhausted excellencies and generals. Only men of action . . . can help us—only the young and the front-fighters who are . . . filled with patriotism and fanaticism." Von Killinger caught the spirit of the age in his single phrase: "Radicalism is trumps."[29]

With his bloody 1923 Putsch attempt Hitler captivated these "Bolshevists of the Right," for he could live off that one violent episode with them for a long time. But in the 1928–31 period as he reached for power via the electoral process, he bent far to soft-pedal his socialist program and sooth the industrialists and other bourgeois elements. So inevitably Hitler encountered mounting snarls and resistance within the Nazi party from Roehm and his ultraradical S.A., storm-trooper mentalities bent on "permanent revolution" and a total messianic remaking of their world. Ultimately, Hitler responded with his famous blood purge of June 30, 1934, the "Night of the Long Knives," in which reportedly over 5,000 of "the first soldiers of the Third Reich" were slaughtered. Like Karl Ernst, the ex-bouncer in a homosexual bar whom Roehm had made leader of the Berlin S.A., many died believing they were victims of a rightist coup by Goebbels and Goering and proudly shouting, "Heil Hitler!" They were like the communists slaughtered in Stalin's great purges who to the horrible end believed, "Stalin can't know." Yet in both cases the murders were at the direct orders of Hitler and Stalin.

Hitler gave his countermovement the slogan, "No Second Revolution!" His speech to the Reichstag, justifying his blood purge, described his victims, the men who had been largely responsible for the success of his movement, in terms that quite accurately depicted its sociological roots and to a large degree his own roots and mentality:

They are permanent revolutionaries who in 1918 had been shaken in their former relation to the state and uprooted, and had thereby lost all inner contact with the human social order. Men who have no respect for any authority . . . men who found their profession of faith in nihilism . . . moral degenerates . . . constant conspirators incapable of any real cooperation, ready to oppose any order, filled with hatred against all authority, their restless and excited minds find satisfaction only in incessant intellectual and conspiratorial activity aimed at the destruction of all existing institutions. . . . These pathological enemies of the state are the enemies of all authority. . . .[30]

From the lips of the man who ordered the burning of Paris in 1944 and staged the *Götterdämmerung* of 1945, these words we may take as an undiluted and true self-expression. Indeed, eleven years later in March 1945 as the walls of his mighty Thousand-Year Reich tumbled about him, Hitler spoke wistfully and admiringly of these Free Corps mentalities, insisting that in 1919 they had "raised an army of Liberation and for a time saved Germany" and would be "suited for a job like that even today."[31] At heart Hitler and his storm-troopers were true radicals.

THE NAZI-COMMUNIST COMMONALITY   Adolph Hitler himself was among the first to declare that nazism and communism had much in common: "There is more that binds us to Bolshevism than separates us from it," he declared in one revealing conversation.

> There is, above all, *revolutionary feeling.* . . . I have always made allowance for this circumstance, and given orders that former Communists are to be admitted to the party at once. The petit bourgeois Social Democrat and the trade-union boss will never be a National Socialist, but the Communist always will.[32]

"Hitler's high opinion of communist spirit and tactics is manifest throughout *Mein Kampf*," Robert G. Waite points out.

> True to his word, after he seized power, he saw to it that thousands of Communists were enrolled in the NSDAP. They were particularly effective in the Gestapo and in the SA, where they formed perhaps a third of the total membership. Indeed, there were so many of them that they were given a special name. They were known popularly as the "Beefsteak Nazi"—Brown on the outside, Red on the inside . . .
>
> The Communists . . . returned *Der Führer*'s compliment and followed his example. Since 1945, hundreds of former Nazis have joined the Communist-controlled Social Unity Party of East Germany. At first

this was done clandestinely, but it has become open. In July 1950, Otto Grotewohl, the Communist Minister President of East Germany, extended an open invitation to all Germans: "Our National Front is not limited to democratic elements . . . We want everyone including the former Nazis." The so-called People's Police of the Soviet Zone are now [i.e., 1952] officered by former commanders of the Wehrmacht; and the Communist-directed *Freie Deutsche Jugend* who marched into Berlin in May 1950 were led by erstwhile commanders of the *Hitler Jugend.*[33]

As late as 1968 the Nazi influence in the East German communist bureaucracy was evident. That year the Russians sponsored an anti-Jewish drive throughout the communist countries. The East German Communist Party newspaper, *Neues Deutschland,* ran a headline which read: *"Zionists Take Over Power in Prague."* This rang a bell with an official of the Jewish Document Center in Vienna who checked and found, with but a one-word change, the same headline in the Nazi *Voelkischer Beobachter* before Hitler invaded Czechoslovakia in 1939: *"Jews Take Over Power in Prague."* Further research revealed that more than 600 former Nazis were holding jobs in the East German regime, including at least 39 former Nazi propagandists in key positions in the state-controlled press and government policy organizations.[34]

Is it so surprising that communists were able to become Nazis and Nazis communists with such ease?

Stripped to ideological essences, Hitler's national socialism and the Marxian and Leninist socialisms were identical: the elite minority of supermen revolutionaries would destroy the hated bourgeois state in a violent struggle with the forces of evil and lead "the masses" into a utopian New Jerusalem. Both the Leninists and the Hitlerites believed in the organized minority who would impose their leadership on the "broad masses" through organization and propaganda, conquer political power and smash the bourgeois state. Both shared a goal of a Republic of Virtue inhabited by supermen or god-men. Both were revolutionary radical movements.

Chapter 32
REVOLUTIONARY RADICALISM TODAY:
COMPETITIVE SOCIAL DEMOLITION

MOSCOW—Fighting broke out today in Red Square between visiting Chinese students and Soviet policemen and other Russians waiting in line to visit the Lenin Mausoleum.

> —*The New York Times,*
> January 26, 1967

"The Chinese lined up near the mausoleum, took out their pocket booklets with quotations from Mao Tse-tung, and, at command, raised them over their heads and began shouting anti-Soviet slogans," said Lyudmilla Pakhomova, a Moscow University student.

The provocative conduct of the Chinese on this site, which is holy for all Soviet people, aroused the just indignation of Soviet men and women who were in Red Square at the time.

> —TASS, Soviet press agency,
> January 26, 1967

Listen, you handful of filthy Soviet revisionist swine! The Chinese people, who are armed with Mao Tse-tung's thought, are not to be bullied! The blood debt you owe must be paid! We will hit back resolutely at your provocations! How closely your atrocious, bloody suppression of Chinese students resembles the atrocities committed by the Czar, by Hitler and by the Ku Klux Klan! This clearly shows that what you are practicing in the Soviet Union is in fact a most reactionary and most savage fascist dictatorship.

> —*Jenmin Jih Pao*, newspaper of
> the Chinese Communist Party,
> January 27, 1967

COMPETITIVE SUBVERSION   The world revolutionary movement today is a pluralistic, competitive free-for-all, much like Christianity after the Lutheran schism. The revolutionary radicals gather in congregations ranging in grandeur and formality from that of the pope conducting mass in St. Peter's to a holy-roller prayer meeting in the Tennessee bush.

But wherever two or three are gathered together in the name of revolution, there also is the spirit of Lenin, Mussolini, Hitler, and the rest. And present, too, is their combined technology. For

[483]

today each revolutionary combat party may arm itself with the amassed experience of seventy years of sustained social demolition operations. Revolutionaries in every country have at their disposal the full body of tested tactics, political warfare methodology and organizational techniques of recruiting, training and deploying professional revolutionaries. This technology represents the collected wisdom of millions of tactical encounters—demonstrations, strikes, riots, guerrilla actions, parliamentary political maneuverings.

The communist parties, each with seasoned Leninist journeymen, are no longer adolescent colonies dependent on the mother institution's tutelage.

In seventy short years, Lenin's party spread from idea to absolute ruler of a third of mankind, including a firm base 90 miles from the U.S. violating the Monroe Doctrine. Revolutionary radicals professing to be Leninist followers expanded from 22 in 1904 to an estimated fifty million in 1972 in 212 parties and "splinter" groups in 102 countries.

Moreover, like mushrooms new revolutionary organizations spring up, copy the Leninist technology, and mix in their own ideological idioms, usually a mishmash of proto-Marxist and para-Marxist phraseology and categories. And in many cases these new messianic parties and their leaders actually get formal tutelage and technical aid from the old-line Bolshevik parties, even though they may be wild-eyed incendiaries under no communist party discipline in the traditional Leninist or Stalinist sense.

The net result of this schism, variety and competition has not been weakness for the world revolutionary movement, but stimulus. The chief immediate effect, as Undersecretary of State W. Averell Harriman observed early after the Sino-Soviet split became evident, was that "the competition for world leadership of the movement is increasing the dangers of communism to free countries. The communist parties of the Soviet Union and Red China are trying to expand their influence and domination in competition with each other. They are exerting pressure to undermine independent countries wherever weakness appears."[1]

THE MONOLITH SPLINTERS Monolithic Kremlin control was the hallmark of the world revolutionary movement during the 30-year Stalinist phase of global combat party colonization. The power that held the satellite revolutionaries in Russian vassalage was Moscow's money and their own fond hope that they could use it to achieve power for themselves, even as Lenin used Japanese and German gold. Boris Souvarine, who was elected to the Comintern

Presidium at its third and fourth congresses and knew Comintern affairs intimately, declared:

> With rare exceptions, the communist parties of Europe, America and Asia needed financial help from the Comintern, that is, from the Bolshevik Party. To lay down conditions for this form of solidarity is to exercise irresistible pressure.[2]

As late as 1951, Stalin was able to dictate detailed strategy to the Japanese Communist Party, enforce it over internal objections, and excommunicate the objectors.

But Soviet control could last only as long as the Russian communist government was the only one with the resources to pour forth for the global communist parties. With the communist consolidation in China, Moscow's monopoly was broken. "He who pays the piper calls the tune," holds the old aphorism. But after 1959, there were more payers—and hence more pipers and more tunes.

Cracks appeared in the Stalinist monolith as early as 1956, when Italian Communist Party chief Palmiro Togliatti introduced the argument for a "polycentric" communism: each communist party should be free to find its own way to power according to the conditions prevailing in its own country. This was in fact a resurrection of the old heretical Lovestone argument for "American exceptionalism" exorcised by Stalin in 1929, resurrected and modified to apply to the global revolutionary movement. Togliatti, as a longtime servant of Stalin and the Stalinized Comintern, could get away with such heresy among Stalin's less prestigious successors, for indeed, they were themselves recognizing what a deadening influence Stalinism was on their own party, with analogous effects overseas. Far from reducing the effectiveness and usefulness of the overseas communist parties, from the Soviet standpoint, such "heresy" in fact enhanced their value, since the public dissociation from Moscow would improve their effectiveness.

Two events marked the crashing end of Stalinist unity and the "return to normalcy" in the world revolutionary movement, the nineteenth-century condition of free-enterprise "competitive subversion."[3] One event was Fidel Castro's startling revolutionary success in Cuba in 1959, followed by his successful installation of a revolutionary dictatorship and proclamation of his "Marxist-Leninist" faith in 1961. The other epochal event was the Sino-Soviet split.

[485]

The feud between Peking and Moscow grew slowly at first. In 1957 at the Moscow conference of 87 communist parties the Chinese tried to dissuade Khrushchev from proceeding along the "revisionist" path. In 1959 Khrushchev tore up his agreement for nuclear cooperation with China, and the next year he broke agreements on construction and industry and yanked out Soviet technicians. At the 1961 CPSU congress, Chou En-lai headed the Chinese delegation; the Soviets expelled the Albanians, Mao's clients, and public polemics began. More than words were involved; Chinese and Russian troops fought pitched border battles in 1969, and the Soviet army increased its divisions poised on the Chinese frontier from 15 in 1968 to 49 in 1972, one-third of its total troop strength. What had been a monolithic movement became tripolar, with a Moscow-Peking-Havana axis.

Havana and Peking both set up their own academies of revolution, just as Lenin had done under the Comintern in 1920. In 1967, under the aegis of his "Tricontinental Congress," Castro reestablished a Comintern-like permanent secretariat to train and supervise overseas revolutionary elements; its staff was comprised of KGB-trained Cubans. The Chinese operated with a far larger budget, and on a global basis; they did not hesitate to set up revolutionary cartels and directly challenge the pro-Soviet communist parties. Predictably, the Soviets and their subsidiaries squawked at the competition like greedy capitalists.

In his February 1964 report to the CPSU Central Committee, Mikhail Suslov, Soviet ringmaster for the foreign communist parties, complained:

> At this moment, with the blessing and support of Peking, renegade anti-party splinter groups have been created in Belgium, Brazil, Australia, Ceylon, Great Britain, and in certain other countries . . . The chief of these groups have fat sums of money that seem to fall to them from the skies. They found newspapers and reviews, they publish all sorts of calumnious writings, they open libraries and bookstores to sell the output of the Chinese propagandists.

On October 21, 1965, the French Communist Party's central committee addressed a secret letter to the Central Committee of the Chinese Communist Party to "condemn as intolerable your meddling in the internal affairs of our party and the undermining activities conducted against us by these individuals who claim your support and whom you help overtly to find means that the masses refuse to give them." French communist couriers with money received from the Chinese Red ambassador in Berne were arrested by Swiss authorities with large caches of dollars for Maoist organization and propaganda in France.

The Chinese and Cubans were not the only competitors. In 1961 the Algerian National Liberation Front won its seven-year guerrilla war and Algeria emerged as a minor fourth pole. Hanoi and Pyongyang soon joined suit. Indeed, by 1971 Hanoi, Pyongyang and Algiers had become regular Meccas for radical revolutionaries. Algiers was a Switzerland-in-reverse. Revolutionary movements from more than 20 nations had "diplomatic representations" there, plotting downfall of the governments of a large share of the earth's surface. They included six African movements from South Africa, Portuguese Mozambique, Portuguese Angola, Portuguese Guinia, South West Africa, and Rhodesia. Also there were Al Fatah, the Palestine Liberation Movement, and the American Black Panther Party, which received the standing of "consulates" and drew subsidies from the Algerian government.

Nikita Khrushchev came to realize that the Stalinist monolith was dead, that the colonized combat parties had, thanks to China's material support, won new independence. All things considered, Khrushchev tried reasonably effectively to evolutionize and adapt Soviet Communist Party policy to meet this new condition. In his famous "Mein Kampf" speech of January 6, 1961, he proclaimed:

> The Communist Party of the Soviet Union does not lead other parties. There is no superior and subordinate party in the communist movement. It is impossible to lead all communist parties from any single center.

Rather, since they all shared compatible goals, *"We synchronize our watches."*

The revolutionaries simply know their common objectives—the destruction of the "main enemy," the United States and its power—and coordinate their plans as best they can. Ultimately, the Soviet leaders seem to have settled upon the mechanism of the conference —bilateral, multilateral, regional and world conferences—as an organizational principle for the global movement.[4]

The Communist Chinese competition caused Moscow to further

refine interrevolutionary party relations. The Moscow magazine *Kommunist* declared in 1963:

> For a revolution to be accomplished in one country or another a revolutionary situation must exist, the essence of which has been comprehensively defined by Lenin. It is not possible to define from outside, from far away, for instance from Moscow, Peking, or another center, when and how the working class of one country or another must accomplish the socialist revolution.
>
> Our Leninist party is carefully studying the revolutionary processes in every country, big and small. Nevertheless, in principle it refrains from dictating one form or another of revolutionary struggle to fraternal parties, regarding this matter as being within the full competence of each fraternal party.
>
> Indeed, no matter how attentively we may study from the sidelines the course of the class struggle in this or that capitalist state, we cannot determine the ways and forms of the development of the revolutionary process better than the communist party active on the spot and in constant contact with the masses. We cannot know better than such a party the mood of the masses, the readiness of the masses for revolutionary action, the deployment of forces, the state of revolutionary reserves, and so on.
>
> The CPSU sees its international duty not in working out and not in imposing readymade schemes of revolutionary struggle on our foreign comrades, *but in handing over to them its historic experience, in giving them all-out help and active support in realizing the policy they have chosen themselves.*[5]

Moreover, the Russians realized that in many cases they will not even be able to deal with real combat parties—genuine Bolshevik organizations that maintain "democratic centralism" and revolutionary professionalism within their own ranks. Instead, often they must deal with inchoate radical forces such as a Fidel Castro, the wild witch doctors of the eastern Congo, the primitive power-seekers of Zanzibar and the eastern Congo, a megalomanic black caesar like Nkrumah, the Napoleon of the Nile, Nasser, the Castro of Algeria, Ben Bella, the Indonesian demigod Sukarno, or young anarchist firebrands like the Venezuelan student revolutionaries. For diplomatic reasons as well as tactical effectiveness, the Soviets have also learned to use such cat's paws as Hanoi, Pyongyang, Algeria, and Cuba to train foreign revolutionaries such as the American SDS and Black Panthers and the Mexican terrorists who began to operate in early 1971.[6]

Today's global revolutionary movement is a panorama of variety, insanity, fanatical energy, and bureaucratic stolidity.

CUBA Nowhere have the doctrinal distinctions between Leninism and fascism become so vague as in Cuba and Castroism. Fidel Castro is said to be able to deliver by memory some of the speeches of José Antonio Primo de Rivera, founder of Spain's Falangism, so much had they impressed him. Among his "preferred reading" is an eight-volume collection of Mussolini's speeches. Observes one scholar of the contemporary radicalism, "It seems that a Fidel Castro in 1940 would have been identified, without hesitation, as a fascist of sorts. It has only been the world situation and the continued disintegration of fascism that led him to cast his lot with the Marxists of our time."[7]

Castro's "doctrine" is most completely expressed in the book, *Revolution in the Revolution?* written by Régis Debray, a 27-year-old French romantic-radical attracted by the Fidel myth who spent a year teaching at Havana University and conversing with the Maximum Leader. The theory parallel's Mussolini's 1919–21 ideological flux: The revolutionary must make revolution—wage guerrilla warfare and urban terrorism, but above all, *act*, and let the ideology and political organization grow in the wake of the romantic rebel with the gun. He must not wait for a party to assume leadership. He forms "focos" or "nuclei" among middle- and upper-class youth who have no need for "proletarian class consciousness" because they will acquire it through association with peasants and workers during the guerrilla struggle.

Castro by 1965 had failed in at least eight attempts to launch guerrilla wars elsewhere in Latin America. So he sent his "first team" out, headed by his top lieutenant and Minister of Industries, Che Guevara. For twenty months Guevara's disappearance was a global mystery. In March 1967 a guerrilla band ambushed and killed seven Bolivian Army soldiers, and Guevara's presence was suspected. It was confirmed in April when Castro's Boswell, Régis Debray, walked into a small town in the guerrilla zone, was arrested, dropped his masquerade and admitted Guevara was leading the band. Bolivian rangers, trained by U.S. Green Berets, cornered the guerrillas on October 8, 1967, and after a brisk firefight captured and executed Guevara. In running ambushes and attacks Guevara's guerrillas had killed 57 Bolivian soldiers. Of the 15 Cubans known to have been with him, eleven were known to have been killed. They included four Cuban Communist Party Central Committee members and two former vice ministers of governments. Castro himself had started in the Sierra Maestra in Cuba with only 13. Guevara's whole venture ranks with Custer among the great blunders of military history, but ironically, this bungler's book, as well as that of Debray, who "finked" on him, were to become bibles to many young American radicals.

URUGUAY The Castro-Debray example spawned a major urban terrorist organization in this little Swiss-like republic of four million. In 1960 Raul Sendic dropped out of law school, organized a sugar workers union, and in May 1962 launched a "poor people's march" from the countryside to Montevideo that became an annual event. Opposed by the landowners, he resorted to violence, staging a guerrilla raid on a rifle club in July 1963. Police soon identified Sendic as the ringleader, and he fled to Argentina. Sendic slipped back in late 1964, but this time he dropped the rural guerrilla effort to organize urban guerrillas along the lines of the then-successful Castroite student gangs in Caracas. Sendic's group took the name "Tupemaros," after the eighteenth-century Inca prince who led an anti-Spanish revolt; they first signed the name to a manifesto in 1965 justifying the bombing of an American plant to protest U.S. involvement in Vietnam. In 1968 a Tupemaros spokesman explained his group's failure to articulate a detailed political program in words reminiscent of Mussolini's in 1921:

> It is not by carefully elaborating political program that one makes the revolution. The basic principles of a socialist revolution have been established and are being carried further in Cuba. It is sufficient to accept these and to follow the way of armed struggle that will make it possible to put them into practice.

The old-line Uruguayan Communist Party sought to steer a middle course between Havana and Moscow, routinely praising the "courage and sincerity" of the Tupemaros but insisting "we will make the revolution by other means." Not so the Soviets. Moscow in 1971 denounced the Tupemaros as "petty bourgeois pseudo-revolutionaries" and "rollicking loud-mouthed thugs" pursuing "gangster tactics." Petty bourgeois the Tupermaros were, beyond doubt. Police dossiers on the 150-odd Tupes arrested by 1970 reveal clear bourgeois origins for most. Several led double lives as highly regarded professional men—a fine arts professor, a prominent engineer, a police chief's son, a scion of a wealthy family, and numbers of journalists, bank employees and minor bureaucrats. Most had middle-class parents and some university education.[8]

MEXICO   Even as Moscow denounced the Tupemaros for "gangster tactics," the KGB from the Soviet Embassy in Mexico City was spinning out one of its most daring plots—launching exactly the same kind of urban terror movement, designed to "turn Mexico into another Vietnam." Forty young Mexican radical revolutionaries were recruited in 1969, transported secretly through Paris and Moscow to Pyongyang, and given nearly a year of concentrated training by the North Koreans in the full panoply of rural guerrilla organization, urban terror tactics, armed robberies, arms hijacking, riot making, street fighting, and civil warfare. In the fall of 1970 these trained cadres deployed clandestinely across Mexico, set up their own revolutionary training schools, and began recruiting for a "Movement of Revolutionary Action." They doubled their numbers very quickly and began supporting themselves with armed robberies. In March 1971, just as they prepared to announce themselves with simultaneous bombings across Mexico, police intelligence agents arrested 19 of the most important MRA leaders, including the original ringleader. Mexico expelled five KGB officers, and rounded up many other MRA members. Nevertheless, though crippled, the KGB-spawned apparatus was able to begin some robberies, bombings and ambushes in the summer of 1971.[9]

JAPAN   No other communist party so illustrates the invigorating effect of the Sino-Soviet split. Utterly powerless and stagnant during the reign of "monolithic communism," the Japanese Communist Party began to grow rapidly in 1960, just as the Sino-Soviet split was emerging and "crumbling communism" became the accepted myth. Party membership, 45,000 in 1958, virtually doubled to 88,000 in 1961, and when the 11th Congress convened in Tokyo in July 1970 it was 300,000. The party could boast 14 seats in the 486-seat Diet, its vote having jumped a million in two years, to 7 percent of the total. The 1970 Congress attempted to assert independence of both Peking and Moscow, and adapt its strategy and program to the open society of postwar Japan.

SUDAN   By 1970 Sudan's communist party, founded in the 1940s by students who imbibed Marxism while studying in Cairo, numbered 30,000 to 50,000, though only about 5,000 were classified as dedicated Marxist-Leninists. Nevertheless, they built a power base by gaining leadership of the powerful railway union, the farmers union in some areas, and the national organizations of women and youth. This was organizational muscle enough to put crowds in the streets whenever needed. In May 1969 young leftist officers overthrew the sectarian-dominated parliament and offered the communist party a deal in return for support in the streets. The Reds split over the proposition; a slim majority of the 25–member central committee rejected it. They called the takeover premature, and predicted a popular uprising that would topple the military, and declared the communists should not get caught in the wreckage. Twelve committee members bolted, took some cabinet posts, and started their own party, claiming to be a communist party too—"national" communists. Both parties pledged loyalty to Moscow's brand of Marxism, but the larger outside group claimed to be the "orthodox" communists. In 1971 they attempted a coup d'état, overthrew the military regime, but bobbled and the regime recouped. The militarists thereupon executed many top communists. Both the executioners and the executed were getting Soviet aid!

ITALY   The pro-Soviet communist party is the nation's second largest political party, with 1.5 million members. It elects 800 of Italy's 8,000 mayors, including some in the largest cities, and polled 28 percent of the 1968 vote. The party collects a royalty or kickback on all Italian-Soviet trade, paid by the Italian businessmen contracting with Soviet import and export agencies. Its budget is estimated at $25 million, more than half from secret sources. And the party serves as a conduit for Soviet money to "Third World" revolutionaries. An Italian Red courier was caught arriving in Caracas in 1965 with $300,000 cash destined for "National Liberation Front" guerrillas. Italy also had in 1971 an estimated pro-Chinese communists in six groups. One, which split out of the Italian party in 1970, took with it five deputies elected in 1968, reducing the Communist Party delegation to 166 in the 630-seat Chamber. By 1971 it was strong enough to launch its own daily newspaper, which soon claimed a circulation of 70,000. Meantime, still another far-left fringe group emerged calling itself the "Nazi-Maoists," and added a rifle to the traditional hammer-and-sickle symbol on its placards and red banners. Other fringe groups espoused a melange of Maoist or Guevarist "permanent guerrilla warfare" doctrines, and dabbled at bomb-making and terrorism, and even raided Communist Party offices. Ironically, the

Moscow-liners called for police protection—and children tormented them with shouts of "the Chinese are coming!"

INDIA   By 1970 one Maoist terrorist group was strong enough to plunge West Bengal, one of India's largest and richest states, into wholesale terrorism in which over 200 people were killed. In 1964 a large bloc splintered from the Moscow-oriented CPI and formed the Maoist CPI (Marxist), with a more incendiary stance. The two groups number about 60,000 each. The CPI (Marxist) sent organizers, chiefly unemployed college graduates, up to the Naxalbari region of North Bengal to organize peasant guerrillas. But on March 2, 1967, a leftist United Front, of which the CPI (Marxist) was the largest component, won power legally in the state government. Soon afterward, the Naxalbari agents started their uprising. The CPI (Marxist) sent agents to tell the leaders to stop, but they refused. So the "Naxalites" formed their own CPI (Marxist-Leninist). In fact, by 1970 these Naxalites splintered into five different groups, principally in Calcutta, dividing the city up much as New York City's five Mafia families have done in their own domain. The Naxalites grew to an estimated 10,000 by 1970, with 4,000 hardcore terrorists. They translated Che Guevara's guerrilla handbook into their Bengali language, and were strong enough to paralyze the city on occasion.

THE AMERICAN MAOISTS   The splintering of the world communist monolith began to be reflected in the United States at the 1959 Communist Party U.S.A. convention in New York City. Milt Rosen, the communist party's New York state labor director, and Mort Scheer, the party's organizer in the Buffalo area, both 33 years old and impatient with their elders, ran for the national committee, and were defeated. They formed a faction of their followers maintaining the "Albanian line," as Maoism was then known in the global polemics,[10] and began recruiting members from other areas of the country.

Such "factionalism" was certainly a high Leninist heresy—unless of course you happen to be Lenin. The crystallizing issue was over whether the party would register under the Internal Security Act of 1950, which had been affirmed by the U.S. Supreme Court. Scheer and his Buffalo unit resisted the party's plan to dismiss all but three leading members, who would then formally comply. National Committeeman Ben Davis went to Buffalo in October 1961, called a meeting and presented a resolution which he demanded the members endorse. Scheer and two others refused, and were expelled on the spot. (One whined that he had been "born in the Communist Party and would like to die in it," to which Davis replied he wasn't going to die in it unless he fell in line with the national committee.)[11] Later Milton Rosen and about two dozen others were also expelled.

True to their Leninist training, Rosen and Scheer responded predictably: They started a publication, *Progressive Labor*, a monthly, in January 1962. On July 1, 1962, more than fifty delegates from eleven cities met in a Manhattan hotel for an all-day conference and announced formation of the Progressive Labor Movement, with Rosen and Scheer as chairman and vice chairman.[12] The Maoist party in America was underway. Its birth was a result of one of the oldest herd phenomena in nature: the old bull versus the young bull.

The new Maoists quickly contacted the Cuban government, which jumped at the opportunity and offered a half million dollars to finance a proposed trip to Cuba. In the summer of 1965, 59 young radicals sojourned in Cuba, captivated by the romantic image of bearded Castro guerrillas, and many unaware of the Maoist communist sponsorship of their trip. They played ping-pong with the Maximum Leader himself, had a "rap" session with Che Guevara on guerrilla warfare, and met Viet Cong representatives. Selected leaders also conferred with the dictator of Algeria's new guerrilla government, Houari Boumedienne, and the leader of the world's largest nonruling communist party, Indonesian chieftain D.N. Aidit. And the Cubans gave the Progressive Labor leaders $15,000 in cash to smuggle back to finance a propaganda newspaper among collegians, *Free Campus*.[13] (A second group of 84 visited Cuba under Progressive Labor sponsorship in 1964.)

With foreign financing and the typical Leninist sloganeering, hate propaganda, and mass agitation techniques, the Progressive Labor Movement rapidly gained publicity and membership. Its Harlem leader, William Epton, created a block-by-block organizational structure and pumped out inflammatory propaganda that helped create the climate and spark the July 1964 Harlem riots; Epton organized distribution of leaflets on "How to Make a Molotov Cocktail" and otherwise incited the violence so as to get himself indicted and convicted for inciting riot and criminal anarchy.[14] Epton's prosecution, of course, became another *cause célèbre* for more agitation, martyr-manufacture and recruitment.

Scheer moved to San Francisco and the Progressive Labor Movement launched weekly newspapers on the East and West coasts. In

April 1965 it held a four-day convention of 200 delegates in New York and announced the formal founding of a new Maoist Progressive Labor Party. Claimed membership: 1,500. Late that year the Progressive Labor Party dissolved its own campus front, the "May 2 Movement," and ordered its members to infiltrate the Students for a Democratic Society.

Shrewdly, the PLP Maoists did not pull all their sympathizers out of the Communist Party U.S.A. They left some inside, incognito, to form a secret apparatus for manipulating the old-line Reds, hauling them always leftward toward more militant and violent positions.

By 1971 the Progressive Labor Party was strong enough to bring 3,000 demonstrators to Washington from as far away as Boston, Minnesota, and Iowa. Chanting "Same Enemy, Same Fight, Workers of the World Unite!" they picketed the White House demanding an end to unemployment and the Vietnam war. Maoism was alive and growing in America.

"DEVILS CRAWLING ACROSS THE WHOLE WORLD"

UNESCO reports that in 1966 the new translations of Lenin published around the world topped the Bible, 201 to 197. The fissioning of the world revolutionary movement by the early 1970s reached astonishing speed. Few countries outside the communist police states lacked their terrorists, aerial hijackers, political murderers and kidnapers, and organized guerrillas. Moreover, even the most diverse revolutionists began to coalesce into a loosely floating "Terrorist International" of globe-girdling sweep. Libya's radical premier proclaimed in a formal speech to shocked diplomats that his country was sending arms, money and volunteers to Irish terrorists waging urban guerrilla warfare in Ulster; indeed, British soldiers seizing Belfast and Londonderry strongholds of the outlaw Irish Republican Army found secret papers documenting contacts with revolutionary groups in Cuba, North America, France, Holland, Belgium, Scandinavia and the Middle East, including the American Black Panthers, the Maoist "Red Army" of Japan, and the Palestinian guerrilla organization Al Fatah.

The world got a shocking insight into the character of many of these lunatic fringe groups in February 1972 when Japanese police discovered the bodies of a dozen members of the "Red Army," a revolutionary group previously responsible for air hijackings. The victims had been tortured to death in a mountain hideout by members of their own group. After a ten-day siege the others were captured and confessed the torture-slayings were the result of a "people's trial" ordered by the band's leader because the victims had disagreed with his plan to overthrow the Japanese government!

Two months later three terrorists from this same group volunteered and trained with the Al Fatah Palestinian guerrillas, flew into Tel Aviv's airport on an Air France flight from Rome, pulled machineguns from their hand luggage, and mowed down 94 persons in the tourist-packed terminal. Most of the 26 dead, ironically, were not Israelis but poor Puerto Rican Catholics who had scrimped and saved for a pilgrimage to the Holy Land. One of the terrorists, prevented from killing himself along with his two comrades, haughtily proclaimed at his trial:

> My profession is a soldier of the Red Army. I would like to warn the entire world the Red Army will slay anyone who stands on the side of the bourgeoisie. This I do not say as a joke . . . World revolutionary warfare has to be carried out worldwide and should not have regional characteristics . . . We decided to have a relationship with the Popular Front for the Liberation of Palestine to propel ourselves onto the world stage. I am a soldier. I obeyed an order and joined this operation . . . Revolutionary warfare cannot be restricted to the destruction of buildings. The slaughter of people is inevitable.[15]

The raging global epidemic of revolutionary radicalism moved Alexander Solzhenitsyn to invoke the spectre of Nechayev in his 1972 Nobel Prize essay:

> Violence, less and less embarrassed by the limits imposed by centuries of lawfulness, is brazenly and victoriously striding across the whole world, unconcerned that its infertility has been demonstrated and proved many times in history. The world is being inundated by the brazen conviction that power can do anything, justice nothing. Dostoevsky's devils—apparently a provincial nightmare fantasy of the last century—are crawling across the whole world in front of our very eyes, infesting countries where they could not have been dreamed of: And by means of the hijackings, kidnappings, explosions and fires of recent years they are announcing their determination to shake and destroy civilization! And they may well succeed.

Chapter 33
THE "NEW LEFT" IN AMERICA

We are post-communist revolutionaries. We are working to build a guerrilla force in an urban environment. We are actively organizing sedition.

—Greg Calvert, SDS National
Secretary, May 1967

The ability to manipulate people through violence and mass media has never been greater, and the potential for us as radicals has never been more exciting than now.

—Dave Gilbert, Columbia
University SDS, June 1968
SDS National Convention

The revolutionary's sole purpose is to turn the System upside down so that in the end he will be in command.

—Black Panther manual on
"Urban Warfare," 1970

The combined strength of armed underground attacks, propaganda, demonstrations in the cities and campuses, actions by local collectives, all forms of organizing and political warfare, can wreck the Amerikan war machine.

—"Communique No. 8," The Weather
Underground, upon the bombing
of the U.S. Capitol, March 1, 1971

THE CAMPUS RADICALS   The 1960s explosion of revolutionary radicalism in America centered on the college campuses. For the messianic engineers of social demolition, they offered a fertile field. The campus population skyrocketed in just over a decade from 2,-600,000 to 7 million, reflecting the birth-rate shift from Depression lows of the 1930s to the postwar "baby boom" of 1947–55. It was no accident that the explosions began in 1964–65 with the "Berkeley Rebellion," which climaxed with the first mass arrest of 773 students occupying the administration building. It happened exactly 18 years after returning World War II GI's married and began families in record numbers. (The New York City marriage bureau ran out of license forms in 1946.) The "baby boom" hit the campuses with a tidal wave. The July 1, 1964 count of 18-year-olds stood at 2,772,000. Just a year later the figure jumped 35 percent, to 3,743,000.[1] More than any ideological infection, the 1960s generation was "radicalized" by the crush of their own numbers and resultant dilution of mature influence.

Social science surveys showed that only a tiny minority became hard-core "activists." This minority displayed what Yale psychologist Kenneth Keniston called a "protest-prone personality." His and others' research presented a remarkably consistent picture of a highly distinctive background: The fathers tended to be college faculty, lawyers, doctors, rather than businessmen, white- or blue-collar employes. Family incomes above $15,00 were ordinary. Moreover, the activists were *not* rebelling against parental politics; instead, they were pushing an already liberal or leftist attitude to an extreme. They were frustrated by the differences they thought they saw between the high ideals and values their parents espoused and the lives their parents actually lead. They tended to be students of humanities and social sciences, with extraordinary interest in abstract thought and religious liberalism. And they suffered from greater anxieties, a trait with a well-documented tendency to convert to frustration and hate.

From permissive family backgrounds these youngsters came to campus expecting intimate contact with wise professors, deep intellectual stimulation, and exciting student associations, Michigan University psychologist Donald R. Brown found. Instead, they crashed against the increasing impersonality, anonymity and exacting demands of the new mass university of the 1960s. The colleges failed to satisfy their high expectations, not from any perverse "exploiter class" plot, but awash in the simple dynamics of population growth, industrial mass organization and regimentation.

The result was bitterness and a tendency to look for a scapegoat. Professor Lewis Feuer, who quit Berkeley in disgust after campus totalitarians took over, found them "possessed by a terrible, compulsive irrationality that corrupted their idealism." A Philadelphia *Bulletin* reporter found the 1968 members of Students for a Democratic Society "super idealists, unhappy because America fails to live up to its textbook image, upset because life is different from dreams. They are not hippies, not freaks. A generation ago they might have been communists."

THE "RED DIAPER" REVOLUTIONARIES   Bored with the prospect of ordinary careers in the affluent "postindustrial" technocracy, these would-be St. Georges began looking for dragons to slay. And they were led headlong down a historical dead-end trail after that nineteenth-century devil "capitalism." They followed young Marxist revolutionaries, who offered neat packaged thinking that

[498   ]

effortlessly explained all evils, and used all the Leninist organizational weapons in the process. Pollster Samuel Lubell concluded from interviews over four years with more than 1,100 students at 37 college campuses that "sons and daughters of onetime socialists, communists and other leftists" constituted the pacesetters in bringing the "politics of violence" to the campuses. He found 17 percent of the "New Left" students he interviewed reported a radical family upbringing. Typically, a Cornell student said to Lubell: "I was only five when my parents—they were communists—took me to my first demonstration." Such students often called "red diaper" babies, constituted "easily the most important single" influence that brought together the revolutionary student movement, Lubell concluded:

> These students comprised the organizing core for the Students for a Democratic Society; they also supplied the "revolutionary" ideology and tactics . . . Far from being in family revolt, these students were projecting the radicalism of their parents. The sense of grievance that animated these radicals did not originate in any current performance of our society, nor was it caused by the war, nor could any possible restructuring of the universities satisfy them. For them, the specific issue of agitation was less vital then to be "agin" something.[2]

A 22-year-old black student at the University of Chicago who spent four years as an undercover Federal Bureau of Investigation informant within the SDS and the Communist Party testified:

> Those people in the SDS who know what is really happening are the Mark Rudds and Machtingers, and people like that. They have traveled to Cuba and been with members of the Communist Party of Cuba and with members of the Communist Party, U.S.A., and have taken their example and listened to them and talked with them, have been educated, have worked with them in projects, and have learned from them how to develop a movement.
> So, what it amounts to is basically a situation in which the Communist Party, U.S.A., might not have that many members, and it may not have that many young members, but it serves as sort of a Rand Corporation of the left—the think tank.[3]

Consider these four examples, for they tell much about the spread of messianic revolutionary radicalism among the '60s generation: *DOUGLAS WACHTER*, a University of California (Berkeley) sophomore, played the key role in organizing the first mass student political violence of the decade. Though only 18 years old at the time, Wachter was a dedicated Communist Party U.S.A. member,

[499]

thoroughly trained by his party parents in its philosophy and agitational techniques. He had in fact represented the California Communist Party as an official delegate in the December 1959 national party convention in New York City. In May 1960 the House Committee on Un-American Activities scheduled a San Francisco hearing and subpenaed Wachter, among others, to testify. Wachter feigned total innocence and gave an interview in the campus newspaper claiming he was being persecuted for his "civil rights" activity. He sounded all the right slogans to appeal to student idealism. At the City Hall hearing he helped spark-plug the demonstrators and convert a peaceful demonstration into a riot that made front-page headlines across the nation; television films showed him leading charges and pep-talking his fellow demonstrators like a scrappy football linebacker. In fact, 23 of the 70 arrested were either known communists or "red diaper" babies, some of them sons and daughters of Lenin School graduates. After a judge dismissed riot charges against 63 of the arrested demonstrators, saying he did not want to mar their youthful lives with criminal records, 58 of them issued a statement denying communist influence and claiming, "Nobody incited us, nobody misguided us. We were led by our own convictions. . . ." And high on the list was Wachter's name!

BETTINA APTHEKER was the daughter of Communist Party national committeeman Herbert Aptheker, who taught at the Communist Party's annual summer schools for party youths. When Bettina, only 18 years old, left her Brooklyn home in 1962 to enter the University of California at Berkeley, she formally transferred her secret communist membership to the California party, and moved into the home of the party's district chairman. She promptly organized the first chapter of the party's new youth front, the W.E.B. DuBois Clubs, in time to lead a "Hands Off Cuba!" picket line during the missile crisis of October 1962. And in the fall of 1964 she was the organizational quarterback and signal-caller in the "Free Speech Movement's" shadowy nine-man "Steering Committee," which she and a clique of five other Trotskyite, Castroite, and Maoist communists dominated. Using standard Leninist front group and mass manipulation techniques, and calling up the resources of her adult comrades in the San Francisco Bay Area's formidable communist party apparatus, she and her Free Speech Movement cohorts turned the Berkeley campus into a shambles. Moreover they created a "beacon demonstration" —a technique devised by the Comintern's globe-trotting social demolition engineers—that touched off reflective flares all over the nation. With a Trotskyite comrade, the charismatic orator Mario Savio, Bettina led the march into the campus administration building that resulted in the 773 arrests. Not until almost a year later did she admit she had been a Communist Party member all along.

MIKE EISENSCHER, son of the Wisconsin Communist Party chairman, in 1964–65 helped radicalize the University of Wisconsin campus. Though only 20, he spent the summer of 1964 in New York working at Communist Party U.S.A. headquarters and undergoing special training; on the second day of the July 1964 riots he and other young communists hurried up to the Bronx and organized a march of 350 young people down into Harlem. They arrived just in time to fuel the explosion at the funeral of the young black whose killing by a policeman three days earlier triggered the turmoil. Back at Madison in the fall, Eisenscher shared a campus-fringe house with Eugene Dennis, Jr., son of the former Communist Party chieftain convicted in the famed 1948 criminal anarchy prosecution. The two youths called signals for the little "colony" of "red diaper babies" in Madison, manipulated civil rights and antiwar slogans like seasoned Comintern professionals, and staged the largest student political demonstration in Wisconsin history. Concealing their roles behind a front group called "the Ad Hoc Committee Against Extremism," they turned out 1,500 pickets to meet Republican presidential candidate Barry Goldwater. After the "Berkeley Rebellion," they brought Bettina Aptheker, by then a national student celebrity, to Madison. Eisenscher also was an incognito observer at the "Congress of Unrepresented Peoples" in Washington in August 1965, in which a few "old pro" radicals led 200 youthful demonstrators in an attempt to seize the House of Representatives—and into the first mass arrest in Capitol Hill history. Shortly thereafter, in an effort to infuse youth, the Communist Party elevated Eisenscher to its national committee.

HOWIE EMMER was a leading climate-maker and stage-setter for the Kent State tragedy of May 4, 1970, in which National Guardsmen fired on rioting students and onlookers, killing four. That tragedy in turn touched off a nationwide hysteria of campus strikes and riots and the shutdown of 700 colleges. Emmer's parents were old-line Communist Party activists in nearby Cleveland. His dedication and skill in Leninist sloganeering and mass manipulation became evident in novelist-journalist James A. Michener's inquest at Kent State. One student told Michener: "He was fantastic at face-to-face persuasion."

Another, appointed to keep certain slogans and issues before students, reported, "At times I thought it was useless, but Howie and Rick [a cohort] kept telling me that one of these days one of these planks would catch on . . . The intellectual history of Kent Sate for the next two years was Howie and Rick." Said another: "He was much more important on this campus than any of the professors. At any rate, he exercised more leadership." A young reporter who regularly covered the Kent State turmoil saw a different Emmer: "He scared me to death. I always felt he'd just as soon conk me over the head as talk to me." Emmer did not last to participate in the fatal riots. During the long buildup, in April 1969 behind a Viet Cong banner he led a flying column of SDSers in assaulting police and seizing the university's administration building. That got him six months in jail. Another violent mass operation later got him convicted for inciting riot, and more time. Michener summed up Emmer's role:

> The dominant characteristic by which people remembered him was the acuity of his intellect. He was not well versed in a wide subject matter, for in many areas he was deficient, but in revolutionary tactics, he was a master. . . . The powerful personality of Howie Emmer encouraged a speed-up of campus friction, for at every moment when the movement seemed about to perish for lack of steam, he moved in to exert a dynamic leadership which kept it functioning. . . . It was obvious that people around him considered him a leader. . . . Certainly the presence of one dedicated leader like Emmer could draw down the lightning of civil disturbance when otherwise it might have passed by.[4]

STUDENTS FOR A DEMOCRATIC SOCIETY   The SDS was the main transmission belt for radicalizing the campuses. It emerged from the League for Industrial Democracy, a democratic socialist group founded in 1905 by Upton Sinclair in the name of "social justice without violence," rivalling the violence-prone Wobblies. In the 1930s the LID campus arm, the Student League for Industrial Democracy, tried a disastrous merger with the Communist Party's youth front. Despite a name change in 1959 to Students for a Democratic Society, by 1961 the organization had dwindled only two chapters and could not even collect enough members for a national convention.

In December 1961 the SDS executive committee met at the University of Michigan to plan a rejuvenation. Assigned to draft a new "manifesto" for a convention the next June was Tom Hayden, a journalism graduate student and former editor of the campus daily. More than any other activist, Hayden became the tactical and ideological sparkplug of the renascent SDS. Drawn by the May 1960 student riots, Hayden had spent the summer of 1960 in Berkeley, rooming with riot-maker Douglas Wachter. He understudied both Wachter and his senior Communist Party comrade Archie Brown, veteran of the Stalinist brigades in the Spanish Civil War. As part of Hayden's on-the-job training, Brown and Wachter and 25 other Bay Area radicals joined him in a "Hiroshima Day" picketing of the San Francisco Federal Building.

At the June 1961 SDS convention at Port Huron, Michigan, Hayden presented the 59 delegates with a 30,000-word mildly Marxist economic critique of America. The convention unanimously named him SDS chief executive. Present were a number of veterans of Communist Party youth activists, including an official party "observer" from its task force for creating a new youth front, the Progressive Youth Organizing Committee. So flagrant was the communist participation that the parent LID's national board called an emergency session and locked the SDS out of the national headquarters in New York. A truce was arranged, but in 1965 the SDS convention removed the organization's constitutional provision excluding "advocates or apologists for any totalitarian principle." The LID cut off all funds, and the SDS moved its headquarters to Chicago.

By this time, SDS had grown to 44 chapters claiming 1,700 members. Major momentum came from mass media glorification of the 1964–65 Berkeley "Free Speech Movement." The SDS national office exploited the publicity by organizing coast-to-coast "sympathy" demonstrations for the Berkeley radicals. Then with crucial Communist Party organizational support the SDS organized an antiwar "protest march" that brought 17,000 demonstrators to the White House in Washington on Easter weekend, 1965. That vaulted SDS into the national spotlight, and drew television and magazine newsmen flocking to SDS leaders for stories on "the New Left." Tragically, few probed behind the mass media facade. Yet one official analysis showed that a fifth of those attending the September 1965 SDS national council had records of affiliation with the Communist Party or other subversive groups.

REDISCOVERING THE DEVIL   The college student who

walked into an SDS meeting in the 1965–68 era heard messianic Marxist rhetoric often virtually indistinguishable from Radio Moscow's worst Stalinist paranoia. SDS organizers denounced "oppressors," "exploiters" and "the Al Capones who run this country." The university was depicted as a "colony" of "the military-industrial complex" and a "midwife to murder." "Imperialism" was offered as a convenient scapegoat for every frustration and failure: "Almost all students are getting screwed by imperialism somehow—the draft, crappy courses, high tuition, oppressive rituals and requirements, etc.," raged New England SDS organizer Allan Spector. SDS, proclaimed another, "is part of an international force fighting an international capitalist system. We must develop better ties with the revolutionary movements in third world nations exploited by American imperialism." A student did not have to "join" or pay dues—though only by sending $5 to Chicago could he be enrolled, receive the weekly *New Left Notes*, vote at the national convention or be counted in apportioning voting delegates. By merely showing up and cranking the mimeograph, walking the picket lines or attending rallies, he enrolled himself as an "activist." "He is bought by being told he is the agent of history and instrument of human salvation," declared Bonaro Overstreet, coauthor of *The Strange Tactics of Extremism.*

In 1967 the SDS national headquarters was a shabby two-room flat on Chicago's West Madison. Fourteen hirsute young men and braless, stringy-haired women sparked "the movement." A "chapter correspondent" kept files on each chapter and on "contacts" who will "get things done." A "literary secretary" shipped bushels of propaganda. The "Radical Education Center" clipped newspapers and manufactured pamphlets and "spider-web charts" on the interlocking directorates of "The Establishment." Two printers and a photographer ground out 150,000 pamphlets in 1967 plus the weekly *New Left Notes* (circulation 5,000). In the field "regional travelers" visited campus groups to advise on tactics and keep leaders supercharged between the annual conventions and frequent regional meetings over the Thanksgiving, Christmas or Easter holidays.

Sadly, Stephen Kelman, a young Harvard student, noted that two photographs hung in the SDS headquarters—Franklin D. Roosevelt and Lenin—and "sooner or later one will have to come down."

As it happened, both did. In their places went Che Guevara and Mao Tse-tung.

For in 1966 the tiny radical core of SDS had already decided the time was ripe to "radicalize" the movement. While the organization maintained a careful facade of "participatory democracy" and spontaneity, in fact, as Pennsylvania "regional traveler" Neil Buckley complained vocally at the 1968 convention, "Its policy-making apparatus has been dominated by a small group of planners. Most of our prime national program has come from a few individuals." In 1966–68 this cabal installed its new strategy under the slogan: *From protest to resistance.* That, explained the mustachioed vice president, Carl Davidson, constituted "an intermediate strategy" and "prerevolutionary form" leading to revolution. It would move through a four-pronged tactical approach that Davidson labeled, "Desanctify, Disrupt, Dismantle, and Drop Out." Chief strategist Hayden, intoned:

Perhaps the only forms of action appropriate to the angry people are violent. Perhaps a small minority, by setting ablaze New York and Washington, could damage this country forever in the court of world opinion. Urban guerrillas are the only realistic alternative at this time [1967] to electoral politics or mass armed resistance.

Hayden certainly played his part: Working in Newark in 1964–67, he quarterbacked a little gaggle of proto-Leninists who climatized the city, set the stage, and actually instigated the murderous Newark rioting of July 14–16, 1967.[5]

SDSers began openly to talk of themselves as "professional revolutionaries" whose lifetime careers were "committed to the destruction of imperialism and capitalism." Quite naturally, the activists turned to the writings of Lenin, Mao, and Guevara, quoting copiously in their "position papers," internal debates, and publications. Shortly before the 1967 Newark explosion National Secretary Greg Calvert told a visiting New York *Times* man that the SDSers considered themselves "post-communist revolutionaries. We are working to build a guerrilla force in an urban environment. We are actively organizing sedition."

In fact, SDS moved from protest to resistance to terrorism. In late 1967 SDS groups began distributing manuals on how to make and plant incendiary time bombs and explosives in draft headquarters and other government offices. The June 1968 convention at Michigan State University held a workshop on explosives and firebombs, and in the fall at the Boulder, Colorado, SDS national council meeting activists were supplied pamphlets with detailed instructions for making fire bombs, train mines, even antipersonnel grenades to be hurled at police. Such literature circulated widely among SDSers from coast to coast, and predictably, some began putting the technology into practice. At Washington University in St. Louis, a 21-year-old SDSer was convicted in the attempted firebombing of an ROTC building. At Ann Arbor, Michigan, a bomb ripped the local office of the Central Intelligence Agency, and SDS members jubilantly claimed credit. SDSer Cameron Bishop, a 26-year-old Army deserter, became the first campus radical to make the FBI's "Most Wanted" list, charged with dynamiting a defense plant transmission line. "It's not reform we're after," an SDSer at the 1969 Chicago convention told reporters. "It's the destruction of your stinking, rotten society—and you better learn that fast."

The grandest SDS success on the campuses was the wrecking and closure of Columbia University in the spring of 1968, using precisely the same battle plan applied at Berkeley in 1964.[6]

Coming on the tide of publicity from Columbia, the June 1968 convention at East Lansing, Michigan, was the SDS's high-water mark. Without too much exaggeration SDS could claim 6,300 dues-paying members in 250 chapters. A strong communist flavor was vividly apparent in the convention. Delegates marched the red flag of communist revolution and the black flag of anarchy to the dais of the convention hall. (Many—generally the Communist Party's "bloc within"—wore red arm bands.) They spouted the maxims of Che Guevara and paraded in khakis, emulating the romantic image of Castro. Of the three national officers chosen, only one failed to proclaim himself a communist. Mike Klonsky, who became national secretary, was the son of a Communist Party organizer who had been among the party leaders convicted in a 1955 Smith Act prosecution and who had fought with the communist Abraham Lincoln Brigade in Spain in 1937. Before her unanimous election as interorganizational secretary, nonstudent Bernadine Dohrn, 26, was asked if she was a "socialist." Her answer: "I consider myself a revolutionary communist." At that, the audience of 500 rose in cheers, and sang the old Wobbly march, "Solidarity Forever."

THE BLACK PANTHER PARTY   On September 27, 1966, a black ghetto riot erupted in San Francisco. Watching from Oakland were two politically active young blacks, Huey Newton, 24, and Bobby Seale, 29. Seale was the apostle, Newton the leader, though younger. Newton had completed a junior college associate arts degree and taken a few law courses in San Francisco. Both had been inspired by the example of Fidel Castro and the Algerian urban terrorists, and the writings of Che Guevara, Mao Tse-tung, and Frantz Fanon. The mass explosions of Harlem, Watts, Chicago, Cleveland and—at last—San Francisco in the 1964–66 summers spurred the Oakland pair to action.

On October 15, 1966, in the federally-financed antipoverty office where they both worked, they mimeographed 1,000 copies of a ten-point "platform and program" for a "Black Panther Party for Self-Defense" drafted by Newton with Seale's advice. The BPP program was a masterfully simple propaganda document, portraying American blacks as an exploited colony, designating the police as the prime hate target, and calling on "all black people" to "arm themselves for self defense."

For their target audience Newton and Seale drew inspiration from Frantz Fanon, a Martinique-born, French-educated psychiatrist who worked in Algeria and studied the FLN (National Liberation Front) urban guerrilla war there; in his *Wretched of the Earth*, Fanon described the urban blacks uprooted from their rural agrarian cultures and pressed into the cities as a semi-criminal "lumpenproletariat" who could substitute for Marx's beloved proletariat as the base for a radical revolution. Newton, by analogy, saw America's blacks in the urban slums, like the one in Oakland where he and Seale grew up, as a constituency that could become the base for a Castroist-revolutionary guerrilla movement. Indeed, Seale's description of Newton's analysis rings reminiscent of Hitler's "Table Talk" descriptions of the rootless radicals he sought for his own stormtroopers in Munich in 1920–23:

> Huey wanted brothers off the block—brothers who had been out there robbing banks, brothers who had been pimping, brothers who had been peddling dope, brothers who ain't gonna take no s___ . . . Huey knew that once you organize the brothers he ran with, he fought with, he fought against, once you organize those brothers . . . you get revolutionaries who are too much.[7]

Newton proved to be a minor-league Hitler in his flair for mass media propaganda and mass movement construction. As his party symbol he appropriated a crouched, ready-to-spring black panther, devised for a Student Non-Violent Coordinating Committee political campaign in Lowndes County, Alabama, in 1965. And he gave his recruits an appealing uniform: a black leather jacket, symbol of success among "street people" in the ghettoes, topped by a black beret. In November 1966, Newton, Seale, and a handful of recruits began sporadically tailing police officers on patrol in Oakland. They always went heavily armed; carrying loaded weapons was not against California law. On New Year's Day, 1967 they opened a storefront headquarters, where they drilled their half dozen to dozen "regulars" in the legal and technical details of handling weapons.

On May 2, 1967, Newton with a stroke of genius staged a lightning event that put his Black Panther Party on every front page and television newscast in the nation. He sent 30 Panthers, armed to the teeth, to the state capitol in Sacramento and onto the floor of the legislature, where the solons were debating a bill to outlaw carrying loaded weapons within city limits. The news media had been carefully alerted in advance, of course. The Sacramento invasion had the "lightning effect" of instantaneously capturing overwhelming mass media attention, an effect first described by Eugen Hadamovsky, Hitler's chief radio propagandist, in a discourse on properly mixing violence and propaganda. Thereafter the Oakland Panthers, a mere handful really, were national figures, sought constantly for interviews, television appearances, and speaking engagements.

MASS MOTIVATION FOR MURDER   On May 15, 1967, the Black Panther Party launched a newspaper, at first monthly, then weekly; within a year it grew to 30,000 circulation nationally; by 1970 it was up to 140,000, hawked on the streets in scores of cities by black-bereted Panthers. In the fifth issue, Newton outlined a highly sophisticated strategy for a small "vanguard party" to exploit mass media to motivate terrorism:

> When the people learn that it is no longer advantageous for them to resist by going to the streets in large numbers, when they see the advantage in the activities of the guerrilla warfare method, they will quickly follow this example. But first, they must respect the party which is transmitting this message. . . . When the masses hear that a gestapo policeman has been executed while sipping coffee at a counter, and the revolutionary executioners fled without being traced, the masses will see the validity of this type of approach to resistance. It is not necessary to organize thirty million black people in primary groups of two's and three's, but it is important for the party to show the people how to go about the revolution. . . . Millions and millions of oppressed

people might not know members of the vanguard party personally or directly, but they will gain through an indirect acquaintance the proper strategy for liberation via the mass media and the physical activities of the party.[8]

The party newspaper was crammed with instructions on how to use weapons, and make bombs. Every clash between black and police was reported in inflammatory terms. Police were depicted, from the first issue, as "pigs" in outrageous racist drawings that smacked of the worst of Hitler's *Voelkischer Beobachter*. Emory Douglas, BPP "Minister of Culture," who drew the cartoons, proclaimed:

> We, the Black Panther artists, draw deadly pictures of the enemy. ... We try to create an atmosphere for the vast majority of black people —who aren't readers but activists—through their observation of our work, they feel they have the right to destroy the enemy ... We have to begin to draw pictures that will make people go out and kill pigs.[9]

For ideology the Panthers drew on every saint in the revolutionary pantheon: Fanon, Marx, Lenin, Guevara, Castro, Mao, and others. "Minister of Information" Eldridge Cleaver even wrote a preface and reissued in pamphlet form Nechayev's *Catechism of a Revolutionary*. Panther propagandists delighted in quoting for recruits Nechayev's declaration that "a revolutionary is a doomed man." As chapters spread mimeographed "study kits" were sent out; the letter transmitting a kit from party headquarters was copied without attribution and only minor changes from Mao Tse-tung's advice to his Chinese Red Army troops in 1929. The major message: Defeat of an enemy relies not only on military action but on political propaganda and organization.

The Panthers financed their growth in large part by armed robberies. Three robberies in Seattle—two banks and a supermarket—yielded $52,000.[10] In Oakland the Panthers for a time functioned more like an armed robbers' insurance cooperative than a political party; "Chief of Staff" David Hilliard oversaw two or three armed robberies each night. The robbers paid a third of their "take" to the party headquarters in return for a promise of bond money and legal services if caught. Alas, the cooperative defaulted on its "policyholders," and instead denounced members who got caught as "counterrevolutionaries" and worse. The "policyholders" repaid the rhetoric by testifying before a Senate investigation.[11]

[509]

In one of his early homilies on revolutionary social demolition, Newton declared: "The Vanguard Party must provide leadership for the people. It must teach the correct strategic methods of prolonged resistance . . . through educational programs and *certain physical activities the party will participate in.*" On October 28, 1967, two Oakland policemen stopped the auto in which Newton was riding, ostensibly for a routine check. According to later trial testimony, Newton grappled with one officer, wrenched his gun away, and shot both, killing one. Wounded in the stomach himself, and gun in hand, he hailed a passing motorist to take him to the hospital, telling the terrified man, "I've just got me two dudes. I would have kept shooting if the gun hadn't jammed." The prosecution and trial ten months later made Newton a national "martyr" to the left, and drew broad radical support to the Panthers, "victims of repression." (Convicted at the first trial, on appeal Newton won a reversal; two subsequent trials ended in deadlocked juries and ultimately the charge was dismissed.)

Defending Newton was Charles Garry, who had been identified in sworn congressional testimony as a Communist Party member. (Garry dodged behind the Fifth Amendment, and though he later denied membership, never did so under oath.) Garry became the Black Panther Party lawyer in many celebrated trials to follow.

From the start the Bay Area's strong communist organization threw in considerable financial and administrative support and provided a steady flow of propaganda advice and backing, sometimes welcomed, sometimes spurned. With the Panthers on their Sacramento legislative stroke was Mark Comfort, a protégé of Communist Party Central Committee member Roscoe Proctor, an Oakland resident. Comfort had strayed ideologically to the extent of participating in the April 1965 Maoist Progressive Labor Party founding convention, but always stayed close to his Communist Party comrades. The national organization facilitated Panther publicity and organization in other cities, and many black Communist Party members under orders secretly adopted the Panther lifestyle, became Black Panther Party members and organizers.[12] In 1968 the Peace and Freedom Party, an amalgam of pacifists, radical militants, and Communist Party members, nominated Black Panther Party "Minister of Information" Eldridge Cleaver for president and put him on the ballot in California and a number of other states. By 1969 the Panthers were openly billing themselves "a Marxist-Leninist Party."

Though Newton and his high command were rudely blunt in fending off any overt Communist Party control, the old-line Reds had more influence on their party than they or the news media knew.

While riots raged in other cities following Martin Luther King's murder in April 1968, Oakland's Panthers ambushed and badly wounded two policeman on routine patrol. Reinforcing officers cornered Eldridge Cleaver and Bobby Hutton near the scene, and after a 90-minute shootout killed Hutton and captured Cleaver. Eight other Panthers were eventually charged. Cleaver jumped bond and fled to Cuba, later Algeria, where he opened up an official Panther Party "diplomatic mission" financed by the Algerian government. Later that summer Panthers across the nation ambushed, bombed, and shot up police. Some officers were ambushed, and some fired on during encounters with Panthers while carrying out routine patrol duties.

Incredibly, Panther lawyer Garry turned this into a "genocidal conspiracy" against the Panthers. In December 1969 he told newsmen that 28 Panthers had been "murdered by the police." Even more incredibly, the *Washington Post* and *New York Times* printed his assertion, without attribution or question, and reported it as fact to the more than 500 newspapers subscribing to their services. *Time, Newsweek,* and most syndicated columnists repeated the claim. Later, pressed for names, Garry offered 19; two had been killed by fellow black nationalists at the University of California at Los Angeles in a feud over control of a campus black studies program, and one had been tortured to death in New Haven by his fellow Panthers; one of the killers testified he acted on the personal order of visiting national cofounder Bobby Seale. Not until thirteen months later did one magazine, *The New Yorker,*[13] publish a carefully-researched study which showed that *only two Panthers died in encounters with police in which the policemen themselves were not being directly threatened by the victims.*

Conversely, 1969–70, at least ten policemen died at the hands of identified Panthers. The nation experienced not a single instance of an ambush killing of police in 1966 or 1967. Seven such instances occurred in 1968, three in 1969. But in 1970, a year in which the Black Panther newspaper vigorously promoted the notion—and incidentally doubled its circulation to 140,000 in at least 42 cities—police ambush murders soared to 19, many of them traced directly to Panthers. The Panther claim of a national conspiracy of police to kill

Panthers was a highly successful case of the pickpocket yelling, "Stop, thief!"

Nevertheless, transmogrified by the mass media into such proletarian paragons and victims of "fascist repression," the Black Panther Party at the end of its second full year, 1969, had grown to an estimated 1,500 to 2,000 active members in 25 chapters across the nation. In its first four years it had operational groups at one time or other in 61 cities; 48 of these were still active in early 1971, though membership had declined to an estimated 1,000 actives.[14] The Panthers reached their high-water mark in September 1970, when an estimated 5,000 black and white radicals rallied in Philadelphia for a Panther-called "People's Constitutional Convention."

TERRORISM, SELF-DESTRUCTION, AND DISARRAY   The Panthers and SDS foundered on the same dynamic which ultimately destroyed both Leninism and Hitlerism: the social fact that violent rhetoric attracts violent pathotypes, and violent groups consume themselves in their own violence and megalomania. Lenin's violent rhetoric in 1905 created a storm kernel of rabid radicals, messianic extremists, common bank robbers and social firebugs, among them a Drzhezhinsky and a Stalin, who after the 1917 Revolution slaughtered more revolutionaries and good "Leninists" than any "class enemy." In the end Stalin exterminated all the other top Bolshevik lieutenants, including Trotsky, murdered in exile in Mexico.

In America in 1969 the SDS "Weathermen" moved into tiny lunatic fringe "communes" where members were compelled to prove their devotion by submitting to sex relations with every other member of the group, male and female, and where pairs were broken up as "ego trips." And the Panthers started murdering each other. A Gallup Poll shed illumination on the character of the "New Left" extremes. It found that among college radicals of both left and right, extremism had a common appeal for its own sake. A significant proportion of students describing themselves as "far left" gave a highly favorable rating to the John Birch Society and Ku Klux Klan. Similarly, a high proportion of those who classified themselves "far right" gave a very favorable rating to the SDS, the Weathermen and the Black Panthers.[15]

By 1971, the revolutionary left in America was flying apart. The SDS split into five warring factions. The Progressive Labor Party Maoists, infiltrating with quiet discipline since 1965, had grown strong enough by the 1968 convention to cause serious subsurface factional infighting. When the 1,500 delegates from nearly three hundred campuses gathered at Chicago in June 1969, the Progressive Labor faction quickly demonstrated their power and intent to run things. They outvoted the "National Leadership" faction, headed by Mike Klonsky, Bernardine Dohrn, and Mark Rudd, and decided to exclude "the capitalist press."

The Klonsky-Dohrn-Rudd group ultimately marched out of the convention, held their own rump session, and marched back in long enough to "expel" the Progressive Labor faction. They called themselves the "Revolutionary Youth Movement," and assumed as their nickname "Weathermen" or "Weather People," from a popular folksong whose lyrics proclaimed, "You don't have to be a weatherman to know which way the wind is blowing." In December 1969 the "Weather People" held a secret meeting in Michigan in which they decided to "go underground" and launch a nationwide campaign of terror bombings.

On March 6, 1970, a tremendous explosion demolished a fashionable Greenwich Village townhouse, and from the flaming wreckage fled two SDS "Weatherwomen," members of the SDS terrorist faction. In the rubble police found remains of a "bomb factory" and three bodies, including one of the organizers of the 1968 Columbia University rioting and another of a "regional traveler" who had helped spark the Kent State buildup. Four days later in Maryland two close associates of Student Non-Violent Coordinating Committee firebrand "Rap" Brown blew themselves to smithereens while apparently transporting a bomb to the courthouse where their cohort was to stand trial on an inciting riot charge. (Brown himself disappeared, only to be caught some 14 months later in a blazing gunbattle following an attempted holdup of a Manhattan bar.) Also in 1970 a Black Panther carrying a bomb along a Minneapolis street blasted himself to bits. Despite the carnage to themselves, Panther and Weatherman terrorists succeeded in setting off bombs in the New York City police headquarters, the U.S. Capitol, and scores of other public and corporate buildings across the nation.

Yet sometimes the violence to themselves was deliberate. In August 1970 a sensational trial in New Haven, Connecticut, convicted one Panther for the torture-murder of another, suspected (wrongly, as it turned out) of having been a police informer. Among the gruesome details aired was a tape recording of "interrogation" sessions in which the murder victim was beaten and scalded with boiling water.

Six other Panthers pleaded guilty to lesser charges in the case, and party cofounder Bobby Seale, tried on a charge of having ordered the murder, was shown to have been present at part of the dead Panther's ordeal though the jury deadlocked on whether he actually ordered the death. In Baltimore, another Panther was tortured and murdered, and a party comrade convicted for the crime. In southern California four Panthers were killed by members of a rival black militant group, US. US leader Ron Kerenga was convicted and sent to prison for torturing two young women followers he had suspected of plotting to poison him.

In early 1971 the Black Panther Party split into two warring factions. Cofounder Huey Newton, in Oakland, and "Minister of Information" Eldridge Cleaver, in Algeria, ritualistically "expelled" each other and hurled such marvelous Marxist epithets as "Arch Revisionist West Coast Pimps" and "revolutionary cultists" across the Atlantic Ocean. In New York, whose Panther chapter aligned with Cleaver, a party member was gunned down in the street. One month later an Oakland emissary sent to New York was found bound and gagged and shot to death and his body set fire in the Queens, N. Y., Panther headquarters; a woman Panther was left bound and gagged in the burning building, but firemen rescued her. Seven Panthers were indicted on murder and arson charges; one was eventually convicted, one killed in a bank robbery attempt, and four had their first trial end with a deadlocked jury.

Newton's response to all the verbal and actual violence was to make a *hadj* to Peking in October 1971 to see Chairman Mao. Shortly before his departure, in a eulogy for a Panther killed attempting to shoot his way out of San Quentin prison, Newton blended allusions to Karl Marx, Régis Debray, and Mao Tse-tung and soared to a height of revolutionary rhetoric seldom equalled since Robespierre's more megalomanic flights:

> George Jackson showed us how to act. He made a statement that the unjust will be criticized by the weapon. . . . In the name of love and in the name of freedom, with love as our guide, *we'll slit every throat that threatens the people and our children. We'll do it in the name of peace, if this is what we have to do; because as soon as it's over, then we can have the kind of world where violence will no longer exist. . . . We'll change their minds or else in the people's name we'll have to wipe them out thoroughly, wholly, absolutely and completely.*[16]

Such is the contemporary revolutionary radical's "final solution" to the problem of war and peace.

THE ULTIMATE IMPOTENCE   We have no reason to fear that the "Red Decade" of the 1960s in America, the so-called "New Left," will have any different outcome than did the Wobblies, the Leninists of the 1920s, or the Stalinists of the 1930s.

Certainly, by their disruption on the campuses and their incitement in the urban ghettoes, and by their revolutionary defeatism and "mass action" tactics during the Vietnam war, the revolutionary radicals have dealt this nation grievous blows. But the transmogrification of the Weatherman after 1968 into pure Nechayevist terror, and the Stalin-Trotsky replay between Huey Newton and Eldridge Cleaver in the Black Panthers, and a thousand other signs, demonstrate that the innate dynamics of revolutionary radicalism in a basically healthy open society push its groupings toward the lunatic fringe of schism, dogmatism, violence, rage, and utter ultimate impotence.

This passion play offers a lesson to citizens of the Open Society, best spoken by two of its great poets of ordered liberty. It was William Cullen Bryant who said, "Truth, crushed to earth, will rise again." The Leninoids crushed truth to earth in America on the campuses at Columbia, Harvard, Berkeley, Madison, Cornell, and a dozen others in the 1964–71 era. But the battered lady was able to rise again, with a helping hand from many gallant knights of the Open Society. And it will always be so if we remember the injunction of Justice Oliver Wendell Holmes: "It takes a heap of sweat, toil and tears to bring about the inevitable."

EPILOG: THE PRICE OF THE DREAM

Marx is God, Marcuse is his Prophet, and Mao is his sword!
—Rioting students, Rome, 1968

"The tragedy of man is that he can conceive of self-perfection but cannot achieve it," declared Reinhold Niebuhr, the late Protestant liberal theologian.

Man's condition is inherently sinful, in Niebuhr's view. And his original and largely ineradicable sin is his pride, or egotism. It is idolatry to suggest that human beings can blueprint and create the Kingdom of God on earth, Niebhur held.

The effort to import dreams into reality is man's divine trait, the source of human advancement that sets him apart from the other apes. Yet as we have seen it also may be a maddening drive that plunges him to savageries no ordinary baboon would dream of committing.

That is because the sin of pride prevents the revolutionary radical from seeing his own idolatry and accepting his own limitations. He suffers from a runaway ego and a runaway imagination. An intellectual thinking about reality is like an architect thinking about a building. He can think up more changes and "ideal societies" in a minute than the construction engineer can execute in a century. He can change whole designs with a few brush strokes or sweeps of an eraser. But the builder works in concrete and steel, and change is not so easy.

Life is not dreams, and never can be. Dreams change with the haste of the summer sky, while earthly reality changes slowly, like the growth of the summer garden. At age 18 Karl Marx professed himself "greatly disturbed by the conflict between what is and what ought to be." The same theme reappears strikingly 130 years later, in a policy statement prepared by several SDS organizers and delivered by Greg Calvert in 1968: "The radical's world-view begins with an individual's perception of the gap between the actual conditions of his daily life and his awareness of the potential for human fulfillment and freedom frustrated by the existing order. The tension, the contradiction, originating in *the gap between what is and what ought*

[517]

to be, forms the beginning of the radical's consciousness . . ."[1] [Emphasis added.]

For every Marxist, every revolutionary radical, this naive idealism is the starting point. (We should never forget that it also happens to be the starting point for every human advance.) The intellectual idealist, by virtue of the ease of his *ought*, of the mercurial nature of his imagination, is apt in his flights of fancy to forget or ignore the relative immalleability of reality. His very frustration may turn from creative impetus to raging, nihilistic hate. And so he may doom himself, as Marx did, to a life of anger and perpetual war with the intractable world in which he lives.

He also condemns himself to a jungle war of "might makes right" against his fellow radicals, and their individual dreams of the road to revolution and the post-revolutionary utopia. The very phrase "a perfect society" is as senseless and empty of real extension as the terms "centaur" or "unicorn" or "fried ice." The notion of "perfection" varies inside each man's head, from man to man and even from minute to minute. Tom Hayden's dream of "the new man" in 1961 at Port Huron differs drastically from Tom Hayden's dream of "the new man" at Berkeley in 1971. And both dreams differ from Mark Rudd's as well as from Richard Nixon's. Sooner or later Hayden and Rudd must either compromise or fight, just as did Stalin and Trotsky, over the issues of who will run the revolution and where he will aim it. Neither can ever fully realize his dream of "a perfect society" or "the new man."

Why do some idealists develop this tragic malignancy in their idealism?

Only a closed mind can swallow the radical package of thought. It is a mind fleeing from reality, from freedom, from ambiguity, from the necessity of independent thinking and evaluation of evidence. Its flight takes the form of the dream of utopia. As we have seen with Marx and Lenin the dream becomes a part of an ego defense mechanism that pre-selects the evidence, blots out large portions of reality, and admits to consciousness only those portions that fit the closed, comforting mental cocoon. The cocoon world of Marxism is actually a terrible black dungeon, womb-like in comfort yet in turmoil from the constant intrusions from outside that must be fought off with terrible contortions. Thus, the rigid demand for absolute faith, and absolute dehumanization of all opposition, and total hate for all nonconforming real-

[518]

ity. These poor pitiable slaves become *prisoners of the dream*—an awful, pathetic picture of ideological slavery!

Roy A. Medvedev, the son of a Marxist philosopher executed in Stalin's 1938 purge, shook the Soviet regime with his probing 566-page study published in the West in 1971 under the title, *Let History Judge: The Origins and Consequences of Stalinism*. Medvedev concludes:

> The closed mind, the refusal to think independently, was the epistemological basis of the cult of personality. It was not only degenerates and careerists who supported the cult; there were also sincere believers, genuinely convinced that everything they did was necessary for the revolution.

In 1971 Red China's Premier Chou En-lai, then 73 years old, during dinner with a *New York Times* correspondent, admitted a bit wistfully that during his youth he had imagined that "the revolution" would automatically produce victory. He thought revolution was quite simple. Only after years of suffering and setbacks, he said, had he learned from "Marxist-Leninist principles and Chairman Mao's thoughts that the revolution must be carried on continuously to win complete victory over the reactionaries."

Chou was a 20-year-old student in Europe when he became a committed communist; he was a 50-year-old man when his party finally took power in China. It was too late for him and his peers to make basic revisions to accommodate the conflict between their faith and reality as they found it. Result: perennial purges, Maoist "struggle" and exhortation and hate and war without end against human nature. And, by one competent scholar's estimate, the price of the dream has been in the range of 35 to 63 million dead, including the 1966–70 orgy of teen-age gangs of lynchers known as the "Great Cultural Revolution."[2] In Russia, another respected scholar estimates the minimal and most conservative death toll for the Soviet regime, not counting the civil war dead, to be 21,500,000; and the real total may very well be half again greater, around 32 million.[3] Medvedev's calculations are numbing. In 1937–38, he concludes, Stalin killed more Communist Party members than had been lost in all the years of underground struggle, three revolutions and the Civil War. He estimates that a minimum of 4 to 5 million persons went to concentration camps between 1936–39, many to die of starvation and disease and at least 500,000, most of them higher ranking individuals, were shot. Executions in Moscow alone ran at a rate of 1,000 a day. "These were not streams, these were rivers of blood, the blood of honest Soviet people," writes Medvedev. "The simple truth must be stated: not one of the tyrants and despots of the past persecuted and destroyed so many of his compatriots."And of course there are— minor by comparison—the butcheries in Poland, East Germany, and Hungary. All in the name of building a perfect world!

From the Russian past one hears the melancholy counterpoint of Dostoyevsky's Brothers Karamazov, as Ivan asks:

> "Tell me yourself, I challenge you—answer. Imagine that you are creating a fabric of human destiny with the object of making men happy in the end, giving them peace and rest at last. Imagine that you are doing this but that it is essential and inevitable to torture to death only one tiny creature—that child beating its breast with its fist, for instance—in order to found that edifice on its unavenged tears. Would you consent to be the architect on those conditions? Tell me. Tell me the truth."
>
> "No, I wouldn't consent," said Alyosha softly.
>
> "And can you accept the idea that the men for whom you are build-ing would agree to receive their happiness from the unatoned blood of a little victim? And accepting it would remain happy forever?"
>
> "No, I can't admit it," said Alyosha.

One thinks sadly of Alyosha's answer, and of the scholar's estimates of tens of millions slaughtered in pursuit of the dream, upon reading such reports from sojourners in Red China as that of historian Bar-bara W. Tuchman on the New York *Times* front page (September 4, 1972):

> In a country where misery and want were the foundation of the social structure, famine was periodic, death from starvation common, disease pervasive, thievery normal and graft and corruption taken for granted, the elimination of these conditions in China is so striking that negative aspects of the new rule fade in relative importance.

One wonders: would the "negative aspects" fade if those giving such testimonials had ever witnessed the Red Guards burying or skinning alive any of the hated "class enemy" or sympathizers with "revisionism"?

And from our own time we hear the embittered protest of a young Czech student in the United States expressing his disgust with our own brand of New Left radicals after the Soviet tanks in 1968 crushed the Czech experiment in "socialism with a human face":

> They are the pampered children of your permissive, affluent society, throwing tantrums because father gave them only education, security and freedom—but not Utopia. . . . What surprises me most is not that they take themselves seriously—students always do, and we are no exception—but that their elders take them seriously. In the West it seems possible to grow quite old without having to grow up—you have so much slack, so much room, so much padding between yourselves and reality . . . You simply haven't faced up to the fact that you can't build a Utopia without terror, and that before long, terror is all that's left. We've had our fill of utopia.

Efforts to remake the world to fit the radical dream must inevitably end in Robespierrism, Leninism, Stalinism, Hitlerism, Castroism, Maoism, simply because the process of remaking requires imposition of one radical's dream, plus savage force. It mattered little whether Stalin or Trotsky or some other radical revolutionary won out in Russia after Lenin's death. The dominant radical, be he Chairman Robespierre or Chairman Mao, must obliterate by violence all the variegated traits of humankind that do not fit the noble dream. Men who do not, will not, or cannot conform to the design must be exterminated; they cannot be admitted to the utopia. The death camps and slave camps thus are integral parts of the process of radical creation. Mass murder is an integral part of the notion of "the man of virtue" or "the new soviet man" or "Maoist man," since there is no room for any other kind of man. Even if the dream be abandoned, the dreamer and his successors will not abandon power, so they must use the tools of tyranny to preserve their "revolutionary dictatorship."

Young radicals never dwell on the fact that, in order to create "the new man" they must shoot a lot of the old ones; they are seldom very aware of this terrorist aspect of their dream themselves until they come to power and face the practicalities of retaining that power and wielding it to reshape reality according to the dream. Yet from Robespierre to Rudd, the revolutionary radicals have had to confront the innate dialectic of reality that ultimately radical idealism means choosing between unthinkable "compromise" with the world as it is, or—murder.

Eugene Loebl was one of the Czech Communist Party leaders who in 1948 helped destroy his nation's democratic regime and install the "dictatorship of the proletariat." Loebl was arrested in 1949, tortured and beaten and tried in the 1952 Stalinist purge trial of 14 high Czech Red leaders, 11 of whom were hanged. Loebl spent 14 years in prison before his "rehabilitation," and became once more a minister in the "Prague spring" government that sought to liberalize the one-party rule. After the 1968 Soviet invasion, Loebl broke with communism and sought refuge in the United States. In 1971 he made a speech in Washington, at a time when the theaters were showing the dramatic movie, "The Confession," based on the book by another of the three purge-trial survivors, Arthur London. Despite the torture and imprisonment that nearly killed him, London still professed to be a communist, to believe that the atrocities were all somehow an accident and it would be different "next time." Loebl was asked: "Why?" His answer:

> I had a discussion with him in prison after the trial. I had the impression then that he would not take the easy course of excusing our whole experience as a mistake of the underlings or *apparatchiki*, but would instead see that it is inherent in the system: see that all that happened under Stalin was not a deviation but is theoretically built into the concepts of Marx. But it seems my impression was wrong.
>
> To apply to the world a theory developed before 1850, even if it were correct at that time, when all social problems have changed—all of us who advocated the theory in *this* century bear a grave moral responsibility, even though we have suffered terribly for our mistake. To face this fact, to question this dream, is a painful experience, and some of us can go through the pain—and some cannot.

In America Loebl was free to give his answer and to return to his comfortable post as a professor of economics on a U.S. college campus. But half a world away in a Siberian slave camp the Russian writer Andrei Sinyavsky languished for his "crime" of writing these words in his essay, "On Socialist Realism":

> We did not want salvation for ourselves, but for all of humanity . . . We set about to correct the universe according to the best of all models, the shining model of the Purpose which we approached ever more closely.
>
> So that prisons should vanish forever, we built new prisons. So that all frontiers should fall, we surrounded ourselves with a Chinese Wall. So that work should become a rest and a pleasure, we introduced forced labor. So that not one drop of blood be shed anymore, we killed and killed and killed . . . O Lord, O Lord—pardon us our sins!

ACKNOWLEDGEMENTS

An old country-lawyer friend of mine, the late Roy Friedin of the Dooly County, Georgia, bar, once propounded this rule: "If you steal from one, that's plagiarism. If you steal from two, that's research. If you steal from ten, that's creativity."

That seems to be a fair summary of both the law and the reality of the case. Obviously, in this book I have drawn on the works of many scholars and memoirists, and I owe them one and all a debt of gratitude which I have tried to acknowledge in the attributions and footnotes; but a truly complete bibliography and footnotes would have required another book as thick as this one.

To Stefan T. Possony, director of international studies of the Hoover Institution on War, Revolution and Peace at Stanford University, I owe special thanks. He gave generously of his own deep historical insight and knowledge, and guided me in fruitful directions, during my early research and planning.

Harry and Bonaro Overstreet, authors of such pioneering works on political extremism as *What We Must Know About Communism* and *The Strange Tactics of Extremism*, gave their own precious time to read and criticize an early version of the manuscript and above all to encourage its discouraged author to keep digging, cutting, polishing and plugging away. Isaac Don Levine, whose pioneering personal investigations make him a preeminent authority on the psychology and practice of Twentieth Century terrorism and radicalism, likewise gave his time, guidance and encouragement. Eugene Lyons, a senior editor of the *Reader's Digest,* gave not only encouragement but valuable personal insight from his own years as a youthful radical in New York and a steadily disillusioned correspondent in the Moscow of the late 1920s and early 1930s. Richard H. Sanger, veteran of 25 years in the U.S. Foreign Service, shared his personal experiences in Moscow in the 1930s with Mikhail Borodin and other international communist veterans. Such Comintern veterans and Lenin School alumni as Joseph Z. Kornfeder and Leonard Patterson, and erstwhile U.S. Communist Party members Benjamin Mandel and Frank S. Meyer, and many others, contributed freely from their personal insights and experiences.

In 1960 the Foreign Languages Publishing House in Moscow began publishing a new English translation of the fourth enlarged Russian edition of Lenin's *Collected Works,* prepared by the Communist Party Central Committee's Institute of Marxism-Leninism, the "holy of holies" of Leninism. The project took ten years, the 45th and final volume appearing in 1970. The 45 volumes contain millions of words written or spoken by Lenin between his 23d birthday in 1893 and his death in 1924. They embrace speeches; letters to family, friends and comrades; telegrams to Soviet officialdom; his polemical essays and newspaper writings. Many are available for the first time in English. In the interest of clarity and reader understanding, I have taken some liberties in editing and condensing and translating from Lenin's writings. For the scholar who may wish to see context and precise language I cite the original source in *Collected Works*. But as with the Bible, translations of Lenin are many and varied. Some are better and more meaningful to the contemporary American reader than others. Some are obscure. In some instances the recent Soviet translators have deliberately tried to fog Lenin's meaning; and in some cases they have dishonestly censored him to make him look less savage to civilized audiences. I have compared other translations and in a very few instances substituted words in the *Collected Works* version to achieve a more clear rendering of Lenin's concepts. And I have chosen in most instances not to burden the general reader with the confusing typography of brackets and elisions. I believe any scholar who wishes to compare my rendering with the *Collected Works* version and other English renderings will find it fair, accurate, and an honest service to modern readers. And to Alexander Barmine, a former Soviet diplomat who escaped the Stalinist death squads in 1938 and now works for the U.S. Information Agency, I owe thanks for checking some of these renderings and pointing out many instances where the Moscow translators have deliberately obscured the savagery in Leninist writings.

In 1964 and 1965, four major new biographies of Lenin appeared by distinguished scholars: Fischer, Payne, Ulam, and Possony. In addition, Angelica Balabanoff published her illuminating personal memoir, *Impressions of Lenin*. Possony's biography tapped for the first time many of the Okhrana police files in the Hoover Institution on War, Revolution and Peace. In 1968 and 1969 two memoirs by Nikolai Valentinov-Volsky, who died at age 85 in 1964, were published posthumously in English. He had known Lenin personally and intimately in the crucial 1904 period when Lenin was rethinking and rebuilding his Bolshevik organization. In an introduction to the second volume, Lenin's earlier biographer and certainly one of the most perceptive, Bertram D. Wolfe, writes: "Valentinov has been able to tell us things that no one else could. He has made the spirit of this man live . . . for he possessed the gift of making Lenin talk of things that he would not discuss with any other observer." Moreover, Valentinov-Volsky had grown up in the same Russian radical milieu that spawned Lenin; he possessed a mastery of Russian literature and radical thought, a first-hand experience with the principals, plus a long life in which to gain perspective and conduct deep, detailed research. And so he was able to present both new information and new insights that give us an unprecedented understanding of the psychodynamics and thinking of Lenin.

Thus my presentation of the personality and plans of Lenin draws on a whole range of historical resources that became available for the first time in the last decade. If I have been able to put together the picture with more clarity than before, it is because I have more pieces of the puzzle. I believe readers will find that I have succeeded, and of course I owe a deep debt to the scholars who have worked the field before me: Levine, Shub, Wolfe, Payne, Ulam, Fischer, Possony, Balabanoff and Valentinov-Volsky.

Here I want to add a personal note. I approached Lenin with genuine puzzlement after researching and writing the chapters on Robespierre, Marx, and the others. I had studied Lenin's writings and his public life, but Lenin personally was to me a complete mystery. My only predisposition was to believe that he was truly different, perhaps unique, and certainly not cut from the pattern I had seen so often in the Young Marx and in first-hand acquaintances with our own contemporary "New Left" nihilists: the comfortable bourgeois family with a peaceful facade masking volcanic subterranean compulsions, which worked themselves out in personality structures integrated around hate ideologies, political hate-mongering, and messianic-apocalyptic "struggle" packages.

In January and February 1971 I read and re-read all the major biographies of Lenin, hunting and answer to the Lenin enigma. The earlier biographers presented the peaceful facade of his youth, and Payne, Ulam, and the others generally followed that picture. But it turned out to be a false picture, accepting too uncritically the legend of the rational revolutionary. Two biographers split this front and left it in shattered rubble: Possony and Valentinov-Volsky. They present compelling evidence which, when combined with the tidbits offered by the others, fall into place. And to my genuinely unexpected astonishment, Lenin's pattern turned out to be perfectly congruent with the others. Indeed, even to the utterly amazing disillusionment in the last days before death, Robespierre and Lenin match. (Marx never gained power and never had to cope first-hand with intractable reality as he sought to procrusteanize the world on his own bed of utopian dreaming.)

NOTES

INTRODUCTION

1. Trotsky himself shrank not the slightest from such a conclusion. On the fifth anniversary of the Bolsheviks' Sverdloff University, on June 18, 1923, to the younger generation he offered this moral thesis: "A revolutionary is he who is not afraid to 'uproot' and put into practice the most merciless oppression. In these actions the moral ones . . . Comrads! Existing conditions already present too many handicaps for a true revolutionary to allow himself the luxury of multiplying objective obstacles by subjective ones. Consequently subjective obstacles (religion, morals, legal rights, etc.) which prevent this merciless oppression. That is why we consider atheism, which is an inherent element of materialism, an indispensible ingredient of a terroristic revolutionary education." It would be hard to imagine a more bloody-minded, egotistical justification for what came to be known as Stalinism; one can hardly help thinking, remembering the ax murder that ended his life, that Trotsky got what he deserved. The quote is from Sorokin, Pitirim A., *The Sociology of Revolution* (New York: Fertig, 1967—1925 Lippincott edition reissued), p. 362.

2. *The Decline of Radicalism, Reflections on America Today* (New York: Random House, 1969), pp. 121–126. I do not mean to single out Dr. Boorstin as a whipping boy, but simply as a recent representative of the kind of definitional debater I am talking about.

3. Ulam, Adam, *The Bolsheviks* (New York: Collier edition, 1968), p. 514.

4. *Karl Marx, Early Writings* (New York: McGraw-Hill), p. 52. Emphasis in original. Note that these sentences come from the same paragraph Marx began by declaring: "It is clear that the weapon of criticism cannot replace the criticism of weapons," the very defining characteristic of Marxian radicalism that Boorstin would surely reject. Cf. Boorstin, *op. cit.*, p. 122.

5. *Virginia Quarterly Review*, Summer 1970, p. 389.

6. *Op. cit.*, pp. 395–397.

7. Address at the Eleanor Roosevelt Memorial Foundation Luncheon, New York Hilton, April 9, 1964.

CHAPTER 1   THE MALIGNANT DREAM

1. See, e.g., Glenn Negley and J. Max Patrick, *The Quest for Utopia, an Anthology of Imaginary Societies* (New York: Doubleday Anchor, 1962).

2. J.O. Hertzler, *The History of Utopian Thought* (New York: Macmillan, Company, 1926), pp. 7–12.

3. Isaiah 53:17; 41: 18–19; 43:19; 51:2; 65: 23; 60:20.

4. R.H.S. Crossman, *Plato Today* (Rev. ed., New York: Oxford University Press, 1959), p. 9.

5. Karl R. Popper, *The Open Society and Its Enemies* (New York: Harper Torchbooks, 1963), p. 14.

6. Ibid., p. 17.

7. Ibid., p. 171.

8. Ibid., pp. 148, 173, 194.

9. Ibid., p. 201.

10. Op. cit. (New York: Harper Torchbooks, 1961), pp. xv, 3. Cohn summarizes his conclusions on pages 21–32 and 307–319. Compare R.A. Knox's excellent parallel study, *Enthusiasm* (New York: Oxford University Press, 1950). Knox explores the groups within and without the Catholic church that over the centuries denounced the Establishment in the name of a private vision and perfervid revivalism-revolutionism.

11. Hanser, Richard, *Putsch! How Hitler Made Revolution* (New York: Wyden, 1970), p. 8.

12. Ibid., p. xiv.

13. Ibid.

14. Ibid., pp. 32, 314–315.

15. Ibid., pp. 70–71

16. Ibid., pp. 318–319.

17. One such behavioral scientist is Anthony Storr. See his book, *Human Aggression* (New York: Atheneum, 1968), chapter 6.

18. Karl Stern, *The Flight From Woman* (London: Allen and Unwin, 1966).

19. Alexander Herzberg, *The Psychology of Philosophers* (New York: Harcourt, Brace and Company, 1929).

20. See, Storr, op. cit., and Lionel Tiger, *Men In Groups* (New York: Random House, 1969).

21. Knox, op. cit., pp. 581–582.

CHAPTER 2   ROUSSEAU: THE IGNOBLE SAVAGE

1. Letter to Malesherbes, January 12, 1762. Emphasis added.

2. Jean Francois Marmontel, *Memoirs,* many editions. One translation is the 1903 edition of Merrill and Baker, New York, in which this episode is recounted in Volume II, pp. 322–323. Marmontel recounts the story as it was told to him by Diderot, whose reliability may be generally credited in such matters, while Rousseau's is not.

3. Isaiah Berlin, *Karl Marx, His Life and Times* (New York: Oxford University Press, 1959), p. 42.

4. *Les Reveries d'un promeneur solitaire,* Book VI.

5. Correspondence, August 30, 1755.

6. Ibid., March 1765.

7. C. Sainte-Beuve, *Portraits of the Eighteenth Century* (New York: 1905), Vol. 1, p. 230.

8. Book One.

9. G. Crocker, Lester *Jean-Jacques Rousseau* (New York: Macmillan Company, 1968), 1:14. This is the latest and best psychoanalytic study of Rousseau. See especially pp. 11–16, 186–188, 194, 356.

10. Will Durant, *The Story of Philosophy* (Pocket Library edition; New York: Simon and Schuster, 1926), p. 259–260.

11. Book VI.

12. Book VI.

13. Book I (emphasis added).

14. Book II.

15. Book IX.

16. Book I.

17. Durants, *Rousseau And Revolution*, p. 211.

18. Confessions, Second Part, Vol. IV.

19. Jean Francois Marmontel, *Memoirs*, (London: John Murray, 1805), 3:-10–12.

20. Book IV.

21. *Emile.*

22. In *The Federalist*, No. 6, Madison wrote: "A man must be far gone in Utopian speculations . . . to forget that men are ambitious, vindictive, and rapacious . . . Have we not already seen enough of the fallacy and extravagance of those idle theories which have amused us with promises of an exemption from the imperfections, weaknesses, and evils incident to society in every shape? Is it not time to awake from the deceitful dream of a golden age and to adopt as a practical maxim for the direction of our political conduct that we, as well as other inhabitants of the globe, are yet remote from the happy empire of perfect wisdom and perfect virtue?" (Some scholars attribute this essay to Hamilton.)

23. Bertrand Russell, *A History Of Western Philosophy* (New York: Simon and Schuster, 1946), p. 684–685.

24. J.B. Bury, *The Idea of Progress, and Inquiry Into Its Growth and Origin* (New York; Macmillan Company, 1932), p. 193 in Dover edition of 1955.

CHAPTER 3   ROBESPIERRE: DEMON CERTITUDE STALKS THE EARTH

1. J.M. Thompson, *Robespierre* (New York: Appleton-Century Company, 1936), 1:8.

2. John Morely, *Biographical Studies* (London: Macmillan Ltd., 1923), p. 313.

3. George Rudé, *The Crowd in the French Revolution* (New York: Oxford University Press, 1959), p. 56.

4. Ibid., pp. 11–12.

5. Morley, op. cit., pp. 262–263.

6. Rudé, op. cit., pp. 109–110.

7. Thompson, op. cit., 1: 289–290.

8. J.L. Talmon, *The Origins of Totalitarian Democracy* (New York: Praeger, 1960), pp. 135–137.

9. Thompson, op. cit., 1: 20.

10. Ibid., 2: 218.

11. Thompson, op. cit. 1: 298–299.

12. Compare Robespierre's rationalization for dispensing with a popular vote to Radio Havana's 168 years later. Before succeeding Batista, Fidel Castro promised elections within a year or two from the dictator's overthrow. Castro took power in January 1959. Three years later overseas listeners wrote Radio Havana asking about the promised elections. On July 23, 1962, Radio Havana broadcast this answer:

> It is quite true that Fidel expected that there would be elections in Cuba within a year or two after the downfall of Batista, and he said so . . . Nobody in Cuba is opposed to elections on principle. We think Cuba is democratic, that power is in the hands of the people, basically of the working class . . . Our democracy is not now expressed through a congress or parliament with regular national elections, but that does not mean it is any the less real and less democratic. Cuba is going through a transitional stage in which our institutions have not caught up with the big changes that have taken place. We are operating under the constitution of 1940 with a number of amendments, but very soon we will have to adopt a new constitution for a socialist Cuba. You cannot write a constitution overnight. A country that is facing an emergency such as a threatened invasion cannot afford to have an election just for the sake of having an election when there is no difference of opinion on the main issue. We do not have differences about

our future, but we do have to win our struggle against outside intervention, that is, the intervention sponsored by U.S. interests. And even if we wanted one right now, it would be a luxury we could not afford.

People here are convinced, and show it in their actions, that Fidel Castro and the team with him are the best leaders Cuba can produce, and that they are going in the direction we want to go in. An election just to settle that would be useless and would only give the enemies of the revolution a chance to try and create divisions when none now exist. We think the essential thing for us today is political unity around the achievements and aims of the revolution. So, no one here is opposed to elections on principle. But we are going to be the ones to decide when we have them and how they are organized.

Ten years later, Cubans are still waiting for the Castro regime to reckon the time ripe for an election. The people of Russia are waiting after 55 years for either the promised elections or withering away of the Soviet state.

13. *The Rebel* (New York: Random House-Vintage, 1956), p. 120.

CHAPTER 4 ROBESPIERRE: FROM IDEALIST TO TYRANT

1. J.M. Thompson, *Robespierre* (New York: Appleton, Century Company, 1936), 1: 34–35.

2. Ibid., 2: 66–67.

3. Ibid. 2: 140.

4. Ibid., 2: 143

5. Ibid., 2: 182–184.

6. In 1793 the Jacobins instituted a new calendar, free of Christian "superstitions." The month of May became "Prairial."

7. Ibid., 2: 203.

8. John Morley, *Biographical Studies* (London: Macmillan Ltd., 1923), p. 343 Cf. figures cited by Hilaire Belloc, p. 323.

9. Thompson, op. cit., 2: 247.

10. Ibid., 2: 248.

11. Ibid., 2: 249–50.

12. Ibid., 2: 266.

13. Lippmann, Walter, *The Public Philosophy* (New York: Mentor, 1956 ed.), p. 71.

CHAPTER 5   BABEUF: THE RISE OF HATE MEDIA

1. Philippe Buonarroti, trans. Bronterre O'Brien, *History of Babeuf's Conspiracy For Equality*, (London: H. Hetherington, 1836), pp. 38–39n.

2. Ibid., p. 43.

3. Milton Rokeach, *The Open and Closed Mind* (New York: Basic Books, 1960).

4. Buonarroti, op. cit., pp. 38–39n.

5. N. L. Talmon, *The Origins of Totalitarian Democracy* (New York: Praeger, 1960), p. 317.

6. Ibid., p. 207.

7. Ibid., p. 169.

8. Ibid., pp. 169–170.

9. Buronarroti, op. cit., p. 62.

10. Ibid., p. 80.

11. Ibid. p. 76.

12. Josette Lepine, *Babeuf* (Paris: Editions Heir et Aujourd 'hui, 1949), p. 185.

13. Ibid., p. 186.

14. Buonarroti, op. cit., pp. 88–89.

15. Ibid., pp. 302–303.

CHAPTER 6   BABEUF: FOUNDING THE TECHNOLOGY OF SOCIAL DEMOLITION

1. See my *The Riot Makers, The Technology of Social Demolition* (New Rochelle, N. Y.: Arlington House, 1970), Chapter V, "The Riot Makers in History."

2. Josette Lepine, *Babeuf* (Paris: Editions Heir et Aujourd 'hui, 1949), p. 192.

3. Philippe Buonarroti, *History of Babeuf's Conspiracy for Equality,* trans. Bronterre O'Brien (London: H. Hetherington, 1836), p. 93.

4. Ibid., p. 123.

5. Elizabeth L. Eisenstein, *The First Professional Revolutionist: Filippo Michele Buonarroti (1761–1837)* (Cambridge: Harvard University Press, 1959), p. 27.

6. Buonarroti, op. cit., p. 304.

7. Ibid., pp. 310–311.

8. Ibid., p. 311.

9. Buonarroti, p. 311.

10. Lepine, op. cit., p. 190.

11. Buonarroti, op. cit., p. 391.

12. J.M. Thomson, *Robespierre* (New York: Appleton-Century Company, 1936), 1: 26–27).

13. Buonarroti, op. cit., p. 95.

14. Lepine, op. cit., p. 192.

15. Gerard Walter, *Babeuf et la Conjuration des Egaux* (Paris: Payot, 1937), p. 125.

16. The classic case of revolutionary radical propaganda in the military is the French Communist Party's work in the French Army in the 1936–40 period before the fall of France. See my *The Riot Makers*, p. 295.

17. Walter, op. cit.

18. Lepine, op. cit. pp. 195–196.

19. Buonarroti, p. 146.

20. Ibid., p. 102n. (Emphasis added.)

21. Buonarroti, op. cit., pp. 135–6, 139 and 142–3. (This estimate was doubtless high; for example, it included 6,100 members of the Legion of Police, 1,000 of the Grenadiers of the Legislature's protective guard, and 1,000 revolutionists from the provinces.)

22. Ibid., p. 131.

23. Ibid., p. 136.

24. Thomson, op. cit., pp. 53–56.

25. Buonarroti, p. 260.

CHAPTER 7   BUONARROTI: THE ORGANIZATIONAL SPIDER

1. Franco Venturi, *Roots of Revolution* (New York: Alfred A. Knopf, 1960), p. 74.

2. Réne Fulop-Miller, *The Jesuits, A History of the Society of Jesus* (New York: Capricorn Books, 1963), p. 435.

3. Elizabeth L. Eisenstein, *The First Professional Revolutionist: Filippo Michele Buonarroti, 1761–1837* (Cambridge, Mass.: Harvard University Press, 1959), pp. 11, 39–43.

4. Abbe Barruel, *Memoires Pour Servir a L'Histoire du Jacobinisme* (London, 1797).

5. Eisenstein, op. cit., p. 12.

6. Ibid., p. 18. Cf. Arthur Lehning, "Buonarroti's Ideas on Communism and Dictatorship," *International Review of Social History*, 2 (1957), 268n.

7. Eisenstein, op. cit., p. 32.

8. Ibid., p. 45.

9. Arthur Lehning, "Buonarroti and His Secret Societies," *International Review of Social History*, 1 (1956), 135. This essay and the one on Buonarroti's ideas, Ibid., p. 6, were published in a collection of Lehning's essays under the title, *From Buonarroti to Bakunin* (Leiden: A. J. Brill, 1970).

10. Eisenstein, op. cit., p. 37.

11. Ibid., p. 40. (Emphasis added.)

12. Ibid., p. 83.

13. Quoted in Ibid., p. 34.

14. Alexander Andryane, *Souvenirs De Geneve* (Brussels, 1839), 1: 120, quoted in Eisenstein, op. cit., p. 50.

15. Ibid.

16. Arthur Lehning, "Buonarroti and His Secret Societies," p. 129.

17. Carl F. Wittke, *The Utopian Communist, A Biography of Wilheim Weitling, Nineteenth-Century Reformer* (Baton Rouge: Louisiana State University Press, 1950), p. 20.

18. See generally, Max Nomad, *Apostles of Revolution* (New York: Crowell-Collier, 1961), p. 26.

CHAPTER 8   "NEW GODS FOR THE VACANT SHRINE"

1. Robert C. Tucker, *Philosophy and Myth in Karl Marx* (New York: Cambridge University Press, 1961), pp. 41–44.

2. Lorenz von Stein, *Socialismus und Communismus Des Heutigen Frankreichs. Ein Beitrag Zur Zeitgeschichte* (Leipzig; Otto Wigand, 1842), cited

in Auguste Cornu, *Karl Marx Et Friedrich Engles*, (Paris: Presses univer-
sitaire de France, 1958), 2: 166.

3. Von Stein, op. cit.

4. Ibid., pp. 28 and 4, Cf. 31 & 64 (Emphasis added.)

5. Ibid., p. 28 (emphasis added.)

BIBLIOGRAPHICAL NOTE: Many biographies have been written on Marx.
The most readable and objective, by far, for a beginning student is Leopold
Schwarzschild's *The Red Prussian: The Life and Legend of Karl Marx*, trans.
from the German by Margaret Wing (New York: Charlles Scribneer's Sons,
1947). In depth of scholarship and independence I would rank first Boris
Nikolaevsky and Otto Maenchen-Helfen, *Karl Marx, Man and Fighter*
(Philadelpia: J. B. Lippincott Company, 1936). Also valuable is E. Carr, *Karl
Marx, A Study in Fanaticism* (London: J. M. Dent and Sons, 1934). Otto
Ruhle's *Karl Marx, His Life and Work* (London: Allen and Unwin, 1928) falls
in the category of worshipful hagiography, but less so than Franz Mehring's
1918 biography, reissued in 1962 by the University of Michigan Press. Robert
Payne's 1970 biography (Simon and Schuster) is readable but less reliable in
some respects than Schwartzschild; it gives the first complete account in
English of Marx's illegitimate son, a story first told in Werner Blumenberg's
Marx (Hamburg: Rowohlt, 1962), which is not available in English. —FHM

CHAPTER 9   PROCRUSTEAN PHILOSOPHY ORGANIZES
THE WORLD

1. Otto Ruhle, *Karl Marx, His Life and Work* (London: Allen and Unwin,
1928), pp. 57–58.

2. *Karl Marx, Early Writings*, T. B. Bottomore, trans. and ed. (New York:
McGraw-Hill Book Company, 1964), p. 46.

3. *Collected Works* (Moscow: Progress Publishers, 1964), 21: 58; from a 1914
encyclopedia article on Marxism.

4. *Complete Works*, 19: 27–28. *Cf. The Teachings of Karl Marx*, (New York:
International Publishers, 1964), pp. 47–48, for a slightly different translation.

5. The full texts of these manuscripts and of *The German Ideology* were not
published until 1932. Plekhanov, Lenin, Kautsky, and Rosa Luxemburg were

unaware of their existence. The 1844 manuscripts, vital though they are for an understanding of Marx's early development, did not appear in English until 1961.

6. Robert Tucker, *Philosophy and Myth in Karl Marx* (Cambridge University Press, 1961), p. 189.

7. Erich Fromm, *Marx's Concept of Man* (New York: Frederick Ungar, 1961), p. 49.

8. *Das Kapital*, 1: 461–462.

9. Fromm, op. cit., pp. 98–99.

10. Karl Marx and Friedrich Engels, *The German Ideology* (New York, International Publishers, 1947), p. 22.

11. They selected that name to avoid confusion with a socialist party founded by Louis Blanc, although they both considered "socialism" and "communism" interchangeable.

12. This significant letter was discovered in Proudhon's archievs and was published in the new edition of Proudhon, *Confessions D'une Revolutionnaire* (Paris: 1929), pp. 432–433.

13. Pierre Joseph Proudhon, *Correspondence*, 2: 198 et seq.

14. Letter to Marx, November 24, 1847, *Marx-Engels Correspondence* (New York: International Publishers, 1935), p. 20.

15. *Collected Works*, 21: 58 (from a 1914 encyclopedia article on Marxism).

CHAPTER 10   PHILOSOPHY ON THE BARRICADES—AND IN EXILE

1. *Rapport de la commission d'enquete sur l'ensurrection qui a eclate dans la journee du 23 Juin et sur les evenements du 15 mai*, 2: 93, 277, et seq.

2. Karl Marx, *Selected Works*, 2: 289, 293.

3. Alphonse Lucas, *Les Clubs Et Les Clubistes*, p. 114; cited by Samuel

Bernstein, "Marx In Paris, 1848: A Neglected Chapter," *Science & Society, A Marxist Quarterly*, Summer 1939, p. 323.

4. Friedrich Engels, "Zur Geschichte Des Bundes Der Kommunisten," p. 13.

5. Marx-Engels Gasamt-Ausgabe, Erstc Abteilung, Band 7, pp. 115–118.

CHAPTER 11   WHAT MADE MARXISM TICK?

1. Alfred G. Meyer, *Marxism, The Unity of Theory and Practice* (Cambridge, Mass.: Harvard University Press, 1954), p. 49.

2. H.H. Hart, "Masochism, Passivity, and Radicalism," *Psychoanalytic Review*, October 1952.

3. Letter of July 23, 1877.

4. Letter of August 17, 1877.

5. See H.S. Wolff, *Headache and Other Head Pain* (New York: Oxford University Press, 1950), Chapter IX. Also Wolf and Marcussen, "A Formulation of the Dynamics of the Migraine Attack," *Psychosomatic Medicine*, September-October 1949, pp. 252–256. There may be a hereditary linkage that creates a congenital predisposition to migraine.

6. Flanders Dunbar, *Emotions and Bodily Changes* (4th ed.: New York: Columbia University Press, 1954), p. 380. See also Seymore L. Lustman, "The Headache as an Internalized Rage Reaction," *Psychiatry*, November 1959, pp. 433–438. Also N.F. Vincent, "Psychodynamics of a Patient with Migraine," *American Journal of Psychotherapy*, 14 (1960): 589, 603–604.

7. Dunbar, op. cit., p. 596. One researcher was able to produce and eliminate skin eruptions by hypnotic suggestion. Often he could reinduce the eruptions by posthyptomic suggestion after as long as a year. In one case he eliminated furunculosis hypnotically. He could even establish the specific psychogenesis of psychosomatic furunculosis by telling patients in deep hypnosis if the symptom had a connection with some particular experience in memory they would dream about it and relate the dream the following morning.

8. Ruhle, pp. 377–378.

9. See Else Frenkel-Brunswik, "A Study of Prejudice in Children," *Human Relations*, 1: 295–306; also to Adorno *et al.*, *The Authoritarian Personality* (New York: Harper & Brothers, 1950); and Milton Rokeach, *The Open and Closed Mind* (New York: Basic Books, 1960).

10. Ibid., p. 302.

CHAPTER 12   CHERNYSHEVSKY: THE GREAT PREDECESSOR

1. Nikolai Valentinov (N.V. Volsky), *The Early Years of Lenin* (Ann Arbor: University of Michigan Press, 1969), p. 130. Hereafter cited as II Valentinov.

2. Nikolai Valentinov (N.V. Volski), *Encounters With Lenin* (Ann Arbor: University of Michigan Press, 1968), p. 70. Hereafter cited as I Valentinov.

3. II Valentinov, 267–268.

4. David Shub, *Lenin* (Baltimore: Pelican Books, 1967), p. 22. Hereafter cited as Shub.

5. I Valentinov, pp. 72–73.

CHAPTER 13   NECHAYEV: "THE REVOLUTIONARY CATECHISM"

1. Rene Cannac, *Netchaiev, du nihilisme au terrorisme* (Paris: Payot, 1961), p. 31.

2. Z. K. Ralli, "S. G. Nechayev" (*Byloe*, 1906, No. Vii), cited in Franco Venturi, *Roots of revolution* (New York: Alfred A. Knopf, 1960), pp. 359, 772. Ralli was a member of Nechayev's circle in Petersburg, and later became a well-known anarchist.

3. Venturi, op. cit., p. 362.

4. In 1917 a note was found in police archives stating that Nechayev had indeed been interrogated in February 1869. Police agents had earlier been instructed to establish who the speakers and organizers of the student assemblies were, and on January 30, the police received information that the day before a conspiracy meeting had occurred in Nechayev's room at a parish

school. See Michael Prawdin, *The Unmentionable Nechayev* (New York: Roy, 1964), pp. 19–20, 25.

5. Cannac, op. cit., pp. 35–38. Cannac bases his account on Vera Zazulitch's "Souvenirs," published in *Byloe* No. 14, Petrograd, 1919; and her "The Nechayev Affair" in *Gruppa Osvobojdenia Pruda*, No. 2, Moscow, 1924.

6. Avrahm Yarmolinsky, *Road to Revolution, a Century of Russian Radicalism* (New York: MacMillan Company, 1956), p. 149 (Collier edition). See Robert Payne, *The Terrorists* (New York: Funk and Wagnalls, 1957), p. 9.

7. E. H. Carr, *Bakunin* (New York: Vintage Books, 1961), p. 391.

8. Warren Rogers, New York *Herald Tribune* correspondent in interview with the author in 1962.

CHAPTER 14   NECHAYEV: "THE POSSESSED"

1. In his feud with Bakunin, Marx reported this episode with relish on page 79 of his pamphlet, *L'Alliances*—but pulled deals just as sordid himself when it suited his purpose.

2. K. J. Kenafick, *Michael Bakunin and Karl Marx* (London: Freedom Press, 1948), pp. 132–133.

3. Michael Prowdin, *The Unmentionable Nechayev* (New York; Roy, 1964), pp. 98–99.

4. Ibid., pp. 92–93.

5. Yarmolinsky, *Road to Revolution, A Century of Russian Radicalism* (New York: Macmillan Company, 1956), p. 157.

6. Cited in E. Lampert, *Studies in Rebellion* (London: Routledge and Kegan Paul, 1957), p. 152.

7. Mikhail Sazhin, Ibid.

8. Franco Venturi, *Roots of Revolution* (New York: Alfred A. Knopf, 1960), p. 377.

9. Max Nomad, *Apostles of Revolution* (New York: Crowell-Collier, 1961), pp. 233–234.

10. Alexander Gambarov, *The Dispute Over Nechayev* (Moscow: 1926), cited in Prawdin, pp. 189–190.

11. Bonch-Bruyevich's memoirs, cited in David Shub, *Lenin, A Biography* (Baltimore: Penquin Books, 1967), p. 422 and Robert Payne, *The Life and Death of Lenin* (New York: Simon & Schuster, 1964), p. 34.

CHAPTER 15   TKACHEV: THE JACOBIN

1. Weeks, Albert L., *The First Bolshevik* (New York: New York University Press, 1968), pp. 48–50, 67n.

2. Ibid., p. 57.

3.Ibid., p. 58.

4. Ibid., pp. 4–5.

5. Ibid., p. 86. See translation (followed here) in Weeks' article by the same title in *Problems of Communism*, November-December 1967, p. 100. (Emphasis added.)

6. Weeks, op. cit., p. 87.

7. David Shub, *Lenin* (Baltimore: Penquin Books, 1967), p. 73. (Emphasis in original.)

8. Bertram Wolfe, *Three Who Made a Revolution* (Boston: Beacon Press, 1955 paperback reprint of 1948 Dial Press edition), p. 156.

9. Adam B. Ulam, *The Bolsheviks* (New York: Macmillan Company, 1965), p. 121. Ulam erroneously attributes the formulation originally to Plekhanov. (All citations are to the 1968 Collier Books edition.)

10. Weeks, op. cit., pp. 88–89.

11. Michael Karpovich, "A Forerunner of Lenin—P.N. Tkachev," *Review of Politics*, (July 1944): 336–350. (Emphasis added.)

12. Weeks, op. cit., p. 121.

13. P.B. Alexrod, *Perezhitoe I Peredumannoe* (Berlin, 1923), pp. 198.

14. Quoted in Karpovich, op. cit. p. 343.

15. Nikolai Valentinov, *Encounters With Lenin* (New York-London: Oxford University Press, 1968), p. 118.

CHAPTER 16   THE DIE IS CAST

1. Unpublished manuscript, "Lenin's Great Mistake," by Max Eastman. (After the first citation in this and succeding chapters, all biographies of Lenin will be cited by author's last name. In the case of Valentinov's two biographies, *Encounters with Lenin* will be referred to as Valentinov I; *The Early Years of Lenin*, as Valentinov II. Lenin's *Collected Works* was pub lished in English translation in 45 volumes by the Foreign Languages Publishing House, Moscow, from 1960 to 1970. These volumes will be cited by volume number, title and page number, e.g., 21 *Collected Works* 215. Most quotations are verbatim, but occasionally I have taken the liberty of changing the translation in the interest of clarity and comprehension for the American reader, relying on a comparison with earlier translations of Lenin andy my own insight into his concepts.)

2. Stefan T. Possony, *Lenin: The Compulsive Revolutionary* (Chicago: Henry Regnery Company, 1964), p. 380.

3. Nikolai Valentinov, *The Early Years of Lenin* (Ann Arbor: University of Michigan Press, 1969), p. 196.

4. II Valentinov, p. 251–252.

5. Ibid., pp. 241–242.

6. Ibid., p. 232.

7. Adam B. Ulam, *The Bolsheviks* (Collier Books ed.; New York: Macmillan Company, 1965), p. 19. Quotings Soviet source.

8. II Valentinov, pp. 276–275.

9. Cf. I Valentinov, pp. 63–65; II Valentinov, pp. 194–196.

CHAPTER 17   CREATING THE SOCIOLOGY OF
DISCONTENT

1. II Valentinov, pp. 68, 143.

2. 1 *Collected Works*, p. 236. Insofar as possible Lenin's quotations are drawn from the *Collected Works* 45-volume edition issued from 1960 to 1970 by the Foreign Languages Publishing House-Progress Publishers in Moscow.

3. See Lenin's revealing 1907 response to the RSDLP party commission, *infra*, page 315.

4. See generally T. Adorno et al., *The Authoritarian Personality* (New York: Harper & Row, 1950) and Milton Rokeach, *The Open and Closed Mind* (New York Basic Books, 1960).

5. II Valentinov, p. 186.

6. Ibid., pp. 185–187, 213.

7. Stefan T. Possony, *Lenin: The Compulsive Revolutionary* (Chicago: Henry Regnery Company, 1964), p. 92.

8. II Valentinov, p. 188. Translation slightly modified for clarity.

9. 14 *Collected Works*, p. 143. Here we follow the more readable translation in II Valentinov, p. 187.

10. Unpublished manuscript, "Lenin's Great Mistake," by Max Eastman.

11. Possony, op. cit., p. 26.

12. I Valentinov, pp. 73–74.

13. Ibid., pp. 118, 127–30n, 173–174.

14. Valentinov, p. 171, emphasis added. Vodovozov was generally an independent and objective—even a bit hostile—observer, though not inclined in 1925 to emphasize his hostility. Vodovozov may have been in error in placing Lenin's detailed mastery of Marx in 1891, or he may have predated it to conform to the Soviet mythology of making him a teen-age whiz-kid of revolution. Possony, p. 32, points out correctly that

Lenin's first published writing, a long book review written in the spring of 1893, did not quote Marx once, a remarkable omission. The second work, written that fall, abounded with quotes from *Das Kapital.* In March 1893 he met his first real Marxist, Lalayants. The omission of Marx quotations from the 1893 book review may not signify that Lenin began his study of Marx only afterwards; since Lenin intended the review for legal publication, he may have omitted mentioning Marx deliberately, seeking to foil the censors.

15. II Valentinov, p. 156.

16. Ibid.

17. Ibid, pp. 172–173.

18. Possony, op. cit., pp. 24–25.

19. Louis Fischer, *The Life of Lenin* (New York: Harper and Row, 1964), p. 21.

20. 1 *Collected Works,* p. 511.

21. Possony, op. cit., p. 35.

22. 1 *Collected Works,* pp. 235–236.

23. Ibid., p. 236. Italics in original.

24. Ibid., p. 184.

25. Ibid., p. 185.

26. Ibid., p. 286. (Emphasis added.) Cf. translation in II Valentinov, pp. 237–238.

27. Ibid., pp. 296–297.

28. Ibid., pp. 298–299. (Italics added.)

29. Ibid., p. 300. Translation altered slightly for clarity. See Payne, p. 102.

30. Ibid., p. 320.

31. Ibid., pp. 327–328. The quote is Marx's September 1843 letter to Ruge. This is the second time Lenin quotes it in his book. See p. 184.

CHAPTER 18   BUILDING HATE MEDIA

1. N. K. Krupskaya, *Reminiscences of Lenin* (Moscow: Foreign Languages Publishing House, 1959), p. 18.

2. Ibid., pp. 23–24. Also 1 *Collected Works*, p. 543.

3. Ibid., pp. 23–24. Also 1 *Collected Works*, p. 543.

4. Ibid., pp. 24–25.

5. Quoted in Stefan T. Possony, *Lenin: The Compulsive Revolutionary* (Chicago: Henry Regnery Company, 1964), p. 37.

6. 1 *Collected Works*, pp. 333–508.

7. II Valentinov, pp. 244–245.

8' *"Ob Agitatsii"* ("On Agitation"). S. Poslesloviem, p. Akselroda. Geneva, 1896, p. 21.

9. Krupskaya, op, cit., p. 19.

10. 5 *Collected Works* 376.

11. 2 *Collected Works* 81, p. 543, n28.

12. 34 *Collected Works*, p. 22.

13. 5 *Collected Works*, pp. 377, 378.

14. 3 *Collected Works*, p. 599. Emphasis added.

15. 5 *Collected Works* 430. Translation varied slightly, conforming with other English versions.

16. "The Hannibals of Liberalism," written in June 1901 and published in the theoretical magazine *Dawn*. Also "What is To Be Done? Burning Questions," a hefty booklet written in late 1901 and published in March 1902, and

named after the Chernyshevsky novel that "plowed over" the 17-year-old Lenin. Also "A Letter to a Comrad on Our Organizational Tasks," written in September 1902.

17. Krupskaya, op. cit., p. 45.

18. 5 *Collected Works* 370–371.

CHAPTER 19   THE AT&T OF HATE

1. 5 *Collected Works*, p. 355.

2. Ibid., pp. 508–509.

3. David Shub, *Lenin, A Biography* (Baltimore: Penguin Books, 1967), p. 68.

4. Ibid., pp. 389–390.

5. Ibid., pp. 374–375.

6. Ibid., p. 384.

7. Ibid., p. 464.

8. Ibid., p. 430.

9. Ibid., pp. 430, 420.

10. Ibid., p. 422.

11. Ibid., pp. 424–425.

12. See Eugene H. Methuin, *The Riot Makers* (New Rochelle,) N.Y.: Arlington House, 1970), Chapters VIII, IX.

13. 5 *Collected Works*, p. 402.

14. Ibid., p. 410.

15. Ibid., p. 412.

16. Ibid., p. 500.

17. Ibid., pp. 400–401.

18. Ibid., p. 414.

19. Methvin, op. cit., Chapters I, IV, VIII, XII.

20. 5 *Collected Works*, pp. 431–432.

21. Ibid., p. 440.

22. Ibid., p. 512. See Translation by International Publishers, New York, 1929.

23. Ibid., p. 440

24. Ibid., pp. 502–508.

25. Ibid., p. 514. (Emphasis added.)

26. Ibid., p. 489.

27. Ibid., p. 499.

28. Ibid., p. 501.

29. Ibid., p. 500.

30. Ibid., p. 488.

31. 5 *Collected Works* 316, "A Talk with Defenders of Economism," an article Lenin published in *Iskra*, No. 12, December 6, 1901, during the period in which he was writing "What Is To Be Done?"

33. Ibid., p. 505.

34. Ibid., pp. 506–508.

35. Ibid., p. 492.

36. Ibid.

37. 6 *Collected Works*, p. 236, "Letter to a Comrade on Our Organizational Tasks," September 1902. "What Is To Be Done?" created a sensation among

Russian Marxists, already split as they were between "revisionists" and "revolutionists." After Lenin's 1895 arrest, the St. Petersburg group had fallen to the revisionists. But in June 1902 the Party central committee voted to go over to the *Iskra*-ists, as the Leninists were now called. A fierce struggle broke out in the ranks between "economists" and *Iskra*-ists. One comrade wrote Lenin—in London by now—discussing the problems they faced in creating a local organization to fit within the grand design Lenin had laid out for the nationwide structure. Lenin gave the question great thought, and in September 1902 answered with his "Letter to a Comrade on our Organizational Tasks." With "What Is To Be Done?" it became one of the two books known as "the bible of the master mold bolshevism," used to stamp out professional revolutionaries in communist training schools the world over.

38. Ibid., p. 24.

39. Ibid., p. 245.

40. Ibid.

41. Ibid., p. 247.

42. Ibid., p. 242.

43. Ibid., pp. 240–241.

44. Ibid., p. 247.

45. Ibid., p. 246.

46. Ibid.

47. Ibid., p. 247.

48. Ibid., p. 244.

49. Ibid., p. 249.

50. Ibid., p. 248.

51. Ibid., p. 242.

52. Ibid., p. 250.

53. Ibid.,

54. 5 *Collected Works*, p. 69. This is Lenin's essay entitled "The Hannibals of Liberalism."

55. 31 *Collected Works*, p. 99, "Left-Wing Communism—An Infantile Disorder," written in 1920. We quote it though 18 years had elapsed, because it shows how Lenin was still true to the principles of his 1902 essay; and as in the earlier case, he was writing to instruct neophytes in his grand design —in this instance, some overzealous British comrades.

CHAPTER 20   THE MAGNETISM OF THE DREAM

1. 5 *Collected Works*, pp. 509–510.

2. Ibid., pp. 501–502.

3. Bertram D. Wolfe, *Three Who Made A Revolution* (Boston: Beacon, 1955 edition), p. 147.

4. One crucial retreat was on slaughtering the Kulaks. See II Valentinov.

5. 5 *Collected Works* 452, 453, 454.

CHAPTER 21   BUILDING THE AT&T OF HATE

1. 7 *Collected Works*, p. 453. See p. 461.

2. I Valentinov, pp. 232–233.

3. Theodore Abel, *The Nazi Movement (Why Hitler Came To Power)* (New York: Atherton, 1966), pp. 65–67, 181–182.

4. I Valentinov, pp. 183, 202.

5. Ibid., pp. 128–129.

6. Stefan T. Possony, *Lenin: The Compulsive Revolutionary* (Chicago: Henry Regnery Company, 1964), p. 80. Emphasis added.

7. 7 *Collected Works*, p. 453. See p. 461.

8. Possony, op. cit., p. 80.

9. Letter to S. I. Gusev, February 15, 1905.

10. 8 *Collected Works* 113. See translation in earlier edition, *Works,* Vol. 8, p. 93, quoted in Adam Ulam, *The Bolsheviks* (New York: Collier Books edition, 1968), p. 206.

11. 8 *Collected Works*, p. 104.

12. 9 *Collected Works* 345–346. See translations in David Shub, *Lenin, A Biography* (Baltimore: Penguin Books, 1967), pp. 101–102, and Robert Payne, *The Life and Death of Lenin* (New York: Simon & Schuster, 1964), p. 189.

13. Possony, op. cit., pp. 93–94.

14. Ibid., p. 98. On the importance of the Lenin's training school innovation, see my *The Riot Makers* (New Rochelle, N. Y.: Arlington House, 1971), pp. 132–136.

15. Bertram D. Wolfe, *Three Who Made A Revolution* (Boston: Beacon, 1955 edition), p. 375.

16. Possony, op. cit., p. 388.

17. 12 *Collected Works*, pp. 424–425.

CHAPTER 22   COLONIZING LENINIST HATE MEDIA CARTELS

1. 28 *Collected Works*, p. 241. 29 *Collected Works*, p. 485.

2. David Shub, *Lenin, A Biography* (Baltimore: Penguin Books, 1967), p. 304.

3. 31 *Collect Works*, p. 207.

4. 33 *Collected Works*, p. 358. The English translation decrees death for "propaganda or agitation that objectively serves the interests" of the anti-

communist bourgeoisie. The 1951 Russian edition contains the even more brutal version reported here, which was softened in the Moscow-published translation.

5. 30 *Collected Works*, p. 327.

6. 31 *Collected Works*, p. 353.

7. In a March 27, 1922 speech defending his New Economic Policy, Lenin boldly warned the Mensheviks and Social Revolutionaries who heckled it as a retreat to capitalism:

> Permit us to put you before a firing squad for saying that. Either you refrain from expressing your views, or if you insist . . . then you will have only yourselves to blame. . . . The Mensheviks and Social Revolutionaries, all of whom preach this sort of thing, are astonished when we declare that we shall shoot people for such things." 33 *Collected Works*, pp. 282–283.

8. Quoted in H. L. Mencken, ed., *New Dictionary of Quotations* (New York: Alfred A. Knopf, 1952), p. 966. I have been unable to find this quote in *Collected Works*, volumes 30 and 31, covering 1920. But these volumes have been edited by Moscow's propagandists to avoid embarrassing Lenin. Moreover, many valid Lenin quotes are not included in those volumes for they are to be found in the papers, memoirs, and verbal reports of many who knew him personally as associate or antagonist. In any case, the quote is certainly an accurate representation of Lenin's view, expressed on hundreds of occasions over 20 years. See, e.g., 28 *Collected Works*.

9. J. M. Thompson, *Robespierre* (New York: Appleton-Century Company, 1936), 2:41. April 24, 1793.

10. *Marx-Engels Correspondence* (New York: International Publishers, 1935), p. 160.

11. Ibid., p. 161.

12. William Z. Foster, chairman of the U.S. Communist Party, so declared in his *History of the Three Internationals* (New York: International Publishers, 1955), p. 50.

13. *Marx-Engels Correspondence*, p. 162.

14. R. N. Carew Hunt, *The Theory and Practice of Communism* (New York: Macmillan Company, 1957), p. 113.

15. *Marx-Engels Correspondence*, p. 227. (Italics in original.)

16. Olga Hess Gankin and H. H. Fisher, *The Bolsheviks and the World War* (Stanford, Calif.: Stanford University Press, 1940), pp. 64–65, 71.

17. 21 *Collected Works*, p. 16.

18. Possony, op. cit., p. 138.

19. Ibid., p. 144.

20. 22 *Collected Works*, p. 124.

21. 21 *Collected Works*, p. 40.

22. Gankin and Fisher, op. cit., p. 347.

23. Ibid., p. 315.

24. Ibid., p. 346.

25. Franz Borkenau, *European Communism* (New York: Harper & Brothers, 1953), p. 33.

26. Gankin and Fisher, op. cit., pp. 479, 559.

27. Angelica Balabanoff, *Impressions of Lenin* (Ann Arbor: University of Michigan Press, 1964), p. 103.

28. Ibid., p. 104.

29. Ibid., p. 104

30. Gankin and Fisher, op. cit., p. 572. At one meeting of German socialists in Milwaukee, Kollontay got a resolution introduced favoring the Bolshevik position, but after heated debate it was defeated. See p. 566.

31. Theodore Draper, *The Roots of American Communism* (New York: Viking Press, 1957), p. 76.

32. Ibid., pp. 26–69.

33. *The Letters of Lenin,* trans. and ed., Elizabeth Hill and Doris Mundie (New York: Harcourt, Brace and Company, 1937), pp. 390–391; and Lenin, *The Imperialist War,* in 18 *Collected Works,* pp. 374–376. Cited in Draper, op. cit., pp. 74, 409 n. Only part of Lenin's letter has been preserved and Lenin himself suspected it had been confiscated by French authorities and never reached Boston.

34. Stefan T. Possony, *Lenin: The Compulsive Revolutionary* (Chicago: Henry Regnery Company, 1964), p. 211.

35. According to the Menshevik Dallin, cited in Jules Monnerot, *Sociology and Psychology of Communism* (Boston: Beacon Press, 1960), p. 85 n.

36. Quoted by Colonel Theodore H. Markhins, *L'armee Rouge, La Puissance Militaire de L'U.R.S.S.* (Paris: Payot, 1938), pp. 261–262.

37. Shub, op. cit., p. 387.

38. E. N. Korn, *The Technique of Revolution,* unpublished dissertation No. 330, Georgetown University Library, Washington, D.C., vol. 2, p. 967.

39. The plan seemed to involve a two-pronged Russian attack through Poland and Rumania. (The Soviets actually declared war on Rumania on May 18, 1919.) The northern drive was to link up with a simultaneous German Bolshevik uprising and move to the Rhine against France. The southern prong was to unite with Kun's forces in Hungary, then strike south into Bulgaria, Yugoslavia and Italy. When Radek was arrested in Berlin in February 1919 he had with him a plan for the general communist offensive, scheduled for that very spring. Moreover, the commander of the Ukrainian Red Army, Antonov-Ovsienko, records in his memoirs that on May 5, 1919, he received direct orders from the Communist Party Central Committee and "commander-in-chief" to free forces for a breakthrough and unification with Hungary, and "we prepared to send them to the aid of Red Hungary." (V. Antonov-Ovsienko, *Reminiscences About The Civil War,* IV, 330, quoted by Shub, op. cit., p. 342.)

40. Quoted in Shub, op. cit., p. 342, citing Paul Millukov.

41. Ruth Fischer, *Stalin and German Communism* (Cambridge: Harvard University Press, 1948), pp. xvi-xvii.

42. Ibid., p. 109.

43. Ibid.

44. Kaas and Lazarovics, *Bolshevism in Hungary: The Bela Kun Period* (London: Grant Richards, 1931), pp. 68–69.

45. Ibid., p. 92.

46. Ibid., pp. 153–155.

CHAPTER 23   THE FIRST GLOBAL MEDIA CONGLOMERATE

1. 29 *Collected Works* 506, 508.

2. 31 *Collected Works,* p. 189.

3. James W. Hulse, *The Forming of the Communist International* (Stanford, Calif.: Stanford University Press, 1964), pp. 8–15.

4. Theodore A. Draper, *Roots of American Communism* (New York: Viking Press, 1957), p. 148.

5. Ibid., pp. 148–149.

6. Hulse, op. cit., pp. 15–16.

7. Ibid., p. 211.

8. Arthur Ransome, *Russia In 1919* (New York: B. W. Huebach, 1919), p. 214. "Albrecht" was the same person referred to as "Eberlin," the balky Spartacist representative.

9. Franz Borkenau, *World Communism: A History of the Communist International* (Ann Arbor: University of Michigan Press, 1962), pp. 162–163.

10. Angelica Balabanoff, *My Life As a Rebel* (New York: Harper and Brothers, 1938), pp. 215–216; see Angelica Balabanoff, *Impressions of Lenin* (Ann Arbor: University of Michigan Press, 1964), p. 70.

11. Balabanoff, *My Life As A Rebel,* p. 216.

12. Balabanoff, *Impressions of Lenin*, pp. 72–73.

13. Draper, op. cit., pp. 231–232.

14. Balabanoff, *My Life As A Rebel*, p. 223.

15. Eric Hass, *The Socialist Labor Party and the Internationals* (New York: New York Labor News Company, 1949), pp. 160–161.

16. Eudocio Ravines, *The Yeman Way* (New York, Charles Scribner's Sons, 1951), pp. 12–13. (Emphasis added.)

17. Balabanoff, *Impressions of Lenin*, pp. 105–106.

18. Michael T. Florinsky, *World Revolution and the U.S.S.R.* (New York: Macmillan Company, 1933), pp. 42–43.

19. Boris Souvaraine, "La Scission de Tours," *Est & Ouest* (Paris), December 16–31, 1970, p. 7. Souvarine, a participant in the 1920 Congress of the French Socialist Party at Tours, at which Lenin's agents split off the most radical elements and formed the French Communist Party, obtained this report from Salevski, to whom Lenin was responding.

20. 31 *Collected Works* 23, 24.

21. 31 *Collected Works*, p. 237.

22. 31 *Collected Works*, p. 238. The organizational structure of a Communist Party is compared in detail to that of a conventional military organization (the United States Army) in William R. Kintner, *The Front Is Everywhere!* (Norman: University of Oklahoma Press, 1950).

CHAPTER 24   LENINIZING THE BOLSHEVIK MEDIA AFFILIATES

1. 31 *Collected Works*, pp. 195–197.

2. 32 *Collected Works*, p. 476.

3. *Selected Works*, Vol. X, pp. 95–96; see also pp. 100–101; see translation in 31 *Collected Works*, p. 77.

4. 31 *Collected Works*, pp. 70, 76, 85, 95–97, 99, 102.

5. "Theses on the Fundamental Tasks of the Second Congress," 31 *Collected Works*, pp. 191–192. Nechayev is clearly the source of this concept.

6. Stefan T. Possony, *Lenin: The Compulsive Revolutionary* (Chicago: Henry Regnery Company, 1964), pp. 306–311.

7. Quoted by Michael T. Florinsky, *World Revolution and the U.S.S.R.* (New York: Macmillan Company, 1953), p. 52.

8. Martin Ebon, *World Communism Today* (New York: McGraw-Hill Book Company, 1948), p. 20.

9. This speech of Lenin's was not published until 1959. It appeared in *Einheit*, the theoretical periodical of the German Communist Party, East Berlin, March 1959, p. 308. Cited in Gunther Nollau, *International Communism and World Revolution* (New York: Praeger, 1961), p. 70.

10. Swearingen and Langer, *Red Flag In Japan: International Communism In Action, 1919–1951* (Cambridge: Harvard University Press, 1952), p. 8.

11. Speech to Second Congress, July 19, 1920, "Fundamental Tasks of the Comintern," 31 *Collected Works*, 215; see June 20 speech on Irish, Indonesians, American Negroes.

12. Ruth Fischer, *Stalin and German Communism* (Cambridge: Harvard University Press, 1948), p. 526. See Jane Degras, *The Communist International, 1919–1943*, (New York: Oxford University Press, 1956–65), p. 105. Degras's three volumes cover 1919–22, 1923–28, and 1929–43.

13. Swearingen and Langer, op. cit., p. 16.

14. Stefan T. Possony, *Century of Conflict* (Chicago: Henry Regnery Company, 1953), pp. 118–119.

15. Ebon, op. cit., p. 394.

16. U.S. Senate, Internal Security Subcommittee, *Communist Leadership, "Tough Guy" Takes Charge* (Washington: Government Printing Office, 1960), pp. 14–15, 35–44.

17. U.S. Senate, Internal Security Subcommittee, *Freedom Commission and*

Freedom Academy (Washington: Government Printing Office, 1959), pp. 113–114. Though the Lenin School was certainly the most notorious and the one reserved for the elite, the other institutes of revolutionary engineering made valuable contributions. There was an Academy of Red Professors, the leading theoretical and scientific school of the world communist superstructure, whose nine-year program put it in a class with the highest theological seminaries of traditional religion—and only a shade behind the Jesuits whose study course lasts 14 years. The Central European School was set up primarily for the Balkan and Baltic countries, but some Americans attended it. Far Eastern University and Sun Yat-sen University together had around 5,000 Chinese students and others from the colonial nations. Both placed heavy emphasis upon guerrilla fighting and military training; Benjamin Gitlow called them "a miniature Chinese West Point". (Benjamin Gitlow, *The Whole of Their Lives* (New York: Charles Scribner's Sons, 1948, p. 250.)

18. E. N. Korn, *The Technique of Revolution*, unpublished dissertation No. 330, Georgetown University Library, Washington, D.C., vol. 2, pp. 999–1000. See also Korn's thesis No. 337, *The Violent Seizure of State Power.*

19. Nollau, op. cit., p. 131.

20. Theodore Draper, *American Communism and Soviet Russia* (New York: Viking, 1960), pp. 158–159.

21. Benjamin Gitlow, op. cit., p. 246; and Louisiana Joint Legislative Committee, *Subversion In Racial Unrest*, Part I (Baton Rouge, 1957), p. 19.

22. U.S. Government, *The Operational Pattern of International Communism In Latin America* (Washington: monograph, 1956), p. 5.

CHAPTER 25   CASE STUDIES IN LENINIST COLONIZATION

1. *Marx-Engels Correspondence* June 9, 1864 (New York: International Publishers, 1935).

2. Ibid., September 7, 1864.

3. Gustav Mayer, *Friedrich Engels* (New York: Alfred A. Knopf, 1936), p. 184.

4. Stefan T. Possony, *Lenin: The Compulsive Revolutionary* (Chicago: Henry Regnery Company, 1964), p. 298.

5. H. A. Taylor, *Communism in Great Britain, A Short History Of The British Communist Party* (London: Conservative Political Center, 1951), p. 11.

6. Allen Hutt, *The Postwar History of the British Working Class* (New York: Coward-McCann, 1938), pp. 57–58.

7. Henry B. Pelling, "The Early History of the Communist Party of Great Britain, 1920–1929," *Transactions of the Royal Historical Society*, 8 (1958), 43–44.

8. "Memoirs," *Radical Humanist*, February 1, 1953, p. 55.

9. Theodore A. Draper, *The Roots of American Communism* (New York: Viking Press, 1957), p. 236.

10. *Radical Humanist*, August 16, 1953, pp. 390–391. But see Draper, op. cit., pp. 239–41, who offers three other possible endings to the intriguing jewel story.

11. Carlton Beals, *Glass Houses* (Philadelphia: J. B. Lippincott Company, 1938), p. 50.

BIBLIOGRAPHICAL NOTE: In addition to those works cited, the following are useful regarding the Comintern era: Merle Fainsod, *International Socialism and the World War* (Cambridge: Harvard University Press, 1935, reissued by Doubleday Anchor in 1969); Joseph Rothschild, *The Communist Party of Bulgaria, Origins and Development, 1883–1936* (New York: Columbia University Press, 1959); Robert A. Scalapino, *The Japanese Communist Movement, 1920–1966* (Berkeley: University of California Press, 1967); George M. Beckmann, and Okupo Genji, (Stanford, Calif.: Stanford University Press, 1969); Justus M. Van Der Kroef, *The Communist Party of Indonesia, Its History, Program and Tactics* (Vancouver: University of British Columbia, 1965); Ruth T. McVey, *The Rise of Indonesian Communism* (Ithaca: Cornell University Press, 1965). Helmut Gruber, *International Communism in the Era of Lenin, A Documentary History* (Ithaca: Cornell University Press, 1967), traces with interpretation and narrative and documents the Second International to the Third; the Lenin-Luxemburg debate over centralism; Zimmerwald and Kienthal conferences; the 1919 Comintern Congress; 1919 in Berlin, Budapest, Munich and Vienna; the Italian split,

1923 German uprising and the Bulgarian uprising—world revolution's last gasps before "socialism in one country" set in.

CHAPTER 26   COLONIZING LENINIST CARTELS IN ASIA

1. David N. Druhe, *Soviet Russia and Indian Communism* (New York: Bookman, 1959), p. 33. Druhe says the British War Office had detected the activity of this school training agents for work in India as early as January 15, 1920. See *London Times*, February 25, 1930, p. 15.

2. Philip Spratt, *Blowing Up India, Reminiscences of a Former Comintern Emissary* (Calcutta: Prachi Prakashan, 1955), p. 34.

3. M. D. Kennedy, *A History of Communism in East Asia* (New York: Frederick A. Praeger, 1957), p. 204.

4. *Fourth Congress of the Communist International*, abridged report (Moscow, 1923), pp. 13–26.

CHAPTER 27   COLONIZING LENINISM IN CHINA

1. C. Martin Wilbur, and Julie L. How, *Documents On Communism, Nationalism and Soviet Advisers In China, 1918–1927, Papers Seized In the 1927 Peking Raid* (New York: Columbia University Press, 1956), p. 42. See Georgi Paloczi-Horvath, *Mao Tse-Tung, Emperor of the Blue Ants* (New York: Doubleday and Company, 1963), pp. 56–59. Communist sources maintain there Marxist study societies as early as 1918 are wrong, according to Paloczi-Horvath, who makes a compelling case. But see also Maurice Meisner, *Li Ta-Chao and the Origins of Chinese Marxism* (Cambridge: Harvard University Press, 1967) on this issue and date of Voitinsky's arrival—page 116. Also Lucien Bianco, *Origins of the Chinese Revolution, 1915–1949* (Stanford, Calif.: Stanford University Press, 1970).

2. Chow Tse-Tung, *The May Fourth Movement, Intellectual Revolution In Modern China* (Cambridge: Harvard University Press, 1960), p. 245n.

3. Meisner, op. cit., pp. 71, 90–91.

4. Ibid., pp. 72–73, 116.

5. Ibid., pp. 115–116.

6. See Paloczi-Horvath, p. 58, and Chow Tse-Tung, p. 244n.

7. O. Edmund Clubb, *Twentieth Century China* (New York: Columbia University Press), p. 111.

8. *Youth* (later *New Youth*), Vol. 1, No. 1 (September 15, 1919), quoted in Chow Tse-Tung, op. cit., p. 74. (Emphasis added.)

9. Wilbur and How, op. cit., p. 42.

10. Ibid., p. 49.

11. Paloczi-Horvath, op. cit., p. 58. See Meisner, op. cit., p. 91, on Li Ta-Chao's initial reaction to Marx's theoretical mumbo-jumbo.

12. In later years, Ch'en, Li, Mao Tse-Tung and the Chinese and Russian communist historials all tried to push back their conversions to a much earlier date. They all were eager to preserve the fiction that the CCP was a spontaneous and native movement, not one spawned by agents from Moscow. The official Comintern representative reports to Moscow claimed that the first Marxist study societies were formed in 1918, and Ch'en and Li claimed they were Marxists by then. But in fact the only mention made of Marxism in their writings as late as 1919 was to denounce it and rebut it. They didn't see the Marxist light until the Comintern representatives got there in 1920 with all that Moscow cash. See Paloczi-Horvath, op. cit., pp. 56–58; Chow Tse-Tung, op. cit., pp. 245–248; and Wilbur and How, op. cit., pp. 47–48.

13. Chow Tse-Tung, op. cit., p. 248.

14. Martin Ebon, *World Communism Today* (New York: McGraw-Hill Book Company, 1948), p. 366.

15. Wilbur and How, op. cit., p. 49.

16. Chow Tse-Tung, op. cit., p. 250.

17. Ibid., p. 249.

18. Wilbur and How, op. cit., pp. 50–51.

19. Ibid., pp. 51–52.

20. Robert S. Elegant, *The Center of the World, Communism and the Mind of China* (New York: Doubleday and Company, 1964), p. 118. See Meisner, op. cit., p. 119.

21. Paloczi-Horvath, op. cit., p. 62. Mao told Edgar Snow there were 12 present; others speak of 9, 11, 13, or 15.

22. Ibid., pp. 119–121. Note that Elegant minimizes the role of the Soviet agents in organizing the CCP. This is because of the main thesis of this excellent book and because for his account of this meeting he relied upon the unpublished memoirs of one of the participants, Chang Kuo-Tao, who was obviously seeking for reasons of nationalistic pride to play down the Russian contribution to getting the Chinese together. The weight of evidence and independent scholarship is against this interpretation, however. For example, see Elegant's footnote on p. 121.

23. Hugh Seton-Watson, *From Lenin to Khrushchev: The History of World Communism* (New York: Praeger, 1960), p. 138–139. Chow Tse-Tung, op. cit., p. 246n.; Clubb, op. cit., p. 119; and finally Wilbur and How, op. cit., pp. 138–140, trace Dr. Sun's contacts with Bolshevik representatives. All vary on dates of the Sneevliet-Sun meeting, ranging from August to November 1921.

24. In Amsterdam in 1935 Sneevliet told the story to Harold R. Isaacs. See Isaacs, *The Tragedy of the Chinese Revolution* (London: Secker and Warburg, 1938), pp. 61–62.

25. Wilbur and How, op. cit., pp. 64, 84, 493.

26. See Isaacs, op. cit. Though Sneevliet, to maintain the Moscow myth that the fledgling communist parties colonized around the world were indeed spontaneous movements, denied he had invoked Comintern authority to enforce his proposal, Ch'en Tu-hsiu, CCP general secretary who was present gave the other version. Ch'en is corroborated by a letter which Radek wrote the Sixth Congress of the Comintern in 1928. See dossier No. 6 Trotsky Archives, Houghton Library, Harvard University, cited in C. Brandt et al., *A Documentary History of Chinese Communism* (London: George Allen and Unwin, 1952), pp. 52, 486n. See also Wilbur and How, op. cit., pp. 83–84, 493.

27. Isaacs, op. cit., p. 66.

28. New York *Times,* July 22, 1923.

29. See Ebon, op. cit., p. 366 and Paloczi-Horvath, op. cit., p. 67, who gives October as date of Borodin's arrival.

30. Wilbur and How, op. cit., p. 64.

31. Ebon, op. cit., p. 368.

32. Clubb, op. cit., p. 129.

33. Wilbur and How, op. cit., p. 94.

34. Ibid., p. 97.

35. Ibid., pp. 97–98, 124.

36. *The Autobiography Of Mao Tse-Tung* (Canton: Truth Book Company, 1949), pp. 2–3.

37. Siao-Yu, *Mao Tse-Tung and I Were Beggars* (Syracuse, N.Y.: Syracuse University Press, 1959), chapters 14, 15. This is a fascinating and insightful account by Mao's fellow student and cofounder of the "New People's Study Society," a close friend during several crucial years. Note parallel to Chernyshevsky's "new people" concept in the novel that so influenced the 17-year-old Lenin. Mao was 20 at the time.

38. Emi Siao, *Mao Tse-Tung, His Childhood and Youth* (Bombay: People's Publishing House, 1955), p. 30.

39. Mildred G. and Victor Goertzel, *Cradles of Eminence* (Boston: Little, Brown and Company, 1962).

40. Richard Nice, *A Handbook Of Abnormal Psychology* (New York: Philosphical Library, 1959), pp. 156–157.

41. Frank S. Meyer, *The Moulding of Communists, The Training of the Communist Cadre* (New York: Harcourt, Brace and Company, 1961).

42. Lucian W. Pye, "Hostility and Authority in Chinese Politics," *Problems of Communism,* May-June 1968, p. 10 ff. (For a panoramic study of this oedipal impulse in student extremist movements, compare Lewis Feuer, *The Conflict of Generations* (New York: Basic Books, 1969), especially pp. 529–

531.) Pye developes some of the themes of his article in his book, *The Spirit of Chinese Politics* (Cambridge: M.I.T. Press, 1968).

CHAPTER 28   RADICAL FORERUNNERS IN THE UNITED STATES

1. John C. Miller, *Crisis in Freedom* (Boston: Little, Brown and Company), pp. 115, 119, 220.

2. Theodore Draper, *The Roots Of American Communism* (New York: Viking Press, 1957), pp. 11–13.

3. Max Nomad, *Apostles of Revolution* (New York: Collier Books, 1961), Chapter 5.

4. *Bill Haywood's Book* (New York: International Publishers, 1929), p. 7.

5. Clarence Darrow, *The Story Of My Life* (New York: Charles Scribner's Sons, 1932), p. 60.

6. Draper, op. cit., p. 26.

7. Ibid., p. 22.

8. William Z. Foster and E. C. Ford, *Syndicalism* (Chicago: n.p., 1912), pp. 43–44.

9. Draper, op. cit., p. 46.

10. Ibid., pp. 46–47.

11. Ibid., pp. 74–75.

12. Ibid., pp. 76–77.

13. Ibid., pp. 80–82.

14. Olga Gankin and Harold Fisher, *The Bolsheviks in the World War* (Stanford, Calif.: Stanford University Press, 1940). Note that Kollontay's letter is dated January 11, 1917, while Trotsky did not arrive until January 14. Possibly Kollontay was wrong on her dates.

15. *The New International,* May 5, 1917, p. 3. cited in Draper, op. cit., p. 88.

CHAPTER 29   THE COMINTERN SUBSIDIARY IN AMERICA

1. Theodore Draper, *The Roots of American Communism* (New York: Viking Press, 1957), p. 107.

2. Theodore Draper, *American Communism and Soviet Russia* (New York: Viking Press, 1960), p. 17.

3. Ibid., p. 9.

4. Draper, *The Roots of American Communism,* p. 139.

5. Ibid., pp. 156–7, 165.

6. Ibid., p. 158.

7. Ibid., pp. 181–182. Note: At this time the FBI was known simply as the Bureau of Investigation, forerunner of J. Edgar Hoover's agency.

8. Ibid., p. 190.

9. Ibid., p. 187.

10. J. Edgar Hoover, *Masters of Deceit* (New York: Pocket Books, 1959), p. 54.

11. Draper, *American Communism and Soviet Russia,* p. 20.

12. See Gitlow, *I Confess* (New York: E. P. Dutton and Company, 1940), p. 561, and Bertram Wolfe, interview cited by Draper, *American Communism and Soviet Russia,* pp. 422, 526.

13. Draper, op. cit., pp. 423, 526.

14. Gitlow, op. cit., p. 561.

15. Draper, *American Communism and Soviet Russia,* p. 430.

CHAPTER 30   MUSSOLINI: THE ITALIAN LENINOID

1. "The Totalitarian Age," book review, *Trans-Action*, October 1969. The book under review was S. V. Woolf, ed., *European Fascism* (New York: Random House, 1968).

2. Gaudens Megaro, *Mussolini in the Making* (New York: Fertig, 1967), pp. 187, 304. Megaro wrote this in 1935, an especially discerning observation for its time.

3. Georges Sorel, *Saggi Di Critica Del Marxismo* (Milan: Sandron, 1903), pp. 16f, 59–94.

4. A. James Gregor, *Contemporary Radical Ideologies* (New York: Random House, 1968), pp. 129, 132.

5. *I Discorsi della Rivoluzione*, 1925, p. 15.

6. *Hitler's Table Talk* (London; 1953), p. 266.

CHAPTER 31   HITLER: THE ELECTRONIC LENINOID

1. T. W. Adorno et al., *The Authoritarian Personality* (New York: Harper and Row, 1960), p. 767. The Adorno book has been criticized on methodological and other grounds, and should be read with care; see the analysis of Christie and Jahoda, editors, *Studies In the Scope and Method of "The Authoritarian Personality"* (Glencoe: Free Press, 1954.)

2. Georg's "acknowledgment" of paternity came when he was 84. The baby Alois was born in 1837, and Georg did not marry the mother until 1842; she died in 1847 and Georg left the boy to be raised by his settled, married brother Johann. Not until 1876 did Georg appear before a notary to declare himself Alois's father. Why did he not acknowledge paternity in 1842 and give the baby his name? Probably because he was not the child's father, some scholars maintain. Werner Maser has made a case that brother Johann was actually the father; since he wanted to remember the child he raised in his will, he wanted to endow him with the family name as well and persuaded the brother to file the legal affidavit to avoid scandalizing his own wife and children. See Werner Maser, *Hitler's Mein Kampf: An Analysis* (London: Faber and Faber, 1970), p. 81. See Konrad Heiden, *Der Fuhrer* (Boston: Houghton Mifflin Company, 1944), p. 41. Others have made a case that Alois

Schicklgruber Hitler was the bastard son of the Jewish man in whose home the mother was serving as a maid at the time she conceived. The man did pay mother and child support money; whether from benevolence or guilt is moot. What is not open to doubt is that Adolf Hitler always suspected that his grandfather may have been a Jew—and thus under his own Nuremburg laws he could not establish that he was a non-Jew since those laws required certification that all four grandparents were non-Jews! In 1930 when an anonymous letter threatened blackmail, he had his personal lawyer investigate his ancestry and confirm what he already suspected—that his "Aryan" purity could not be proven. The best single brief analysis of Adolf Hitler is a paper entitled, "The Historian's Use of Psychology: Adolf Hitler as a Case Study," by Professor Robert G. L. Waite of Williams College, which was delivered at the American Historical Association meeting in San Francisco on December 30, 1965. It provides a wealth of detail on the pathology of Hitler's family constellation and individual personality. Professor Waite concludes that Hitler's suspicion over his own possible Jewish grandfather contributed heavily to his fanatical anti-Semitism.

3. *Mein Kampf*, Chapter 1. Emphasis added.

4. For a discussion of the lasting power of such an adolescent "militant enthusiasm" see Konrad Lorenz, *On Aggression* (New York: Harcourt, Brace and World, 1966). Lorenz maintains (p. 265): "The urge to become a member of a group is certainly something that has been programmed in the prehuman phylogeny of man," and it takes hold primarily and lastingly in the adolescent stage.

5. See A. James Gregor, *Contemporary Radical Ideologies* (New York: Random House, 1968), pp. 171–214, for a discussion of Hitler's ideology and its sources.

6. *Hitler's Table Talk* (London; 1953), pp. 413–414, published under the title *Hitler's Secret Conversations* (New York: Farrar, Straus, 1953). Hereinafter the citation *Table Talk* refers to the London edition.

7. Quoted in Heiden, op. cit., p. 314.

8. Ibid., pp. 315–316.

9. Max Weber, *Gemeinschaft Und Gesellschaft* (Tubingen: Mohr, 1922), p. 140.

10. Theodore Abel, *The Nazi Movement, Why Hitler Came To Power* (New York: Atheling, 1966), p. 66.

11. Richard Hanser, *Putsch! How Hitler Made Revolution* (New York: Wyden, 1970).

12. Heiden, op. cit., pp. 34, 106.

13. Abel, op. cit., p. 120.

14. F. L. Schuman, *The Nazi Dictatorship* (New York: Alfred A. Knopf, 1963), p. 93.

15. *Mein Kampf.*

16. Op. cit., p. 141.

17. See Goering's testimony, *The Trial of German Major War Criminals,* part 9, p. 64, English report. Quoted in Charles Bewley, *Herman Goring And the Third Reich* (New York: Devin-Adair, 1962), p. 45.

18. *Table Talk*, p. 108.

19. Heiden, op. cit., p. 94.

20. Abel, op. cit., p. 173.

21. *Table Talk*, p. 176.

22. Hermann Rauschning, *Hitler Speaks* (London: Thornton Butterworth, 1940), p. 247.

23. *Table Talk*, pp. 335–336.

24. Heiden, op. cit., p. 311.

25. Op. cit., p. 138. (Emphasis added.)

26. Waite, op. cit., p. 271.

27. Ibid., p. 42.

28. Ibid., p. 272.

29. Ibid., pp. 276, 42.

30. Reichstag speech of July 13, 1934, printed in the *Volkischer Beobachter,* July 14, 1934. Cited in Waite, op. cit., pp. 280–281.

31. Quoted in Waite, op. cit., p. 281.

32. Hermann Rauschning, *The Voice of Destruction* (New York; 1940), p. 131.

33. G. L. Waite, *Vanguard of Nazism, The Free Corps Movement in Postwar Germany, 1918–1923* (New York: W. W. Norton Company, 1969), p. 274.

34. London *Sunday Times* News Service dispatch, January 5, 1969.

CHAPTER 32   REVOLUTIONARY RADICALISM TODAY: COMPETITIVE SOCIAL DEMOLITION

1. Speech, February 6, 1965, to the Fellows of the American Bar Foundation, New Orleans, Louisiana.

2. Gunther Nollau, *International Communism and World Revolution* (New York: Praeger, 1961), p. 167.

3. The phrase was coined by Brian Crozier. See *Since Stalin* (New York: Coward-McCann, 1970).

4. Whelan, Joseph G., *World Communism, 1967–1969* (Washington: Senate Internal Security Subcommittee-Government Printing Office, 1970).

5. *Kommunist,* September 1963. (Emphasis added.)

6. See John Barron, "The Soviet Plot to Destroy Mexico," *Reader's Digest,* November 1971.

7. A. James Gregor, *Contemporary Radical Ideologies* (New York: Random House, 1968), pp. 163–164.

8. Robert Moss, "Urban Guerrillas in Uruguay," *Problems of Communism,* September-October 1971, pp. 14–23.

9. John Barron, *KGB* (New York: Reader's Digest Press, 1973).

10. Phillip Abbott Luce, *The New Left, The Resurgence of Radicalism Among American Students* (New York: McKay, 1960), p. 83.

11. U.S. House Committee on Un-American Activities, *Communist Activities In The Buffalo N.Y., Area.* (Washington: Government Printing Office, 1964), pp. 1544–1549.

12. U.S. House Committee on Un-American Activities, 1963 *Annual Report* (Washington: Government Printing Office, 1964), p. 13.

13. Luce, op. cit., supplemented in interview with the author.

14. Eugene H. Methvin, *The Riot Makers,* (New Rochelle, N.Y.: Arlington House, 1971), pp. 94–95, 374–378.

15. Associated Press, July 13, 1972.

CHAPTER 33   THE "NEW LEFT" IN AMERICA

1. U.S. Census Bureau estimate of the number of 18-year-olds on July 1 in each year.

2. Samuel Lubell, *The Hidden Crisis in American Politics* (New York: W. W. Norton Company, 1970), pp. 182–183, 186–187, 188.

3. U.S. Senate Internal Security Subcommittee, *Testimony of Gerald Wayne Kirk* (Washington: U.S. Government Printing Office, 1970), p. 40.

4. James A. Michener, *Kent State, What Happened and Why* (New York: Reader's Digest Press-Random House, 1971), pp. 84–85, 105–106, 141–144, 162.

5. For a full account see Eugene H. Methvin, *The Riot Makers* (New Rochelle, N.Y.: Arlington House, 1971), Chapter 1.

6. See Ibid., Chapter 14, for full account.

7. Bobby Seale, *Seize the Time* (New York: Random House, 1970), p. 64.

8. *The Black Panther,* July 20, 1967. The reference to the killing of a policeman sipping coffee adverts to an episode in a movie about the Algerian urban terror campaign used in Panther training sessions, "The Battle of Algiers."

9. Ibid., May 18, 1968.

10. U.S. House Internal Security Committee, 1970 *Annual Report* (Washington: Government Printing Office, 1970), p. 51.

11. U.S. Senate Permanent Investigations Subcommittee, *Riots Civil and Criminal Disorders*, Part 19 (Washington, Government Printing Office, 1969), Testimony of Larry Powell, pp. 3783 ff. See especially pp. 3823–3824.

12. U.S. Senate Internal Security Subcommittee, *Testimony of Gerald Wayne Kirk*, Part 1 (Washington: Government Printing Office, 1970), pp. 21, 29, 132.

13. Edward Jay Epstein, "The Panthers and the Police A Pattern of Genocide?" *New Yorker*, February 13, 1971, pp. 45–77.

14. U.S. House Internal Security Committee, *Gun-Barrel Politics: The Black Panther Party, 1966–1971* (Washington: Government Printing Office, 1971), pp. 69–70.

15. Gallup Poll report, New York *Times*, February 7, 1971

16. *The Black Panther Supplement*, September 4, 1971. (Emphasis added.)

EPILOG: THE PRICE OF THE DREAM

1. Quoted by Carl Davidson in *The Guardian*, March 3, 1968.

2. Walker, Richard L., *The Human Cost of Chinese Communism* (Washington: Senate Internal Security Subcommittee, 1971).

3. Conquest, Robert, *The Great Terror* (New York: Macmillan, 1968); cf. his *The Human Cost of Soviet Communism* (Washington: Senate Internal Security Subcommittee, 1970).

INDEX

Socialist Party of America, 332, 388, 418, 421–426, 428–432
Socialist Propaganda League, 331, 332, 341, 388, 389, 424–426, 428
Socialist Youth Corps (China), 401–403
Society for the Liberation of the People, 217
Society for the Study of Journalism, 413
Society for the Study of Marxism, 397
Society for the Study of Russia, 397
Society for the Study of Socialism, 397
Society of Exiles, 130, 131
Society of the Pantheon, 94, 96, 97
Society of the Rights of Man, 163
Solzhenitsyn, Alexander, 69, 496
Sorel, Georges, 442, 444, 450, 456n
Sorokin, Pitirim, 21
South Wales Socialist Society (Britain), 371
Souvarine, Boris, 484, 485
Soviet Union, Communist Party of the, 295, 314, 337, 339, 345, 407, 484–488, 491–493, 519, 523, 524; see also Bolshevism, Communism, etc.
Soviet Union, see also Russia
Soviet World, 429
Soyecourt, Marquis of, 90
Spartacist League, 333, 334, 341, 368, 369
Spector, Allan, 504
Spinoza, Baruch, 442
Stalin, Joseph V., 13, 15, 18, 30, 55–58, 69, 84, 180, 218, 275, 291, 295, 297, 298, 309, 316, 355, 357–362, 378n, 379, 392, 409, 410, 414, 434–437, 480, 484, 485, 487, 503, 504, 512, 515, 518, 519, 521, 522, 524
Stampa, La, 455
Starkov, Vasili, 228
State and Revolution, 449, 452
Steffens, Lincoln, 427
Stein, Lorenz von, 142–146, 174, 365, 449
Stern, Karl, 37
Stevenson, Adlai, 22, 252
Strange Tactics of Extremism, The, 504, 523
Strauss, David Friedrich, 151
Struve, Peter, 260, 261, 270, 274, 292
Student League for Industrial Democracy, 502
Student Nonviolent Coordinating Committee, 14, 404n, 507, 508, 513
Students for a Democratic Society, 14, 22, 404n, 453, 488, 495, 497–499, 502–506, 512, 513, 517, 518
Sublime Maitres Parfaits, 123, 124, 129, 130

Sudan, communism in, 491
Sukarno, 488
Sun Yat-sen, 394–396, 399, 404–409, 413
Sun Yat-sen University, 358, 409
Suslov, Mikhail, 486
Syndicalism, 421

Table Talk, 476
Talmon, J. L., 65
Tanchelm, 33
Taratuta, Victor, 316
"Tasks of Revolutionary Propaganda in Russia," 219, 220
TASS, 483
Tate, Sharon, 35n
Ten Days That Shook the World, 428
Ter-Petrossian, Semyon A. (Kamo), 315, 316
Thaelmann, Ernst, 359
Theot, Catherine, 79, 80
"Theses on Comintern Fundamental Tasks," 350
Third International, 328, 337–349, 371, 423, 429; see also Comintern
Thompson, J. M., 71
Thorez, Maurice, 359, 387
"Tiger, The," 190
Time, 511
Timon, 45
Tito, Marshal, 360, 438
Tkachev, Peter, 192, 193, 216–222, 242, 267, 272, 278
Togliatti, Palmiro, 362, 375, 485
Toilers of the East, Congresses of the, 392
Toilers of the East, University of the, 358, 384, 392, 401, 409
Tolstoy, Leo, 182
Trade Union Educational League (TUEL), 421
Trent, Evelyn, 377
Tribuna, La, 443
Tribune of the People, 86, 93, 95, 96, 104
Tricontinental Congress, 486
Trotsky, Leon, 15, 18, 230, 242, 301, 302, 309, 333, 339, 341–343, 345, 356, 359, 380, 389, 390, 425–429, 431, 434, 436, 479, 500, 501, 512, 515, 518, 521
Tuchman, Barbara W., 520
Tukhachevsky, Marshal, 359
Tulin, K., 261
Tupemaros, 490, 491
Turati, Filippo, 340, 373–375
Turgenev, Ivan Sergeyevich, 182, 185, 186
"21 Conditions," 348, 350, 364

Ulam, Adam B., 524, 525
Ulbricht, Walter, 435

[583]